Authors
Robert Rueda
Tina Saldivar
Lynne Shapiro
Shane Templeton
C. Ann Terry
Catherine Valentino
Shelby A. Wolf

Consultants
Jeanneine P. Jones
Monette Coleman McIver
Rojulene Norris

HOUGHTON MIFFLIN BOSTON

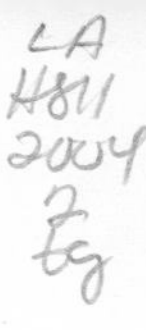

Credit

Special Character *W.R.* by Anne Kennedy.

Teacher Advisory Panel

Karen Brohaugh
Scandia Elementary School
Scandia, MN

Sybil Bynum-Williams
Bonaire Middle School
Bonaire, GA

Ann Clayton
Rockway Middle School
Miami, FL

Yvette Colyer
Bel-Air Elementary School
Albuquerque, NM

Charlene Cook
Belair Elementary School
Jefferson City, MO

Brenda Dukes
Aycock Middle School
Greensboro, NC

Sharon Fiske
Meadlowlark School
Great Falls, MT

Peggy Gallo
Upper Dublin School District
Dresher, PA

Ann Hoffmeister
Verona Public Schools
Verona, IL

Gerri McManus
Stanley School
Swampscott, MA

Sissy Othicke
Los Ranchos Elementary School
Albuquerque, NM

Rosa Maria Peña
Rodriguez Elementary School
Austin, TX

Connie Rupp
Stukey Elementary School
Northglen, CO

Marge Segal
Holcomb Bridge Middle School
Alpharetta, GA

Judy Thomas
Meadowview Elementary School
Meadowview, VA

Carolyn Tucker
Dixon Elementary School
Dixon, KY

Alfie Turner
Colton Elementary School
Spring Valley, NY

Ginger Verrill
Bush Elementary School
Idaho Falls, ID

Linda Wallis
Madison Elementary School
Riverside, CA

Printed in the U.S.A.

ISBN: 0-618-31009-6

1 2 3 4 5 6 7 8 9 10-B-11 10 09 08 07 06 05 04 03 02

HOUGHTON MIFFLIN

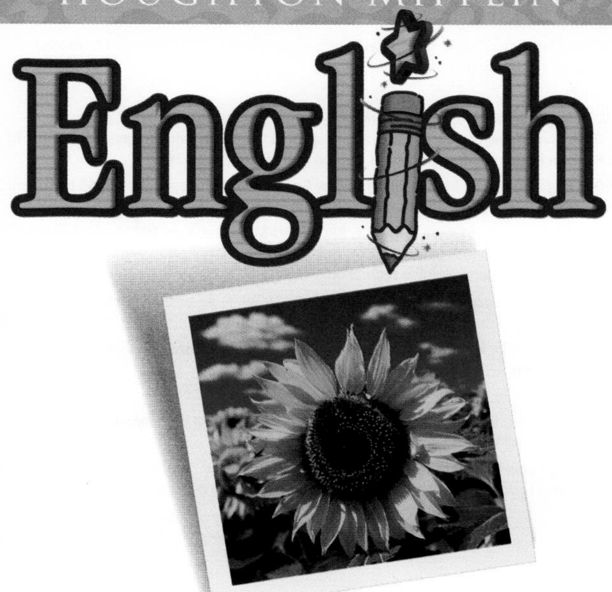

Authors
Robert Rueda
Tina Saldivar
Lynne Shapiro
Shane Templeton
C. Ann Terry
Catherine Valentino
Shelby A. Wolf

Consultants
Jeanneine P. Jones
Monette Coleman McIver
Rojulene Norris

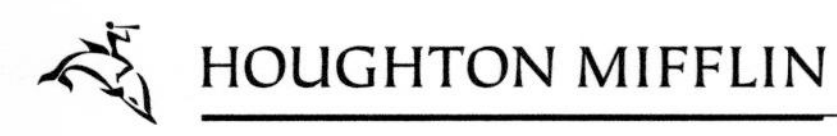

BOSTON

Acknowledgments

For each of the selections listed below, grateful acknowledgment is made for permission to excerpt and/or reprint original or copyrighted material as follows:

Published Models

From "Gloria Who Might Be My Best Friend" from THE STORIES JULIAN TELLS by Ann Cameron. Copyright ©1981 by Ann Cameron. Cover illustration copyright ©1981 by Ann Strugnell. Reprinted by permission of Random House Children's Books, a division of Random House, Inc.

From HIDE AND SEEK FOG by Alvin Tresselt, illustrated by Roger Duvoisin. Copyright ©1965 by Lothrop, Lee & Shepard Co., Inc. Used by permission of HarperCollins Publishers.

From "How to Make a Bag of Rain" from YOUR BIG BACKYARD Magazine, June 1999 issue, a publication of the National Wildlife Federation. Copyright ©1999 by National Wildlife Federation. Reprinted by permission of National Wildlife Federation.

"My Life in the Country" by Tomie dePaola. Copyright ©2001 by Tomie dePaola. Reprinted by permission of the author.

THE WOLF'S CHICKEN STEW by Keiko Kasza. Copyright ©1987 by Keiko Kasza. Reprinted by permission of Putnam & Grosset Group, a division of Penguin Putnam Inc.

Poetry

"Commas" from BING BANG BOING by Douglas Florian. Copyright ©1994 by Douglas Florian. Reprinted with permission of Harcourt, Inc.

"Fishes' Evening Song" from WHISPERING AND OTHER THINGS by Dahlov Ipcar. Copyright ©1967 by Dahlov Ipcar. Published by Alfred A. Knopf, Inc. Reprinted by permission of McIntosh and Otis, Inc.

Acknowledgments are continued at the back of the book following the last page of the Index.

Printed in the U.S.A.

ISBN: 0-618-30998-5

1 2 3 4 5 6 7 8 9 10-VH-11 10 09 08 07 06 05 04 03 02

TABLE OF CONTENTS

Table of Contents

Lesson Objective

Children will:

- use a table of contents

Focus on Instruction

- Tell children that a table of contents helps a reader know what is in a book. Explain that it shows how the book is organized, such as by chapters or by units.
- Explain that some books, such as story books with chapters, have tables of contents that only list the chapter number, chapter title, and first page. Tell children that books with many different parts or with a great deal of information may have longer, more detailed tables of contents. For example, a book about weather might have chapters on such things as hurricanes, thunderstorms, and tornadoes. Help children understand that all of these elements would be listed in the table of contents, which might be several pages long.
- Explain that one way to use the contents is by finding the largest sections of the book first. Then look at the elements in each section. Are there chapters or special features? Ask children how a table of contents might help them in using this book.
- Have children find the answers to these questions.
  1. How many units are in this book? (10) What is the name of the section that comes before Unit 1? (Getting Started)
  2. On what page does Unit 2 begin? (62) What is the Special Focus about? (Narrating; Writing a Friendly Letter)
  3. On what page does Unit 5 begin? (162) What are the five special features at the end of the unit? (Enrichment, Checkup, Test Practice, Cumulative Review, Extra Practice)
  4. On what page does the Tools and Tips section begin? (H2) What comes after the last Tools and Tips section? (Index) How many sections are in Tools and Tips? (7)

Unit 2 Writing a Personal Narrative 62

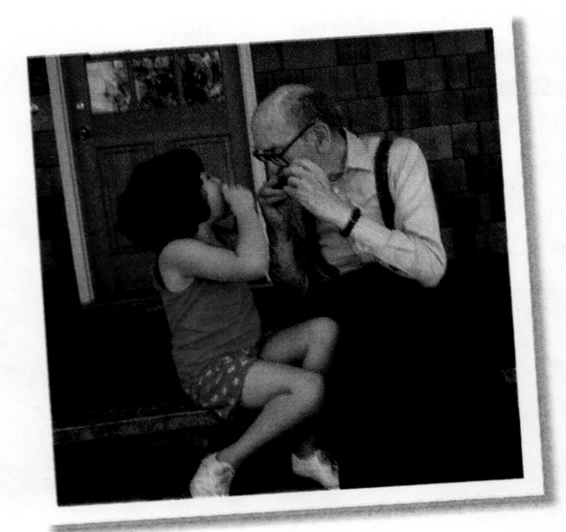

Unit 3 Nouns and Pronouns 92

Unit 4 Writing a Story 134

Table of Contents v

Unit 5 Verbs 162

Unit 6 Writing Instructions 206

Unit 7 Adjectives 238

Table of Contents vii

Unit 8 Writing a Description 266

Unit 9 More Capitalization and Punctuation 296

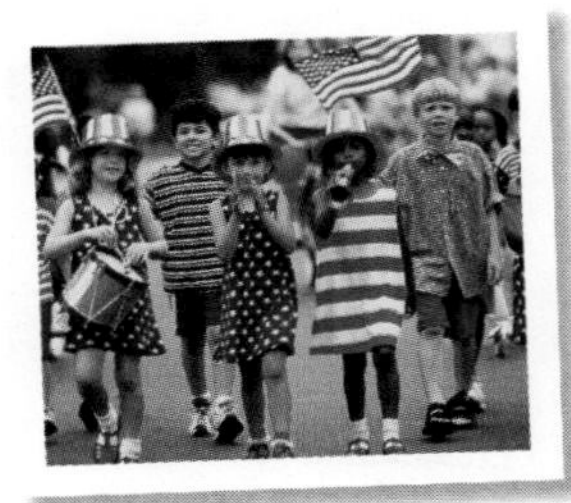

Unit 10 Writing to Express an Opinion 340

Table of Contents ix

Tools and Tips H2

Getting Started Planning Guide

2 weeks

	Blackline Masters (TE)
LISTENING, SPEAKING, AND VIEWING	
Learning Together *(2)*	
Being a Good Listener *(3)*	
Being a Good Speaker *(4)*	
Having a Conversation *(5)*	
Having a Discussion *(6–7)*	GS–1
Being a Good Viewer *(8)*	GS–2
Viewing: Looking and Thinking *(9–10)*	
THE WRITING PROCESS	
What Is the Writing Process? *(12–13)*	
THE WRITING PROCESS: WRITING A CLASS STORY	
Choosing a Topic for a Class Story *(14–15)*	
Exploring a Topic for a Class Story *(16)*	
Organizing Details for a Class Story *(17)*	
Drafting a Class Story *(18–19)*	
Revising a Class Story *(20–21)*	
Proofreading a Class Story *(22–23)*	
Publishing a Class Story *(24–25)*	

Tools and Tips

- **Using the Dictionary,** *pp. H3–H12*
- **Using Technology,** *pp. H21–H30*
- **Writer's Tools,** *pp. H31–H34*
- **Spelling Guide,** *pp. H40–H44*
- **My First Thesaurus,** *pp. H45–H56*

All audiotape recordings are also available on CD.

Getting Started

Additional Resources

Teacher's Resource Book

Posters, Getting Started

Technology Tools

TEACHER'S RESOURCE DISK (for handwriting support)

CD-ROM: *Sunbuddy® Writer
Paint, Write & Play! (published by The Learning Company)
*Type to Learn Jr.™

INTERNET: http://www.eduplace.com/kids/hme/ or http://www.eduplace.com/rdg/hme/

Visit Education Place for these additional support materials and activities:

- student writing models
- graphic organizers

Keeping a Journal

Discuss with children the value of keeping a journal as a way of promoting self-expression and fluency. Encourage children to record their thoughts and ideas in a notebook. Inform students whether the journal will be private or will be reviewed periodically as a way of assisting growth. The following prompts may be useful for generating writing ideas.

Journal Prompts

- Where would you go, if you could go anywhere?
- What is your favorite story? What makes it special?
- What meal do you like best? What meal do you like least?

Meeting Individual Needs

▶ **FOR SPECIAL NEEDS/INCLUSION:** *Houghton Mifflin English* Audiotape

▶ **FOR STUDENTS ACQUIRING ENGLISH:**
- Notes and activities are included in this Teacher's Edition throughout the unit to help you adapt or use pupil book activities with students acquiring English.
- Students acquiring English can listen to the published and student models on audiotape.

▶ **ENRICHMENT:** See *Teacher's Resource Book.*

School-Home Connection

Suggestions for informing or involving family members in classroom activities and learning related to this unit are included in the Teacher's Edition throughout the unit.

Listening, Speaking, and Viewing

Every day you listen, speak, and view things. What do you think these people are listening to, saying, or viewing?

1

Listening, Speaking, and Viewing

Lesson Objective

Children will:

- identify and discuss everyday activities that involve listening, speaking, and viewing

Note to Softbound Users The Grade 2 student book is available in both hardbound and consumable formats. This Teacher's Edition shows the student pages for the hardbound format, but the Teacher's Edition is designed to be used with either format. Except for slight variations in direction lines necessitated by the format, the student book text in both formats is the same. If you are using the consumable format, please check the student book for exact wording of direction lines.

Focus on Instruction

- Direct children's attention to the pictures. Discuss with children what information the people might be sharing in each scene. Then have volunteers tell whether it is being shared through listening, speaking, or viewing.
- Ask children which pictures show informal situations, such as talking with a friend or a family member. Explain that this is when people may use slang or other informal language. However, in school or when they are speaking with people they don't know or with other adults, children should remember to use more formal speech and to follow all the rules of grammar.

Learning Together

Lesson Objectives

Children will:

- identify purposes for listening, speaking, and viewing in daily activities
- cite occasions for using listening, speaking, and viewing to communicate in their lives

Focus on Instruction

Read aloud the first paragraph. Ask volunteers to talk about some of the things they see and do every day. Have them tell how sharing this information might help someone else. (Sample answer: It could help someone learn more about the community; it could help someone learn more about the person who is sharing the information.)

Think and Discuss

Have partners take turns reading aloud the items on the posters. Then discuss some of the similarities children notice among the posters.

Try It Together

Note children's responses on the board or on chart paper. Then work together to match their responses with some of the items on the posters. For example:

Why We Speak
help a newcomer to the school
give facts or directions.

Learning Together

Each one of you is special. You share "pieces of yourself" with others when you **speak**. You learn from others when you **listen** or **view**.

Think and Discuss

These children made posters about why people listen, speak, and view. Read their posters.

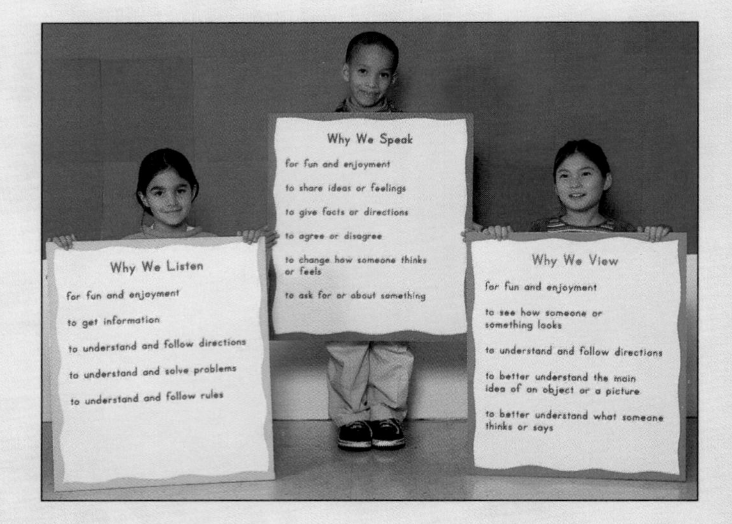

Try It Together

Make a class list of times and places that you have used listening, speaking, and viewing.

Being a Good Listener

Every day you hear sounds, music, and words. Read how listening is more than just hearing!

Think and Discuss

Read the Listening Tips. Which tips are these children following? Most are looking at the speaker, paying attention; some are thinking, one has a question

Listening Tips

- Look at the speaker.
- Pay attention.
- Think about what the speaker is reading or saying.
- Ask questions if you do not understand.

Try It Together

Listen as your teacher reads a story aloud. Then answer the questions.

Being a Good Listener

Lesson Objectives

Children will:

- discuss guidelines for good listening
- use the guidelines when listening to a story

Focus on Instruction

Ask volunteers to name some people whom they listen to every day. Have them tell who they might listen to very closely and who they might not listen to closely and ask them to explain their responses.

Think and Discuss

- Have different volunteers read each item on the Listening Tips list. After each item is read, ask the class to identify children in the picture who are following that tip.
- To extend the activity, read each tip aloud and have children pantomime the action mentioned.

Try It Together

Read this story aloud. Then have volunteers answer the questions that follow.

Pedro has two cats. He named one cat Sneakers and the other cat Socks. Socks has white paws that look just like white socks. Both cats are very playful. They love to chase balls of yarn. Every time Pedro sits down, Sneakers crawls into his lap. Sneakers is so happy that he purrs loudly.

Pedro helps to take good care of his cats. He puts out fresh water every day. He feeds them twice a day. He brushes their fur. Pedro says his cats are just like best friends.

- What kind of pets does Pedro have? (cats)
- What are their names? (Sneakers and Socks)
- What do both cats like to do? (chase balls of yarn)
- How does Pedro take good care of his cats? (He gives them water and food; he brushes their fur.)
- What does Pedro say about his cats? (They are just like best friends.)
- How do you think Socks got his name? (Sample answer: His paws look like white socks.)

Alternatively, children can listen to the story on audiotape.

 The tips on this page are also available as a poster.

Being a Good Speaker

Lesson Objectives

Children will:
- discuss guidelines for good speaking
- use the guidelines when telling a story

Focus on Instruction

- Have volunteers list some of the people they speak to every day. As you write their responses on the board, ask them to tell whether they use language for friends or more formal language.
- After a number of volunteers have contributed responses, compare and discuss the kind of language children seem to use most often every day,

Think and Discuss

- Ask volunteers to read each tip. Then have them act out how they would follow each tip. Ask the class to act out how they might follow the same tip.

Try It Together

- If some children need extra support, have them work with a partner and practice one or two sentences in each mode before they tell their stories to a larger group.

 The tips on this page are also available as a poster.

Being a Good Speaker

When you speak, you want people to hear and think about what you say.

When you speak to friends, you might use different words and sentences than you would use if you were speaking to an adult.

Think and Discuss

Read the Speaking Tips. Which tip is this child following? **She's looking at her listeners.**

Speaking Tips
- Think about what you will say.
- Speak clearly and loudly enough for your audience.
- Use words and sentences that "fit" your listeners.
- Look at your listeners.

Try It Together

Draw a picture of an animal. Think of a short story about it. Tell it to your classmates as if you are talking to friends. Then tell it again as if you are talking to adults.

Having a Conversation

A conversation is a friendly talk. You can talk about many different things.

In a conversation, take turns listening and speaking. Ask or answer questions, share ideas, or tell how you feel.

Think and Discuss

In what ways are these children being good listeners and speakers? They're taking turns. One is telling how he feels and asking a question.

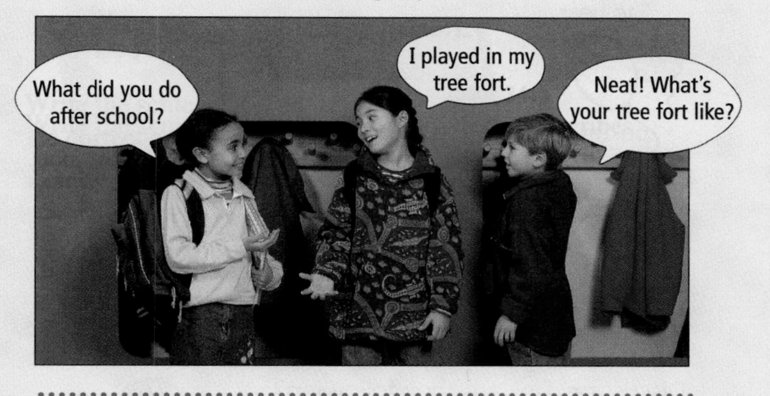

Try It Together

With a group, have a conversation about what each of you did yesterday after school.

Having a Conversation

Lesson Objectives

Children will:

- use listening and speaking guidelines in a conversation

Focus on Instruction

Discuss with children when they might have had a conversation today. Ask volunteers to tell with whom they had a conversation. Then discuss why the guidelines for both listening and speaking are important in a conversation.

Think and Discuss

- Have children share their responses. Then discuss how asking a good question can keep a conversation interesting. Point out that by answering a question, new information is shared and may spark other questions or responses.

Try It Together

- Suggest that one member of each group read aloud the Listening Tips and the Speaking Tips before beginning the conversation.

Having a Discussion

Lesson Objectives

Children will:
- discuss guidelines for having a discussion
- use the guidelines in a group discussion

Focus on Instruction

- Point out that a discussion is like a conversation, in that people are speaking, listening, and sharing ideas. Help them understand that a conversation can change topics often, but a discussion is about one topic.
- Have volunteers read aloud each item in the Discussion Tips. Ask children to tell which tips are also used in conversation. (Sample answer: share ideas; take turn; ask questions)

Think and Discuss

- Help children see that the child who talked about a family picnic is not really keeping to the topic. Explain that while everyone is talking about a picnic, the topic is planning a class picnic.

Having a Discussion

A discussion is a talk in which people share their ideas on one main topic. To have a good discussion, follow these tips.

Discussion Tips

- Share your ideas. They are important!
- Take turns. Wait for others to finish speaking before you begin.
- Speak clearly and loudly enough for everyone to hear.
- Keep to the topic.
- Let others share their ideas. Don't do all the talking.
- Look at the person speaking.
- If you do not agree with someone, say so politely.
- Think about what each person says. Ask questions if you do not understand.

Think and Discuss

Look at the photo on the next page. The children are discussing a class picnic! Which Discussion Tips are they following?

sharing ideas; taking turns; keeping to the topic; letting others share; disagreeing politely; asking questions

Try It Together

With a group, have a discussion about places to go on a class field trip.

Try It Together

- Suggest that one or two members of each group be note-takers and write down some of the group's ideas.
- Circulate among the groups to make sure children are following the Discussion Tips and other listening and speaking guidelines.
- Blackline Master GS–1 provides checklists children can use to assess their speaking and writing skills.

Being a Good Viewer

Lesson Objectives

Children will:
- identify ways in which they learn by viewing
- identify ways to be a good observer

Focus on Instruction

- Have volunteers tell how they use viewing to get information. Discuss things such as bus numbers, restroom signs, and the color of traffic lights. Ask children to share any other ways that come to mind.
- Have volunteers read aloud the Viewing Tips. Discuss each item on the list. Be sure children understand the meanings of *main idea* and *theme*.
- Display a large travel poster and have children look at it for a minute or so. Then place the poster face down. Begin a discussion about what the children saw first, what ideas the picture made them think of, and any other details or thoughts related to the picture. Write children's responses on the board.

Think and Discuss

- Ask volunteers to read aloud each tip one at a time. Then have children identify the people in the picture who are following that particular tip.

Try It Together

- After children complete the activity, ask volunteers to share their responses with the class. Compare and discuss the types of things children saw in their pictures.
- Blackline Master GS–2 provides a checklist children can use to assess their viewing skills.

 The tips on this page are also available as a poster.

Being a Good Viewer

All day long you see pictures and objects. Read how viewing is more than just seeing!

Think and Discuss

Read the Viewing Tips. Which tips are these children following?

looking at whole object; taking a closer look at one part

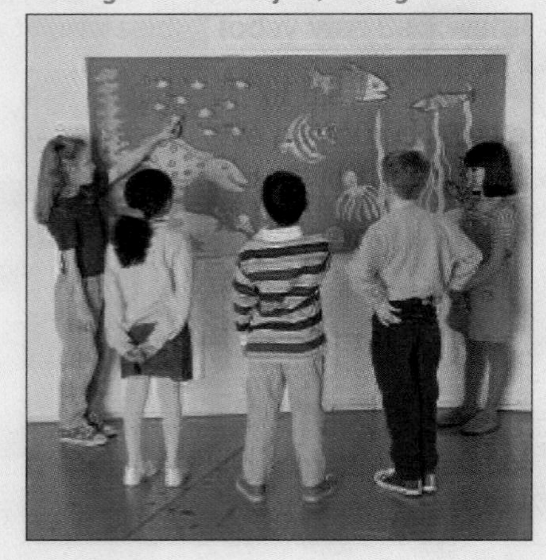

Viewing Tips
- First, look at the whole picture or object.
- Then take a longer, closer look at each part.
- Ask yourself questions.
- Think about the message, main idea, or theme.

Try It Together

View a picture from a magazine. Tell a classmate exactly what you see. Then tell how the picture makes you feel or explain the message you get from the picture.

Viewing: Looking and Thinking

Pictures help you understand what you read. News videos help you understand what you hear. Posters, signs, and displays send messages.

Think and Discuss

How are the parts of this display alike? How are they different? Think about what you already know about its main idea. What message do you think it sends?

They show children with pets; they show different children and animals; sample answer: Love and care for your pets.

Viewing: Looking and Thinking

Lesson Objective

Children will:

- use the guidelines for viewing to find main ideas and messages in visual materials

Focus on Instruction

- Help children understand that sometimes pictures alone can have strong messages. Point out that other times, words and pictures work together to send a strong message or deliver information.
- Discuss such varying viewing opportunities as picture books, photos with captions, and story illustrations accompanied by text. Talk about ways in which pictures work alone effectively and how they work with words in these examples.

Think and Discuss

- Before children begin the activity, review the Viewing Tips on page 8.

Viewing: Looking and Thinking *continued*

Focus on Instruction

- Ask children how else Lynn could have shared this information with her classmates. Help them see that she could have written the information and then read it aloud to the class. Have volunteers tell which guidelines children might use if Lynn had chosen this method. (listening tips)

Try It Together

- If children need extra support, you can do this as a whole-class activity. Be sure children recognize that all the pictures show food, but that all the foods are different. Help them see that the topic is about a balanced, healthful diet.

Viewing continued

Lynn learned about something that she wanted to share with her classmates. She made a poster with pictures to help her classmates understand it.

Try It Together

With a classmate, view Lynn's poster. What is the same in each picture? What is different? What is the main idea of the poster? How do Lynn's pictures help her classmates understand what she wrote?

Each shows food; each shows different kinds of food; eat different kinds of food every day; they can see what she means

The Writing Process

Every day children and adults write at home, in school, at work, and at play! Look at these pictures. What do you think these people are writing?

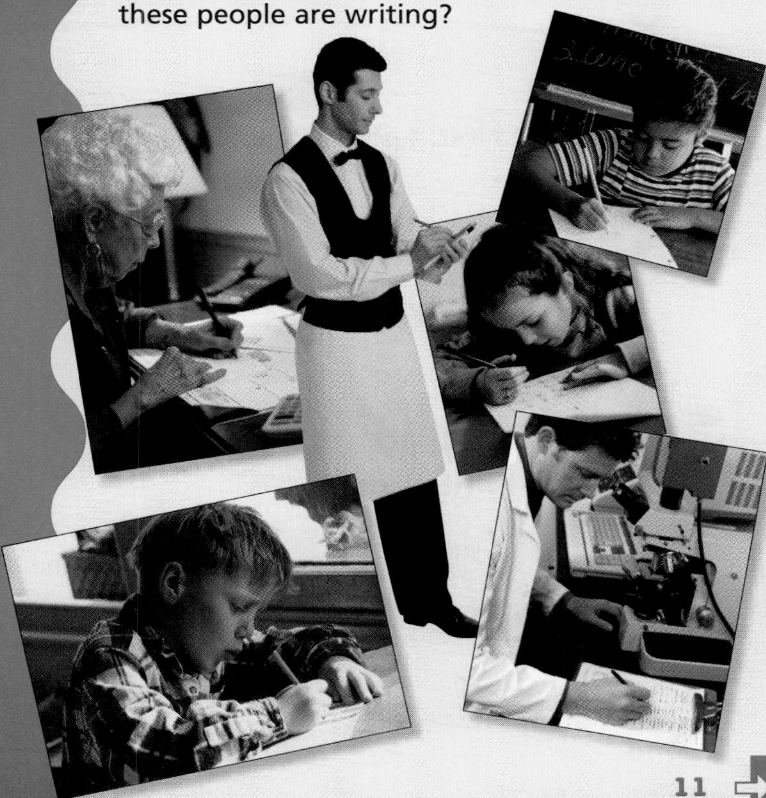

11

The Writing Process

Lesson Objective

Children will:
- identify and discuss everyday activities that involve writing

Focus on Instruction

- Ask children what kind of writing each picture shows. (Sample answers: paper for a class assignment, such as a report or a story; order in a restaurant; notes for a job assignment; letter; homework; writing for fun at home)
- Explain to children that people write for different purposes and that not all writing activities require the same amount of attention to detail. Explain that when they are writing just for themselves, such as when they write lists or notes to themselves, they do not need to be as exact or to check for spelling, capitalization, punctuation, or other rules because they know what they mean.
- Explain that when they are doing more formal writing, such as letters, instructions for other people to follow, or assignments in school, children need to be sure that their writing is clear and correct.

Looking Ahead Tell children that in this section they will learn how to use a series of steps called the writing process. Using the writing process will help them make their papers clear and correct so that other people can understand and enjoy what they have written.

What Is the Writing Process?

Lesson Objective

Children will:
- discuss the steps of the writing process

Focus on Instruction

- Call children's attention to the cartoon dinosaur, W.R. Explain that W.R. will give them writing tips and point out important things to remember as they learn to write.
- Tell children that they are going to look at pictures that model a story that W.R. wrote, using the writing process. Explain that the writing process is a step-by-step writing plan that professional writers use when they write too. Even though these writers know all about writing, they don't usually write what they have to say perfectly the first time. They go back and reread it and work through it several, sometimes many, times before they are happy with it. Explain to children that the writing process will help them know when it is time to think about different parts of writing.
- Discuss with children the graphics that model each stage of the writing process.

  Prewriting Explain that in this first stage, a writer chooses what to write about and lists details about that topic. Point out that one way to think about and list details is in a word web like the one in the picture. Ask children to look at the web to see what topic W.R. chose. (class visit by a police officer)

  Drafting Ask children what the model shows. (a sentence about the police officer's visit) Have a volunteer read the sentence aloud. Have children look back to the details in the web and compare those details with the ones in the Drafting model. Ask how they are alike or different. (The details are the same but now they are written as a complete sentence.) Explain that in this second stage, W.R. wrote a sentence, using the details he listed in Prewriting.

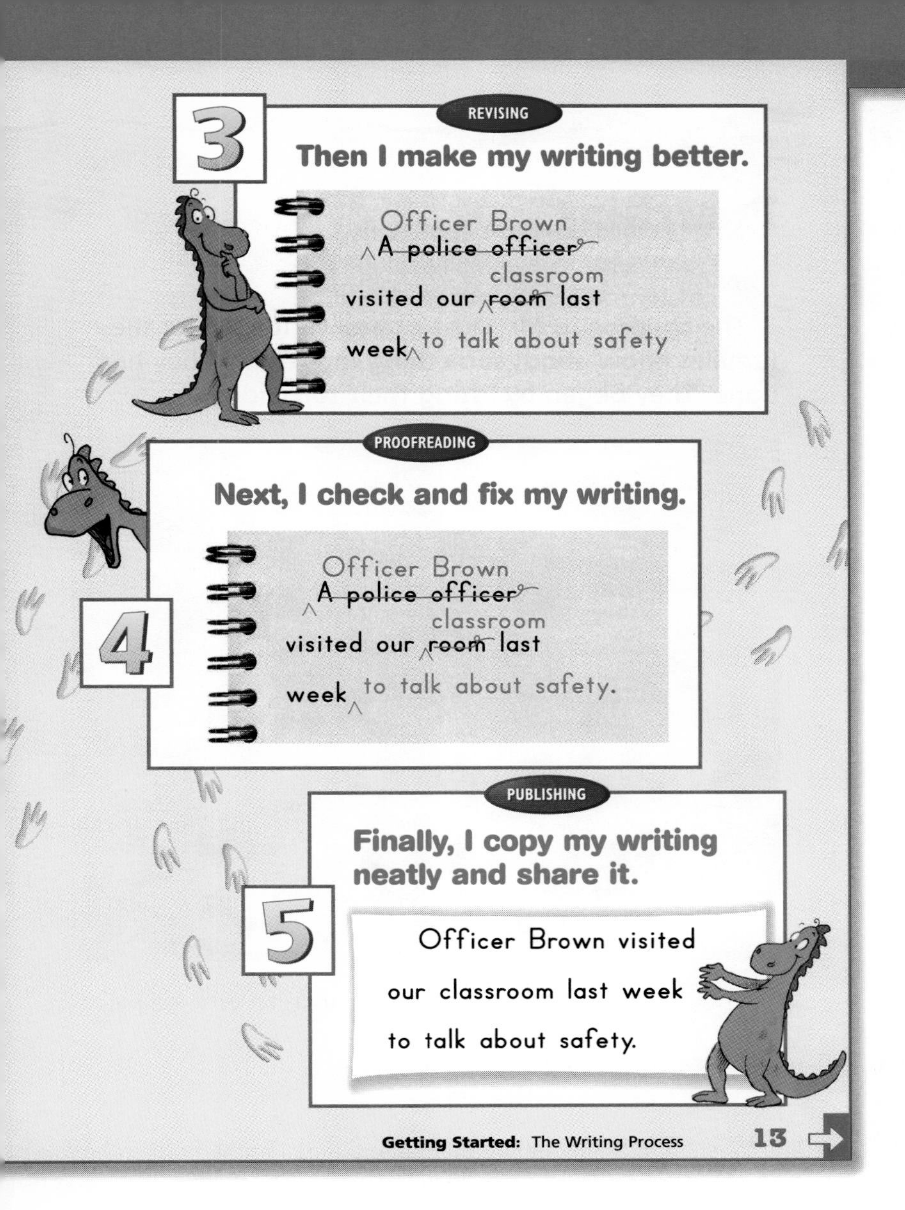

Revising Ask children what the model shows. (changes made to the sentence shown in the drafting stage) Explain that in this third stage, the writer often makes changes to make the writing clearer. Ask children what changes W.R, made. (He named the police officer; he used a more exact noun, *classroom;* he added facts that told what Officer Brown talked about.) Explain the use of the caret (to add) and the delete mark (to take out).

Proofreading Ask children what new changes in red that the model shows. (A period was added after *safety.*) Explain that in this fourth stage, the writer checks for and corrects any mistakes in using capital letters, end marks or other punctuation marks, spelling, or incorrect words. Ask children how W.R. made his correction. (He wrote in a period.)

Publishing Ask children what the model shows. (a neat final copy of W.R.'s story) Have a volunteer read aloud the sentence. Explain that after making all the changes and corrections, a writer makes a clean final copy to share with someone else, or the **audience.** Ask children who will be W.R.'s audience. (his class) Ask how W.R. might share his story. (Sample answers: He might read it aloud. He might put it a special place for his classmates to read on their own.)

Looking Ahead Tell children that they will read about how one class used the writing process to write a class story and that they will also follow these steps to write their own class story.

These pages are available as posters.

FOR STUDENTS ACQUIRING ENGLISH

Most children who are acquiring English will think of writing as a very formal process. In their previous school experience, they may have been assigned topics for compositions that were graded on the first attempt. To emphasize that the writing process is a series of *choices* that writers make in order to share ideas, review with students the numbered stages of the writing process, stressing the idea of steps, not end product.

Prewriting

Choosing a Topic for a Class Story

Lesson Objectives

Children will:
- list topics for a class story
- select a topic to write about

Focus on Instruction

- Remind children that the first stage of the writing process is called prewriting. Ask children if anyone remembers the first thing to do during prewriting. (choose a topic)
- Have volunteers read aloud page 14. Ask children who would be reading the class story that Mr. Ortiz's class was going to write. (their families) Explain that the children's families are their audience.
- Ask children why Mr. Ortiz's class wanted to write a class story. (They wanted to let their families know about something interesting they had done.) Explain that this is their **purpose,** or reason, for writing. Mr. Ortiz's class wanted to inform their families about something they had done.
- Explain to children that a writer always needs to think about his or her audience and purpose when writing.

Focus on the Model

- Have volunteers read aloud the topics in the model. Ask children what four topics Mr. Ortiz's class thought of. (visit from the fire department, bicycle and bus safety, trip to the library, visit from the school nurse)
- Ask why Mr. Ortiz made the list of topics. (to help the children remember and think about their ideas) Ask how Mr. Ortiz showed which topic the class decided to write about. (He circled it.)

Prewriting

Choosing a Topic for a Class Story

The children in Mr. Ortiz's class wanted to let their families know about something interesting they had done. They began by listing their topic ideas.

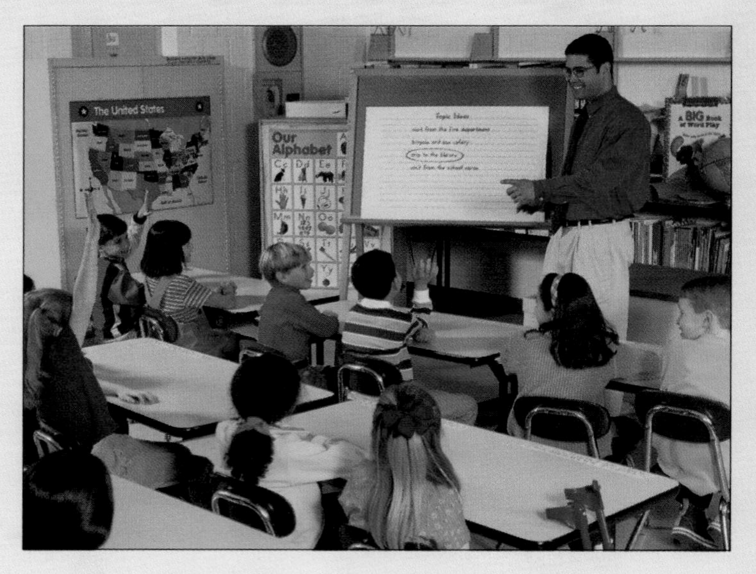

They discussed the topics and chose to write about their trip to the library.

Topic Ideas

visit from the fire department

bicycle and bus safety

trip to the library

visit from the school nurse

Choose Your Topic

1. **Write** something that your class has done that you would like to write about.
2. **Make** a class list of everyone's ideas. Discuss the ideas with your class.
3. **Choose** one idea to write about as a whole class.
4. **Copy** and complete these sentences. Name your topic and audience.

   We will write about _____.

   _____ will read or hear our story.

Choose Your Topic

Help with Choosing a Topic

As a group, have children think about experiences they have shared as a class. If they have difficulty, suggest these categories:

- class visitors
- school assemblies
- classroom activities
- field trips
- a funny or unusual school event

- Accept and list all ideas for a class story. List them on the chalkboard, on an overhead transparency, or on chart paper. Topics that are not suitable may spark other ideas that will make an interesting story.
- Emphasize that choosing an idea is a very important part of writing a story. If an idea is not interesting, the class will not enjoy writing about it.
- Select five topics that would make the best stories. Then write the three questions shown in W.R.'s thought balloon on the board or a transparency. For each topic, guide the class through the questions. For every affirmative answer, put a check mark beside that topic. When children are finished, each topic will have one, two, three, or no check marks beside it. Encourage discussion and summarize children's conclusions about each story idea. If children are unable to agree on a topic, you could have them vote. Have a volunteer circle the chosen topic.
- Write the sentences to be completed in step 4 below the chosen topic. Have children fill in their audience and purpose.

Exploring a Topic for a Class Story

Lesson Objectives

Children will:

- discuss their story topic
- list details for their story
- make a word web

Focus on Instruction

Have a volunteer read the introductory paragraph aloud.

Focus on the Model

- Ask children to look at the model and tell what Mr. Ortiz's class used to help them explore their topic. (a word web) Explain that a word web is a tool that helps writers to think of details about their topics.
- To help children understand how a word web is structured, have them find the words circled in red. *(trip to library)* Remind them that this is the topic that Mr. Ortiz's class is going to write about.
- Then have them find the words circled in purple. Explain that these are the parts about the trip to the library that the class will tell about. Last, have children find the words circled in yellow. Point out that these words have lines connecting them to words circled in purple. Explain that the words circled in yellow give details about the words circled in purple. Tell children that they can keep adding words to tell more details.

Explore Your Class Story Topic

- Help children to explore their topic and make a word web. Tell them to think about what their audience would like to know about their experience. To help them generate details about their topic, ask questions that begin with *who, what, where, when, why,* and *how.* Examples:

  What happened?

  What did we see?

  What did we do?

  Who was there?

  What was the person's name?

  When did this happen?

  Record their responses in a word web on the chalkboard, on an overhead transparency, or on chart paper.
- Ask questions to elicit the major ideas about the topic, then ask questions about each of those ideas to generate more and more specific details. Continue asking questions to elicit details until you think you have enough information for children to write an interesting story.
- Keep the word web for use in the next lesson.

Prewriting continued

Exploring a Topic for a Class Story

The children thought about their trip to the library. Then they used a word web to explore their topic.

Learning from a Model

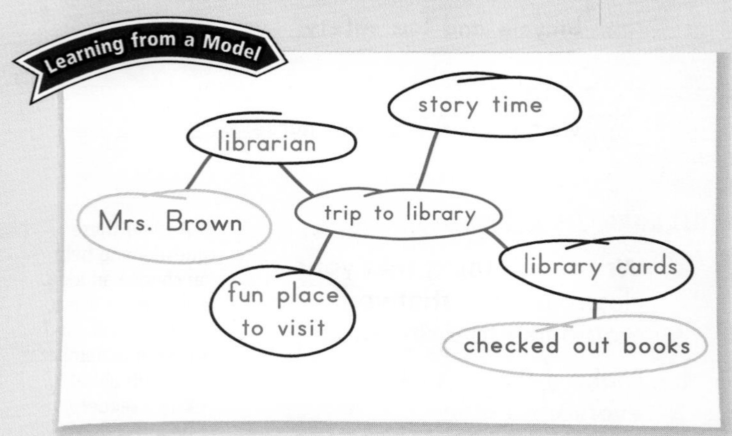

Explore Your Class Story Topic

1. **Explore** your topic with your class.
2. **Tell** your teacher important details that should be included in your story. Your teacher will record your details in a word web.

FOR STUDENTS ACQUIRING ENGLISH

Tell students there are many ways to think about subjects to write about. Explain that the word web in their book is one way to explore topics. Draw a simple word web on the board, emphasizing the importance of the central circle by drawing over its outline with colored chalk. Refer students to the web shown in their books and explain that the words in the smaller circles connect to the main circle or topic but are not as important as the words in the central circle.

Organizing Details for a Class Story

The children looked at their word web. Then they told Mr. Ortiz what happened on their trip in the order that it happened. He wrote the details in a Sequence Chart.

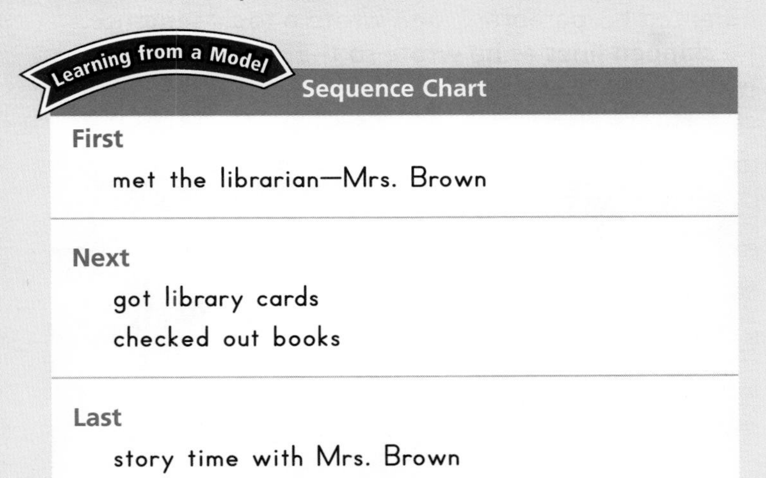

Organize Your Details

1. **Discuss** your topic and details from your word web.
2. **Help** your teacher make a Sequence Chart.

FOR STUDENTS ACQUIRING ENGLISH

Have students identify which words from the word web appear again in the Sequence Chart (almost all). Ask what is different about the words as they appear in the word web and the words in the chart. (The chart shows the ideas in order or **sequence.**) Have children name the order words in the chart (*First, Next, Last*).

Organizing Details

Lesson Objectives

Children will:
- discuss their topic and details
- make a Sequence Chart to organize the details

Focus on Instruction

- Have a volunteer read aloud the first paragraph. Ask children in what order Mr. Ortiz's class decided to tell the details about their trip to the library. (in the order they happened) Ask what would happen if they told the details in a mixed-up order. (Their families would not be able to follow the story as well. They might even be confused about what happened.)
- Summarize that Mr. Ortiz's class organized their details in an order that made sense. They decided what they would tell first, next, and last.

Focus on the Model

- Discuss the Sequence Chart with children. Ask what are the three parts of the chart. (First, Next, Last)
- Ask children what detail Mr. Ortiz's class put in the first part. *(met the librarian—Mrs. Brown).* Then ask what details the class put in the next part *(got library cards, checked out books)* and the last part *(story time with Mrs. Brown).*

Organize Your Details

- Display the word web from the previous lesson.
- Discuss with children the order in which they should present the details of their story. Explain that for a story, telling events in the order they happened is usually a good way to organize them. Number the major parts of the web in the order that they will be presented in the story.
- Create a Sequence Chart on the chalkboard, on an overhead transparency, or on chart paper. Have volunteers write the details from the word web in the appropriate section of the Sequence Chart.
- Summarize by telling children that they have done a very good job of getting ready to write their class story. They have thought of a topic, listed interesting details about it, and have put those details in order. Now they are ready to write their story.
- Keep the Sequence Chart for the next lesson.

Drafting

Lesson Objectives

Children will:

- write a topic sentence to begin their class story
- write a working draft of their story

Focus on Instruction

- Explain to children that they are now ready to write their class story and that this is the second stage of the writing process, drafting.
- Have a volunteer read aloud the paragraph on page 18. Explain that a working draft is their first try at writing the story. Writers just try to get their ideas on paper during the drafting stage. Then they work with that paper to make it clearer and more interesting for their audience.

Focus on the Model

- Ask a volunteer to read the model aloud.
- Ask children which line is indented and how they know. (the first; starts in a few spaces)
- Ask children why they think Mr. Ortiz crossed out some words. (because the children changed their mind about what to say) Explain that since this is a working draft, not a final copy, he didn't bother to start over again. Reinforce that it is OK for a working draft to be a little messy.

Reading As a Writer

Reread the first sentence. Ask children what they found out about the story. (The class went to the library, and they had a great time.) Explain that the beginning sentence should introduce the topic. It should also tell the main idea of the piece of writing. Tell children that the topic for this story is the class's visit to the library and that the main idea is that the children had a great time.

Drafting

Drafting a Class Story

Mr. Ortiz wrote the working draft of the class story, as the children told him what to write. Mr. Ortiz indented his paragraph and wrote a topic sentence. He skipped lines as he wrote so that the class could make changes later.

Learning from a Model

Our class had a great time when we visited the library! First, we met the librarian. Her name is Mrs. Brown. Next, she gave each of us a library card. ~~We read~~ Then we checked out books. ~~Finally~~ Before we left, Mrs. Brown read us a story. Our library is a fun place to visit.

Draft Your Class Story

1. **Write** a topic sentence that makes a good beginning for your class story.
2. **Share** your sentence. As a class, choose one topic sentence to begin your class story.
3. **Use** the details in your Sequence Chart to tell your story to your teacher. Your teacher will write the working draft. You can fix mistakes and make changes later.

Drafting Your Class Story

- Display the Sequence Chart from the last lesson.
- Have children write some topic sentences on their own, or work with the class to generate possibilities. Ask students what the topic is for their class story. Ask them what is the one big, or main, idea of their story. Then tell them to write a sentence that states the topic and that main idea. Explain that there is no one perfect sentence, that there will always be more than one good way to begin a story or piece of writing.
- Have children use the details in their Sequence Chart to draft their story. Write the draft on the chalkboard, on an overhead transparency, or on chart paper. **Note:** Skip lines to leave room for revisions in the next lesson.
- As you write, make some wording suggestions, write them, and then cross them out, explaining that you changed your mind.

Note About Proofreading

There are several options for modeling proofreading in the forthcoming Proofreading stage.

- One option is to include a few simple mistakes in capitalization, punctuation, usage, or spelling in this draft of the class story so that there will be some errors to correct at the proofreading stage. To do this, ask children to tell you where to put capital letters and punctuation marks as they suggest the sentences for the story or to write some of the sentences themselves. They will undoubtedly make some mistakes! You could also ask them to spell some hard words, telling them to spell the words as best they can for now and that they can check the spellings later.
- For other options, see Teacher's Edition page 23.

- Save the draft for the next lesson.

Revising

Lesson Objectives

Children will:
- list changes to improve their class story
- discuss their suggested changes
- decide which revisions to make and revise the story

Focus on Instruction

- Explain to children that the revising stage is the time to make their writing say what they want it to say. Explain that *revise* means "to change." They should think about words or sentences to add or change that would make their class story clearer and more interesting for their audience.
- To explain the process of revising, show children a lump of clay. Ask what they would need to do to mold it into an animal. (Samples: Take some clay away, add more clay, and shape the clay better.) Explain that just as they add or take away bits of clay to make a better animal, writers add and cross out ideas to make a clearer, more interesting story.
- Have a volunteer read aloud the introductory paragraph.

Focus on the Model

- Read aloud the model with the revisions.
- Point out that this model shows the working draft of Mr. Ortiz's class story plus some revisions his class made. Explain that the words in blue show their revisions.
- Write a caret on the chalkboard and introduce the term *caret.* Have children find that mark in the model and tell what it is used for. (to show where to add new words)
- Ask children why was it a good idea for Mr. Ortiz to skip lines when he wrote his class's story. (It left room for revisions.)

Revising

Revising a Class Story

The children read their working draft aloud. They talked about how to make it clearer and more interesting for their families. Then the class decided on some changes to make. Mr. Ortiz made the changes to the working draft.

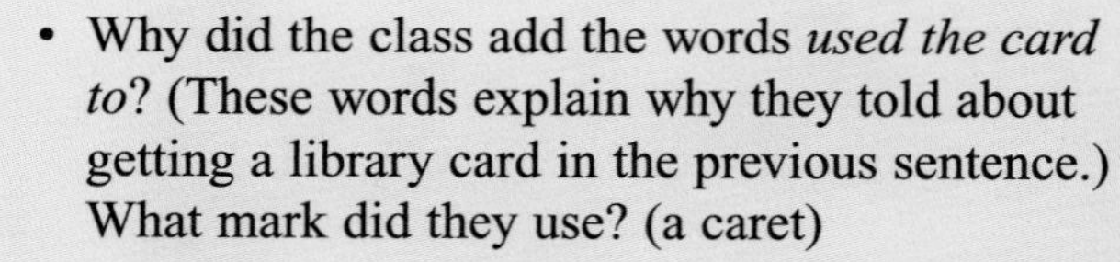

Reading As a Writer

Ask children these questions about the model.

- Why did the class add the words *used the card to*? (These words explain why they told about getting a library card in the previous sentence.) What mark did they use? (a caret)
- Why did they add the sentence *It was called Amos and Boris*? (It tells exactly which story the librarian read.) Explain that naming the story adds details and tells their audience more about what happened.
- Is there anything else you would have wanted to know about this story? What other details could the class have added? (Answers will vary.)

Our class had a great time when we visited the library! First, we met the librarian. Her name is Mrs. Brown. Next, she gave each of us a library card. ~~We read~~ Then we ^used the card to^ check~~ed~~ out books. ~~Finally~~ Before we left, Mrs. Brown read us a story. ^It was called Amos and Boris.^ Our library is a fun place to visit.

Revise Your Class Story

1. **Read** your class story aloud.
2. **Write** two things that you would like to change to make the story better.
3. **Talk** with your class about changes you think would make the story better. Together, decide which changes to make.
4. **Help** your teacher revise your class story.

Revise Your Class Story

- Display the working draft of your class's story from the previous lesson.
- Have children work independently, or work with them as a class to list changes to improve their class story. Ask these questions to focus their thinking.

Revising Questions

- What else would my audience want to know?
- What other details could we add to tell who, what, where, when, why, or how?
- Where do we need to add words such as *first, next,* or *last* to tell when things happened?
- Do we need a more interesting beginning?
- Do we need an ending?
- Are there any sentences that don't keep to the topic that should come out?

- Write children's suggestions on the chalkboard or on an overhead transparency but not in the draft. After five or six suggestions, discuss which ones would make the story clearer or more interesting for their audience. If someone suggests correcting a mistake, explain that they should focus for now on saying what they want to say.
- If children suggest adding events that do not keep to their topic, explain that these are good ideas but that they do not belong in this story.
- If children suggest adding irrelevant details, help them think of interesting ones by asking focused questions, such as " What did __________ look like?," "What was special about __________?," or "What happened after that?"
- Identify vague or overused verbs, nouns, or adjectives in the story, and help children think of more exact and vivid replacements. Direct their attention to My First Thesaurus in the Tools and Tips at the back of this book as a place to find exact words.
- Have volunteers make the desired revisions to the draft, using carets and delete marks.
- Save the revised story for the next lesson.

Proofreading

Lesson Objectives

Children will:

- make their own copies of the class story
- proofread their copies

Focus on Instruction

- Tell children that they revised their class story so that it describes their experience clearly and in an interesting way. Now it is time to check for mistakes. Explain that to proofread means to check that they used and spelled all words correctly and used capital letters, end marks, and other punctuation marks correctly.
- Explain that writers use proofreading marks to show how to fix their mistakes. Write the following sentences, including the errors, on the chalkboard or an overhead transparency. Model how to use proofreading marks to make the corrections. Use the terms *caret, delete mark,* and *slash mark.*

  Mr. smith lives next door.
  (Use three underlines to show that the *s* on *smith* should be a capital letter.)

  Jerry got a new Puppy.
  (Use a slash mark to show that the *P* on *Puppy* should be a small letter.)

  Did you see my shoe?
  (Insert *blue* before *shoe* with a caret.)

  Do you hav a pen?
  (Cross out *hav* with a delete mark.
  Write *have* above it.)

- Have a volunteer read the introductory paragraph aloud.

Focus on the Model

- Explain that this model is the working draft with both the revisions and the proofreading corrections on it. The blue revisions are the same ones shown in the previous lesson. The red changes are proofreading corrections. Point out that working drafts often look a little messy after all the changes and corrections have been made but that this is all right as long as the writer can read them to make a final copy.
- Suggest to children that it is helpful to mark proofreading corrections with a pen or a pencil that is a different color from the one used for revisions. This will help them see the different kinds of changes more easily.

Proofreading

Proofreading a Class Story

Each child in Mr. Ortiz's class copied the revised class story. Then the children used proofreading marks to fix mistakes. Look at Nita's proofread story.

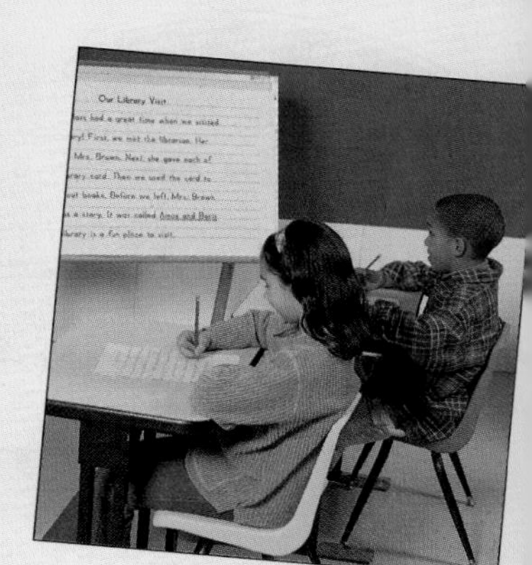

Learning from a Model

Our class had a great time when we visited the library! First, we met the librarian. Her name is Mrs. brown. Next, she gave each of us a library card. Then we used the card to check out ~~boks~~ books. Before we left, Mrs. Brown read us a story. It was called Amos and Boris. Our Library is a fun place to visit.

Reading As a Writer

Ask children these questions about the model. You can have them refer to the Proofreading Marks box on the next page.

- Why are there three underlines under the *b* in *brown* in the third sentence? (They show that the *b* should be a capital letter.)
- Which word did Nita not spell correctly? (*books*) How did she correct it? (She used a delete mark to cross out the wrong spelling and wrote the correct one above it.)
- What mark is through the *L* in *Library* in the last sentence? (a slash mark) What does that mark mean? (The *L* should be a small letter.)

Proofread Your Class Story

1. **Write** your own copy of your class story.
2. **Proofread** your class story. Use the Proofreading Checklist and Proofreading Marks.

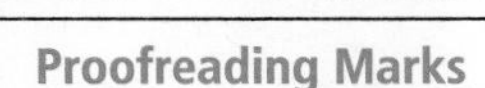

Proofreading Checklist

- Each sentence begins with a capital letter.
- Each sentence ends with the correct mark.
- Each word is spelled correctly.

Point to each word as you proofread.

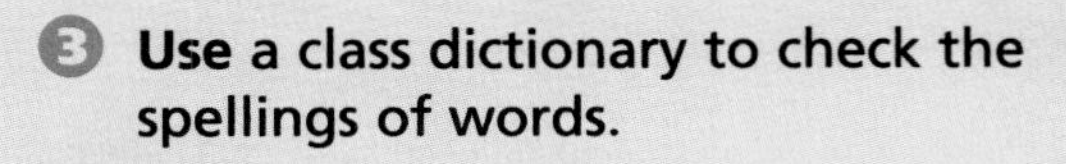

Proofreading Marks

∧ Add	≡ Capital letter
Delete	/ Small letter
¶ Indent for new paragraph	

3. **Use** a class dictionary to check the spellings of words.

See the Spelling Guide on page H40.

Proofread Your Class Story

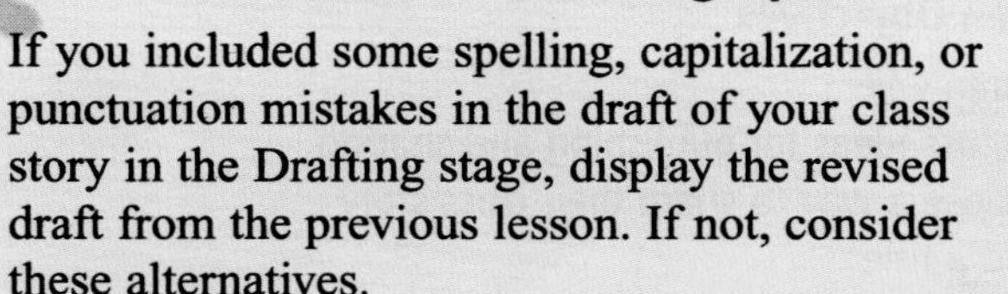

Note About Proofreading Options

If you included some spelling, capitalization, or punctuation mistakes in the draft of your class story in the Drafting stage, display the revised draft from the previous lesson. If not, consider these alternatives.

1. Copy the revised draft on the chalkboard, on an overhead transparency, or on chart paper. Include some simple capitalization and punctuation mistakes that your students would know how to correct. Also misspell a few words that your students can spell correctly or other words that they could check in a dictionary. Have the class proofread the story and mark the corrections.
2. Have each child copy the class story on a sheet of paper and proofread it.

- Review and discuss the Proofreading Checklist with children. Then reread the class story (or their own copies) with children, looking for one kind of mistake at a time. When a mistake is found, have children tell you which proofreading mark to use, or ask a volunteer to make the correction with the appropriate mark.
- Help children find the spellings of misspelled words in a class dictionary or other classroom resources.

Publishing

Lesson Objectives

Children will:

- discuss ideas for publishing and sharing
- choose a way to share their class story
- add a title
- reflect on their writing experience

Focus on Instruction

- Have a volunteer read the introductory paragraph. Discuss different ways to publish or share writing, such as illustrated papers or booklets, reading aloud, recording on audiotape, dramatizing, and making a poster.
- Explain that the first step for publishing or sharing is to make a neat, corrected final copy. Point out that it would be too hard for a writer's audience to read a draft with all its changes. Explain that making a neat, correct final copy shows respect for their readers.
- Explain that making the final copy involves copying the first draft but leaving out parts that have been crossed out and incorporating new words and sentences; making any wording changes; and correcting all mistakes.

Publish Your Class Story

- Discuss with children which publishing and sharing ideas would work for their audience.
- Ask children to think of some book, story, or movie titles and to tell why they are good titles. (Sample answers: The title lets the reader know what the writing or movie is about, uses only a few words, or arouses curiosity in some way.)
- Decide how your class will publish and share their story. Consider these options:
  1. Make a final copy on chart or poster paper, and have the class illustrate it. They could post it for their audience to see or, if the audience is one person, present it to the audience.
  2. Type the class story and duplicate individual copies for each child. They can add their own illustrations.
  3. If children made individual copies for proofreading, have them make their own final copies if they are willing to copy them again. If not, type and duplicate individual copies.

Publishing

Publishing a Class Story

Mr. Ortiz's class thought of a good way to publish the class story for their families. Mr. Ortiz made a neat final copy, and the children drew pictures to go with it. They displayed them for Parents Night.

FOR STUDENTS ACQUIRING ENGLISH

Emphasize that there are many ways to "publish." Brainstorm with students other ways to share the story about the class visit to the library (making a picture book with simple captions; assigning roles and acting out a simple version of the event; designing a poster about story time; reading aloud the final draft to classmates or parents).

Publish Your Class Story

1. **Talk** with your class about different ways to share your story.
2. **Choose** a special way to share your class story with your audience.
3. **Make** a neat final copy of your class story. Be sure you wrote your letters correctly and used good spacing.
4. **Write** an interesting title. Be sure to begin the first, last, and each important word with a capital letter.

Reflect

Together, talk about these questions.

- What was easy about writing this class story?
- What was hard?
- What did you learn about the writing process?

- If you want one final class copy, you or an aide may want to make the copy to be sure it is correct.
- If children make their own final copies, remind them to form their letters correctly, use correct letter and word spacing, and use margins on their papers. Check that they hold their pencils correctly, put their papers in the correct position, and use correct posture. For handwriting instruction and practice, use the handwriting masters on the Teacher's Resource Disk.

SCHOOL-HOME CONNECTION
Post children's copies of their class stories for Parents Night, or send final copies home with children to read aloud to their families.

Reflect

Tell children that one thing to do that will help them become better writers is to reflect on, or think about, what they learned about writing after they complete their papers. Discuss the questions for reflection shown in the pupil book.

Creating a Writing Portfolio

Consider having each child create a writing portfolio, a selective collection of the child's writing compiled over the school year. The writing portfolio can be used to determine writing strengths and weaknesses, to monitor growth, to inform instruction, and to set goals. It should *not* be a place to store all of the child's writing.

- **Selection:** A paper might be selected because it is generally noteworthy, a good example of a particular aspect of writing, an example of a particular kind of writing, representative work at a particular point in the school year, or a typical example of the child's work.
- **Appearance and format:** The portfolio can be an expandable file folder, or it can be more elaborate, such as a three-ring binder with multiple sections. If the portfolio will be passed on to next year's teacher, it may include a table of contents that lists the papers in the order they were written or groups them by type or special quality, such as good examples of word choice.
- **Use:** Children select papers for their portfolios, often completing a form for each paper, explaining why they chose it. Children should periodically review their portfolios to determine strengths and weaknesses and to set goals as writers.

Unit 1 Planning Guide

The Sentence

2 $\frac{1}{2}$ weeks

		Checkup (PE)	Extra Practice (PE)	Graphic Organizer (BLM)	Writing Wrap-Up (BLM)	More Practice (TE)	Workbook Plus	Reteaching Workbook	Students Acquiring English Practice Book
1	What Is a Sentence? *(27–28)*	48	53	1–1	1–3	53	1–2	1	1–2
2	Naming Part *(29–30)*	48	54	1–1	1–3	54	3–4	2	3–4
3	Action Part *(31–32)*	48	55	1–1	1–3	55	5–6	3	5–6
4	Is It a Sentence? *(33–34)*	48	56	1–1	1–3	56	7–8	4	7–8
	Revising Strategies: Sentence Fluency Writing Complete Sentences *(35–36)*						9–10	5–6	
5	Telling Sentences *(37–38)*	49	57	1–2	1–4	57	11–12	7	9–10
6	Questions *(39–40)*	49	58	1–2	1–4	58	13–14	8	11–12
7	Which Kind of Sentence? *(41–42)*	49	59		1–4	59	15–16	9	13–14
8	Commands *(43–44)*	49	60	1–2	1–4	60	17–18	10	15–16
9	Exclamations *(45–46)*	49	61	1–2	1–4	61	19–20	11	17–18
	Enrichment *(47)*								
	Test Practice *(51–52)*								19–20

Tools and Tips

- **Grammar Glossary,** *pp. H35–H39*

School-Home Connection

Suggestions for informing or involving family members in classroom activities and learning related to this unit are included in the Teacher's Edition throughout the unit.

Meeting Individual Needs

- **FOR SPECIAL NEEDS/INCLUSION:** *Houghton Mifflin English* Audiotape See also Reteaching.
- **FOR STUDENTS ACQUIRING ENGLISH:**
  - Notes and activities are included in this Teacher's Edition throughout the unit to help you adapt or use pupil book activities with students acquiring English.
  - Additional support is available for students at various stages of English proficiency: **Beginning/Preproduction, Early Production/Speech Emergence,** and **Intermediate/ Advanced**. See Students Acquiring English Practice Book.
  - Students can listen to the Try It Out activities on audiotape. 
- **ENRICHMENT:** *p. 47*

All audiotape recordings are also available on CD.

Daily Language Practice

Each sentence or group of words includes one error based on skills taught in this Grammar unit. Each day write one item on the chalkboard. Have children find the error and write the sentence correctly on a sheet of paper. To make the activity easier, identify the kind of error.

1. The gray pony. Gallops. Sample: The gray pony gallops. **(complete sentences)**
2. The duck swims toward the boat Sample: The duck swims toward the boat. **(end punctuation/ telling sentences)**
3. The hungry baby bird. Chirps for food. Sample: The hungry baby bird chirps for food. **(complete sentences)**
4. Squeaks and runs. Sample: The little mouse squeaks and runs. **(complete sentences)**
5. The dog chews the bone The dog chews the bone. **(end punctuation/telling sentences)**
6. How many days are in a year How many days are in a year? **(end punctuation/questions)**
7. What city is the capital of your country. What city is the capital of your country? **(end punctuation/questions)**
8. return the books to the library. Return the books to the library. **(capitalization)**
9. The soup is boiling over? The soup is boiling over! **(end punctuation/exclamations)**
10. someone is knocking at the back door. Sample: Someone is knocking at the back door. **(capitalization)**

Additional Resources

Workbook Plus, Unit 1
Reteaching Workbook, Unit 1
Students Acquiring English Practice Book, Unit 1
Teacher's Resource Book
Audiotapes

Technology Tools

TEACHER'S RESOURCE DISK (for handwriting support)
INTERNET: http://www.eduplace.com/kids/hme/ or http://www.eduplace.com/rdg/hme/
Visit Education Place for an interactive quiz.

Assessment

Test Booklet, Unit 1

Keeping a Journal

Discuss with children the value of keeping a journal as a way of promoting self-expression and fluency. Encourage children to record their thoughts and ideas in a notebook. Inform students whether the journal will be private or will be reviewed periodically as a way of assisting growth. The following prompts may be useful for generating writing ideas.

Journal Prompts

- What kind of decorations would you plan for the table at a birthday party?
- Where do you like to sit when you ride in a bus?
- Do you have a favorite ice cream flavor? Why do you like that flavor?

Introducing the Unit

Using the Photograph

- Have children look at the photograph. Ask a volunteer to read the caption. What animals are in the photograph? (two polar bears) Discuss with children where they think this might be taking place. (near the North Pole, where polar bears live, in a cold place) Write responses in complete sentences on the board.
- Have children tell what happens in the photograph, for example, "The two bears play." Point out that the bears seem to be playfully hugging one another and suggest, "The two bears are together." Write this sentence on the board above the previous responses.
- Point out that each response on the board is a sentence and that a sentence tells what someone or something did or does. Briefly explain that a sentence has two parts. The naming part of a sentence tells who or what did or does something. The action part of a sentence tells what the naming part did or does.

Grammar Song

See Blackline Master G-1 for a song to help children remember the concepts and rules taught in this unit.

Independent Writing

Children can benefit by having time each day or several times a week to write in their journals or do self-selected writing activities. Remind children to think about purpose and audience and choose an appropriate format for both.

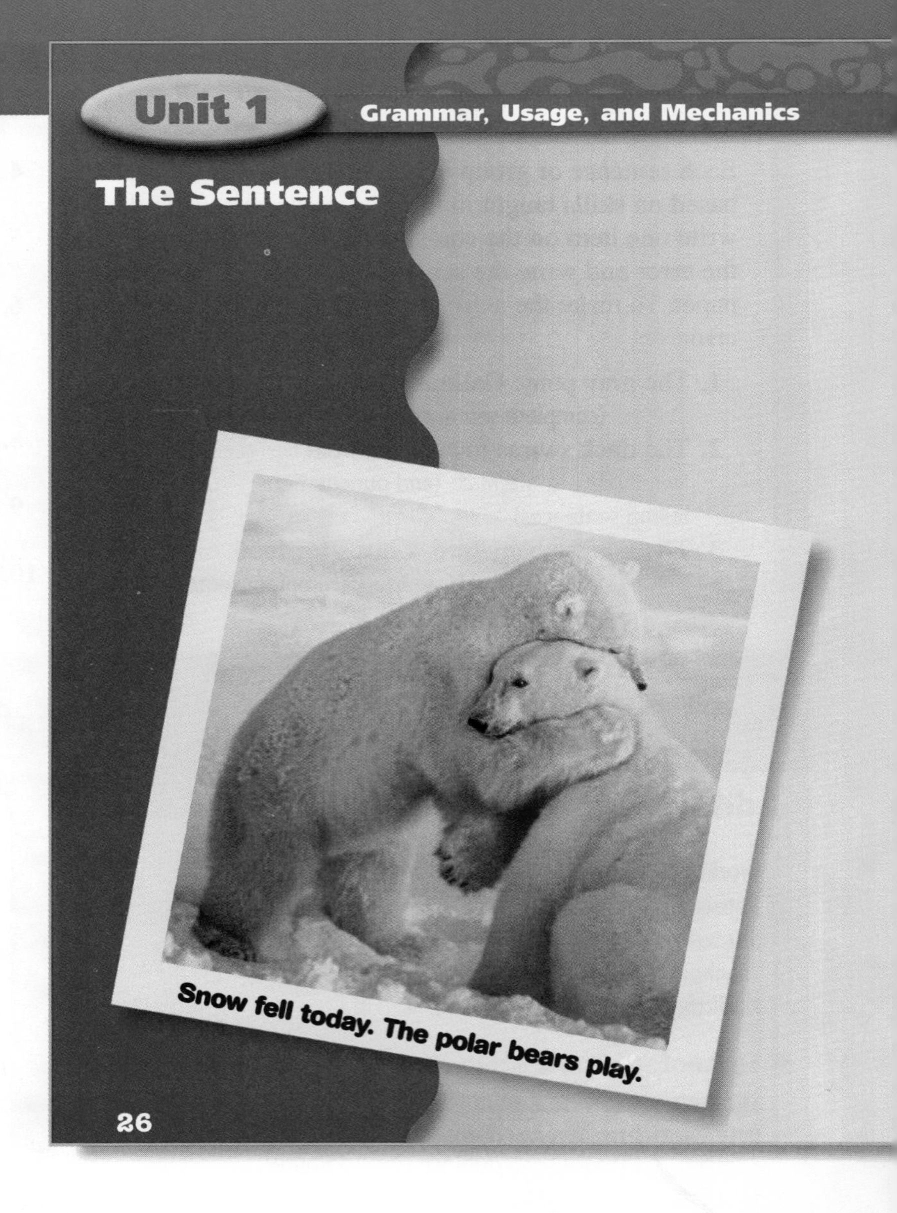

Shared Writing Activity

Work with children to write sentences with a naming part and an action part.

1. Write this column heading on the chalkboard: *Who or What*. Have children tell who or what is in the photograph. (Samples: two polar bears, one polar bear) Write their responses under the heading.
2. Write this column heading on the chalkboard: *Did or Does*. Have children tell what someone or something in the photograph did or does. (Samples: play, snuggle, rests its head, stands) Write their responses under the heading.
3. Discuss again that a complete sentence has a naming part that tells who or what and an action part that tells what the naming part did or does. Work with children to make sentences from the items listed in the two columns. Have them write the sentences.
4. As children work, give individuals help with capitalizing the first word of their sentences and with end punctuation.
5. Suggest that children illustrate one or two of their sentences. Then ask volunteers to use the illustration to identify the *who* or *what* and the *did* or *does* parts of their sentences.

Grammar 1

What Is a Sentence?

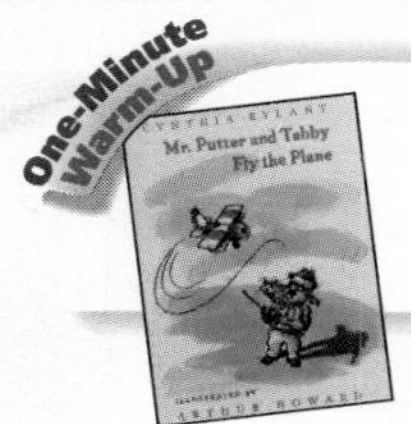

Who did something? What did that person or animal do?

Mr. Putter cheered. Tabby purred and hiccuped.

—from Mr. Putter and Tabby Fly the Plane, by Cynthia Rylant

who: Mr. Putter, Tabby; did what: cheered, purred and hiccuped

A **sentence** tells what someone or something did or does. Who played? What do the blocks do?

The boy played. The blocks fall.

Try It Out

Speak Up Match the groups of words to say sentences about the picture.

1. A balloon — rings.
2. The train — popped.
3. The bell — goes fast.

Write It Now write the sentences.

Example The girl ran. / smiled.

The girl smiled.

A balloon popped.

The train goes fast.

The bell rings.

What Is a Sentence?

Lesson Objectives

Children will:

- identify sentences
- write sentences
- write a description of a toy, using complete sentences

One-Minute Warm-Up Write the quoted sentences on the board. Have volunteers underline once the part that tells who or what. *(Mr. Putter, Tabby)* Then have them underline twice the part that tells what Mr. Putter and Tabby did. *(cheered; purred and hiccuped)* Have them tell which words helped them with their answers.

Focus on Instruction

Point out that the first word of a sentence always begins with a capital letter. Explain also that the words in a sentence must tell who or what did or does something.

Try It Out

VIEWING Have children suggest complete sentences about the picture. Record the sentences on a chart. (Sample responses are shown.)

Who or What	Did or Does
The train	runs.
The girl	watches.
One balloon	broke.

Meeting Individual Needs

RETEACHING

ALTERNATIVE STRATEGY

- On the board, write this sentence: *The train stops.*
- Tell children this is a sentence. It has two parts. One part tells *who* or *what*; the other part tells what someone or something did or does. Ask children which part tells who or what. *(The train)* Ask which part tells what it does. *(stops)*

CHALLENGE

Have children write three sentences about their day. Each sentence should tell who or what does something. For example: *Dad bakes. My kitten slept.*

FOR STUDENTS ACQUIRING ENGLISH

Make sure children know how we make the letters, where we write in relation to the line, and that we write from left to right. Demonstrate cheering and how a cat purrs and hiccups. Show blocks falling. Point to the words in the book.

FOR STUDENTS ACQUIRING ENGLISH

- Have children listen to the Try It Out sentences on the audiotape. Distribute the SAE Practice page for Unit 1, Lesson 1. 
- Help children describe the art in the book and then the art on the Practice page. Assist with vocabulary as needed. Write children's ideas on the board as complete sentences; tell them that these are sentences they made about the pictures. Have volunteers act out the verbs *smile, ring, pop, toot.* Provide props such as bells or horns where possible. Next, children listen and match the sentence with the picture. Then they copy the sentence.

Summing Up Help children summarize these key points about the lesson:

A **sentence** tells what someone or something did or does.

You may want to have children complete the parts related to this lesson on Blackline Master 1-1.

On Your Own

Have children test each sentence by asking:

Does the sentence have one part that tells **who** or **what** and another part that tells what someone or something **did** or **does**?

FOR STUDENTS ACQUIRING ENGLISH

Distribute the SAE Practice page for Unit 1, Lesson 1. Have volunteers use props or act out *fly, play, walk, float, roll.* Children draw a line to the word that completes the sentence. Then they copy the complete sentence. Help children begin to distinguish between present and past as what is happening now and what happened before.

Writing Wrap-Up

Writing Tip: Suggest that children first create a list of words or phrases that tell about the toy, such as *green, on six wheels* and *plastic front.* See Blackline Master 1-3 for a sample description.

TECHNOLOGY CONNECTION

Children may want to use grade-appropriate thesaurus software for words to describe their toys.

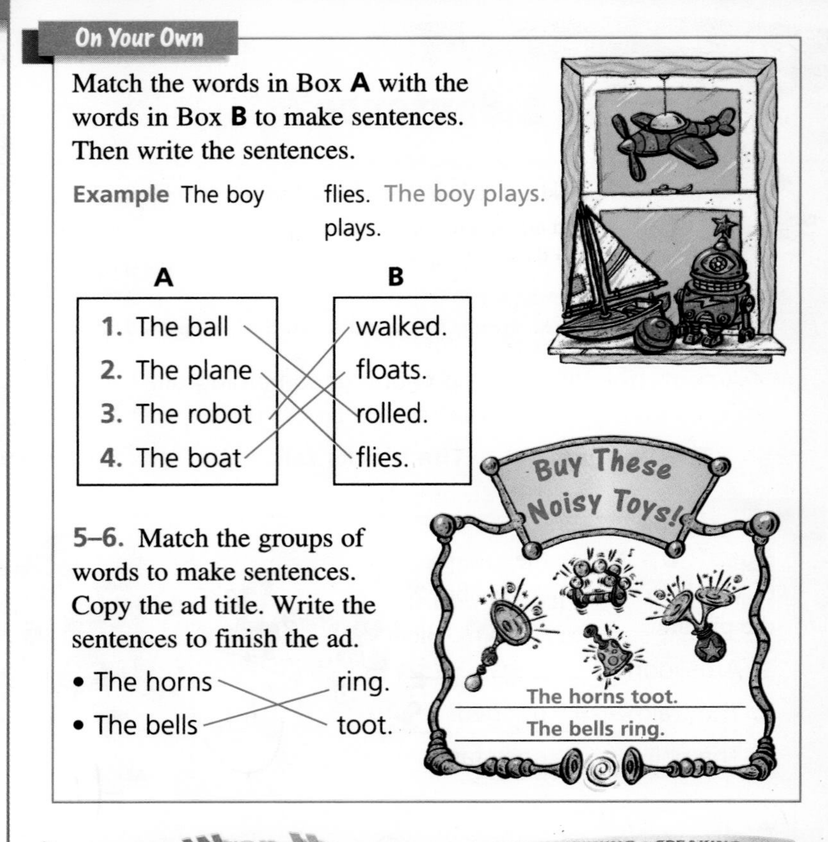

On Your Own

Match the words in Box **A** with the words in Box **B** to make sentences. Then write the sentences.

Example The boy — flies. plays. The boy plays.

A	B
1. The ball	walked.
2. The plane	floats.
3. The robot	rolled.
4. The boat	flies.

5–6. Match the groups of words to make sentences. Copy the ad title. Write the sentences to finish the ad.

- The horns — ring.
- The bells — toot.

Writing Wrap-Up WRITING • THINKING • LISTENING • SPEAKING

DESCRIBING

Write Sentences

Write sentences that tell about a toy. Draw a picture of it. Then read your sentences aloud. Have classmates tell what the toy can do or what you do with the toy.

Sentences will vary.

28 What Is a Sentence? For Extra Practice, see page 53.

Meeting Individual Needs

● RETEACHING WORKBOOK, page 1

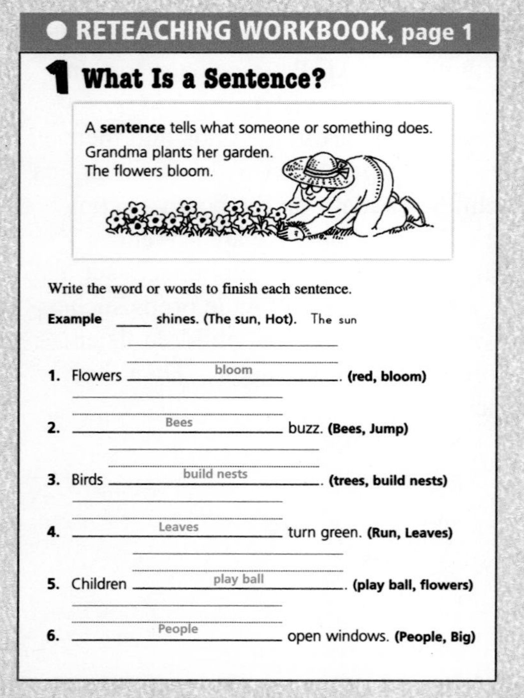

1 What Is a Sentence?

A **sentence** tells what someone or something does.
Grandma plants her garden.
The flowers bloom.

Write the word or words to finish each sentence.

Example ____ shines. (The sun, Hot). The sun

1. Flowers ___bloom___. **(red, bloom)**
2. ___Bees___ buzz. **(Bees, Jump)**
3. Birds ___build nests___. **(trees, build nests)**
4. ___Leaves___ turn green. **(Run, Leaves)**
5. Children ___play ball___. **(play ball, flowers)**
6. ___People___ open windows. **(People, Big)**

▲■ WORKBOOK PLUS, pages 1–2

1 What Is a Sentence?

The children open their eyes.
The morning begins.

Draw lines to match the groups of words to make sentences. Then write the sentences.

1. The sun — barks.
2. The dog — rises.
3. Dad — hurry.
4. We — calls.
5. Breakfast — tastes good.

1. The sun rises.
2. The dog barks.
3. Dad calls.
4. We hurry.
5. Breakfast tastes good.

1 What Is a Sentence? (continued from page 1)

Challenge

Draw lines to match the groups of words to make sentences. Then write the poem.

1. I — are baking.
2. The day — grins.
3. Rolls — am waking.
4. Everyone — begins.

I am waking.
The day begins.
Rolls are baking.
Everyone grins.

Writing Application: A Sentence NARRATING

Write a sentence about what you like to eat for breakfast.

Answers will vary.

Grammar

2 Naming Part

Responses will vary but might include a clown, tightrope walker, ringmaster, lion, tiger, elephant, dog, and bear.

Think of a person or animal that you could find at the circus. Act out something it does. Have a classmate name the person or animal.

The **naming part** of a sentence tells who or what did or does something. Read the sentences. Who went to the circus? What jumps through a hoop?

Jason went to the circus.

A dog jumps through a hoop.

Try It Out

Speak Up Say a naming part from the Word Box to begin each sentence about the picture.

A bear	A girl	The clown

1. ___ (The clown) holds the hoop.
2. ___ (A girl) stood on a horse.

Write It Now write each sentence. Draw a line under the naming part.

Example ___ sat on a ball.
A bear sat on a ball.

The clown holds the hoop.
A girl stood on a horse.

Meeting Individual Needs

RETEACHING
ALTERNATIVE STRATEGY

- Name an animal category, such as circus animals, farm animals, or pets.
- Ask a volunteer to name an animal in that category. Have another volunteer use the word in a sentence by telling something the animal does.
- Write the sentence on the board. Underline and identify the naming word or words as the naming part of the sentence.

CHALLENGE

Help children write riddles about people or animals in a circus. Have children write sentences to answer each other's riddles. Each sentence should tell who or what does something. Ask children to underline the naming parts of their sentences.

FOR STUDENTS ACQUIRING ENGLISH

Do a practice dictation. Say *dog*, for example, and then repeat it after ten or fifteen seconds. Have children check their work as you spell the words letter by letter. Alternatively, call on children to spell the words aloud.

Naming Part

Lesson Objectives

Children will:
- identify the naming parts of sentences
- write sentences
- write informative sentences for a circus poster

One-Minute Warm-Up Have children create sentences about what they acted out. Write the sentences on the board. Ask volunteers to underline the name of the person or animal that did or does something. (For example: *The clown* waves or *The tiger* sits.)

Focus on Instruction

Point out that the naming part of a sentence may be one word or more than one word. Use examples, such as *Dogs jump*, *The tall clown* cried, or *The big brown bear* stands.

Try It Out

VIEWING Have children suggest naming parts by identifying things in the illustration. Then use the naming parts in sentences about the illustration. Record children's sentences on a chart. (Sample responses are shown.)

Naming Part	Did or Does
Two dogs	jump through a hoop.
A girl	rides on a horse.
The clown	smiles.

FOR STUDENTS ACQUIRING ENGLISH

- Have children listen to the Try It Out sentences on the audiotape. Distribute the SAE Practice page for Unit 1, Lesson 2.
- Ask if anyone has been to the circus. List words relating to the circus on the board. Then discuss and help children label the art on the Practice page. Dictate words for the labels, spelling them letter by letter if needed. Ask children for their names; explain that every sentence has a naming part that tells who or what. Children listen and choose the naming word from the box to complete each sentence. Then they write the sentence again and underline the naming part.

4. _____ sat on a ball. (A tiger)
5. _____ stood on an elephant. (A girl)

Summing Up Help children summarize these key points about the lesson:

The **naming part** of a sentence tells **who** or **what** did or does something. It may be one word or more than one word.

You may want to have children complete the parts related to this lesson on Blackline Master 1-1.

On Your Own

Have children test each sentence by asking:

Does the sentence have a naming part that tells who or what did or does something?

FOR STUDENTS ACQUIRING ENGLISH

Distribute the SAE Practice page for Unit 1, Lesson 2. Review capital and lower case letters. Act out the vocabulary on the Practice page as needed. Children choose the naming word from the box to complete the sentence.

1. _____ juggle. (Clowns)
2. _____ roar. (Lions)

Writing Wrap-Up

Writing Tip: Suggest that children first draw and label pictures of people and animals that perform in a circus, such as *clowns, elephants,* and *monkeys.* See Blackline Master 1-3 for a sample poster.

TECHNOLOGY CONNECTION

Children may want to use available software to illustrate their posters using clip art.

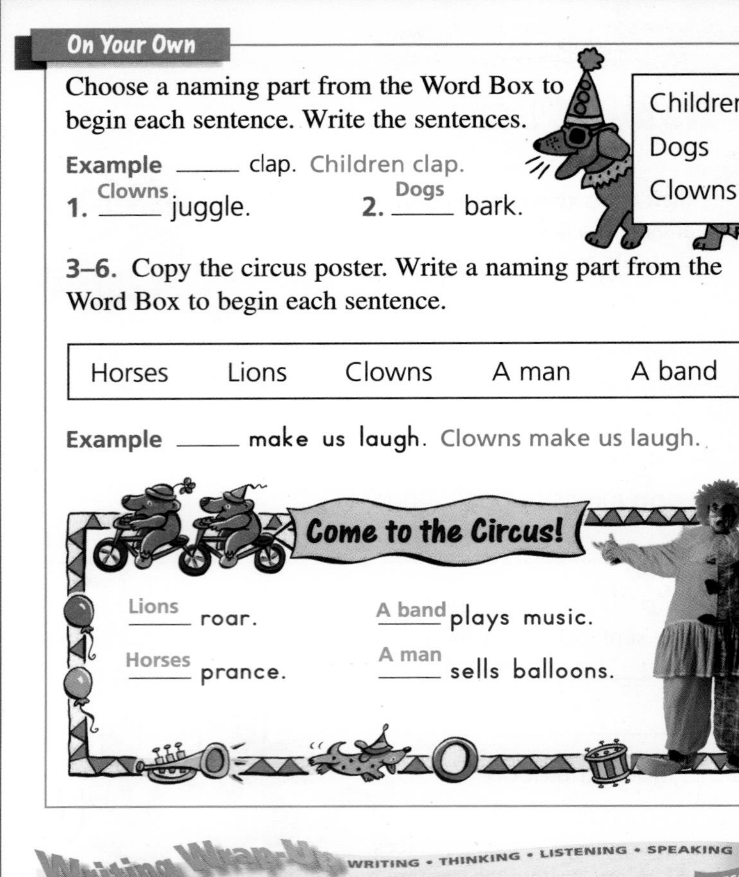

On Your Own

Choose a naming part from the Word Box to begin each sentence. Write the sentences.

Children
Dogs
Clowns

Example _____ clap. Children clap.

1. Clowns juggle.
2. Dogs bark.

3–6. Copy the circus poster. Write a naming part from the Word Box to begin each sentence.

Horses	Lions	Clowns	A man	A band

Example _____ make us laugh. Clowns make us laugh.

Writing Wrap-Up WRITING • THINKING • LISTENING • SPEAKING

DESCRIBING

Write Circus Poster Sentences

Make your own circus poster. Tell what people and animals do at a circus. Add pictures. Show your poster and read the sentences. Have a classmate say the naming part of each sentence.

Posters will vary.

30 Naming Part

For Extra Practice, see page 54.

Meeting Individual Needs

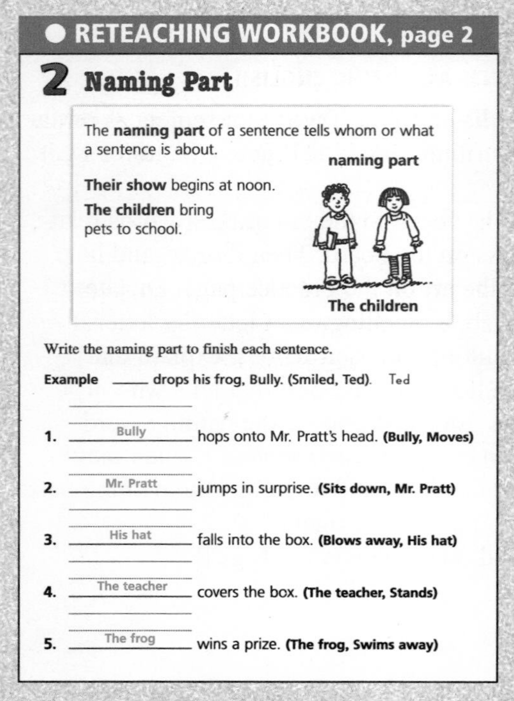

● RETEACHING WORKBOOK, page 2

2 Naming Part

The **naming part** of a sentence tells whom or what a sentence is about.

Their show begins at noon.

The children bring pets to school.

Write the naming part to finish each sentence.

Example _____ drops his frog, Bully. (Smiled, Ted). Ted

1. Bully hops onto Mr. Pratt's head. **(Bully, Moves)**
2. Mr. Pratt jumps in surprise. **(Sits down, Mr. Pratt)**
3. His hat falls into the box. **(Blows away, His hat)**
4. The teacher covers the box. **(The teacher, Stands)**
5. The frog wins a prize. **(The frog, Swims away)**

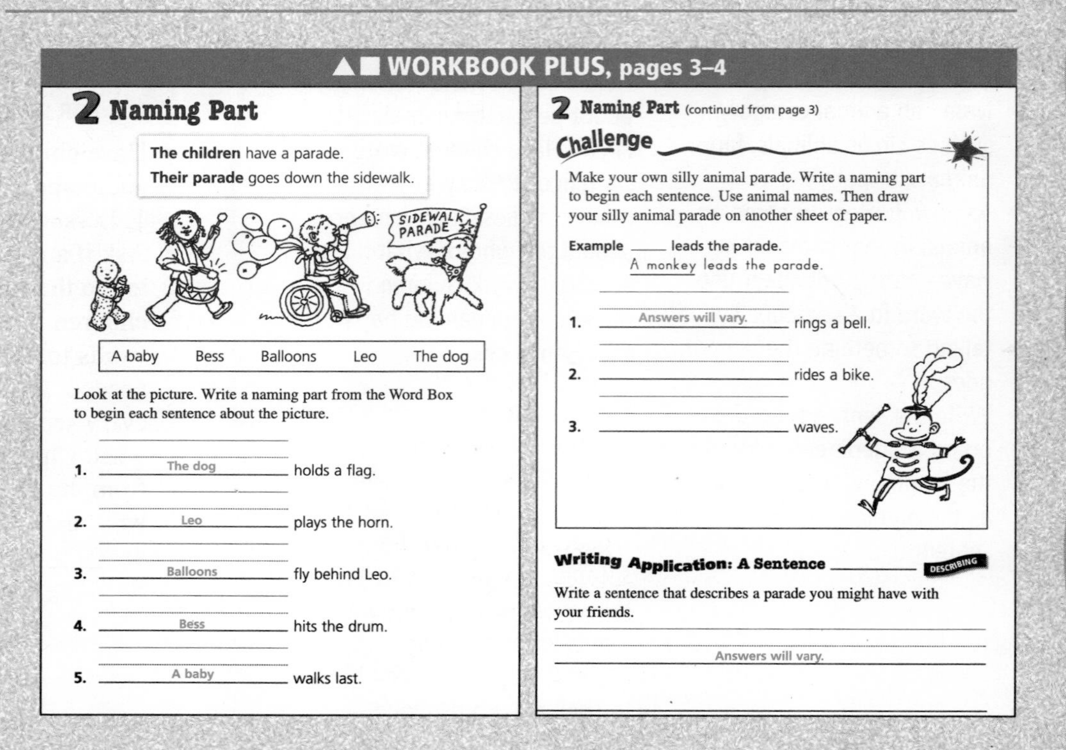

▲■ WORKBOOK PLUS, pages 3–4

2 Naming Part

The children have a parade.

Their parade goes down the sidewalk.

A baby	Bess	Balloons	Leo	The dog

Look at the picture. Write a naming part from the Word Box to begin each sentence about the picture.

1. The dog holds a flag.
2. Leo plays the horn.
3. Balloons fly behind Leo.
4. Bess hits the drum.
5. A baby walks last.

2 Naming Part (continued from page 3)

Challenge

Make your own silly animal parade. Write a naming part to begin each sentence. Use animal names. Then draw your silly animal parade on another sheet of paper.

Example _____ leads the parade.
A monkey leads the parade.

1. Answers will vary. rings a bell.
2. _____ rides a bike.
3. _____ waves.

Writing Application: A Sentence DESCRIBING

Write a sentence that describes a parade you might have with your friends.

Answers will vary.

Grammar

3 Action Part

Act out something you can or like to do. Have classmates guess the action you are doing.
Actions will vary.

The **action part** of a sentence tells what the naming part did or does. Tell what Ken did or does.

Ken **followed the signs**. Ken **slides**.

Try It Out

Speak Up Say an action part from the Word Box to finish each sentence.

showed what to do	climbed a pole
walked on a log	watched

1. Ken climbed a pole.
2. Anna walked on a log.
3. A chipmunk watched.

Write It Now write the sentences.

Example The signs ____.
The signs showed what to do.

Ken climbed a pole.
Anna walked on a log.
A chipmunk watched.

Action Part

Lesson Objectives

Children will:
- identify the action parts of sentences
- write sentences
- write informative sentences about school-related jobs

One-Minute Warm-Up Have children say the words that name the actions they performed. List the words on the board. For each word, have children add their names to the verbs to make a sentence, such as *Adam jumps*.

Focus on Instruction

Point out that the action part of a sentence may be more than just the action word itself. Provide examples such as *Ken climbs the rope.*

Try It Out

LISTENING AND SPEAKING Write these questions on the board, saying each aloud: What did Ken do? *(Ken climbed a pole.)* What did Anna do? *(Anna walked on a log.)* What did a chipmunk do? *(A chipmunk watched.)*

Call on a volunteer to say a question. Have another child answer the question, using a sentence from Try It Out. Continue until all children have a turn.

FOR STUDENTS ACQUIRING ENGLISH

- Have children listen to the Try It Out sentences on the audiotape. Distribute the SAE Practice page for Unit 1, Lesson 3.
- Write and say *slide*, *sign*, *climb*, *pole*, *log*; say that the *g* in *sign* and the *b* in *climb* are silent. Have children say the words. Then write several action verbs such as *walk*, *stand*, *talk*, *sing*, *drink*. Point to the verb and have the first child who can read the word say it and perform the action. Next have the class perform actions together as you point to the words on the board. Then say that most sentences have an action part. Children listen and choose the action part from the box. Then they write the sentence. Example: Maria ____. (jumped)

Meeting Individual Needs

RETEACHING
ALTERNATIVE STRATEGY
- Have children act out different ways they could cross the room, such as walk, twirl, skip, or crawl.
- Record the word for each action on the board, writing the name of the person who acted it out in front of the word. Have children identify the words as a sentence and underline the action part of the sentence.

CHALLENGE
Have children cut out magazine pictures that show actions and paste each on a separate paper. Have them write a sentence under each picture, telling what is happening, and then underline the action part.

FOR STUDENTS ACQUIRING ENGLISH
Perform actions such as *jump*, *sing*, *write*, *walk* and have children say what you are doing. Have children continue as classmates guess what they are doing. Write the verbs on the board; say that these are actions.

Summing Up Help children summarize these key points about the lesson:

The **action part** of a sentence tells what the naming part **did** or **does**.

You may want to have children complete the parts related to this lesson on Blackline Master 1-1.

On Your Own

Have children test each sentence by asking:

Does the sentence have an action part that tells what the naming part did or does?

FOR STUDENTS ACQUIRING ENGLISH

Distribute the SAE Practice page for Unit 1, Lesson 3. Have children read aloud the names of each of the jobs. Discuss what each person does. Have the children cut out the sentence strips and match the naming and action parts.

Writing Wrap-Up

Writing Tip: Suggest that children first make a list of the different workers in their school, for example, *teacher, teacher's helper, librarian* and *principal*. See Blackline Master 1-3 for a sample of informative writing.

SCHOOL-HOME CONNECTION

Suggest that children read their sentences to family members. Then have them discuss other school-related jobs.

On Your Own

Choose an action part from the Word Box to finish each sentence. Write the sentences.

writes books	makes bread	makes us well

Example A baker_____. A baker makes bread.

1. A doctor _____. makes us well
2. An author _____. writes books

3–4. Choose an action part from the Word Box to finish each sentence on Rosa's list. Write the title and sentences.

grows food	flies a jet	fixes teeth

Example A dentist _____. A dentist fixes teeth.

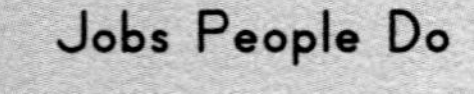

Jobs People Do

A pilot ___flies a jet___.

A farmer ___grows food___.

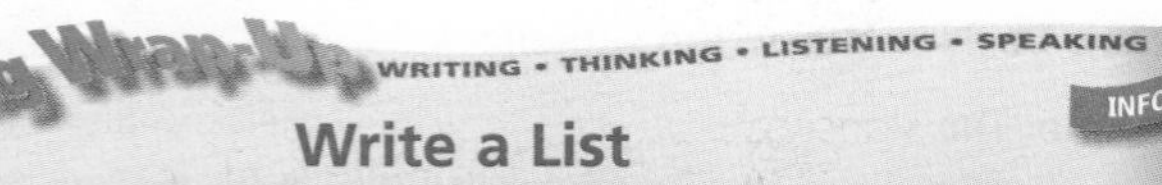

Write a List

Write three sentences about jobs people do in your school or class. Read your sentences. Have a classmate name the action parts. Discuss if you would like to do these jobs. Lists will vary.

32 Action Part For Extra Practice, see page 55.

Meeting Individual Needs

● RETEACHING WORKBOOK, page 3

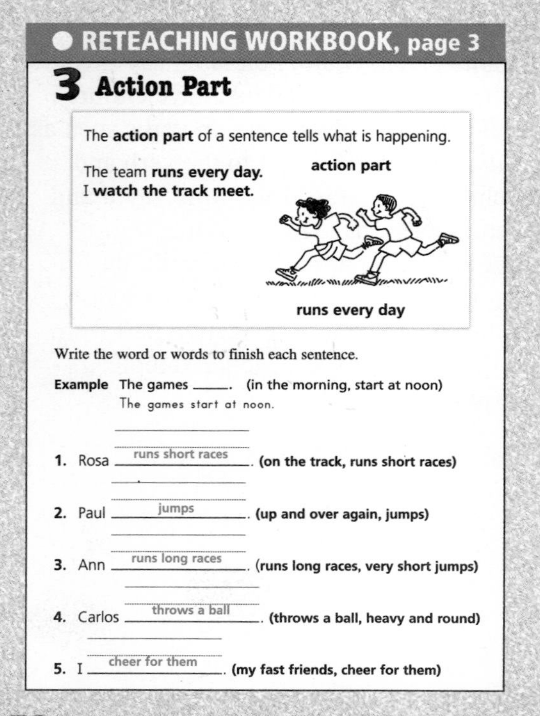

3 Action Part

The **action part** of a sentence tells what is happening.

The team **runs every day.**
I **watch the track meet.**

action part

runs every day

Write the word or words to finish each sentence.

Example The games _____. (in the morning, start at noon)
The games start at noon.

1. Rosa __runs short races__. (on the track, runs short races)
2. Paul __jumps__. (up and over again, jumps)
3. Ann __runs long races__. (runs long races, very short jumps)
4. Carlos __throws a ball__. (throws a ball, heavy and round)
5. I __cheer for them__. (my fast friends, cheer for them)

▲■ WORKBOOK PLUS, pages 5-6

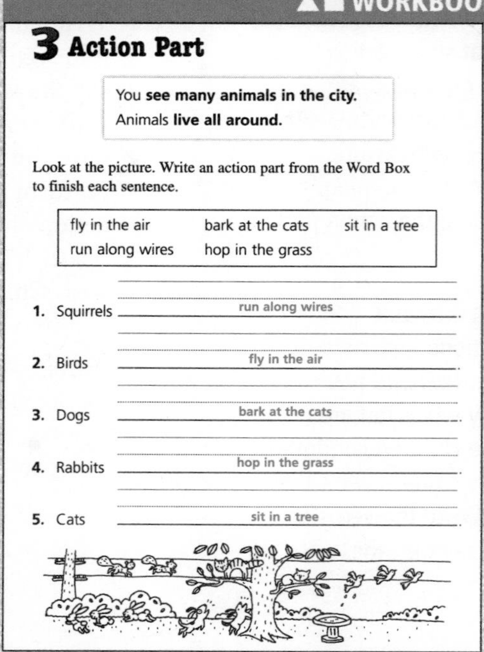

3 Action Part

You **see many animals in the city.**
Animals **live all around.**

Look at the picture. Write an action part from the Word Box to finish each sentence.

fly in the air	bark at the cats	sit in a tree
run along wires	hop in the grass	

1. Squirrels __run along wires__.
2. Birds __fly in the air__.
3. Dogs __bark at the cats__.
4. Rabbits __hop in the grass__.
5. Cats __sit in a tree__.

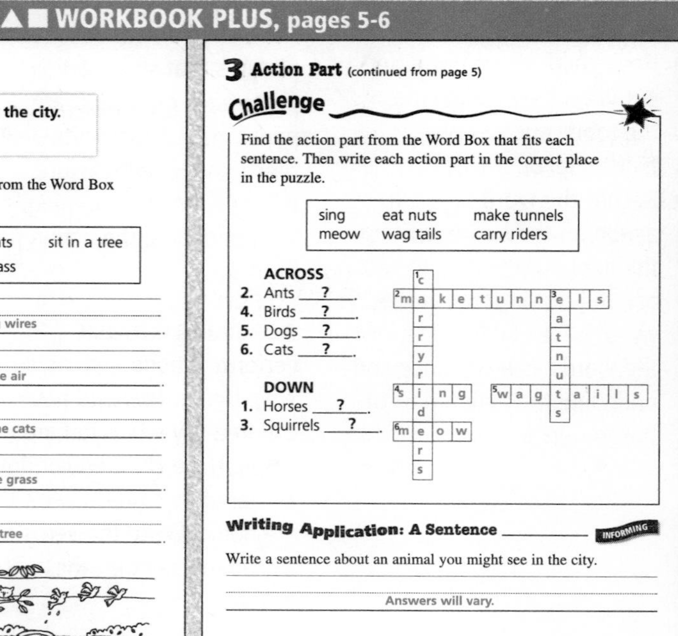

3 Action Part (continued from page 5)

Challenge

Find the action part from the Word Box that fits each sentence. Then write each action part in the correct place in the puzzle.

sing	eat nuts	make tunnels
meow	wag tails	carry riders

ACROSS
2. Ants __?__.
4. Birds __?__.
5. Dogs __?__.
6. Cats __?__.

DOWN
1. Horses __?__.
3. Squirrels __?__.

Writing Application: A Sentence INFORMING

Write a sentence about an animal you might see in the city.

Answers will vary.

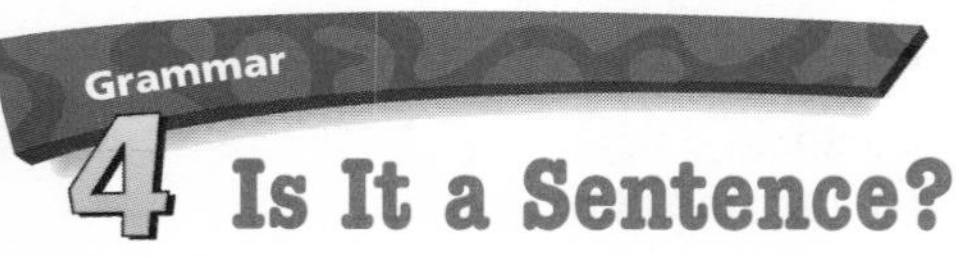

4 Is It a Sentence?

Naming parts: *Father, Mother, They*: Action parts: *kissed her again, closed the door.*

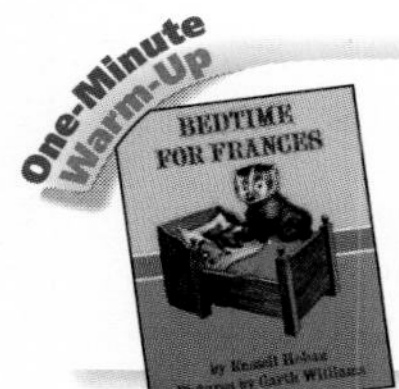

Say the naming part and the action part in each sentence.

Father kissed her again. Mother kissed her again.
They closed the door.

—from Bedtime for Frances, by Russell Hoban

A complete sentence has a **naming part** and an **action part**. Read this sentence. Say the naming part. Say the action part.

A big frog jumps off a rock.

Try It Out

Speak Up Which two word groups are complete sentences? Read them aloud and tell why.

1. Sleeps on a log.
2. Fish swim in the water.
3. Three birds sing.
4. The green frog.

Sentences 2, 3; each has a naming part and an action part.

Write It Now write the two complete sentences.

Example Floats on the pond. A lily pad floats.
A lily pad floats.

Fish swim in the water.
Three birds sing.

Meeting Individual Needs

RETEACHING
ALTERNATIVE STRATEGY

- Write this sentence on the board: *A squirrel eats nuts.*
- Tell children this is a complete sentence. It has a naming part and an action part. Ask children which part is the naming part. *(A squirrel)* Ask which part is the action part. *(eats nuts).*
- Continue with these sentences: *The rabbit hops away. A deer leaps over a fence.*

CHALLENGE

Direct children to write a sentence on a cardboard strip. Cut each strip in half between the subject and the predicate. Then give each child a sentence part. Tell children to add a new subject or predicate to make a new sentence.

FOR STUDENTS ACQUIRING ENGLISH

Give a sentence with only the naming part and ask children to complete it any way they wish. To review, use some of the naming parts from the previous lesson. For example, *A farmer ______. A baker ______. A dentist ______.*

Is It a Sentence?

Lesson Objectives

Children will:

- distinguish between sentences and word groups that are not sentences
- write informative sentences for a sign

One-Minute Warm-Up Write the quoted sentences on the board. Have volunteers underline each naming part once and say the word that tells *who* or *what*. Have them underline each action part twice and say the word that tells what the naming part *did*.

Focus on Instruction

Point out that beginning a group of words with a capital letter and ending it with a period does not make it a sentence. To be a sentence, the group of words also must have a naming part and an action part.

Try It Out

LISTENING AND SPEAKING Have a volunteer read the group of words in item 1 while the class listens. Ask what part is missing to make the group of words a sentence. *(the naming part)* Have children use the pictures to add a naming part and then say the sentence. *(A turtle sleeps on a log.)* Repeat the procedure using item 4, having children add an action part to complete the sentence. *(The green frog jumps.)*

FOR STUDENTS ACQUIRING ENGLISH

- Have children listen to the Try It Out sentences on the audiotape. Distribute the SAE Practice page for Unit 1, Lesson 4.
- Have children identify the *frog*, *tree*, and *fish* in the drawing in the book. Write the words and have children say them. Listen for the correct pronunciation of *fr* and *tr*. Remind children that every sentence in English must have a naming part and an action part. Keep in mind that in languages such as Spanish, the verb carries ample information and the noun is not repeated. Children listen and write **yes** if the word groups make sentences and **no** if they do not. Later, talk about why.
  1. Frogs jump. (yes)
  2. Sing in the tree. (no)

Summing Up Help children summarize these key points about the lesson:

A complete sentence has a **naming part** and an **action part.** Each part may be one word or more than one word.

You may want to have children complete the parts related to this lesson on Blackline Master 1-1.

On Your Own

Suggest that children test each word group by asking:

Does the word group have a naming part and an action part?

FOR STUDENTS ACQUIRING ENGLISH

Distribute the SAE Practice page for Unit 1, Lesson 4. Review by presenting either naming parts or action parts and having children make complete sentences. Children write **yes** if the word groups make sentences and **no** if they do not. Help children find the naming and action parts. Example: Next to the water. (no)

Writing Wrap-Up

Writing Tip: Suggest that children make a list of people who would see their sign and then write the information they want these people to know. See Blackline Master 1-3 for a sample of informative writing.

TECHNOLOGY CONNECTION

Children may use a computer to add bold type to certain words or to add a border to their signs.

On Your Own

Read and copy each word group. Write **yes** after each complete sentence. Write **no** after the other word groups.

Example The seeds open. yes

1. Plants grow. yes
2. Floats away. no
3. Deep water. no
4. It falls down. yes

5–6. Read each word group. Write the two complete sentences to make a sign like the one below.

Example Ducks live here. Ducks live here.
A big lake.

- Children swim here.
- Swims and runs.
- Little children and dogs.
- All boats stay out.

Writing Wrap-Up

WRITING • THINKING • LISTENING • SPEAKING

INFORMING

Write Sentences for a Sign

Write two complete sentences to make a sign for your bedroom door. Read them to a classmate. Have the classmate say each naming part and action part. Sentences will vary.

34 Is It a Sentence? For Extra Practice, see page 56.

Meeting Individual Needs

● RETEACHING WORKBOOK, page 4

4 Is It a Sentence?

A sentence has a naming part and an action part.
naming part action part
The baseball game + begins.
The baseball game begins.

Write **yes** beside each group of words that is a sentence.
Write **no** beside each group of words that is not a sentence.

Example Rico bats. yes

1. the players no
2. The ball flies high. yes
3. keeps running no
4. Pam catches the ball. yes
5. Her team wins. yes
6. The game ends. yes

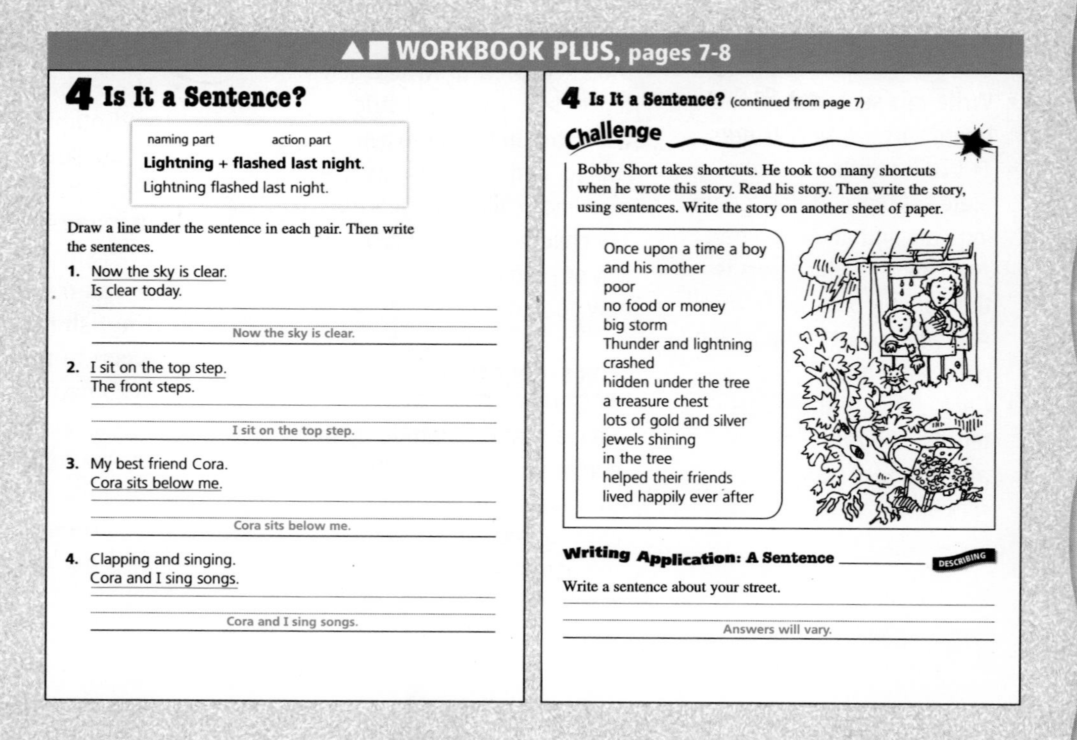

▲■ WORKBOOK PLUS, pages 7-8

4 Is It a Sentence?

naming part action part
Lightning + flashed last night.
Lightning flashed last night.

Draw a line under the sentence in each pair. Then write the sentences.

1. Now the sky is clear.
Is clear today.
Now the sky is clear.
2. I sit on the top step.
The front steps.
I sit on the top step.
3. My best friend Cora.
Cora sits below me.
Cora sits below me.
4. Clapping and singing.
Cora and I sing songs.
Cora and I sing songs.

4 Is It a Sentence? (continued from page 7)

Challenge

Bobby Short takes shortcuts. He took too many shortcuts when he wrote this story. Read his story. Then write the story, using sentences. Write the story on another sheet of paper.

Once upon a time a boy
and his mother
poor
no food or money
big storm
Thunder and lightning
crashed
hidden under the tree
a treasure chest
lots of gold and silver
jewels shining
in the tree
helped their friends
lived happily ever after

Writing Application: A Sentence DESCRIBING

Write a sentence about your street.

Answers will vary.

Revising Strategies — Sentence Fluency

Writing Complete Sentences

Completing Sentences Write complete sentences. Each one must have a **naming part** and an **action part.**

Monkeys play in the jungle.

Try It Out

Speak Up Look at each picture and the word group under it. Add a naming part or an action part to the word group to say a complete sentence about the picture.

Sample answer: The monkey climbs on a branch.

1. The monkey.

Sample answer: The monkey eats corn.

2. Eats corn.

Sample answer: The monkey rubs its head.

3. Rubs its head.

Sample answer: The monkeys hold hands.

4. The monkeys.

Write It 1–4. Now write the four complete sentences. Begin and end them correctly.

Example That monkey. That monkey jumps.

See sample sentences above.

Writing Complete Sentences

Lesson Objective

Children will:

- say and write complete sentences

Focus on Instruction

Remind children that a complete sentence must have a naming part and an action part.

Try It Out

SPEAK UP Go over the examples with children. Be sure they understand that they must use the picture to supply the missing part of the sentence.

WRITE IT Explain to children that they should write the four complete sentences that they said in Speak Up. Have them reread their sentences and check that they have used correct capitalization and punctuation.

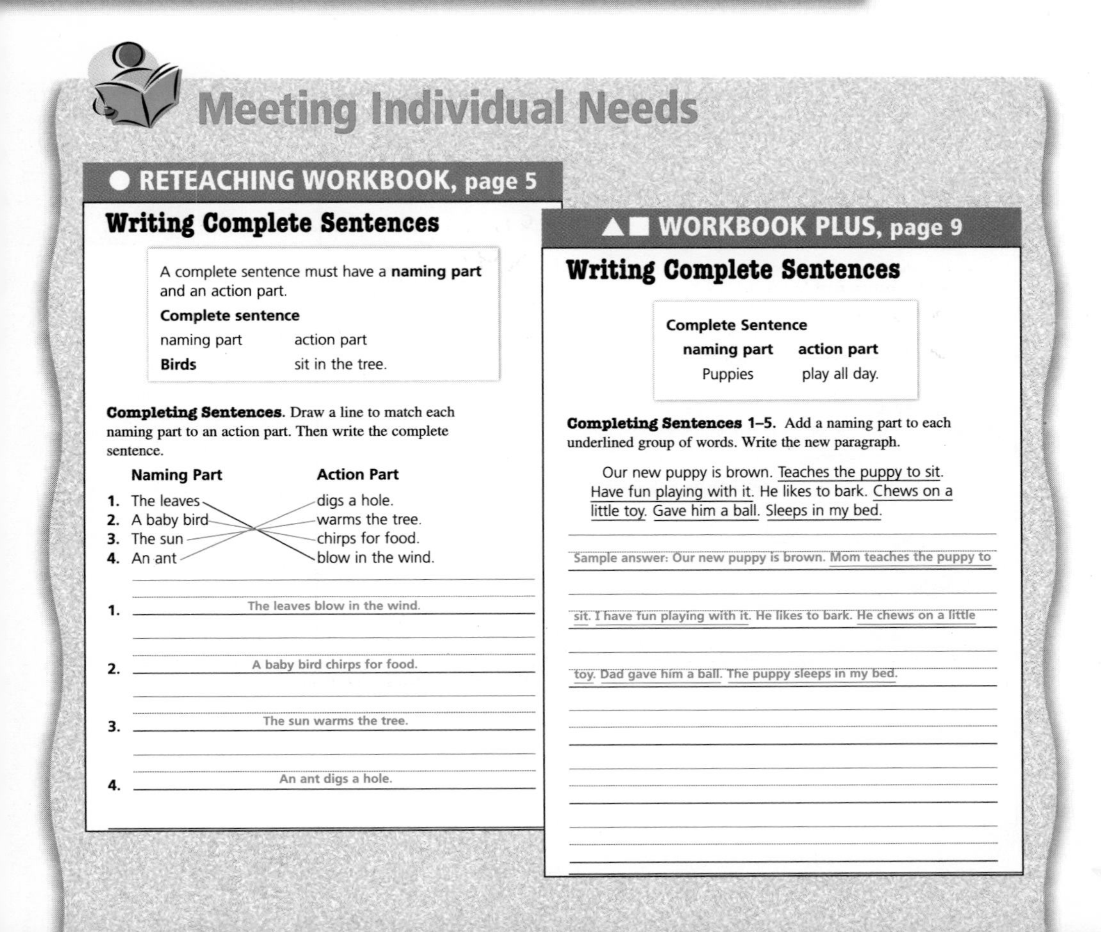

Meeting Individual Needs

● RETEACHING WORKBOOK, page 5

Writing Complete Sentences

A complete sentence must have a **naming part** and an action part.

Complete sentence

naming part	action part
Birds	sit in the tree.

Completing Sentences. Draw a line to match each naming part to an action part. Then write the complete sentence.

Naming Part	Action Part
1. The leaves	digs a hole.
2. A baby bird	warms the tree.
3. The sun	chirps for food.
4. An ant	blow in the wind.

1. The leaves blow in the wind.
2. A baby bird chirps for food.
3. The sun warms the tree.
4. An ant digs a hole.

▲■ WORKBOOK PLUS, page 9

Writing Complete Sentences

Complete Sentence

naming part	action part
Puppies	play all day.

Completing Sentences 1–5. Add a naming part to each underlined group of words. Write the new paragraph.

Our new puppy is brown. Teaches the puppy to sit. Have fun playing with it. He likes to bark. Chews on a little toy. Gave him a ball. Sleeps in my bed.

Sample answer: Our new puppy is brown. Mom teaches the puppy to sit. I have fun playing with it. He likes to bark. He chews on a little toy. Dad gave him a ball. The puppy sleeps in my bed.

Writing Complete Sentences

Apply It

Go over the example with children. Point out that there can be more than one correct answer. Then have them complete the revising activity independently.

Have children find places in their own writing in progress where they can make complete sentences from word groups.

FOR STUDENTS ACQUIRING ENGLISH

To help students decide what part of the sentence is missing in the *Speak Up* activity, ask: *What does the monkey do? Who eats corn?* etc. For Write It, make a template with blanks for the students to fill in. Sample item: The monkey_____. For *Apply It*, read the journal aloud. Pause at each phrase and ask, *Who?; Did what?*

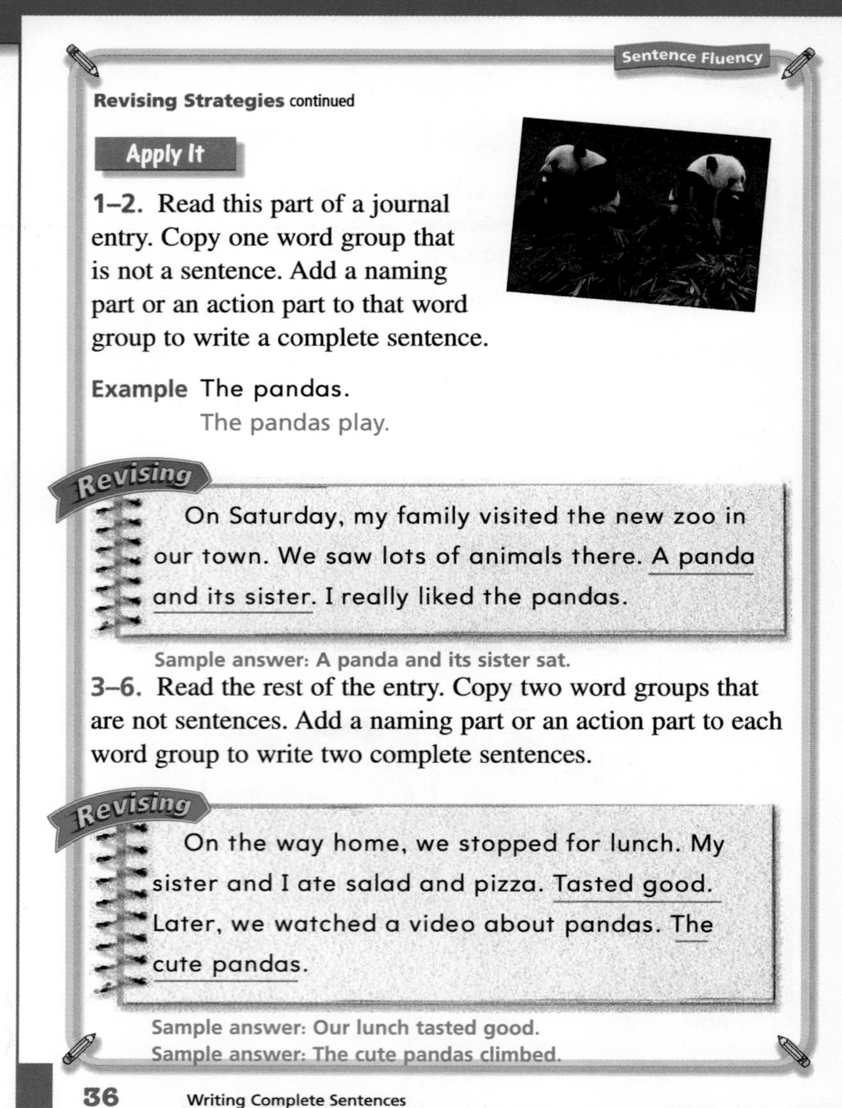

Sentence Fluency

Revising Strategies continued

Apply It

1–2. Read this part of a journal entry. Copy one word group that is not a sentence. Add a naming part or an action part to that word group to write a complete sentence.

Example The pandas.
The pandas play.

Revising

On Saturday, my family visited the new zoo in our town. We saw lots of animals there. A panda and its sister. I really liked the pandas.

Sample answer: A panda and its sister sat.

3–6. Read the rest of the entry. Copy two word groups that are not sentences. Add a naming part or an action part to each word group to write two complete sentences.

Revising

On the way home, we stopped for lunch. My sister and I ate salad and pizza. Tasted good. Later, we watched a video about pandas. The cute pandas.

Sample answer: Our lunch tasted good.
Sample answer: The cute pandas climbed.

36 Writing Complete Sentences

Meeting Individual Needs

● RETEACHING WORKBOOK, page 6

Writing Complete Sentences

A complete sentence must have a naming part and an **action part**.

Complete sentence

naming part	action part
My parakeet	**sits on my hand.**

Completing Sentences. Complete each sentence. Use the words in ( ) to tell you which part to add. Sample answers

1. This bird eats little seeds. **(naming part)**
2. The bird cage swings in the window. **(action part)**
3. My brother feeds the bird. **(action part)**
4. My sister cleans the cage. **(naming part)**
5. Our bird plays in his cage. **(action part)**
6. Mom teaches the bird tricks. **(naming part)**

▲■ WORKBOOK PLUS, page 10

Writing Complete Sentences

Complete Sentence

naming part	**action part**
The circus	starts at 7 o'clock.

Completing Sentences Add an action part to each underlined group of words. Write the new sentences.

The tall clown danced in the ring. The circus horses. Then a man. He rode the horses all around. A big elephant. The elephant. The circus.

1. The circus horses ran in.
2. Then a man rode the horses.
3. A big elephant lifted his trunk.
4. The elephant made a big sound.
5. The circus comes here every year.

Grammar / Mechanics

5 Telling Sentences

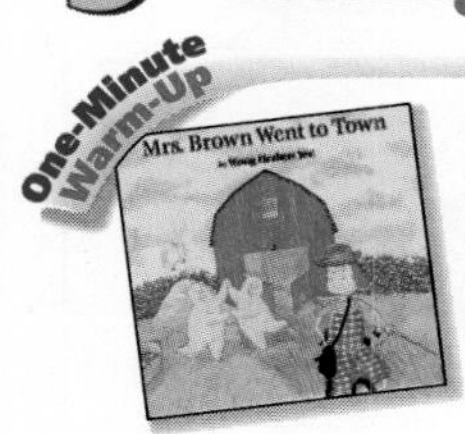

Read these sentences. What place do they tell about? Tell what you know about that place.

Life on the farm wasn't always this way. Everything changed just last Saturday. a farm; answers will vary.

—from Mrs. Brown Went to Town, by Wong Herbert Yee

A **telling sentence** tells something. It begins with a **capital letter**. It ends with a **period**.

Some animals live on farms.

Horses live there.

Try It Out

Speak Up Tell how to make each sentence correct.

1. the sheep are in a pen. *Change t to T in the.*
2. Pigs roll in the mud *Add a period after mud.*
3. cows eat grass *Change c to C in cows; add a period after grass.*

Write It Now write the sentences correctly.

Example chickens lay eggs
Chickens lay eggs.

The sheep are in a pen.
Pigs roll in the mud.
Cows eat grass.

Meeting Individual Needs

RETEACHING
ALTERNATIVE STRATEGY

- Write telling sentences about farm life on strips of oaktag, some with a lowercase initial letter and/or a missing period. Hold up a strip with a correct sentence and point out the capital letter and the end mark.
- Call on a volunteer to take a sentence, read it, show it to the class, and tell why it is correct or incorrect. If it is incorrect, have the child correct it with a marker, and then stamp it with a sticker and mail it in a box resembling a rural mailbox.

CHALLENGE
Have children write telling sentences about things that happen at school during the day. Suggest that children share their day with someone at home by reading their sentences aloud to that person.

FOR STUDENTS ACQUIRING ENGLISH
Review capital and lower case letters. Explain that all sentences in English begin with a capital letter and end with a period. Go back through the previous lesson and have children find the capital letters and periods.

Telling Sentences

Lesson Objectives

Children will:
- identify telling sentences
- capitalize and punctuate telling sentences correctly
- proofread for capital letters and periods
- write descriptive sentences for a post card

One-Minute Warm-Up Write the first quoted sentence on the board and read it aloud. Ask if you are asking something or telling something. Then invite children to identify the first letter and to locate and circle the end mark. Repeat with the second sentence.

Focus on Instruction

Point out that beginning a telling sentence with a capital letter and ending the sentence with a period helps show when one idea ends and another idea begins.

Try It Out

VIEWING Have children suggest telling sentences about the illustration. Record the sentences in a chart. Have volunteers circle the capital letters and the periods in the sentences. Then discuss why these are important. (Sample responses are shown.)

Telling Sentences
1. The chicken sits on a nest.
2. Two sheep stand by the fence.
3. A cow walks to the barn.

FOR STUDENTS ACQUIRING ENGLISH

- Have children listen to the Try It Out sentences on the audiotape. Distribute the SAE Practice page for Unit 1, Lesson 5.
- Print several letters on lines on the board, some capital letters and some lower case. Call on children to come up and mark capital letters with one color chalk and lower case with another. Then ask which letters can begin sentences. Write two-word sentences and call on children to use the lines to show how to make the mark that ends a sentence. Make sure each period is where it should be in relation to the line. Children listen and fix capital letters or add periods. They write the sentences.
  1. Sheep eat grass (grass.)
  2. pigs like mud. (Pigs)

Summing Up Help children summarize these key points about the lesson:

A **telling sentence** tells something. It begins with a **capital letter.** It ends with a **period.**

You may want to have children complete the parts related to this lesson on Blackline Master 1-2.

On Your Own

Have children test each telling sentence by asking:

Does the sentence tell something? Does it begin with a capital letter and end with a period?

FOR STUDENTS ACQUIRING ENGLISH

Distribute the SAE Practice page for Unit 1, Lesson 5. Children underline the correct telling sentence. Then they write the sentence again.

1. The dog sleeps   The dog sleeps.
2. The cows eat grass.   the cows eat grass

Writing Wrap-Up

Writing Tip: Suggest that children organize their ideas in a web. For example, they would write *Lincoln Park* in the center of the web, connected to *zoo, flower beds, playground,* and *farm*. See Blackline Master 1-4 for a sample of descriptive writing.

TECHNOLOGY CONNECTION

Children may be able to use the Internet to refer to photos of the place they visited as they draw a picture.

On Your Own

Write each sentence correctly.

Example the sun shines
The sun shines.

1. It is hot — It is hot.
2. the cat naps — The cat naps.

3–6. Proofread this post card. Find four mistakes with capital letters and periods. Write the message correctly.

Example we swam in the pond
We swam in the pond.

Dear Mom and Dad,

~~we~~ We fed the chickens.

We rode the horses.

~~the~~ The farm is very busy.

Tim and Pam

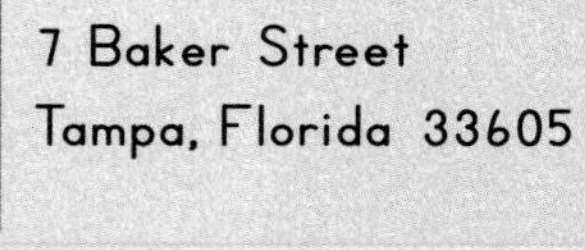

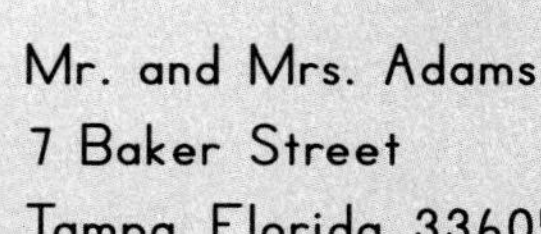

Mr. and Mrs. Adams
7 Baker Street
Tampa, Florida 33605

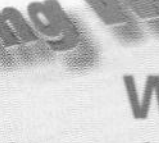

Writing Wrap-Up WRITING • THINKING • LISTENING • SPEAKING

DESCRIBING

Write a Post Card Message

Write and draw about a place. Read your sentences to a classmate. Together, check for capital letters and periods. Messages will vary.

 For Extra Practice, see page 57.

Meeting Individual Needs

● RETEACHING WORKBOOK, page 7

5 Telling Sentences

A **telling sentence** tells something. It begins with a capital letter. It ends with a period.
My friends come for dinner.
Everyone helps.

Write each correct telling sentence.

Example Dad cooks fish Dad cooks fish. Dad cooks fish.

1. Aunt Ida bakes apples. aunt Ida bakes apples.
   Aunt Ida bakes apples.
2. the kitchen smells good. The kitchen smells good.
   The kitchen smells good.
3. Abe sets the table. Abe sets the table
   Abe sets the table.

▲■ WORKBOOK PLUS, pages 11–12

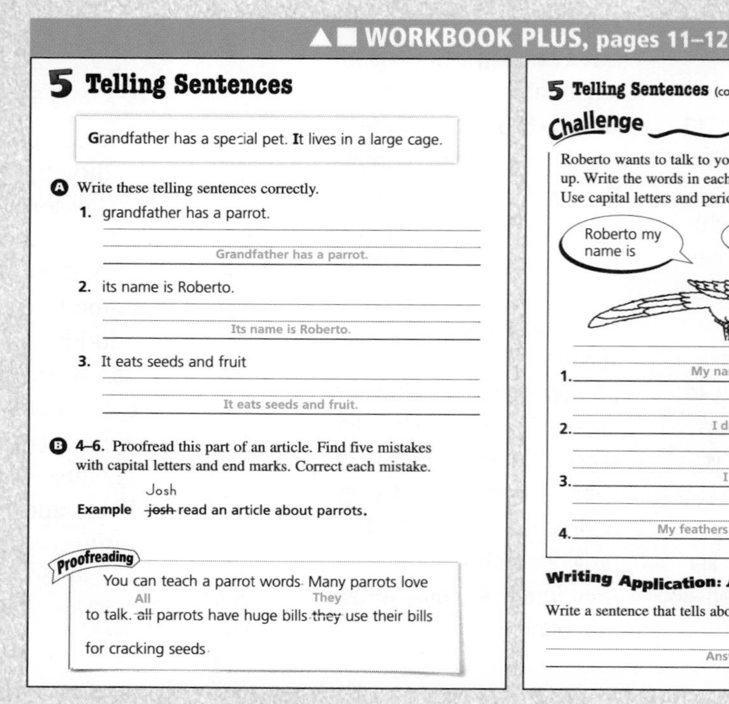

5 Telling Sentences

Grandfather has a special pet. It lives in a large cage.

A Write these telling sentences correctly.

1. grandfather has a parrot.
   Grandfather has a parrot.
2. its name is Roberto.
   Its name is Roberto.
3. It eats seeds and fruit
   It eats seeds and fruit.

B 4–6. Proofread this part of an article. Find five mistakes with capital letters and end marks. Correct each mistake.

Example ~~josh~~ Josh read an article about parrots.

Proofreading

You can teach a parrot words. Many parrots love to talk. ~~all~~ All parrots have huge bills. ~~they~~ They use their bills for cracking seeds.

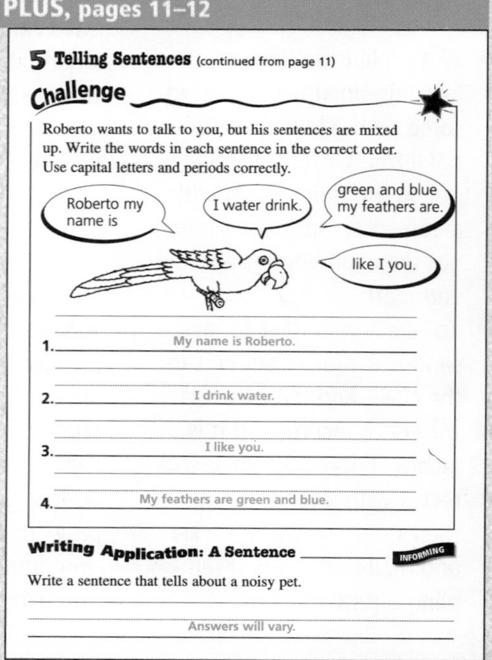

5 Telling Sentences (continued from page 11)

Challenge

Roberto wants to talk to you, but his sentences are mixed up. Write the words in each sentence in the correct order. Use capital letters and periods correctly.

1. My name is Roberto.
2. I drink water.
3. I like you.
4. My feathers are green and blue.

Writing Application: A Sentence INFORMING

Write a sentence that tells about a noisy pet.

Answers will vary.

Grammar / Mechanics

6 Questions

Look at the picture. What is the squirrel looking at? What might it be thinking? Say a sentence that the squirrel might ask if it could talk.
Answers will vary.

A **question** is a sentence that asks something. A question begins with a **capital letter** and ends with a **question mark**.

What is your name?

Do you like trees?

Try It Out

Speak Up Tell how to make each question correct.

1. will it eat seeds? (Will it eat seeds?)
2. is the squirrel red (Is the squirrel red?)
3. Where does it live (Where does it live?)

Write It Now write the questions correctly.

Example did it find acorns
Did it find acorns?

Will it eat seeds?
Is the squirrel red?
Where does it live?

Questions

Lesson Objectives

Children will:

- identify questions
- capitalize and punctuate questions correctly
- proofread for capital letters and question marks
- write questions that are expressed clearly

One-Minute Warm-Up Write the children's questions on the board. Have volunteers tell how each question begins and ends.

Focus on Instruction

Point out that in saying a question, a person's voice rises toward the end of the question.

Try It Out

VIEWING Have children suggest questions about the picture. Record the questions on a chart. Have volunteers circle the capital letters and the question marks in the sentences. Then discuss what the capital letter and the end mark show. (Sample responses are shown.)

Questions
1. Does the squirrel make a sound?
2. Is the squirrel frightened?
3. Will the squirrel run up the tree?

Meeting Individual Needs

RETEACHING
ALTERNATIVE STRATEGY

- Ask several simple questions; for example, *Does a squirrel eat corn?* Explain that each sentence is called a question. Write the questions on the board and point out that each begins with a capital letter and ends with a question mark.
- Have volunteers ask questions. Write them on the board and have children tell how each question begins and ends.

CHALLENGE

Have children pretend they are calling in to a radio show to ask questions about wild animals. Have them write three questions they would ask the veterinarian who is hosting the show.

FOR STUDENTS ACQUIRING ENGLISH

Write groups of words on the board and ask children what they need to change to make them questions. Then have partners write a question of their own. You may want to give them some words to choose.

FOR STUDENTS ACQUIRING ENGLISH

- Have children listen to the Try It Out sentences on the audiotape. Distribute the SAE Practice page for Unit 1, Lesson 6.
- Have children work in groups of three to write their own questions. Give the students a drawing to write about or have them use the art in the previous lesson. Write a question mark on the board and ask what this is. Then help children describe the art in the book. Ask questions: *What is this animal? What is the squirrel doing? Can squirrels read signs?* Point out that you asked questions and that all questions end with the mark on the board. Children listen and fix capital letters or add question marks. They write the questions. Example: Does the squirrel live in a tree (tree?)

Summing Up Help children summarize these key points about the lesson:

A **question** is a sentence that asks something.

A question begins with a **capital letter** and ends with a **question mark.**

You may want to have children complete the parts related to this lesson on Blackline Master 1-2.

On Your Own

Have children test each question by asking:

Does the sentence ask something? Does it begin with a capital letter and end with a question mark?

FOR STUDENTS ACQUIRING ENGLISH

Distribute the SAE Practice page for Unit 1, Lesson 6. Make sure children understand that a question is a type of sentence. Review periods and question marks. Children circle the questions on this page.

Writing Wrap-Up

Writing Tip: Suggest that children read their questions to themselves to make sure they have expressed themselves clearly. See Blackline Master 1-4 for a sample of informative writing.

SCHOOL-HOME CONNECTION

Children may want to test family members to see whether they can answer the questions.

On Your Own

Write the correct question in each pair.

Example what is that in the sky. What is that in the sky?
What is that in the sky?

1. Is the moon up there?
   is the moon up there?
2. Do you see the stars
   Do you see the stars?
3. Is that a rocket?
   Is that a rocket
4. where is it going?
   Where is it going?

5–8. Proofread Jan's science questions. Find four mistakes with capital letters and end marks. Write each question correctly.

Example what do I want to know.
What do I want to know?

How
~~how~~ big are rockets?
Are all rockets the same size?
Can a rocket reach Mars?
Where
~~where~~ are rockets built?

Write Questions

Write three questions that you can answer correctly. Read your questions to classmates. Have them try to answer the questions.
Questions will vary.

 For Extra Practice, see page 58.

Meeting Individual Needs

● RETEACHING WORKBOOK, page 8

6 Questions

A **question** asks something. It begins with a capital letter. It ends with a question mark.
What things make you laugh**?**
Do you laugh at a funny story**?**

Write the correct questions.

Example Do you tell jokes? do you tell jokes?
Do you tell jokes?

Who likes riddles?

1. Do you smile at a surprise Do you smile at a surprise?
   Do you smile at a surprise?
2. What surprises do you like? what surprises do you like?
   What surprises do you like?
3. do cartoons make you smile? Do cartoons make you smile?
   Do cartoons make you smile?

▲■ WORKBOOK PLUS, pages 13–14

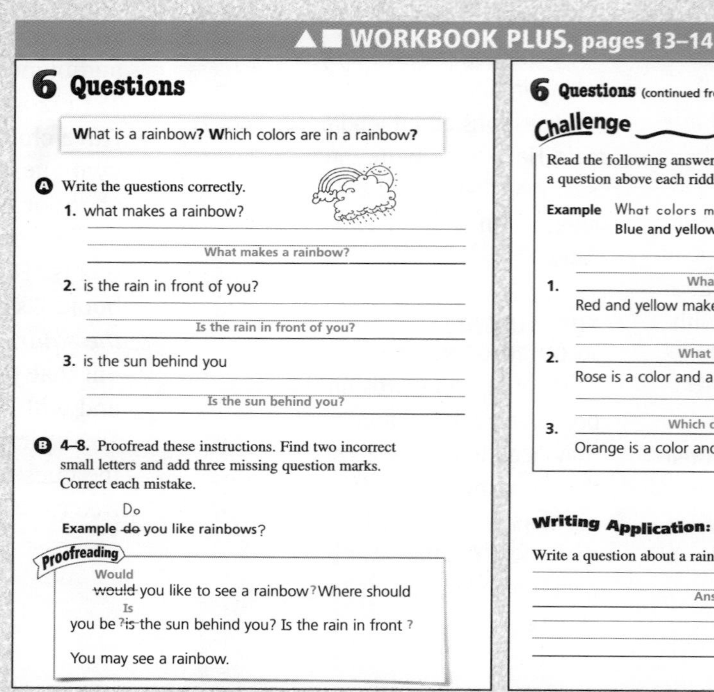

6 Questions

What is a rainbow? Which colors are in a rainbow?

A Write the questions correctly.

1. what makes a rainbow?
   What makes a rainbow?
2. is the rain in front of you?
   Is the rain in front of you?
3. is the sun behind you
   Is the sun behind you?

B **4–8.** Proofread these instructions. Find two incorrect small letters and add three missing question marks. Correct each mistake.

Example Do ~~do~~ you like rainbows?

Proofreading

Would ~~would~~ you like to see a rainbow? Where should you be? Is ~~is~~ the sun behind you? Is the rain in front? You may see a rainbow.

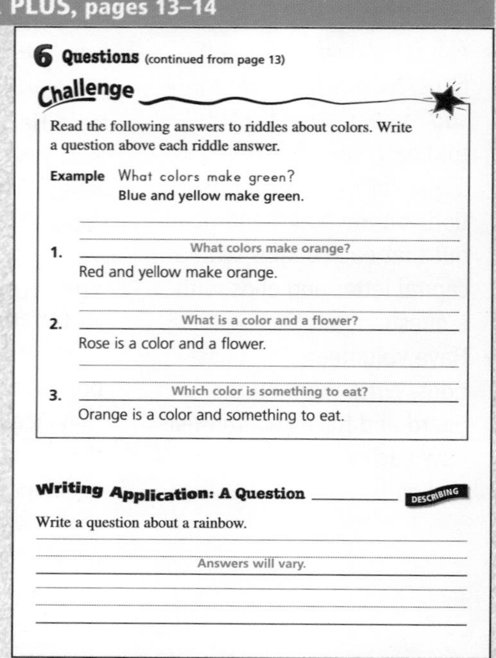

6 Questions (continued from page 13)

Challenge

Read the following answers to riddles about colors. Write a question above each riddle answer.

Example What colors make green?
Blue and yellow make green.

1. What colors make orange?
   Red and yellow make orange.
2. What is a color and a flower?
   Rose is a color and a flower.
3. Which color is something to eat?
   Orange is a color and something to eat.

Writing Application: A Question DESCRIBING

Write a question about a rainbow.
Answers will vary.

Grammar / Mechanics

7 Which Kind of Sentence?

One-Minute Warm-Up

Look at the picture below. Ask questions about it. Invite classmates to answer with telling sentences.
Questions and answers will vary.

A sentence can ask a question or tell something. A **question** ends with a question mark. A **telling sentence** ends with a period. Read the question. Then read the telling sentence that answers it.

What is in the balloon?

Pets are in the balloon.

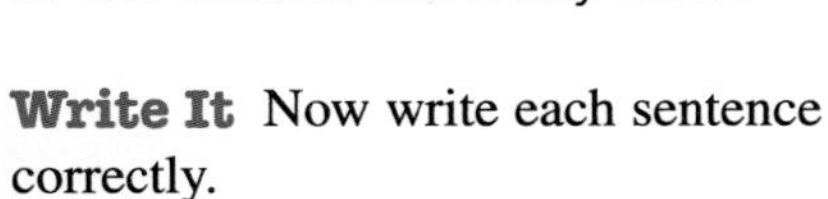

Try It Out

Speak Up Read each sentence and say if it is a telling sentence or a question. Tell what end mark should be added.

question; question mark
1. What color is the balloon

telling sentence; period
2. The balloon has many colors

Write It Now write each sentence correctly.

Example where will the balloon go
Where will the balloon go?

What color is the balloon?
The balloon has many colors.

Meeting Individual Needs

RETEACHING
ALTERNATIVE STRATEGY

- Make two columns, wide enough for sentences, on the board. Write *Telling Sentence* and *Question* as headings. Have children dictate sentences for you to write. For each, have them say in which column a sentence belongs and what end mark each should use.
- Ask children how the written sentences are alike. (Each begins with a capital letter.)

CHALLENGE
Have children make a "Telling" box or a "Question" box. Then ask them to write a telling sentence and a question in the correct box. Have volunteers read a sentence aloud and say whether it is in the correct box.

FOR STUDENTS ACQUIRING ENGLISH
Ask questions such as *Is this a book? Is his name Marcos? Does Ana have brown hair?* Call attention to the rising intonation in these yes-no questions. Model and have children repeat.

Which Kind of Sentence?

Lesson Objectives

Children will:
- distinguish between telling sentences and questions
- correctly punctuate telling sentences and questions
- proofread sentences for capital letters and end marks
- write informative questions and answers for a nature guide, using end marks correctly

One-Minute Warm-Up Write on the board children's questions and answers about the picture omitting the end punctuation. Have volunteers add end punctuation to each sentence and tell why they used that kind of mark.

Focus on Instruction

Tell children that all sentences begin with a capital letter, but not all sentences end with a period. Explain that a question is a sentence that ends with a question mark.

Try It Out

LISTENING AND SPEAKING Have pairs of children take turns saying the question *"What color is the balloon?"* and answering the question with the telling sentence *"The balloon has many colors."* Ask children to substitute other words for color, for example: *What shape is the balloon?* Suggest that children stress the word shape in the question and the word relating to shape in the answer.

FOR STUDENTS ACQUIRING ENGLISH

- Have children listen to the Try It Out sentences on the audiotape. Distribute the SAE Practice page for Unit 1, Lesson 7.
- Ask a variety of questions: *Do you have a dog? What day is it? Am I [your name]?* Write the questions on the board without punctuation. Ask how children know these are questions. Call attention to the falling intonation of *wh-* questions and the rising intonation of yes-no questions. Ask for more examples from children. Listen for correct intonation. Then children listen and add end punctuation. Then discuss which are telling sentences and which are questions.
  1. Is the balloon big (big? – question)
  2. The boys and girls watch (watch. – telling sentence)

Summing Up Help children summarize these key points about the lesson:

A sentence can ask a question or tell something. A **question** ends with a question mark. A **telling sentence** ends with a period.

You may want to have children complete the parts related to this lesson on Blackline Master 1-2.

On Your Own

Have children test each sentence by asking:

Does this tell something or does this ask something? Which end mark does this sentence need?

FOR STUDENTS ACQUIRING ENGLISH

Distribute the SAE Practice page for Unit 1, Lesson 7. Ask children to describe the art. Help them label the art. Children add punctuation and write **T** for telling sentences and **Q** for questions.

1. Bees buzz (buzz. T)
2. Do bees make honey (honey? Q)

Writing Wrap-Up

Writing Tip: Tell children that using words such as *what*, *where*, or *when* are good ways to begin questions that ask for information about something. See Blackline Master 1-4 for a sample of questions and answers.

TECHNOLOGY CONNECTION

Children may want to use an encyclopedia to gather information, including illustrations.

On Your Own

Write each sentence. Add the correct end mark. Write **T** after each telling sentence and **Q** after each question.

Example A bee is a bug
A bee is a bug. T

1. Do bees buzz? Q
2. Bees make honey. T
3. Bees have wings. T
4. Is honey sweet? Q

5–8. Proofread these sentences from a nature guide. Find four mistakes with capital letters and end marks. Write each sentence correctly.

Example is this a spider Is this a spider?

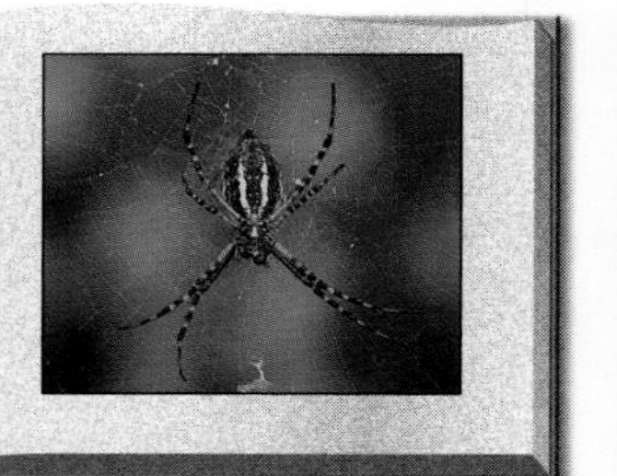

Writing Wrap-Up

WRITING • THINKING • LISTENING • SPEAKING

INFORMING

Write a Nature Guide Page

Write two questions about a bug. Write the answers and draw a picture. Read your questions and answers. Have a classmate check that you used end marks correctly. Questions and answers will vary.

 For Extra Practice, see page 59.

Meeting Individual Needs

● RETEACHING WORKBOOK, page 9

7 Which Kind of Sentence?

A **telling sentence** begins with a capital letter and ends with a period.
We visited a sheep farm**.**
A **question** begins with a capital letter and ends with a question mark.
Have you been to a sheep farm**?**

Write **telling** after each telling sentence. Write **question** after each question.

Example Where do we get wool? question

1. Wool comes from sheep. telling
2. A sheep's wool grows thick. telling
3. Do people cut the wool? question
4. Does that hurt the sheep? question
5. The sheep does not feel it. telling
6. How do we use wool? question

▲■ WORKBOOK PLUS, pages 15–16

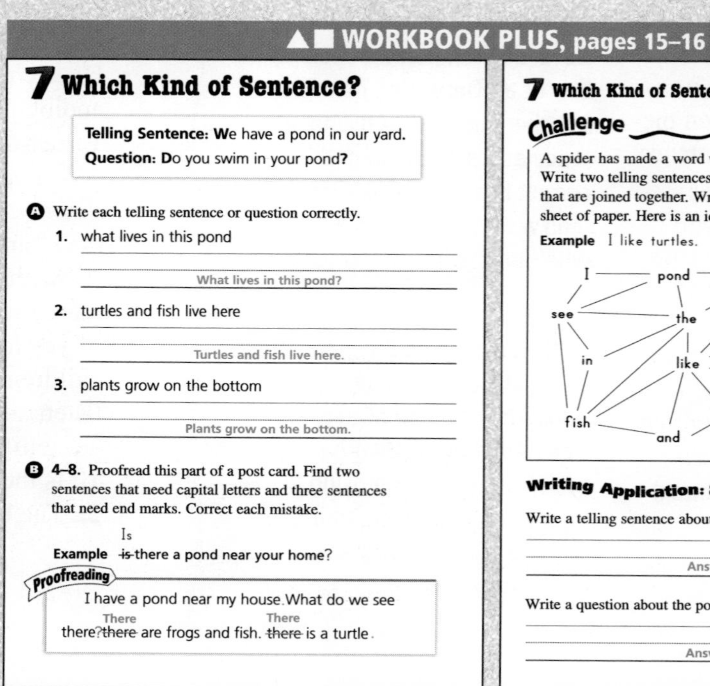

7 Which Kind of Sentence?

Telling Sentence: **W**e have a pond in our yard**.**
Question: **D**o you swim in your pond**?**

A Write each telling sentence or question correctly.

1. what lives in this pond
What lives in this pond?
2. turtles and fish live here
Turtles and fish live here.
3. plants grow on the bottom
Plants grow on the bottom.

B **4–8.** Proofread this part of a post card. Find two sentences that need capital letters and three sentences that need end marks. Correct each mistake.

Example Is is there a pond near your home?

Proofreading

I have a pond near my house. What do we see there? There there are frogs and fish. There there is a turtle.

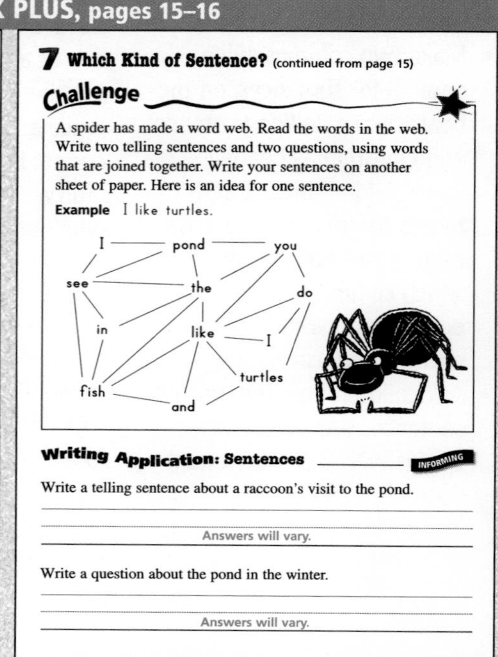

7 Which Kind of Sentence? (continued from page 15)

Challenge

A spider has made a word web. Read the words in the web. Write two telling sentences and two questions, using words that are joined together. Write your sentences on another sheet of paper. Here is an idea for one sentence.

Example I like turtles.

Writing Application: Sentences INFORMING

Write a telling sentence about a raccoon's visit to the pond.
Answers will vary.

Write a question about the pond in the winter.
Answers will vary.

Grammar / Mechanics

8 Commands

Do what this sentence tells you to do.

Close your eyes and count to four.

—from Clap Your Hands, by Lorinda Bryan Cauley

Children should do what the sentence says.

A telling sentence ends with a period. A question ends with a question mark. Another kind of sentence is a **command**. A command tells a person or animal to do something. A command begins with a **capital letter** and ends with a **period**. A command often begins with an action word.

Play this game with me. Listen to the rules.

Try It Out

Speak Up Tell how to make each command correct.

1. Hide 3. count to ten.

Add a period after sentences 1, 2, and 4.

2. be quiet 4. Look around

Begin sentences 2 and 3 with a capital letter.

Write It Now write the sentences correctly.

Example close your eyes
Close your eyes.

Hide.
Be quiet.
Count to ten.
Look around.

Meeting Individual Needs

RETEACHING
ALTERNATIVE STRATEGY

- Say several commands, for example, *Follow the rules* or *Play quietly*. Explain that each one is called a **command.** Write them on the board, pointing out that each begins with a capital letter and ends with a period.
- Have volunteers say commands. Write them on the board. Have children tell how each command should begin and end.

CHALLENGE

Have a volunteer say commands that are rules for a familiar game. Have the other children guess the name of the game. The first one to give the answer is the next one to give rules for a game.

FOR STUDENTS ACQUIRING ENGLISH

Give children a series of simple classroom commands to follow such as *sit down, stand up, touch your nose, clap your hands*. Children perform these actions in unison. Then they take turns giving some themselves.

Commands

Lesson Objectives

Children will:

- identify commands
- capitalize and punctuate commands correctly
- proofread for capital letters and periods
- write informative commands for a game

One-Minute Warm-Up Have children obey the command. Ask several volunteers to give other simple commands. Explain that these sentences are commands because they tell the listener to do something.

Focus on Instruction

Point out that in saying a sentence that is a command, the naming part is you, although it is not usually said in the sentence. Use the lesson sentences as examples: *(You) Play this game with me. (You) Listen to the rules.*

Try It Out

Listening and Speaking Have children listen as you ask each question about the rules in the exercise. Then have them say the rule that answers the question.

- Which rule tells how long to wait for the other players to hide? *(Count to ten.)*
- Which rule tells what to do to find the other players? *(Look around.)*
- Which rule tells what the players who are hiding should do? *(Be quiet.)*

FOR STUDENTS ACQUIRING ENGLISH

- Have children listen to the Try It Out sentences on the audiotape. Distribute the SAE Practice page for Unit 1, Lesson 8.
- Write the word *command* on the board. Say and write examples such as *Open the door. Tell me your name.* Remind children that a command does not have *you* as the naming part because this word is understood. Say that this is the only type of sentence in English that does not have a naming part. Ask what the command begins with. (a capital letter) Ask what a command ends with. (usually a period) Children listen, correct capital letters where needed, and add a period to each command.
  1. Sit down, please (please.)
  2. Spell your name for me (me.)
  3. open your books (Open - books.)

Summing Up Help children summarize these key points about the lesson:

A **command** is a sentence that tells a person or animal to do something. A command begins with a **capital letter** and ends with a **period**.

You may want to have children complete the parts related to this lesson on Blackline Master 1-2.

On Your Own

Have children ask these questions about each command: Where does it begin? Where does it end?

FOR STUDENTS ACQUIRING ENGLISH

Distribute the SAE Practice page for Unit 1, Lesson 8. Ask if children know the games of tug of war and Simon Says. Have volunteers describe them. Assist with vocabulary. Children add capital letters and add a period to each command.

1. pull the rope (Pull – rope.)
2. take two steps back (Take – back.)

Writing Wrap-Up

Writing Tip: Suggest that children visualize each command to make sure they have included enough information. See Blackline Master 1-4 for a sample of possible commands for the game.

SCHOOL-HOME CONNECTION

Have children work with family members to think of commands for favorite family games.

On Your Own

Write each command correctly.

Example stand here
Stand here.

1. take this rope — Take this rope.
2. pull hard — Pull hard.
3. do not let go — Do not let go.

4–6. Proofread this chart of commands. Find three mistakes with capital letters and end marks. Write the commands correctly.

Example line up at the door? Line up at the door.

Proofreading

Fire Drill Rules

~~do~~ Do not talk.

Please walk quickly?.

Follow your teacher.

Writing Wrap-Up

WRITING • THINKING • LISTENING • SPEAKING

INFORMING

Write Commands

Write commands to use while playing Simon Says. Work with a classmate to check that your commands begin and end correctly. In pairs, read and act out the commands.

Commands will vary.

 For Extra Practice, see page 60.

Meeting Individual Needs

● RETEACHING WORKBOOK, page 10

8 Commands

A **command** tells someone to do something. It begins with a capital letter. It ends with a period.
Brush your teeth now.
Turn off the water.

Write these commands correctly.

Example wash your face well — Wash your face well.

1. pick up the towel — Pick up the towel.
2. climb into bed now — Climb into bed now.
3. choose a story for tonight — Choose a story for tonight.
4. give me a good-night hug — Give me a good-night hug.

▲■ WORKBOOK PLUS, pages 17–18

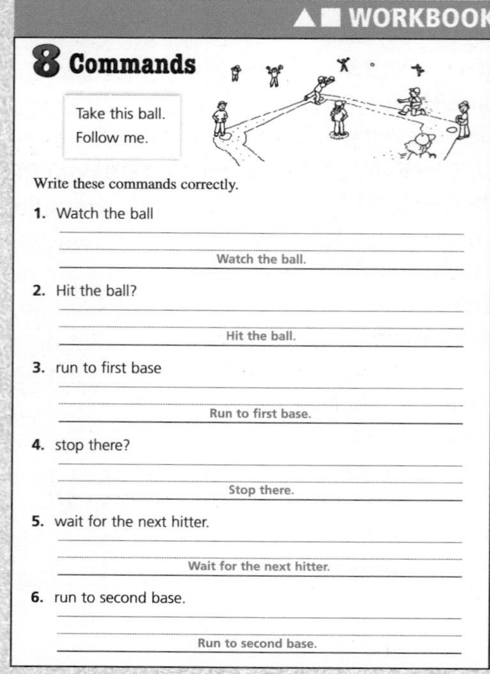

8 Commands

Take this ball.
Follow me.

Write these commands correctly.

1. Watch the ball — Watch the ball.
2. Hit the ball? — Hit the ball.
3. run to first base — Run to first base.
4. stop there? — Stop there.
5. wait for the next hitter. — Wait for the next hitter.
6. run to second base. — Run to second base.

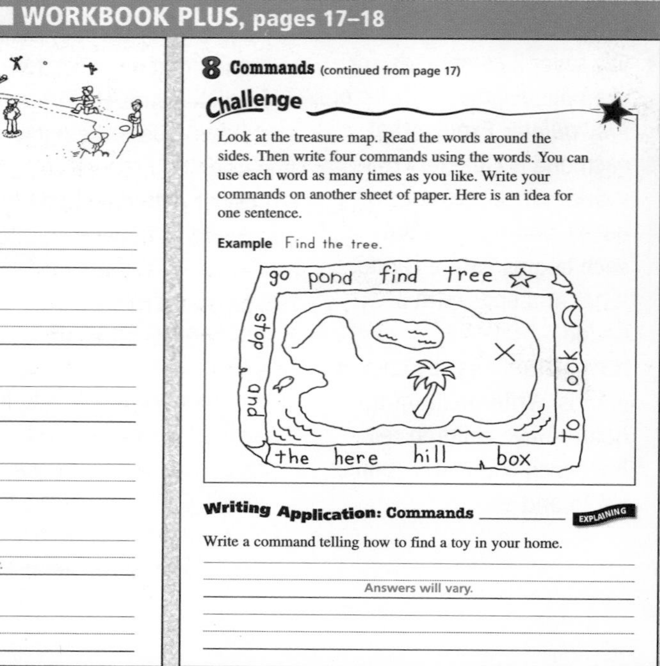

8 Commands (continued from page 17)

Challenge

Look at the treasure map. Read the words around the sides. Then write four commands using the words. You can use each word as many times as you like. Write your commands on another sheet of paper. Here is an idea for one sentence.

Example Find the tree.

Writing Application: Commands EXPLAINING

Write a command telling how to find a toy in your home.

Answers will vary.

Grammar / Mechanics

9 Exclamations

One-Minute Warm-Up

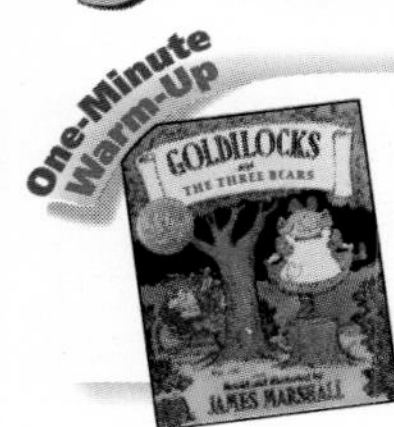

Say this sentence with surprise or anger in your voice.

"Somebody has been lying in my bed!"

—from Goldilocks and the Three Bears, by James Marshall

Responses will vary.

All sentences begin with a **capital letter**. A telling sentence and a command end with a period. A question ends with a question mark. Another kind of a sentence is an **exclamation**. It ends with an **exclamation point** (!). An exclamation shows a strong feeling such as excitement, surprise, or fear.

Someone broke my chair! There she is!

Try It Out

Speak Up Tell how to make each exclamation correct. Read each sentence with strong feeling.

1. help me!
2. I am afraid
3. I must run home now

Add an ! after sentences 2 and 3. Begin sentence 1 with a capital letter.

Write It Now write the exclamations correctly.

Example This bed is too hard This bed is too hard!

Help me!
I am afraid!
I must run home now!

Exclamations

Lesson Objectives

Children will:

- identify exclamations
- capitalize and punctuate exclamations correctly
- proofread for capital letters and exclamation points
- write creative exclamations about a fanciful picture

One-Minute Warm-Up Write the quoted sentence on the board without any end punctuation. Have volunteers say it as a statement and as a question and write the appropriate end mark. Then add an exclamation point and have children say it.

Focus on Instruction

Point out that in saying an exclamation the tone of voice brings out the strong feeling intended.

Try It Out

LISTENING AND SPEAKING Have children listen as you ask a question about the exclamations in the exercise. Then call on individuals to say the exclamation that answers the question, prompting them to use the same tone of voice as Goldilocks.

- What does Goldilocks say when she sees the bears and cries out for help? *(Help me!)*
- How does Goldilocks say she feels? *(I am afraid!)*
- What does Goldilocks say she must do? (*I must run home now!*)

FOR STUDENTS ACQUIRING ENGLISH

- Have children listen to the Try It Out sentences on the audiotape. Distribute the SAE Practice page for Unit 1, Lesson 9.
- Make an exclamation point on the board. Ask what it is called and how it is used. Model the strong stress on a key word in an exclamation. Have children practice saying sentences after you. Ask if children know the story of "Goldilocks and the Three Bears." If not, tell the story or have volunteers take turns telling parts of it. Tell children to listen for strong stress in the exclamations. Children listen and add capital letters and exclamation points.
  1. this chair is too big (This – big!)
  2. I'm tired (tired!)

Meeting Individual Needs

RETEACHING

ALTERNATIVE STRATEGY

- Say several exclamations, for example, *I'm so hungry!* or *My slipper is gone!* Explain that each statement is called an **exclamation**. Write them on the board, pointing out that each begins with a capital letter and ends with an exclamation point.
- Have volunteers say exclamations. Write them on the board and ask how each should begin and end.

CHALLENGE

Have a volunteer say exclamations for a particular situation. Have the other children guess what the situation is. The first one to give the answer is the next one to say an exclamation.

FOR STUDENTS ACQUIRING ENGLISH

With strong feeling say, for example, *I'm cold!* (or *I'm hot!*) *I'm so hungry! That's a great story!* Write the phrases without the exclamation point. Use the first one to show how the mark is made. Call on children to make it on the others.

Summing Up Help children summarize these key points about the lesson:

An **exclamation** shows strong feeling. It begins with a **capital letter** and ends with an **exclamation point.**

You may want to have children complete the parts related to this lesson on Blackline Master 1-2.

On Your Own

Have children test each exclamation by asking:

Does it show a strong feeling? Should it begin with a capital letter and end with an exclamation point?

FOR STUDENTS ACQUIRING ENGLISH

Distribute the SAE Practice page for Unit 1, Lesson 9. Find out if children know the nursery rhymes in this lesson. If not, plan a reading. Review strong stress. Children add capital letters and exclamation points.

1. you are a big wolf (You – wolf!)
2. that's a big spider (That's – spider!)

Writing Wrap-Up

Writing Tip: Have children think of a fairy tale that makes them laugh or feel afraid. See Blackline Master 1-4 for a sample of an exclamation.

SCHOOL-HOME CONNECTION

Have children play a game with family members by saying an exclamation from or about a familiar story and having others guess the name of the story.

On Your Own

Write the correct exclamation in each pair.

Example close the door Close the door!
Close the door!

1. the wolf is after us!
   The wolf is after us!
2. I will blow your house down?
   I will blow your house down!
3. Go away.
   Go away!
4. I am not afraid!
   I am not afraid.

5–8. Proofread this page from a class book. Find four mistakes with capital letters and end marks in these exclamations. Write the title and sentences correctly.

Example spider scares little girl.
Spider scares little girl!

Proofreading

Nursery Rhyme News
~~cow~~ Cow jumps over the moon!
~~big~~ Big egg falls off the wall!
Mouse runs up the clock~~?~~!

Writing Wrap-Up

WRITING • THINKING • LISTENING • SPEAKING

CREATING

Write Exclamations

Draw a picture of a nursery rhyme or fairy tale. Write an exclamation about the picture. Read your exclamation with expression to a classmate. Add it to a class book.
Exclamations will vary.

 For Extra Practice, see page 61.

Meeting Individual Needs

● RETEACHING WORKBOOK, page 11

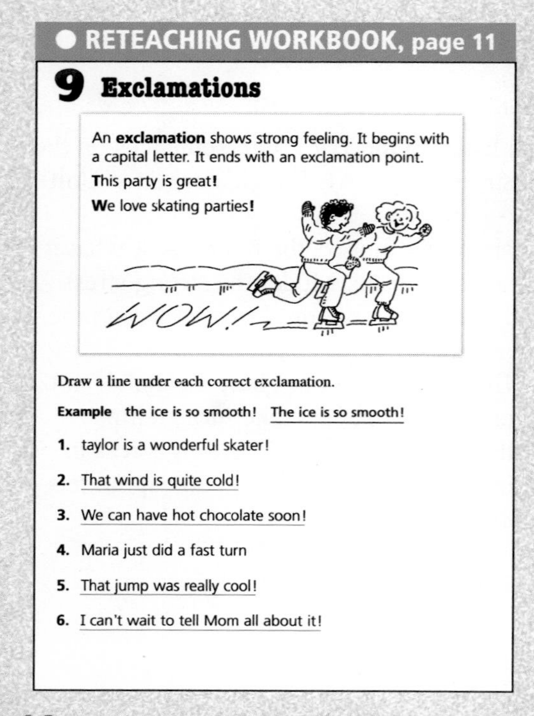

9 Exclamations

An **exclamation** shows strong feeling. It begins with a capital letter. It ends with an exclamation point.
This party is great**!**
We love skating parties**!**

Draw a line under each correct exclamation.

Example the ice is so smooth! The ice is so smooth!

1. taylor is a wonderful skater!
2. That wind is quite cold!
3. We can have hot chocolate soon!
4. Maria just did a fast turn
5. That jump was really cool!
6. I can't wait to tell Mom all about it!

▲■ WORKBOOK PLUS, pages 19-20

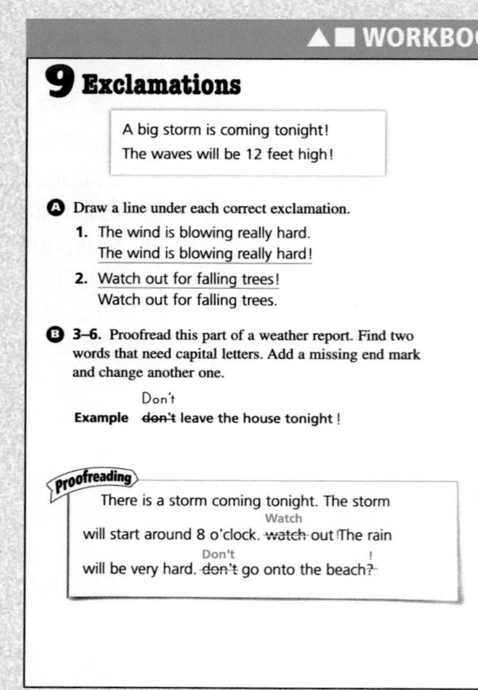

9 Exclamations

A big storm is coming tonight!
The waves will be 12 feet high!

A Draw a line under each correct exclamation.

1. The wind is blowing really hard.
   The wind is blowing really hard!
2. Watch out for falling trees!
   Watch out for falling trees.

B 3–6. Proofread this part of a weather report. Find two words that need capital letters. Add a missing end mark and change another one.

Example ~~don't~~ Don't leave the house tonight !

Proofreading

There is a storm coming tonight. The storm will start around 8 o'clock. ~~watch~~ Watch out ! The rain will be very hard. ~~don't~~ Don't go onto the beach~~?~~ !

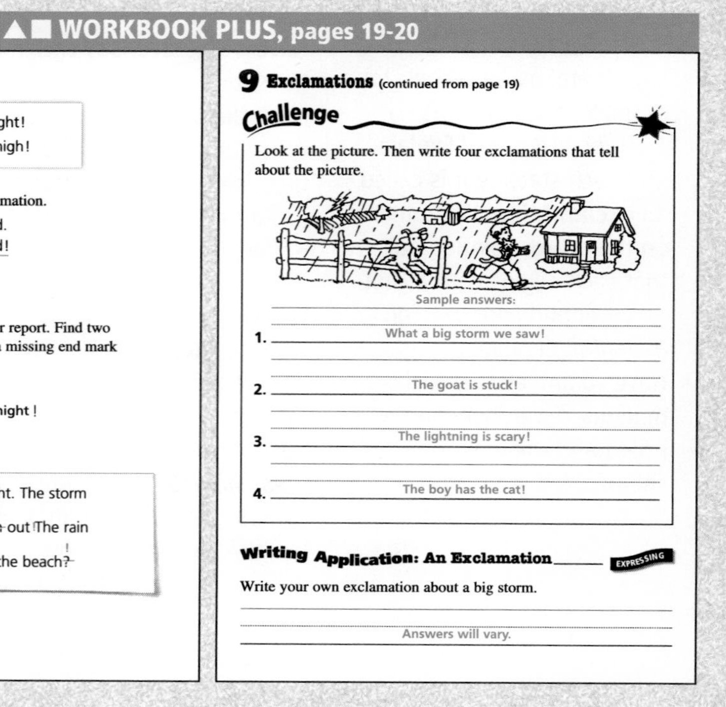

9 Exclamations (continued from page 19)

Challenge

Look at the picture. Then write four exclamations that tell about the picture.

Sample answers:
1. What a big storm we saw!
2. The goat is stuck!
3. The lightning is scary!
4. The boy has the cat!

Writing Application: An Exclamation EXPRESSING

Write your own exclamation about a big storm.

Answers will vary.

Enrichment

The Sentence!

Silly Animals

- Fold a sheet of paper. Draw the front part of an animal on the left and the back part of another animal on the right.
- Name your animal and write a sentence about it. Write the naming part on the left and the action part on the right.

Challenge Write a story about your animal. Have a classmate say the naming part and action part of each sentence.

The Sentence Game

Get Ready You will need some paper and 4 blank cards for each player. Write a spelling word on each card. Then write T for telling sentence or Q for question.

How to Play Mix and stack the cards face down. Choose a card and read the word and the letter aloud. Another player writes the word and uses it in a telling sentence or question. Score 1 point for each word spelled correctly. Score 1 point for each complete sentence.

Enrichment

Objectives

Children will:
- generate sentences by drawing silly animals
- identify naming and action parts of sentences
- generate telling sentences and questions by playing a card game

Using the Activities

The Enrichment page provides fun, creative activities that reinforce children's understanding and use of sentences. The activities are designed to be enjoyed by all children. Here are some ideas for using the activities.

- Pair children who need extra support with more capable classmates.
- Children can work with these activities in class after they have completed other assignments.
- Activities that can be completed individually can be assigned as homework.

Notes on the Activities

SILLY ANIMALS

- Before you begin, be sure that each child has drawing materials.
- You might have children work in pairs. Each child can draw one half of the silly animal. Then partners can work together to make up a name.

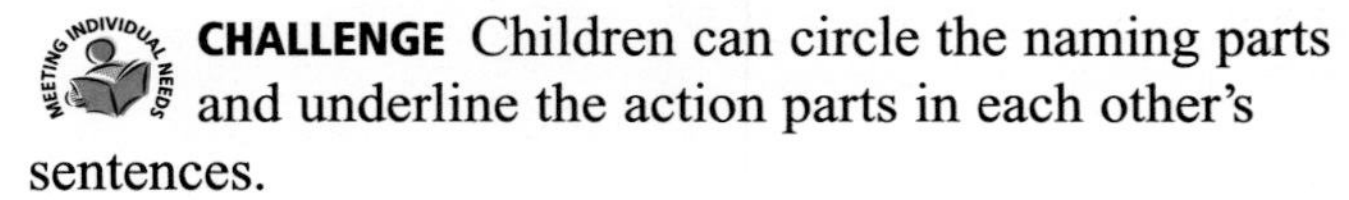

CHALLENGE Children can circle the naming parts and underline the action parts in each other's sentences.

THE SENTENCE GAME

This is a good game to put in a learning center.

- Introduce this game by drawing two blanks on the chalkboard. Fill them in with spelling words. Then ask children to say a telling sentence and a question for each word.
- You can make cards in advance and store them in a learning center with paper and pencils.

FOR STUDENTS ACQUIRING ENGLISH

For the activity *Silly Animals*, model an animal and then do a few as a class before asking children to work alone or in pairs. For *The Sentence Game*, model making the cards, then ask each child to make a few. Play as a class or in teams of two. If the class has no appropriate spelling words, use the ones from this unit.

Checkup

Objectives

Children will:
- make complete sentences
- finish sentences by writing a naming part or an actionpart
- identify complete sentences

Using the Checkup

Use the Checkup exercises as assessment, as review for the unit test, as extra practice, or as a diagnostic aid to help determine those children who need reteaching.

INTERNET CONNECTION
Children can take an interactive quiz for this unit at www.eduplace.com /kids/hme/ and then get immediate feedback.

What Is a Sentence? (page 27)
Write sentences by matching the words in Box A with the words in Box B.

A	B
1. The plane	tasted good.
2. The ride	liked the ride.
3. The food	took off.
4. All of us	was bumpy.

Naming Part and Action Part (pages 29, 31)
Choose a naming part or an action part from the Word Box to finish each sentence. Write the sentences.

The plane	was setting

5. The sun ____. was setting
6. ____ landed. The plane

Is It a Sentence? (page 33)
Copy each group of words. Write **yes** after each complete sentence. Write **no** after each group of words that is not a sentence.

7. Bright lights. no
8. The city was hot. yes
9. I walked home. yes
10. Made a loud noise. no

48 Checkup

Which Kind of Sentence? (pages 37, 39, 41)

Write each sentence. Add the correct end mark. Write **T** after each telling sentence. Write **Q** after each question.

11. I like the park . T
12. Will you come ? Q
13. Is it fun ? Q
14. Children ride bikes . T

Telling Sentences, Questions, Commands, and Exclamations

(pages 37, 39, 43, 45)

Write each sentence correctly. Add a capital letter and end mark.

Can we go to the parade?
15. can we go to the parade

Hold my hand.
16. hold my hand

That balloon is huge!
17. that balloon is huge

A band plays music.
18. a band plays music

Objectives

Children will:

- identify telling sentences and questions
- use capital letters and end marks correctly in telling sentences, questions, commands, and exclamations

Objectives

Children will:

- proofread a report for mistakes in capital letters, end marks, and to combine a naming part and an action part into one sentence

Mixed Review 19–25. Proofread this report. Find seven mistakes with capital letters and end marks. Be sure to make two word groups into one sentence. Then write the report correctly.

Proofreading Checklist

- ✔ Do sentences have a naming part and an action part?
- ✔ Do sentences begin with capital letters?
- ✔ Do telling sentences and commands end with periods?
- ✔ Do questions end with question marks?
- ✔ Do sentences that show strong feeling end with exclamation points?

Example do all birds build nests
Do all birds build nests?

Proofreading

Is It a Bird?

I love birds! Do you like birds. ? Guess what a bird is. Is a bird an animal that flies?

Not all birds fly. An ostrich and penguin do not fly?. An ostrich runs very fast. A penguin. swims ~~Swims~~ with its short wings.

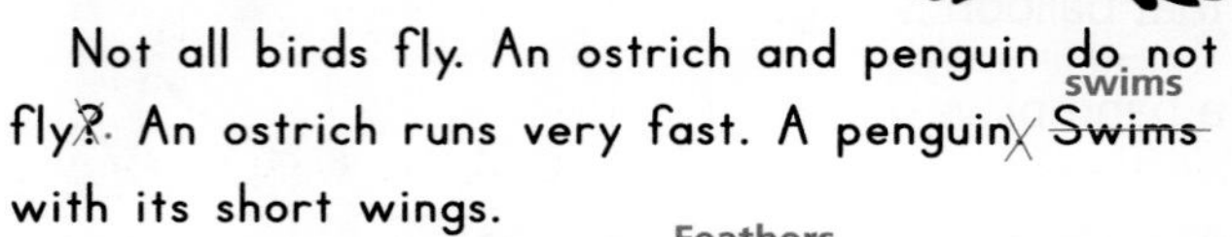

All birds have feathers. Feathers ~~feathers~~ keep a bird warm and dry. No other animals have feathers.

All birds lay eggs. Do ~~do~~ you want to know more about birds? Look in a bird book.

See www.eduplace.com/kids/hme/ for an online quiz.

Test Practice

Number a sheet of paper from 1 to 6. Read each sentence in 1, 2, and 3. Write the letter for the sentence that has the **naming part** underlined. Then read each sentence in 4, 5, and 6. Write the letter for the sentence that has the **action part** underlined.

1 **A** Kittens sit in a box.
(B) Ducks swim by.
C Birds fly in the air.
D Tom pats a brown dog.

2 **A** I drank cold water.
B Carlos rode his bike.
C The man sang a song.
(D) A girl swam in the pool.

3 (A) Jim played a drum.
B Lee ate some popcorn.
C Dad packed his lunch.
D A cloud hid the sun.

4 **A** Steve plays baseball.
B Two girls ate snacks.
C Jenny lost her hat.
(D) Snow covered the field.

5 **A** They fixed the lamp.
B Andy set the table.
(C) Mike went to the store.
D A glass broke.

6 **A** We went to a movie.
(B) Elena watched TV.
C The twins did a dance.
D A big storm began.

Test Practice

Objective

Children will:

- practice completing a test format that requires them to choose the correct item among four

Using the Test Practice

These Test Practice pages provide practice with common formats used in standardized or multiple-choice tests.

These two pages work with skills taught in the basic lessons in Unit 1.

Notes on the Test Format

- Ask a volunteer to read the directions aloud. If necessary, review that the naming part of a sentence tells *who* or *what* in a sentence. Point out that there will be only one correct answer.
- Then have children carefully read each sentence in Item 1. Explain that they should read all four possible answers before choosing the one that has the naming part underlined.

FOR STUDENTS ACQUIRING ENGLISH

Begin by reviewing what a sentence is, the types of sentences—telling sentences, questions, or exclamations—and the three types of end marks. Write sentences and have children add the correct punctuation. Then ask the children to find the naming part and the action part. Distribute the SAE Test Practice pages for Unit 1. Read the directions aloud for each section; show children how to circle the correct answers. Tell children to read all of the answers before choosing their responses and to look for clues such as word order.

Objective

Children will:

- practice completing a test format that requires them to choose the correct item from among three

Notes on the Test Format

- Have children discuss the directions and determine what to do. Then have a volunteer read aloud the sentence in Item 7. Tell children that reading aloud may give them clues about the type of sentence it is.
- Go over the responses to Item 7. Point out that there are only three possible end marks from which to choose. You may wish to review each of the marks.
- Ask children to try reading the sentence with the sound that each end mark would require. Then have them choose the correct answer.

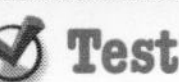

Test Practice continued

Write the numbers 7 to 18 on your paper. Read each sentence. Choose the mark that belongs at the end of the sentence. Write the letter that is under the correct end mark.

7 Choose a book to read
. Ⓐ ? B ! C

8 What time is it
. A ? Ⓑ ! C

9 Ben likes to play music
. Ⓐ ? B ! C

10 I love that song
. A ? B ! Ⓒ

11 A friend can come too
. Ⓐ ? B ! C

12 Where are we going
. A ? Ⓑ ! C

13 That is good news
. A ? B ! Ⓒ

14 Please close the door
. Ⓐ ? B ! C

15 What is the weather
. A ? Ⓑ ! C

16 What do you want to eat
. A ? Ⓑ ! C

17 I like to go to school
. Ⓐ ? B ! C

18 You did a great job
. A ? B ! Ⓒ

Extra Practice

1 What Is a Sentence? (pages 27–28)

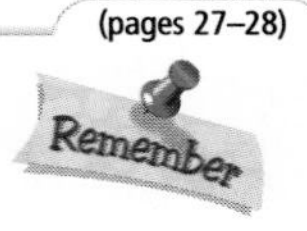

- A sentence tells what someone or something did or does.

●▲ Make sentences by matching sentence parts. Write the sentences.

Example The boy wagged its tail. drew a dog. The boy drew a dog.

A	B
1. Kate	crossed the sky.
2. The rainbow	were red and blue.
3. The colors	painted a picture.

■ Write each sentence, using a sentence part from the Word Box to complete it.

Ryan	swims	kitten
barks	crawls	

Example The puppy ____. The puppy barks.

4. Ryan has a turtle.
5. His pet turtle crawls.
6. My kitten has whiskers.
7. Her fish swims fast.

What Is a Sentence?

Objectives

Children will:

- combine naming and action parts to make sentences
- identify and write sentence parts to complete sentences

Using the Extra Practice

The Extra Practice activities provide two levels of additional practice for the basic lesson: Easy/Average (●▲), and Challenging (■).

The Extra Practice activities can be used in the following ways.

- Assign activities according to children's needs and abilities as homework after children have completed the basic lesson.
- Assign the Easy/Average activities after using the lesson Reteaching instruction.
- Assign the Challenging exercises as a Bonus activity.
- Assign the Easy/Average activities to prepare children for the Checkup.
- Assign the Easy/Average activities to children who had difficulty with specific lessons on the Checkup.

Meeting Individual Needs — More Practice for Lesson 1

● EASY ▲ AVERAGE

Draw lines to make sentences.

1. Rob — fell from the sky.
2. The rain — hangs on the wall.
3. The painting — sang a song together.
4. The girls — went fishing.
5. The fisherman — went to school.
6. My brother — is full of vegetables.
7. The garden — barks a lot.
8. The beach — helps me with my chores.
9. The lions — is a fun place to play with sand.
10. My dog — roared in the jungle.

■ CHALLENGING

Add a sentence part to make each group of words a sentence. (Answers will vary.)

1. The cat ____.
2. ________ fell asleep.
3. My sister ________.
4. The car __________.
5. _______ went shopping.
6. Bobby and Marie _______.
7. ________ took a trip.
8. The doctor ____________.
9. The teacher ____________.
10. My friend ____________.

Naming Part

Objective

Children will:
- identify and write the naming parts of sentences

Extra Practice

(pages 29–30)

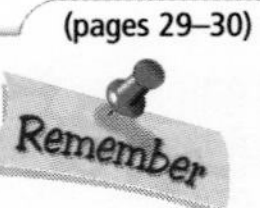

2 Naming Part
- The naming part of a sentence tells who or what did or does something.

●▲ Choose a naming part from the Word Box to begin each sentence. Write the sentences.

Chicks	Bees	Birds	Frogs	Lions

Example _____ peep. Chicks peep.

1. Frogs leap.
2. Birds sing.
3. Bees sting.
4. Lions roar.

■ Write each sentence. Draw a line under the naming part.

Example Those snakes hiss. Those snakes hiss.

5. Babies sleep.
6. Children skip.
7. Raindrops drip.
8. Most kittens play.
9. The goat eats hay.
10. Bears growl.
11. Those monkeys howl.
12. Roosters crow.
13. Some farmers hoe.
14. Cows moo and chew.

Meeting Individual Needs — More Practice for Lesson 2

● **EASY** ▲ **AVERAGE**

Choose one of these naming parts to begin each sentence: sun, water, grass, kittens, dogs, clowns, kids, balls, babies, pencils

1. _____ write. Pencils
2. _____ shines. Sun
3. _____ grows. Grass
4. _____ drips. Water
5. _____ play. Kids
6. _____ cry. Babies
7. _____ meow. Kittens
8. _____ bounce. Balls
9. _____ joke. Clowns
10. _____ bark. Dogs

■ **CHALLENGING**

Draw a line under each naming part.

1. The girls played.
2. Manny sat down.
3. Frank and June ate lunch.
4. Most boys go to school.
5. Some people like apples.
6. Those kids have a new ball.
7. Cats meow.
8. Many birds can fly.
9. Parents help their children.
10. Horses trot.

Extra Practice

3 Action Part (pages 31–32)

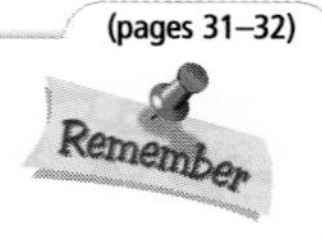

- The action part of the sentence tells what the naming part did or does.

●▲ Write each sentence, using an action part from the Word Box.

naps	shines	hops
chirps	bloom	

Example The rabbit ____.
The rabbit hops.

1. The flowers bloom.
2. The sun shines.
3. The robin chirps.
4. The cat naps.

■ Write each sentence, adding your own action part.

Example Flowers ____.
Flowers grow in my garden.

5. Bees ____. Answers will vary.
6. Birds ____. Answers will vary.
7. My friend and I ____. Answers will vary.

Action Part

Objective

Children will:

- Identify and write the action parts of sentences

Meeting Individual Needs

More Practice for Lesson 3

● **EASY** ▲ **AVERAGE**

Choose one of these action parts to finish each sentence: growls, jumps, smiles, rings, honks, moos, purrs, falls, rips, bakes

1. The bell ______. rings
2. The happy girl ______. smiles
3. The car horn ______. honks
4. The cow ______. moos
5. The snow ______. falls
6. The paper ______. rips
7. The tiger ________. growls
8. The grasshopper ______. jumps
9. The baker ______. bakes
10. The cat ______. purrs

■ **CHALLENGING**

Write an action part to finish each sentence. (Answers will vary.)

1. Some people ______.
2. Those girls ________.
3. The mean dog _______.
4. The happy fish ________.
5. Kate _________.
6. Snakes ________.
7. Willy and Joe _______.
8. The snowman _________.
9. My bicycle ___________.
10. Turtles __________.

Is It a Sentence?

Objectives

Children will:
- identify sentences
- identify naming and action parts
- write naming and action parts in the correct order to make sentences

Extra Practice

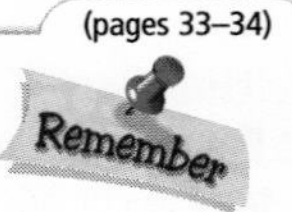

(pages 33–34)

4 Is It a Sentence?
- A complete sentence has a naming part and an action part.

●▲ Copy each word group.
Write **yes** if the word group is a sentence.
Write **no** if it is not a sentence.

Example A big park.
A big park. no

1. Children played. yes
2. Two happy boys. no
3. Sat on swings. no
4. We ran home. yes

■ Put the naming part and the action part together in the correct order. Write each sentence.

Example loves the rain.
Brad
Brad loves the rain.

5. Pam
wears red boots. Pam wears red boots.
6. fall on us.
Big raindrops
Big raindrops fall on us.

Meeting Individual Needs

More Practice for Lesson 4

● **EASY** ▲ **AVERAGE**

Write **yes** if the words make a sentence. Write **no** if the words do not make a sentence.

1. mice in the house no
2. to get a book no
3. People laughed. yes
4. We found you. yes
5. you found no
6. Missy went to sleep. yes
7. four little dogs no
8. Charlie and no
9. rode the bus no
10. Julie rides her bicycle. yes

■ **CHALLENGING**

Write **N** if the words are a naming part. Write **A** if the words are an action part. Put the naming part and the action part together in the correct order to make sentences.

1. has a kitten. A	Beth N	Beth has a kitten.
2. found a key. A	Sally N	Sally found a key.
3. George and Sam N	talked. A	George and Sam talked.
4. had a good time. A	Bruce N	Bruce had a good time.
5. fly at night. A	Bats N	Bats fly at night.
6. The sisters N	share a room. A	The sisters share a room.
7. My teddy bear N	is brown. A	My teddy bear is brown.
8. Gina N	wants to play. A	Gina wants to play.
9. stands over there. A	The teacher N	The teacher stands over there.
10. has many friends. A	She N	She has many friends.

Extra Practice

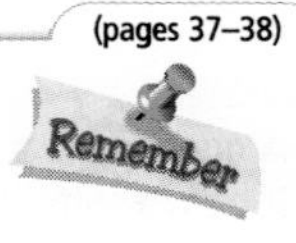

(pages 37–38)

5 Telling Sentences

- A telling sentence tells something.
- It begins with a capital letter.
- It ends with a period (.).

●▲ Write the correct telling sentence in each pair.

Example I have a fish. I have a fish.
I have a fish

1. it lives in a fishbowl
   It lives in a fishbowl.
2. The fish has blue stripes
   The fish has blue stripes.
3. It is a zebra fish.
   it is a zebra fish.
4. i like my pet
   I like my pet.

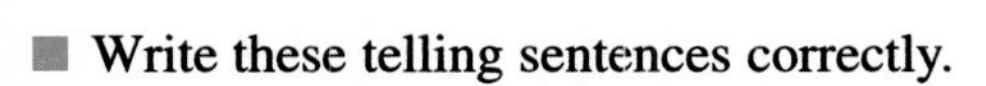

■ Write these telling sentences correctly.

Example joe has a parrot
Joe has a parrot.

5. it has green wings It has green wings.
6. the parrot talks The parrot talks.
7. it walks up a ladder It walks up a ladder.

Telling Sentences

Objective

Children will:

- identify and write telling sentences

Meeting Individual Needs — More Practice for Lesson 5

● **EASY** ▲ **AVERAGE**

Write **yes** if the sentence is a correctly written telling sentence. Write **no** if the sentence is not a correctly written telling sentence.

1. Mark has a blue shirt. yes
2. I want to go no
3. She lives in a pink house. yes
4. Bears like to eat honey. yes
5. rabbits hop in the grass no
6. The sun is shining today. yes
7. no one is at home no
8. everybody claps no
9. Susan read the book no
10. Many kids like the movie. yes

■ **CHALLENGING**

Write these telling sentences correctly.

1. the parrot can sing
   The parrot can sing.
2. the cage is big
   The cage is big.
3. we feed it seeds
   We feed it seeds.
4. my bird is pretty
   My bird is pretty.
5. our bird talks a lot
   Our bird talks a lot.
6. the two birds sing
   The two birds sing.
7. her name is Polly
   Her name is Polly.
8. his name is Mike
   His name is Mike.
9. they drink water
   They drink water.
10. birds fly in the sky
    Birds fly in the sky.

Questions

Objective

Children will:

- identify and write questions

Extra Practice

(pages 39–40)

6 Questions

- A question is a sentence that asks something.
- It begins with a capital letter.
- It ends with a question mark (?).

●▲ Write the correct question in each pair.

Example where is the dog Where is the dog?
Where is the dog?

1. Is it under the bed?
   is it under the bed?
2. did you call the dog
   Did you call the dog?
3. Did you hear a bark?
   Did you hear a bark
4. is it in the back yard
   Is it in the back yard?

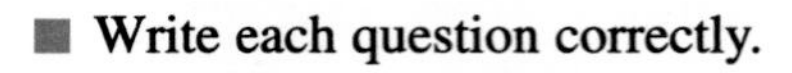

■ Write each question correctly.

Example Do you have a pet
Do you have a pet?

5. Is it a dog **Is it a dog?**
6. what is its name **What is its name?**
7. can it do tricks **Can it do tricks?**

58 Extra Practice

Meeting Individual Needs

More Practice for Lesson 6

● **EASY** ▲ **AVERAGE**

Write **yes** if the sentence is a correctly written question. Write **no** if the sentence is not a correctly written question.

1. is it in the house? no
2. Are you hiding? yes
3. Did you fall asleep no
4. Do you hear the birds no
5. Will you bake a cake? yes
6. please close the door no
7. When did the cat go out? yes
8. How do you do this? yes
9. who is in the house no
10. where are my socks no

■ **CHALLENGING**

Write these questions correctly.

1. did you find the puppy
   Did you find the puppy?
2. who wants to see my dog
   Who wants to see my dog?
3. are you happy to see it
   Are you happy to see it?
4. is that your puppy
   Is that your puppy?
5. does he belong to you
   Does he belong to you?
6. can he shake my hand
   Can he shake my hand?
7. will he eat this bone
   Will he eat this bone?
8. when does he go to sleep
   When does he go to sleep?
9. where does he play
   Where does he play?
10. May I take him home
    May I take him home?

Extra Practice

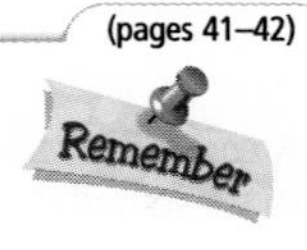

(pages 41–42)

7 Which Kind of Sentence?

Remember

- A sentence can tell something or ask a question.
- A telling sentence ends with a period.
- A question ends with a question mark.

●▲ Write each sentence. Add an end mark. Write **T** after each telling sentence. Write **Q** after each question.

Example Do you like kittens
Do you like kittens? Q

1. Lee has a kitten . T
2. Would you like one ? Q
3. Dogs are good pets . T
4. Do you have a pet ? Q
5. What color is your fish ? Q
6. It is orange and black . T

■ Write these as sentences. Use capital letters and end marks correctly.

Example we walk in the woods
We walk in the woods.

7. i like trees in the fall
I like trees in the fall.
8. what colors are the leaves
What colors are the leaves?

Which Kind of Sentence?

Objective

Children will:

- identify and write telling sentences and questions

Meeting Individual Needs

More Practice for Lesson 7

● **EASY** ▲ **AVERAGE**

Circle the **T** after each telling sentence. Circle the **Q** after each question. Add an end mark.

1. Chris has a fish. (T) Q
2. Some fish eat worms. (T) Q
3. Are all fish blue? T (Q)
4. That is a nice color. (T) Q
5. How many fish do you have? T (Q)
6. Seth has nine fish. (T) Q
7. That is a big fish tank. (T) Q
8. Do you like my new fish? T (Q)
9. Will you keep them in your room? T (Q)
10. I like all my fish. (T) Q

■ **CHALLENGING**

Write each group of words correctly as a telling sentence or a question.

1. will you take a hike
Will you take a hike?
2. he will pack us a lunch
He will pack us a lunch.
3. what would you like to eat
What would you like to eat?
4. we will eat fruit and cheese
We will eat fruit and cheese.
5. how far is the mountain
How far is the mountain?
6. will we get cold Will we get cold?
7. where is the cabin Where is the cabin?
8. we can see deer We can see deer.
9. did you see that bear
Did you see that bear?
10. what is that sound What is that sound?

Commands

Objective

Children will:
- identify and write commands

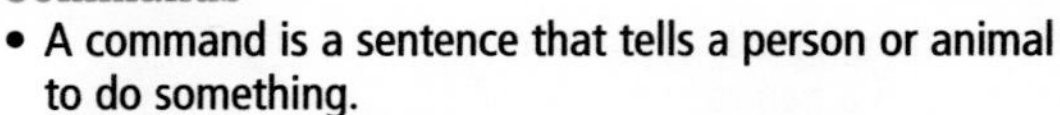

Extra Practice

(pages 43–44)

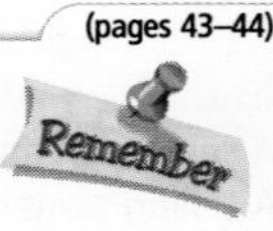

8 Commands
- A command is a sentence that tells a person or animal to do something.
- It begins with a capital letter and ends with a period.

●▲ Write the correct command in each pair.

Example Listen to the rules. Listen to the rules.
listen to the rules.

1. put the ball here.
   Put the ball here.
2. Dribble the ball.
   Dribble the ball?
3. Run as fast as you can.
   Run as fast as you can
4. aim for the goal
   Aim for the goal.

■ Write the commands correctly.

Example draw some squares.
Draw some squares.

5. toss a stone in a square. **Toss a stone in a square.**
6. hop on one foot **Hop on one foot.**
7. Pick up your stone **Pick up your stone.**

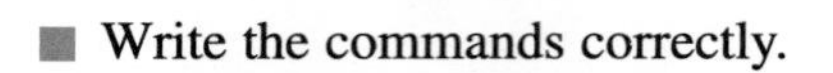

Meeting Individual Needs — More Practice for Lesson 8

● EASY ▲ AVERAGE

Write **yes** if the sentence is a correctly written command. Write **no** if the sentence is not a correctly written command.

1. Give me the book. yes
2. Can I have that? no
3. see the dog run no
4. I want to go home. no
5. Put the book over there. yes
6. Sit in that chair. yes
7. Did you eat breakfast? no
8. Do not walk on the grass. yes
9. Will you walk on the sidewalk? no
10. Look at the picture. yes

■ CHALLENGING

Write the commands correctly.

1. dance very fast Dance very fast.
2. sing as loud as you can Sing as loud as you can.
3. eat all your lunch Eat all your lunch.
4. go to bed early Go to bed early.
5. skip down the street Skip down the street.
6. jump up and down Jump up and down.
7. use this pencil Use this pencil.
8. do not break it Do not break it.
9. find your sister Find your sister.
10. listen to me Listen to me.

Extra Practice

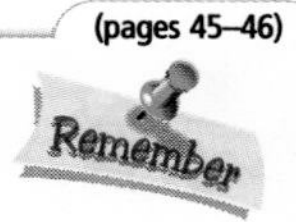

(pages 45–46)

9 Exclamations

- An exclamation is a sentence that shows a strong feeling.
- It begins with a capital letter and ends with an exclamation point (!).

●▲ Write the correct exclamation in each pair. Read the sentence with strong feeling in your voice.

Example I love scary stories I love scary stories!
I love scary stories!

1. this book is great!
   This book is great!
2. I am so afraid?
   I am so afraid!
3. What a neat picture!
   what a neat picture
4. I am so proud of you.
   I am so proud of you!

■ Write each sentence as an exclamation.

Example This story is exciting This story is exciting!

5. the woods are dark The woods are dark!
6. the girl is lost The girl is lost!
7. A storm is coming A storm is coming!

Exclamations

Objective

Children will:

- identify and write exclamations

Meeting Individual Needs — More Practice for Lesson 9

● **EASY** ▲ **AVERAGE**

Write **yes** if the sentence is a correct exclamation. Write **no** if the sentence is not a correct exclamation.

1. what are you doing? no
2. I like that very much! yes
3. Who is that? no
4. What a great movie! yes
5. I found the treasure! yes
6. I love that song no
7. Look out! yes
8. watch where you are going no
9. I have a surprise for you. no
10. You are great! yes

■ **CHALLENGING**

Write each sentence as an exclamation.

1. be careful with that knife Be careful with that knife!
2. do not go in there Do not go in there!
3. this ride is so much fun This ride is so much fun!
4. my house is on fire My house is on fire!
5. the glass is going to fall The glass is going to fall!
6. it is raining so hard It is raining so hard!
7. I lost my little sister I lost my little sister!
8. that movie is exciting That movie is exciting!
9. he is so sad He is so sad!
10. I miss my mother I miss my mother!

Unit 2 Planning Guide

Writing a Personal Narrative

Writing a Personal Narrative: ***2 weeks***
Special Focus and Communication Links: ***1 week (optional)***

	Blackline Masters (TE)	Workbook Plus	Reteaching Workbook
A Published Model "Gloria," by Ann Cameron *(63–66)*			
What Makes a Great Personal Narrative? *(67)*			
Student Model Working Draft *(68)*	2–1		
Final Copy *(69)*			
The Writing Process Write a Personal Narrative			
Prewriting Focus Skill: Telling Enough Details *(71)*	2–2	21	12
Focus Skill: Keeping to the Topic *(72)*		22	
Plan Your Personal Narrative *(73)*	2–3		
Drafting Write Your Personal Narrative *(74)*		21	12
Revising How Good Is Your Personal Narrative? [rubric] *(75)*	2–4	23	14
Writing Conference *(76)*	2–5		
Revising Strategies *(78)*		24	15
Proofreading *(79)*			
Publishing and Reflecting *(80)*			
Writing Prompts and Test Practice *(82–83)*			
SPECIAL FOCUS ON NARRATING			
Writing a Friendly Letter *(84–87)*			
COMMUNICATION LINKS			
Speaking: Telling a Story About Yourself *(88–89)*			
Listening/Speaking: Retelling a Spoken Message *(90–91)*			

Unit 2

Tools and Tips

- **Using the Dictionary,** *pp. H3–H12*
- **Using Technology,** *pp. H21–H30*
- **Writer's Tools,** *pp. H31–H34*
- **Spelling Guide,** *pp. H40–H44*
- **My First Thesaurus,** *pp. H45–H56*

School-Home Connection

Suggestions for informing or involving family members in classroom activities and learning related to this unit are included in the Teacher's Edition throughout the unit.

Meeting Individual Needs

- **FOR SPECIAL NEEDS/INCLUSION:** *Houghton Mifflin English* Audiotape
- **FOR STUDENTS ACQUIRING ENGLISH:**
  - Notes and activities are included in this Teacher's Edition throughout the unit to help you adapt or use pupil book activities with students acquiring English.
  - Students aquiring English can listen to the published and student models on audiotape.
- **ENRICHMENT:** See *Teacher's Resource Book.*

All audiotape recordings are also available on CD.

Daily Language Practice

Each sentence or group of words includes one error based on skills presented in the Grammar and Spelling Connections in this unit or from Grammar Unit 1. Each day write one sentence on the chalkboard. Have children find the error and write the sentence correctly on a sheet of paper. To make the activity easier, identify the kind of error.

1. The caterpillar crawls on the sidewalk The caterpillar crawls on the sidewalk. (end punctuation/telling sentences)
2. what is the name of your school? What is the name of your school? (capitalization)
3. Please pay for your food here! Please pay for your food here. (end punctuation/commands)
4. I have lost my money? I have lost my money! (end punctuation/exclamations)
5. The little boy falls down in the mude. Sample: The little boy falls down in the mud. (spelling/short *u* sound)
6. Mrs. Parks pays for the groceries Mrs. Parks pays for the groceries. (end punctuation/telling sentences)
7. How happy everyone is How happy everyone is! (end punctuation/exclamations)
8. keep this door closed! Keep this door closed! (capitalization)
9. How much ise this pair of shoes? How much is this pair of shoes? (spelling/short *i* sound)
10. The girl at the table reads a book? Sample: The girl at the table reads a book. (end punctuation/telling sentences)

Additional Resources

Workbook Plus, Unit 2
Reteaching Workbook, Unit 2
Teacher's Resource Book
Transparencies, Unit 2
Posters, Unit 2
Audiotapes

Technology Tools

TEACHER'S RESOURCE DISK (for handwriting support)

CD-ROM: *Sunbuddy® Writer
Paint, Write & Play! (published by The Learning Company)
*Type to Learn Jr.™

INTERNET: http://www.eduplace.com/kids/hme/ or http://www.eduplace.com/rdg/hme/

Visit Education Place for these additional support materials and activities:

- author biographies
- student writing models
- graphic organizers
- an interactive rubric
- writing prompts

Assessment

Test Booklet, Unit 2

Keeping a Journal

Discuss with children the value of keeping a journal as a way of promoting self-expression and fluency. Encourage children to record their thoughts and ideas in a notebook. Inform students whether the journal will be private or will be reviewed periodically as a way of assisting growth. The following prompts may be useful for generating writing ideas.

Journal Prompts

- What kinds of stories do you like best? Why?
- Tell something special about your last birthday.
- What is something that happened one time on your way home from school?

Introducing the Unit

Using the Photograph

- Have children look at the photograph, and ask a volunteer to read the caption. What are the girl and her grandfather doing? (They are each blowing on something, perhaps whistles that he has made.) Where are they? (sitting on a doorstep)
- How do you think the girl feels about being with her grandfather? (She likes it.) How do you know? (In the caption she says they have fun together. She is sitting close to him, watching what he is doing.)
- Suggest that the girl might write a story that tells about a time when she and her grandfather were having fun together. Explain that this kind of story is called a personal narrative. A **personal narrative** tells about something that really happened to the writer. Tell children that they will learn about writing a personal narrative in this unit.

Independent Writing

Children can benefit by having time each day or several times a week to write in their journals or do self-selected writing activities. Remind children to think about purpose and audience and choose an appropriate format for both.

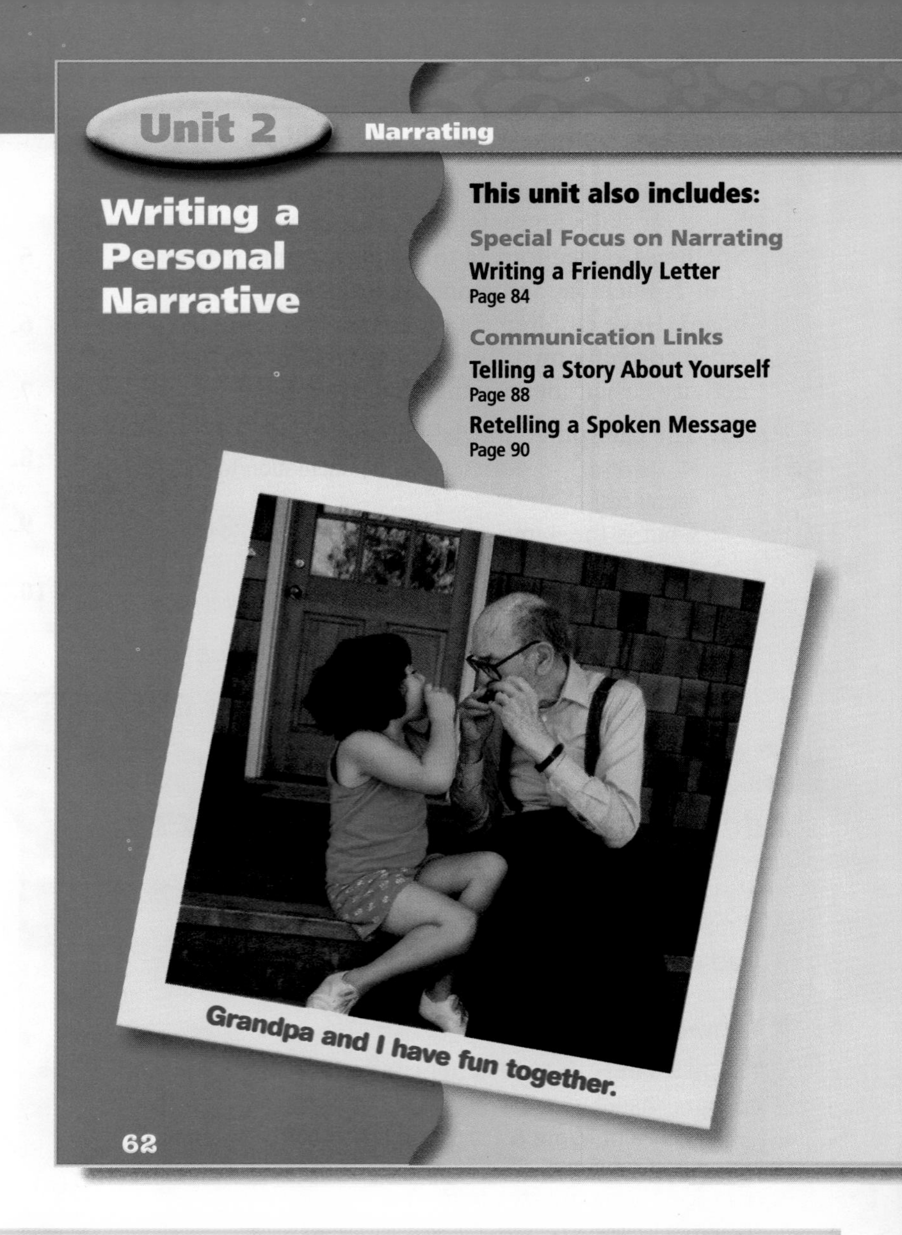

Grandpa and I have fun together.

Shared Writing Activity

Work with children to write sentences that would appear in a personal narrative.

1. Have children choose some special thing that happened to them that they think would make a good story. They may want to write about a good time with a family member. Write volunteers' suggestions on the chalkboard.
2. Chose one of the volunteers' suggestions and work together to decide how they might begin the story. Write this sentence on the board or on an overhead transparency.
3. Ask the child whose suggestion is being developed to tell three things that happened. Note the details on the board. Then work as a class to develop them into detail sentences.
4. As you write them, place them in a logical order. Then read the final sentences together.

A Published Model

Listening to a Personal Narrative

"Gloria" is a personal narrative about making a new friend. What happened first, next, and last on the day that Julian met Gloria?

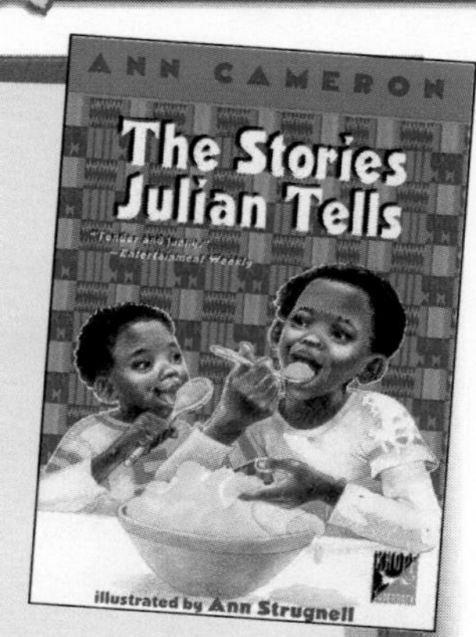

Gloria

from The Stories Julian Tells, by Ann Cameron

It happened one afternoon when I was walking down the street by myself. My mother was visiting a friend of hers, and Huey was visiting a friend of his. Huey's friend is five and so I think he is too young to play with. And there aren't any kids just my age. I was walking down the street feeling lonely. (first)

A block from our house I saw a moving van in front of a brown house, and men were carrying in chairs and tables and bookcases and boxes full of I don't know what. I watched for a while, and suddenly I heard a voice right behind me.

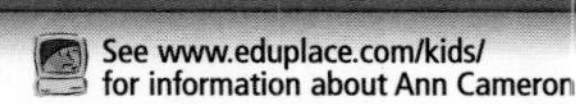

See www.eduplace.com/kids/ for information about Ann Cameron.

About the Author

INTERNET CONNECTION Send children to www.eduplace.com/kids/ for information about Ann Cameron.

Bibliography

Here are other books that model this type of writing that children may enjoy reading.

- ***Secret Place*** by Eve Bunting
- ***Owl Moon*** by Jane Yolen
- ***My Rotten, Red-Headed Older Brother*** by Patricia Polacco
- ***The Rainbow Tulip*** by Pat Mora

"Gloria"

Lesson Objectives

Children will:

- read a published model of a personal narrative
- identify characteristics of personal narratives
- identify well-crafted character descriptions
- use illustrations to enhance meaning of story
- write personal and critical responses

Focus on the Model

Note: The selection, "Gloria," is not a true personal narrative because it is fiction, but it represents the characteristics of a personal narrative.

Building Background

Ask children to discuss their experiences making friends with someone for the first time. What happened? How did they feel? Tell children that they will read a personal narrative that tells about that kind of experience.

Introducing Vocabulary

Introduce key vocabulary words by writing this sentence on the board. Ask children to explain the bold face word.

Julian's family used a **moving van** to move all of their furniture to their new house.

Reading the Selection

- Discuss with children the general purpose for listening or reading personal narratives. Explain that we read personal narratives to find out how writers feel about an experience that happened to them.
- Read aloud the introduction to the selection and the purpose-setting question. Tell children to read or listen for the answer to the question.
- Read aloud or have volunteers read aloud the selection if you wish to reinforce listening skills or if children need extra support.

   Alternatively, children can listen to the selection on audiotape.
- The call outs highlight characteristics of a personal narrative that are addressed in the questions at the end of this selection.

FOR STUDENTS ACQUIRING ENGLISH

Encourage children to look at the pictures and guess the plot of the narrative. After reading through once, act out the scene with volunteers reading and playing the roles of the two children.

next

"Who are you?"

I turned around and there was a girl in a yellow dress. She looked the same age as me. She had curly hair that was braided into two pigtails with red ribbons at the ends.

"I'm Julian," I said. "Who are you?"

"I'm Gloria," she said. "I come from Newport. Do you know where Newport is?"

I wasn't sure, but I didn't tell Gloria. "It's a town on the ocean," I said.

"Right," Gloria said. "Can you turn a cartwheel?"

She turned sideways herself and did two cartwheels on the grass.

I had never tried a cartwheel before, but I tried to copy Gloria. My hands went down in the grass, my feet went up in the air, and — I fell over.

personal pronouns — I looked at Gloria to see if she was laughing at me. If she was laughing at me, I was going to go home and forget about her.

But she just looked at me very seriously and said, "It takes practice," and then I liked her.

—last

Focus on Instruction

Ask volunteers to retell the selection. Write their responses on the board or on an overhead transparency and help them develop a summary of the selection.

Answers to Reading As a Writer

The Think About the Personal Narrative questions highlight criteria listed on the "What Makes a Great Personal Narrative?" and "How Good Is Your Personal Narrative?" pages in the pupil book.

Think About the Personal Narrative

- First, Julian was feeling lonely. Next, Julian met Gloria. Last, Julian and Gloria did cartwheels, and Julian decided he liked Gloria.
- The story told about the day Julian met Gloria.
- Julian used the words *I* and *me* .

Think About Writer's Craft

- A picture of Gloria is created by the words *girl in a yellow dress* and *She had curly hair that was braided into two pigtails with red ribbons at the ends.*

Think About the Picture

- Julian looks nervous.

More About Writer's Craft

- Other Writer's Craft techniques or grammar elements that you can point out in "Gloria" include the use of interrogative and declarative sentences, the use of quotation marks that set off a character's exact words, and the use of capital letters with proper nouns.

Notes on Responding

Personal Response

Have children share their responses and relate any experiences they have had with making new friends.

Critical Thinking

Ask children to suggest what else Gloria could have said or done to encourage Julian to like her. (Answers will vary.) Have children explain their answers.

A Published Model

Reading As a Writer See TE margin for answers.

Think About the Personal Narrative

- What happened first, next, and last on the day Julian met Gloria?
- What one experience did the story tell about?
- What words did Julian use to name himself in the story?

Think About Writer's Craft

- On page 64, which words give you a picture of what Gloria looks like?

Think About the Picture

- What does the picture on pages 64–65 tell you about what Julian is thinking or feeling as Gloria does a cartwheel?

Responding See TE margin for answers.

Write an answer to this question on another sheet of paper.

- **Personal Response** How did you feel as you read the story? Why?

66 A Published Model

Mapping the Selection

After children have read the personal narrative, draw the following sequence chart on the chalkboard. Have children fill in the chart to answer each question about what happens first, next, and last in the story.

Sequence Chart
What happened to Julian?
First
Next
Last

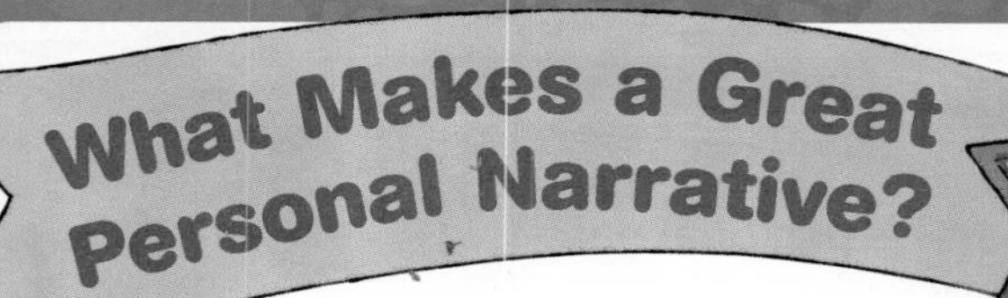

A **personal narrative** is a story about you. It tells about something that really happened. When you write a story about yourself, remember to do these things.

- Use I and me.
- Write about only one thing that happened.
- Write enough details to help your reader imagine what happened.
- Write about the events in order: first, next, last.
- Begin your story in an interesting way. Finish by telling how the story ends or how you felt.

What Makes a Great Personal Narrative?

Lesson Objective

Children will:

- discuss the characteristics of a well-written personal narrative

Focus on Instruction

- Explain to children that "Gloria" was a great example of a well-written personal narrative. Ask volunteers to read aloud the definition as well as the characteristics of a personal narrative. Review which characteristics Ann Cameron used in "Gloria." (used *I*, told mainly about one thing, told events in order, began in an interesting way)
- Have children read the Grammar Check at the bottom of the page. Tell them that the Grammar Check is a reminder that a great personal narrative must also be written correctly. Explain that in the proofreading stage they will be asked to check their papers for correct sentences and punctuation.

If this is children's first encounter with the cartoon dinosaur, explain that this is W.R., the writing star. W.R. will help children learn to write great personal narratives.

Connecting to the Rubric

- These criteria are tied to the rubric on page 75.
- Explain to children that they will be writing their own personal narratives and that they will learn how to include these characteristics. Let children know that after they write their narratives, they will use these characteristics to help them evaluate their writing.

 This page is available as a poster.

Looking Ahead Tell children that they will next see how the characteristics listed on this page are applied in one child's working draft and final copy of a personal narrative.

FOR STUDENTS ACQUIRING ENGLISH

Based on the model, have children define *personal narrative* in their word logs (a story from the author's life that describes one moment). After reading and defining words in the rubric, return to the model and find examples of each item. Be sure to write the item and example on the board or on an overhead transparency.

A Student Model: Working Draft

Lesson Objectives

Children will:
- read a working draft of a student-written personal narrative
- discuss the ways the model meets the criteria for a well-written personal narrative and ways that it could be improved

Focus on the Model

- Tell children that they will read a working draft of a personal narrative written by a real student, Sarah Rose Manning. Remind children that a working draft is a work in progress. This means that the writer writes his or her story without taking time for revisions, knowing that she will make revisions later.
- Have volunteers read the model aloud.

 Alternatively students can listen to it read by a student (although not the student writer) on audiotape.

- Tell children to note which characteristics of a great personal narrative Sarah included. Explain that the speech balloons show W.R.'s thoughts about the personal narrative and that children will discuss his ideas after they read.

> - Reading the draft aloud gives children practice listening and responding to a writer's work in progress and provides practice for peer conferences.
> - This working draft does not include any usage, capitalization, or punctuation mistakes so that children can focus on the content.

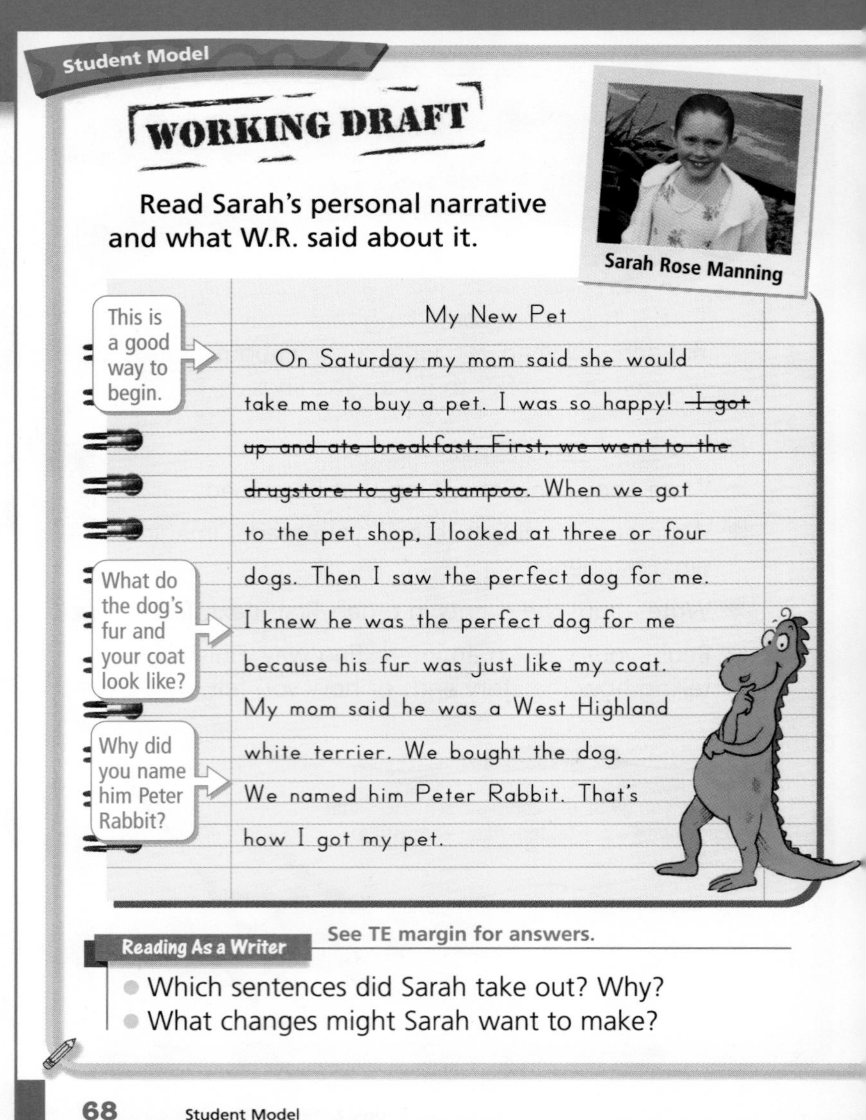

Reading As a Writer See TE margin for answers.
- Which sentences did Sarah take out? Why?
- What changes might Sarah want to make?

68 Student Model

Answers to Reading As a Writer

- She took out the sentences: I got up and ate breakfast. First, we went to the drugstore to get shampoo. She took these sentences out because they weren't about the topic.
- Sample answer: Sarah may want to add more details about the dog.

Read Sarah's final copy and what W.R. said about it. What did Sarah do to make it better?

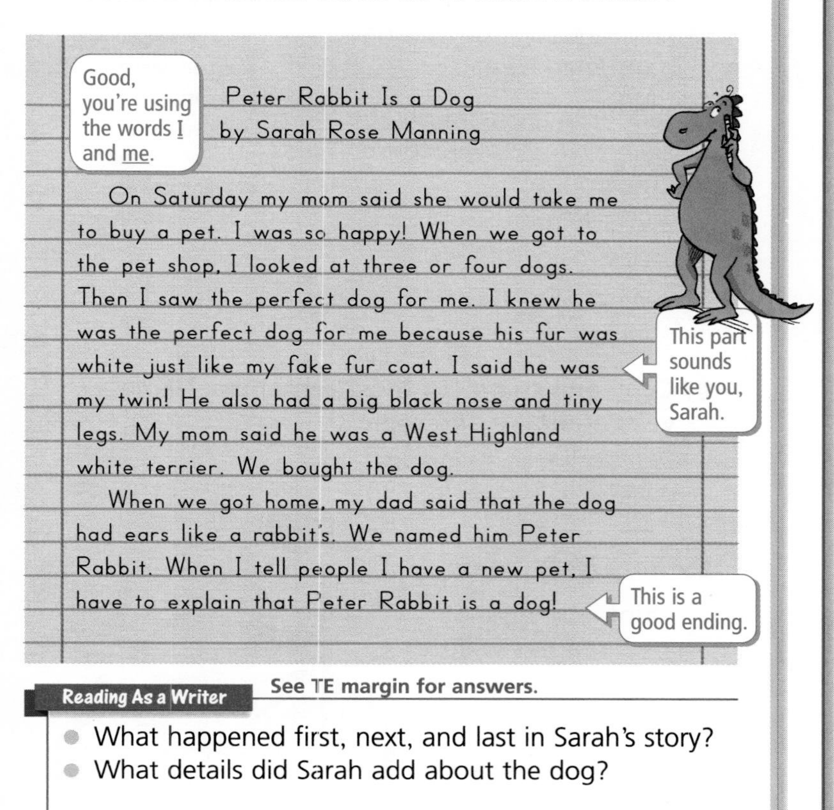

Peter Rabbit Is a Dog
by Sarah Rose Manning

On Saturday my mom said she would take me to buy a pet. I was so happy! When we got to the pet shop, I looked at three or four dogs. Then I saw the perfect dog for me. I knew he was the perfect dog for me because his fur was white just like my fake fur coat. I said he was my twin! He also had a big black nose and tiny legs. My mom said he was a West Highland white terrier. We bought the dog.

When we got home, my dad said that the dog had ears like a rabbit's. We named him Peter Rabbit. When I tell people I have a new pet, I have to explain that Peter Rabbit is a dog!

Reading As a Writer See TE margin for answers.

- What happened first, next, and last in Sarah's story?
- What details did Sarah add about the dog?

See www.eduplace.com/kids/hme/ for more examples of student writing.

A Student Model: Final Copy

Lesson Objectives

Children will:

- read a well-written final copy of a student's personal narrative
- note and compare the revisions that improved the first draft

Focus on the Model

SUMMARY OF REVISIONS In the final copy, Sarah took out sentences that didn't keep to the topic, added details, and wrote an ending that makes a personal comment. Blackline Master 2-1 provides a copy of the student's working draft, showing the revisions that were made.

Have volunteers read the model aloud. Alternatively, children can listen to it read by another student (although not the student writer) on audiotape.

- Point out the comment that W.R. makes about part of the final copy sounding like Sarah. Tell children that W.R. is referring to the writer's (Sarah's) voice. Explain that voice is the personality of the writer in his or her writing. Readers can "hear" Sarah's voice in the words she uses to tell what she thinks about her dog.

Answers to Reading As a Writer

- First, Sarah and her mom went to the pet store and looked at dogs. Next, they picked out a dog and took it home. Last, the family named the dog.
- She added that he had white fur, a big black nose, and tiny legs.

Connecting to the Rubric

- Review with children how Sarah's final copy addressed the characteristics on page 67.
- Reinforce the Grammar Check by having children check that Sarah used complete sentences beginning with capital letters and ending with the correct mark.

More About Writer's Craft

- Discuss with children why Sarah wrote two paragraphs instead of one. (One paragraph tells what happened at the store; the other tells what happened at home.)

Looking Ahead Tell children that they will next write their own personal narratives, using the writing process. As they go along, they will learn how to choose and add details that tell about one main event.

FOR STUDENTS ACQUIRING ENGLISH

Before reading, define *pet* as "an animal that lives with you at home." Then ask children to generate a list of pets. As you read, encourage children to ask questions about the paragraph. Often, comprehension questions can be used as revision questions.

INTERNET CONNECTION Send your children to www.eduplace.com/kids/hme/ to see more models of student writing. You can also find and print these models at www.eduplace.com/rdg/hme/.

Write a Personal Narrative

Lesson Objectives

Children will:
- list their ideas for audience, purpose, and publishing/sharing formats
- list ideas for a personal narrative
- discuss their ideas with a partner
- choose an appropriate topic to write about

Start Thinking

Focus on Instruction

- Ask children how a personal narrative written for their teacher might be different from one for their best friend. (The teacher's would probably use more formal language.)
- Discuss how the purpose for writing might affect the story. (A story written to entertain might be funny, one written as a warning might be serious.)
- Ask how writing the narrative to show with pictures might differ from writing to record on audiotape. (They might break up the text to match the pictures.)

Choose a Topic

Focus on Instruction

Point out the Help box to children for assistance in thinking of ideas. Draw children's attention to the Writing Prompts on page 82.

- Suggest to children that they choose two topics so that if one does not work out, they can use the other and won't have to start all over.
- Remind children to choose a topic that they enjoy.
- Review children's final choices. If a topic is too general, ask children to focus on one detail or experience.

Have each child make his or her own writing folder and title it *My Personal Narrative*. Explain that they will keep notes, organizers, and drafts in this folder. Have children put their papers with their thoughts about their audience, purpose, and publishing format in their writing folder.

SCHOOL-HOME CONNECTION Tell children to ask family members to help brainstorm ideas for a possible topic.

Write a Personal Narrative

Choose Your Topic

1. **List** three things that have happened to you.
2. **Talk** with a classmate about each idea. Answer these questions.
   - Which idea does your classmate like best?
   - Which idea do you remember best?
3. **Copy and complete** these sentences. Name your audience and topic.

   _____ will read or hear my story.

   I will write about _____.

Stuck for an Idea?
- When were you surprised?
- When did you make a friend?
- When did you learn something new?

See page 82 for more ideas.

Explore Your Topic

1. **Think** about what your readers will want to know.
2. **Draw** pictures showing what you will write about.

Help with Choosing a Topic

MORE TOPIC IDEAS

Suggest that children:
- think of a friend and how they met,
- look at the things they own that they like best and think back to how they got them, or
- write the words *The Most Exciting Day* on a piece of paper and then list events that have happened to them that they found most exciting.

TECH TIP

Children can refer to Using the Computer on page H23.

PREWRITING DRAFTING REVISING PROOFREADING PUBLISHING

Focus Skill

Telling Enough Details

When you write your story, help your readers imagine what happened by telling enough details. The words what, who, why, when, and where can help you think of details.

Try It Together

Answers will vary.

Talk with your class about something special that has happened at your school. List details that tell what, who, why, when, and where.

Explore Your Story Idea

1. **Look** back at the pictures you drew for your story. Circle the picture that shows the most important idea.
2. **Make** a Five W's Chart like this one for your story. Write details to answer the questions.

Five W's Chart
What happened?
Who was there?
Why did it happen?
When did it happen?
Where did it happen?

See www.eduplace.com/kids/hme/ for graphic organizers.

Telling Enough Details

Lesson Objectives

Children will:

- identify the most important idea in their story
- list story details that tell what, who, why, when, and where

Focus on Instruction

- Write the five W's on the chalkboard. Point out that the five W's help writers tell enough details to make their story interesting.
- Write on the board: *We had a party*. Ask children to use the five W's to ask questions about the sentence.

Try It Together

As you write student responses on the board, ask children to add enough details to make the event clear.

Explore Your Story Idea

- Review each child's choice of an important event and its accompanying list of details. Make sure that children have enough details to elaborate their event successfully in a written personal narrative.
- Help children elaborate their topics by asking questions such as these using the five W's:

What happened? What made it happen? What did you do or say when this happened? Who else was there? What did they say or do? Why did it happen? When did it happen? Where did it happen?

- Use Blackline Master 2-2 to help children explore their topics. Children can also use appropriate graphic organizers on page H17.

INTERNET CONNECTION

Send students to www.eduplace.com/ kids/hme/ for graphic organizers. You can also find and print these organizers at www.eduplace.com/rdg/hme/.

Meeting Individual Needs

● RETEACHING WORKBOOK, page 12

Telling Enough Details

Tell enough details so readers will know what happened.

Not enough: I went away.
Enough: I went away with Mom.

Read this story. Does it tell enough?

Henry and I took a trip. We saw things. A woman told us a lot about animals.

Who is Henry? What did the people see on their trip? What animals did they learn about? Add details to make the story tell enough. Answers will vary.

My ______ Henry and I took a trip to ______.

We saw ______

A woman told us about ______

▲■ WORKBOOK PLUS, page 21

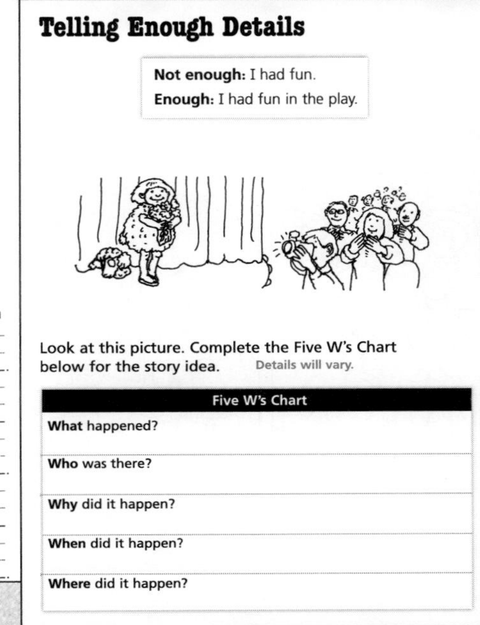

Telling Enough Details

Not enough: I had fun.
Enough: I had fun in the play.

Look at this picture. Complete the Five W's Chart below for the story idea. Details will vary.

Five W's Chart
What happened?
Who was there?
Why did it happen?
When did it happen?
Where did it happen?

FOR STUDENTS ACQUIRING ENGLISH

In addition to the Five W's Chart, ask children to make a Five Senses Chart. Children should fill in phrases or words, responding to the questions, *What did you see? What did you hear? What did you touch?*, etc. Provide sentence starters or templates like these: I saw _______. I heard _______.

Keeping to the Topic

Lesson Objectives

Children will:
- identify details that are unimportant to a topic
- add details that are important to the topic of their story

Focus on Instruction

- Ask children why it is important to identify details that don't have anything to do with their subject. (Those details should be removed from the story.)

Try It Together

- Discuss the four pictures with children. After children identify the inappropriate picture, ask them why they should not include an event that happened on another day at a different park. (It would be confusing to the reader. It would not be important to the story about the water park.)
- Have children look back at Sarah's working draft. Point out the crossed-out sentences. Discuss with children why these sentences don't keep with the topic.

Explore Your Story

Telling their stories to classmates taps into children's oral language and helps them think about words and details to use in their narratives.

FOR STUDENTS ACQUIRING ENGLISH

Encourage children to write notes after telling their stories to their partners. Ask beginners to write words or phrases below each of their own pictures and to share them with a partner. Model listening skills: Look at the pictures being described or at the person who is talking and offer suggestions.

Focus Skill

Keeping to the Topic

Write only about events that are important to the main part of your story. Don't write about things that do not belong in your story.

Try It Together **The third picture does not show one of the activities at a water park. It shows someone riding a horse.**

Write the number of the picture that doesn't show one of the activities at a water park. Talk with your class about how you chose that picture.

1. water slide

2. wave pool

3. 
horseback riding

4. 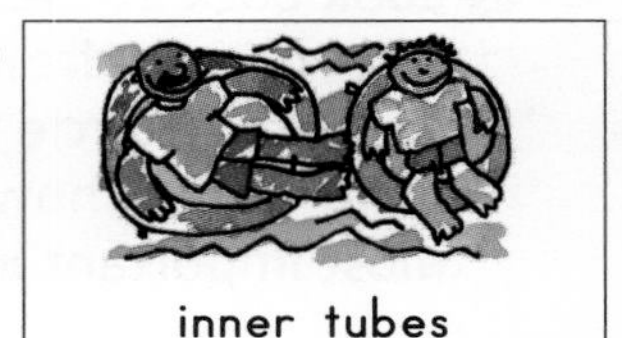
inner tubes

Explore Your Story

1. **Use** your Five W's Chart to tell your story to a classmate.
2. **Cross out** details that do not belong.

Meeting Individual Needs

● RETEACHING WORKBOOK, page 13

Keeping to the Topic

Keep to the topic when you write your story.
We like buses and trains. We like shopping. ~~Plums are sweet.~~

Cross out the picture that does not tell about a day in the city. Write a sentence that tells why you chose that picture.

▲■ WORKBOOK PLUS, page 22

Keeping to the Topic

The picnic was fun. We played lots of games. ~~Dad is tall.~~ The hot dogs were tasty.

Read this list. Cross out things that do not belong. Write a sentence that tells why you chose these things.

What Happened at the Picnic

played softball
ate hamburgers
~~made my bed~~
sat in the grass
~~washed the windows~~
smelled the flowers

Plan Your Personal Narrative

1 Look at how Sarah organized her details.

Five W's Chart
What happened?
picked out a dog
named him Peter Rabbit
went to buy a pet

Sequence Chart
First went to buy a pet
Next picked out a dog
Last named him Peter Rabbit

2 Make a chart like the one below. Write details from your Five W's Chart in the boxes, showing the order in which the events happened. Include all of your details.

Sequence Chart
First
Next
Last

See www.eduplace.com/kids/hme/ for graphic organizers.

Lesson Objectives

Children will:

- write details from their Five W's Chart
- organize their details into a time-order sequence

Plan Your Personal Narrative

Focus on Instruction

- Review each child's Sequence Chart. Make sure that children have included all of the details from their Five W's Chart.
- Children can check each detail in their Five W's Chart as they add it to their Sequence Chart.
- A copy of the organizer appears on Blackline Master 2-3. You can find other graphic organizers in the Tools and Tips section of the pupil book.

INTERNET CONNECTION Send your students to www.eduplace.com/kids/hme/ for graphic organizers. You can also find and print these organizers at www.eduplace.com/rdg/hme/.

MEETING INDIVIDUAL NEEDS

FOR STUDENTS ACQUIRING ENGLISH

Encourage children who have trouble organizing their narratives to cut and paste their pictures onto a new sheet. Provide a sheet with spaces labeled *First*, *Next*, and *Last*. Practice with cut-up newspaper comic strips and have children work in small groups to paste them in order.

Help with Sequencing Events

MORE IDEAS FOR PLANNING

- Have children number the details in their Five W's Chart in the order they happened.
- Have children circle in one color the details that happened first. Have them circle in another color the details that happened next, and use a third color to circle those that happened last.

TECH TIP

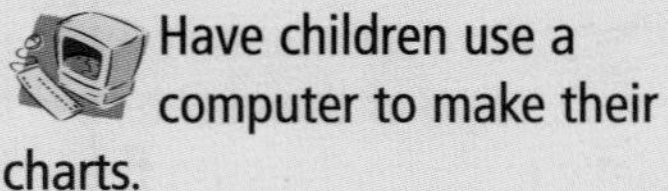

Have children use a computer to make their charts.

Lesson Objective

Children will:
- use details from their Sequence Chart to draft their narrative

Write Your Personal Narrative

Focus on Instruction

- Point out Sarah's details and the sentence she wrote from her details. Tell children that one way to work on their sentences is to play an unscrambling game with their details. Ask a volunteer to show how to unscramble Sarah's details to match her sentence.
- Ask children to suggest other sentences Sarah could have written, using those details. (Sample answer: My mom and I went to buy a pet on Saturday.)
- Ask a volunteer to write some details from his or her Sequence Chart on the board.
- Lead the class in discussing how the volunteer can unscramble the details to make sentences.

Drafting Reminders

- Tell children that they should just get their ideas on paper. They should not worry about mistakes.
- Tell children if they don't know how to spell a word, they should spell it as best they can and go on. They can fix the spelling later.
- Tell children to skip every other line to leave room for changes.
- Remind children just to cross out words they don't like if they change their minds. They should not start over.

FOR STUDENTS ACQUIRING ENGLISH

Have children return to their pictures for detail ideas. They can also re-enact their scene to gain more ideas. As they write, encourage them to concentrate on the ideas and not the grammar. At first, what they say is more important than how they say it.

Write Your Personal Narrative

Sometimes you write one sentence for each detail. Other times you put more details into one sentence.

Sarah used details from her Sequence Chart to write her story.

1. **Use** your Sequence Chart to help you write your story. Use some of the details in your First box to write your beginning sentence.
2. **Use** your other details to help you write the rest of your story. You can write one sentence for each detail or put more details into one sentence.
3. **Use** some of the details in your Last box to write your ending sentence.

Help with Writing Your Personal Narrative

MANAGEMENT TIP

Have the children read some of their sentences quietly to themselves. Do their written words sound as if they were speaking them? Does their voice come through?

TECH TIP

Suggest that children write their details and then use the Cut and Paste functions to unscramble them.

How Good Is Your Personal Narrative?

- **Read** your draft.
- **Copy** the sentences below that describe your personal narrative.

Superstar

- My beginning is interesting.
- I wrote many details that tell what, who, why, when, and where.
- All of my sentences are in order and tell about one main idea.
- The last part tells how the story ended, how I felt, or what I learned.
- My writing has only a few mistakes.

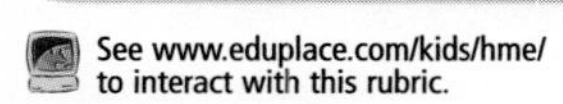

Rising Star

- My beginning could be more interesting.
- I need more details that tell what, who, why, when, and where.
- Some sentences are out of order or do not tell about my main idea.
- The story needs a better ending.
- My writing has many mistakes.

See www.eduplace.com/kids/hme/ to interact with this rubric.

How Good Is Your Personal Narrative?

Lesson Objective

Children will:
- evaluate their personal narratives, using a rubric

Connecting to the Criteria

Have children reread the characteristics of a personal narrative listed on page 67. Then explain that the rubric shown on this page refers to those characteristics. Tell them that the rubric will help them decide what parts of their narratives meet the standards of a great personal narrative and what parts they think still need more work.

Focus on Instruction

- Review the rubric with children. Have volunteers read aloud pairs of related characteristics. Discuss with children the differences between the sentences in each pair.
- Blackline Master 2-4 provides a copy of the rubric as a checklist for children using the hardbound editions. Alternatively they can write the sentences that describe their narratives.
- See the Teacher's Resource Book for scoring rubrics.

INTERNET CONNECTION Have children go to www.eduplace.com/kids/hme/ to use an interactive version of the rubric shown in the pupil book. Children will get feedback and support depending on how they mark the rubric items.

This page is also available as a poster.

Meeting Individual Needs

● RETEACHING WORKBOOK, page 14

Revising a Personal Narrative

Have I	yes
• written an interesting beginning?	☐
• added enough details?	☐
• kept to the topic?	☐
• ended in an interesting way?	☐

Revise this narrative to make it better. Check off each box to be sure. You can write your changes in the spaces above each line, on the sides, and below the paragraph.

What a day at the stables! ~~I like Annie's horse.~~ One morning Diamond was acting funny. Annie told her mother. Annie's mother said not to worry. She said there would be a surprise. That afternoon, Diamond had a new baby with her! ~~I brought my books in my pack.~~ The baby was so funny and skinny. He hopped around on the grass. Now we know why Diamond was acting funny!

▲■ WORKBOOK PLUS, page 23

Revising a Personal Narrative

Have I	yes
• written an interesting beginning?	☐
• added enough details	☐
• kept to the topic?	☐
• ended in an interesting way?	☐

Revise this narrative to make it better. Check off each box to be sure. You can write your changes in the spaces above each line, on the sides, and below the paragraph. Sample answers

What a wet adventure I had! ~~I had an adventure.~~ Where I live, it rains a lot. One year, it rained so much that it flooded. The rivers rose higher than the road. We live on a hill and we got trapped. The first day, my dad ~~he~~ rowed the canoe to the store to get food. ~~I think that store is pretty good.~~ Then a helicopter came to rescue us. I was very relieved. We stayed at my cousins' house for a week.

FOR STUDENTS ACQUIRING ENGLISH

Encourage children to consider both categories of the evaluation rubric and steer them away from becoming too critical of themselves. Remind them that they will have help fixing each area of weakness that they find. Before they begin evaluating, model how to review by using your own or a volunteer's story: *Does my beginning really grab someone's attention? How else could I write this? Wait! I didn't tell who was acting here*, etc. Give children time and an audience to practice speaking their own thoughts.

Lesson Objective

Children will:

- revise their working drafts, based on their evaluations

Revise Your Personal Narrative

Focus on Instruction

Revising Reminders

Remind children that revising focuses on making their personal narratives clearer and more interesting. They should not worry about correcting mistakes at this stage.

- Review each child's evaluation of his or her personal narrative, and discuss what revisions the child could make to improve it. As they revise each part, have them check off the appropriate sentence from the rubric. When they are finished revising, ask them to read their narratives again to be sure the papers are clear.

FOR STUDENTS ACQUIRING ENGLISH

Children usually need a lot of practice conferencing in order to know how to ask helpful questions. Model conferencing with a few different volunteers, then ask children to hold a simple conference in which they read their narratives to each other, listen and tell two good points, and ask questions about two confusing points. Have the whole class "confer" after listening to a volunteer, listing questions on the board. Finally, point out positive listening habits.

Revise Your Personal Narrative

1. **Look** at the sentences from page 75 that you wrote about your personal narrative. What can you do to make your story better?

- Cross out sentences that aren't needed.
- Write another ending. Do you like it better?

2. **Have a writing conference.**

When You're the Writer

- Write a question about a part of your story that you want help with.
- Read your story to a classmate. Ask your question.

When You're the Listener

- Tell two things you like about the story.
- Ask questions about parts that aren't clear or that could be more interesting.
- Look at the next page for some other ideas.

3. **Revise** your story.

Think about what you and your classmate talked about. Make changes to your draft. The Revising Strategies on page 78 may help you.

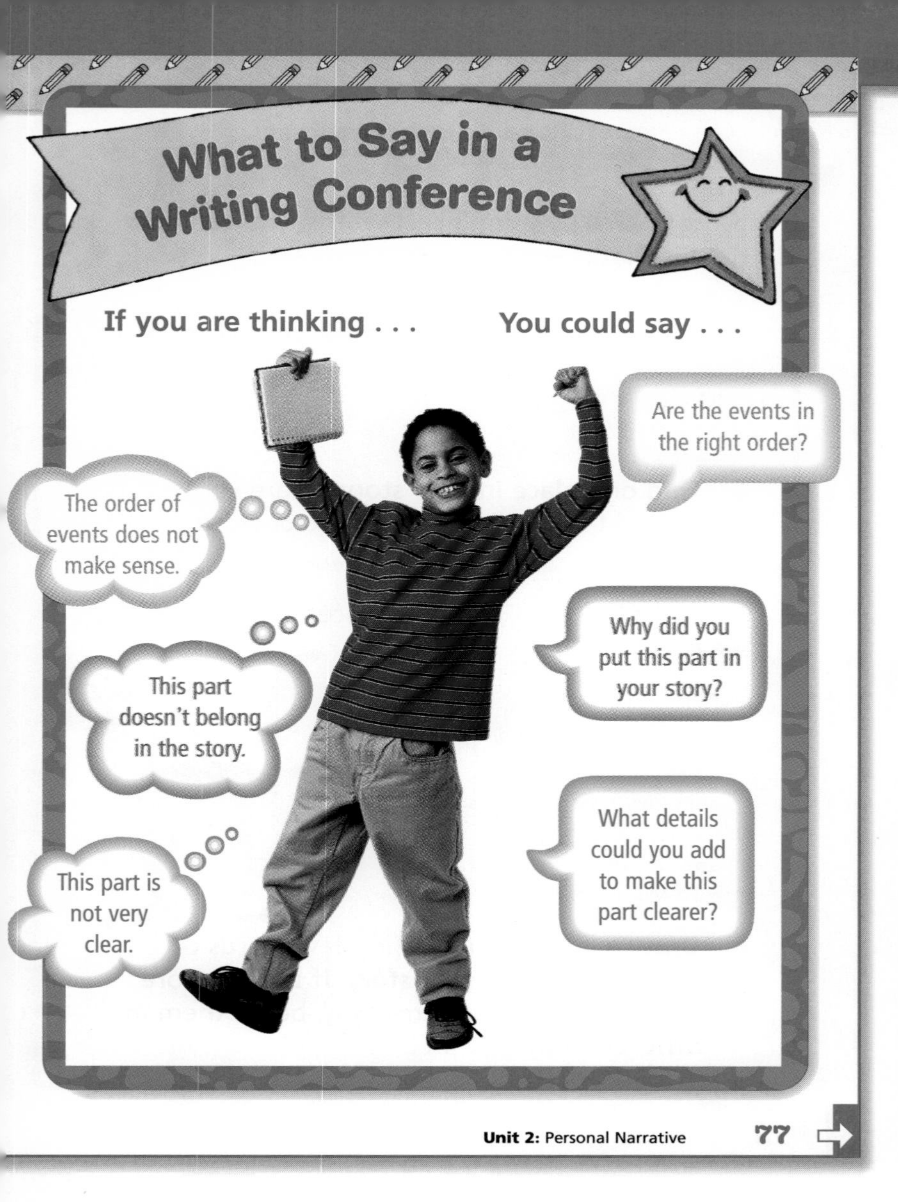

Help with Conferencing

ADDITIONAL CONFERENCING QUESTIONS

These questions may be useful during teacher-student conferences.

- What is the main thing that happened?
- Can you elaborate about ___ so an audience can picture it clearly?
- What happened *first*, *next*, *before*, or *after*?
- What did you learn from this experience? Can you include those ideas in your ending?
- How did you feel when this was over? Could you tell about those feelings in your ending?

EVALUATION TIP

Be sensitive about pairing children. Take extra time to see how children interact before assigning them.

What to Say in a Writing Conference

Lesson Objectives

Children will:

- have a writing conference
- retell a spoken message by summarizing or clarifying

Read aloud and discuss with children the text in the thought and speech balloons. Explain that the thought balloons show what a listener might think while listening to a personal narrative. The speech balloons show what the listener could ask to help the writer know what parts might not be clear or could be revised.

Writing Conference Reminders

- Tell children to read their papers aloud to their partners rather than have their partners read the papers. Unclear handwriting and mistakes in spelling can interfere with the partner's ability to respond to the content of the paper.
- Tell children to do these things when they are the listeners:

Always compliment the writer about something they like in the paper. Discuss with children some possibilities, such as the topic is a good one or the details are interesting.

Retell what they have heard after listening to their partner's paper. They should tell what the personal narrative is about and include the important ideas and details.

- Remind children to choose their words carefully. They want to be helpful, not make the writers feel bad.
- Direct children to speak slowly and clearly when they read their papers. They should speak softly if reading to a partner and louder if reading to a larger group.
- Tell children that they don't have to take all of their partner's suggestions, but they should think about them.

 This page is also available as a poster.

- Children can use Blackline Master 2-5 during their writing conferences.

Revising Strategies

Lesson Objectives

Children will:
- vary the beginnings of their sentences
- replace weak words with exact ones

Focus on Instruction

Word Choice

- Write the following sentence pairs on the board:

  The cold water splashed around.

  The freezing water splashed around.

  The ice cream tasted good.

  The ice cream tasted creamy.

- Discuss with children the different images that are evoked by the weak and the exact words. (cold/freezing, good/creamy) Summarize that using exact words will help readers have a clearer picture of the story events.
- Introduce *My First Thesaurus* at the back of the pupil book. Explain how to use it, and tell them they can use it when they write to find exact words.

Sentence Fluency

- Write the following sentences on the board:

  I went to a farm. I went with my brother.
  I went in a big train with my brother.

- Ask volunteers to suggest new beginnings for each sentence. (I went to a farm. My brother went, too. We went in a big train.)
- Explain that readers will find a story more interesting if the sentences begin in different ways.

FOR STUDENTS ACQUIRING ENGLISH

As a class, practice finding exact words for a volunteer's narrative. Review thesaurus use. If necessary, sing the alphabet song while writing it on the board. Finally, brainstorm a list of overused and weak words such as *said*, *went*, *go* and try out alternatives such as *whispered*, *flew*, *run*, etc.

Revising Strategies

Word Choice By using exact words, you can add details that make your writing clearer.

Maria and I ~~went~~ ran inside when it started to rain.

My shirt was ~~wet~~ soaked.

▶ **Find** one place in your story where you can add details by using an exact word.

Use My First Thesaurus on page H45 to find exact words.

Sentence Fluency Begin sentences in different ways.

I ~~was~~ played an elf in a show at summer camp. I ~~was supposed to sneak~~ sneaked into the shoemaker's shop.

▶ **Draw** a line under the first few words of each sentence in your story. If two or more sentences start the same way, begin them in different ways.

78 Revising

Meeting Individual Needs

● RETEACHING WORKBOOK, page 15

Revising Strategies: Sentence Fluency

When you have two sentences that begin the same way, begin one in a new way.

I swam across the pool. I ~~swam~~ paddled to the ladder.

Change one sentence in each pair so the sentences begin in different ways. Sample answers

1. The pool was not too deep. The pool had a big ladder.
   The pool was not too deep. It had a big ladder.
2. My mom is a good swimmer. My mom is in races.
   My mom is a good swimmer. She swims in races.
3. I know how to dive. I know diving is hard work.
   I know how to dive. I learned that diving is hard work.

▲■ WORKBOOK PLUS, page 24

Revising Strategies: Sentence Fluency

I went to visit Aunt Carole. I visited ~~I went to see~~ my four cousins.

Revise one sentence in each pair, so the sentences have different beginnings. Sample answers:

1. Orin wanted to work on his tree house. Orin wanted to buy nails at the hardware store.
   Orin wanted to work on his tree house. He bought nails at the hardware store.
2. I was helping Orin all day. I was using a hammer and a saw.
   I helped Orin all day. I was using a hammer and a saw.
3. Orin had finished his plans. Orin had some friends help.
   Orin finished his plans. He had some friends help.

Proofread Your Personal Narrative

1. **Proofread** your draft. Use the Proofreading Checklist and the Proofreading Marks.
2. **Use** a class dictionary to check spellings.

Proofreading Checklist

- Each sentence begins with a capital letter.
- Each sentence ends with the correct end mark.
- Each sentence has a naming part and an action part.
- Each word is spelled correctly.

Proofreading Marks

∧	Add	≡	Capital letter
⌐	Delete	/	Small letter
¶	Indent for new paragraph		

Using the Proofreading Marks

Do you know what happened next. ? i called Home.

3. **Review** these rules before you proofread.

Grammar and Spelling Connections

Sentences Begin and end sentences correctly.

I was really scared when I moved to our new house. Who would play with me?

Short Vowel Sounds A short vowel sound may be spelled **a**, **e**, **i**, **o**, or **u**.

hat pet pin top fun

See the Spelling Guide on page H40.

See www.eduplace.com/kids/hme/ for proofreading practice.

Help with Proofreading

MANAGEMENT TIPS

Have each child keep a personal checklist of skills that he or she needs to proofread for. Staple the list to the child's folder.

- Offer children extra help proofreading by having partners exchange papers.

TECH TIP

Children can underline those words that they are unsure of and then look up their correct spelling in a dictionary. The underlining can be removed later.

Lesson Objective

Children will:

- proofread their personal narrative

Proofread Your Personal Narrative

Focus on Instruction

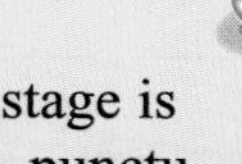

Proofreading Reminders

- Remind children that the proofreading stage is when they correct capitalization, usage, punctuation, and spelling.
- Review with children how and when to use the proofreading marks.
- Have children use the Proofreading Checklist in the pupil book. Review and clarify each item in the checklist, using any related Grammar and Spelling Connections. If children need extra support, review the related grammar lessons with them.
- Provide dictionaries for children to check spellings. Tell them to circle any words they think are misspelled and check them in a dictionary after they have finished circling.
- For proofreading practice, see the usage and mechanics lessons in the Grammar units and the Mixed Review practice in each Grammar unit Checkup.

FOR STUDENTS ACQUIRING ENGLISH

Give a mini-lesson on end marks. Ask the class to write the different marks on the board, then make a game of reviewing their use. Split the class into small groups and ask them to write as many sentences with different end marks in five minutes. Share the results. Give special recognition to the funniest examples of end mark use.

Lesson Objectives

Children will:

- make neat final copies of their personal narratives
- choose a way to publish or share their narratives
- reflect on their writing experience
- evaluate the writing in comparison to others in their writing portfolio

Publish Your Personal Narrative

Focus on Instruction

- Have children decide how they'll share their writing, as it may affect the form of their final copy.
- Ask children to make neat corrections on their final copies, if they find mistakes, rather than recopy their papers again.
- Observe the way children hold their pencils and position their papers when they make their final copies. Check that they are gaining handwriting proficiency. Remind children to use word and letter spacing and margins to make their papers readable.
- For handwriting instruction and practice, see Teacher's Resource Disk for printable blackline masters.

Keeping a Writing Portfolio

A writing portfolio is where students can keep samples of their writing. Here are suggestions for creating and using writing portfolios.

- **Selection** A paper might be selected because it is
  - ✓ generally noteworthy
  - ✓ a good example of a particular criterion
  - ✓ an example of a certain kind of writing
  - ✓ from a certain time in the school year
  - ✓ a typical example of the student's work
- **Labeling:** For every paper, have students complete a cover sheet giving the title, date of completion, and reason for inclusion.
- **Review:** Have students remove papers that no longer reflect their best work or aren't needed as baselines.
- **Evaluation:** Review students' portfolios with them to discuss growth and areas that need improvement.

SCHOOL-HOME CONNECTION Have children share their personal narratives with a family member. Ask children to discuss if the family member remembered the details of the event.

Publish Your Personal Narrative

1. **Make** a neat final copy of your story.
2. **Write** an interesting title.
3. **Look** at Ideas for Sharing on the next page.
4. **Publish** or share your story in a way that works for your audience.

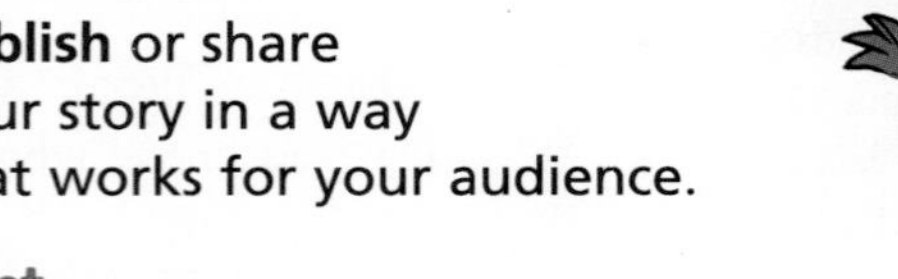

- Be sure you wrote all letters correctly and used good spacing. Check that you fixed every mistake.
- Begin the first, last, and each important word in your title with a capital letter.

Reflect

Answer these questions about your personal narrative.

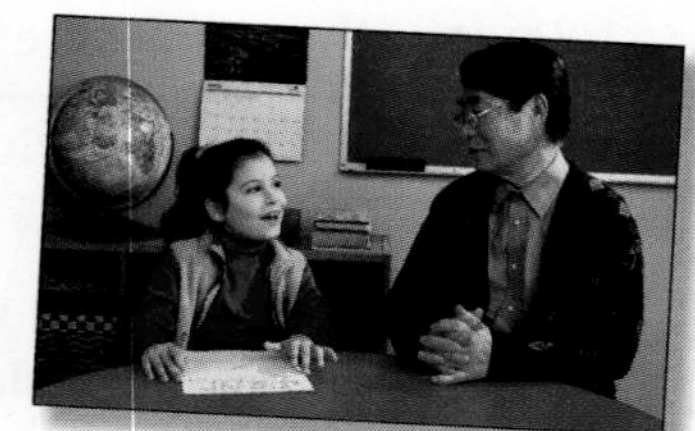

- What was easy about writing this story? What was hard?
- What did you learn about writing a story about yourself?

- Do you like this paper better than other papers you have written? Why or why not?

Tech Tip If you wrote your story on a computer, fix all mistakes. Then print out a final copy.

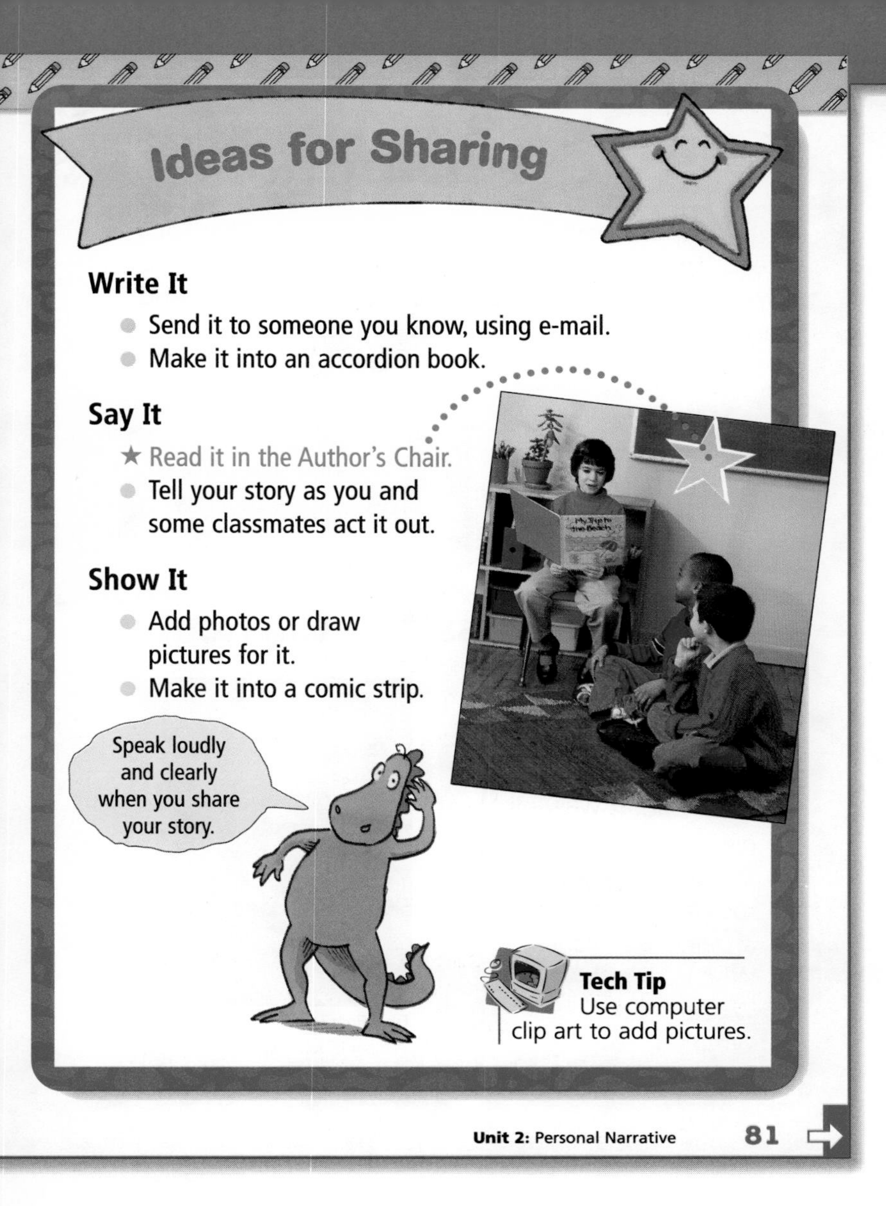

Ideas for Sharing

Write It

- Send it to someone you know, using e-mail.
- Make it into an accordion book.

Say It

★ Read it in the Author's Chair.
- Tell your story as you and some classmates act it out.

Show It

- Add photos or draw pictures for it.
- Make it into a comic strip.

Speak loudly and clearly when you share your story.

Tech Tip Use computer clip art to add pictures.

Unit 2: Personal Narrative 81

Help with Publishing

Directions for Making an Accordion Book

Provide children with an 11x17 inch sheet of paper. Have children hold the paper horizontally and fold the short ends in so they meet in the center. Then have children turn over the folded piece of paper and fold it in half again. When they open the paper they will have an accordion book.

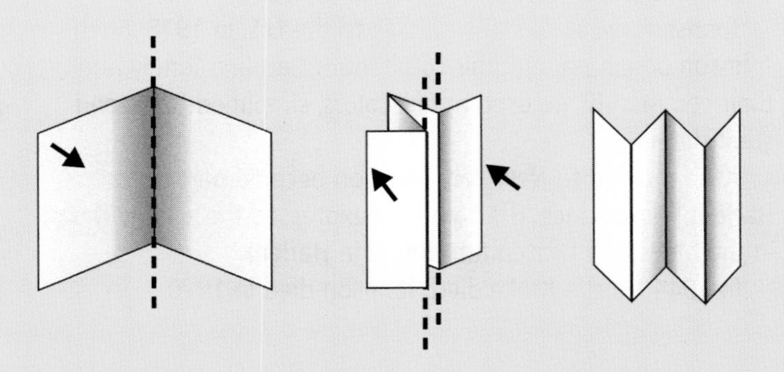

Ideas for Sharing

- **E-Mail** Refer children to the lesson on page H25 for tips on using e-mail.

TECH TIP Direct children to a school or community website to post their writing.

- **Accordion Book** See the Help with Publishing box for directions.
- **Read It Aloud** Read a different story every day and let the student writers be the Author of the Day.
- **Act It Out** Remind children to use the appropriate volume and rate for their audience, their purpose, and the occasion. Help them decide on appropriate props and motions to clarify and support their presentations.
- **Add Pictures** Provide various art supplies so children can illustrate their narratives.

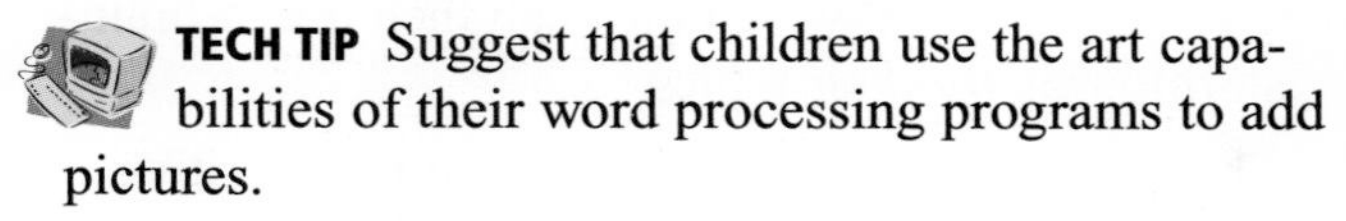

TECH TIP Suggest that children use the art capabilities of their word processing programs to add pictures.

- **Comic Strip** Help children break down their stories into scenes that can be illustrated in each cell of their comic strip.

This page is available as a poster.

Writing Prompts

Objectives

Children will:

- review prompts for choosing a topic or to practice for a writing test
- view critically a work of fine art and use it to write instructions

Using the Prompts

You can use the prompts on this page in several ways.

- Encourage children to review the prompts to help inspire them as they are choosing their topics for a personal narrative. Suggest that children use prompts that interest them, which they can then use to brainstorm ideas for their topics.
- Choose a prompt to provide practice for a writing test. Use it with the Test Practice on the next page.
- Choose a prompt that fits with a related topic in another subject to integrate writing a personal narrative across the curriculum.
- Have children look carefully at the painting. Ask them these questions:

How did William Johnson show how the children feel about their ferry boat trip? (They are holding hands and seem to be talking and having a good time.)

Ask volunteers to tell what things the children see on the trip. (They see a bridge, buildings, and a tugboat.)

INTERNET CONNECTION Send your students to www.eduplace.com/kids/hme for more writing ideas. You can also find and print these prompts at www.eduplace.com/rdg/hme/.

FOR STUDENTS ACQUIRING ENGLISH

Some particularly useful prompts with children acquiring English are: *What is your favorite spot/place in the whole world? Write about a time you spent there. Write about a sad moment during your trip to the United States. Write about a funny moment on your first day of school in the U.S. Write about a special holiday you spent with your family.*

Assessment Link

Use these prompts for ideas or to practice for a test. Decide who your audience will be and write your narrative in a way that they will understand and enjoy.

1. When did you solve a problem? Write a personal narrative telling about the problem and how you solved it.

2. Write a personal narrative about helping someone. Whom did you help? How? Why? Where and when did you help?

Writing Across the Curriculum

3. **FINE ART** The people in this painting are riding on a ferry boat. Write a personal narrative about a time you rode on a boat, a bus, a train, or a plane. Who was with you? Where did you go? What did you do?

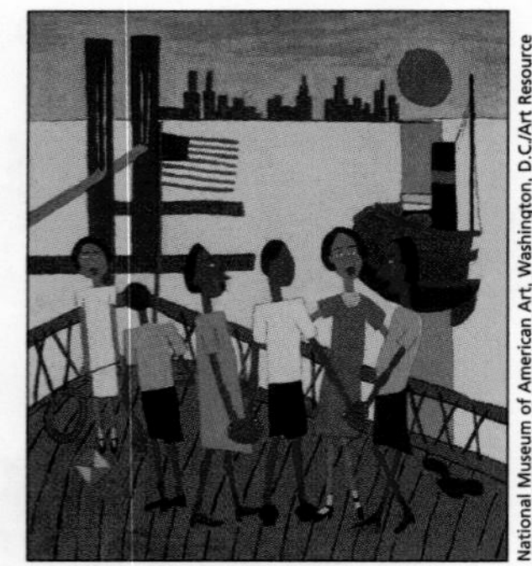

National Museum of American Art, Washington, D.C./Art Resource

Ferry Boat Trip
William H. Johnson
ca. 1943–1944

82 Writing Prompts

See www.eduplace.com/kids/hme/ for more prompts.

About the Artist

William Johnson

William Henry Johnson was born in 1901. He moved to New York at age seventeen. Johnson attended the National Academy of Design, where he won many awards.

Johnson studied the techniques of modernism in France in the late 1920s. There he married Danish artist Holcha Krake. They lived in Scandinavia during the 1930s. Here Johnson became interested in folk expression in art.

Johnson and Krake moved back to the U.S. in 1938. Soon Johnson began painting his rural South Carolina family and their community. He used bright colors, simplified form, and stark detail.

After moving to New York Johnson became part of the Harlem Renaissance. His paintings expressed the energy found in the blues and jazz culture found in Harlem.

In 1944 Holcha Krake died. Johnson died in 1970.

Assessment Link

Test Practice

Read this writing prompt.

Write a personal narrative about helping someone. Whom did you help? How? Why? Where and when did you help?

Follow these steps for writing to a prompt.

1. **Look** for clues that tell you what to write about. The words helping someone are clues.
2. **Look** for questions that you should answer. What questions are in the prompt above?
3. **Plan** your writing. Make and fill in a chart like the one at the right.
4. **Look** at page 75. What makes a Superstar?
5. **Write** your personal narrative.

Answering a Writing Prompt

Clue words: helping someone

My topic:

Whom did you help?

How did you help?

Why did you help?

Where did you help?

When did you help?

See www.eduplace.com/kids/hme/ for graphic organizers.

Test Practice

Objective

Children will:

- learn strategies for evaluating a writing prompt and writing a personal narrative for a test

Using the Test Practice

- Read through the page with children, discussing the strategies for evaluating and responding to a prompt to write a personal narrative.
- Review the rubric on page 75 with children before they write their practice test.
- Have children write a personal narrative in response to the prompt on this page or to one of the prompts on the previous page. Impose time limitations or other qualifications specific to the testing requirements of your school.

INTERNET CONNECTION Send children to www.eduplace.com/kids/hme/ for graphic organizers. You can also find and print these organizers at www.eduplace.com/rdg/hme/.

FOR STUDENTS ACQUIRING ENGLISH

Offer children more than one prompt from which to choose. This will enable children to feel confident about and connected to their topic. Before beginning, guide children to list from memory the rubric for a great personal narrative. Then read the test steps, helping children understand each one.

Writing a Friendly Letter

Lesson Objective

Children will:
- read a model of a friendly letter and identify its parts

Focus on the Model

- Ask children to explain the purpose of a friendly letter. Guide them to see that it is to share news, thoughts, or experiences with friends and family. Explain that writing a friendly letter is similar to writing a personal narrative because both include interesting details about the writer's life.
- Tell children that they will read Adam's friendly letter about his vacation in Florida.
- Point out the blue call outs. Explain that they highlight the five parts of a friendly letter. Tell the class that they will learn about these elements after they read the letter.
- Ask volunteers to read the letter aloud.

Alternatively, children can listen to the model on audiotape.

Focus on Instruction

- Point out the boldfaced words in the call outs. Be sure children understand that they are the key parts of the letter.
- Discuss with the class the explanation of the call outs given in the Reading As a Writer section. Have volunteers answer the questions.

Answers to Reading As a Writer

- The writer's street address is on the first line. The city, state, and ZIP Code are on the second line. The date the letter was written is on the third line.
- Jonathan will get Adam's letter.
- Adam wrote about his trip to a state park in Key Largo. He wrote about what he did and what he ate during his trip.
- Adam used *Your friend* for a closing. He began them with a capital letter.
- Adam wrote his signature below the closing.

FOR STUDENTS ACQUIRING ENGLISH

Have children find and say the boldfaced words in Reading As a Writer. Show how a date is written in English; stress the order of month, day, and year and the capital letter on the month. Have children work with partners to practice writing headings using their own addresses and the current date. Then discuss when to use the different closings.

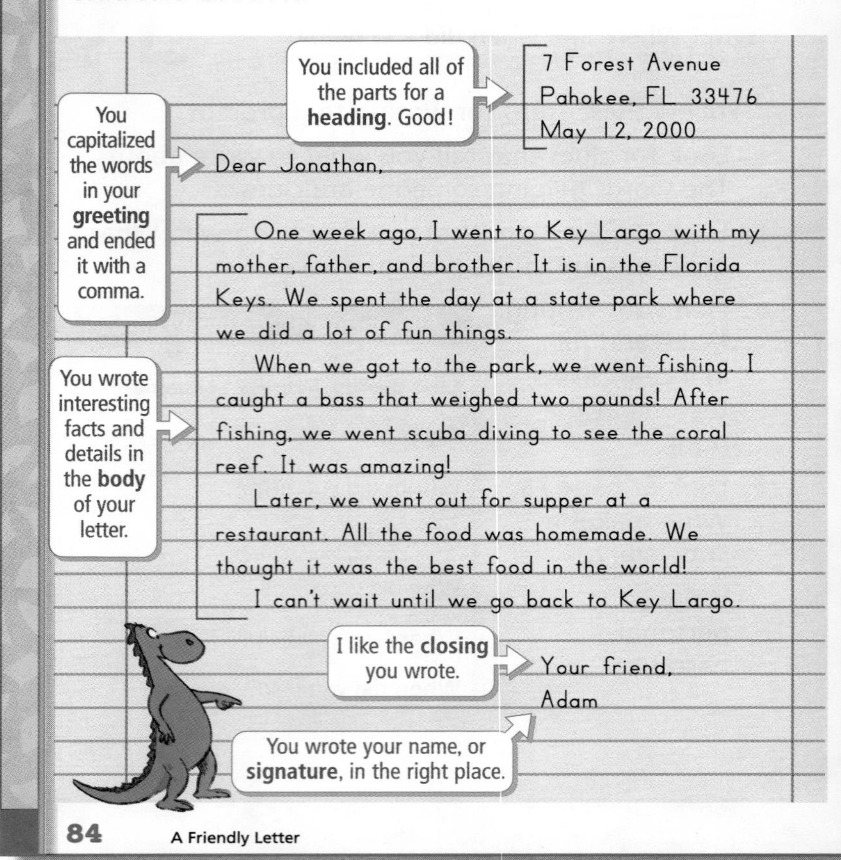

Special Focus on Narrating

Writing a Friendly Letter

You write a **friendly letter** to someone you know. Read Adam's friendly letter and what W.R. said about it.

You included all of the parts for a **heading**. Good!

7 Forest Avenue
Pahokee, FL 33476
May 12, 2000

You capitalized the words in your **greeting** and ended it with a comma.

Dear Jonathan,

One week ago, I went to Key Largo with my mother, father, and brother. It is in the Florida Keys. We spent the day at a state park where we did a lot of fun things.

When we got to the park, we went fishing. I caught a bass that weighed two pounds! After fishing, we went scuba diving to see the coral reef. It was amazing!

Later, we went out for supper at a restaurant. All the food was homemade. We thought it was the best food in the world!

I can't wait until we go back to Key Largo.

You wrote interesting facts and details in the **body** of your letter.

I like the **closing** you wrote.

Your friend,
Adam

You wrote your name, or **signature**, in the right place.

84 A Friendly Letter

Reading As a Writer

See TE margin for answers.

- What information is on each line of the **heading**?
- Who will get Adam's letter?
- What did Adam write about in the **body** of his letter?
- What words did Adam use for a **closing**? How did he begin them?
- Where did Adam write his **signature**?

How to Write a Friendly Letter

1. **Choose** a person you want to write to.
2. **List** what you could say in your letter. Circle what you will say and number your ideas in the order you will write about them.
3. **Write** your letter. Include all five parts.

A friendly letter has five parts.
- heading
- greeting
- body
- closing
- signature

4. **Proofread** your letter. Use the Proofreading Checklist on page 79. Use a class dictionary to check your spelling.

Help with Writing a Friendly Letter

TOPIC IDEAS
Suggest these possibilities:
- A letter explaining a class activity, such as a science experiment or class play.
- A letter describing an after-school activity, such as an athletic event.
- A letter telling a friend about a significant family event, such as the birth of a sibling, an important family outing, or a holiday celebration.

DRAFTING TIP
Suggest that children begin by selecting an interesting event from their own lives that would also be of interest to the recipient. Ask children to include questions about the other person's life and interests as well.

Lesson Objectives:

Children will:
- write a friendly letter
- revise and proofread a friendly letter

How to Write a Friendly Letter

Focus on Instruction

- Discuss why people write friendly letters. Ask children to brainstorm a short list of people to whom they might send a friendly letter. Make sure they can spell the names of the people on their list.
- Remind children that correct order helps their reader understand what happened. Suggest that children keep their order list on hand as they write their letters.
- Before children begin their work, have them share their ideas for friendly letters with partners. Suggest that they discuss the people receiving the letters and the ideas that will go in the letters.
- Remind children to use words that sound as if they were telling the events in person.

SCHOOL-HOME CONNECTION Ask children to think of a school event or experience that they enjoyed. Then have them write about it in a friendly letter to someone at home.

How to Write a Friendly Letter *continued*

Lesson Objectives:

Children will:
- make a neat final copy of a letter
- address an envelope correctly

Focus on Instruction

- Review with children the Proofreading Checklist on page 79 and the use of proofreading marks. Stress the importance of proofreading a letter several times so their reader understands all their words.
- Explore with children why it is important to write the main address and the return address correctly. Go over the information on each line. Point out that if an apartment number is included in the address, it follows the street address on the same line.
- Be sure children understand that a return address helps ensure that the letter can be returned to the writer if the recipient has moved or there is some other problem with delivery. Again, discuss the contents of each line and the placement of the return address on the envelope.

Connecting to the Criteria

- Remind children to check that their letters contain all five parts and that the information in each part is correct. Also have children check their envelopes to make sure both addresses are written and placed correctly. Have children look back at the Reading As a Writer section to help them.

Discuss with each child whether this paper should go into the portfolio. Consider these possible reasons: (1) It is an especially good piece of writing; (2) it reflects a particular aspect of writing that the child did well; (3) it shows an aspect of writing that needs more work and could be used as a baseline for measuring growth.

FOR STUDENTS ACQUIRING ENGLISH

Provide blank envelopes for practice. Explain that a letter cannot be mailed without correct postage; show where to put the stamp(s). Say what postage is needed for letters mailed to addresses in the United States and to countries where children have family or friends. You may want to get list of current rates from the post office.

5. **Make** a neat final copy of your letter.
6. **Address** the envelope. Remember to add a postage stamp. Look at this envelope that Hannah addressed to her friend.

7. **Mail** your letter.

Remember, you can mail your letter at a post office or in a nearby mailbox.

Other Types of Friendly Letters

You write an **invitation** to ask someone to come to a party or other event. The invitation tells the kind of event and gives the date, time, and place.

Write a **thank-you letter** to thank someone for a gift or for doing something for you.

Read the invitation and the thank-you letter on the next page.

Help with Writing a Friendly Letter

TECH TIPS

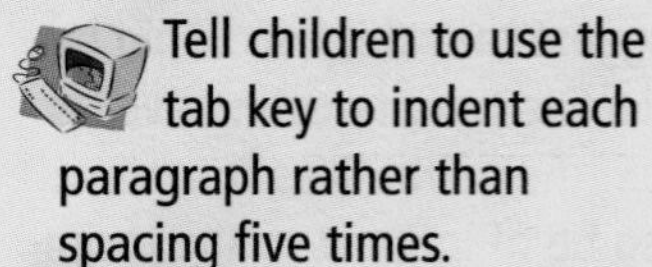

Tell children to use the tab key to indent each paragraph rather than spacing five times.
- Children might also be able to use a template to help them correctly format their letters.

Invitation

63 Dewey Street
Round Rock, TX 78681
October 1, 2000

Dear Auntie Marie,

Please come to my birthday party. I will be seven years old this year.

The party will be at my house on Friday, October 22, at 6:00 in the evening. Please call me to let me know if you can join us.

I hope you can come!

Love,
Bethanie

Thank-you Letter

16 Lime Lane
Boston, MA 02116
August 24, 2000

Dear Max,

Thank you for teaching me how to use my camera last Saturday. I really enjoyed our time together. I have a very funny picture of you at the beach. I will put it in a frame and mail it to you soon.

Sincerely,
Kimi

Help with Writing a Friendly Letter

TOPIC IDEAS

Use these suggestions as ideas for a thank-you letter:

- receiving a special book
- being taught how to make a family recipe
- being taken on a trip to a museum, the zoo, or other special or interesting place

Use these suggestions as ideas for an invitation:

- a school art show
- a family celebration
- a visit during a school break

Lesson Objectives

Children will:

- study a model of a thank-you letter and an invitation
- write a class thank-you letter and a class invitation

Other Types of Friendly Letters

Focus on Instruction

- Ask a volunteer to read the invitation to the class. Work together to find the key elements in an invitation, such as date, time, and place.
- Have children work with partners to discuss events for which they would like to write invitations. Tell children to share with each other the key information that they would include.
- Work together to choose one school event and write a class invitation for that event.
- Have a volunteer read the thank-you letter to the class. Guide children to find the words and phrases that describe the gift. Use this information to reinforce the idea that an effective thank-you letter acknowledges the giver's kindness by pointing out why it was meaningful.
- Ask volunteers to suggest what they would write in a thank-you letter for a similar favor, such as a family friend teaching them how to swim.
- As a class, write a thank-you letter to someone who has visited the class (such as a speaker), given a gift, or done some other kindness.

FOR STUDENTS ACQUIRING ENGLISH

Ask children to brainstorm a list of events for which one might send invitations. Review months of the year, days of the week, and how to write dates in English. Ask children to compare the invitation and thank you letter. How are they the same? How are they different?

Telling a Story About Yourself

Lesson Objectives

Children will:

- tell a story about themselves
- choose and adapt spoken language for different audiences
- vary speaking volume and rate to show feeling

Focus on Instruction

- Ask children if they have heard family members tell stories about their own childhoods or other events. Have volunteers tell what makes these stories interesting to hear. Talk about the kinds of words, expressions, and body movements storytellers use.
- Remind children that they should use complete sentences when they tell their stories. Review the four kinds of sentences and point out that people vary the inflection and tone of their voices when speaking different kinds of sentences. When asking a question, the voice rises at the end; a command is given in an even and strong voice; an exclamation may be shouted or whispered in a forceful voice.
- Read aloud the text in the speech balloon, demonstrating changes in inflection, volume, and tone. Tell children they should vary their inflections and their sentences while telling a story about themselves.

Think and Discuss

- Before discussing the questions, ask children to tell what they liked about Lisa's story and what they noticed about the way she told it.
- Point out the hand gestures in the pictures and ask how they help the listeners understand Lisa's story. (The size of the space between Lisa's hands helps the other children see the sizes of the tiny puppy and the large dog.)
- Ask children what kinds of visual clues storytellers might use besides hand gestures. (They might use body movements or facial expressions.)

Telling a Story About Yourself

Lisa told a story about herself. What important things did she do with her voice, face, and hands?

Answers will vary but should include points in Tips on page 89.

Think and Discuss

- How often should a speaker look at the audience? most of the time
- What kinds of words and details should a speaker use to make a story clear? words that explain what he or she means
- How can a speaker use his or her voice to make a story interesting? whisper, talk loudly to emphasize certain words, pause
- How can a speaker use his or her face, hands, and body to keep the audience interested? look at the audience, use facial expressions, use hands to show sizes, make gestures, act the story out

Tips for Telling a Story About Yourself

- Look at your audience.
- Speak clearly and loudly enough for everyone to hear.
- Use words that tell exactly what you want to say.
- Include details that tell who, what, where, when, why, and how.
- Speak with feeling.
- Use body language to show how you felt.

Apply It

Plan and tell your classmates a story about something that happened to you. Write your story idea. Make sure you use the tips listed above as you tell your story.

Focus on Instruction

- Have volunteers read aloud the Tips for Telling a Story About Yourself, and discuss them with the class. Ask how speakers vary their voices when speaking to small groups or the entire class. (Speakers will speak more loudly when telling a story to a large group.)
- Remind children to tell their story in a logical order. Tell what happened *first* and *next*; save the final event for *last*.
- Have volunteers demonstrate changing their voices to show different feelings. Remind them that they can change the tone of their voice as well as how quickly or slowly they speak. Discuss the different words they might choose to express different events and feelings. For example, if they were happy about being out in the snow they might say *The snowflakes tickled my nose*; if they were unhappy they might instead say *The snowflakes froze my nose.*
- Help children practice the range of body motions that can express feeling and mood. Write the words *happy*, *sad*, *angry*, *tired*, and *grumpy* on the board. Ask volunteers to use body language to express each feeling. You can extend this activity by asking children to pantomime a brief activity and asking the class to guess what they are doing.

Apply It

- Tell children to choose a story that will be interesting to their classmates and to stick to their topics while they speak. Remind them to think about logical order of events as they plan their stories.
- While children are practicing their stories, remind them to vary the speed and pitch of their voices to make their stories interesting. Before each child begins speaking, remind him or her to speak clearly.
- Remind listeners to be polite and attentive.

FOR STUDENTS ACQUIRING ENGLISH

To help children answer the Think and Discuss questions, write an answer key on the board (*often, exact words...*). Suggest topics by asking, "What was your favorite gift ever? Has anything funny happened to you this week?" Have children web their ideas to organize them.

Retelling a Spoken Message

Lesson Objectives

Children will:
- tell and retell messages
- choose and adapt spoken language for different audiences
- listen for the purpose of remembering and retelling

Focus on Instruction

- Point out that people send and receive messages every day. Have volunteers describe everyday situations in which someone might send or carry a message. (Sample answer: A teacher might send a message home about a field trip; a child might tell another child where and when to meet him or her.) Then ask children to share their own experiences of sending a message to someone, or retelling someone else's message. Ask if children have a method for remembering the important details.
- Ask children why it is important to retell a message correctly. (Sample answer: If you deliver a wrong or incomplete message, people can become confused.)

Try It Together

- Have volunteers read aloud the text that accompanies the pictures. Use questions such as these to prompt the discussion:

  What kinds of information do the important details tell? (who, where, and when)

  What would happen if the child forgot one detail? (The mother would have to call Carol to check the day or time.)

  How do you think the child remembered the details of the message? (Answers will vary.)
- Explain that asking questions and retelling a message in complete sentences will help children remember them.

Retelling a Spoken Message

Have you ever listened to a message and then had to retell it to a friend or family member? If so, could you remember the whole message?

When you hear a message, listen carefully for important facts such as names, times, and places.

Try It Together

Discuss with your class what the child says and does.

1

listens to the message

2

asks question; listens to answer

3

repeats message

4

retells the message

Tips for Retelling a Spoken Message

- ▶ Listen to the whole message.
- ▶ Listen for important facts and details.
- ▶ Ask questions about facts that are not clear.
- ▶ Repeat the message right away.
- ▶ Retell the message to the right person.

Apply It

Work with a small group. First, write a short message. Then tell your message quietly to one person. Listen as he or she asks questions and repeats the message to you. Then listen as he or she retells it to the whole group.

Focus on Instruction

- Ask volunteers to read aloud the Tips for Retelling a Spoken Message. Discuss each item that needs clarification. Emphasize repeating the message immediately to be sure all the details are correct.
- Ask children what kind of facts might be missing from a message or might be unclear. (Sample answers: the exact time, the place, the people involved)

Apply It

- Remind children to include only important details in their messages. Suggest they begin with simple messages, then experiment with longer and more difficult ones.
- Discuss how the four types of sentences can be useful when retelling a message. Point out that asking questions will help clarify details. Explain that, while listening to a message, children should listen for exclamatory or imperative sentences and repeat them with the same language and tone of voice. Tell children to use complete sentences as they tell their messages, and monitor their use of complete sentences, naming parts, and action parts.
- Stress that children not interrupt one another. Have them wait until the speaker is finished before talking about any missing details.
- Remind children to vary the volume of their voices as they retell the message to the group. Tell them to speak loudly enough for children in their group to hear them, and quietly enough so they do not disturb the rest of the class.

FOR STUDENTS ACQUIRING ENGLISH

To introduce the topic of Retelling a Spoken Message, dictate simple sentences to children and ask them to repeat them. Then form pairs of mixed proficiencies and ask children to do the Apply It activity. The beginning children can read a scripted message you have written.

Unit 3 Planning Guide

Nouns and Pronouns

3 weeks

	Lesson	Checkup (PE)	Extra Practice (PE)	Graphic Organizer (BLM)	Writing Wrap-Up (BLM)	More Practice (TE)	Workbook Plus	Reteaching Workbook	Students Acquiring English Practice Book
1	Nouns *(93–94)*	119	124	3–1	3–6	124	25–26	16	21–22
2	More Nouns *(95–96)*	119	125	3–1	3–6	125	27–28	17	23–24
3	One and More Than One *(97–98)*	119	126	3–2	3–6	126	29–30	18	25–26
	Revising Strategies: Sentence Fluency Combining Sentences *(99–100)*						31–32	19–20	
4	Nouns with *es (101–102)*	119	127	3–2	3–6	127	33–34	21	27–28
5	Nouns That Change Spelling *(103–104)*	119	128	3–2	3–7	128	35–36	22	29–30
6	Special Nouns *(105–106)*	120	129	3–3	3–7	129	37–38	23	31–32
7	Pronouns *(107–108)*	120	130	3–4	3–7	130	39–40	24	33–34
	Revising Strategies: Sentence Fluency Writing Clearly with Nouns and Pronouns *(109–110)*						41–42	25–26	
8	Naming Yourself Last *(111–112)*	120	131		3–7	131	43–44	27	35–36
9	Nouns Ending with *'s (113–114)*	120	132	3–5	3–8	132	45–46	28	37–38
10	Nouns Ending with *s' (115–116)*	120	133	3–5	3–8	133	47–48	29	39–40
	Revising Strategies: Vocabulary Exact Nouns *(117)*						49	30	
	Enrichment *(118)*								
	Test Practice *(122–123)*								41–42

Tools and Tips

▶ **Grammar Glossary,** *pp. H35–H39*

School-Home Connection

Suggestions for informing or involving family members in classroom activities and learning related to this unit are included in the Teacher's Edition throughout the unit.

Meeting Individual Needs

▶ **FOR SPECIAL NEEDS/INCLUSION:** *Houghton Mifflin English* Audiotape See also Reteaching.

▶ **FOR STUDENTS ACQUIRING ENGLISH:**

- Notes and activities are included in this Teacher's Edition throughout the unit to help you adapt or use pupil book activities with students acquiring English.
- Additional support is available for students at various stages of English proficiency: **Beginning/Preproduction, Early Production/Speech Emergence,** and **Intermediate/ Advanced**. See Students Acquiring English Practice Book.
- Students can listen to the Try It Out activities on audiotape.

▶ **ENRICHMENT:** *p. 118*

All audiotape recordings are also available on CD.

Daily Language Practice

Each sentence or group of words includes two errors based on skills taught in this or previous Grammar units. Each day write one item on the chalkboard. Have children find the errors and write the sentence correctly on a sheet of paper. To make the activity easier, identify the kinds of errors.

1. My mother sings a Birthday song My mother sings a birthday song. (capitalizing nouns; end punctuation/telling sentences)
2. Did Dave take home a Book to read. Sample: Did Dave take home a book to read? (capitalizing nouns; end punctuation/questions)
3. Two girl are playing on the slide Two girls are playing on the slide. (plural nouns with *-s*; end punctuation/telling sentences)
4. The books in three box. Sample: The teacher put the books in three boxes. (plural nouns with *-es*; complete sentences)
5. All child must fasten their seatbelts? All children must fasten their seatbelts. (irregular plural nouns; end punctuation/commands)
6. Today my sister marie. Sample: Today my sister Marie went to the zoo. (capitalizing proper nouns; complete sentences)
7. Ray said it wants to help make breakfast Ray said he wants to help make breakfast. (pronouns; end punctuation/telling sentences)
8. I and judy feed the pony. Judy and I feed the pony. (naming yourself last; capitalizing proper nouns)
9. Neds pet rabbit is gone? Ned's pet rabbit is gone! (possessive nouns ending with *'s*; end punctuation/exclamations)
10. The two girls bedroom. Is very clean. Sample: The two girls' bedroom is very clean. (possessive nouns ending with *s'*; complete sentences)

Additional Resources

Workbook Plus, Unit 3
Reteaching Workbook, Unit 3
Students Acquiring English Practice Book, Unit 3
Teacher's Resource Book
Audiotapes

Technology Tools

TEACHER'S RESOURCE DISK (for handwriting support)
INTERNET: http://www.eduplace.com/kids/hme/ or http://www.eduplace.com/rdg/hme/
Visit Education Place for an interactive quiz.

Assessment

Test Booklet, Unit 3

Keeping a Journal

Discuss with children the value of keeping a journal as a way of promoting self-expression and fluency. Encourage children to record their thoughts and ideas in a notebook. Inform students whether the journal will be private or will be reviewed periodically as a way of assisting growth. The following prompts may be useful for generating writing ideas.

Journal Prompts

- What is your favorite toy? Why do you like it?
- What holiday is really special for you?
- Tell about something you did this morning before school.

Introducing the Unit

Using the Photograph

- Have children look at the photograph and name some of the things that are pictured. (Sample responses: children, faces, puppets, smiles) Explain that a word that names a person, an animal, a place, or a thing is a **noun**.
- Have a volunteer read the caption aloud. Who is saying it? (the children holding their puppets) How can you tell they are saying it? Help children understand that the word *we* talks about more than one person. It can be used instead of all of the children's names. Explain that the word *we* is a **pronoun** and that a pronoun is a word that can take the place of a noun.
- How do you think the children feel about the puppets they made? (They like them.) How can you tell? (by the looks on their faces and what they are saying) Have several volunteers read the caption in unison, the way they think the children would have said it.

Grammar Song

See Blackline Master G-1 for a song to help children remember concepts and rules taught in this unit.

Independent Writing

Children can benefit by having time each day or several times a week to write in their journals or do self-selected writing activities. Remind children to think about purpose and audience and choose an appropriate format for both.

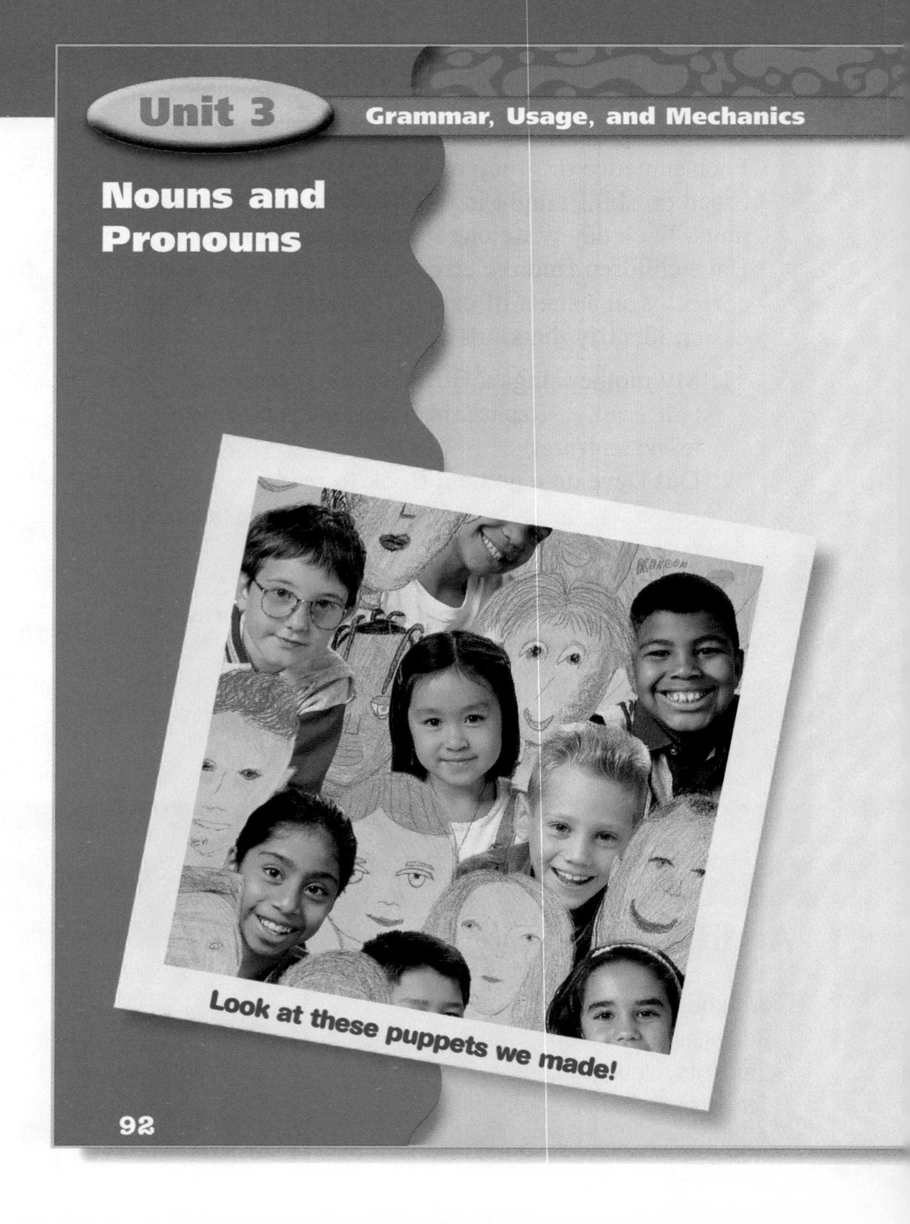

Look at these puppets we made!

Shared Writing Activity

Work with children to write sentences using nouns and pronouns, as prompted by the photograph.

1. Have children say nouns that name things they see in the photograph. Which nouns name one? Which nouns name more than one? List the nouns under the headings *One* and *More than One* on the chalkboard.
2. Work with children to write sentences about the photograph, using nouns from the lists on the chalkboard. Write the sentences on the board or on an overhead transparency.
3. Have children generate sentences, similar to the following, that describe particular children in the photograph and other things shown in the photograph. Write the sentences and underline the nouns in each sentence.
   A boy wears glasses.
   A girl has a red clip in her hair.
   The puppets have hair colored on them.
   Two boys have big smiles.
   A puppet has red hair.
4. Write these pronouns on the chalkboard: *It, They, She, He.* Work with children to change each sentence, using a pronoun in place of one underlined word in each sentence.
5. As children write sentences, reinforce what children have learned about using capital letters and end marks.

1 Nouns

Say the words that name people in this sentence.

Our family and friends begin to arrive too. *family, friends*

—from A Birthday Basket for Tía, by Pat Mora

A word that names a person is called a **noun**. Read these sentences. Say the nouns that name people.

My **father** is a **teacher**.

My **mother** is a **dentist**.

Try It Out

Speak Up Tell which words are nouns.

1. The girl claps.
2. A boy cheers.
3. The baby laughs.

Write It Now write the sentences and draw a line under each noun.

Example The mother smiles.
The mother smiles.

The girl claps.
A boy cheers.
The baby laughs.

Meeting Individual Needs

RETEACHING
ALTERNATIVE STRATEGY

- Write groups of three nouns on the board, one of which names a person; for example, *desk, father, car.*
- Have a volunteer underline the noun that names a person. Have children use each underlined noun in a sentence.
- Write children's sentences on the board. Have volunteers underline each noun that names a person.

CHALLENGE

Have children tell what they might be when they grow up. Write their suggestions on the board. Ask each child to select one of the nouns and write a sentence telling what that person does.

FOR STUDENTS ACQUIRING ENGLISH

Make sets of naming cards that say *girl, boy, teacher.* These can be 3 x 5 cards or sticky tabs. Have children place the naming cards on or in front of classmates or you, or place the cards in the wrong places and have children fix.

Nouns

Lesson Objectives

Children will:

- identify words that name people as nouns
- write nouns in sentences
- write sentences describing things people like to do

One-Minute Warm-Up Copy on the board this sentence from the lesson: *Our family and friends begin to arrive too.* Erase the word *friends*. Have volunteers take turns substituting names of other persons, such as *cousins*. Ask children to tell what kinds of things these words name. (people)

Focus on Instruction

Make sure children understand that the noun alone is the naming word — and not the article *a*, *an*, or *the* before it.

Try It Out

VIEWING Have children suggest sentences about the people shown in the picture. Record the sentences in a chart. Call on volunteers to write each noun that names a person. (Sample responses are shown.)

Nouns that Name a Person	
The boy shouts.	*boy*
The girl smiles.	*girl*
The mother claps.	*mother*

FOR STUDENTS ACQUIRING ENGLISH

- Have children listen to the Try It Out sentences on the audiotape. Distribute the SAE Practice page for Unit 3, Lesson 1. 
- Help children suggest sentences about the photo in the book and the art on the Practice page. Help children label the art on the Practice page. Remind children about naming parts of sentences. Say that words that name people are called nouns. Write *noun* on the board. Ask children to point to classmates and say *girl* or *boy*. For extra practice, place naming cards for people in the wrong places and have children fix the mistakes. Children listen and say which words are nouns. Then they write the nouns.
Example: The baby hides.

Summing Up Help children summarize these key points about the lesson:

A word that names a person is called a **noun.**

You may want to have children complete the parts related to this lesson on Blackline Master 3-1.

On Your Own

Have children test each noun they underlined by asking:

Who does this name? Is this a person?

FOR STUDENTS ACQUIRING ENGLISH

Distribute the SAE Practice page for Unit 3, Lesson 1. Ask children to name words for family members; write their ideas on the board. Assist with additional vocabulary for family members; give examples children can relate to. Then children underline the nouns for people and write the nouns. Example: My sister had a party. (sister)

Writing Wrap-Up

Writing Tip: Have children use a web for each person, writing the name of the person and connecting to it words that describe what the person likes to do. See Blackline Master 3-6 for sample sentences.

SCHOOL-HOME CONNECTION

Have children use the sentences they wrote as riddles. They should leave out the name of the person and have a family member guess who the sentence describes.

On Your Own

Write these sentences. Draw a line under each noun that names a person.

Example The girl has a birthday party.
The girl has a birthday party.

1. The father serves cake. father
2. The friends bring gifts. friends

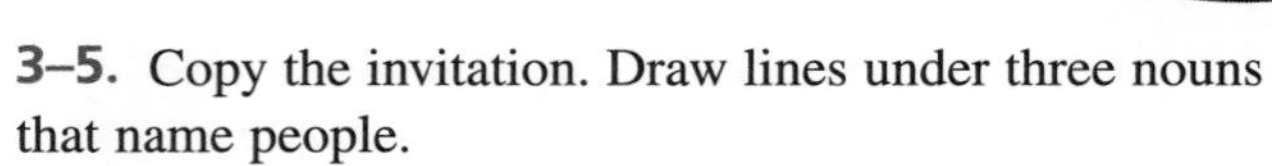

3–5. Copy the invitation. Draw lines under three nouns that name people.

Example My grandpa chooses songs.
My grandpa chooses songs.

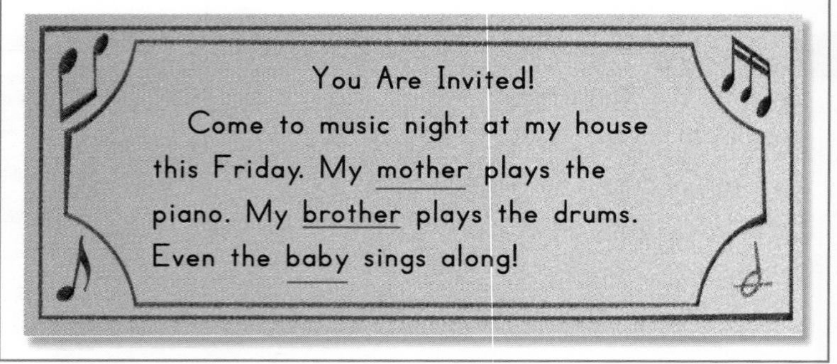

Writing Wrap-Up

WRITING • THINKING • LISTENING • SPEAKING

INFORMING

Write Sentences

Write sentences about what two or more people in your family like to do. Read the sentences to a classmate. Have the classmate say each noun that names a person.

Sentences will vary.

94 Nouns For Extra Practice, see page 124.

Meeting Individual Needs

● RETEACHING WORKBOOK, page 16

1 Nouns

A word that names a person is called a **noun**.
My **mother** drives a school bus.

Write the noun that names a person in each row. Draw a picture of the noun in the box.

Example ask boy make — boy

1. clown in tell — clown
2. happy are teacher — teacher
3. baby need just — baby
4. doctor funny in — doctor

▲■ WORKBOOK PLUS, pages 25-26

1 Nouns

A **writer** can write about many things.

Write the noun that names a person in each sentence.

1. My grandmother writes stories. grandmother
2. A sailor might cross a stormy sea. sailor
3. A boy might win a contest. boy
4. A king might rule a strange land. king
5. A girl could meet a friendly lion. girl
6. My brother loves the stories. brother
7. My friend reads the stories. friend
8. My father tells good stories too. father

1 Nouns (continued from page 25)

Challenge

Some nouns are missing from Emma's letter. Write a noun that names a person on each line. Use the nouns from the Word Box or your own words. Answers will vary.

brother	aunt	friend	doctor	painter
sister	dentist	sailor	teacher	grandfather

Dear Marcos,

Please come to my costume party. My little ______ is dressing up as a ______. My ______ is going to be a ______. I will be a ______. I'll see you there.

Your ______,
Emma

Writing Application: Sentences NARRATING

Write four sentences that tell about exciting story ideas. Use a noun that names a person in each sentence.
Students to respond on separate paper. Answers will vary.

Grammar

2 More Nouns

Sentences will vary. Children should use nouns naming the animal, place, and thing.

Make up sentences about the picture. Name at least one animal, one place, and one thing.

A noun names a person. A **noun** can also name an animal, a place, or a thing. Read the sentences. Which noun names a place? Which noun names a thing? Which noun names an animal?

Tom went to the **lake**.

A **fish** swam near the **dock**.

Try It Out

Speak Up Read each sentence. Say the noun that names an animal, a place, or a thing.

1. The farm was huge. farm
2. We saw a horse. horse
3. Dan drove a truck. truck
4. I dug up a carrot. carrot

Write It Now write each sentence. Draw a line under the noun that names an animal, a place, or a thing.

Example The barn was red. The <u>barn</u> was red.

farm, horse, truck, carrot

Meeting Individual Needs

RETEACHING

ALTERNATIVE STRATEGY

- Write these sentences on the board: *My dog plays with a bone in the yard; The kitten found a ball on the porch; A squirrel in the tree was eating a nut.*
- Tell children each sentence contains a word that names an animal, a place, and a thing, and that these words are called nouns.
- Have volunteers take turns drawing a line under the noun in each category.

CHALLENGE

Have children write these "place" nouns: *country, ocean, school.* Ask them to write another noun that names something which might be in that place. Have them write sentences using the noun pairs.

FOR STUDENTS ACQUIRING ENGLISH

Make sets of naming cards for things in the classroom. These can be 3 x 5 cards or sticky tabs. Have children place the naming cards on or in front of things with those names, or place the cards in the wrong places and have children fix.

More Nouns

Lesson Objectives

Children will:

- identify words that name animals, places, or things as nouns
- write nouns in sentences
- write a journal entry expressing ideas about a place

One-Minute Warm-Up Have volunteers take turns writing one of the sentences on the board. Have them underline the noun or nouns in each sentence and tell what each noun names — an animal, a place, or a thing.

Focus on Instruction

Remind children that only the naming word is the noun, not the article *the* and *a* or *an* before it.

Try It Out

VIEWING Have children say nouns that name the animal, a place, or a thing in the picture and then use each noun in a sentence. Record the sentences in a chart. Have children underline the noun in each sentence and write what the noun names—an animal, a place, or a thing. (Sample responses are shown.)

Noun	What It Names
The horse is big.	*animal*
The farm is fun.	*place*
The truck goes fast.	*thing*

MEETING INDIVIDUAL NEEDS — FOR STUDENTS ACQUIRING ENGLISH

- Have children listen to the Try It Out sentences on the audiotape. Distribute the SAE Practice page for Unit 3, Lesson 2.
- Help children suggest sentences about the art in the book and on the Practice page. Help children label the art on the Practice page. Remind children about naming parts of sentences. Say that words that name animals, places, and things are also called nouns. Write *noun* on the board. Ask children to say and point to examples of nouns in the classroom. For extra practice, place naming cards in front of the wrong nouns and have children fix the mistakes. Children listen and tell which words are nouns. They say what the nouns name and write the nouns. Example: The <u>cow</u> is black and white.

Summing Up Help children summarize these key points about the lesson:

A **noun** names a person. A noun can also name an animal, a place, or a thing.

You may want to have children complete the parts related to this lesson on Blackline Master 3-1.

On Your Own

Have children test each noun they have underlined by asking:

Does the noun name a place or a thing? Does it name an animal?

FOR STUDENTS ACQUIRING ENGLISH

Distribute the SAE Practice page for Unit 3, Lesson 2. Children draw a line under each noun that names a place or thing. Then children choose a noun from the box to complete each sentence.

1. We go to the park.
2. I play with my _____. (dog)

Writing Wrap-Up

Writing Tip: Suggest that children first create a list of people, animals, places, or things that were a part of the place they visited, such as *farmer, lamb, shed,* and *pigs*. See Blackline Master 3-6 for a sample journal entry.

TECHNOLOGY CONNECTION

Children may want to use available software to add clip art to their journal entries.

On Your Own

Write the sentences. Draw a line under each noun that names a place or a thing.

Example I have a baseball.
I have a baseball.

1. Emma has the bat.
Emma has the bat.
2. We play at school.
We play at school.

3–5. Copy Karen's journal entry. Write a noun from the Word Box to finish each sentence.

dog
school
park
kite

Example There is a park near my _____.
There is a park near my school.

I went to the (3) today. I took a (4) to fly. My (5) came along to chase squirrels. park, kite, dog

Writing Wrap-Up

WRITING • THINKING • LISTENING • SPEAKING

EXPRESSING

Write a Journal Entry

Write about a place that your family likes. Read your entry aloud. Have a classmate say the nouns and tell whether they name people, animals, places, or things.

Journal entries will vary.

96 More Nouns For Extra Practice, see page 125.

Meeting Individual Needs

● RETEACHING WORKBOOK, page 17

2 More Nouns

A noun names a person, a place, or a thing.

person thing place
The **teacher** hung my **picture** in the **hall**.

person

Write the noun that names a place or a thing in each sentence.

Example Our school is red. school

1. Our room is sunny. room
2. My desk is clean. desk
3. I sit next to the window. window
4. The sun keeps me warm. sun
5. I can see my house. house
6. I see the bus come. bus

▲■ WORKBOOK PLUS, pages 27-28

2 More Nouns

person thing place
Cleo lives in a **building** near the **park**.

A Write the nouns that name places or things.

1. We live in the city. city
2. Our apartment is big. apartment
3. My room is sunny. room
4. I love the big window. window

B Write the noun in each row.

5. add cat sad cat
6. then tall cave cave
7. fork far first fork
8. open late home home

2 More Nouns (continued from page 27)

Challenge

Finish this list for Lin. Look at the words in the Word Box. Write the names of the three places under PLACES TO GO. Then write the things that Lin needs to get under the name of the correct place.

bread	leaves	market	library
bookmark	rocks	acorns	milk
park	cheese	books	tapes

PLACES TO GO

market	library	park

THINGS TO GET

bread	books	leaves
milk	bookmark	rocks
cheese	tapes	acorns

Writing Application: A Description DESCRIBING

Write a description of a strange land. What is it like? What things are in it?

Students to respond on separate paper. Answers will vary.

Grammar

3 One and More Than One

One-Minute Warm-Up

List things in your classroom. Which words on your list name more than one thing?
Answers will vary.

A noun can name **more than one** person, animal, place, or thing. Add **s** to most nouns to name more than one. Look at the underlined nouns. Which noun names one? Which noun names more than one?

A swimmer is in the pool.

Two swimmers are racing.

Try It Out

Speak Up Read the sentences. Say the two nouns in each sentence. Tell which one names more than one.

1. The swimmers are at the pool.
   swimmers, pool; swimmers
2. Two teams will have a race.
   teams, race; teams
3. The racers dive into the water.
   racers, water; racers
4. The winners get a prize.
   winners, prize; winners

Write It Now write each sentence. Draw a line under the noun that names more than one.

Example Two flags are by the pool.
Two flags are by the pool.
swimmers, teams, racers, winners

Meeting Individual Needs

RETEACHING
ALTERNATIVE STRATEGY

- Write these words in three lists on the board: *doll, puzzle, game; egg, apple, cake; shirt, coat, cap.*
- Have volunteers add an s to each word to make it name more than one.
- Have children tell what is added to most nouns to name more than one. (*s*)

CHALLENGE

On slips of paper write singular nouns whose plurals are formed by adding *s*. Have children choose a slip and write a sentence using the noun to name more than one by adding s to the noun.

FOR STUDENTS ACQUIRING ENGLISH

Point out multiple objects that take *-s*. Children repeat after you, then continue on their own. Check for correct voicing on *-s* ending. Be sure that children are not inserting extra vowels to break up clusters as in *girls* or *desks*.

One and More Than One

Lesson Objectives

Children will:

- distinguish between singular nouns and plural nouns ending with *s*
- form plural nouns by adding *s*
- write plural nouns in sentences
- proofread for plural nouns by adding *s*
- write informative sentences stating rules

One-Minute Warm-Up Use a response to write a sentence such as *I have one book* on the board. Erase *one* and write *four*. Have a volunteer read the sentence aloud. Discuss what needs to be changed to make sense. Change the noun to name more than one by adding *s*. Continue with other nouns.

Focus on Instruction

Tell children that not all nouns take an *s* to name more than one. They will learn about some nouns that do not add *s* to name more than one in later lessons.

Try It Out

LISTENING AND SPEAKING Write these questions on the board, saying each aloud. Have a volunteer repeat a question. Have another child use a Try It Out sentence to answer it. (Sample responses are shown.)

Where are the swimmers? *(The swimmers are at the pool.)*

Who will have a race? *(Two teams will have a race.)*

What do the racers do? *(The racers dive into the water.)*

Who gets prizes? *(The winners get a prize.)*

FOR STUDENTS ACQUIRING ENGLISH

- Have children listen to the Try It Out sentences on the audiotape. Distribute the SAE Practice page for Unit 3, Lesson 3.
- First, have children look at the drawings to see how many of these nouns they can identify on their own. Call on children to tell you what they think the drawings are. Write their ideas on the board, encouraging more than one response and making sure use of singular and plural reflects the actual drawings. Then have children listen to the tape and circle the drawing in the pair that corresponds to what they hear on tape.
  1. cat cats (cats)
  2. boy boys (boys)
  3. flag flags (flags)

Summing Up Help children summarize these key points about the lesson:

A noun can name **more than one** person, animal, place, or thing. Most nouns add *s* to name more than one.

You may want to have children complete the parts related to this lesson on Blackline Master 3-2.

On Your Own

Have children test each noun by saying the word *one* before each noun.

FOR STUDENTS ACQUIRING ENGLISH

Distribute the SAE Practice page for Unit 3, Lesson 3. Help children suggest sentences for the art. Assist with vocabulary. Then children draw a line under each noun that names more than one.

1. The (swimmer, swimmers) race.
2. The (boys, boy) dive well.

Writing Wrap-Up

Writing Tip: Suggest that children first make a list of places in the school where different rules apply, for example, *halls, classroom,* or *cafeteria.* See Blackline Master 3-6 for a sample of rules.

TECHNOLOGY CONNECTION

Children may wish to use a computer to print some words in their rules in bold type.

On Your Own

Write the sentences. Complete each one with the noun that names more than one.

Example The (girl, girls) dive in.
The girls dive in.

1. The (racers, racer) swim fast. racers
2. The (parent, parents) cheer. parents

3–6. Proofread this sign. Find four nouns that should name more than one. Write the sign correctly.

Example People must wear cap.
People must wear caps.

Proofreading

Obey All Pool ~~Rule~~ Rules

~~Swimmer~~ Swimmers must hang their ~~towel~~ towels on hooks.

No ~~ball~~ balls are allowed in the pool.

Do not run near the pool.

Writing Wrap-Up

WRITING • THINKING • LISTENING • SPEAKING

INFORMING

Write School Rules

Write two rules to follow at school. Read your rules to a classmate. Have the classmate tell which nouns name one and which nouns name more than one. Rules will vary.

98 One and More Than One

For Extra Practice, see page 126.

Meeting Individual Needs

● RETEACHING WORKBOOK, page 18

3 One and More Than One

Add s to most nouns to name more than one.

one hill	two **hills**
a river	many **rivers**

Write the sentences. Use the nouns that name more than one.

Example The (riders, rider) go west. The riders go west.

1. Their (horse, horses) are tired. Their horses are tired.
2. The (wagon, wagons) bump along. The wagons bump along.
3. The (days, day) are long and dusty. The days are long and dusty.
4. The (animal, animals) want to rest. The animals want to rest.

▲■ WORKBOOK PLUS, pages 29–30

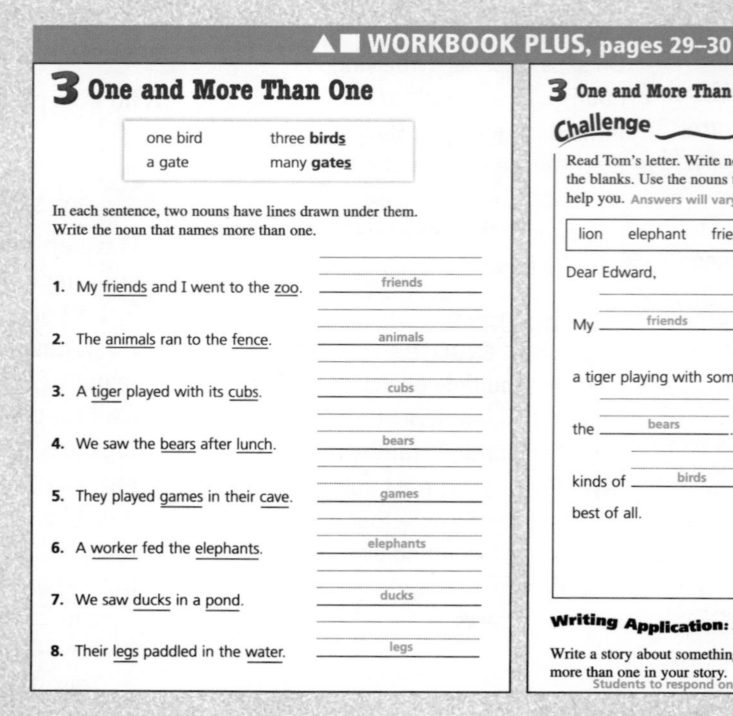

3 One and More Than One

one bird	three **birds**
a gate	many **gates**

In each sentence, two nouns have lines drawn under them. Write the noun that names more than one.

1. My friends and I went to the zoo. friends
2. The animals ran to the fence. animals
3. A tiger played with its cubs. cubs
4. We saw the bears after lunch. bears
5. They played games in their cave. games
6. A worker fed the elephants. elephants
7. We saw ducks in a pond. ducks
8. Their legs paddled in the water. legs

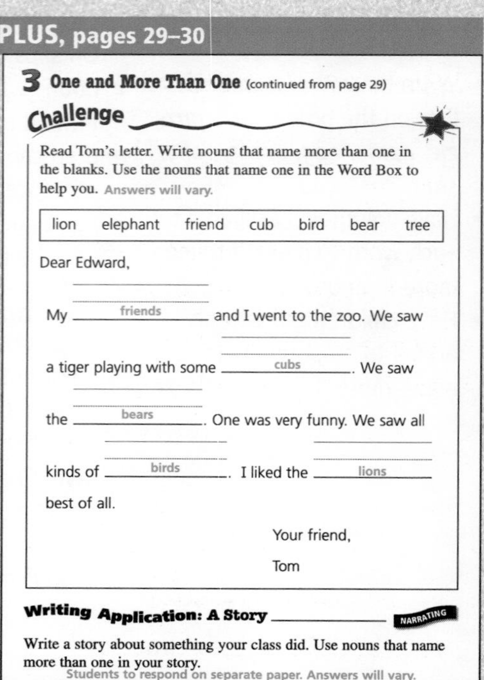

3 One and More Than One (continued from page 29)

Challenge

Read Tom's letter. Write nouns that name more than one in the blanks. Use the nouns that name one in the Word Box to help you. Answers will vary.

lion elephant friend cub bird bear tree

Dear Edward,

My friends and I went to the zoo. We saw a tiger playing with some cubs. We saw the bears. One was very funny. We saw all kinds of birds. I liked the lions best of all.

Your friend,

Tom

Writing Application: A Story NARRATING

Write a story about something your class did. Use nouns that name more than one in your story.
Students to respond on separate paper. Answers will vary.

Revising Strategies — Sentence Fluency

Combining Sentences: Naming Parts

Joining Naming Parts You may write two sentences that have the same action part. Join them to make one longer sentence. Write and between the two **naming parts** and then write the action part.

Tasha went to the pool.
Deb went to the pool.
Tasha and Deb went to the pool.

Try It Out

Speak Up/Write It Read each pair of sentences. Use and to join their naming parts. Then say and write the new longer sentence.

Example The glasses are on the table.
The books are on the table.
The glasses and the books are on the table.

1. Tasha jumped into the pool.
   Deb jumped into the pool.
   Tasha and Deb jumped into the pool.
2. The books got wet.
   The glasses got wet.
   The books and the glasses got wet.

Combining Sentences: Naming Parts

Lesson Objective

Children will:

- use *and* to join the naming parts of two sentences to form one new sentence

Focus on Instruction

- Review with children that the naming part of a sentence tells *who* or *what*, and the action part tells what is happening.

Try It Out

SPEAK UP/WRITE IT Read the example with the class. Help children identify the naming and action parts of each sentence. Point out that they are going to join the two naming parts in the new sentence.

- When children understand the example, explain that the exercises follow the same pattern.
- Be sure children use correct capitalization and punctuation when they write the sentences.

Meeting Individual Needs

● RETEACHING WORKBOOK, page 19

Combining Sentences: Naming Parts

When two sentences have the same action part, you can join the naming parts. Use and to join the naming parts.

Two sentences: Lea played baseball. Shawn played baseball.
One sentence: Lea **and** Shawn played baseball.

Joining Naming Parts Read each sentence pair. Join the naming parts. Complete the new sentence.

Example: The balls were new. The bats were new.
The balls and the bats were new.

1. Jayson ran to first base. Annie ran to first base.
   Jayson and Annie ran to first base.
2. My ball got dirty. My shoes got dirty.
   My ball and my shoes got dirty.
3. The sun felt warm. The breeze felt warm.
   The sun and the breeze felt warm.
4. Ted hit the ball hard. Alexis hit the ball hard.
   Ted and Alexis hit the ball hard.

▲■ WORKBOOK PLUS, page 31

Combining Sentences: Naming Parts

Two sentences: Nina looked at the snow. Luc looked at the snow.
One sentence: **Nina** and **Luc** looked at the snow.

Joining Naming Parts 1–4. Look at the underlined sentence pairs. Join the naming parts in each pair. Write the new paragraph.

The snow fell. The sleet fell. Nina wanted to go out to play. Luc wanted to go out to play. Mom said no. Dad said no. Nina asked again. Luc asked again. The weather was fine now!

The snow and sleet fell. Nina and Luc wanted to go out to play. Mom and Dad said no. Nina and Luc asked again. The weather was fine now!

Combining Sentences: Naming Parts

Apply It

- Go over the example with children. Have volunteers identify the naming parts in each sentence. Then ask a child to make one sentence out of the two by joining the naming parts with *and*.
- Have children complete the revising activity independently. Be sure they understand that they will be joining the underlined pairs of sentences. Point out that in the e-mail letter, unlike other letters, the paragraphs are not indented.

Have children find places in their own writing in progress where they can join the naming parts of two sentences to form one longer sentence.

FOR STUDENTS ACQUIRING ENGLISH

For the section *Try It Out*, do each step as a class, asking volunteers to read aloud, join the naming parts, say the new sentence, and even come to the board to write it. This will involve the whole class. For *Apply It*, ask a volunteer to define *e-mail*. Do all these steps together as well and use computers for fun and reinforcement of vocabulary.

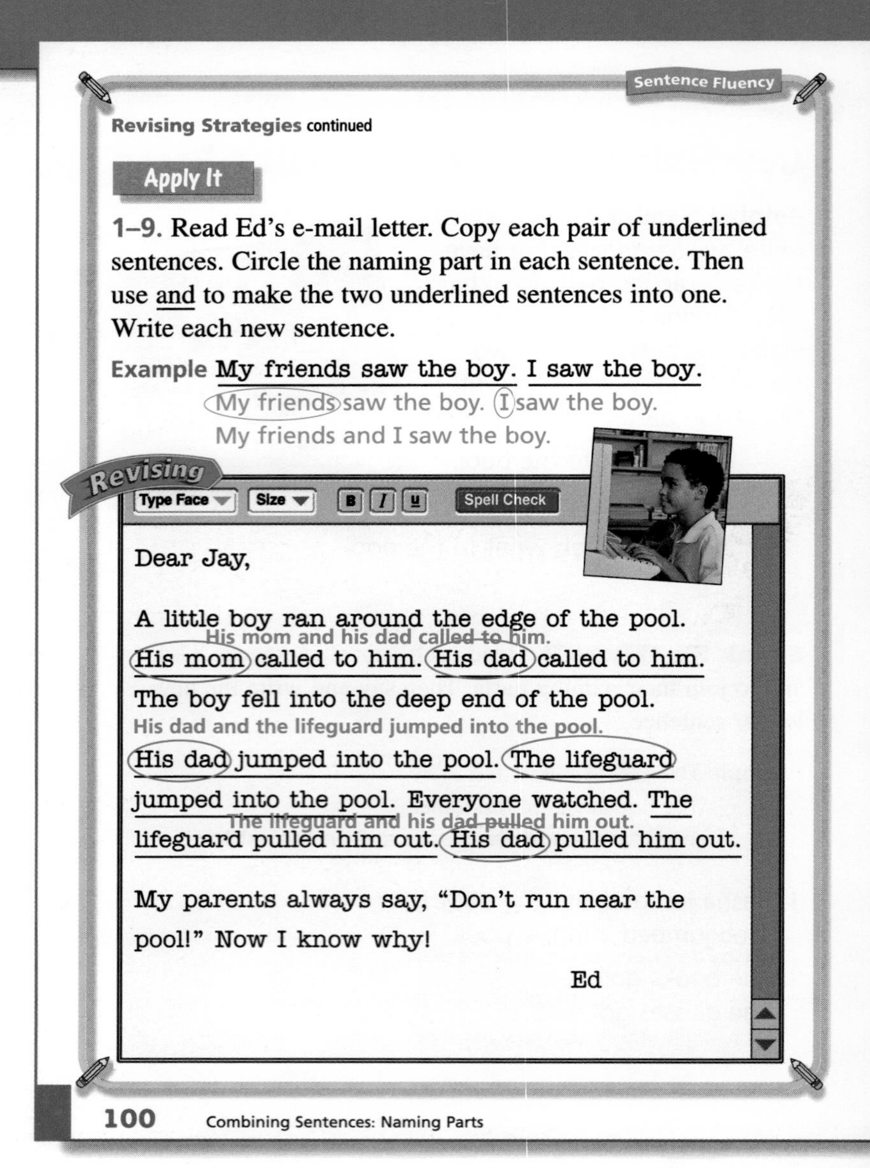

Sentence Fluency

Revising Strategies continued

Apply It

1–9. Read Ed's e-mail letter. Copy each pair of underlined sentences. Circle the naming part in each sentence. Then use and to make the two underlined sentences into one. Write each new sentence.

Example My friends saw the boy. I saw the boy.
(My friends) saw the boy. (I) saw the boy.
My friends and I saw the boy.

Revising

Type Face | Size | B | I | U | Spell Check

Dear Jay,

A little boy ran around the edge of the pool. (His mom) called to him. (His dad) called to him. [His mom and his dad called to him.] The boy fell into the deep end of the pool. [His dad and the lifeguard jumped into the pool.] (His dad) jumped into the pool. (The lifeguard) jumped into the pool. Everyone watched. The lifeguard pulled him out. (His dad) pulled him out. [The lifeguard and his dad pulled him out.]

My parents always say, "Don't run near the pool!" Now I know why!

Ed

100 Combining Sentences: Naming Parts

Meeting Individual Needs

● RETEACHING WORKBOOK, page 20

Combining Sentences: Naming Parts

When you join two naming parts, use and between the two naming parts.

Two sentences: The water spilled. The soil spilled.
One sentence: **The water** and **the soil** spilled.

Joining Naming Parts Read each sentence pair. Use and to join the naming parts. Write the new sentence.

Example Each pot had a plant. Each dish had a plant.
Each pot and each dish had a plant.

1. The pots in the window are pretty. The plants in the window are pretty.
   The pots and the plants in the window are pretty.
2. Marta watered each plant. Rashid watered each plant.
   Marta and Rashid watered each plant.
3. The plants grew tall. The flowers grew tall.
   The plants and flowers grew tall.
4. My cat sniffed the flowers. My dog sniffed the flowers.
   My cat and my dog sniffed the flowers.

▲■ WORKBOOK PLUS, page 32

Combining Sentences: Naming Parts

Two sentences: The squirrel ate nuts. The bird ate nuts.
One sentence: **The squirrel** and **the bird** ate nuts.

Joining Naming Parts Read each underlined sentence pair. Join the naming parts. Write the new sentences.

Different animals eat different kinds of foods. Nuts are good for birds. Seeds are good for birds. Mice like acorns. Squirrels like acorns. Turtles eat bugs. Frogs eat bugs. Horses eat hay. Goats eat hay. I like milk and cereal.

1. Nuts and seeds are good for birds.
2. Mice and squirrels like acorns.
3. Turtles and frogs eat bugs.
4. Horses and goats eat hay.

Grammar

4 Nouns with es

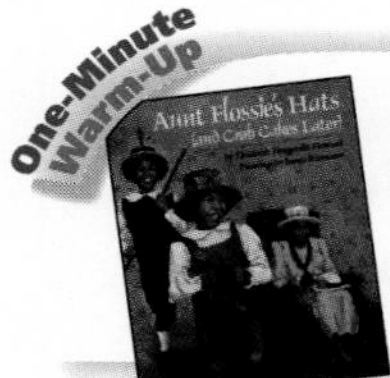

One-Minute Warm-Up

Which words name more than one? How do they end?

. . . and boxes and boxes and boxes of hats! *boxes* and *hats*; *es* and *s*

—from Aunt Flossie's Hats (and Crab Cakes Later), by Elizabeth Fitzgerald Howard

Add s to most nouns to name more than one. Add **es** to nouns that end with s, x, ch, and sh to name **more than one**. Say the nouns that name more than one.

class	fox	beach	wish
classes	foxes	beaches	wishes

Try It Out

Speak Up Say each sentence, using the noun that names more than one.

1. Maria likes the (dress, dresses).
2. Roberto sees four (watches, watch).
3. Here are some blue (dishes, dish).

Write It Now write the sentences correctly.

Example I see two (box, boxes). I see two boxes.

dresses
watches
dishes

Meeting Individual Needs

RETEACHING
ALTERNATIVE STRATEGY

- Have children make a chart by writing the three headings *Name One*, *Name More Than One*, and *Rule*.
- List these words on the board: *glass*, *fox*, *match*, and *wish*. In the first column have children write the word *glass*, in the second column *glasses*, and in the third column *add es to name more than one*.
- Have children continue with the remaining words.

CHALLENGE

Have children complete the sentences, adding *es* to the missing words *box*, *guess*, *wish*. *Three clams made two___.*
They hid gold in six ___.
A clam made two ___ to find it. (wishes, boxes, guesses)

FOR STUDENTS ACQUIRING ENGLISH

Say and have children repeat *cat/cats, pen/pens, boy/boys*. Then say and have children repeat *box/boxes, lunch/lunches, class/classes*. Ask what the difference is. Have children tap out the syllables with you. Add more examples.

Nouns with es

Lesson Objectives

Children will:

- distinguish between singular nouns and plural nouns ending with *es*
- form the plural of nouns that end with *x, ch, sh*, or *s*
- write plural nouns in sentences
- proofread for plural nouns by adding *es*
- write a narrative, using plural nouns by adding *es*

One-Minute Warm-Up Write the quoted sentence on the board. Have children name kinds of hats that might be in boxes. Write the nouns on the board and discuss the different plural noun endings.

Focus on Instruction

Remind children that *s* is added to most nouns to name more than one. Explain that with some nouns, another rule applies.

Try It Out

VIEWING Have children say nouns suggested by the illustration. Record the nouns on a chart, listing nouns naming one in column one and nouns naming more than one in column two. Continue with other nouns. (Sample responses are shown.)

Nouns for One	Nouns for More Than One
watch	watches
dish	dishes
dress	dresses
box	boxes

FOR STUDENTS ACQUIRING ENGLISH

- Have children listen to the Try It Out sentences on the audiotape. Distribute the SAE Practice page for Unit 3, Lesson 4.
- First, have children look at the drawings to see how many of these nouns they can identify on their own. Call on children to tell you what they think the drawings are. Write children's ideas on the board, making sure use of singular and plural reflects the actual drawings. Then have children listen to the tape and circle the drawing in the pair that corresponds to what they hear on tape.

1. box boxes (boxes)
2. fox foxes (foxes)
3. watch watches (watches)

Summing Up Help children summarize these key points about the lesson:

> Most nouns add *s* to name more than one. Nouns that end with *s*, *x*, *ch*, and *sh* add *es* to name **more than one.**

You may want to have children complete the parts related to this lesson on Blackline Master 3-2.

On Your Own

Have children test each noun by asking:

> Does the noun need *s* or *es* added to name more than one?

FOR STUDENTS ACQUIRING ENGLISH

Distribute the SAE Practice page for Unit 3, Lesson 4. Help children suggest sentences for the art. Assist with vocabulary. Then children draw a line under each noun that names more than one.

1. We ate our (lunch, lunches).
2. Do you like (peaches, peach)?

Writing Wrap-Up

Writing Tip: Suggest that children list details about the picnic in three columns: *When/Where*, *Who*, *What*. See Blackline Master 3-6 for a sample of a story.

SCHOOL-HOME CONNECTION

Children may want to talk to family members about the things they most like about picnics.

On Your Own

Write each noun to name more than one.

Example porch porches

1. bench — benches
2. box — boxes
3. bush — bushes
4. class — classes

5–8. Proofread Suelin's letter. Find four nouns that should end in es. Write the letter correctly.

Example Mom made two lunch.
Mom made two lunches.

Proofreading

Dear Grandma,
Mom and I had a picnic at the beach. We took two buses to get there. We packed four ~~sandwich~~ sandwiches, three ~~peachs~~ peaches, two ~~glass~~ glasses, and two ~~dishs~~ dishes. We had fun!
Suelin

NARRATING

Write a Story Stories will vary.

Write about a picnic you would like to have with friends. Tell what you would eat and do. Use words such as lunches, peaches, and sandwiches. Read your story to a classmate.

 For Extra Practice, see page 127.

Meeting Individual Needs

● RETEACHING WORKBOOK, page 21

4 Nouns with es

Add es to nouns that end with x, ch, sh, or s to name more than one.

a dress	two **dresses**
one fox	four **foxes**
a branch	some **branches**
one brush	many **brushes**

Write the noun that names more than one to finish each sentence.

Example Polly's and Gil's ____ went on a picnic. (class, classes)
Polly's and Gil's classes went on a picnic.

1. Their picnic was packed in boxes. **(box, boxes)**
2. They sat on benches. **(bench, benches)**
3. Gil and Polly ate their lunches. **(lunches, lunch)**
4. They used paper dishes. **(dishes, dish)**
5. Gil poured milk into all the glasses. **(glass, glasses)**

▲■ WORKBOOK PLUS, pages 33-34

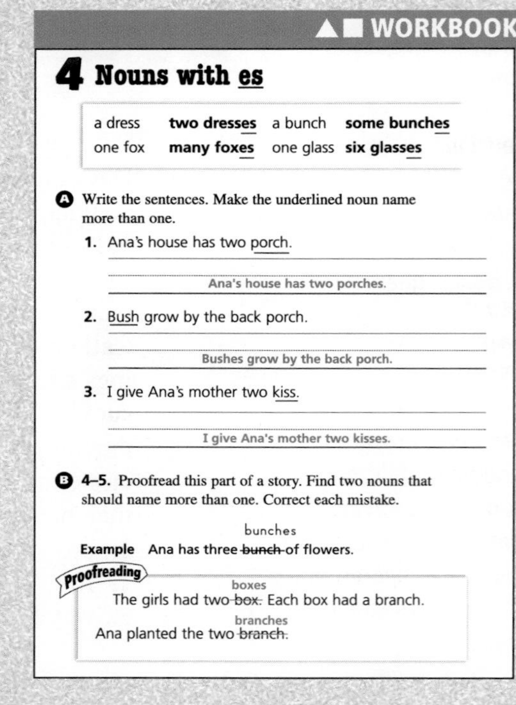

4 Nouns with es

a dress	**two dresses**	a bunch	**some bunches**
one fox	**many foxes**	one glass	**six glasses**

A Write the sentences. Make the underlined noun name more than one.

1. Ana's house has two porch.
Ana's house has two porches.
2. Bush grow by the back porch.
Bushes grow by the back porch.
3. I give Ana's mother two kiss.
I give Ana's mother two kisses.

B 4–5. Proofread this part of a story. Find two nouns that should name more than one. Correct each mistake.

Example Ana has three ~~bunch~~ bunches of flowers.

Proofreading

The girls had two ~~box~~ boxes. Each box had a branch.
Ana planted the two ~~branch~~ branches.

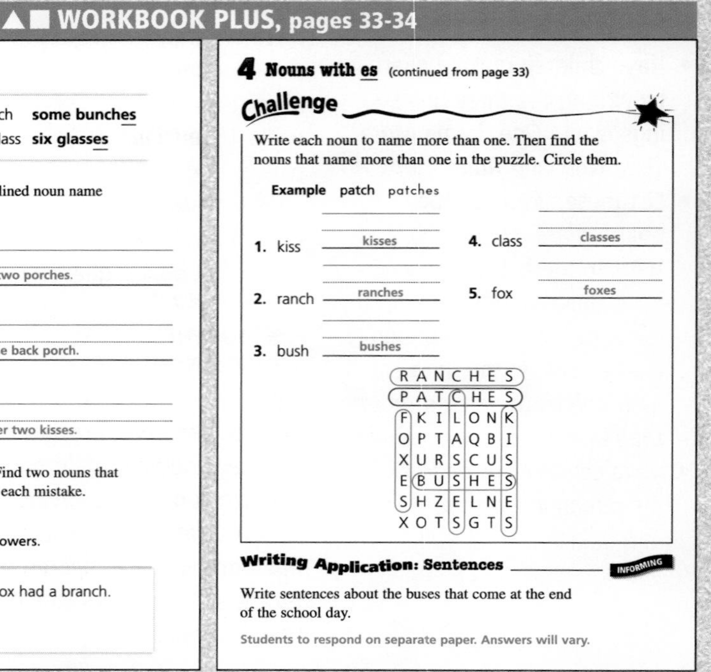

4 Nouns with es (continued from page 33)

Challenge

Write each noun to name more than one. Then find the nouns that name more than one in the puzzle. Circle them.

Example patch patches

1. kiss — kisses
2. ranch — ranches
3. bush — bushes
4. class — classes
5. fox — foxes

R	A	N	C	H	E	S
P	A	T	C	H	E	S
F	K	I	L	O	N	K
O	P	T	A	Q	B	I
X	U	R	S	C	U	S
E	B	U	S	H	E	S
S	H	Z	E	L	N	E
X	O	T	S	G	T	S

Writing Application: Sentences INFORMING

Write sentences about the buses that come at the end of the school day.

Students to respond on separate paper. Answers will vary.

5 Nouns That Change Spelling

mountains, children; children

One-Minute Warm-Up

Read the sentence. Which nouns name more than one? Which noun does not add s or es to name more than one?

There are many mountains where the children live.
—from Children Around the World, by Lynda Snowdon

Add s or es to most nouns to name more than one. Change the spelling of some nouns to name **more than one**. Look at the pictures and words below. Which nouns name more than one?

child	children	man	men	woman	women

Try It Out

Speak Up Name the group of people in each picture.

1. women

2. men

3. children

Write It Now write these nouns. women, men, children

Meeting Individual Needs

RETEACHING
ALTERNATIVE STRATEGY

- Write on the board: woman—women; man—men; child—children.
- Write this story: *A ___ and a ___ sat by a lake. Along came a ___ and three ___ on bikes. A crowd of ___ and ___ arrived in a boat.*
- Read the story, pausing at each blank. Ask volunteers to choose a word that fits in the blank. Have them tell whether it names one or more than one. Cross out each word as it is used. (Answers will vary.)

CHALLENGE

Display several pictures that show action, and that have more than one man, woman, or child. Have children choose a picture and write three sentences telling what the people are doing.

FOR STUDENTS ACQUIRING ENGLISH

Show drawings and write the following on the board: *child, man, woman.* Say the word. Write and say *children, men, women.* Repeat, but this time have children come to the board to write the plural as you spell it. Then lead the children in saying the word.

Nouns That Change Spelling

Lesson Objectives

Children will:

- distinguish between the singular and plural forms of irregular nouns
- form the plural of irregular nouns
- write sentences using plural forms of irregular nouns
- write a persuasive ad, using irregular nouns

One-Minute Warm-Up Write the literature quotation on the board and underline *children*. Ask volunteers to find the smaller noun in *children*. (*child*) Then ask them how the word changes to name more than one.

Focus on Instruction

Have children check their spelling by comparing their words with those on page 103.

Try It Out

VIEWING Have children say the nouns *women, men,* and *children*. Record the nouns on a chart. (Sample responses are shown below.) Then have volunteers say sentences using the plural and then singular forms of the noun.

More than one	Sentences
men	Three men smiled. One man smiled.
women	All the women looked. One woman looked.
children	The children laughed. One child laughed.

FOR STUDENTS ACQUIRING ENGLISH

- Have children listen to the Try It Out sentences on the audiotape. Distribute the SAE Practice page for Unit 3, Lesson 5.
- First, have children look at the drawings to see how many of these nouns they can identify on their own. Call on children to tell you what the drawings are. Write children's ideas on the board. Continue until someone gives you the noun that will have the irregular plural. Ask what they think the plural will be. Have children listen to the tape and circle the drawing in the pair that corresponds to what they hear on tape. Then they write the word.

1. child children (children)
2. woman women (women)

Summing Up Help children summarize these key points about the lesson:

> Most nouns add *s* or *es* to name more than one.
> Some nouns change their spelling to name **more than one.**

You may want to have children complete the parts related to this lesson on Blackline Master 3-2.

On Your Own

Have children test each noun by asking:

> Does the noun change its spelling to name more than one?

FOR STUDENTS ACQUIRING ENGLISH

Distribute the SAE Practice page for Unit 3, Lesson 5. Help children suggest sentences for the art. Also make sure children know what a mule is. Children underline the noun that belongs in each sentence. Then children write the sentence.

1. Two (women, woman) chased the dog.
2. Four (child, children) watched.

Writing Wrap-Up

Writing Tip: Suggest that children draw and label things people could do to help in the class. See Blackline Master 3-7 for a sample advertisement.

TECHNOLOGY CONNECTION

Children may want to use available software to incorporate bold type and decorative fonts in their ads.

On Your Own

Write the sentences correctly.

Example Two (child, children) saw a mule.
Two children saw a mule.

1. Three (man, men) chased the mule.
2. Two (woman, women) caught it.

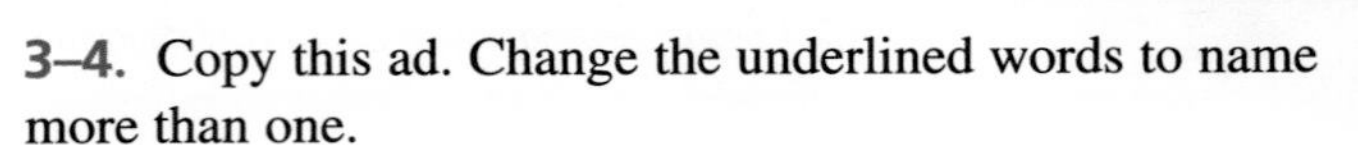

3–4. Copy this ad. Change the underlined words to name more than one.

Example We need man. We need men.

WANTED: MULE RIDERS
We need child (children) and woman (women).
YOU MUST LIKE ANIMALS!

Writing Wrap-Up

WRITING • THINKING • LISTENING • SPEAKING

PERSUADING

Write an Ad

Write an ad for men, women, or children to help in your class. Tell why it would be fun to help. Read your ad to classmates. Discuss if what you wrote would make someone want to answer the ad. Ads will vary.

104 Nouns That Change Spelling For Extra Practice, see page 128.

Meeting Individual Needs

● RETEACHING WORKBOOK, page 22

5 Nouns That Change Spelling

Some nouns change spelling to name more than one.

one man	many **men**
one child	six **children**
a woman	two **women**

Write the noun that names more than one in each sentence.

Example Three ____ are shopping. (children, child)
Three children are shopping.

1. Two children want red caps. **(child, children)**
2. Four men are looking at ties. **(men, man)**
3. Those two women need new shoes. **(woman, women)**
4. Those men are buying belts. **(man, men)**
5. Two women are trying on dresses. **(women, woman)**

▲■ WORKBOOK PLUS, pages 35-36

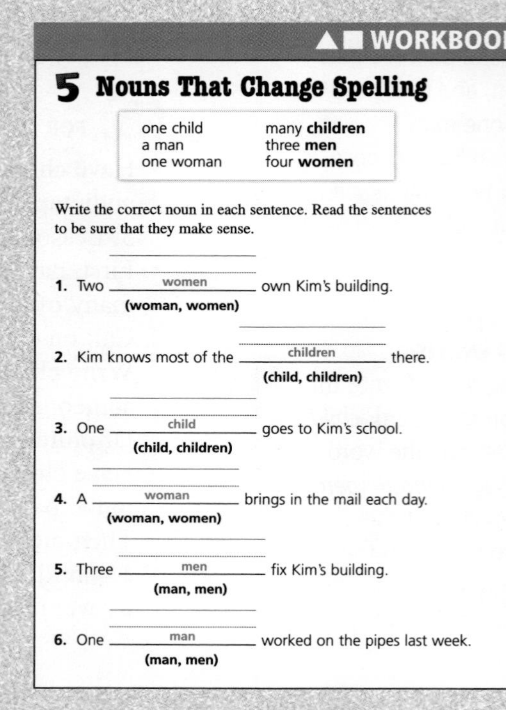

5 Nouns That Change Spelling

one child	many **children**
a man	three **men**
one woman	four **women**

Write the correct noun in each sentence. Read the sentences to be sure that they make sense.

1. Two women own Kim's building. **(woman, women)**
2. Kim knows most of the children there. **(child, children)**
3. One child goes to Kim's school. **(child, children)**
4. A woman brings in the mail each day. **(woman, women)**
5. Three men fix Kim's building. **(man, men)**
6. One man worked on the pipes last week. **(man, men)**

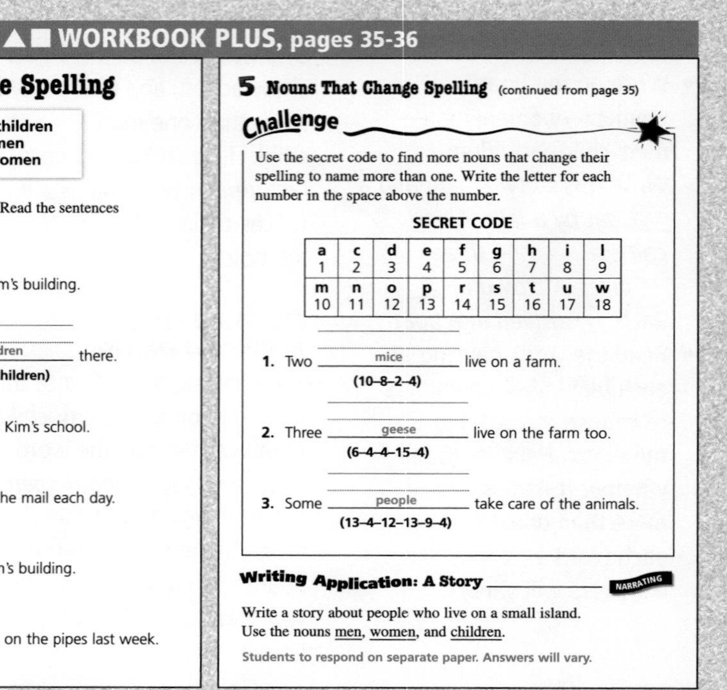

5 Nouns That Change Spelling (continued from page 35)

Challenge

Use the secret code to find more nouns that change their spelling to name more than one. Write the letter for each number in the space above the number.

SECRET CODE

a	c	d	e	f	g	h	i	l
1	2	3	4	5	6	7	8	9
m	**n**	**o**	**p**	**r**	**s**	**t**	**u**	**w**
10	11	12	13	14	15	16	17	18

1. Two mice live on a farm. **(10–8–2–4)**
2. Three geese live on the farm too. **(6–4–4–15–4)**
3. Some people take care of the animals. **(13–4–12–13–9–4)**

Writing Application: A Story NARRATING

Write a story about people who live on a small island. Use the nouns men, women, and children.

Students to respond on separate paper. Answers will vary.

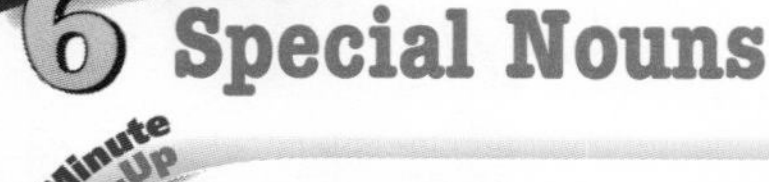

Grammar / Mechanics

6 Special Nouns

Chants will vary.

One-Minute Warm-Up

Name an alphabet letter. Think of a special person, place, and pet name that begin with that letter. Make up a chant like this one.

A, my name is Ann.
I live in Appleton.
My pet's name is Amos.

Some nouns name special people, animals, places, or things. These **special nouns** begin with **capital letters**.

Nouns	Special Nouns
man	Dean
street	Elm Street
town	Lakewood
pet	Wags

Try It Out

Speak Up Tell which nouns name special people, animals, or places. How do they begin?

1. Deven lives in Farwell.
   Deven, Farwell; with a capital letter
2. His sister Cora has a cat, Fluffy.
   Cora, Fluffy; with a capital letter

Write It Write the sentences. Begin each special noun correctly.

Example I live in vermont. I live in Vermont.

3. My friend marta writes to me. Marta
4. She moved to texas last year. Texas

Meeting Individual Needs

RETEACHING
ALTERNATIVE STRATEGY

- Have children address an envelope to themselves. Demonstrate each step on the board, using a familiar address. Point out that names of people and special places begin with capital letters.
- Mix up and pass out the envelopes. Have children draw a picture, write a sentence about it, sign it, put it in the envelope, and give it to the addressee.

CHALLENGE

Have children copy the following and fill in the blanks: A fire truck stopped at 850 ___ Street in the town of ___. The owner of the house, ___, ran out with his cat, ___. (Answers will vary.)

FOR STUDENTS ACQUIRING ENGLISH

Have children write the letters of the alphabet, showing both capitals and lower case letters. You may want to have children work with partners so that they can help each other. Circulate as they work. If needed, children can copy the alphabet.

Special Nouns

Lesson Objectives

Children will:

- identify proper nouns
- capitalize proper nouns
- write proper nouns in sentences
- proofread for capital letters in proper nouns
- write informative sentences for a lost-animal poster

One-Minute Warm-Up Have children repeat the chant, substituting other people, places, and things. Write the nouns on the board and have volunteers tell what kinds of things are named.

Focus on Instruction

Point out that some special nouns, such as *Elm Street*, are made up of two words, and that each word begins with a capital letter.

Try It Out

VIEWING Have children suggest sentences about the illustration. Record the sentences in a chart, omitting capital letters. (Sample responses are shown.) Have children copy each sentence, capitalizing the special nouns.

Special Nouns
1. One day aunt bonnie came to farwell for a visit.
2. She took a picture of Deven and Cora.
3. One of the children was holding fluffy.

FOR STUDENTS ACQUIRING ENGLISH

- Have children listen to the Try It Out sentences on the audiotape. Distribute the SAE Practice page for Unit 3, Lesson 6.
- Have children write their complete names; check that capital and lower case letters are correct. As a group think of special names for people, places, or animals for each letter: *A* is for *Ana*. *Ana* is a *girl*. *B* is for *Barney*. *Barney is a big, purple dinosaur*. *C* is for *Canada*. *Canada is a country*. If necessary, give children clues for local sites or point at a map. Write the words on the board; have children mark the capital letters. Children say which are proper nouns and point out capital letters.
  1. His name is José.
  2. He is from Florida.

Summing Up Help children summarize these key points about the lesson:

Some nouns name special people, animals, places, or things. These **special nouns** begin with **capital letters.**

You may want to have children complete the parts related to this lesson on Blackline Master 3-3.

On Your Own

Have children test each noun by asking:

Does the noun name a special person, animal, place, or thing. Should it begin with a capital letter?

FOR STUDENTS ACQUIRING ENGLISH

Distribute the SAE Practice page for Unit 3, Lesson 6. Children rewrite sentences, correcting capital letters on proper nouns. Children may need assistance with names, including whether they are girls' names or boys' names.

1. My friend is carol. (My friend is Carol.)
2. Her cat is named fawn. (Her cat is named Fawn.)

Writing Wrap-Up

Writing Tip: Display lost-and-found ads from a local newspaper to see what information is included. See Blackline Master 3-7 for a sample poster.

TECHNOLOGY CONNECTION

Children may wish to use computers to highlight some information in bold print on their posters.

On Your Own

Write the sentences. Begin each special noun correctly.

Example Where is eric today?
Where is Eric today?

1. He went to dallas. **Dallas**
2. He took his dog, chip. **Chip**

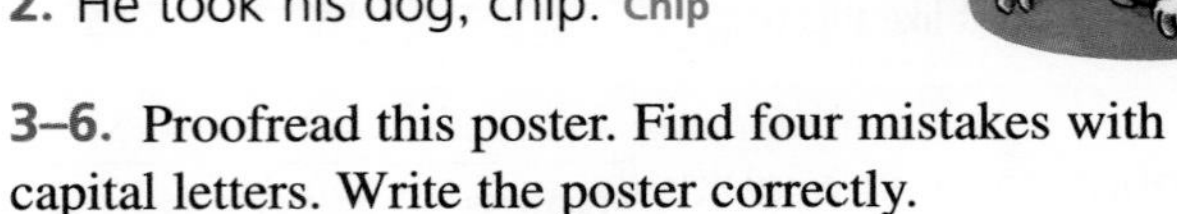

3–6. Proofread this poster. Find four mistakes with capital letters. Write the poster correctly.

Example We looked all over portland.
We looked all over Portland.

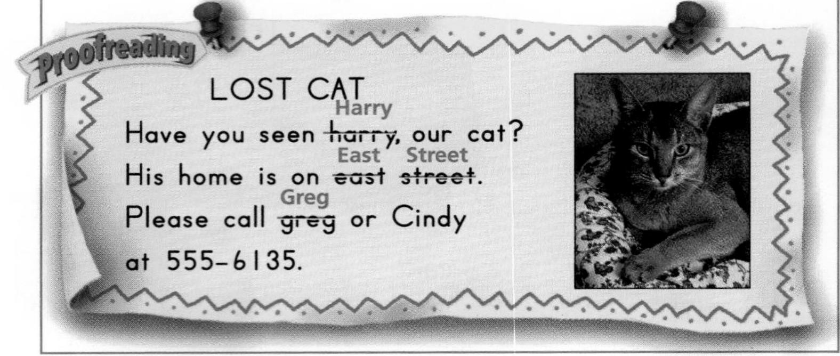

Writing Wrap-Up

WRITING • THINKING • LISTENING • SPEAKING

INFORMING

Write Sentences for a Poster

Make a poster for a lost animal. Write the animal's name and where it lives. Draw a picture. Show and read your poster. Have classmates name the special nouns. Posters will vary.

106 Special Nouns For Extra Practice, see page 129.

Meeting Individual Needs

● RETEACHING WORKBOOK, page 23

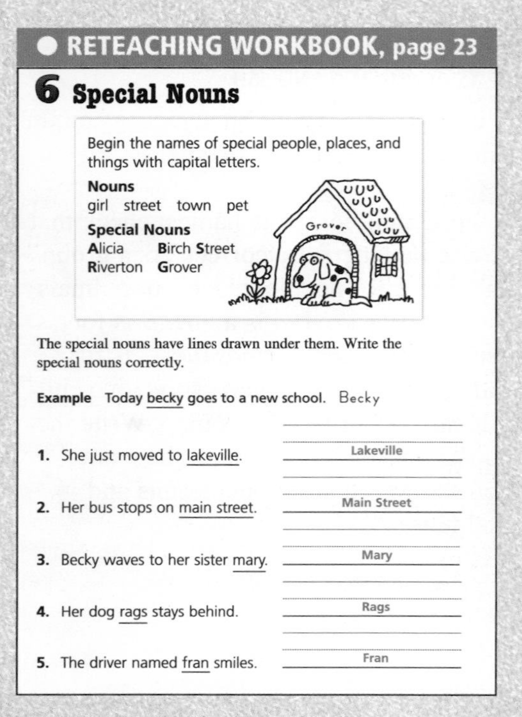

6 Special Nouns

Begin the names of special people, places, and things with capital letters.

Nouns
girl street town pet

Special Nouns
Alicia Birch Street
Riverton Grover

The special nouns have lines drawn under them. Write the special nouns correctly.

Example Today becky goes to a new school. Becky

1. She just moved to lakeville. Lakeville
2. Her bus stops on main street. Main Street
3. Becky waves to her sister mary. Mary
4. Her dog rags stays behind. Rags
5. The driver named fran smiles. Fran

▲■ WORKBOOK PLUS, pages 37-38

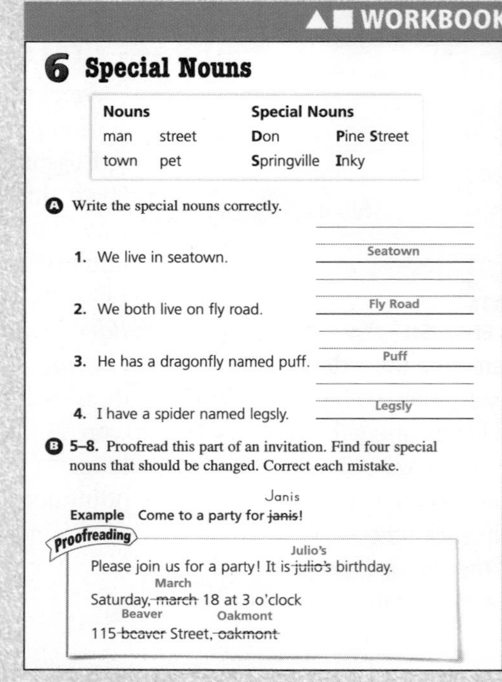

6 Special Nouns

Nouns		Special Nouns	
man	street	Don	Pine Street
town	pet	Springville	Inky

A Write the special nouns correctly.

1. We live in seatown. Seatown
2. We both live on fly road. Fly Road
3. He has a dragonfly named puff. Puff
4. I have a spider named legsly. Legsly

B **5–8.** Proofread this part of an invitation. Find four special nouns that should be changed. Correct each mistake.

Example Come to a party for ~~janis~~ Janis!

Proofreading

Please join us for a party! It is ~~julio's~~ Julio's birthday.
Saturday, ~~march~~ March 18 at 3 o'clock
115 ~~beaver~~ Beaver Street, ~~oakmont~~ Oakmont

6 Special Nouns (continued from page 37)

Challenge

Finish these sentences with your own special nouns.
Answers will vary.

1. My full name is ______.
2. If I could change my name, I would change it to ______.
3. I live on ______.
4. I live in ______.
5. If I could live anywhere, I would live in ______.
6. If I had a pet grasshopper, I would name it ______.

Writing Application: A Story NARRATING

Write a story about going with a friend to a special street in another town. Tell what happens. Be sure to use special nouns. Students to respond on separate paper. Answers will vary.

Grammar / Usage

7 Pronouns

Play the game I Spy. Think of clues like the ones on the poster. Use he, she, it, and they in your clues.

I spy somebody.
She has brown hair.
She is wearing jeans.
Who is she?

Clues and answers will vary.

A **noun** names a person, an animal, a place, or a thing. A **pronoun** can take the place of a noun.

The **plane** lands.	**Jill** looks.	**Jeff** stands.	**Jeff** and **Jill** go.
It lands.	**She** looks.	**He** stands.	**They** go.

Try It Out

Speak Up Name the pronoun in the Word Box that can take the place of the underlined noun or nouns in each sentence.

It	She
They	He

1. Steve and Betsy made bread. They
2. Betsy warmed milk. She
3. Steve added flour. He
4. The bread baked in the oven. It

Write It Now write each sentence, using a pronoun from the Word Box in place of the underlined noun or nouns.

Example Betsy likes bread. She likes bread. They, She, He, It

Pronouns

Lesson Objectives

Children will:

- identify pronouns
- write pronouns correctly
- write sentences with pronouns
- proofread for use of pronouns
- write an informative phone message, using pronouns

One-Minute Warm-Up Write the children's clues on the board. Have volunteers locate and identify the pronouns in each set of clues and then try to find the answer to the clues.

Focus on Instruction

Point out that using pronouns avoids the need to repeat the same nouns over and over again, which can be boring.

Try It Out

VIEWING Have children suggest sentences about the illustration — two about Betsy, two about Steve, and two about both Betsy and Steve. Record the sentences in a chart. (Sample sentences are shown.) Have children name the pronoun in the word box that can take the place of the underlined word or words in the second sentence of each pair. (She; He; They)

They	She	He
1. Betsy added milk. Betsy put the dough in a pan.		
2. Steve turned on the oven. Steve set the clock.		
3. Betsy and Steve sat down at the table. Betsy and Steve waited for the bread to bake.		

Meeting Individual Needs

RETEACHING
ALTERNATIVE STRATEGY

- Tell children that a pronoun is a word that can take the place of a noun.
- Write these sentences on the board, underlining the pronouns: Nan asked Maria to go to the store with *her. Maria said she would go. The girls decided they would walk.*
- Have children decide which noun the underlined pronoun takes the place of. (Nan; Maria; girls)

CHALLENGE

Have children write riddles using the pronouns *he, she, it,* or *they.* Write this example on the board: *They swim in ponds. They have feathers. They quack. What are they?* (ducks)

FOR STUDENTS ACQUIRING ENGLISH

Give each child a set of 3 x 5 cards with the pronouns *he, she, it, they.* Call on each child to place the four cards by appropriate individuals or objects. Then call out people or objects and have children see who can place the correct card first.

FOR STUDENTS ACQUIRING ENGLISH

- Have children listen to the Try It Out sentences on the audiotape. Distribute the SAE Practice page for Unit 3, Lesson 7.
- Help children suggest sentences about the art in the book and on the Practice page; assist with vocabulary. Tell children that most of the time we call animals he or she. Also make sure children know that they is the only word for the plurals; this is in contrast to languages that have gender distinctions for plurals. Children say which pronoun in the box can take the place of the underlined word or words. You may need to assist children with gender for names.
  1. Jill and Eduardo made muffins. (They)
  2. Jill got the flour. (She)

Summing Up Help children summarize these key points about the lesson:

A **noun** names a person, an animal, a place, or a thing. A **pronoun** can take the place of a noun.

You may want to have children complete the parts related to this lesson on Blackline Master 3-4.

On Your Own

Have children test each pronoun by asking:

Should this pronoun take the place of this noun?

FOR STUDENTS ACQUIRING ENGLISH

Distribute the SAE Practice page for Unit 3, Lesson 7. Children choose a noun from the box and rewrite each sentence. Then they circle errors in pronouns in pairs of sentences and fix the errors.

1. Susan and Bill clean the house. (They)
2. Bill helped. It washed the dishes. (He)

Writing Wrap-Up

Writing Tip: Suggest that children reread their phone messages to make sure the meaning is clear and the information is correct and complete. See Blackline Master 3-7 for a sample phone message.

TECHNOLOGY CONNECTION

Have children talk to family members to get their ideas about how phone messages should be taken.

On Your Own

Write each sentence. Use a pronoun from the Word Box to take the place of the underlined noun.

They
She
He

Example Toys are on the rug.
They are on the rug.

1. Tony picks up toys. **He picks up toys.**
2. Lucy cleans the rug. **She cleans the rug.**

3–4. Proofread Emily's note. Find two mistakes in using pronouns. Copy the note correctly.

Example Matt swept the floor. It used a broom.
Matt swept the floor. He used a broom.

Proofreading

Mom,

Tim put the dishes away. ~~They~~ He was careful. The kitchen is clean now. ~~He~~ It looks spotless.

Emily

Writing Wrap-Up

WRITING • THINKING • LISTENING • SPEAKING

INFORMING

Write a Message

Write a phone message. Tell who called, for whom, and what he or she wanted. Use he, she, it, or they. Read the message aloud. Have a classmate name the pronouns. **Messages will vary.**

 For Extra Practice, see page 130.

Meeting Individual Needs

● RETEACHING WORKBOOK, page 24

7 Pronouns

A **pronoun** is a word that can take the place of a noun. He, she, it, and they are pronouns.

Matt called the cat.	**He** called the cat.
Jan reached for the cat.	**She** reached for the cat.
The cat was up a tree.	**It** was up a tree.
Matt and Jan called for help.	**They** called for help.

Write each sentence. Use the pronoun that can take the place of the underlined word or words.

Example Our neighborhood is very noisy. **(It, They)**
It is very noisy.

1. Todd and Pam have a pet duck. **(She, They)**
   They have a pet duck.
2. The duck quacks all day long. **(It, They)**
   It quacks all day long.
3. Willie wants a duck too. **(It, He)**
   He wants a duck too.
4. Mom says that one duck is enough. **(She, He)**
   She says that one duck is enough.

▲■ WORKBOOK PLUS, pages 39-40

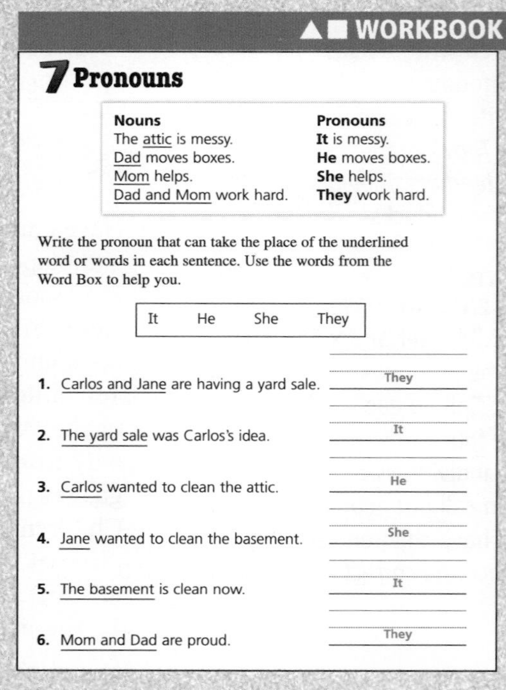

7 Pronouns

Nouns	Pronouns
The attic is messy.	**It** is messy.
Dad moves boxes.	**He** moves boxes.
Mom helps.	**She** helps.
Dad and Mom work hard.	**They** work hard.

Write the pronoun that can take the place of the underlined word or words in each sentence. Use the words from the Word Box to help you.

It	He	She	They

1. Carlos and Jane are having a yard sale. They
2. The yard sale was Carlos's idea. It
3. Carlos wanted to clean the attic. He
4. Jane wanted to clean the basement. She
5. The basement is clean now. It
6. Mom and Dad are proud. They

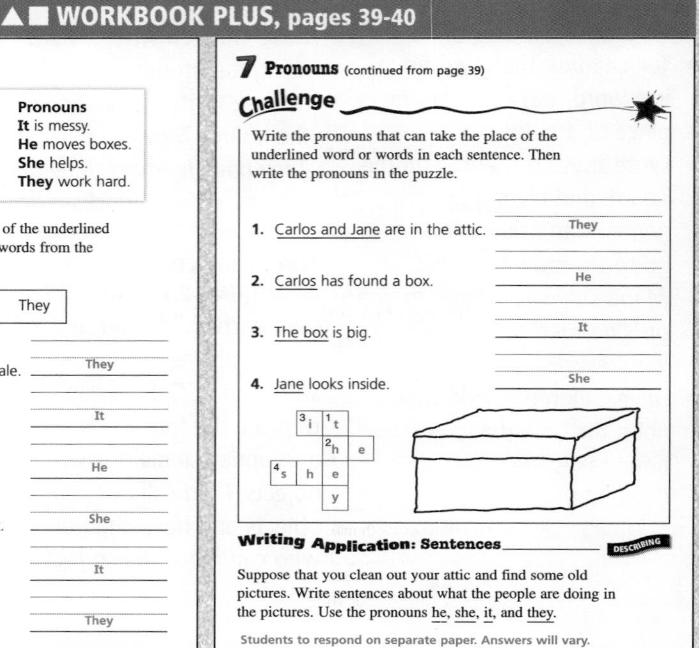

7 Pronouns (continued from page 39)

Challenge

Write the pronouns that can take the place of the underlined word or words in each sentence. Then write the pronouns in the puzzle.

1. Carlos and Jane are in the attic. They
2. Carlos has found a box. He
3. The box is big. It
4. Jane looks inside. She

Writing Application: Sentences DESCRIBING

Suppose that you clean out your attic and find some old pictures. Write sentences about what the people are doing in the pictures. Use the pronouns he, she, it, and they.

Students to respond on separate paper. Answers will vary.

Revising Strategies — Sentence Fluency

Writing Clearly with Nouns and Pronouns

Using Pronouns When you write, try not to use the same **naming part** over and over again. Use a **pronoun** to take its place. This will make your writing better.

Gina and Ben do jobs. **Gina and Ben** help.

Gina and Ben do jobs. **They** help.

Try It Out

Speak Up Read the poster. Find the naming part that is repeated in each numbered pair of sentences. Use a pronoun in place of the naming part in the second sentence. Say the new sentence.

Write It 1–2. Now write the two new sentences you said. They will wax it too! It will look like new.

Example Ben drew the poster.
Ben painted it.
He painted it.

Writing Clearly with Nouns and Pronouns

Lesson Objective

Children will:
- use pronouns to avoid repeating nouns

Focus on Instruction

- Remind children that pronouns are words that take the place of nouns. You might review *he*, *she*, *it*, and *they*, and then ask children to identify the nouns and pronoun in the example.
- Use the example to show how repeating a noun can make writing uninteresting. Have children make up several sentences that begin with *Gina and Ben*. Then, have them replace the nouns with the pronoun, *they*.

Try It Out

SPEAK UP Go over the poster with children. Help them find the repeated naming part in each pair of sentences. Point out that the pronoun children choose must have the same meaning as the noun or nouns it replaces.

WRITE IT When children write each sentence, remind them to use the same pronoun they used when saying it aloud. Have them double-check their writing for errors in spelling and punctuation.

Meeting Individual Needs

● RETEACHING WORKBOOK, page 25

Writing Clearly with Nouns and Pronouns

Use a pronoun to take the place of a naming part that is repeated.

With nouns: **The cake** was almost ready. **The cake** smelled good.

With pronouns: **The cake** was almost ready. **It** smelled good.

Using Pronouns Draw a line under the pronoun in ( ) that should take the place of the underlined naming part. Write the new sentence.

Example: My mitt is big. My mitt covers my hand. (It, He)
It covers my hand.

1. The oven is hot. The oven has been on a long time. **(She, It)**
   It has been on a long time.
2. Mom made the frosting. Mom is a good baker. **(She, He)**
   She is a good baker.
3. Paul is waiting for cake. Paul likes cake with milk. **(It, He)**
   He likes cake with milk.
4. Mom and Paul smile. Mom and Paul eat cake. **(They, He)**
   They eat cake.

▲■ WORKBOOK PLUS, page 41

Writing Clearly with Nouns and Pronouns

With nouns: **The flowers** are on the table. **The flowers** are in the bowl.

With pronouns: **The flowers** are on the table. **They** are in the bowl.

Using Pronouns 1-5. Find the sentences with naming parts that are repeated. Use a pronoun in place of one of the naming parts. Write the new paragraph.

Grandma has a nice garden. Grandma works in it every day. Uncle Dave mows the lawn on Sunday. Uncle Dave rakes the leaves. Lila helps pull the weeds. Lila trims the bushes. The robins use the birdbath. The robins eat the worms. Mom and Dad like this garden. Mom and Dad started a garden, too.

Grandma has a nice garden. She works in it every day. Uncle Dave mows the lawn on Sunday. He rakes the leaves. Lila helps pull the weeds. She trims the bushes. The robins use the birdbath. They eat the worms. Mom and Dad like this garden. They started a garden, too.

Writing Clearly with Nouns and Pronouns

Apply It

- Read the example aloud to the class. Explain that children can use the pronoun *He* in the second sentence in place of *Mr. Smith*.
- Have children complete the revising activity independently. Suggest that they begin by finding the repeated noun or nouns in the ad.

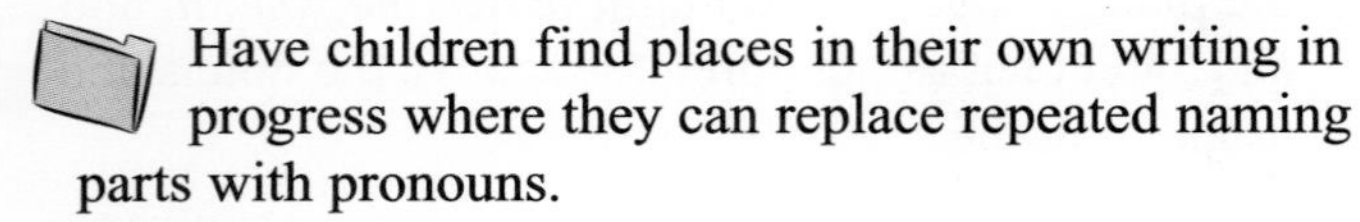

Have children find places in their own writing in progress where they can replace repeated naming parts with pronouns.

FOR STUDENTS ACQUIRING ENGLISH

Before beginning, brainstorm a list of pronouns. Have children do each activity in a small group. Walk around helping with writing and pronunciation. When all have finished, share as a class by asking each group to write an answer on the board and read it, so children can practice reading and writing.

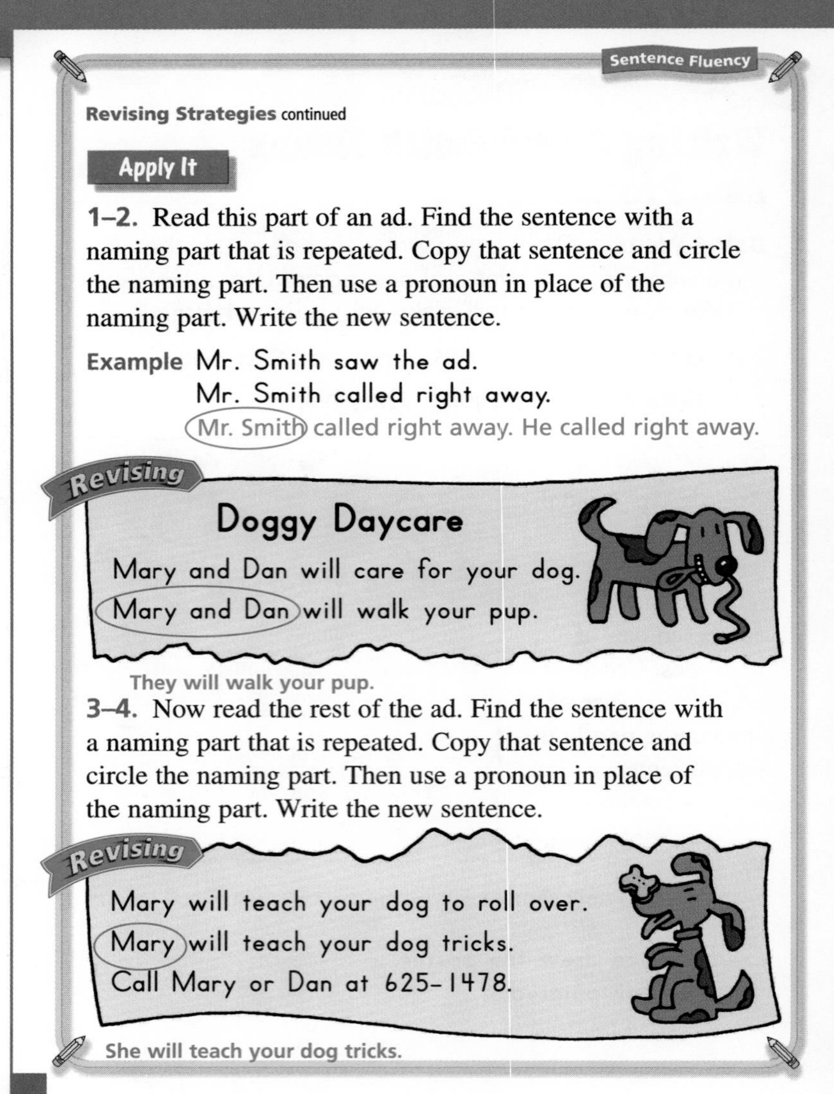

Sentence Fluency

Revising Strategies continued

Apply It

1–2. Read this part of an ad. Find the sentence with a naming part that is repeated. Copy that sentence and circle the naming part. Then use a pronoun in place of the naming part. Write the new sentence.

Example Mr. Smith saw the ad.
Mr. Smith called right away.
Mr. Smith called right away. He called right away.

Revising

Doggy Daycare
Mary and Dan will care for your dog.
Mary and Dan will walk your pup.

They will walk your pup.

3–4. Now read the rest of the ad. Find the sentence with a naming part that is repeated. Copy that sentence and circle the naming part. Then use a pronoun in place of the naming part. Write the new sentence.

Revising

Mary will teach your dog to roll over.
Mary will teach your dog tricks.
Call Mary or Dan at 625-1478.

She will teach your dog tricks.

110 Writing Clearly With Nouns and Pronouns

Meeting Individual Needs

● RETEACHING WORKBOOK, page 26

Writing Clearly with Nouns and Pronouns

Do not repeat naming parts over and over again.
Use a pronoun instead.

With nouns: **My shoes are very wet.**
My shoes are on the mat.
With pronouns: **They** are on the mat.

Using Pronouns Use a pronoun from the word box to replace the repeated naming part. Write the new sentence.

he	she	it

Example The rain started falling. The rain made big puddles.
It made big puddles.

1. Shira did not have an umbrella. Shira was getting wet.
   She was getting wet.
2. Dad had a big umbrella. Dad opened the umbrella quickly.
   He opened the umbrella quickly.
3. The umbrella was very handy. The umbrella kept everyone dry.
   It kept everyone dry.

▲■ WORKBOOK PLUS, page 42

Writing Clearly with Nouns and Pronouns

With nouns: **Paula and Rob** were outside.
Paula and Rob took a walk.
With pronouns: **Paula and Rob** were outside.
They took a walk.

Using Pronouns Find the sentences with naming parts that are repeated. Use a pronoun in place of one of the naming parts. Write the new sentence.

Marc likes to ski. Marc goes skiing with his family. The skis are new. The skis are bright and shiny. Marc and his dad ski together. Marc and his dad have fun. Skiing is not hard to learn. Skiing is a great sport.

1. He goes skiing with his family.
2. They are bright and shiny.
3. They have fun.
4. It is a great sport.

Grammar / Usage

8 Naming Yourself Last

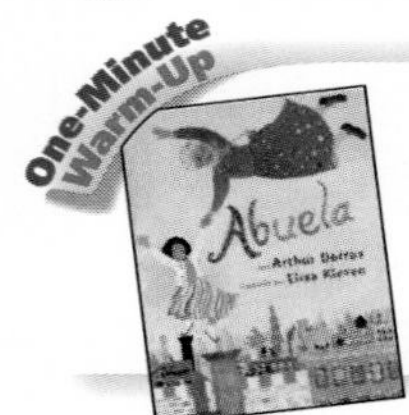

One-Minute Warm-Up

Say the naming part of the sentence. What person is named last? Say another sentence, using Abuela and I.

Abuela and I are always going places.

—from Abuela, by Arthur Dorros

Abuela and I; I; responses will vary.

When you write or talk about another person and yourself, **name yourself last**. Always use the word I in the naming part of the sentence.

Tina and **I** rode our new bikes.

Try It Out

Speak Up Tell how to make the sentences correct.

1. I and Carl ran a race. *Carl and I*
2. Me and Amy jumped rope. *Amy and I*
3. I and Chen flew a kite. *Chen and I*

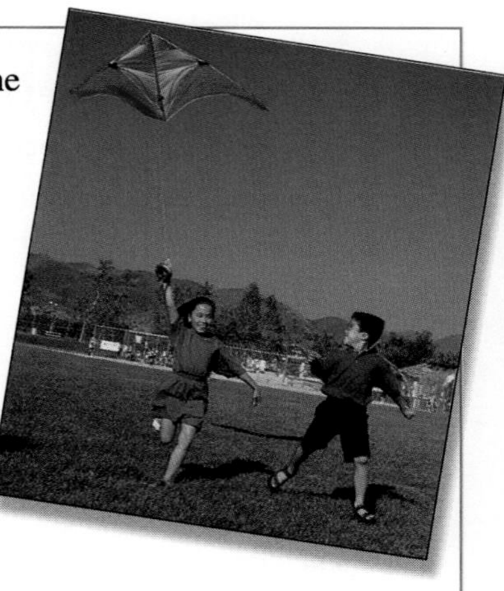

Write It Now write the sentences correctly.

Example Ann and me played.
Ann and I played.

Carl and I ran a race.
Amy and I jumped rope.
Chen and I flew a kite.

Meeting Individual Needs

RETEACHING
ALTERNATIVE STRATEGY

- Write each child's name followed by *and* I on a strip of paper. Have a child draw a strip. Have that child and the child whose name is on the strip pantomime an action.
- Have the class guess the action. Then write one child's name plus *and I* plus the action to form a sentence.
- Remind children that *I* is always last—you name yourself last.

CHALLENGE

Have children say sentences telling an action they can do that can also be done by animals or objects, for example, *A duck, a boat, and I can ___.* (float) Have other children guess the action.

FOR STUDENTS ACQUIRING ENGLISH

Ask children what to do when two people want to go through a door at the same time or when two people want the last cookie. Is it good manners to go first? Is it good manners to take the last cookie? Compare this to naming oneself last. Give examples with *I*.

Naming Yourself Last

Lesson Objectives

Children will:

- name others before themselves
- write a sentence in which they name themselves last
- proofread for use of pronouns
- write a poem, using pronouns

One-Minute Warm-Up Copy on the board the quoted sentence and underline the pronoun *I*. Then reread the sentence using *I* first. Ask children why they think this is not correct. Have children then substitute the name of a family member for *Abuela* and read the sentence correctly.

Focus on Instruction

Remind children that a pronoun is used to take the place of a noun. Tell children that when the pronoun *I* is used, it takes the place of the name of the person speaking.

Try It Out

LISTENING AND SPEAKING Copy this example sentence from the lesson on the board: *Ann and* (me, I) *played.* Tell children that when they are unsure which pronoun to use, they should try the pronoun alone. Point out that when they say the sentence without *Ann and*, their ear will tell them that *I* is the correct word. (*I played*, not *me played*).

FOR STUDENTS ACQUIRING ENGLISH

- Have children listen to the Try It Out sentences on the audiotape. Distribute the SAE Practice page for Unit 3, Lesson 8.
- Ask what the children in the photo are doing. Help children suggest sentences about the art on the Practice page. Children complete the following any way they wish: _____ *and I like* _____. If they complete it with a simple verb, tell them to use *to*. Remind children that it is good manners to name themselves last, no matter how many people are in the naming part. Also, they must always use *I*, not *me*, in the naming part. Children listen and say how to fix the naming part. Then they write the corrected sentence.
  1. I and Karin played. (Karin and I)
  2. Me and James raced cars. (James and I)

Summing Up Help children summarize these key points about the lesson:

When you write about or talk about another person and yourself, **name yourself last**. Always use the word *I* in the naming part of the sentence.

You may want to have children complete the parts related to this lesson on Blackline Master 3-4.

On Your Own

Have children test each sentence by asking:

Did I name myself last? Did I use the word *I* in the naming part of the sentence?

FOR STUDENTS ACQUIRING ENGLISH

Distribute the SAE Practice page for Unit 3, Lesson 8. Remind children that the word they must use for themselves in the naming part is always *I*, not *me*. Children say how to fix the naming part.

1. Me and Laura like cats. (Laura and I)
2. I and Felipe play soccer. (Felipe and I)

Writing Wrap-Up

Writing Tip: Have children make a web of things they do with friends and then choose those to include in their poems. See Blackline Master 3-7 for a poetry sample.

SCHOOL-HOME CONNECTION

Suggest that children find poems they like in books at home and read them together with their family.

On Your Own

Write the sentences correctly.

Example I and Jane paint. Jane and I paint.

1. Taro and me sing. **Taro and I sing.**
2. I and Liz run. **Liz and I run.**

3–6. Proofread this poem. Find four mistakes in using pronouns. Write the poem correctly.

Example Me and Carlos play ball.
Carlos and I play ball.

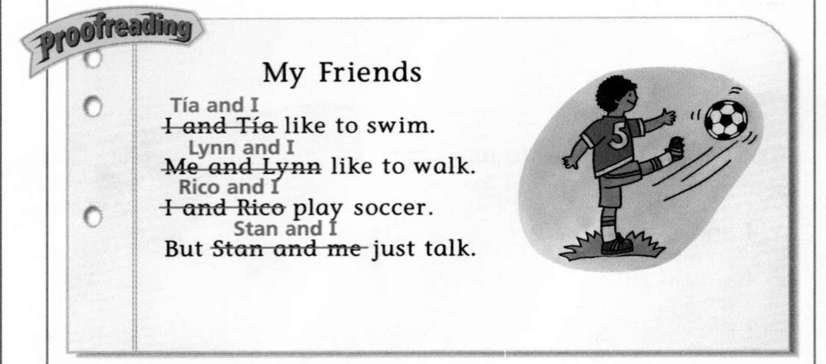
Proofreading

My Friends

~~I and Tía~~ Tía and I like to swim.
~~Me and Lynn~~ Lynn and I like to walk.
~~I and Rico~~ Rico and I play soccer.
But ~~Stan and me~~ Stan and I just talk.

Writing Wrap-Up WRITING • THINKING • LISTENING • SPEAKING

CREATING

Write a Poem

Write a poem about what you do with friends. Use each friend's name and then I. Listen as classmates read their poems. Did they name themselves last?

Poems will vary.

 For Extra Practice, see page 131.

Meeting Individual Needs

● RETEACHING WORKBOOK, page 27

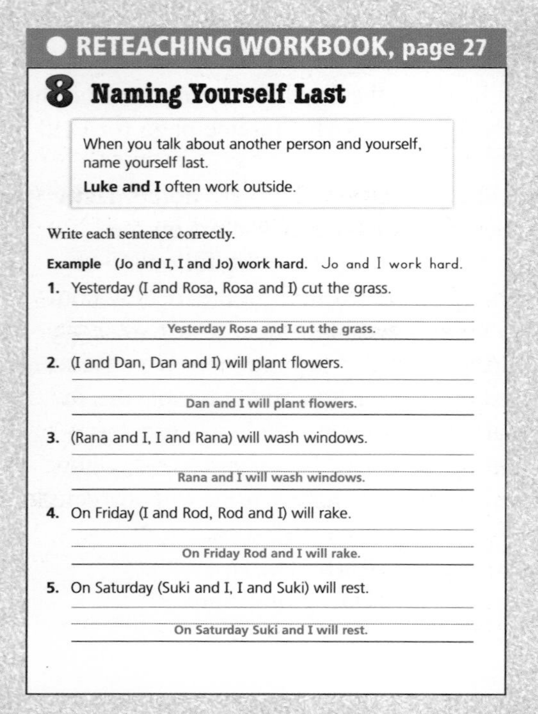

8 Naming Yourself Last

When you talk about another person and yourself, name yourself last.
Luke and I often work outside.

Write each sentence correctly.

Example (Jo and I, I and Jo) work hard. Jo and I work hard.

1. Yesterday (I and Rosa, Rosa and I) cut the grass.
   Yesterday Rosa and I cut the grass.
2. (I and Dan, Dan and I) will plant flowers.
   Dan and I will plant flowers.
3. (Rana and I, I and Rana) will wash windows.
   Rana and I will wash windows.
4. On Friday (I and Rod, Rod and I) will rake.
   On Friday Rod and I will rake.
5. On Saturday (Suki and I, I and Suki) will rest.
   On Saturday Suki and I will rest.

▲■ WORKBOOK PLUS, pages 43-44

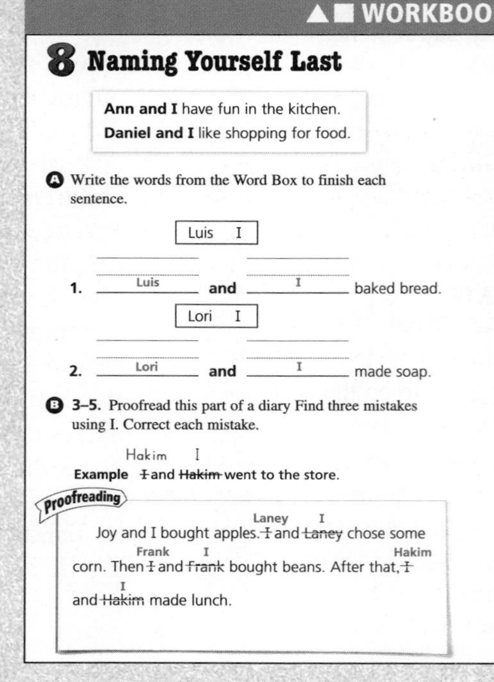

8 Naming Yourself Last

Ann and I have fun in the kitchen.
Daniel and I like shopping for food.

A Write the words from the Word Box to finish each sentence.

Luis I

1. Luis and I baked bread.

Lori I

2. Lori and I made soap.

B 3–5. Proofread this part of a diary Find three mistakes using I. Correct each mistake.

Example ~~I~~ Hakim and ~~Hakim~~ I went to the store.

Proofreading

Joy and I bought apples. ~~I~~ Laney and ~~Laney~~ I chose some corn. Then ~~I~~ Frank and ~~Frank~~ I bought beans. After that, ~~I~~ Hakim and ~~Hakim~~ I made lunch.

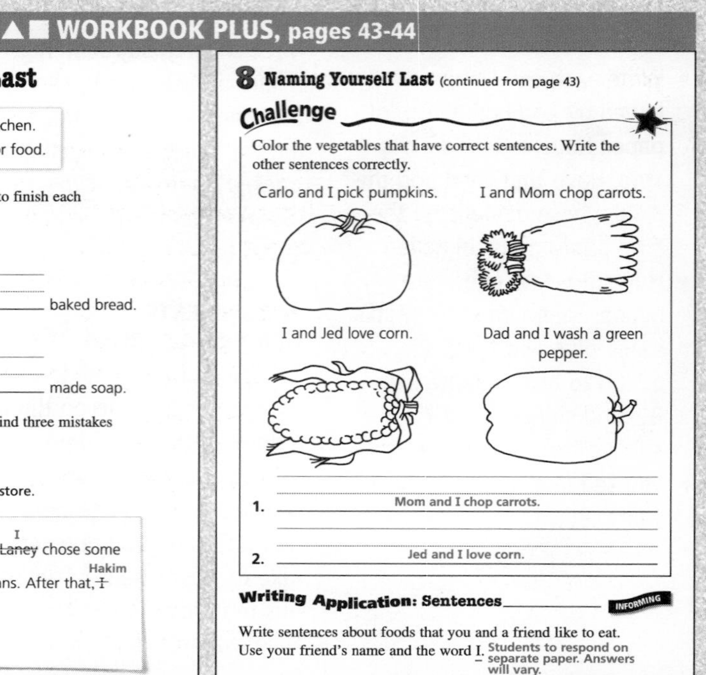

8 Naming Yourself Last (continued from page 43)

Challenge

Color the vegetables that have correct sentences. Write the other sentences correctly.

Carlo and I pick pumpkins. I and Mom chop carrots.

I and Jed love corn. Dad and I wash a green pepper.

1. Mom and I chop carrots.
2. Jed and I love corn.

Writing Application: Sentences INFORMING

Write sentences about foods that you and a friend like to eat. Use your friend's name and the word I. Students to respond on separate paper. Answers will vary.

Grammar / Mechanics

9 Nouns Ending with 's

One-Minute Warm-Up

Read the sentence. Whose parents are named? Julius is a pig that Maya owns. What two words could you say to show this? *Maya's parents*; *Maya's pig*

Maya's parents didn't think that they would like Julius.

—from Julius by Angela Johnson

Some nouns show that a person or animal owns or has something. When a noun names one person or animal, add an **apostrophe** (') and **s** to that noun to **show ownership**.

girl's pet   Sam's hamster   owl's wing

Try It Out

Add an apostrophe and *s* to the first noun.

Speak Up Tell what to add to each noun in ( ) to make it correctly show ownership. Read each pair of nouns.

1. (bird) cage **bird's cage**
2. (Sara) puppy **Sara's puppy**
3. (owl) beak **owl's beak**
4. (dog) nose **dog's nose**

Write It Now write each pair of nouns correctly. **bird's cage, Sara's puppy, owl's beak, dog's nose**

Example (dog) leash dog's leash

Meeting Individual Needs

RETEACHING
ALTERNATIVE STRATEGY

- Have children write their names and the name of something they own on a slip of paper, for example, Katy baseball cap.
- Have children trade papers and add an apostrophe and *s* to the name of the person. Call on children to say the words on their papers.
- Remind children that when a noun names one person, add an apostrophe and *s* to show ownership.

CHALLENGE
Have children find magazine or newspaper pictures that show one person who has something, for example, a girl holding a kite. Have children write words to show what the person has: *girl's kite.*

FOR STUDENTS ACQUIRING ENGLISH
Point out objects and ask, for example, *Whose hat is this?* Say and write, *It's Jana's hat.* Show how to make an apostrophe. Have children practice making *'s* with their own names. Make sure the apostrophe is positioned correctly in relation to the letters.

Nouns Ending in 's

Lesson Objectives

Children will:

- identify nouns that show ownership of one
- form nouns that show ownership of one by adding *'s*
- proofread for nouns that show ownership of one by adding *'s*
- write a paragraph of comparison and contrast, using nouns that show ownership of one

One-Minute Warm-Up Write the quoted sentence on the board and underline *Maya's parents*. Ask volunteers to tell whose parents the sentence is about. Then have volunteers point out the special mark that lets them know.

Focus on Instruction

Point out that the use of an apostrophe to show ownership is different from its use in contractions.

Try It Out

LISTENING AND SPEAKING Write the example pair of nouns from the lesson, *dog leash*, on the board and have children listen as you say the words. Call on a volunteer to say the words to show that the leash belongs to the dog. (*dog's leash*) Add *'s* to the word *dog* on the board and repeat the words. Follow the same procedure with each pair of nouns in the lesson: *bird cage*, *Sara puppy*, *owl beak*, *dog nose*.

FOR STUDENTS ACQUIRING ENGLISH

- Have children listen to the Try It Out sentences on the audiotape. Distribute the SAE Practice page for Unit 3, Lesson 9.
- Help children suggest sentences about the photo in the book. Ask, *What is this baby animal called? Whose puppy is it?* Next help children name the animals on the Practice page. Write out the words on the board as needed. Make sure children understand that no matter how the name is spelled, ownership is always *'s* for singular naming words. Children listen and write the name of the child to show who owns the pet.

1. _____ rabbit (Andrea's rabbit)
2. _____ hamster (Luis's hamster)

Summing Up Help children summarize these key points about the lesson:

Some nouns show that one person or animal owns or has something. Add an **apostrophe** and **s** to show **ownership.**

You may want to have children complete the parts related to this lesson on Blackline Master 3-5.

On Your Own

Have children test each noun that shows ownership of one by asking:

Has an apostrophe and s been added to the noun?

FOR STUDENTS ACQUIRING ENGLISH

Distribute the SAE Practice page for Unit 3, Lesson 9. For extra practice, have children sit in a circle with each child in turn identifying something belonging to the next child. For example, *Diana's sweater*. Then children underline the sentence that is correct in each pair. Example: Carlos dog is brown. Carlos's dog is brown.

Writing Wrap-Up

Writing Tip: Suggest that children think about pets they are familiar with and their characteristics. See Blackline Master 3-8 for a sample paragraph.

TECHNOLOGY CONNECTION

Children may wish to set up a three-column table to compare and contrast the characteristics of the pets.

On Your Own

Write the sentence in each pair with a noun that correctly shows ownership.

Example Sue mice are cute. Sue's mice are cute.
Sue's mice are cute.

1. A boy's bird got loose.
   A boy bird got loose.
2. Toms dog did tricks.
   Tom's dog did tricks.

3–6. Proofread these judge's notes. Find four nouns with mistakes in showing ownership. Write the notes correctly.

Example Pablo fish won second prize.
Pablo's fish won second prize.

The best trick was done by ~~Megs~~ Meg's puppy.
~~Ben~~ Ben's kitten has the softest fur.
The prize for the biggest pet should go to ~~Marco~~ Marco's dog.
~~Kims~~ Kim's snake is the longest pet.

Write a Paragraph

Write about two children and the pets they own. Tell how the pets are alike and different. Read your paragraph. Have a classmate tell which nouns show ownership. Paragraphs will vary.

114 Nouns Ending with 's For Extra Practice, see page 132.

Meeting Individual Needs

● RETEACHING WORKBOOK, page 28

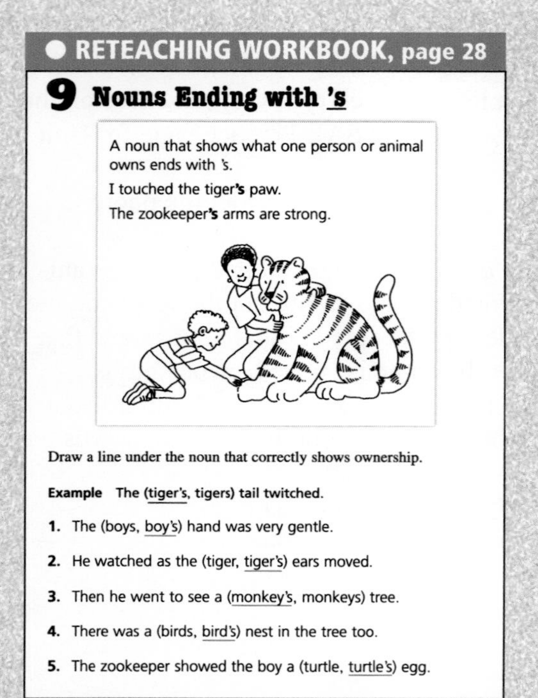

9 Nouns Ending with 's

A noun that shows what one person or animal owns ends with 's.
I touched the tiger**'s** paw.
The zookeeper**'s** arms are strong.

Draw a line under the noun that correctly shows ownership.

Example The (tiger's, tigers) tail twitched.

1. The (boys, boy's) hand was very gentle.
2. He watched as the (tiger, tiger's) ears moved.
3. Then he went to see a (monkey's, monkeys) tree.
4. There was a (birds, bird's) nest in the tree too.
5. The zookeeper showed the boy a (turtle, turtle's) egg.

▲■ WORKBOOK PLUS, pages 45-46

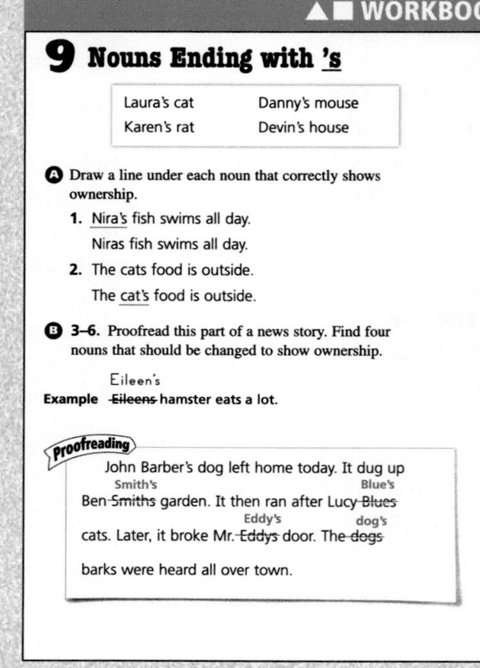

9 Nouns Ending with 's

Laura's cat	Danny's mouse
Karen's rat	Devin's house

A Draw a line under each noun that correctly shows ownership.

1. Nira's fish swims all day.
   Niras fish swims all day.
2. The cats food is outside.
   The cat's food is outside.

B **3–6.** Proofread this part of a news story. Find four nouns that should be changed to show ownership.

Example ~~Eileens~~ Eileen's hamster eats a lot.

Proofreading

John Barber's dog left home today. It dug up Ben ~~Smiths~~ Smith's garden. It then ran after Lucy ~~Blues~~ Blue's cats. Later, it broke Mr. ~~Eddys~~ Eddy's door. The ~~dogs~~ dog's barks were heard all over town.

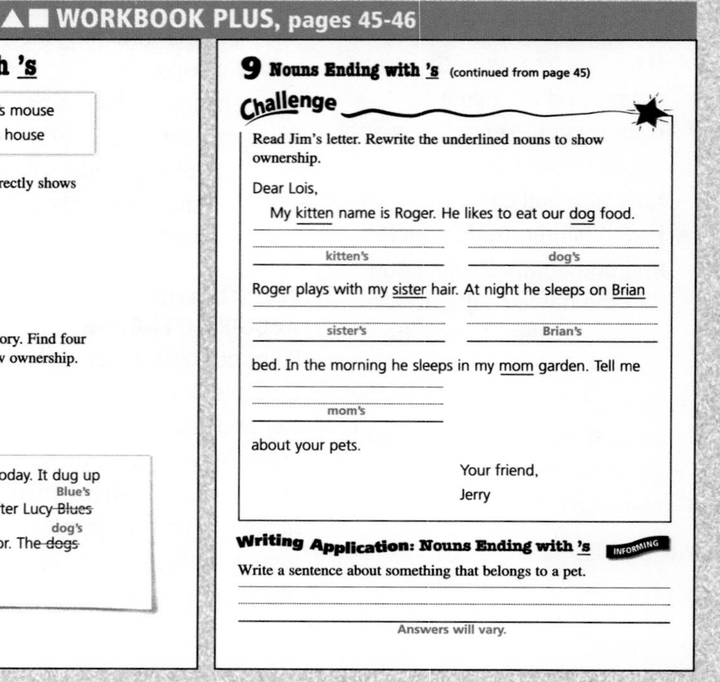

9 Nouns Ending with 's (continued from page 45)

Challenge

Read Jim's letter. Rewrite the underlined nouns to show ownership.

Dear Lois,
My kitten name is Roger. He likes to eat our dog food.
kitten's dog's
Roger plays with my sister hair. At night he sleeps on Brian
sister's Brian's
bed. In the morning he sleeps in my mom garden. Tell me
mom's
about your pets.
Your friend,
Jerry

Writing Application: Nouns Ending with 's INFORMING

Write a sentence about something that belongs to a pet.

Answers will vary.

Grammar / Mechanics

10 Nouns Ending with s'

boys, girls, birds; sentences will vary.

One-Minute Warm-Up

Read the words. To whom do the kites belong? Who owns the books? To whom do the nests belong? Use the words in sentences.

boys' kites
girls' books
birds' nests

A noun that names one person or animal ends with an apostrophe and s to show ownership. When a noun names more than one and ends in s, add just an **apostrophe** (') after the s to **show ownership**. The underlined nouns name more than one. What was added to show ownership? Where was it added?

two boys' closets birds' nests twins' room

Try It Out Add an apostrophe after s in each underlined noun.

Speak Up Each underlined noun names more than one. Tell what you must add to make these nouns show ownership. Read the word groups.

1. four boys caps
2. kittens box
3. friends books
4. cousins dogs

Write It Now write each group of words above. Make the underlined noun show ownership.

boys', kittens', friends', cousins'

Example two girls dresses two girls' dresses

Meeting Individual Needs

RETEACHING
ALTERNATIVE STRATEGY

- Write the *two friends' tapes* on the board. Have children tell whether the underlined noun names more than one (yes), with what letter it ends (*s*). Ask what was added to show ownership ('), and where it was added (after the *s*).
- Remind children that a noun that names more than one and ends in *s* takes only an apostrophe after the *s* to show ownership.

CHALLENGE
Have children draw pictures that show two or more people who have something, for example, three boys wearing cowboy boots. Have children write words to show what the people have: *boys' boots.*

FOR STUDENTS ACQUIRING ENGLISH
Review singular possessives using children's names. Then use gestures to indicate multiple girls and their books and write *the girls'* books on the board. Continue with *boys'*, *friends'*, and other examples. Ask what is different.

Nouns Ending with s'

Lesson Objectives

Children will:
- identify nouns that show ownership of more than one and end in *s*
- form nouns that show ownership of more than one and end in *s* by adding an apostrophe
- proofread for nouns that show ownership of more than one and end in *s* by adding an apostrophe
- write a narrative, using nouns that show ownership of more than one and end in *s*

One-Minute Warm-Up Write the children's sentences on the board. Have them identify the words that show ownership.

Focus on Instruction

Point out that children must decide whether the noun to show ownership names one or more than one.

Try It Out

LISTENING AND SPEAKING Write *two girls dresses* on the board and have children listen as you say the words. Call on a volunteer to say the words to show that the dresses belong to the two girls. *(two girls' dresses)* Add an apostrophe to the word *girls* on the board and repeat the words. Follow the same procedure with each numbered item in the lesson.

FOR STUDENTS ACQUIRING ENGLISH

- Have children listen to the Try It Out sentences on the audiotape. Distribute the SAE Practice page for Unit 3, Lesson 10. 
- Help children suggest sentences about the photo in the book. For example, ask, "What color are the players' uniforms?" (The players' uniforms are yellow.) Review plurals, including plurals that change spelling. Then have children describe the drawings on the Practice page. Help children name and count the farm animals as well as associated objects such as nests and eggs. Children listen and add an apostrophe to make the plural possessive.
  1. the hens eggs (the hens' eggs)
  2. the cows ears (the cows' ears)

Summing Up Help children summarize these key points about the lesson:

A noun that names one person or animal ends with an apostrophe and an s to show ownership. When a noun names more than one and ends in *s*, add just an apostrophe after the *s* to show ownership.

You may want to have children complete the parts related to this lesson on Blackline Master 3-5.

On Your Own

Have children test each possessive noun by asking:

Does the noun end in *s* and have an apostrophe after the *s*?

FOR STUDENTS ACQUIRING ENGLISH

Distribute the SAE Practice page for Unit 3, Lesson 10. Children circle the nouns that show ownership.

1. Paul makes his sisters beds. (sisters')
2. Amy puts her brothers toys away. (brothers')

Writing Wrap-Up

Writing Tip: Suggest use of words such as *first, next,* and *then* to keep the order of what happens clear. See Blackline Master 3-8 for a sample story.

SCHOOL-HOME CONNECTION

Children may want to work with family members to write a new "chapter."

On Your Own

The underlined nouns name more than one. Write the sentences, adding an apostrophe to each underlined noun to show ownership.

Example My <u>aunts</u> barn is full. My aunts' barn is full.

1. The <u>hens</u> cages are in one corner. **hens'**
2. My <u>brothers</u> bikes are here too. **brothers'**

3–5. Proofread Tanya's list. Find three mistakes with nouns that name more than one and that show ownership. Write the list correctly.

Example I will pick up my brothers books.
I will pick up my brothers' books.

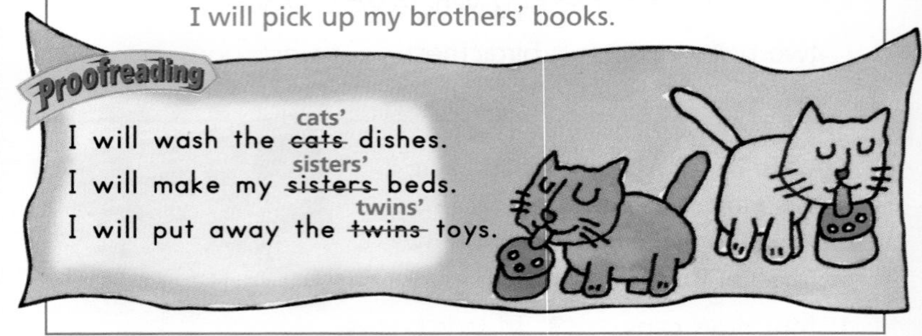

Writing Wrap-Up

WRITING • THINKING • LISTENING • SPEAKING

NARRATING

Write a Story

Write about girls' pets, friends' kites, or boys' hats. Read your story. Have a classmate draw a picture of it. Name the nouns that show ownership in each of your stories.

Stories will vary.

 For Extra Practice, see page 133.

Meeting Individual Needs

● RETEACHING WORKBOOK, page 29

10 Nouns Ending with s'

When a noun names more than one and ends in s, add ' to show ownership.
My brothers' beds are very neat.
Our birds' cages are kept very clean.

Draw a line under the noun that names more than one and shows ownership correctly.

Example The (birds <u>birds'</u>) perches are smooth.

1. Our (sisters, <u>sisters'</u>) beds have lots of toys on them.
2. We visit our (<u>grandmothers'</u>, grandmother's) houses and see their kittens.
3. We take care of their (<u>kittens'</u>, kittens) food and water.
4. My brothers play in our (<u>cousins'</u>, cousins) back yard.

▲■ WORKBOOK PLUS, pages 47-48

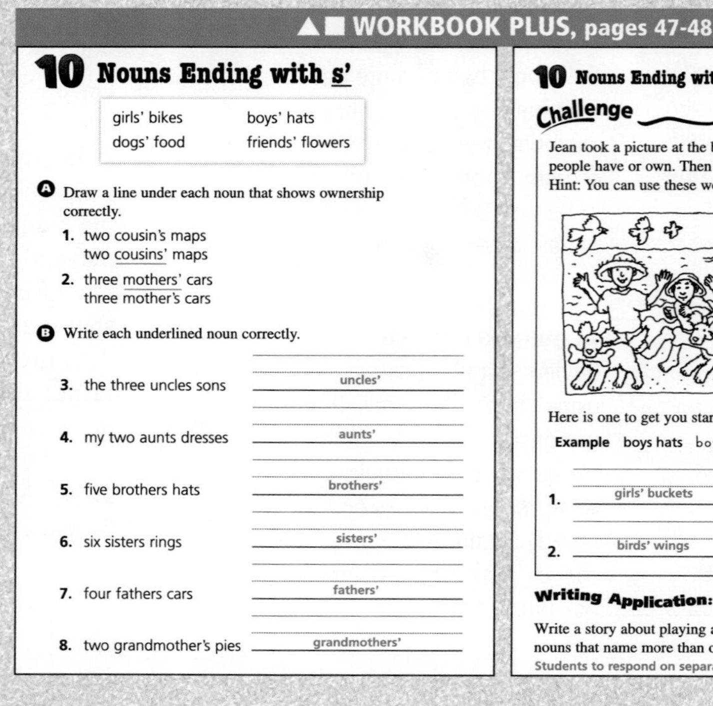

10 Nouns Ending with s'

girls' bikes	boys' hats
dogs' food	friends' flowers

A Draw a line under each noun that shows ownership correctly.

1. two cousin's maps
   two <u>cousins'</u> maps
2. three <u>mothers'</u> cars
   three mother's cars

B Write each underlined noun correctly.

3. the three uncles sons — uncles'
4. my two aunts dresses — aunts'
5. five brothers hats — brothers'
6. six sisters rings — sisters'
7. four fathers cars — fathers'
8. two grandmother's pies — grandmothers'

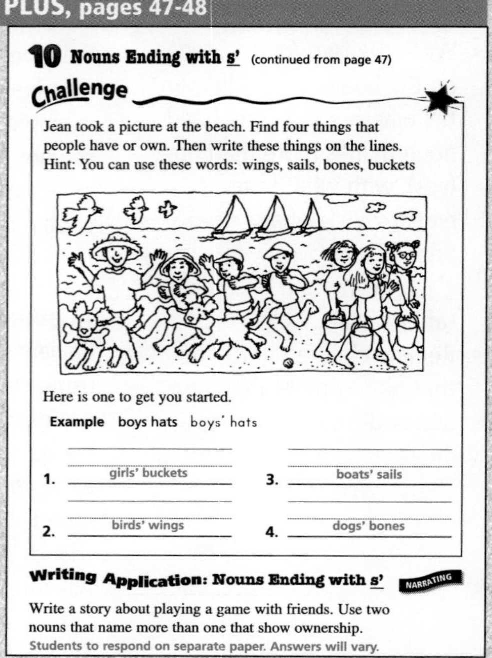

10 Nouns Ending with s' (continued from page 47)

Challenge

Jean took a picture at the beach. Find four things that people have or own. Then write these things on the lines.
Hint: You can use these words: wings, sails, bones, buckets

Here is one to get you started.

Example boys hats boys' hats

1. girls' buckets
2. birds' wings
3. boats' sails
4. dogs' bones

Writing Application: Nouns Ending with s' NARRATING

Write a story about playing a game with friends. Use two nouns that name more than one that show ownership.

Students to respond on separate paper. Answers will vary.

Revising Strategies | Vocabulary

Exact Nouns

Nouns name people, animals, places, and things. When you write, choose nouns that give lots of information. Use **exact nouns** to paint a picture in your reader's mind and to make your writing more interesting.

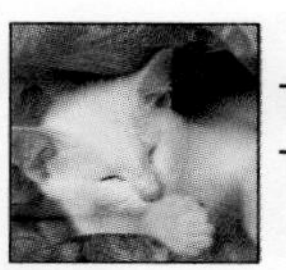

The animal sleeps.
The **kitten** sleeps.

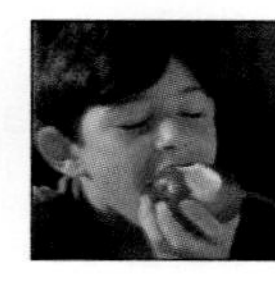

I eat fruit.
I eat an **apple**.

Apply It

Writing Exact Nouns 1–3. Read and copy this poster. Write an exact noun from the box in place of each underlined noun. Use your dictionary for help.

goldfish
pony
puppy
parrot

Example You will see a horse.
You will see a pony.

parrot, puppy, goldfish

Exact Nouns

Lesson Objective

Children will:
- replace weak nouns with exact ones
- use a dictionary

Focus on Instruction

- Ask children to say how the nouns *apple* and *kitten* give more information than *fruit* and *animal*. (*Apple and kitten* tell exactly what kind of fruit or animal.) Discuss why the exact nouns improve the sentences. (They more clearly describe the naming part of the sentence.)
- Have children give other examples of general and exact nouns. Begin by writing these words on the chalkboard: *food/pizza drink/milk game/baseball*

Apply It

- Go over the example with children. Have them look at the words in the box and choose the best one. Point out that while any of the words will complete the sentence, they want to choose the word that best replaces *horse*. Then have them complete the activity independently.

Have children who need more support work with partners.

Have children find places in their own writing in progress where they can use exact nouns.

Meeting Individual Needs

● **RETEACHING WORKBOOK, page 30**

Exact Nouns

Use **exact nouns** to make your writing clearer and more interesting.
baby toys
This person has many things.

Revising Change each underlined noun to an exact noun. Choose words from the word box. Write the new sentence.

puppy	bedroom	bananas	clothes

1. The baby's things are soft and cuddly.
The baby's clothes are soft and cuddly.
2. My place is next to the baby's room.
My bedroom is next to the baby's room.
3. Our pet loves the baby.
Our puppy loves the baby.
4. Dad gives the baby mashed fruit to eat.
Dad gives the baby mashed bananas to eat.

▲■ **WORKBOOK PLUS, page 49**

Exact Nouns

kitchen pots
This room is full of things.

Revising 1-5. Change each underlined noun to a more exact noun. Choose words from the word box. Sample answers

apples	painter	green beans	cats	statues
lamps	babies	shoes	robot	roses

Revising

My cousin Julio is a worker (painter). He likes to paint pictures of people (babies). Sometimes, Julio draws pictures of fruit (apples). Other times, he paints pictures of flowers (roses). He also likes to draw colorful pictures of animals (cats). I like to watch Julio work. His paintings are beautiful.

FOR STUDENTS ACQUIRING ENGLISH

Define noun as "the title for all the words that are people, places, and things" to enable comprehension. Use magazine pictures to practice exact nouns. You give a general noun, the class gives a specific one. Try to include the Apply It words in the magazine picture exercise.

Enrichment

Objectives

Children will:

- generate nouns by identifying them in pictures
- write addresses for an address book

Using the Activities

The Enrichment page provides fun, creative activities that reinforce children's understanding and use of sentences. The activities are designed to be enjoyed by all children. Here are some ideas for using the activities.

- Pair children who need extra support with more capable classmates.
- Children can work with these activities in class after they have completed other assignments.
- Activities that can be completed individually can be assigned as homework.

Notes on the Activities

PICTURE NAMES

- Collect magazines and store them in a learning center. Children can do this activity independently.
- Have children look at the example. Ask them to name the nouns they see.
- As an alternative, you could have children make their own drawings and include as many nouns in them as they can. Then they can trade drawings with a partner and write the nouns they see in each other's pictures.

BUDDY BOOKS

- You will need blank paper for the book pages.
- Tell children that they are looking at pages from a book about where friends live. Ask a volunteer to read the sentence. Then tell children that they will be making their own book pages.
- Help children spell street or town names.
- Children can add pages for future entries.

CHALLENGE Some children may need help using the telephone book. Remind them to look in alphabetical order of the person's last name.

FOR STUDENTS ACQUIRING ENGLISH

Use the magazine pictures you brought in for the lesson on page 117. Make lists for the first few as a class, then split into two teams. Have each team list nouns for a photo, exchange and then award points for the most nouns, most original, funniest, etc.

Enrichment

Nouns and Pronouns!

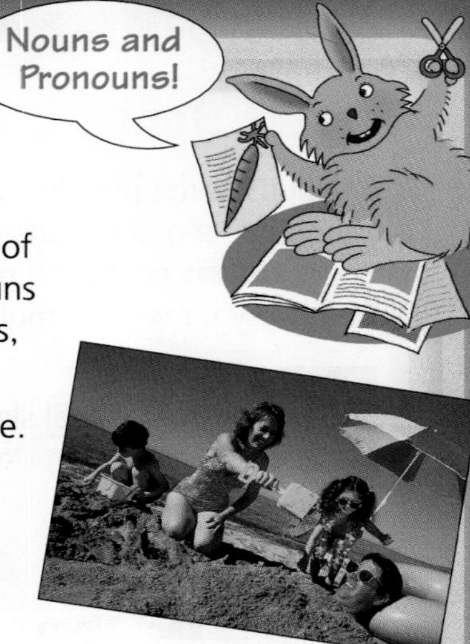

Picture Names

- Cut out a picture from a magazine. Paste it on a sheet of paper. On the back, write nouns for the people, animals, places, and things in the picture.
- Trade pictures with a classmate. Make a list of nouns in your classmate's picture. Look at your classmate's list. Did you both write the same nouns?

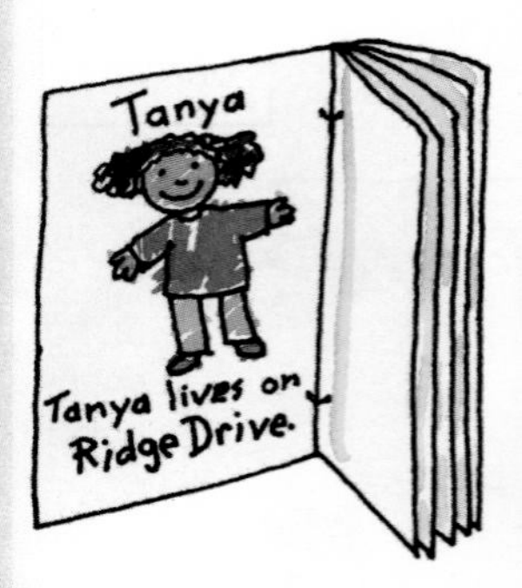

Buddy Books

Make a book with three sheets of paper. Write a friend's name on each page. Draw a picture of the friend. Then write a sentence under the picture that tells where your friend lives.

Challenge Use the telephone book to find your friends' telephone numbers. Add them to your buddy book.

118 Enrichment

Nouns (pages 93, 95)
Write the sentences. Draw a line under each noun. Tell if the noun names a person, an animal, a place, or a thing.

1. We swam in the lake. place
2. We slept in a tent. thing
3. My father cooked. person
4. Our dog went with us. animal

One and More Than One (page 97)
Write each sentence, using the noun that names more than one.

5. Three (boats, boat) went by.
6. I ate two (apple, apples).
7. We read some (book, books).

Nouns with es (page 101)
Write each noun to name more than one.

8. dish dishes
9. bus buses
10. fox foxes
11. lunch lunches

Nouns That Change Spelling (page 103)
Write each noun to name more than one.

12. child children
13. man men

Checkup

Objectives

Children will:
- identify nouns in sentences
- choose correct plural nouns in sentences
- write correct plural nouns

Using the Checkup

Use the Checkup exercises as assessment, as review for the unit test, as extra practice, or as a diagnostic aid to help determine those children who need reteaching.

INTERNET CONNECTION
Children can take an interactive quiz for this unit at www.eduplace.com /kids/hme/ and then get immediate feedback.

Objectives

Children will:

- capitalize special nouns in sentences
- use pronouns correctly in sentences
- use nouns and pronouns correctly in a sentence
- write nouns to show ownership

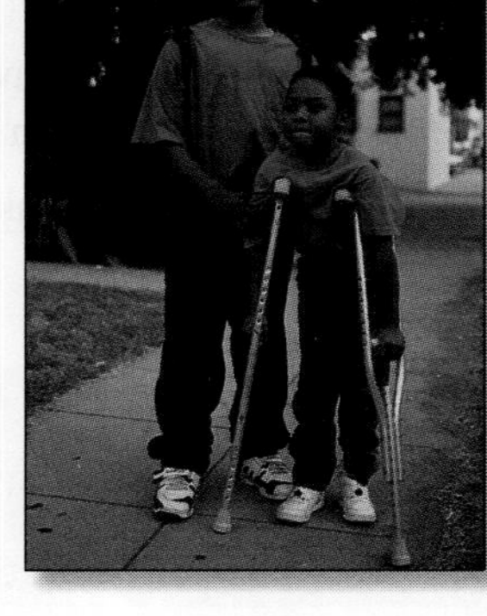

Special Nouns (page 105)

Write the sentences, using a capital letter for each special noun.

14. My brother is called rusty.
Rusty

15. Our house is on oak road.
Oak Road

Pronouns (page 107)

Write each sentence. Use one of the pronouns in ( ) to take the place of the underlined words.

16. Jenny and Paul hiked up the hill. (It, She, They)

17. The hill was very high. (He, It, They)

Naming Yourself Last (page 111)

Write the sentences correctly.

18. (Lee and I, I and Lee) ran in a race.

19. (Ed and me, Ed and I) read books.

Nouns Ending with 's and s' (pages 113, 115)

Write each word group. Make the first noun show ownership.

20. mom pan **mom's pan**

21. two boys kites **two boys' kites**

Mixed Review

22–28. Proofread this sports article. Find five mistakes with nouns, one mistake with pronouns, and one mistake with naming yourself last. Write the article correctly.

Proofreading Checklist

- ✔ Do the names of special people and places begin with capital letters?
- ✔ Do nouns that name more than one end with s or es?
- ✔ Are the correct pronouns used to take the place of nouns?
- ✔ Is an apostrophe and s added to a noun that names one to show ownership?
- ✔ When naming another person and yourself, is the word I used last?

Example Davids goal won the game.
David's goal won the game.

Proofreading

Our soccer team's first game was last week. We played a team from ~~oakville~~ Oakville. It was a close game. Our team won! David scored the winning goal. ~~It~~ He was very happy. ~~Me and Carmen~~ Carmen and I also scored goals. All the children played hard.

Our team has two new ~~coach~~ coaches and a new goalie named ~~sandra~~ Sandra. Our ~~teams~~ team's next game is on Saturday at the field on Main ~~street~~ Street. Come and watch us play.

See www.eduplace.com/kids/hme/ for an online quiz.

Objective

Children will:

- proofread an article and correct errors in nouns, pronouns, and word order

Test Practice

Objective

Children will:

- practice completing a test format that requires them to choose the correct item among three

Using the Test Practice

These Test Practice pages provide practice with common formats used in standardized or multiple-choice tests.

These pages work with skills taught in the basic lessons in Unit 3.

Notes on the Test Format

- Read the directions aloud to the class. Then have them look at Item 1.
- Have children read all three possible answers. Point out that two of the answers are spelled incorrectly. Tell children to find the two wrong answers before choosing the correct one. Explain that all the items require the correct spelling of a noun that names more than one.

FOR STUDENTS ACQUIRING ENGLISH

Review singular and plural nouns, including capital letters and spelling changes for plurals and irregulars. Then review possessives. Distribute the SAE Test Practice pages for Unit 3. Read the directions aloud for each section. Explain that in the first section children are to circle the noun that is correct. In the second they are to circle the pronoun that can replace the underlined words. Remind children to read all of the answers before choosing their responses.

Assessment Link

Test Practice

Number a sheet of paper from 1 to 8. Read each sentence. A noun is missing. Choose the correct noun to go in the blank. Write the letter for that answer.

1 I see three park ____.

- **A** benchs
- **B** bench
- Ⓒ benches

2 Four ____ fished.

- Ⓐ men
- **B** man
- **C** mans

3 Lynn read four ____.

- **A** book
- Ⓑ books
- **C** bookes

4 My uncle is ____.

- Ⓐ Ron
- **B** ron

5 The school is on ____.

- **A** oak street
- Ⓑ Oak Street
- **C** Oak street

6 ____ walked to school.

- Ⓐ Mark and I
- **B** Mark and me
- **C** I and Mark

7 I had fun at ____ birthday party.

- **A** my brothers
- **B** my brother
- Ⓒ my brother's

8 Two ____ kites are lost.

- **A** boys
- Ⓑ boys'
- **C** boy's

122 Test Practice

Test Practice continued

Now write the numbers 9 to 14 on your sheet of paper. Read each sentence. Choose the pronoun that you can use to take the place of the underlined words. Write the letter for that answer.

9 The girl jumped over the stream.

A It
(B) She
C They
D He

10 Kim and Alex read that book.

A She
B He
C It
(D) They

11 A red car zoomed by.

(A) It
B They
C She
D He

12 Mom and Dad went out for dinner.

A He
B She
C It
(D) They

13 Anna sent me a card.

A He
B It
(C) She
D They

14 The man cut the grass.

A It
B They
(C) He
D She

Objective

Children will:
- practice completing a test format that requires them to choose the correct item from among four

Notes on the Test Format

- Have a child read the directions aloud. Then ask another child to explain what the directions ask them to do. Direct their attention to Item 9. Point out that the naming part of the sentence is underlined.
- Then go over the possible answers. Be sure children understand that the correct answer has to have the same meaning as the underlined words.
- Have children read each of the answers before choosing the correct one. Point out that the order of pronoun answers is different in most of the items.

Nouns

Objective

Children will:
- identify and write nouns that name people

Using the Extra Practice

The Extra Practice activities provide two levels of additional practice for the basic lesson: Easy/Average (●▲), and Challenging (■).

The Extra Practice activities can be used in the following ways.

- Assign activities according to children's needs and abilities as homework after children have completed the basic lesson.
- Assign the Easy/Average activities after using the lesson Reteaching instruction.
- Assign the Challenging exercises as a Bonus activity.
- Assign the Easy/Average activities to prepare children for the Checkup.
- Assign the Easy/Average activities to children who had difficulty with specific lessons on the Checkup.

Extra Practice

(pages 93–94)

1 Nouns

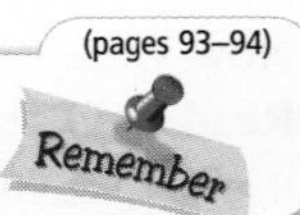

- A word that names a person is called a noun.

●▲ Write the sentences. Draw a line under each noun that names a person.

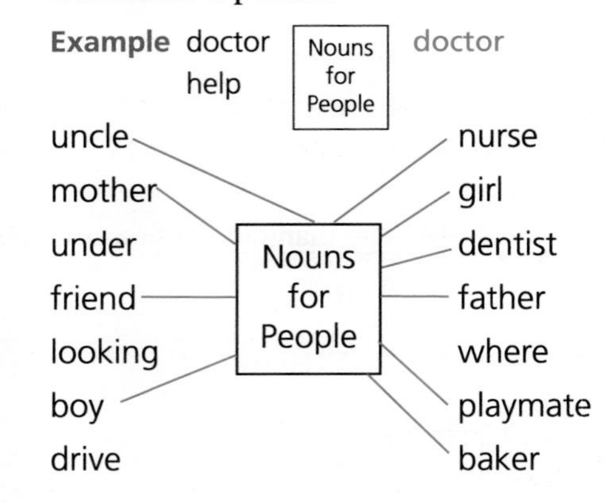

Example A dancer leaped.
A dancer leaped.

1. The teacher watched.
2. A man played music.
3. The baby clapped.

■ **4–13.** Copy the box. Around the box, write each noun that names a person.

Example doctor help | Nouns for People | doctor

uncle, mother, under, friend, looking, boy, drive

Nouns for People

nurse, girl, dentist, father, where, playmate, baker

Meeting Individual Needs — More Practice for Lesson 1

● **EASY** ▲ **AVERAGE**

Draw a line under each word that names a person. Write the word.

1. The man ran.
2. The boy played a game.
3. A girl skipped rope.
4. The pilot flew the plane.
5. Her baby cried.
6. His mother laughed.
7. The policewoman gave a ticket.
8. The firefighter helped us quickly.
9. A lady told me her name.
10. That woman lives near here.

■ **CHALLENGING**

Write a noun that names a person to finish each sentence. (Answers will vary.)

1. A ______ came to my house.
2. The ______ gave me a gift.
3. That ______ was singing.
4. This ______ told a story.
5. The ______ will buy a car.
6. That ______ is a friend of mine.
7. A ______ sat on the steps.
8. The ______ writes a letter.
9. A ______ helped everyone.
10. This ______ is a nice person.

Extra Practice

2 More Nouns

(pages 95–96)

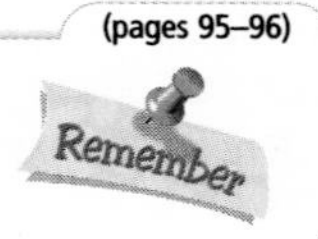

- A noun can name a person, an animal, a place, or a thing.

●▲ Write the sentences. Draw a line under each noun that names an animal, a place, or a thing.

Example We went to a farm.
We went to a farm.

1. We saw farmers and cows. cows
2. We walked by a huge field. field
3. The corn grew tall. corn

■ Write the noun in each row.

Example take glass sit glass

4.	go	like	pig
5.	town	eat	small
6.	send	football	over
7.	bed	keep	hear
8.	see	street	live
9.	three	ate	mom
10.	egg	brown	was

More Nouns

Objective

Children will:
- identify and write nouns that name a person, an animal, a place, or a thing

Meeting Individual Needs

More Practice for Lesson 2

● **EASY** ▲ **AVERAGE**

Write each noun that names an animal, a place, or a thing.

1. I saw a pig. pig
2. We grew pumpkins. pumpkins
3. The barn was red. barn
4. The horses ran fast. horses
5. The apples tasted good. apples
6. There was a big tractor. tractor
7. She gave us a pie. pie
8. We went into the house. house
9. The farm was nice. farm
10. I petted a woolly sheep. sheep

■ **CHALLENGING**

Draw a line under the noun in each row.

1.	were	going	house
2.	city	pink	played
3.	table	look	big
4.	little	bird	white
5.	ran	took	street
6.	and	is	snake
7.	sleep	book	funny
8.	gift	listen	sad
9.	come	sit	father
10.	baker	hot	sweet

One and More Than One

Objective

Children will:
- identify and write nouns that name more than one

Extra Practice

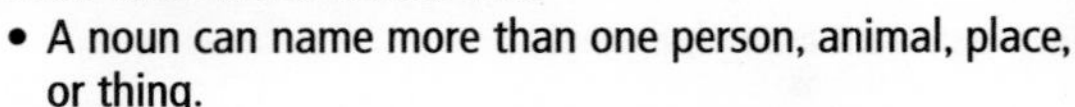

(pages 97–98)

3 One and More Than One

Remember

- A noun can name more than one person, animal, place, or thing.
- Add s to most nouns to name more than one.

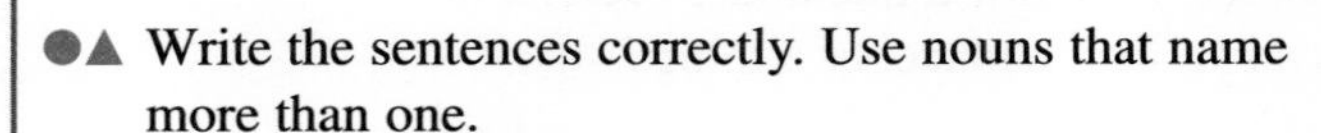

●▲ Write the sentences correctly. Use nouns that name more than one.

Example We have two (garden, gardens)
We have two gardens.

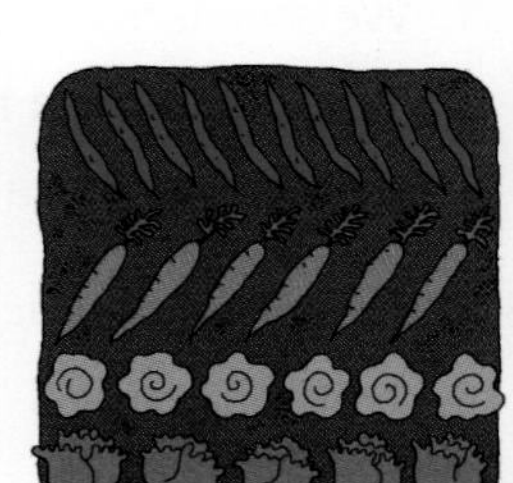

1. Many (plants, plant) grow there.
2. One garden has (bean, beans).
3. The other one has (flowers, flower).
4. Chris and Rob grow (tulip, tulips).
5. Lisa grows (carrots, carrot).
6. Does your garden have (weed, weeds)?

■ Write each noun to name more than one.

Example car cars

7. desk desks
8. clock clocks
9. lamp lamps
10. chair chairs
11. cat cats
12. pond ponds
13. boy boys
14. girl girls

126 Extra Practice

Meeting Individual Needs — More Practice for Lesson 3

● **EASY** ▲ **AVERAGE**

Draw a line under each noun in ( ) that names more than one.

1. We have two (horse, horses).
2. Our (cow, cows) are sleeping.
3. Three (pig, pigs) are playing.
4. My (cats, cat) see a mouse.
5. Are the (ponds, pond) cold?
6. The pond is full of (frogs, frog).
7. The (rivers, river) are near the pond.
8. How many (pear, pears) grow on that tree?
9. She has four pear (tree, trees).
10. Dad made us some (pies, pie).

■ **CHALLENGING**

Write each noun to name more than one.

1. snake snakes
2. table tables
3. pen pens
4. turtle turtles
5. home homes
6. road roads
7. skirt skirts
8. shoe shoes
9. orange oranges
10. balloon balloons

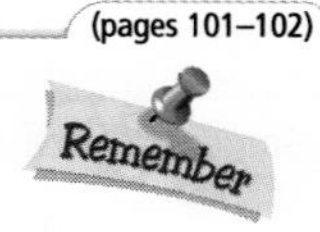

(pages 101–102)

4 Nouns with es

- Add es to nouns that end in x, ch, sh, or s to name more than one.

●▲ Write each sentence, using the noun that names more than one.

Example The (box, boxes) were stacked.
The boxes were stacked.

1. The workers ate their (lunch, lunches).
2. They painted two (benches, bench).
3. They painted three (porches, porch).
4. Then they cleaned all the (brush, brushes).

■ Write each noun to name more than one.

Example one bus two ____ buses

5. one fox two foxes
6. one dish five dishes
7. one patch three patches
8. one glass four glasses
9. one inch ten inches

Nouns with es

Objective

Children will:

- identify and write nouns that end in *x*, *ch*, *sh*, or *s* and name more than one

Meeting Individual Needs

More Practice for Lesson 4

● EASY ▲ AVERAGE

Draw a line under each noun in ( ) that names more than one.

1. The (watch, watches) were broken.
2. Those (peach, peaches) are sweet.
3. My arm has two (scratches, scratch).
4. The ball is in the (bush, bushes).
5. Her (guess, guesses) were correct.
6. Those (fox, foxes) are smart.
7. Do you have many (dresses, dress)?
8. Give me those (box, boxes).
9. The door has two (latches, latch).
10. The curtains have red (sashes, sash).

■ CHALLENGING

Write each noun to name more than one.

1. one box four ____ boxes
2. one hatch two ____ hatches
3. one peach five ____ peaches
4. one bush six ____ bushes
5. one dress ten ____ dresses
6. one guess nine ____ guesses
7. one wish three ____ wishes
8. one scratch two ____ scratches
9. one fox seven ____ foxes
10. one crash four ____ crashes

Nouns That Change Spelling

Objective

Children will:
- identify and write nouns that change spelling

Extra Practice

(pages 103–104)

5 Nouns That Change Spelling
- Some nouns change their spelling to name more than one.

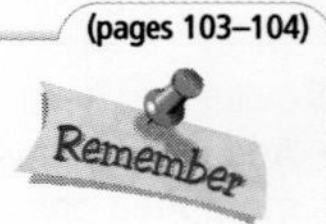

●▲ Write each sentence, using the correct noun.

Example All of the (child, children) watched the game.
All of the children watched the game.

1. Today two (man, men) played tennis.
2. One (man, men) kept score.
3. Four (woman, women) played later.
4. Some (child, children) will play tomorrow.

■ Write each sentence, using the correct noun from the Word Box.

Example man / men Two of my teachers are ____.
Two of my teachers are men.

man / men
5. My art teacher is a man.

child / children
6. Many children like art class.

woman / women
7. Men and women are artists.

128 Extra Practice

Meeting Individual Needs — More Practice for Lesson 5

● **EASY** ▲ **AVERAGE**

Draw a line under the noun in ( ) that belongs in each sentence.

1. Many (child, children) go to school.
2. One (woman, women) drives that car.
3. Six (man, men) play soccer.
4. That (children, child) is my friend.
5. Who is that (men, man)?
6. Tell those (women, woman) to come here.
7. Twelve (children, child) are in my class.
8. How many (men, man) live here?
9. A (child, children) can go first.
10. Do you know that (women, woman)?

■ **CHALLENGING**

Choose one of these words to finish each sentence: man, men, woman, women, child, children (Answers will vary; accept all that agree in number)

1. That ____ is my friend.
2. A ____ eats lunch here.
3. This ____ lives next door.
4. Two ____ are in the car.
5. My dog likes that ____.
6. Those ____ are nice.
7. Five ____ play ball.
8. Where did that ____ go?
9. Ask those ____ a question.
10. One ____ gave me a gift.

Extra Practice

(pages 105–106)

6 Special Nouns

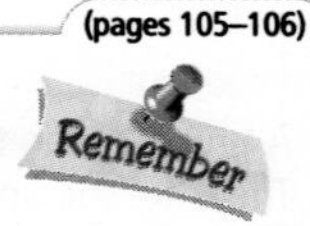

- Begin the names of special people, animals, places, and things with capital letters.

●▲ Write each sentence, using a capital letter to begin each special noun.

Example We moved to elm lane.
We moved to Elm Lane.

1. We live in wilton. Wilton
2. My new friend is ben. Ben
3. His pony is named blaze. Blaze

■ Write the sentences correctly.

Example My pen pal is john.
My pen pal is John.

4. He lives in dallas. He lives in Dallas.
5. His house is on park road. His house is on Park Road.
6. His fish is named goldie. His fish is named Goldie.

Special Nouns

Objective

Children will:

- identify and write nouns that name special people, animals, places and things

Meeting Individual Needs

More Practice for Lesson 6

● EASY ▲ AVERAGE

Draw a line under each special noun. Then write each one correctly.

1. I live on carlton street.
2. My name is betty brown.
3. I have a dog named ralph.
4. I have a brother named mick.
5. He lives with his wife sandy.
6. They live in topeka.
7. They have a son named brett.
8. He has a pet pig named franklin.
9. They found the pig on powder lane.
10. They also have an alligator named denise.

■ CHALLENGING

Write these sentences correctly.

1. My friend is todd martle.
   My friend is Todd Martle.
2. He lives in iowa. He lives in Iowa.
3. His house is on red road.
   His house is on Red Road.
4. He has a dog named bop.
   He has a dog named Bop.
5. I have a sister named lou.
   I have a sister named Lou.
6. She visits her friend on star street.
   She visits her friend on Star Street.
7. They play with their friend dan.
   They play with their friend Dan.
8. He lives on frog avenue.
   He lives on Frog Avenue.
9. I want to go to texas.
   I want to go to Texas.
10. My cousin gina lives there.
    My cousin Gina lives there.

Pronouns

Objective

Children will:
- identify and write pronouns

Extra Practice

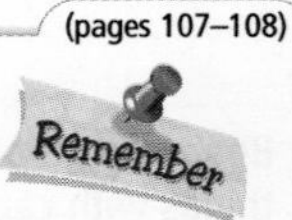

(pages 107–108)

7 Pronouns
- A pronoun can take the place of a noun.
- They, he, she and it are pronouns.

Remember

●▲ Chose the correct pronoun to take the place of the underlined word or words. Write each sentence.

Example Stan drove his car.
He They It
He drove his car.

1. Mary went with him.
   She He It
2. The car had a flat tire.
   He She It
3. Stan and Mary fixed it.
   It They He

■ Write each sentence, using a pronoun from the Word Box to take the place of the underlined word or words.

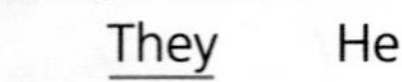

He	She	It	They

Example Raul and Maria visited me.
They visited me.

4. Maria enjoyed the visit. She enjoyed the visit.
5. Raul wrote a thank-you note. He wrote a thank-you note.

Meeting Individual Needs — More Practice for Lesson 7

● **EASY** ▲ **AVERAGE**

Draw a line under each pronoun that can take the place of the underlined word or words.

1. Fred went to the store. She He It
2. The store was big. She He It
3. Pat and Peter drove the car. She They He
4. The road was bumpy. He She It
5. A dog was hurt. It They He
6. Paula helped her. He She They
7. Kate and Tom saw it. They He It
8. John told them. He She It
9. The sky was dark. It They She
10. Rain fell down. They She It

■ **CHALLENGING**

Write each sentence, choosing one of these pronouns to replace the underlined words in each sentence: He, She, It, They

1. José and Marta are friends.
   They are friends.
2. Tony goes to my school.
   He goes to my school.
3. Our school is big. It is big.
4. The teacher holds her pen.
   She holds her pen.
5. Sue reads the book.
   She reads the book.
6. Jill and Joan go to lunch.
   They go to lunch.
7. Rob plays the flute. He plays the flute.
8. That drum is loud. It is loud.
9. The drum and the flute sound pretty.
   They sound pretty.
10. The sun is shining. It is shining.

Extra Practice

(pages 111–112)

8 Naming Yourself Last

- When you write or talk about another person and yourself, name yourself last.
- Use the word I in the naming part of the sentence.

●▲ Choose the words in ( ) that are correct. Then write each sentence.

Example (I and Alice, Alice and I) fish.
Alice and I fish.

1. (Kate and I, I and Kate) skate.
2. (Me and Nora, Nora and I) play ball.
3. (Pablo and I, Pablo and me) collect stamps.
4. (I and Randy, Randy and I) go swimming.
5. (Carmen and I, I and Carmen) ride bikes.

■ **6–8.** Find three sentences that are not correct. Write them correctly.

Example I and Doug go shopping.
Doug and I go shopping.

I and my sister like horses. **My sister and I like horses.**
Sarah and I play the piano.
Ben and me are friends. **Ben and I are friends.**
Me and Paulo have pet birds. **Paulo and I have pet birds.**

Naming Yourself Last

Objectives

Children will:

- identify and write the correct way to name themselves in sentences when talking about another person and themselves
- correctly use the word I in the naming part of sentences

Meeting Individual Needs

More Practice for Lesson 8

● **EASY** ▲ **AVERAGE**

Draw a line under the words in ( ) that are correct in the sentence.

1. (Mark and me, Mark and I) go swimming.
2. (I and Ted, Ted and I) play cards.
3. (Carla and I, I and Carla) ride the bus.
4. (Jorge and me, Jorge and I) eat dinner.
5. (Polly and me, Polly and I) watch birds.
6. (Ruby and I, I and Ruby) draw pictures.
7. (Carol and I, me and Carol) sing songs.
8. (I and Ellen, Ellen and I) have money.
9. (I and Andy, Andy and I) write poems.
10. (Me and June, June and I) see clouds.

■ **CHALLENGING**

Write the sentences correctly.

1. Sara and me are pals.
   Sara and I are pals.
2. I and Tino play music.
   Tino and I play music.
3. Me and Dirk eat apples.
   Dirk and I eat apples.
4. Dom and me write stories.
   Dom and I write stories.
5. I and Harry go to the zoo.
   Harry and I go to the zoo.
6. I and Mia have fun.
   Mia and I have fun.
7. Pat and me do the dishes.
   Pat and I do the dishes.
8. I and you like to run.
   You and I like to run.
9. Me and Juan found the cat.
   Juan and I found the cat.
10. Trish and me slept over.
    Trish and I slept over.

Nouns Ending with 's

Objective

Children will:

- correctly add apostrophes and the letter *s* to nouns to show ownership

Extra Practice

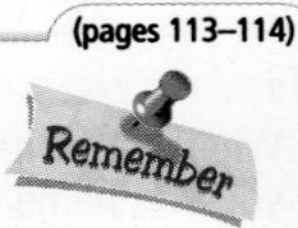

(pages 113–114)

9 Nouns Ending with 's

- When a noun names one person or animal, add an apostrophe (') and s to that noun to show ownership.

●▲ Change each underlined noun to show ownership. Then write each group of words correctly.

Example Jack sister Jack's sister

1. horse saddle horse's
2. girl boots girl's
3. boy food boy's
4. Carla brush Carla's

■ Change the noun in ( ) to show ownership. Write each sentence correctly.

Example A (cat) paw is hurt. A cat's paw is hurt.

5. (Emma) uncle is a vet. Emma's uncle is a vet.
6. Her (uncle) office is busy. Her uncle's office is busy.
7. A (boy) dog had puppies. A boy's dog had puppies.

132 Extra Practice

Meeting Individual Needs — More Practice for Lesson 9

● EASY ▲ AVERAGE

Write each underlined noun correctly to show ownership.

1. girl book girl's
2. Tom house Tom's
3. dog bowl dog's
4. Lee sister Lee's
5. Rob job Rob's
6. man car man's
7. woman skirt woman's
8. Cindy hammer Cindy's
9. boy game boy's
10. cat toy cat's

■ CHALLENGING

Change the noun in the ( ) to show ownership. Write each sentence correctly.

1. (Ned) cat is lost. Ned's cat is lost.
2. Jim found the (cat) collar. Jim found the cat's collar.
3. The cat went to the (dog) house. The cat went to the dog's house.
4. (Bill) dog likes cats. Bill's dog likes cats.
5. The dog licked the (cat) paw. The dog licked the cat's paw.
6. The (dog) tail wagged. The dog's tail wagged.
7. (Jim) dog does not like cats. Jim's dog does not like cats.
8. (Marie) cat does not like dogs. Marie's cat does not like dogs.
9. I threw the (dog) ball. I threw the dog's ball.
10. It landed in the (cat) bed. It landed in the cat's bed.

Extra Practice

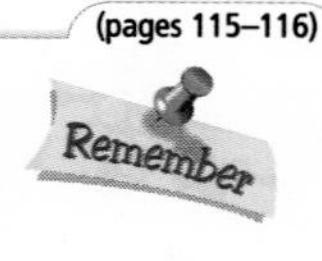

10 Nouns Ending with s'

(pages 115–116)

- When a noun ends in s and names more than one person or animal, add just an apostrophe (') to that noun to show ownership.

●▲ Write the group of words that has a noun that names more than one and that shows ownership.

Example fathers books fathers' books
fathers' books

1. cousins' football
   cousins football
2. monkey tails
   monkeys' tails
3. friends' party
   friends party
4. foxes dens
   foxes' dens

■ Each noun in ( ) names more than one. Change this noun to show ownership. Write each sentence correctly.

Example I found the (twins) ball. I found the twins' ball.

5. Have you seen my (parents) keys? Have you seen my parents' keys?
6. We searched my (sisters) room. We searched my sisters' room.
7. Did they fall in the (dogs) bowl? Did they fall in the dogs' bowl?

Unit 3: Nouns and Pronouns 133

Nouns Ending with s'

Objective

Children will:

- correctly add apostrophes to nouns that name more than one person or animal to show ownership

Meeting Individual Needs — More Practice for Lesson 10

● EASY ▲ AVERAGE

Draw a line under each group of words that has a noun naming more than one and shows ownership.

1. boys' room — boy's room
2. cows milk — cows' milk
3. girls' crayons — girls crayons
4. parrot's cage — parrots' cage
5. lions' manes — lions manes
6. rabbit's hole — rabbits' hole
7. aunt's house — aunts' house
8. grandmothers chairs — grandmothers' chairs
9. horses' saddles — horse's saddles
10. bear's honey — bears' honey

■ CHALLENGING

Each noun in ( ) names more than one. Write each sentence correctly to show ownership.

1. Who took my (sisters) books?
   Who took my sisters' books?
2. They are not in my (brothers) rooms.
   They are not in my brothers' rooms.
3. Where are my (cousins) toys?
   Where are my cousins' toys?
4. I found them in my (uncles) house.
   I found them in my uncles' house.
5. Have you seen my (friends) lunches?
   Have you seen my friends' lunches?
6. They lost them on my (parents) street.
   They lost them on my parents' street.
7. I found them by the (dogs) house.
   I found them by the dogs' house.
8. I found the (cats) toys there, too.
   I found the cats' toys there, too.
9. The dogs stole the (kids) lunches.
   The dogs found the kids' lunches.
10. I took away the (dogs) stolen food.
    I took away the dogs' stolen food.

Unit 4 Planning Guide

Writing a Story

Writing a Story: ***2 weeks***
Special Focus and Communication Link: ***1 week (optional)***

	Blackline Masters (TE)	Workbook Plus	Reteaching Workbook
A Published Model "The Wolf's Chicken Stew," by Keiko Kasza *(135–137)*			
What Makes a Great Story? *(139)*			
Student Model Working Draft *(140–141)* Final Copy *(142–143)*	4–1A, 4–1B		
The Writing Process Write a Story			
Prewriting Choosing a Problem *(145)* Focus Skill: Developing Characters *(146)* Focus Skill: Mapping Your Story *(147)*	 4–2 4–3	50 51 52	31 32 33
Drafting Focus Skill: Beginning Your Story *(148)*		53	34
Revising ✓ How Good Is Your Story? [rubric] *(149)* Writing Conference *(150)* **Revising Strategies** *(152)*	4–4 4–5 	54 55	35 36
Proofreading *(153)*			
Publishing and Reflecting *(154)*			
✓ **Writing Prompts and Test Practice** *(156–157)*			
SPECIAL FOCUS ON EXPRESSING **Writing a Book Report** *(158–159)*			
COMMUNICATION LINK **Viewing/Media: Different Forms of Stories** *(160–161)*			

Tools and Tips

- **Using the Dictionary,** *pp. H3–H12*
- **Using Technology,** *pp. H21–H30*
- **Writer's Tools,** *pp. H31–H34*
- **Spelling Guide,** *pp. H40–H44*
- **My First Thesaurus,** *pp. H45–H56*

School-Home Connection

Suggestions for informing or involving family members in classroom activities and learning related to this unit are included in the Teacher's Edition throughout the unit.

Meeting Individual Needs

- **FOR SPECIAL NEEDS/INCLUSION:** *Houghton Mifflin English* Audiotape
- **FOR STUDENTS ACQUIRING ENGLISH:**
  - Notes and activities are included in this Teacher's Edition throughout the unit to help you adapt or use pupil book activities with students acquiring English.
  - Students aquiring English can listen to the published and student models on audiotape.
- **ENRICHMENT:** See *Teacher's Resource Book.*

All audiotape recordings are also available on CD.

Daily Language Practice

Each sentence or group of words includes two capitalization, punctuation, usage, or spelling errors based on skills presented in the Grammar and Spelling Connections in this unit or from Grammar Units 1 and 3. Each day write one item on the chalkboard. Have children find the errors and write the sentence correctly on a sheet of paper. To make the activity easier, identify the kinds of errors.

1. My Sister takes mee to swimming lessons. Sample: My sister takes me to swimming lessons. (capitalizing proper nouns; spelling/long *e*)
2. the boys say they are starting a hobby club? The boys say they are starting a hobby club. (capitalization; end punctuation/statements)
3. I and Les see a dogs' tracks in the snow. Les and I see a dog's tracks in the snow. (naming yourself last; possessive nouns ending with *'s*)
4. Every morning nell sings while it makes breakfast. Every morning Nell sings while she makes breakfast. (capitalizing proper nouns; pronouns)
5. The two woman in the picture. Are dancing. Sample: The two women in the picture are dancing. (irregular plural nouns; complete sentences)
6. Who lives in the new house on King Streat! Who lives in the new house on King Street? (spelling/long *e*; end punctuation/questions)
7. Those two bike are going to crash. Those two bikes are going to crash! (plural nouns with s; end punctuation/exclamations)
8. Put two stamps on Marys' letter? Put two stamps on Mary's letter. (possessive nouns ending with *'s*; end punctuation/commands)
9. the book is not. In my book bag. Sample: The book is not in my book bag. (capitalization; complete sentences)
10. The three man in the boat. Sample: The three men in the boat are fishing. (irregular/plural nouns; complete sentences)

Additional Resources

Workbook Plus, Unit 4
Reteaching Workbook, Unit 4
Teacher's Resource Book
Transparencies, Unit 4
Posters, Unit 4
Audiotapes

Technology Tools

TEACHER'S RESOURCE DISK (for handwriting support)

CD-ROM: *Sunbuddy® Writer
Paint, Write & Play! (published by The Learning Company)
*Type to Learn Jr.™

INTERNET: http://www.eduplace.com/kids/hme/ or http://www.eduplace.com/rdg/hme/

Visit Education Place for these additional support materials and activities:

- author biographies
- student writing models
- graphic organizers
- an interactive rubric
- writing prompts

Assessment

Test Booklet, Unit 4

Keeping a Journal

Discuss with children the value of keeping a journal as a way of promoting self-expression and fluency. Encourage children to record their thoughts and ideas in a notebook. Inform students whether the journal will be private or will be reviewed periodically as a way of assisting growth. The following prompts may be useful for generating writing ideas.

Journal Prompts

- Do you know a story or a poem about the moon? Tell about it.
- Have you ever heard the whistle of a train? What does the sound make you think of?
- What is a funny riddle that you have heard?

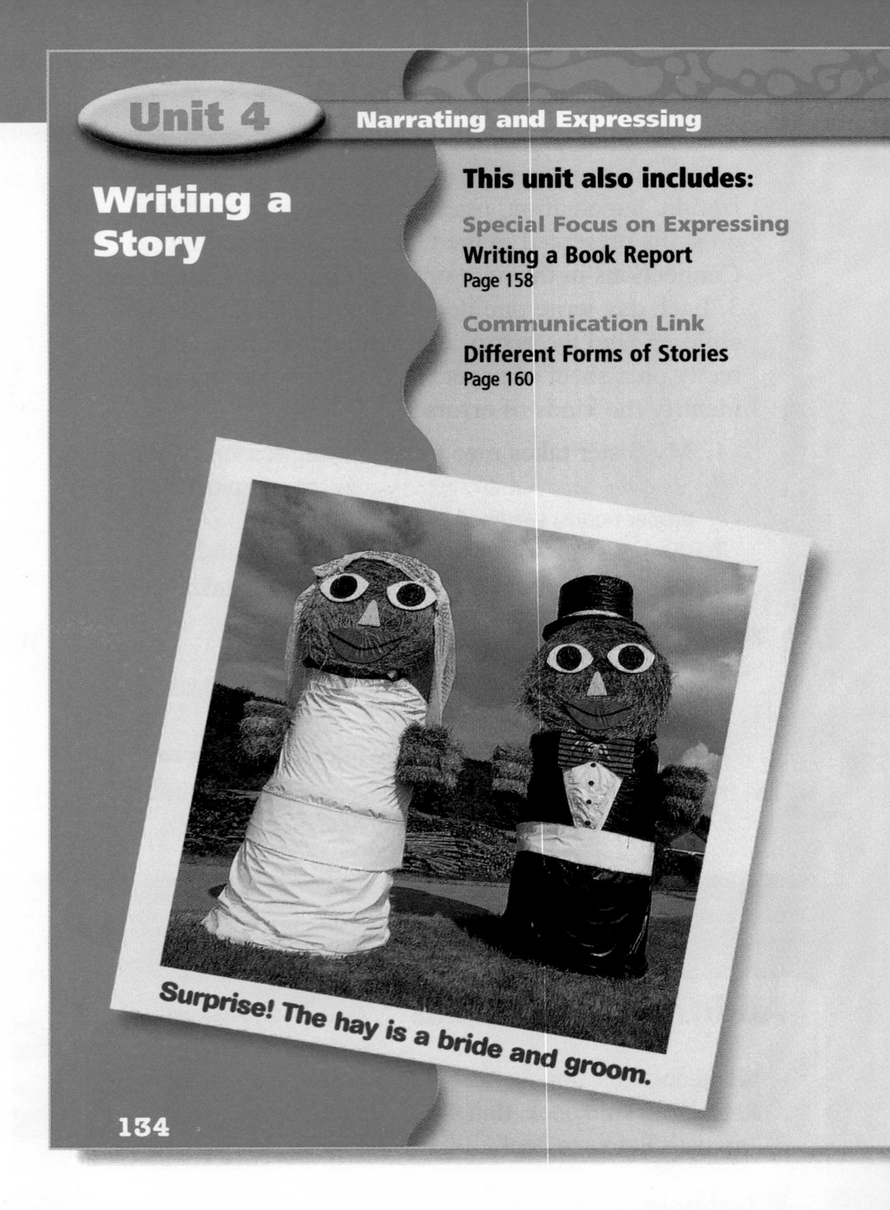

Unit 4 Narrating and Expressing

Writing a Story

This unit also includes:

Special Focus on Expressing
Writing a Book Report
Page 158

Communication Link
Different Forms of Stories
Page 160

Surprise! The hay is a bride and groom.

134

Introducing the Unit

Using the Photograph

- Have children look at the photograph, and ask a volunteer to read the caption aloud. What are the bride and groom made out of? (Their heads and bodies are round bales of hay. Their arms are square bales of hay.) If necessary, explain that hay is made from dried grasses and is usually used as animal food.
- If this photograph were an illustration for a story, would it be a story about real people or would it be a make-believe story? (Answers will vary.)
- Point out to children that writers often write a **story** about things that have happened to them. Sometimes a story is made up but it could really happen. Other times writers write a story that is a completely make-believe story. Tell children that they will develop a story based on the photograph.
- Ask volunteers to tell the names of their favorite books. Have them tell where the story took place, who was in the story, and what happened. Explain that this information identifies the setting, characters, and plot of the story.

Independent Writing

Children can benefit by having time each day or several times a week to write in their journals or do self-selected writing activities. Remind children to think about purpose and audience and choose an appropriate format for both.

Shared Writing Activity

Work with children to develop a story suggested by the photograph.

1. Have children identify the characters in the picture. (bride and groom) Tell children to decide on names for these characters. Write the names on the board.
2. Ask volunteers for ideas as to where the story might take place. Note these ideas on the board and then as a class choose one to be the story setting.
3. Have volunteers tell what might happen to the characters. What problem might they have to solve? Write the suggestions on the board. As a class, choose the story events that work best.
4. Together, develop these ideas into story sentences. Use the information about setting and character to develop detail sentences for the story. Read the the completed sentences aloud and work as a class to order them correctly as you write them on the board.
5. Then read the story together as a class.

A Published Model

Listening to a Story

The Wolf's Chicken Stew is a story about a character with a problem. Who is the character? What is the problem?

The Wolf's Chicken Stew

by Keiko Kasza

beginning

There once lived a wolf who loved to eat more than anything else in the world. As soon as he finished one meal, he began to think of the next.

wolf's problem

One day the wolf got a terrible craving for chicken stew.

All day long he walked across the forest in search of a delicious chicken. Finally he spotted one.

"Ah, she is just perfect for my stew," he thought.

The wolf crept closer. But just as he was about to grab his prey . . . he had another idea.

"If there were just some way to fatten this bird a little more," he thought, "there would be all the more stew for me."

So . . . the wolf ran home to his kitchen and he began to cook.

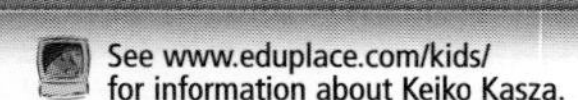

See www.eduplace.com/kids/ for information about Keiko Kasza.

About the Author

INTERNET CONNECTION Send children to www.eduplace.com/kids/ for information about Keiko Kasza.

Bibliography

Here are other books that model this type of writing that children may enjoy reading.

- ***Three Stories You Can Read to Your Dog*** by Sara Swan Miller
- ***Frog and Toad Are Friends*** by Arnold Lobel
- ***Once in a Wood: Ten Tales from Aesop*** by Eve Rice
- ***Moose Tales*** by Nancy Van Laan

"The Wolf's Chicken Stew"

Lesson Objectives

Children will:

- read a published model of a story
- identify characteristics of a story
- use repetition to emphasize plot development
- use illustrations to evaluate character's feelings
- write personal and critical responses

Focus on the Model

Building Background

Ask children if they like to read stories and why. Ask if they remember how a problem in a favorite story was solved. How did the characters use their courage, strength, or wits to solve the problem? Tell children they will be reading a story about a clever solution to a problem.

Introducing Vocabulary

Introduce key vocabulary words by writing these sentences on the board. Have a volunteer read each sentence aloud. Ask children to explain the meaning of the bold face words.

Most pizza is delicious. Pizza with pineapple is **scrumptious**.

The hawk swooped down to the field for his dinner. His **prey** was a green snake.

Reading the Selection

- Discuss with children the general purpose for listening to or reading stories. Explain that we read stories to find our how characters solve an interesting problem.
- Read aloud the introduction to "The Wolf's Chicken Stew." Tell children that the purpose-setting question focuses on a characteristic of stories. Direct children to read to learn how the character solves a problem.
- Read aloud or have volunteers read aloud the selection if you wish to reinforce listening skills or if children need extra support.

Alternatively, children can listen to the selection on audiotape.

- The call outs highlight key characteristics of a story that are addressed in the Thinking About the Story questions at the end of this selection.

FOR STUDENTS ACQUIRING ENGLISH

Using the pictures, have children work in pairs to tell each other the story. Share group versions as a class, then read the story. As a read-aloud, ask volunteers to read the characters' lines.

A Published Model

middle

First he made a hundred scrumptious pancakes. Then, late at night, he left them on the chicken's porch.

"Eat well, my pretty chicken," he cried. "Get nice and fat for my stew!"

The next night he brought a hundred scrumptious doughnuts.

"Eat well, my pretty chicken," he cried. "Get nice and fat for my stew!"

And on the next night he brought a scrumptious cake weighing a hundred pounds.

"Eat well, my pretty chicken," he cried. "Get nice and fat for my stew!"

At last, all was ready. This was the night he had been waiting for. He put a large stew pot on the fire and set out joyfully to find his dinner.

"That chicken must be as fat as a balloon by now," he thought. "Let's see."

But as he peeked into the chicken's house . . . the door opened suddenly and the chicken screeched, "Oh, so it was you, Mr. Wolf!"

end

136 A Published Model

"Children, children! Look, the pancakes and the doughnuts and that scrumptious cake . . . All those presents were from Uncle Wolf!"

The baby chicks jumped all over the wolf and gave him a hundred kisses.

"Oh, thank you, Uncle Wolf! You're the best cook in the world!"

Mrs. Chicken helped solve the problem.

Uncle Wolf didn't have chicken stew that night but Mrs. Chicken fixed him a nice dinner anyway.

"Aw, shucks," he thought, as he walked home, "maybe tomorrow I'll bake the little critters a hundred scrumptious cookies!"

end

Focus on Instruction

Ask volunteers to retell the selection. Write their responses on the board or on an overhead transparency and help them develop a summary of the selection.

Answers to Reading As a Writer

The Think About the Story questions highlight criteria listed on the "What Makes a Great Story?" and "How Good Is Your Story?" pages in the pupil book.

Think About the Story

- The wolf had a problem. He had a craving for chicken stew.
- Mrs. Chicken made Mr. Wolf a nice dinner.
- **Beginning**: The wolf had a craving for chicken stew and decided to fatten up the chicken. **Middle**: The wolf baked and delivered sweets to Mrs. Chicken to fatten her up. **End**: Mrs. Chicken surprised the wolf by showing him all of the children that she had been feeding with his sweets. Then Mrs. Chicken made dinner for the wolf.

Think About Writer's Craft

- He places quotation marks around the character's exact words. ("Eat well my pretty chicken," he cried. "Get nice and fat for my stew!" Sample answer: Repeating the sentence helps the reader feel the excitement building in the story.)

Think About the Picture

- He looks very surprised.

More About Writer's Craft

- Other Writer's Craft techniques or grammar elements that you can point out in "The Wolf's Chicken Stew" include the use of declarative sentences and the use of quotation marks that set off a character's exact words.

Notes on Responding

Personal Response

Ask children to participate in discussing what they found most interesting or exciting in the story. Ask if they know real people who have solved problems with cleverness or kindness.

Critical Thinking

Ask children if they think the wolf still wanted chicken stew at the end of the story. Why or why not? (Sample answer: No, the wolf liked all of the chickens and wanted to bake cookies for the little ones.)

A Published Model

Reading As a Writer

See TE margin for answers.

Think About the Story

- Which character had a problem? What was the problem?
- How did Mrs. Chicken help the character solve the problem?
- What happened at the beginning, in the middle, and at the end of the story?

Think About Writer's Craft

- How does the writer show you the exact words the characters say?
- What does Mr. Wolf say three times? Why?

Think About the Picture

- How does the picture on page 137 help you know how Mr. Wolf is feeling as Mrs. Chicken opens the door?

Responding

See TE margin for answers.

Write an answer to this question.

- **Personal Response** What part of the story did you find most interesting or exciting? Why?

138 A Published Model

Mapping the Selection

MAPPING THE STORY

Mapping is an excellent way for children to see the structure of a piece of writing. When children have finished reading the story, draw the following map on the board. Have them complete the map by answering the questions.

The Wolf's Chicken Stew
Beginning: What problem does Wolf have?
Middle: How does he try to solve it?
End: How does Chicken help him solve it?

What Makes a Great Story?

A **story** is a tale with a beginning, a middle, and an end. Stories are make-believe, but they may seem real. When you write a story, remember to do these things.

- ▶ Write an interesting beginning sentence.
- ▶ Make sure that your story has a beginning, middle, and end, and that the events are in order.
- ▶ Include interesting details about the setting, characters, and their problem.
- ▶ Finish your story by telling how the problem is solved and how the story ends.

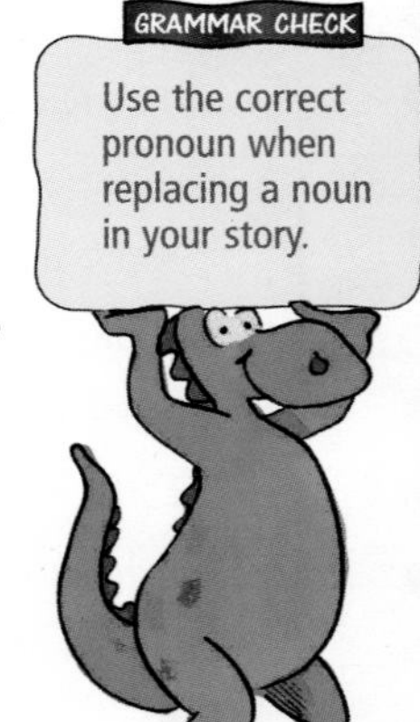

What Makes a Great Story?

Lesson Objective

Children will:

- discuss the characteristics of a well-written story

Focus on Instruction

- Tell children that "The Wolf's Chicken Stew" was an excellent example of a well-written story. Have children read aloud the definition and characteristics of a story. Ask them to name the ones that they found in the published model, "The Wolf's Chicken Stew." (enjoyable characters and setting; interesting problem; clear beginning, middle, and end; order makes sense; story has interesting beginning and ends by telling the solution and how the story ends)
- Have children read the Grammar Check. Tell them that the Grammar Check reminds them to use the correct pronoun when replacing a noun in their stories. Explain that they will be asked to check their papers for correct pronouns when they proofread them.

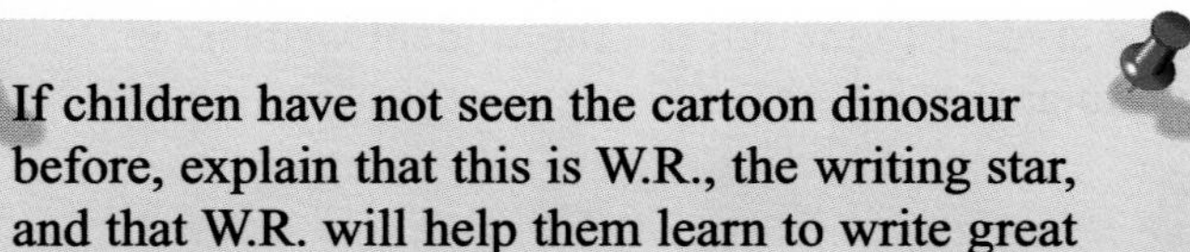
If children have not seen the cartoon dinosaur before, explain that this is W.R., the writing star, and that W.R. will help them learn to write great stories.

Connecting to the Rubric

- These criteria are tied to the rubric on page 149.
- Explain to children that they will be writing their own stories and that they will learn how to include these characteristics. After they write their stories, they will use these characteristics to help them evaluate their papers.

 This page is available as a poster.

Looking Ahead Tell children that they will next see how the characteristics listed on this page are applied in one student's working draft and final copy of a story.

FOR STUDENTS ACQUIRING ENGLISH

Before looking at the text, ask children to tell you what a story is. Write their ideas on the board, then have them compare these ideas to the text. As you read aloud the rubric, define these words: *characters*, *setting*, *problem*, *beginning*, *middle*, and *end*. Ask children to offer definitions, then decide on the best ones together.

A Student Model: Working Draft

Lesson Objectives

Children will:
- read a working draft of a student-written story
- discuss the ways the model meets the criteria for a well-written story and ways that it could be improved

Focus on the Model

- Tell children that they will read a working draft of a story written by a real student, Kelly O'Masta. Remind children that this working draft is a work in progress that will be revised later. At this point the writer is simply trying to get ideas on paper.
- Have children read the model aloud. Tell children to think about whether Kelly included the important elements of a story. Explain that the speech balloons show W.R.'s thoughts about the story and that children will discuss his ideas after they read.

 Alternatively, children can listen to the draft read by a student (although not the student writer) on audiotape.

- Reading the draft aloud gives children practice listening and responding to a writer's work in progress and provides practice for peer conferences.
- This working draft does not include any usage, capitalization, or punctuation mistakes so that children can focus on the content.

Student Model

WORKING DRAFT

Read Kelly's make-believe story and what W.R. said about it.

Kelly O'Masta

This is a good beginning!

Super Soccer Star

It had been a long, tough season for the Cavalier soccer team. The coach kept reminding the kids to watch the ball and the other team members at all times. He wanted the players to spread out and pass the ball. The players didn't listen to him. They weren't even paying attention to the game. ~~Instead, many of them played with the team mascot.~~

Can you tell more about the characters?

Kelly and Elizabeth were good players. Keegan was a good player too, but he did not like being the goalie.

Before the last game, the coach got the Cavaliers in a huddle on the soccer field. He told them to play like a team and they would do fine. The team they were playing was big and fast. They quickly scored a goal.

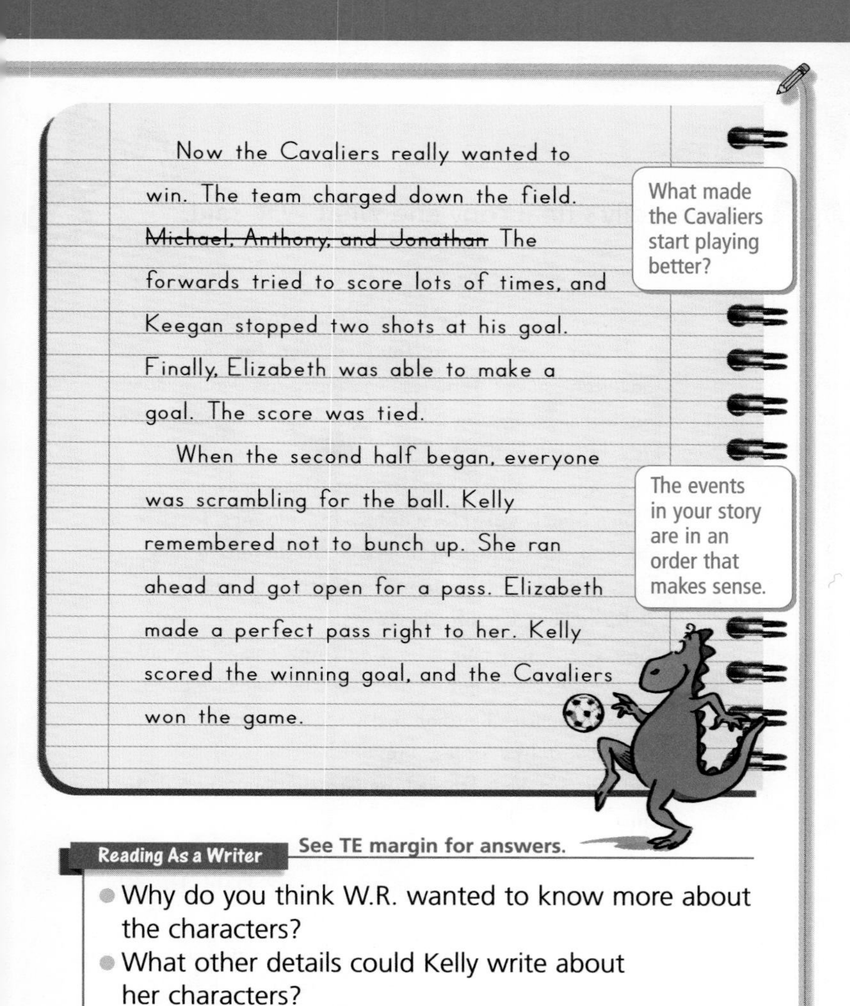

Now the Cavaliers really wanted to win. The team charged down the field. ~~Michael, Anthony, and Jonathan~~ The forwards tried to score lots of times, and Keegan stopped two shots at his goal. Finally, Elizabeth was able to make a goal. The score was tied.

When the second half began, everyone was scrambling for the ball. Kelly remembered not to bunch up. She ran ahead and got open for a pass. Elizabeth made a perfect pass right to her. Kelly scored the winning goal, and the Cavaliers won the game.

Reading As a Writer See TE margin for answers.

- Why do you think W.R. wanted to know more about the characters?
- What other details could Kelly write about her characters?
- Where does Kelly's story take place?

Answers to Reading As a Writer

- Sample answer: Kelly didn't tell much about what her characters were like or what they did.
- She could add more details telling what they look like, what they do, what they say, or how they feel.
- The setting is a soccer field.

A Student Model: Final Copy

Lesson Objectives

Children will:
- read a well-written final copy of a student's story
- note and compare the revisions that improved the first draft

Focus on the Model

SUMMARY OF REVISIONS In her final copy, Kelly added supporting details to give more information about the problem; added details to make the characters more interesting; added information to expand the middle of the story; added an ending that summarized the story. Blackline Master 4-1 provides a copy of the student's working draft, showing the revisions that were made.

Have volunteers read the model aloud. Alternatively, children can listen to it read by a student (although not the student writer) on audiotape.

Student Model

FINAL COPY

Read Kelly's final copy and what W.R. said.

Playing Like a Team
by Kelly O'Masta

It had been a long, tough season for the Cavalier soccer team. They had played nine games but hadn't won any. The coach kept reminding the kids to watch the ball and the other team members at all times. His favorite words were, "Don't bunch up!" He wanted the players to spread out and pass the ball. They didn't listen to him. They weren't even paying attention to the game.

Knowing more about the characters helps me understand the story better.

Kelly and Elizabeth were good players, but they spent too much time talking. They laughed loudly, did cartwheels, danced, and chased each other around. Keegan was a good player too, but he did not like being the goalie. He was tall enough, but he often played with the net and did chin-ups on the bar.

Before the last game, the coach got the Cavaliers in a huddle on the soccer field. He told them to play like a team and they would do fine. The team they were playing was big and fast. They quickly scored a goal. It seemed that things couldn't get worse, but they did.

Just before halftime, the coach tripped and fell. Everyone thought he had broken his ankle. An ambulance came. Before the coach was put in the ambulance, he asked the team to gather around him. He said, "Play like a team and you will be fine."

> You added interesting information here telling why the team began to play better.

Now the Cavaliers really wanted to win. The team charged down the field. They tried to remember to spread out and pass the ball. The forwards tried to score lots of times, and Keegan stopped two shots at his goal. Finally, Elizabeth was able to make a goal. The score was tied.

When the second half began, everyone was scrambling for the ball. Kelly remembered not to bunch up. She ran ahead and got open for a pass. Elizabeth made a perfect pass right to her. Kelly scored the winning goal, and the Cavaliers won the game. Playing like a team really paid off!

> I like the sentence you added to end your story.

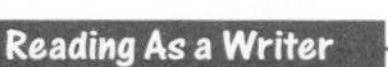

See TE margin for answers.

- What did W.R. like about Kelly's final copy?
- What was the team's problem? How did they solve it?
- Why is the last sentence a good ending?

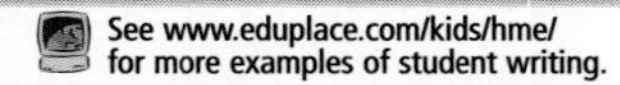

Answers to Reading As a Writer

- Sample answer: W.R. liked Kelly's ending, the details she added about her characters, and the information she added about why the team began to play better.
- Sample answer: The Cavaliers were having a terrible season. They hadn't won any games. After the coach broke his ankle, the players started playing together as a team and they won the game.
- Sample answer: The last sentence explains why Kelly's team won and proved that the coach was right.

Connecting to the Rubric

- Have children look again at the list of characteristics on page 139 and review with them how Kelly's final copy addressed each one.
- Reinforce the Grammar Check by pointing out how Kelly substitutes the pronoun *they* for *the players* when the noun is repeated in the same paragraph.

More About Writer's Craft

- Explain that writers begin new paragraphs for each new main idea. Kelly's story tells events in order. Point out the opening sentence of each paragraph, and discuss how each new paragraph discusses a new time in the story.

Looking Ahead Tell children that they will next write their own stories, using the writing process. As they go along, they will learn how to choose a problem, develop their characters, map their story, and write a good beginning.

FOR STUDENTS ACQUIRING ENGLISH

Have children work in small groups to compare the student model to the rubric. They should decide what parts need work and then rewrite them. Ask them to be innovative, to try dialogue, and to think about their experiences playing sports. Have children read the second draft of the model to see the actual changes.

INTERNET CONNECTION Send your children to www.eduplace.com/kids/hme/ to see more models of student writing. You can also find and print these models at www.eduplace.com/rdg/hme/.

Write a Story

Lesson Objectives

Children will:
- list their ideas for audience, purpose, and publishing/sharing formats
- list ideas for a main character and setting
- discuss their ideas with a partner
- choose an appropriate topic to write about

Start Thinking

Focus on Instruction

- Ask how a story written for a classmate differs from one written for an adult. (It needs simpler language; characters and problems children would enjoy.)
- Have children discuss their purpose for writing a story. Suggest making someone laugh or sharing an experience.
- Ask children how a story read aloud is different from one that is written. Ask how pictures help tell a story. (A written story can be re-read and easily shared. Pictures can add details.)

Choose Your Main Character and Setting

Focus on Instruction

- Point out the Help box to children. Explain that characters can be animals that talk or creatures that are made up. Remind children to choose a main character that they will really like.
- Suggest children choose make-believe settings or real places that they might like to visit. Tell them to imagine places where their characters might live or visit. For additional help, children can turn to the Writing Prompts on page 156.
- Review children's final choices. Ask for a description of the character and its name. Ask for a description of the setting and why the child finds it interesting.

Have children start a writing folder titled *My Story*. Explain that they will keep notes, organizers, and drafts in this folder. Children can put papers with their thoughts about audience, purpose, and publishing in their writing folder.

SCHOOL-HOME CONNECTION Tell children to ask family members to help brainstorm ideas for main character and setting.

Write a Story

Choose Your Main Character

1. **List** three make-believe characters that you could write about in a story.
2. **Think** about the characters you listed.
   - Which character could you write the most interesting story about?
   - Which one would your audience like to read about?
3. **Copy and complete** this sentence.
   My main character will be a _____ named _____.

Stuck for an Idea?
How about these characters?
- a wild animal
- an insect
- a snowman
- a princess

Choose Your Setting

1. **List** two places where your story could take place.
2. **Talk** with a classmate about your main character and the settings you have listed. Decide which setting will work better for your character.
3. **Copy and complete** this sentence.
   My story will take place in a _____ called _____.

Help with Choosing a Topic

MORE TOPIC IDEAS
Suggest that children:
- think of three favorite animals, why they like them, and what they might say if they could talk,
- think of two places they would love to visit, or
- put their character in a strange setting, a place where he or she would find an interesting problem.

TECH TIP
Children who are using a computer can start a folder into which they will put all files related to their story. At this stage, have them make a list of possible topics. Refer children to a Using the Computer on page H23.

Focus Skill

Choosing a Problem

A good story has an interesting problem for the main character to solve. The way a character solves a problem helps to make the story interesting for the reader.

Try It Together Answers will vary.

Plan a story about a child at recess. Talk with your class about different problems that the child might have to solve. How could each problem be solved?

Choose Your Story Idea

1. **Think** about your main character and setting.
2. **Make** a chart like the one below. List two problems you could write about in your story. Then list a way that each problem could be solved.

Possible Problem	Possible Solution

3. **Mark** the problem you will write about.

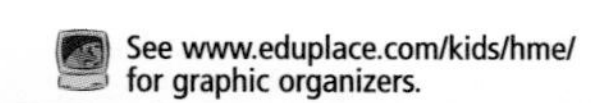
See www.eduplace.com/kids/hme/ for graphic organizers.

Choosing a Problem

Lesson Objective

Children will:
- chart problems and how to solve them

Focus on Instruction

- Discuss with children why most stories have one main character. Point out that readers can imagine they are in the story when they read how one character feels, thinks, and acts.
- Help children understand that telling the way the character solves the problem is what makes any story worth telling.

Try it Together

Ask children to invent problems and solutions. Call on several volunteers to solve one problem.

Choose Your Story Idea

- If children list problems that don't fit their character or setting, suggest they change their earlier ideas. Group discussion may generate new ideas.
- When children share solutions with classmates, ask them to explain steps to check that they make sense.

INTERNET CONNECTION Send your students to www.eduplace.com/kids/hme/ for graphic organizers. You can also find and print these organizers at www.eduplace.com/rdg/hme/.

Meeting Individual Needs

● RETEACHING WORKBOOK, page 31

Choosing a Problem

Every story has a problem for the characters to solve.
Problem: Gino's kitten is in the tree.
Solution: Uncle Jay uses a ladder to get the kitten down.

Look at the picture of this main character and the setting. What problem might this character have? How might he solve his problem?

Complete the chart. List one problem for the main character. Tell how the character could solve the problem. Sample answers

Main Character: Pig	Setting: Pig's new house
Problem: pig has no money; wolves might not build a safe house	
Solution: pig asks other pigs for help	

▲■ WORKBOOK PLUS, page 50

Choosing a Problem

Problem: Theo the cat needs a new home for his family.
Solution: Friendly birds fly over town and find Theo's family a nice warm barn.

Read the main character and setting. Complete the chart by listing two problems for the main character. List one way the character could solve each problem. Answers will vary.

Main Character: a mouse **Setting:** a boat in the ocean

Problem 1:
Solution:
Problem 2:
Solution:

FOR STUDENTS ACQUIRING ENGLISH

In stories, problems often develop around the themes of school, friends, or sports. Write these categories on the board in large circles. Then connect smaller circles to each category, making a web. Ask children to brainstorm specific problems to add to the web. Finally, move on to the planning charts.

Developing Characters

Lesson Objectives

Children will:
- identify characters in their story
- create web with details about characters

Focus on Instruction

- Ask children why it is important for the characters to seem real. (readers want to believe the story)
- As children look at Kelly's character web, ask this question: What kind of information does the detail *chin-ups on the bar* tell about Keegan? (he has strong arm muscles, is fooling around but is not lazy)
- Ask if Kelly's characters remind children of real people they know. Tell them that writers often model main characters after people they know or admire.

Try it Together

Write children's suggestions in character webs on the chalkboard. Show them how to expand the web by adding details and descriptive words to each category.

Explore Your Characters

- The character web will help children list details about their characters. Explain how to create it so children are able to complete one for each character. Use Blackline Master 4-2 to help children explore their characters. You can find other graphic organizers in the Tools and Tips section of the pupil book.
- Explain that notes on a character web can be phrases or single words. Tell children to list descriptive words that tell about the character's strengths and personality traits, as well as the way the character looks, acts, and talks.

INTERNET CONNECTION Send your students to www.eduplace.com/kids/hme/ for graphic organizers. You can also find and print these organizers at www.eduplace.com/rdg/hme/.

FOR STUDENTS ACQUIRING ENGLISH

Another way of helping children develop detailed characters is by creating a *character shield*. Each student folds a paper in quarters, drawing pictures and symbols in each square to represent the characters' beliefs and thoughts, interests/activities, friends, and future.

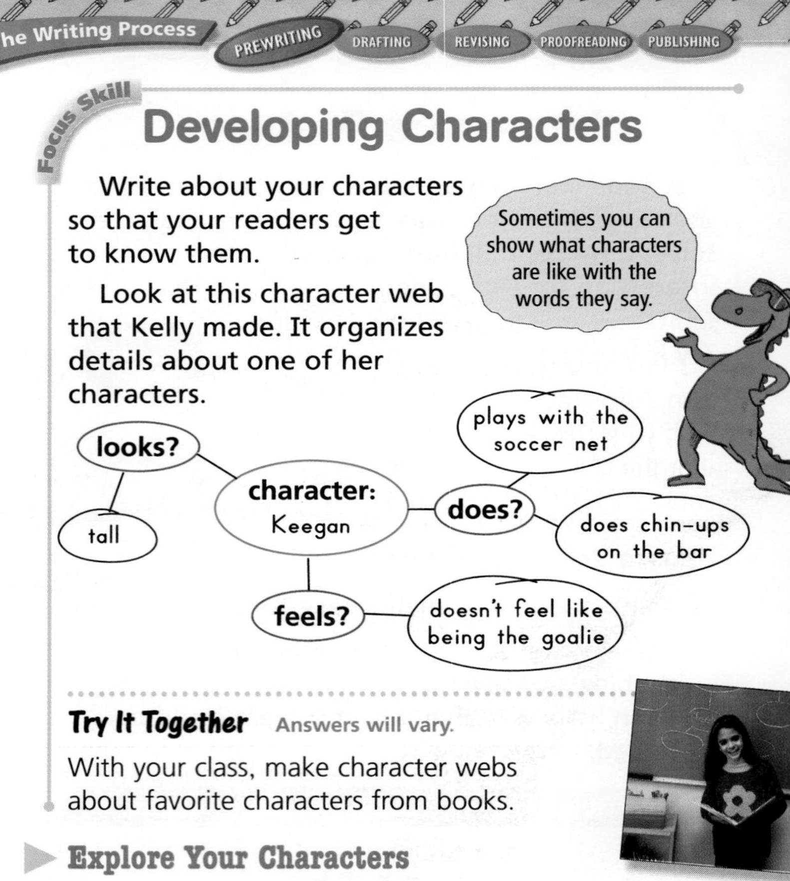

The Writing Process: PREWRITING · DRAFTING · REVISING · PROOFREADING · PUBLISHING

Focus Skill

Developing Characters

Write about your characters so that your readers get to know them.

Look at this character web that Kelly made. It organizes details about one of her characters.

Try It Together Answers will vary.

With your class, make character webs about favorite characters from books.

Explore Your Characters

1. **List** the characters that you will put in your story.
2. **Make** character webs. Write details telling what your characters look like, what they do, and how they feel.

146 Prewriting

See www.eduplace.com/kids/hme/ for graphic organizers.

Meeting Individual Needs

● RETEACHING WORKBOOK, page 32

Developing Characters

Tell facts and details about your characters.
Taylor is a smart boy.
He is a good athlete too.

What if W.R. were a story character? Write details about him in the web. Then write a sentence that tells about W.R. Details and sentences will vary.

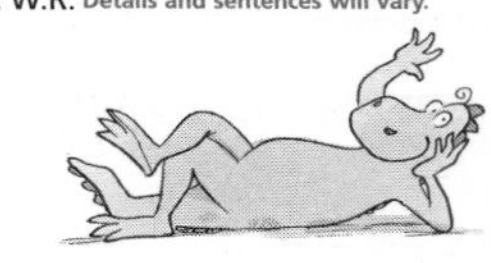

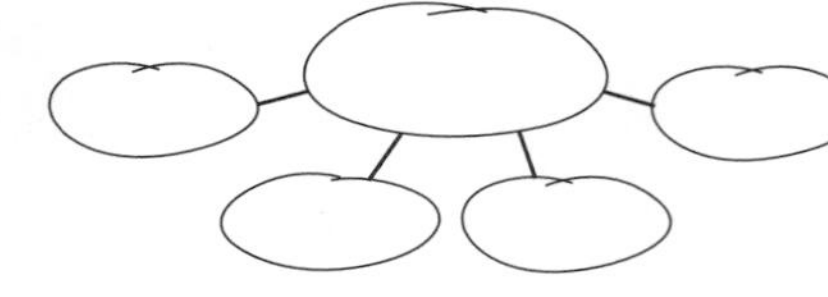

▲■ WORKBOOK PLUS, page 51

Developing Characters

Daisy the Lamb
happy · eats daisies · black and fluffy

Draw a picture of a story character. Complete the web with details about the character. Tell what the character looks like, how he or she feels and thinks, and what he or she does.

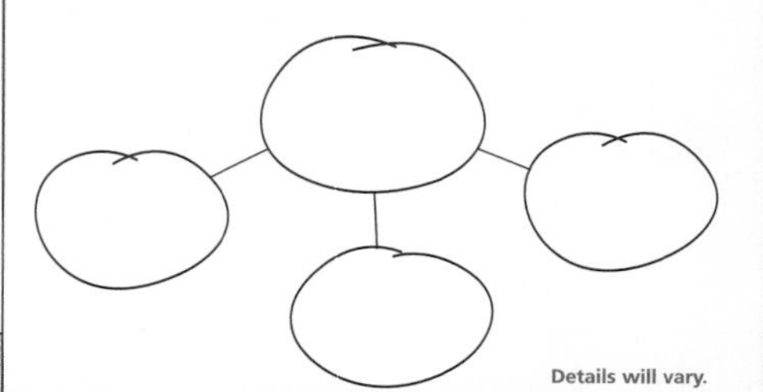

Details will vary.

Focus Skill

Mapping Your Story

Use a story map to plan what will happen at the beginning, middle, and end of your story.

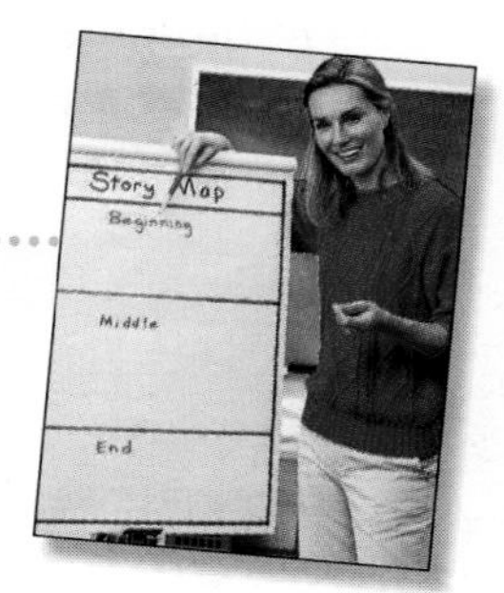

Try It Together Answers will vary.

With your class, make a story map of The Wolf's Chicken Stew.

Plan Your Story

1. **Make** a story map like the one below.
2. **Write** your story events in order.

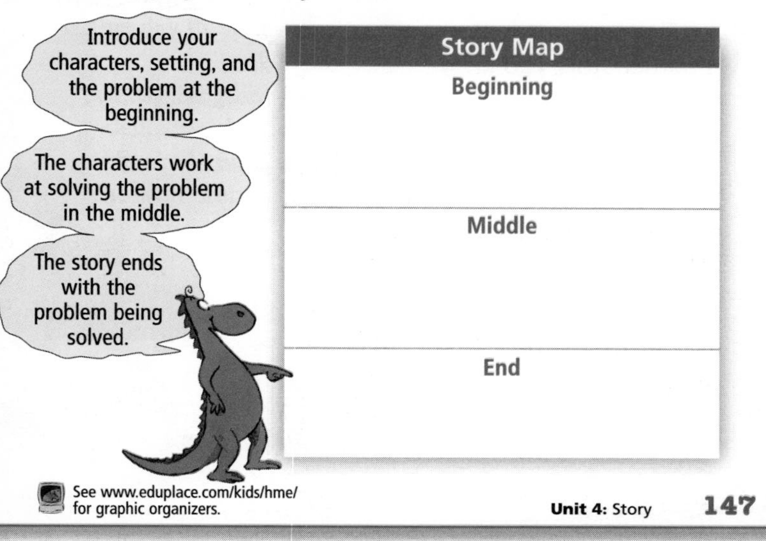

See www.eduplace.com/kids/hme/ for graphic organizers.

Mapping Your Story

Lesson Objectives

Children will:

- chart events that occur in the beginning, middle, and end of the story
- plan the order of story events

Focus on Instruction

- Ask children to think of how they will tell a story about their day. Do they tell it in the order in which it happened? Why? (Stories are easier to understand when things happen in a logical order: the listener can feel like he or she is really there.)
- Ask this question: How would Kelly's story be different if she had written the events from the ending first? Would it be as interesting? (It would not be as interesting because the mystery would be taken out of solving the problem.)

Try it Together

Ask children to review the mapping activity they completed after they read "The Wolf's Chicken Stew." Discuss the fact that this story is easy to understand and to remember because it is written in time order.

Plan Your Story

- Ask children to use pencil when completing their maps so they can easily make changes. Explain that the map is useful for planning and organizing ideas. Children do not have to worry about spelling or writing complete sentences.
- A copy of the organizer appears on Blackline master 4-3. You can find other graphic organizers in the Tools and Tips section of the pupil book.

INTERNET CONNECTION Send your students to www.eduplace.com/kids/hme/ for graphic organizers. You can also find and print these organizers at www.eduplace.com/rdg/hme/.

Meeting Individual Needs

● RETEACHING WORKBOOK, page 33

Mapping Your Story

Every story has a beginning, middle, and end.

Look at the pictures. They tell the beginning and end of a story. Draw a middle for the story in the box.
Drawings will vary.

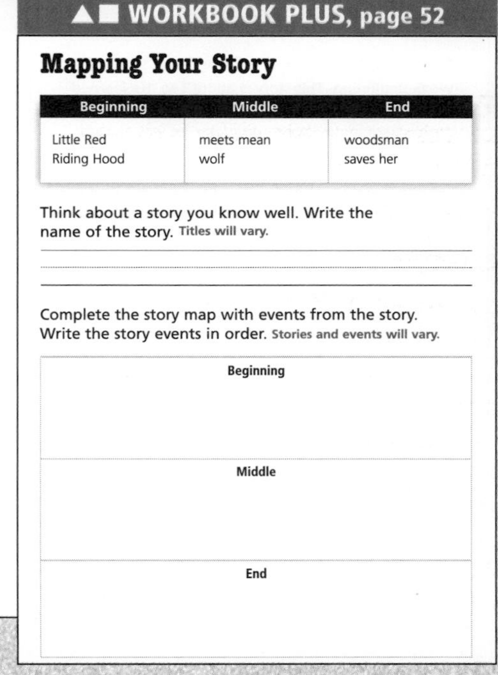

▲■ WORKBOOK PLUS, page 52

Mapping Your Story

Beginning	Middle	End
Little Red Riding Hood	meets mean wolf	woodsman saves her

Think about a story you know well. Write the name of the story. Titles will vary.

Complete the story map with events from the story. Write the story events in order. Stories and events will vary.

Beginning

Middle

End

FOR STUDENTS ACQUIRING ENGLISH

In addition to mapping, have children draw pictures of their characters and scenes to help them expand their details. Bring in newspaper comic strips without captions. Have groups of children write captions for the scenes. Then explain that they will do the same for their stories.

Beginning Your Story

Lesson Objectives

Children will:
- write two beginnings for their stories
- choose their favorite beginning
- use story map and character webs to draft their stories

Focus on Instruction

As children look at the chart, ask this question: What makes the beginning in the chart strong? (The reader is curious about what happens next.) What makes the beginning weak? (There is nothing surprising or puzzling in the beginning.)

Try it Together

Ask children to think of beginnings that seem like riddles or give a hint about the story problem without giving it away. Write children's suggestions on the chalkboard and discuss each beginning.

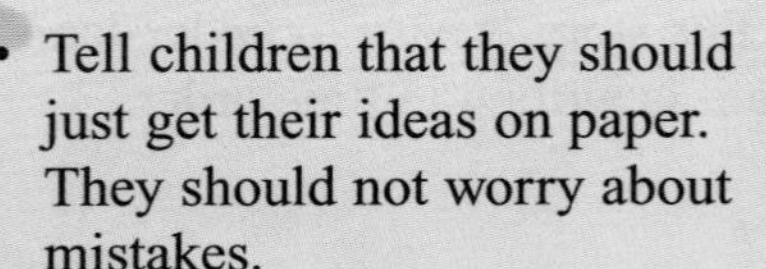

Drafting Reminders

- Tell children that they should just get their ideas on paper. They should not worry about mistakes.
- Tell children if they don't know how to spell a word, they should spell it as best they can and go on. They can fix the spelling later.
- Tell children to skip every other line to leave room for changes.
- Remind children just to cross out words they don't like if they change their minds. They should not start over.

FOR STUDENTS ACQUIRING ENGLISH

Remind children of the different ways to begin a story and give examples such as a character thinking something ("I wonder if I will make it to the moon . . ."), a character doing something ("With a loud blast, the rocket took off."), a character saying something ("Yipee! I made it!").

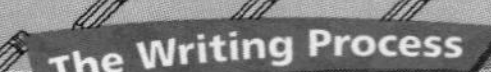

Focus Skill

Beginning Your Story

Beginning your story with something surprising or puzzling will make your readers want to keep reading.

Weak Beginning	Strong Beginning
Mariel and Luís lost their cat.	Yesterday, Mariel and Luís knew something was wrong.

Try It Together Answers will vary.

Work with your class to write a strong beginning for the story of The Three Little Pigs, or another story you know.

Write Your Story

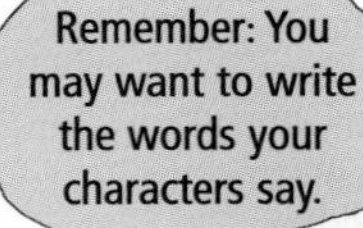

1. **Look** at the first box on your story map. Write two strong beginnings.
2. **Mark** the one you like better.
3. **Copy** the beginning you marked onto another sheet of paper.
4. **Use** your story map and character webs to draft the rest of your story.

Meeting Individual Needs

● RETEACHING WORKBOOK, page 34

Beginning Your Story

A good story beginning can be interesting or surprising.
Weak Beginning: This story is about Leo. He learned to fly.
Strong Beginning: When Leo woke, he was already chirping. Today was the day that he would learn to fly.

What beginning would you write for a story about a friendly, but sad, dragon? Write two different beginnings for the story. Check the one you like better.
Sample beginnings:

☐ Beginning 1. "Where is everyone going?" asked Smoky. "Please wait!"

☐ Beginning 2. Poor Smoky was sad. He had come to town to make friends.

▲■ WORKBOOK PLUS, page 53

Beginning Your Story

Weak Beginning	Strong Beginning
This story is about Jamie. Last week was Jamie's birthday.	When Jamie woke, he was already smiling. Can you imagine the best day of your life?

What beginning would you write for a story about a boy who suddenly became invisible? Write two different beginnings for the story. Check the one you like better.

☐ 1. Sample beginning: No one was looking at Mario. They just walked past him.

☐ 2.

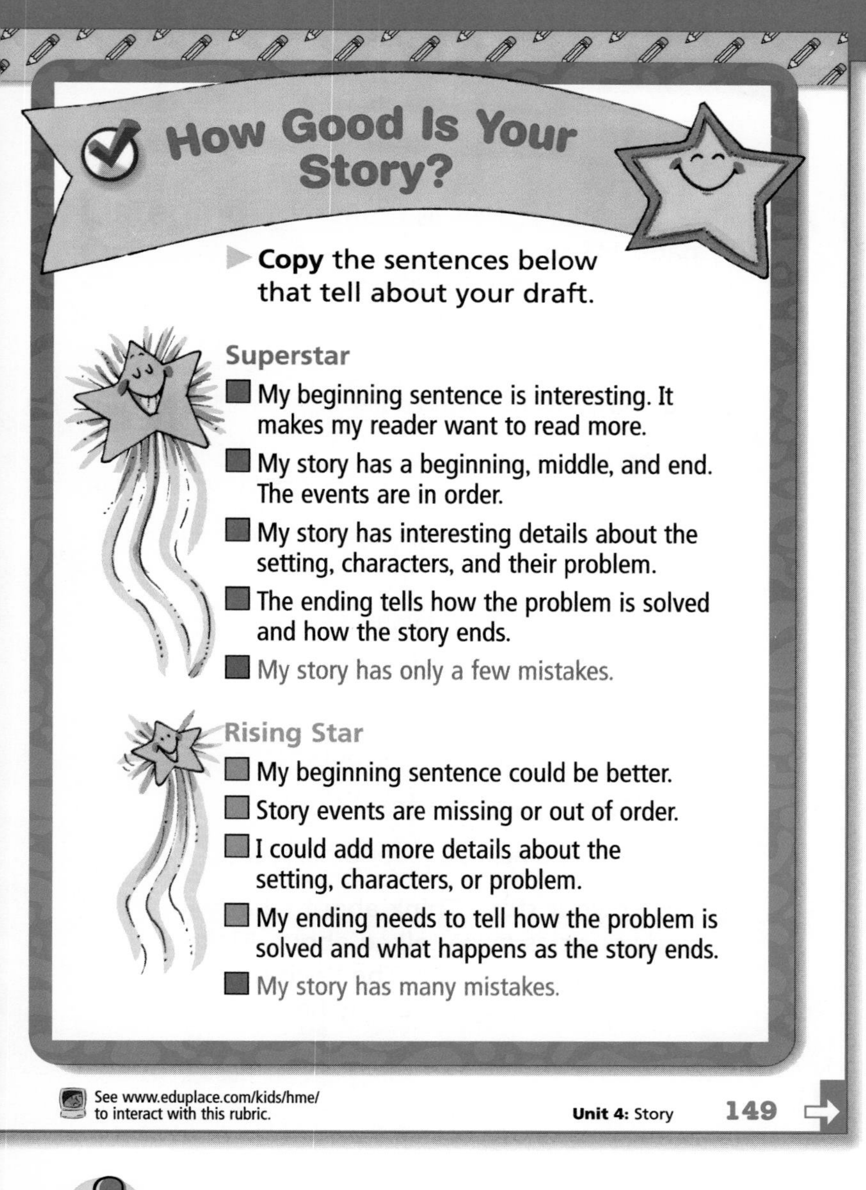

How Good Is Your Story?

Copy the sentences below that tell about your draft.

Superstar

- My beginning sentence is interesting. It makes my reader want to read more.
- My story has a beginning, middle, and end. The events are in order.
- My story has interesting details about the setting, characters, and their problem.
- The ending tells how the problem is solved and how the story ends.
- My story has only a few mistakes.

Rising Star

- My beginning sentence could be better.
- Story events are missing or out of order.
- I could add more details about the setting, characters, or problem.
- My ending needs to tell how the problem is solved and what happens as the story ends.
- My story has many mistakes.

See www.eduplace.com/kids/hme/ to interact with this rubric.

Unit 4: Story 149

How Good Is Your Story?

Lesson Objective

Children will:

- evaluate their story, using a rubric

Connecting to the Criteria

Have children reread the characteristics of a story listed on page 139. Tell them that the rubric shown on this page refers to those characteristics. Explain that they can use the rubric to help them decide which parts of their stories meet the standards of a great story, and which parts they think need more work.

Focus on Instruction

- Review the rubric with children. Have volunteers read aloud the pairs of related characteristics. Discuss with children the differences between the sentences in each pair.
- After children write their criteria, have them circle the ones that indicate aspects of their stories that need revision. Blackline Master 4-4 provides a copy of the rubric as a checklist for children using the hardbound edition. Alternatively they can write the sentences that describe their stories.
- See the Teacher's Resource Book for scoring rubrics.

INTERNET CONNECTION Have children go to www.eduplace.com/kids/hme/ to use an interactive version of the rubric shown in the pupil book. Children will get feedback and support depending on how they mark the rubric items.

This page is available as a poster.

Meeting Individual Needs

● RETEACHING WORKBOOK, page 35

Revising a Story

Have I	yes
• added details about the character and setting?	☐
• written a clear beginning, middle, and end?	☐
• written an interesting beginning?	☐

Revise this story. Check off each box when you have finished revising. Write your changes in the spaces above each line, on the sides, and below the paragraph.
Sample answers

Rita the mouse was very upset.
~~This is about Rita the mouse.~~ Her piece of yarn was her favorite thing. One day, she saw Tiger playing with her yarn. How could she save it? Rita ran out of her mouse hole and
Tiger got tired watching her. He finally fell asleep.
around the kitchen. Then Rita grabbed her yarn and ran
Her yarn was saved!
back into the hole.

▲■ WORKBOOK PLUS, page 54

Revising a Story

Have I	yes
• added details about the character and setting?	☐
• written a clear beginning, middle, and end?	☐
• written an interesting beginning?	☐

Revise this story to make it better. Check off each box when you have finished revising. Write your changes in the spaces above each line, on the sides, and below the paragraph. Sample answers

Ramón was a sad, sad boy.
~~The boy's name was Ramón.~~ He lived in a big house with his mother and sister. When his best friend, Robert,
He had no one to play with.
moved to Seattle, Ramón felt lonely. ~~He asked his sister what to do. She did not know.~~ He asked his mother what to do. She said, "Well, maybe we could get you a
The puppy became Ramón's new best friend.
puppy to keep you company."

FOR STUDENTS ACQUIRING ENGLISH

Remind children that their beginnings may make readers jump right in, but these kinds of beginnings need to be explained quickly. On an overhead transparency, share excellent student examples and show how they fulfill parts of the rubric. Then ask children to read and evaluate one particularly good example. This will connect their listening skills to the writing task, giving them a sense of what needs to improve in the flow of their words.

Lesson Objective

Children will:
- revise their working drafts, based on their evaluations

Revise Your Story

Focus on Instruction

Revising Reminders

Remind children that revisions should focus on the content of their stories, and on making their stories more interesting and organized. Children should not worry about mistakes at this stage.

- Discuss with children the evaluations they made of their own writing, and make any additional suggestions for improvements and revisions.
- Suggest that children look at each part of their story. Have them highlight descriptions of the main character, to check if he or she is described adequately.
- Ask children to number events in sequence, to be sure the steps are in the best order.

FOR STUDENTS ACQUIRING ENGLISH

To help children see the weak points in their stories, ask them to go back and redraw a comic strip based on what they've written. If scenes are missing from the pictures, then something is missing from the story. This exercise is equally effective in peer conferencing: one partner reads his/her story while the other draws scenes. The reader/writer can then see what parts are incomprehensible or missing. Before conferences, model good listening behavior: listening quietly, looking at the reader, and waiting until the reader pauses before asking questions.

Revise Your Story

- Write a new beginning or ending.
- Change the order of events so that they make more sense.
- Add details to help your readers know the characters better.

1. **Look** at the sentences from page 149 that you wrote about your story. What do you need to do to make your story better?
2. **Have a writing conference.**

When You're the Writer

- Write a question about a part of your story that you need help with.
- Share your story and your question with a classmate.

When You're the Listener

- Tell two things you like about the story.
- Ask about parts that are not clear.
- Look at the next page for other ideas.

3. **Revise** your story. Think about what you and your classmate talked about. Make changes to your draft. The Revising Strategies on page 152 may help you.

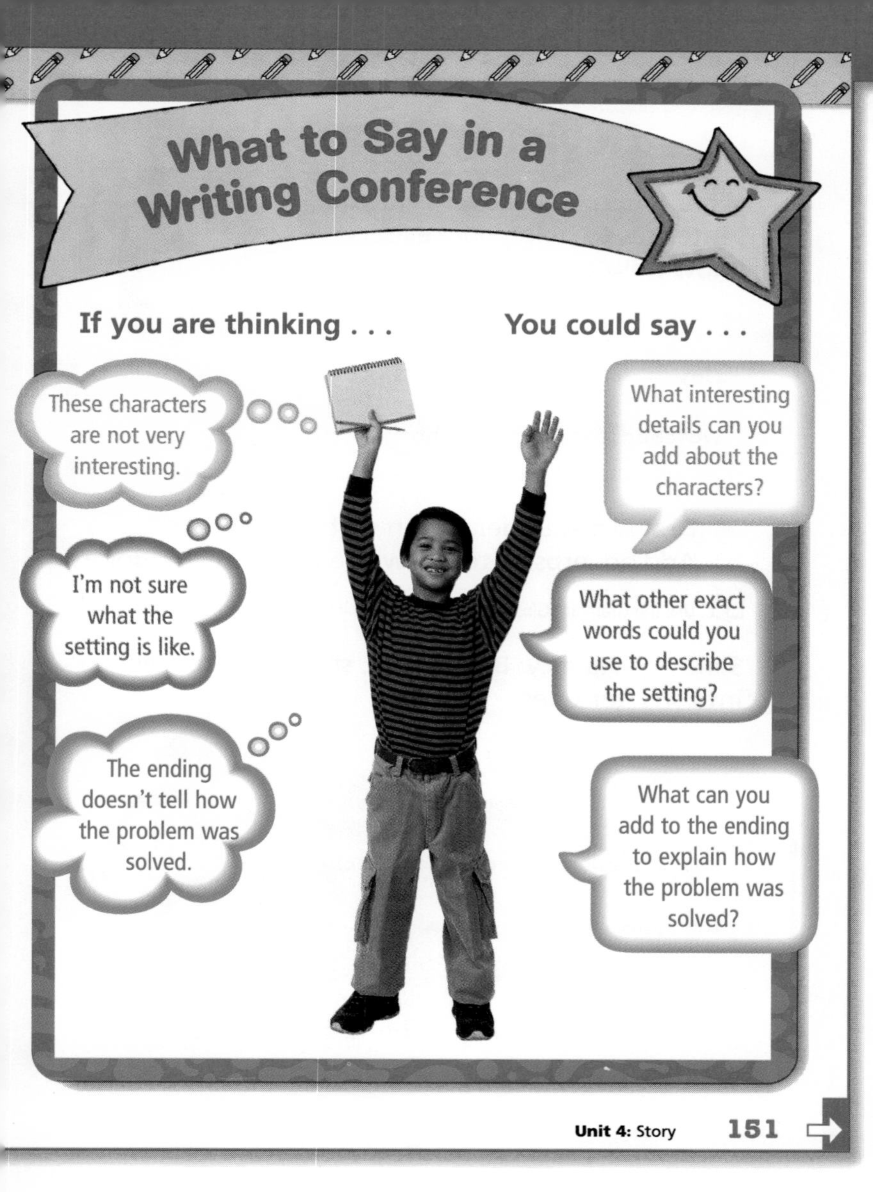

Help with Conferencing

ADDITIONAL CONFERENCING QUESTIONS

These questions may be useful during teacher-student conferences.

- Can your reader see your setting and characters clearly? What might you add to create vivid images?
- Can the reader understand why your characters feel as they do? What can you add to make this clearer?
- Would you like to take out any characters or add a new character who can help solve the problem in the story?
- Are all story events in the correct order?

EVALUATION TIP

As children speak about each other's work, ask the writer to listen to comments without interrupting.

What to Say in a Writing Conference

Lesson Objectives

Children will:

- have a writing conference
- retell a spoken message by summarizing or clarifying

Read aloud and discuss with children the text in the thought and speech balloons. Explain that the thought balloons show what a listener might think while listening to a story. The speech balloons show what the listener could ask to help the writer know what parts might not be clear or could be revised.

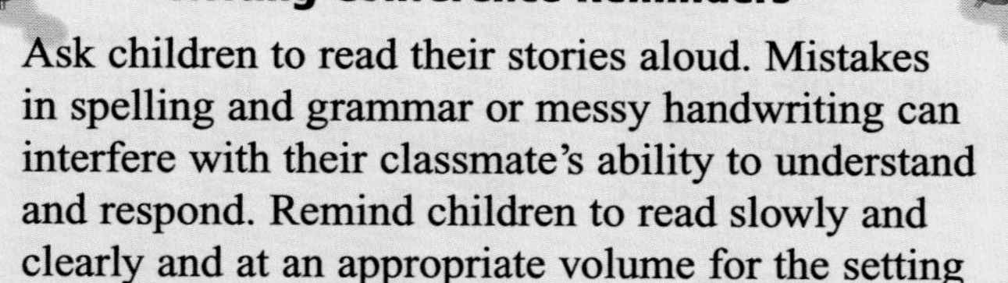

Writing Conference Reminders

- Ask children to read their stories aloud. Mistakes in spelling and grammar or messy handwriting can interfere with their classmate's ability to understand and respond. Remind children to read slowly and clearly and at an appropriate volume for the setting and audience. They should speak softly if reading to a partner and louder if reading to a larger group.
- Tell children to do these things when they are the listeners:

  Always compliment the writer about something they like in the paper. Discuss some possibilities, such as the beginning makes me want to read more or the characters are interesting.

  Retell what they have heard after listening to their partner's paper. They should tell what the story is about and include the important ideas and details.
- Suggest that children choose their words carefully. They don't want to hurt the writer's feelings.
- Explain to children that they don't have to use every one of their classmate's suggestions. Tell them to think about points that their classmate felt were unclear or undeveloped.

 This page is also available as a poster.

- Children can use Blackline Master 4-5 during their writing conferences.

Revising Strategies

Lesson Objectives

Children will:
- use adverbs in sentences
- break long sentences into shorter ones

Focus on Instruction

Word Choice

- Write the following sentences on the board:

  Leo sang with the radio.

  Ash danced around the room.

- Ask volunteers to suggest an adverb for each sentence. (Leo sang loudly with the radio. Ash danced quickly around the room.)
- Suggest children list two or three adverbs for one verb before choosing the best one. Ask them to check for repetition and show them how to write a list of synonyms to replace any overused adverbs.

Sentence Fluency

- Write the following long sentence on the board:

  Gary and Megan went to the pet store and bought cat food and watched the rabbits in their cages.

- Discuss with children how to break the long sentence into two shorter ones. (Gary and Megan went to the pet store and bought cat food. They watched the rabbits in their cages.)

FOR STUDENTS ACQUIRING ENGLISH

Ask children to retell their stories without looking at their papers. Their partners take notes and ask questions, then the teller does so. Based on the verbal retelling and the notes, the student should have more details to add.

Revising Strategies

Word Choice Use adverbs in your sentences to help your readers know **how** an action was done.

Jay walked ^slowly^ past the toy store window. He watched the toy bear bang ^loudly^ on its drum.

▶ Draw lines under action verbs in your story. Add adverbs to tell how the actions were done.

Use the Grammar Glossary on page H35 to learn more about adverbs.

Sentence Fluency Break long, stringy sentences into shorter ones.

Andy and Meg went to the beach and sat on the sand. ~~and~~ ^They^ watched the gulls and the waves.

▶ Find and fix stringy sentences in your story.

152 Revising

Meeting Individual Needs

● RETEACHING WORKBOOK, page 36

Revising Strategies: Sentence Fluency

Adverbs show how an action is done.

I pulled ^carefully^ on my raincoat.

Choose an adverb for each sentence to tell more about the action. Then write the sentence.

happily	loudly	soundly	swiftly	brightly

1. The lions played a game.
   The lions happily played a game.
2. One lion roared.
   One lion roared loudly.
3. A bird flew to the tree.
   A bird flew swiftly to the tree.
4. The stars shone.
   The stars shone brightly.
5. That night, everyone slept.
   That night, everyone slept soundly.

▲■ WORKBOOK PLUS, page 55

Revising Strategies: Sentence Fluency

The owl flew ^swiftly^ over the field.

The mouse ran ^quickly^ under the bush.

Add an adverb to each sentence to tell how the action was done. Answers will vary.

1. The wind blew.
2. The animals waited.
3. The moon rose.
4. The horses raced.
5. The frog croaked.

PREWRITING · DRAFTING · REVISING · PROOFREADING · PUBLISHING

Proofread Your Story

1 **Proofread** your story. Use the Proofreading Checklist and the Proofreading Marks.

2 **Use** a class dictionary to check spellings.

Proofreading Checklist

- Each sentence begins with a capital letter.
- Each sentence ends with the correct end mark.
- Each paragraph is indented.
- Each word is spelled correctly.

Proofreading Marks

∧	Add	≡	Capital letter
⌐	Delete	/	Small letter
¶	Indent for new paragraph		

Using the Proofreading Marks

Sparky is a ~~doge~~ dog. she is Andy's pet.

3 **Review** these rules before you proofread.

Grammar and Spelling Connections

Nouns and Pronouns Use the correct pronoun when replacing one or more nouns.

Dale and Clara weren't home.

They were at the park.

Long Vowel Sounds The long **e** sound may be spelled e, ee, ea, or y.

me green read happy

See the Spelling Guide on page H40.

See www.eduplace.com/kids/hme/ for proofreading practice.

Lesson Objective

Children will:
- proofread their stories

Proofread Your Story

Focus on Instruction

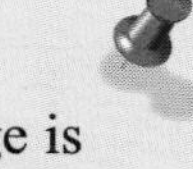

Proofreading Reminders

- Remind children that the proofreading stage is the time to correct capitalization, punctuation, spelling, and usage mistakes.
- Review the use of proofreading marks. Suggest that children use a different color pencil to make their proofreading corrections.
- Have children use the Proofreading Checklist in the pupil book. Review and clarify each item in the checklist, and review the Grammar and Spelling Connections. If children need extra support, review the related grammar lessons on pages 93 and 107 with them.
- Provide dictionaries for children. Have them mark any words they think are misspelled and check them in the dictionary.
- For proofreading practice, see the usage and mechanics lessons in the Grammar units and the Mixed Review practice in each Grammar unit Checkup.

Help with Proofreading

MANAGEMENT TIPS

Have each child keep a personal checklist of skills that he or she needs to proofread for. Staple the list to the child's folder.

- Children can get additional proofreading help by exchanging papers with a partner.

TECH TIP

The computer can help children find overused nouns and replace them with pronouns. Demonstrate using the *find* feature to count the number of times a specific noun or name was used. Then show children how to select a noun and replace it with a pronoun.

MEETING INDIVIDUAL NEEDS — FOR STUDENTS ACQUIRING ENGLISH

Help children make their stories perfect to prepare for hosting and reading aloud to a class of younger students. Invite a kindergarten or pre-school class to your room, ask your class to form small groups, and have them read their short stories to their guests.

Lesson Objectives

Children will:
- make neat final copies of their stories
- choose a way to publish or share their stories
- reflect on the writing experience
- evaluate the writing in comparison to others in their writing portfolio

Publish Your Story

Focus on Instruction

- Have children decide how they will publish their story. Then they can prepare their final copy.
- If children find mistakes on their final copies, help them make neat corrections and not copy the story again.
- Observe the way children hold their pencils and position their papers when they make their final copies. Check that they are gaining handwriting proficiency. Remind children to use word and letter spacing and margins to make their papers readable.
- For handwriting instruction and practice, see the Teacher's Resource Disk for printable blackline masters.

Keeping a Writing Portfolio

A writing portfolio is where students can keep samples of their writing. Here are suggestions for creating and using writing portfolios.

- **Selection** A paper might be selected because it is
  - ✓ generally noteworthy
  - ✓ a good example of a particular criterion
  - ✓ an example of a certain kind of writing
  - ✓ from a certain time in the school year
  - ✓ a typical example of the student's work
- **Labeling:** For every paper, have students complete a cover sheet giving the title, date of completion, and reason for inclusion.
- **Review:** Have students remove papers that no longer reflect their best work or aren't needed as baselines.
- **Evaluation:** Review students' portfolios with them to discuss growth and areas that need improvement.

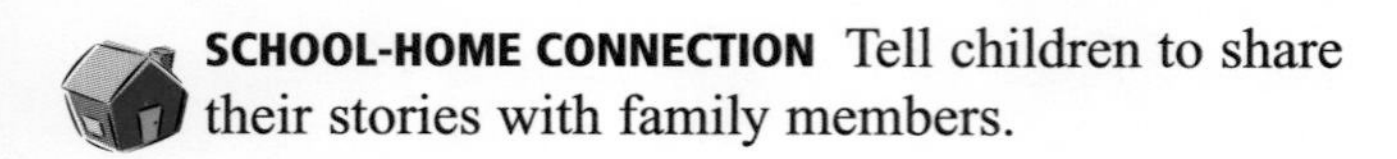

SCHOOL-HOME CONNECTION Tell children to share their stories with family members.

Publish Your Story

1. **Make** a neat final copy of your story.
2. **Write** an interesting title. Tell something about your story, but don't give away what happens.

- Be sure you wrote all letters correctly and used good spacing. Check that you fixed every mistake.
- Begin the first, last, and each important word in your title with a capital letter.

3. **Look** at Ideas for Sharing on the next page.
4. **Publish** or share your story in a way that works for your audience.

Reflect

Answer these questions about your story.

- What is your favorite part of your story? Why?

- Do you like your story better than other papers you have written? Why or why not?

Tech Tip If you wrote your story on a computer, fix each mistake. Then print out a final copy.

154 Publishing

Ideas for Sharing

Write It

- Bind your story with your classmates' stories to make a class book.
- Write your story as a play.

Say It

- ★ Read your story aloud while some classmates act it out.
- Tell your story to a classmate. Use your voice and body movements to make it more interesting.

Change the tone of your voice as you read your story to make it sound more exciting.

Show It

- Make three paintings that show the beginning, middle, and end of your story.
- Present your story, using finger puppets.

Help with Publishing

DIRECTIONS FOR MAKING FINGER PUPPETS
Provide children with scissors, markers, clear tape, and colored construction paper rectangles, 2" x 3". Show them how to wrap the paper around one finger and tape it to create a cylinder. Then ask them to draw faces on their puppets and add colored hats, ears, tails, or clothes.

Ideas for Sharing

- **Class Book** Have children create illustrations, a cover, and a table of contents. Then help children assemble the stories in a binder or bind them inexpensively at a local photocopy shop.

TECH TIP

Children can include tech art with their stories.

- **Play** When children have completed their writing, help them stage a simple reading. Allow children time to practice before reading the play for the class. Help children choose appropriate props to clarify and support their presentations.
- **Read and Act** Help children make simple props out of colored construction paper. Remind readers to speak slowly and clearly.
- **Tell Your Story** Remind storytellers to use appropriate rate and volume for their audience, purpose, and occasion.
- **Paintings** Provide children with three sheets of paper and watercolors or tempera. Tell them to paint the beginning painting first, the middle painting second, and the end painting last. Encourage children to say their stories to themselves as they paint.
- **Finger Puppets** See the Help with Publishing box for directions.

Writing Prompts

Objectives

Children will:
- review prompts for choosing a topic or to practice for a writing test
- critically view a work of fine art and use it to write a story

Using the Prompts

You can use the prompts on this page in several ways.

- Have children review the prompts to help spark ideas when they are choosing their own topics for a story. Suggest that children choose one or two prompts that interest them and brainstorm ideas of their own.
- Choose a prompt to provide practice for a writing test. Use it with the Test Practice on the next page.
- Choose a prompt that fits with a related topic in another subject area to integrate writing a story across the curriculum.
- Direct children attention to the painting. Ask:

  How does the boy feel about the deer? How do you know? (He loves the deer because he is holding it lovingly.)

  Does the yearling seem happy or upset in the boy's arms? How do you know? (He seems happy because he is not struggling.)

INTERNET CONNECTION Send your students to www.eduplace.com/kids/hme for more writing ideas. You can also find and print these prompts at www.eduplace.com/rdg/hme/.

FOR STUDENTS ACQUIRING ENGLISH

The following prompts are particularly useful with children learning English: *What animal stories from your native country are about something in nature? (For example, how the leopard got its spots.) Write about a boy/girl living 100 years from now. What is he/she like? What happens to him/her one day?* Bring in artwork or newpaper photos to generate ideas.

Assessment Link

Use these prompts for ideas or to practice for a test. Write your story in a way that your audience will understand and enjoy.

1. Write a story about a hero. What problem will the hero solve? How does the hero solve the problem?

2. What amazing place can you write about? What adventure could a character have there? Write a story about the adventure.

Writing Across the Curriculum

3. 

What is happening in this painting? Where and how did the boy get the deer? Write an interesting story about the boy and the deer.

Charles Scribner's Sons, Oil on canvas, 45 X 32 in. Private Collection
Photography by Peter Ralston

Jody and Flag, 1939, N.C. Wyeth
The Yearling, by Marjorie Kinnan Rawlings

156 Writing Prompts

See www.eduplace.com/kids/hme/ for more prompts.

About the Artist

N.C. Wyeth

Newell Convers Wyeth was born in 1882. He was raised on a small farm near Boston. Between farm chores, Wyeth practiced drawing. By the time he was sixteen, Wyeth was determined to become an artist.

With professional training, Wyeth's talent blossomed. His first sale was to the Saturday Evening Post for a painting of a bucking bronco and cowboy. Soon he was illustrating young people's books. Between the years 1925 and 1935, Wyeth did his most unique work. His paintings had a feeling of freedom that hadn't been seen before.

Wyeth passed an artistic legacy along in his family. His son and grandson, Andrew and Jamie Wyeth, are accomplished and respected American artists.

Assessment Link

Test Practice

Read this writing prompt.

> Write a story about a hero. What problem will the hero solve? How does the hero solve the problem?

Follow these steps for writing to a prompt.

1. **Look** for clues that tell you what to write.
2. **Look** for questions that you should answer.
3. **Plan** your writing. Copy and fill in this chart.

Answering a Writing Prompt
Clues: **a story about a hero; solve the problem**
Hero:
Problem:
Beginning:
Middle:
End:

4. **Look** at page 149. What makes a Superstar?
5. **Write** your story.

See www.eduplace.com/kids/hme/ for graphic organizers.

Test Practice

Objective

Children will:

- learn strategies for evaluating a writing prompt and writing a story for a test

Using the Test Practice

- Discuss with children the strategies for evaluating and responding to a prompt to write a story.
- Review the rubric on page 149 with children before they write their practice test.
- Have children write a story in response to the prompt on this page or to one of the prompts on the previous page. Impose time limitations or other qualifications specific to the testing requirements of your school.
- Tell children to use the chart on the page to help plan their writing.

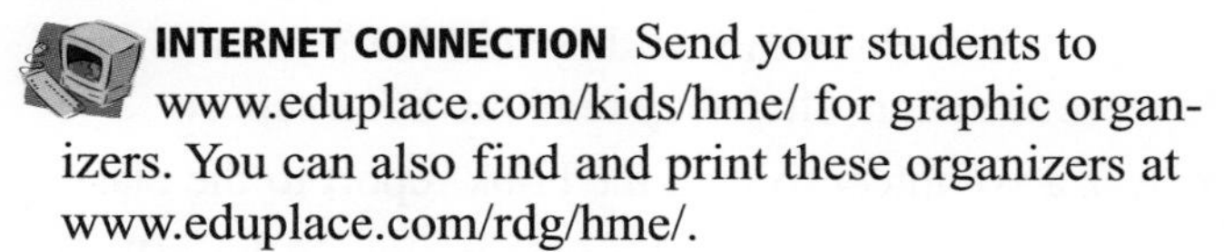

INTERNET CONNECTION Send your students to www.eduplace.com/kids/hme/ for graphic organizers. You can also find and print these organizers at www.eduplace.com/rdg/hme/.

FOR STUDENTS ACQUIRING ENGLISH

Challenge children to name words that describe heroes (*strong, wise, caring, helpful, weak, etc.*). Consider having children work in pairs to write stories or ask the whole class to do so: children brainstorm and vote on characters, setting, problem, ending, etc. Then they pass around the story, with each student adding a sentence or paragraph to make a finished product.

Writing a Book Report

Lesson Objective

Children will:

- read a model of a book report

Focus on the Model

- Ask children to explain the purpose of a book report. Guide them to see that book reports give background information about a book and its author, briefly summarize the book's plot, and express the writer's opinion of the book. Help them understand that the writer's opinion is supported with reasons and examples.
- Explain that writing a book report is similar to writing a narrative because both include interesting details about the topic; in this case, the book.
- Tell the class that they will read Celsey's book report about a book called *I'm Too Big/Je Suis Trop Gros*.
- Before children read the book report, explain that the blue call outs highlight important elements of a book report. Tell children that they will learn more about these elements after they read the book report.
- Ask a volunteer to read the book report to the class.
- Discuss with the class the explanation of the call outs given in the Reading As a Writer section. Have volunteers answer the questions.

Alternatively, children can listen to the story on audiotape.

Answers to Reading as a Writer

- The title is *I'm Too Big/Je Suis Trop Gros.*
- It was written by Lone Morton.
- This book is about an elephant and a giraffe who do not like the way they look. They want to change themselves. At the end of the book, they realize that they are great just the way they are.
- Celsey did like the book because the elephant and giraffe ended up liking themselves. Celsey thinks books like this one help people feel good about their differences.

FOR STUDENTS ACQUIRING ENGLISH

Make sure children understand what a giraffe and an elephant are. Show pictures of each one, and have children talk about where they live, what they eat, and what makes each one special. Help children with vocabulary needed to describe the animals such as *neck*, *spots*, and *trunk*.

INTERNET CONNECTION Send your students to www.eduplace.com/kids/hme/ to see more models of student writing. You can also find and print these models at www.eduplace.com/rdg/hme/.

Writing a Book Report

In a **book report**, you write about a book you have read. You also tell if you liked the book and why. Read Celsey's book report and what W.R. said about it.

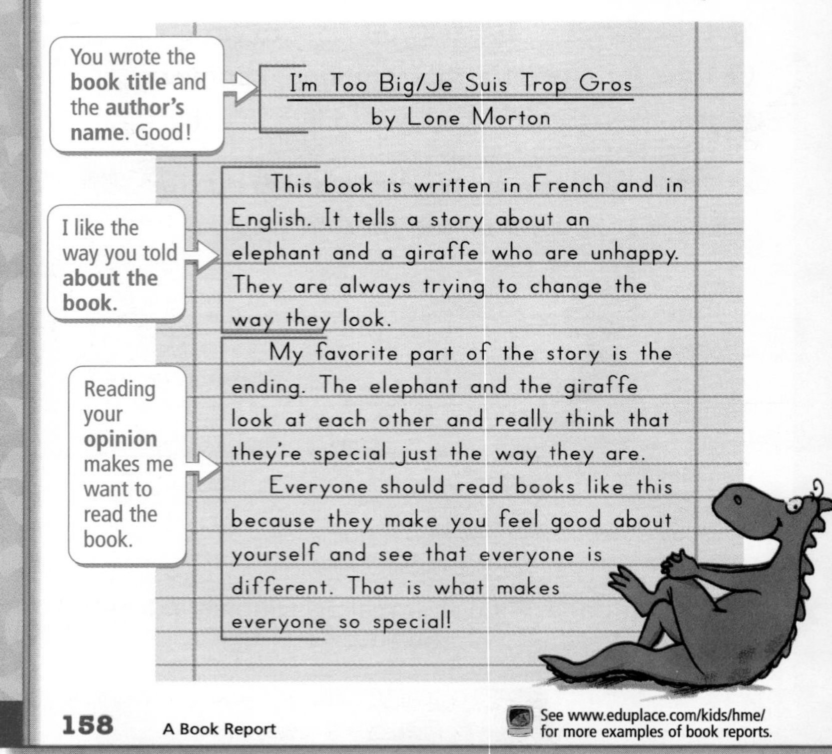

I'm Too Big/Je Suis Trop Gros
by Lone Morton

This book is written in French and in English. It tells a story about an elephant and a giraffe who are unhappy. They are always trying to change the way they look.

My favorite part of the story is the ending. The elephant and the giraffe look at each other and really think that they're special just the way they are.

Everyone should read books like this because they make you feel good about yourself and see that everyone is different. That is what makes everyone so special!

See www.eduplace.com/kids/hme/ for more examples of book reports.

Reading As a Writer See TE margin for answers.

- What is the **title** of the book that Celsey read?
- Who is the **author** of the book?
- What is this **book about**?
- What is Celsey's **opinion** of the book?

How to Write a Book Report

1. **Read** a book that interests you.
2. **Write** the book title and the author's name.
3. **Describe** what the book is about. Write about the main ideas.
4. **Explain** your opinion.
   - Tell if you liked the book or not. Then tell why.
   - If the book has pictures, tell what you think of them. Did they add to the story? How?
5. **Proofread** your book report. Use the Proofreading Checklist on page 153. Use a class dictionary to check your spelling.
6. **Publish or share** your report. Read it aloud or display your final copy.

Capitalize the first, last, and other important words in the book title. Draw a line under the title.

Help with Writing a Book Report

TOPIC IDEAS

Suggest these possibilities:

- a book about a favorite place or person
- a special bedtime book
- a book that has a unique format, such as a pop-up book or tactile book
- a book that has been handed down through the family

TECH TIP

Children may use italic type or underscore whenever they write the title of the book. They may also choose to use clip art to illustrate their descriptions of the book.

Lesson Objectives

Children will:

- write a book report
- revise and proofread a book report
- make a neat final copy of a book report

How to Write a Book Report

Focus on Instruction

- Talk about why people write book reports. Have children create a list of two or three books that they have read or would like to read.
- Suggest that children jot down the major events in the book as they read it. Show children how to record page numbers of passages they might want to refer to.
- Have children talk with partners about their books before they write. This will help them express their ideas and will provide experience with word choice.
- Review with children the Proofreading Checklist on page 153 and the use of proofreading marks.
- Review children's publishing plans with them to help them address any special requirements.

Connecting to the Criteria

Remind children to check that their book reports include the book's title and author, capitalized correctly. Their book reports should also describe the book's plot and explain the writer's opinion of it. Have children look back at the Reading As a Writer section for help.

SCHOOL-HOME CONNECTION Have children read their book reports at home and then ask family to recommend and discuss other books they have read.

Discuss with each child whether this paper should go into the portfolio. Consider these possible reasons: (1) It is an especially good piece of writing; (2) it reflects a particular aspect of writing that the child did well; (3) it shows an aspect of writing that needs more work and could be used as a baseline for measuring growth.

FOR STUDENTS ACQUIRING ENGLISH

Ask children what special thing Celsey did with the title of the book. (underlined it) Explain that this is the way to show a title of a book when one is writing by hand. Then discuss the use of capital letters on all the important words in the title of the book. Have children say who the author is. Ask for examples of other opinions about the book.

Different Forms of Stories

Lesson Objectives

Children will:
- listen to a story and visualize characters and setting
- view illustrations to understand how pictures add information
- listen to music to understand how it can affect the mood of a story

Focus on Instruction

- Read the story below to your class before they open their books to page 160 and see the illustrations. Children are to create their own images of the characters based on what they hear. Read in a monotone. When you have finished reading, lead a class discussion, using the questions that follow the story.

Alternatively, children can listen to the story on audiotape.

> A frog was sitting in front of his house. Along came a rabbit, which had been the frog's neighbor for many years. When the rabbit came close, the frog spoke.
>
> "Good morning, I haven't seen you in a while," said the frog.
>
> "Hello. I've been to town to visit my sister," replied the rabbit.
>
> "Good," croaked the frog, "and how is your garden coming?"
>
> "Well, we picked lots of carrots. But the frost got the cabbages. It may be a hard winter."
>
> "That's too bad," croaked the frog.

Discussion Questions

- What do you think the frog looks like?
- How do you think the frog sounds when he speaks?
- How do you think the rabbit looks and speaks?
- Do you think these characters are friends? Why or why not?
- Would you want to be friends with either of these characters? Why or why not?

Think and Discuss

- Have children compare the pictures they visualized with the pictures in the book. To extend the discussion, ask children how the mood of the story changes with each picture. Have them tell how the drawings change their expectations for the rest of the story.

Different Forms of Stories

Some stories, like the one you just heard, have only words. When you read or hear them, you must create pictures of the characters and places in your mind.

Think and Discuss See TE margin for answers.

What are the frog and rabbit like in this first set of pictures? What are they like in the second set? How do the pictures change your ideas about the setting and the characters in the story your teacher read?

You know that pictures can help you understand a story. They can show you what the weather is like and if a place is cheerful or gloomy. Pictures can also show you what a character looks like or how a character feels.

Music and other sounds can also help you understand a story. They can make a story seem sad, funny, calm, exciting, or even scary. Characters' voices can make them sound nice, mean, happy, or upset.

Apply It See TE margin for answers.

Look at the picture on this book cover.

- What do you think this story might be about?
- Do you think it will be happy, sad, exciting, or scary? Why?

Now listen as your teacher plays some music that goes with this story.

- How did the music make you feel?
- Did the music make you change your mind about the story? Why or why not?

Focus on Instruction

- Ask children to think about their favorite songs and musical pieces. Ask volunteers to tell how music can change a mood or feeling. (Sample answers: Slow music can make us feel sad or calm; bouncy or fast music can give us energy or make us feel happy.)
- Ask how songs or tunes can tell a story. (Songs can tell a real or made-up story; some tunes can make us visualize a person, place, or time.) Play and/or sing some folk songs that tell a story, such as "Sweet Betsy from Pike" or "There Was an Old Woman..." Have volunteers tell the story and share any pictures they thought of as they listened to the song.
- Discuss books that have been made into movies, such as *Winnie the Pooh*, *The Jungle Book*, or *Stuart Little*. Ask volunteers how the pictures in a movie changed their ideas about a character or setting. (Sample answer: Seeing Stuart Little so realistic and so small makes him cuter.) Ask volunteers to explain how the music in a film added feelings to a special scene. (Sample answer: The Winnie the Pooh song creates a happy, silly feeling.)

Apply It

- Have children study the picture silently before responding. To extend the activity, have children write two titles for the book that convey their feelings about the illustration.
- Play music such as Igor Stravinsky's *The Firebird,* Gustav Holst's *The Planets,* John Williams's *Star Wars,* or some birdcalls after your children have expressed what they think the story will be about. Have children look at the picture as they listen.
- Ask volunteers to share both sets of ideas with the class, and compare and contrast them.

FOR STUDENTS ACQUIRING ENGLISH

Have children name different forms of stories. Ask: "What kinds of stories do you know that have music, moving pictures or voices?" (*some songs, movies, plays...*) Provide examples if possible or ask children to give them. Then all can participate in the Apply It activity.

Unit 5 Planning Guide

Verbs

3 weeks

		Checkup (PE)	Extra Practice (PE)	Graphic Organizer (BLM)	Writing Wrap-Up (BLM)	More Practice (TE)	Workbook Plus	Reteaching Workbook	Students Acquiring English Practice Book
1	Verbs *(163–164)*	187	196	5–1	5–4	196	56–57	37	43–44
2	Verbs That Tell About Now *(165–166)*	187	197	5–1	5–4	197	58–59	38	45–46
3	Pronouns and Verbs *(167–168)*	187	198	5–1	5–4	198	60–61	39	47–48
4	Verbs with *ed (169–170)*	187	199		5–4	199	62–63	40	49–50
	Revising Strategies: Sentence Fluency Combining Sentences: Action Parts *(171–172)*						64–65	41–42	
5	*ran, run* and *came, come (173–174)*	188	200	5–2	5–5	200	66–67	43	51–52
6	*saw, seen* and *went, gone (175–176)*	188	201	5–2	5–5	201	68–69	44	53–54
7	*did, done* and *gave, given (177–178)*	188	202	5–2	5–5	202	70–71	45	55–56
8	*is* and *are (179–180)*	188	203	5–3	5–5	203	72–73	46	57–58
9	*was* and *were (181–182)*	188	204	5–3	5–6	204	74–75	47	59–60
10	Contractions *(183–184)*	188	205		5–6	205	76–77	48	61–62
	Revising Strategies: Vocabulary Exact Verbs *(185)*						78	49	
	Enrichment *(186)*								
✓	**Cumulative Review** *(192–195)*								
✓	**Test Practice** *(190–191)*								63–64

Unit 5

Tools and Tips

- **Grammar Glossary,** *pp. H35–H39*

School-Home Connection

Suggestions for informing or involving family members in classroom activities and learning related to this unit are included in the Teacher's Edition throughout the unit.

Meeting Individual Needs

- **FOR SPECIAL NEEDS/INCLUSION:** *Houghton Mifflin English* Audiotape See also Reteaching.
- **FOR STUDENTS ACQUIRING ENGLISH:**
  - Notes and activities are included in this Teacher's Edition throughout the unit to help you adapt or use pupil book activities with students acquiring English.
  - Additional support is available for students at various stages of English proficiency: **Beginning/Preproduction, Early Production/Speech Emergence,** and **Intermediate/ Advanced**. See Students Acquiring English Practice Book.
  - Students can listen to the Try It Out activities on audiotape.
- **ENRICHMENT:** *p. 186*

All audiotape recordings are also available on CD.

Daily Language Practice

Each sentence or group of words includes two or three errors based on skills taught in this or previous Grammar units. Each day write one sentence on the chalkboard. Have children find the errors, and write the sentence correctly on a sheet of paper. To make the activity easier, identify the kinds of errors.

1. Henry feed his two pet goat. Sample: Henry feeds his two pet goats. **(verbs in the present, plural nouns with *s*)**
2. Cindy and Tim calls to the three child in the pool. Cindy and Tim call to the three children in the pool. **(verbs in the present, irregular plural nouns)**
3. each day we waits for the bus. Each day we wait for the bus. **(capitalization; pronouns and verbs)**
4. Last night I and Paul work a puzzle. Last night Paul and I worked a puzzle. **(naming yourself last; verbs in the past with *ed*)**
5. How many children have came to this picnic today. How many children have come to this picnic today? **(helping verbs with *come, came*; end punctuation/questions)**
6. I and Brian have saw that movie two times. Brian and I have seen that movie two times. **(naming yourself last; helping verbs with *saw, seen*)**
7. After school julia done his homework quickly. After school Julia did her homework quickly. **(capitalizing proper nouns; verbs *did* and *done*)**
8. Tobys' books is on the bottom shelf of the book-case. Toby's books are on the bottom shelf of the book-case. **(possessive nouns ending with *'s*; verbs *is* and *are*)**
9. Two clownes was in a purple and yellow car. Two clowns were in a purple and yellow car. **(plural nouns with *s*; verbs *was* and *were*)**
10. The four buss cant go out in the thick fog. The four buses can't go out in the thick fog. **(plural nouns with *es*; contractions with *not*)**

Additional Resources

Workbook Plus, Unit 5
Reteaching Workbook, Unit 5
Students Acquiring English Practice Book, Unit 5
Teacher's Resource Book
Audiotapes

Technology Tools

TEACHER'S RESOURCE DISK (for handwriting support)
INTERNET: http://www.eduplace.com/kids/hme/ or http://www.eduplace.com/rdg/hme/
Visit Education Place for an interactive quiz.

Assessment

Test Booklet, Unit 5

Keeping a Journal

Discuss with children the value of keeping a journal as a way of promoting self-expression and fluency. Encourage children to record their thoughts and ideas in a notebook. Inform students whether the journal will be private or will be reviewed periodically as a way of assisting growth. The following prompts may be useful for generating writing ideas.

Journal Prompts

- What games do you like to play outdoors? How do you play them?
- What would you do if you had a pet and it got lost?
- Tell about something that you like to make and how you make it.

Introducing the Unit

Using the Photograph

- Have children look at the photograph. Ask them what the children are doing in the photograph. (taking part in a sack race) Have a volunteer explain this kind of race. (Each runner has his or her legs in a sack or bag. Each person hops in the sack to try to be the first one to reach the finish line.)
- Ask what the girl in the middle does as she runs in the race. (She opens her mouth wide. She holds tightly to the sack. She jumps hard.)
- Have a volunteer read the caption aloud and act out the action. Remind children that a sentence has an action part. Expain that a **verb** is found in the action part. A verb names an action that someone or something does or did. Tell children that they will write sentences using verbs that describe the actions of these runners.

Grammar Song

See Blackline Master G-1 for a song to help children remember the concepts and rules taught in this unit.

Independent Writing

Children can benefit by having time each day or several times a week to write in their journals or do self-selected writing activities. Remind children to think about purpose and audience and choose an appropriate format for both.

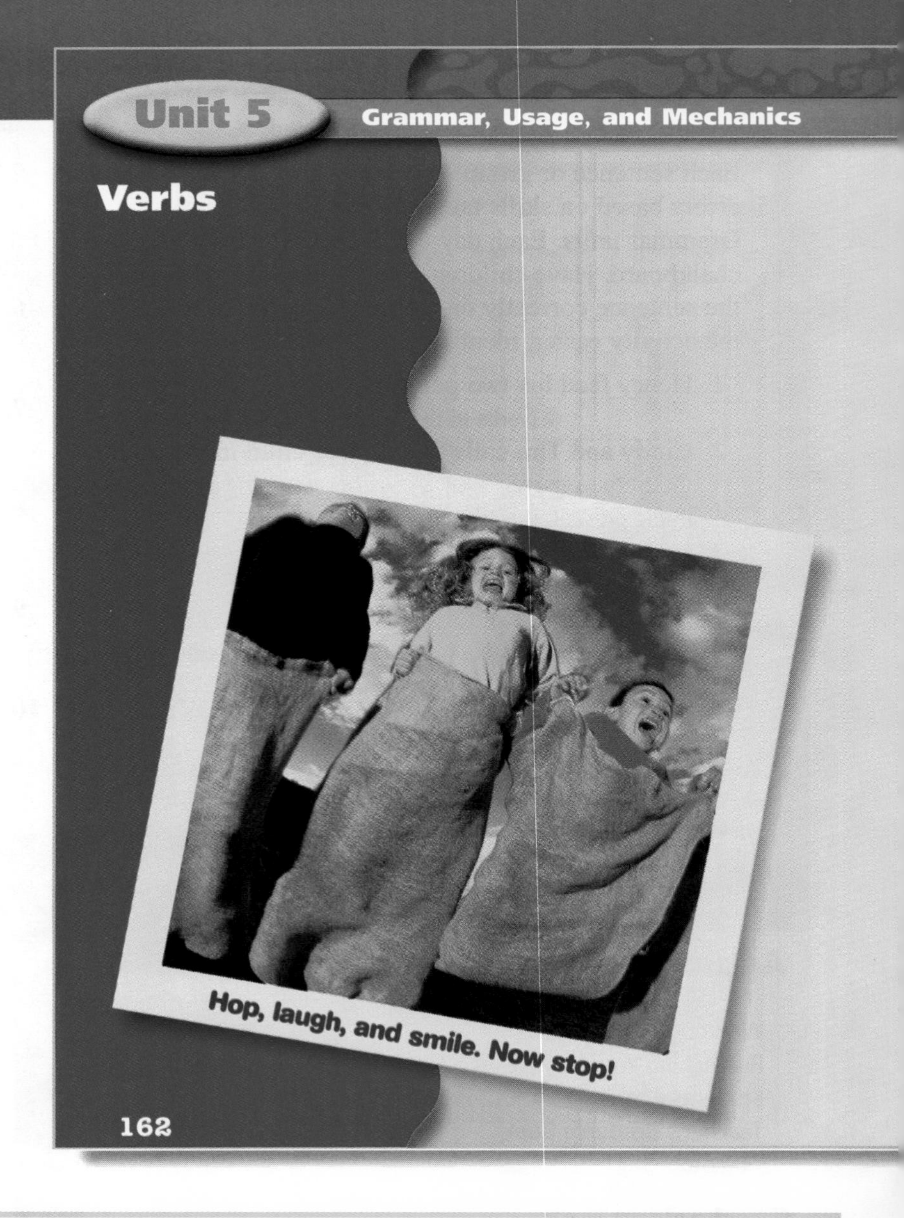

Hop, laugh, and smile. Now stop!

Shared Writing Activity

Work with children to write sentences using verbs that describe the actions of runners in a sack race.

1. Have children suggest verbs and verb phrases to describe the actions of runners in a sack race. Write them on the board, underlining the verbs. Encourage them to also include actions in addition to the ones shown in the photograph.
2. Ask volunteers to act out an action from the list, and have other children guess the pantomimed action.
3. Discuss with children whether some of the actions would be done in a particular order or whether they would be done simultaneously.
4. Work as a class to write sentences using the listed actions to create a paragraph about what runners in a sack race do. Children can give the runners' names to tell who is performing an action. Write the sentences in paragraph form on the chalkboard or on an overhead transparency. As you write, underline each verb and indicate the action part of each sentence.

Grammar 1

Verbs

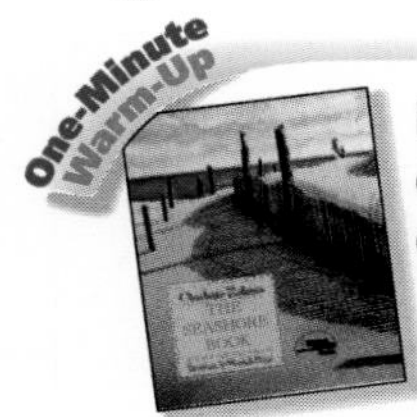

One-Minute Warm-Up

Read the sentence. Which word tells what it does to the cool sand? What do you think it is? What can you do with or on sand?

It warms the cool sand. *warms*; the sun; answers will vary.

—from The Seashore Book, by Charlotte Zolotow

A **verb** names an action that someone or something does or did. A verb is found in the action part of a sentence. What are the verbs in these sentences?

Alex **runs** beside the water. She **played** in the sand.

Try It Out

Speak Up Say each sentence, using a verb from the Word Box.

swim	dig	sails	blows

1. The wind blows.
2. A boat sails.
3. Fish swim.

Write It Now write each sentence and draw a line under the verb.

Example Children ______ in the sand.
Children dig in the sand. blows, sails, swim

Meeting Individual Needs

RETEACHING
ALTERNATIVE STRATEGY

- Write nouns, adjectives, and verbs related to a day at the beach on separate index cards and place them in a pile face down.
- Have each child choose a card from the pile. Ask each to read the card and decide if the word shows an action.
- Ask children to pantomime any words that show action (verbs). Have them say a naming part and add it to any verb they find to make sentences.

CHALLENGE
Have children write a book about an imaginary sea creature. Brainstorm actions the creature may do. Ask each child to choose one action and write a sentence about it. Children can illustrate one another's sentences.

FOR STUDENTS ACQUIRING ENGLISH
Act out verbs such as *sleep, jump, run.* Children guess what you are doing. Write *action verbs.* Call on a child to mime an action. The first child to guess correctly mimes the next action, and so on. Write the action verbs on the board under the heading.

Verbs

Lesson Objectives

Children will:
- identify verbs
- write informing sentences and identify verbs

One-Minute Warm-Up As children respond, list each response on the board. Point out that all the activities are action words.

Focus on Instruction

If children are not sure if a word is a verb, they can ask themselves if that word names a person, place, or thing. If so, the word is not a verb. If they can picture someone or something doing the action the word names, that word is probably a verb.

Try It Out

LISTENING AND SPEAKING Have half the class say the sentences aloud while the other half of the class listens for action words. When children hear an action word, they should pantomime it. Then have the class switch roles.

FOR STUDENTS ACQUIRING ENGLISH

- Have children listen to the Try It Out sentences on the audiotape. Distribute the SAE Practice page for Unit 5, Lesson 1. 
- Help children suggest sentences about the photo in the book. Ask, *What is the boat doing?* (*It is sailing*, or *It is moving*.) Keep in mind that when describing actions, the progressive tense may be the most natural, both for questions and responses. Next ask children to describe the art on the Practice page. Children listen and say the verb that best completes each sentence; check for correct pronunciation of -s endings. Then they write sentences.
  1. The girl _____ in the sand. (digs)
  2. The boys ______ shells. (find)

Summing Up Help children summarize these key points about the lesson: A **verb** names an action that someone or something does or did.

You may want to have children complete the parts related to this lesson on Blackline Master 5-1.

On Your Own

If children need help finding the verbs, have them read each sentence aloud, taking away one word at a time. For each missing word, ask children to notice whether they can still picture an action. If they cannot, then the missing word is the verb.

FOR STUDENTS ACQUIRING ENGLISH

Distribute the SAE Practice page for Unit 5, Lesson 1. Children underline the action verbs. Have children pronounce the verbs; listen for the -s ending in item 5.

1. We swim in the water.
2. The boys play in the sand.
3. They fill the pails with sand.

Writing Wrap-Up

Writing Tip: Have children think about what they did today. Have them make a list of verbs that fit their actions. See Blackline Master 5-4 for sample sentences.

SCHOOL-HOME CONNECTION

Have children interview family members about their day. Children may then choose one action that has been mentioned and use it in a sentence.

On Your Own

Write each sentence. Draw a line under the verb.

Example I make a sand house. I make a sand house.

1. I fill a pail.
2. I swim fast.
3. I eat lunch.
4. Birds fly by.

5–6. Look at Sam's photo album. Write the number of each photo. Next to the number, write the sentence that tells about the photo. Draw a line under the verb.

Example I find shells. I find shells.

- Girls wade in the water.
- Ron and I play in the sand.

5.

Ron and I play in the sand.

6.

Girls wade in the water.

Writing Wrap-Up

WRITING • THINKING • LISTENING • SPEAKING

INFORMING

Write Picture Labels

Draw pictures of yourself doing different things. Write a sentence about each picture. Read your sentences to a classmate. Have the classmate say each verb. Sentences will vary.

164 Verbs

For Extra Practice, see page 196.

Meeting Individual Needs

● RETEACHING WORKBOOK, page 37

1 Verbs

A **verb** names an action.
A mother bear **stands** in the river.

Write the verb that finishes each sentence.

Example The bear ____ for fish. The bear looks for fish. (well, looks)

1. The baby bear watches. (watches, fox)
2. Fish swim by the big bear. (bell, swim)
3. The mother bear waits. (waits, holes)
4. Then she moves fast. (woods, moves)
5. The bear holds up a big fish. (holds, tree)

▲■ WORKBOOK PLUS, pages 56-57

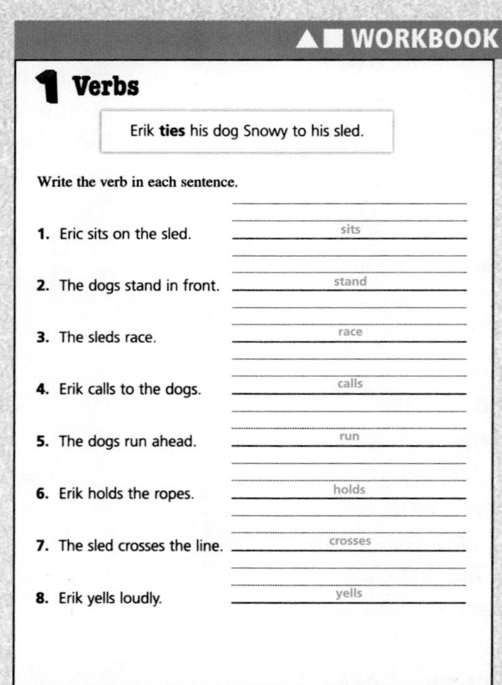

1 Verbs

Erik **ties** his dog Snowy to his sled.

Write the verb in each sentence.

1. Eric sits on the sled. sits
2. The dogs stand in front. stand
3. The sleds race. race
4. Erik calls to the dogs. calls
5. The dogs run ahead. run
6. Erik holds the ropes. holds
7. The sled crosses the line. crosses
8. Erik yells loudly. yells

1 Verbs (continued from page 56)

Challenge

Find the verb in the Word Box that goes with each picture clue. Write the verb in the puzzle.

laugh	hop	plant	shake	sit	eat

ACROSS — Example 1. laugh; 3. shake; 5. plant

DOWN — 2. hop; 3. sit; 4. eat

Writing Application: A Story NARRATING

Write a story about a dog that can talk and fly. Try to use a different verb in each sentence. Circle the verbs.
Students to respond on separate paper. Answers will vary.

Grammar

2 Verbs That Tell About Now

Clap your hands as a classmate watches. Then clap together. For each action, say a sentence to tell what you are doing. Repeat with other actions.

Sentences will vary.

A verb can name an action that is happening now. Add **s** to this kind of a verb when it tells about a noun that **names one**. Read the sentences. Which noun names one? Does the verb end with s?

A **girl** walks. The girls walk.

Try It Out

Speak Up Say each sentence, using the correct verb.

1. The girls (swing, swings) high.
2. Lee (run, runs) very fast.
3. Hannah (jump, jumps) down.

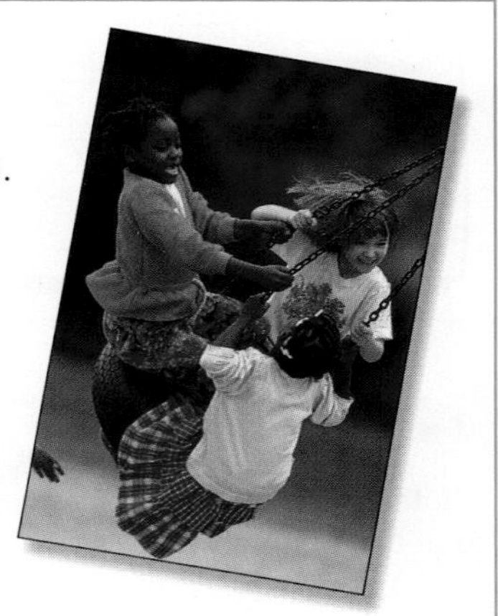

Write It Now write the sentences correctly.

Example Scott (slide, slides).
Scott slides.

The girls swing high.
Lee runs very fast.
Hannah jumps down.

Verbs That Tell About Now

Lesson Objectives

Children will:
- use the correct forms of verbs in the present tense
- write a book summary, and have others identify present-tense verbs

One-Minute Warm-Up Have volunteers name all the actions that are happening now in the classroom. List their responses on the chalkboard.

Focus on Instruction

If children need help choosing the correct verb, ask whether the naming part of each sentence names one or more than one.

Try It Out

VIEWING Have children look at the picture to ask questions about what is happening now. Ask them to include the number of people they are talking about in their questions. Children can write their questions and answers in a chart like the one shown. (Sample sentences are shown)

Questions	Answers
What is one girl doing?	One girl swings.
What are two girls doing?	Two girls swing.

Meeting Individual Needs

RETEACHING
ALTERNATIVE STRATEGY
- Write in red on a strip of paper: *walks, eats, laughs, jumps.* Write in black: *see-saw, dig, sleep, swim.*
- Give a child a verb ending in *s* to pantomime. When others identify the action, write the child's name and the action in a sentence. Underline the verb. Repeat with the other verbs and ask how they are alike.
- Have children pantomime verbs that do not end in *s.* Say that when two people do the action, the verb does not end in *s.*

CHALLENGE
Have children write about two friends that do things together, have a fight and do things alone, and then make up. Children can exchange stories, circle the verbs about one friend with one color, and use another color for verbs about both friends.

FOR STUDENTS ACQUIRING ENGLISH
Prepare verb cards with the *-s* form on one side, the simple form on the other. Have individuals or groups stand. Say a sentence with the verb that fits the number; children repeat. Continue until children can choose the form.

FOR STUDENTS ACQUIRING ENGLISH
- Have children listen to the Try It Out sentences on the audiotape. Distribute the SAE Practice page for Unit 5, Lesson 2.
- Help children suggest sentences about the photo in the book. Rapidly show a verb card and a card with a boy or a girl as you raise your fingers to indicate how many; have children chant along with you as you say, for example, *One boy sings, two boys slide, One girl plays, four girls hide.* Children can choose the verb, person, and number, and lead the chant. Next, have children describe the art on the Practice page; help with vocabulary. Children listen and say the correct verb. Then they write each sentence.
Example: Mary (swings, swing).

Summing Up Help children summarize these key points about the lesson:

When a verb names an action that is **happening now**, add s to that verb to tell about a noun that names **one**.

You may want to have children complete the parts related to this lesson on Blackline Master 5-1.

On Your Own

If children have trouble finding the correct verb, have them ask:

How many people (things) are in the naming part?

FOR STUDENTS ACQUIRING ENGLISH

Distribute the SAE Practice page for Unit 5, Lesson 2. Discuss the art; assist with vocabulary. Explain that we refer to most animals as *he* or *she*. Children underline the correct verb. Then they write each sentence.

1. William (throws, throw) the ball.
2. The dog (gets, get) the ball.

Writing Wrap-Up

Writing Tip: Suggest that children use a simple flow chart to help them list the main events that occur in the book. See Blackline Master 5-4 for a sample summary.

TECHNOLOGY CONNECTION

Children may use available drawing software to add sketches of characters or events to their summaries.

On Your Own

Choose and write the correct verb for each sentence.

Example The ball (roll, rolls) in the lake. rolls

1. A big dog (jump, jumps) into the water.
2. The dog (get, gets) the ball.
3. He (swim, swims) to shore.
4. The girls (thank, thanks) the wet dog.

5–8. Now copy the title and sentence below. Correctly write the sentences above to finish Lily's book summary.

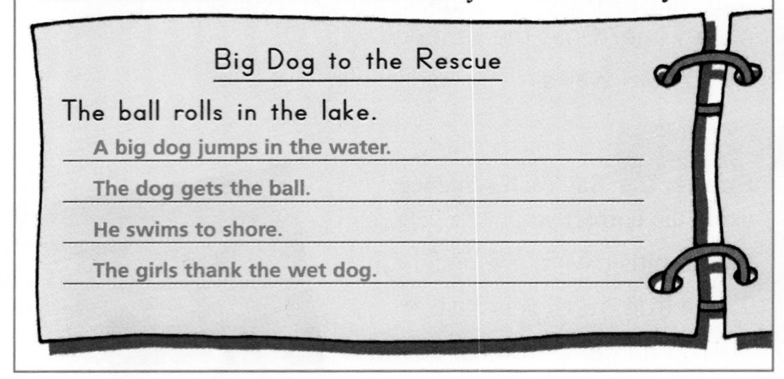

Big Dog to the Rescue

The ball rolls in the lake.

A big dog jumps in the water.

The dog gets the ball.

He swims to shore.

The girls thank the wet dog.

WRITING • THINKING • LISTENING • SPEAKING

SUMMARIZING

Write a Book Summary

Write sentences telling what happens in a book. Use verbs that tell about now. Read your summary to a classmate. Have the classmate name the verbs that tell about now.

 For Extra Practice, see page 197.

Meeting Individual Needs

● RETEACHING WORKBOOK, page 38

2 Verbs That Tell About Now

Add s to a verb that tells about one.
One turtle **swims**. Two turtles **swim**.

Write each sentence. Use the verb that tells about the underlined naming part.

Example Al and Li (bring, brings) food. Al and Li bring food.

1. Li (clean, cleans) the bowl.
   Li cleans the bowl.
2. Al and Li (care, cares) for the turtles.
   Al and Li care for the turtles.
3. Li (put, puts) the turtles in the tub.
   Li puts the turtles in the tub.
4. The three turtles (slide, slides).
   The three turtles slide.
5. Li (place, places) them in the clean bowl.
   Li places them in the clean bowl.

▲■ WORKBOOK PLUS, pages 58–59

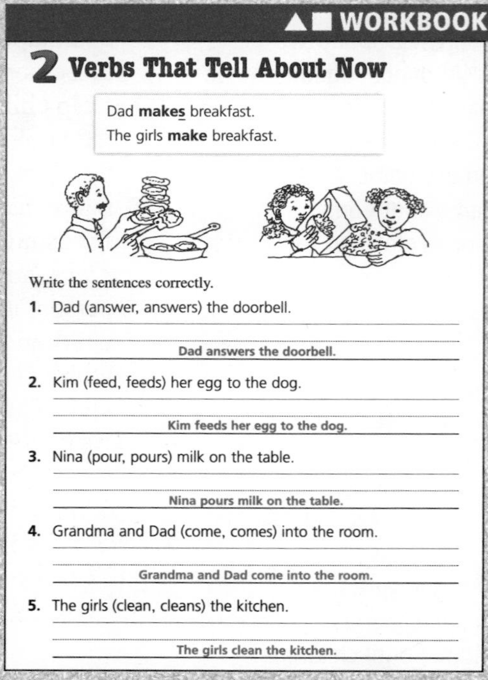

2 Verbs That Tell About Now

Dad **makes** breakfast.
The girls **make** breakfast.

Write the sentences correctly.

1. Dad (answer, answers) the doorbell.
   Dad answers the doorbell.
2. Kim (feed, feeds) her egg to the dog.
   Kim feeds her egg to the dog.
3. Nina (pour, pours) milk on the table.
   Nina pours milk on the table.
4. Grandma and Dad (come, comes) into the room.
   Grandma and Dad come into the room.
5. The girls (clean, cleans) the kitchen.
   The girls clean the kitchen.

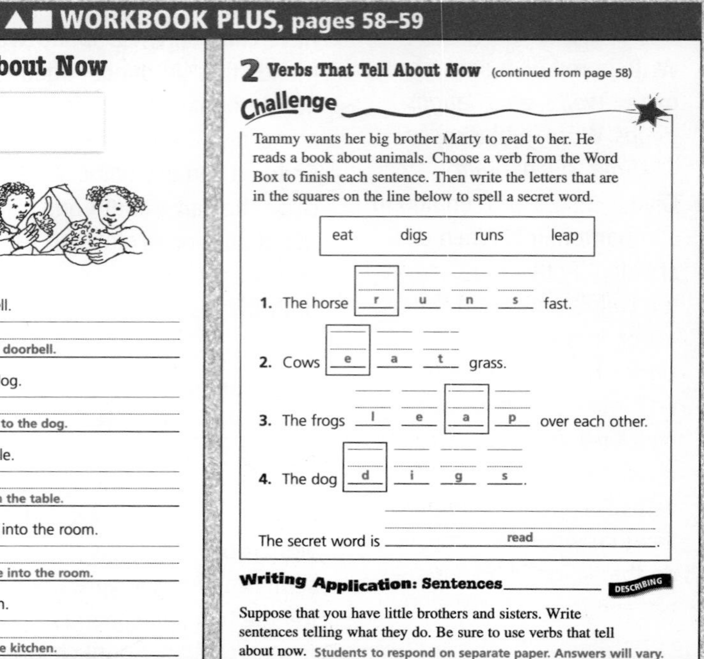

2 Verbs That Tell About Now (continued from page 58)

Challenge

Tammy wants her big brother Marty to read to her. He reads a book about animals. Choose a verb from the Word Box to finish each sentence. Then write the letters that are in the squares on the line below to spell a secret word.

eat	digs	runs	leap

1. The horse r u n s fast.
2. Cows e a t grass.
3. The frogs l e a p over each other.
4. The dog d i g s.

The secret word is read.

Writing Application: Sentences DESCRIBING

Suppose that you have little brothers and sisters. Write sentences telling what they do. Be sure to use verbs that tell about now. Students to respond on separate paper. Answers will vary.

Grammar / Usage

3 Pronouns and Verbs

Sample answers: It drops. They crack. She looks.

One-Minute Warm-Up

Make up three sentences about the picture. Use the words they, it, and she.

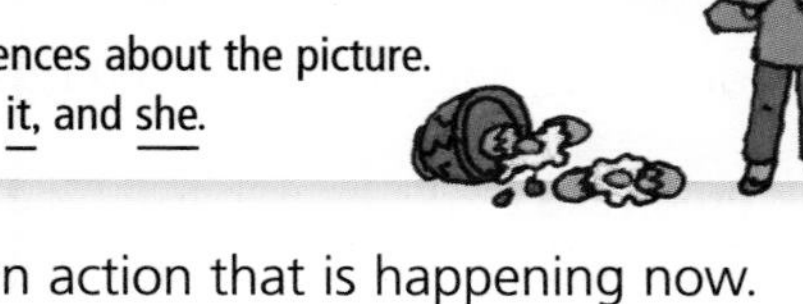

A **verb** can name an action that is happening now. A **pronoun** can tell who or what is doing the action. If the pronoun he, she, or it comes before a verb that tells about now, add s or es to the verb.

She cracks the eggs. **We crack** the eggs.

He mixes the eggs. **You mix** the eggs.

Try It Out

Speak Up Say each sentence, using the correct verb.

1. I (get, gets) paint.
2. She (reach, reaches) for a hammer.
3. He (fix, fixes) the birdhouse.
4. It (look, looks) good.

Write It Now write each sentence, using the correct verb.

Example We (find, finds) some wood.
We find some wood. get, reaches, fixes, looks

Meeting Individual Needs

RETEACHING
ALTERNATIVE STRATEGY

- Draw sketches of people and things in the classroom to represent each pronoun. Group and label the sketches to correspond with the two groups of pronouns.
- Write several verbs on separate cards. Write each verb twice, once with the s or *es* ending, and once without.
- Have children match each verb to a sketch and read the pronoun and verb aloud. Help them focus on which group always takes verbs with *s* or *es* endings and which group does not.

CHALLENGE
List all the pronouns on the chalkboard. Have children write a list of verbs, some with *s* or *es* endings and some without. They can exchange verb lists with a partner and write a story using all the verbs and as many pronouns as they can.

FOR STUDENTS ACQUIRING ENGLISH
Prepare sets of strips with subject pronouns and regular verbs, some with *–s* and some without. Use capital letters on the pronouns and periods after the verbs. Have children work in small groups to combine the strips in as many ways as possible.

Pronouns and Verbs

Lesson Objectives

Children will:

- use the correct forms of verbs with pronouns
- proofread for correct verb usage
- write a narrative using pronouns, and have others identify pronouns and verbs

One-Minute Warm-Up Help volunteers write the sentences on the chalkboard. Have them use one color chalk to underline the action word and another color to underline the word that tells who or what did the action. Have them tell how they knew which color to use.

Focus on Instruction

Have children draw pictures representing the pronouns in each group. For example, they may draw a boy, a girl, and two friends to represent *he*, *we*, and *she*. Have them label their drawings.

Try It Out

LISTENING AND SPEAKING Have a volunteer say aloud one of the sentences. The rest of the class should listen for pronouns and verbs. Ask them to make a two-column chart and list the pronouns and correct verbs they hear.

Pronoun	Verb
I	get
She	reaches
He	fixes
It	looks

FOR STUDENTS ACQUIRING ENGLISH

- Have children listen to the Try It Out sentences on the audiotape. Distribute the SAE Practice page for Unit 5, Lesson 3.
- Help children suggest sentences about the art in the book and on the Practice page. To practice pronouns have children place 3 x 5 cards with pronouns in front of you, themselves, and one or more classmates. Then put the wrong pronouns with individuals or groups and have children fix the mistakes. Ask children to find the difference in the endings for the verbs *cracks* and *mixes*. Tell children to listen for the extra syllable in additional examples such as *splashes*, *watches*, *wishes*, *fishes*. Children say the correct verb and write the sentence.
Example: He (watch, watches) his mother.

Summing Up Help children summarize these key points about the lesson:

A **verb** can name an action that is happening now. When *he*, *she* or *it* comes before a now verb, add *s* or *es* to the verb. When *I*, *you*, *we*, or *they* comes before a now verb, do not add *s* or *es* to the verb.

You may want to have children complete the parts related to this lesson on Blackline Master 5-1.

On Your Own

If children have difficulty identifying the correct verb, suggest that they refer to the drawings they made representing the different pronouns.

FOR STUDENTS ACQUIRING ENGLISH

Distribute the SAE Practice page for Unit 5, Lesson 3. Discuss the art. Ask, *What are they making?* Assist with vocabulary. Children underline the correct verb. Then they write each sentence.

1. She (cut, <u>cuts</u>) the fruit.
2. We (fills, <u>fill</u>) the bowls.

Writing Wrap-Up

Writing Tip: Have children list characters and their corresponding pronouns before they begin writing. See Blackline Master 5-4 for a sample story.

TECHNOLOGY CONNECTION

Children may want to use clip art to illustrate their stories.

On Your Own

Write each sentence, using the correct verb.

Example We (make, makes) a cake. We make a cake.

1. She (mix, mixes) the butter and the sugar. mixes
2. I (add, adds) the milk and the eggs. add

3–6. Proofread Carl's how-to list. Find four mistakes in using verbs with pronouns. Correct the verbs and write the list correctly.

Example I finds the berries. I find the berries.

How We ~~Makes~~ Make Fruit Salad

We ~~brings~~ bring four kinds of fruit.

You chop the fruit.

He ~~mix~~ mixes everything together.

She ~~serve~~ serves the fruit salad.

WRITING • THINKING • LISTENING • SPEAKING

NARRATING

Write a Story

Write about an adventure a boy, a girl, and some animals have. In some sentences use <u>he</u>, <u>she</u>, <u>it</u>, or <u>they</u> instead of nouns. Read your story. Have classmates name the pronouns and verbs.

 For Extra Practice, see page 198.

Meeting Individual Needs

● RETEACHING WORKBOOK, page 39

3 Pronouns and Verbs

When the pronoun <u>he</u>, <u>she</u>, or <u>it</u> comes before a verb that tells about now, add <u>s</u> or <u>es</u> to the verb.

He **rub<u>s</u>** his nose. She **wash<u>es</u>** her hands.

Write each sentence correctly.

Example He (take, takes) a tissue. He takes a tissue.

1. It (feel, feels) as if I have a cold. It feels as if I have a cold.
2. He (coughs, cough) loudly. He coughs loudly.
3. She (sleep, sleeps) all day. She sleeps all day.
4. He (wishes, wish) the cold would go away! He wishes the cold would go away!

▲■ WORKBOOK PLUS, pages 60-61

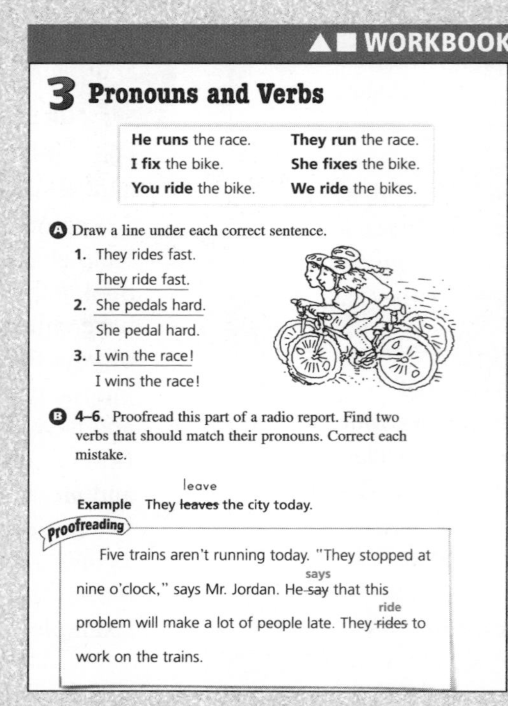

3 Pronouns and Verbs

He runs the race.	**They run** the race.
I fix the bike.	**She fixes** the bike.
You ride the bike.	**We ride** the bikes.

A Draw a line under each correct sentence.

1. They rides fast. <u>They ride fast.</u>
2. <u>She pedals hard.</u> She pedal hard.
3. <u>I win the race!</u> I wins the race!

B 4–6. Proofread this part of a radio report. Find two verbs that should match their pronouns. Correct each mistake.

Example They ~~leaves~~ leave the city today.

Proofreading

Five trains aren't running today. "They stopped at nine o'clock," says Mr. Jordan. He ~~say~~ says that this problem will make a lot of people late. They ~~rides~~ ride to work on the trains.

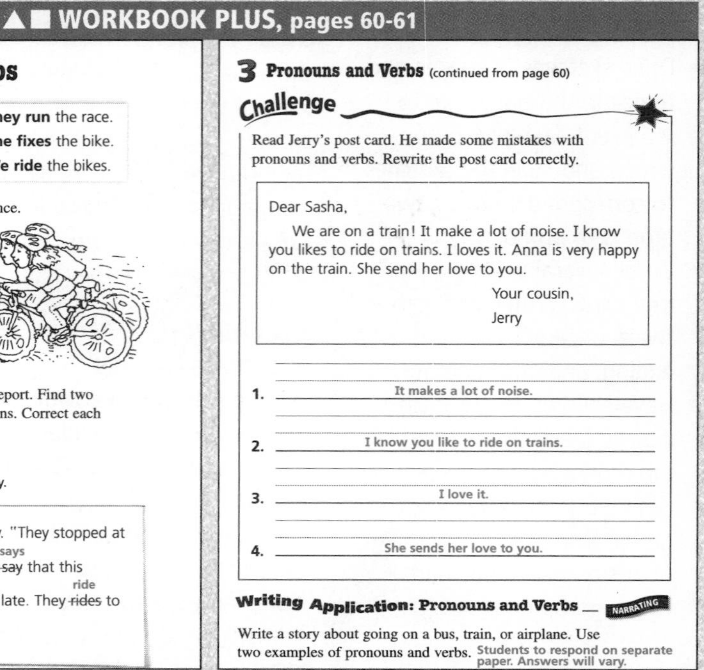

3 Pronouns and Verbs (continued from page 60)

Challenge

Read Jerry's post card. He made some mistakes with pronouns and verbs. Rewrite the post card correctly.

Dear Sasha,
We are on a train! It make a lot of noise. I know you likes to ride on trains. I loves it. Anna is very happy on the train. She send her love to you.
Your cousin,
Jerry

1. It makes a lot of noise.
2. I know you like to ride on trains.
3. I love it.
4. She sends her love to you.

Writing Application: Pronouns and Verbs NARRATING

Write a story about going on a bus, train, or airplane. Use two examples of pronouns and verbs. Students to respond on separate paper. Answers will vary.

Grammar

4 Verbs with ed

One-Minute Warm-Up

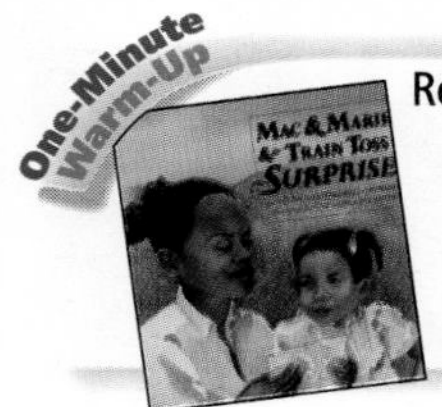

Read the sentences. Which two words tell what Mac did?

Mac listened some more to the ocean sound. He smiled at the beautiful shell.

—from Mac and Marie and the Train Toss Surprise, by Elizabeth Fitzgerald Howard

listened and *smiled*

Some verbs name actions that are happening now. Other verbs name actions that happened before now, or in the **past**. Add **ed** to most verbs to show that the action happened in the past.

We walk on the beach.

Yesterday we walk**ed** on the beach.

Try It Out

Speak Up Say each sentence, using the verb that names a past action.

1. Boats (rocked, rock) in the water.
2. Waves (wash, washed) the rocks.

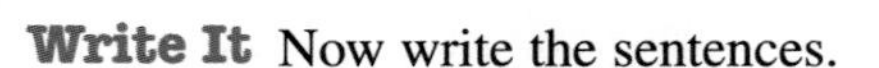

Write It Now write the sentences.

Example We (watch, watched) birds.
We watched birds.

Boats rocked in the water.
Waves washed the rocks.

Verbs with ed

Lesson Objectives

Children will:

- identify verbs in the past tense
- form the past tense of regular verbs correctly
- write a journal entry expressing past events, and have others identify past-tense verbs

One-Minute Warm-Up Have volunteers write on the chalkboard the two words that tell what Mac did. Ask them to circle the smaller verb inside each (listen, smile).

Focus on Instruction

Tell children that clue words in sentences can indicate when actions happen, such as today, now, last night, yesterday.

Try It Out

VIEWING Have children suggest verbs that name a past action that happened in the illustration. Children can then use the verbs in sentences. Record their responses in a chart. (Sample responses are shown.)

Verbs	Sentences
covered	The water covered the sand.
walked	The birds walked on the beach.

Meeting Individual Needs

RETEACHING
ALTERNATIVE STRATEGY

- Ask a volunteer to walk around the room. Meanwhile, write the following on the chalkboard: (child's name) walks *in the room.* Have children identify the verb *walks.* Point out that it tells about an action that is happening now.
- Have the child who is walking sit down. On the chalkboard, write this sentence: (child's name) *walked in the room.* Have children identify the verb *walked.* Explain that *ed* was added to the verb *walk* to show that the action happened in the past.

CHALLENGE

Have children list actions that have happened in the class so far. For example: *walked, looked, talked, listened.* They can exchange papers and write a short play about the class using the past-tense verbs. Model dialogue form on the chalkboard.

FOR STUDENTS ACQUIRING ENGLISH

Perform a series of actions involving regular verbs. Ask *What did I do?* Children respond in the past. For example, *You opened the door.* Write the response. Have a child underline the verbs and mark the endings with colored chalk.

FOR STUDENTS ACQUIRING ENGLISH

- Have children listen to the Try It Out sentences on the audiotape. Distribute the SAE Practice page for Unit 5, Lesson 4.
- Help children suggest sentences about the photo in the book and the art on the Practice page. Write the following: *yesterday, last Friday, last week, this morning*. Ask if these tell an action is happening now or happened in the past. (the past) Use these expressions and regular verbs with things you did. For example, *I visited my aunt yesterday*. Ask children what they did. Next, children listen and choose the past form of the verb. Then they write the sentence.
  1. I (paint, painted) a picture.
  2. My sister (played, play) with blocks.

Summing Up Help children summarize these key points about the lesson:

> Some verbs name actions that happened before now, or in the **past**. Add *ed* to most verbs to show the past.

You may want to have children complete the parts related to this lesson on Blackline Master 5-1.

On Your Own

If children have difficulty, remind them that the ending *ed* signals the past.

FOR STUDENTS ACQUIRING ENGLISH

Distribute the SAE Practice page for Unit 5, Lesson 4. Contrast the vowels in *pecked*, *peeked*, *picked*. To clarify meaning, give examples in context; have children repeat the verbs after you. Children write the verb that tells about the camping trip last weekend.
Example: We _____ next to the lake. (camp) *(camped)*

Writing Wrap-Up

Writing Tip: Suggest that children organize their day in parts, using such phrases as *In the morning*, *After school*, and *At night* to tell what they did. See Blackline Master 5-4 for a sample journal entry.

SCHOOL-HOME CONNECTION

Ask children to interview family members about things they did earlier in the day. Have them write what they learn in a short paragraph using past-tense verbs.

On Your Own

Write each sentence, using the verb that tells about the past.

Example We (look, looked) in the water.
We looked in the water.

1. We (discover, discovered) little fish.
2. Crabs (peeked, peek) out from rocks.
3. Seaweed (float, floated) by.
4. Justin (picked, pick) up a shell.

5–7. Copy Flora's journal entry. Change each verb in ( ) so that the sentences tell about the past.

Example My family (camps) _____ near the beach.
My family camped near the beach.

We (fish) fished from the dock.
We (play) played in the sand.
We (cook) cooked dinner over a campfire.

Writing Wrap-Up

WRITING • THINKING • LISTENING • SPEAKING

EXPRESSING

Write a Journal Entry

Write about what you did yesterday. Use verbs that tell about the past. Read your sentences to a classmate. Have the classmate name the verbs. Compare what you did.
Responses will vary.

 For Extra Practice, see page 199.

Meeting Individual Needs

● RETEACHING WORKBOOK, page 40

4 Verbs with ed

Add ed to a verb to show that something happened in the **past**.
Now I **play** a trick. Yesterday I **played** a trick.

Write the verb that tells about the past to finish each sentence.

Example My brother and sister ____ for me. (look, looked)
My brother and sister looked for me.

1. I waited behind my door. (wait, waited)
2. I stayed very quiet. (stayed, stay)
3. Cal and Beth walked by my door. (walked, walk)
4. I jumped out at them. (jumped, jump)
5. We laughed at my trick. (laugh, laughed)

▲■ WORKBOOK PLUS, pages 62–63

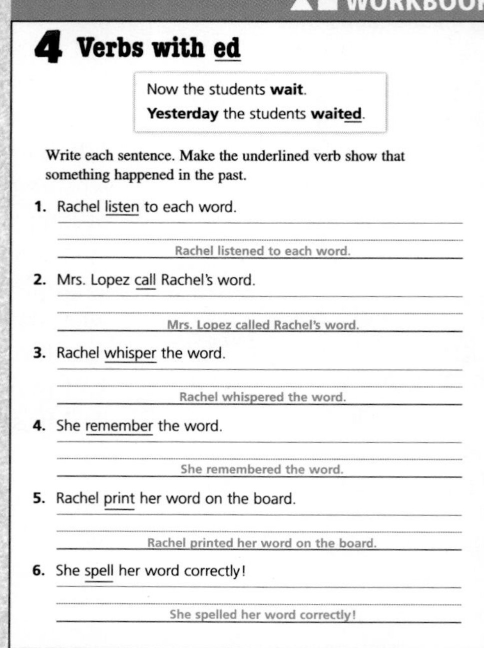

4 Verbs with ed

Now the students **wait**.
Yesterday the students **waited**.

Write each sentence. Make the underlined verb show that something happened in the past.

1. Rachel listen to each word.
   Rachel listened to each word.
2. Mrs. Lopez call Rachel's word.
   Mrs. Lopez called Rachel's word.
3. Rachel whisper the word.
   Rachel whispered the word.
4. She remember the word.
   She remembered the word.
5. Rachel print her word on the board.
   Rachel printed her word on the board.
6. She spell her word correctly!
   She spelled her word correctly!

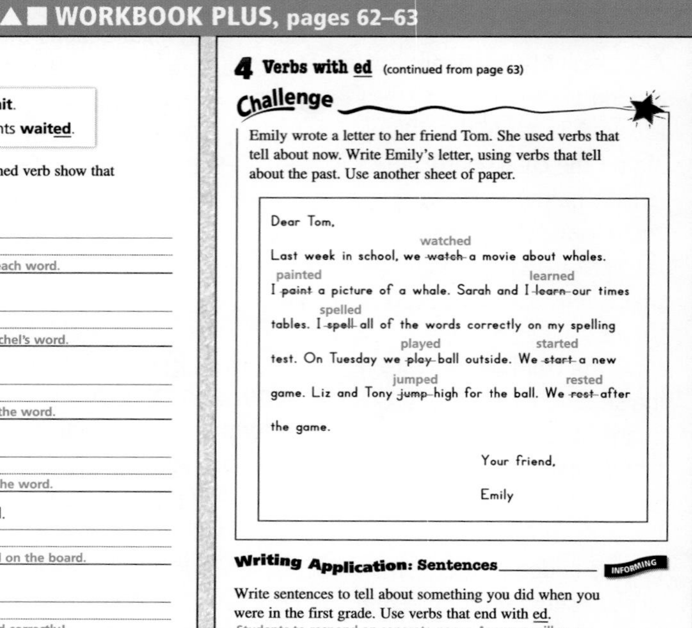

4 Verbs with ed (continued from page 63)

Challenge

Emily wrote a letter to her friend Tom. She used verbs that tell about now. Write Emily's letter, using verbs that tell about the past. Use another sheet of paper.

Dear Tom,

Last week in school, we ~~watch~~ watched a movie about whales. I ~~paint~~ painted a picture of a whale. Sarah and I ~~learn~~ learned our times tables. I ~~spell~~ spelled all of the words correctly on my spelling test. On Tuesday we ~~play~~ played ball outside. We ~~start~~ started a new game. Liz and Tony ~~jump~~ jumped high for the ball. We ~~rest~~ rested after the game.

Your friend,
Emily

Writing Application: Sentences INFORMING

Write sentences to tell about something you did when you were in the first grade. Use verbs that end with ed.
Students to respond on separate paper. Answers will vary.

Revising Strategies — Sentence Fluency

Combining Sentences: Action Parts

Joining Action Parts You may write two sentences that have the same naming part. Join them to make one longer sentence. Write the naming part. Then write the two **action parts** with and between them.

We **went on a walk**.

We **looked at plants**.

We **went on a walk** and **looked at plants**.

Try It Out

Speak Up/Write It Read the two sentences next to each number. Use and to join their action parts. Then say and write the new longer sentence.

Example We took paper. We drew plants.
We took paper and drew plants.

1. Ann saw flowers.
   Ann smelled one.
   Ann saw flowers and smelled one.
2. I drew a fern.
   I colored it.
   I drew a fern and colored it.

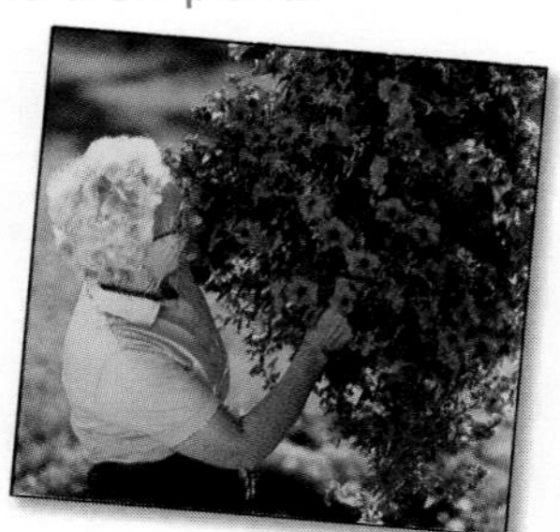

Combining Sentences: Action Parts

Lesson Objective

Children will:

- use *and* to join the action parts of two sentences to form one new sentence

Focus on Instruction

- Remind children that they know how to join two naming parts with *and*. Tell them that now they will do the same thing with action parts of sentences.
- Go over the example with children. Point out that they should look for the words that are the same in both sentences. (We) Explain that these words can become the naming part of a single new sentence.

Try It Out

Speak Up/Write It Read the example with the class. Encourage them to name the repeated naming part in the two sentences. (We) Then have them look at the answer. Point out that the sentence tells the two things that "we" did.

- When children write each sentence, remind them to join the action parts with *and*.

Meeting Individual Needs

● RETEACHING WORKBOOK, page 41

Combining Sentences: Action Parts

When two sentences have the same naming part, you can use and to join the action parts.

Two sentences: This picture **is new**. This picture **is funny**.

One sentence: This picture is **new** and **funny**.

Joining Action Parts Read each sentence pair. Join the action parts. Complete the new sentence.

Example Deena draws comics. Deena paints pictures.
Deena draws comics and paints pictures.

1. Artie helps Deena. Artie mixes the paints.
   Artie helps Deena and mixes the paints.
2. The comics are funny. The comics are colorful.
   The comics are funny and colorful.
3. I laugh at the comics. I read them every day.
   I laugh at the comics and read them every day.
4. Deena is a good artist. Deena is a good friend.
   Deena is a good artist and a good friend.

▲■ WORKBOOK PLUS, page 64

Combining Sentences: Action Parts

Two sentences: My brother **cooks**. My brother **bakes**.

One sentence: My brother **cooks** and **bakes**.

Joining Action Parts 1-4. Read each underlined sentence pair. Join the action parts. Write the new paragraph.

He will bake a big cake. He will frost it. Jana will pour the juice. Jana will serve the cake. Mom will laugh. Mom will smile at us. She will taste her cake. She will enjoy her birthday party. We'll all have a great time!

He will bake a big cake and frost it. Jana will pour the juice and serve the cake. Mom will laugh and smile at us. She will taste her cake and enjoy her birthday party. We'll all have a great time!

Combining Sentences: Action Parts

Apply It

- Read the example aloud to the class. Have children identify the naming part in each sentence. (light) Then ask them to identify the action parts. Point out that they can join the action parts with *and* to make a new sentence.
- Have children complete the revising activity independently. Be sure they understand that they should focus on the pairs of underlined sentences.

Have children find places in their own writing in progress where they can join the action parts of two sentences to form one longer sentence.

FOR STUDENTS ACQUIRING ENGLISH

Distribute two strips of paper to each child. Ask them to write a sentence beginning with *We* on each slip. Then ask them to cut the sentences and add an "and" to make one sentence which they mount on a piece of paper and share with the class. Repeat for all pronouns.

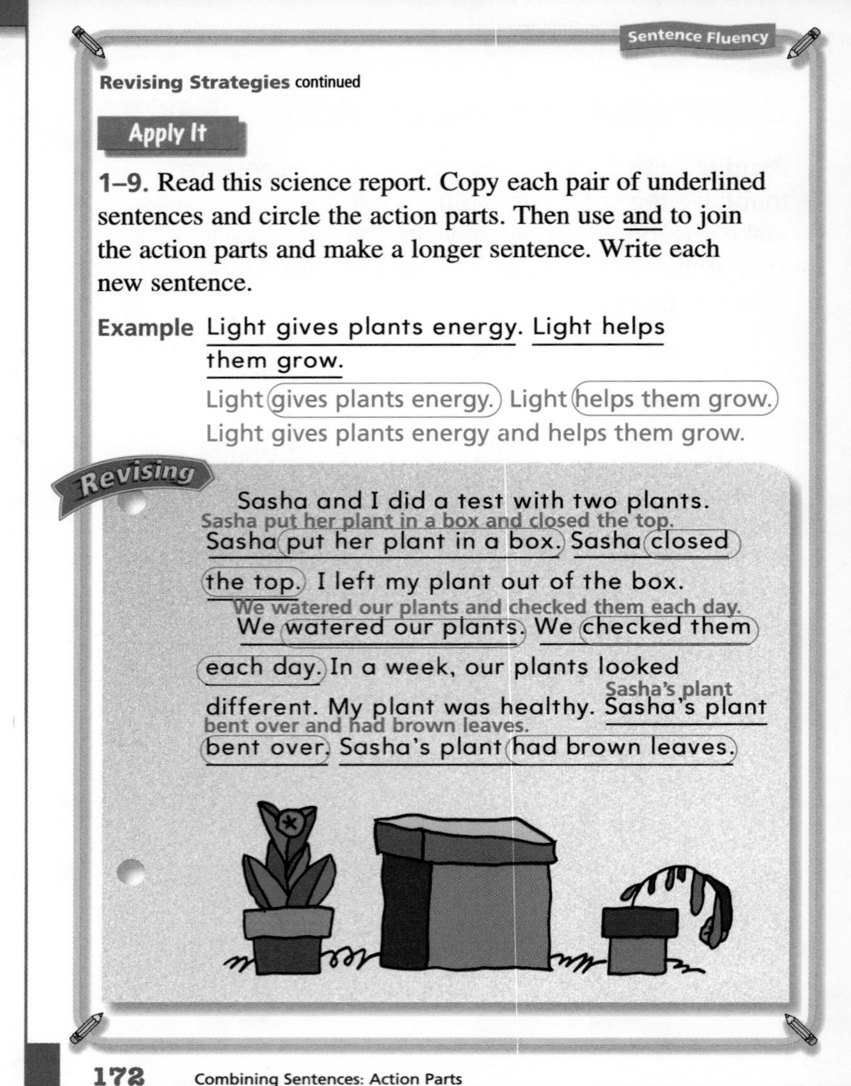
Sentence Fluency

Revising Strategies continued

Apply It

1–9. Read this science report. Copy each pair of underlined sentences and circle the action parts. Then use and to join the action parts and make a longer sentence. Write each new sentence.

Example Light gives plants energy. Light helps them grow.
Light (gives plants energy.) Light (helps them grow.)
Light gives plants energy and helps them grow.

Revising

Sasha and I did a test with two plants. Sasha (put her plant in a box.) Sasha (closed the top.) I left my plant out of the box. We (watered our plants.) We (checked them each day.) In a week, our plants looked different. My plant was healthy. Sasha's plant (bent over.) Sasha's plant (had brown leaves.)

Sasha put her plant in a box and closed the top.
We watered our plants and checked them each day.
Sasha's plant bent over and had brown leaves.

172 Combining Sentences: Action Parts

Meeting Individual Needs

● RETEACHING WORKBOOK, page 42

Combining Sentences: Action Parts

When you join two action parts, use and between the two action parts.

Two sentences:	Martine **swam in the pool**. Martine **splashed me**.
One sentence:	Martine **swam in the pool** and **splashed me**.

Joining Action Parts Read each sentence pair. Use and to join the action parts. Write the new sentence.

Example The town pool is big. The town pool has six lifeguards.
The town pool is big and has six lifeguards.

1. I swim with my sister. I swim with my brother.
   I swim with my sister and my brother.
2. We play water games. We have races.
   We play water games and have races.
3. My aunt takes us swimming. My aunt watches us.
   My aunt takes us swimming and watches us.
4. She tells us when to stop. She tells us when to dry off.
   She tells us when to stop and dry off.

▲■ WORKBOOK PLUS, page 65

Combining Sentences: Action Parts

Two sentences:	Laura sings very well. Laura dances nicely.
One sentence:	Laura **sings very well** and **dances nicely**.

Joining Action Parts Read each underlined sentence pair. Join the naming parts. Write the new sentences.

The thunder was booming. The thunder was crashing. Lightning flashed in my eyes. Lightning scared the dog. This was a bad storm. It flooded the street. It blew down trees. The rain made huge puddles. The rain ran down the street. I was glad when it was over.

1. The thunder was booming and crashing.
2. Lightning flashed in my eyes and scared the dog.
3. It flooded the street and blew down trees.
4. The rain made huge puddles and ran down the street.

Grammar / Usage

5 ran, run and came, come

What is wrong with the answer to this riddle? The verb is incorrect;

How can you fix it? use ran or has run.

Riddle Why did the clock lose the race?

Answer It run out of time.

The **helping verbs** has and have are used with run and come to tell about the past. Has and have are not used with ran and came. These **verbs** already tell about the past.

Dad and Uncle Ed **came** to the race.

They **have come** often.

Uncle Ed **ran** on a team in school.

He **has run** in many races.

Try It Out

Speak Up Say each sentence, using the correct verb.

1. A dog has (ran, run) after Amy.
2. Two kittens have (ran, run) after the dog.
3. Now the kittens have (came, come) back.
4. They (came, come) back a while ago.

Write It Now write the sentences correctly. run, come, run, came

Example Amy (ran, run) to the barn. Amy ran to the barn.

Meeting Individual Needs

RETEACHING
ALTERNATIVE STRATEGY

- Divide the class into four groups (have, has, run, come). Give each group member a card with their group's word on it.
- Explain that the *has* and *have* groups are the helpers. Write cloze sentences on the chalkboard and have the *run* and *come* members put their cards in the blanks. For example: She (come) to the race.
- Ask the *has* and *have* members to add their cards to help make the sentences correct. For example: She (has) (come) to the race.

CHALLENGE

Have one partner be an interviewer and one partner be a runner in a race. Interviewers can make up questions using *has, have, run, come, ran,* and *came.* Runners can make up answers using the same words.

FOR STUDENTS ACQUIRING ENGLISH

Say that some verbs have more than one part. Say and write sentences such as *We have read many books.* Tell children that the extra parts are called helping verbs; mark the main verb in one color and the helping verb in another.

ran, run and came, come

Lesson Objectives

Children will:

- identify helping words
- use the verbs *ran, run* and *came, come* correctly in sentences
- proofread for correct use of *ran, run* and *came, come*
- write an informative article using *ran, run* and *came, come*

One-Minute Warm-Up Have volunteers write the answer to the riddle correctly on the chalkboard. Ask them to explain the difference between *ran* and *run*.

Focus on Instruction

Point out that the verbs *run* and *come* alone tell about actions that happen now. When the helping verbs *has* or *have* are added to these verbs, they tell about actions in the past.

Try It Out

LISTENING AND SPEAKING Have a group slowly say aloud the sentences. Ask another group to raise their hands when they hear a helping verb and to stamp their feet when they hear a past-tense verb.

FOR STUDENTS ACQUIRING ENGLISH

- Have children listen to the Try It Out sentences on the audiotape. Distribute the SAE Practice page for Unit 5, Lesson 5.
- Help children suggest sentences about the art in the book and on the Practice page. Present *has run* and *have run* to show the past participle, but keep in mind that the perfect tenses are challenging and may be unfamiliar to many children. Say that when they see *has* and *have* as helping verbs, they will use *run* and *come,* instead of *ran* and *came.* Tell them that there will be other similar verbs that they will learn. Children listen and say the correct verb. Then they write the sentence.
  1. The kittens have (ran, run) away.
  2. One kitten (came, come) home.

Summing Up Help children summarize these key points about the lesson:

The **helping verbs** *has* and *have* are used with *run* and *come*. They are not used with ran and came. These verbs already tell about the **past**.

You may want to have children complete the parts related to this lesson on Blackline Master 5-2.

On Your Own

Have children test the sentences by saying each with and without the helping verb.

FOR STUDENTS ACQUIRING ENGLISH

Distribute the SAE Practice page for Unit 5, Lesson 5. Ask children which forms to use with *has* and *have*. Make sure children are aware that *come* and *run* are also simple present verbs. Help children suggest sentences for the art. Children draw a line under the correct verb and then write the sentence. Example: The parents have (came, come).

Writing Wrap-Up

Writing Tip: Before they begin, have children brainstorm sentences using *ran, came, has, have, run* and *come* that they could include in their article. See Blackline Master 5-5 for a sample article.

TECHNOLOGY CONNECTION

Children may use a prepared news article format on available software to design and write their articles.

On Your Own

Write each sentence, using the correct verb.

Example: The track team (come, came).
The track team came.

1. The coach has (came, come) too. come
2. The boys (ran, run) last night. ran

3–5. Proofread this sports article. Find mistakes with three underlined verbs. Write the sports article correctly.

Example Sue come to the race last year.
Sue came to the race last year.

Proofreading

Big Race Won by Speedy Sue

Many people have ~~came~~ come to the race today. Sue has ~~ran~~ run in many races. Everyone ran fast. Sue ~~run~~ ran faster than anyone! She won the race.

Writing Wrap-Up WRITING • THINKING • LISTENING • SPEAKING

INFORMING

Write a Sports Article

Write an article about an animal race. Use the verbs ran and came. Use has or have with run and come. Read the article to a classmate. Work together to check that you have used verbs correctly. Articles will vary.

 For Extra Practice, see page 200.

Meeting Individual Needs

● RETEACHING WORKBOOK, page 43

5 ran, run and came, come

Have and has are **helping words.**
Use helping words with run and come.
Do not use helping words with ran and came.
Warm weather **came**. The birds **have come** back.
A lamb **ran** past us. It **has run** to the field.

Write the correct verb to finish each sentence.

Example Guy has ____ to my house. (came, come)
Guy has come to my house.

1. He ran here. (ran, run)
2. A deer came to my yard. (came, come)
3. It ran away from us. (ran, run)
4. It has come back again. (came, come)

▲■ WORKBOOK PLUS, pages 66–67

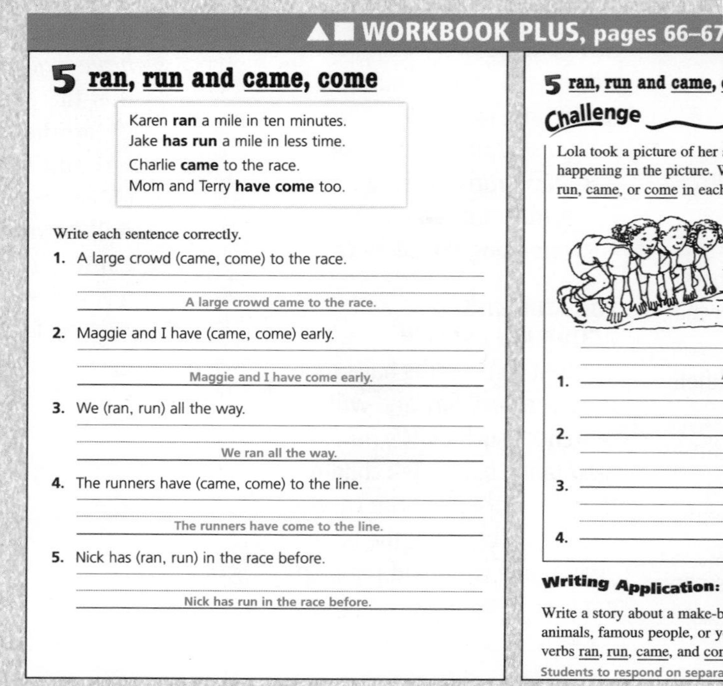

5 ran, run and came, come

Karen **ran** a mile in ten minutes.
Jake **has run** a mile in less time.
Charlie **came** to the race.
Mom and Terry **have come** too.

Write each sentence correctly.

1. A large crowd (came, come) to the race.
A large crowd came to the race.
2. Maggie and I have (came, come) early.
Maggie and I have come early.
3. We (ran, run) all the way.
We ran all the way.
4. The runners have (came, come) to the line.
The runners have come to the line.
5. Nick has (ran, run) in the race before.
Nick has run in the race before.

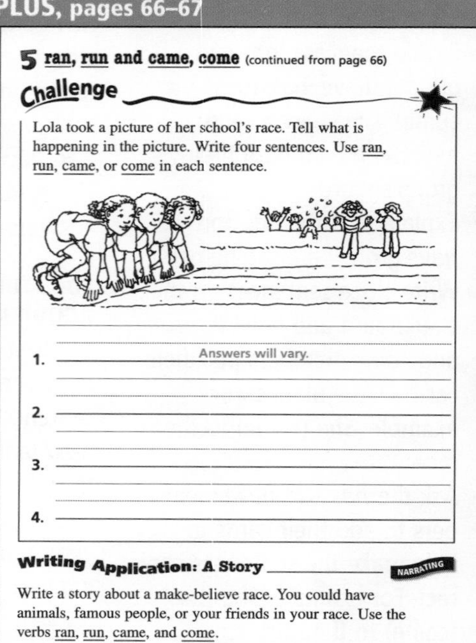

5 ran, run and came, come (continued from page 66)

Challenge

Lola took a picture of her school's race. Tell what is happening in the picture. Write four sentences. Use ran, run, came, or come in each sentence.

1. Answers will vary.
2.
3.
4.

Writing Application: A Story NARRATING

Write a story about a make-believe race. You could have animals, famous people, or your friends in your race. Use the verbs ran, run, came, and come.
Students to respond on separate paper. Answers will vary.

Grammar / Usage

6 saw, seen and went, gone

One-Minute Warm-Up

Read the sentence. Now say a new sentence about what you think Olly saw. Answers will vary.

Instead of frogs he saw something he had never seen before.
—from Olly's Polliwogs, by Anne and Harlow Rockwell

The **helping verbs** has and have are used with seen and gone to tell about the past. Has and have are not used with saw and went. These **verbs** already tell about the past.

Grandpa and Jen **went** to the lake.

They **have gone** there many times.

Jen **saw** some frogs on the rocks.

She **has seen** them under rocks too.

Try It Out

Speak Up Say each sentence, using the correct verb.

1. Jen (saw, seen) two deer today.
2. The two deer have (went, gone) away.
3. They (went, gone) into the trees.

Write It Now write the sentences correctly.

Example Jen has (saw, seen) deer at the lake.
Jen has seen deer at the lake. saw, gone, went

saw, seen and went, gone

Lesson Objectives

Children will:

- use the verbs *saw, seen* and *went, gone* correctly in sentences in a story
- proofread for correct usage of *saw, seen* and *went, gone*
- write a descriptive letter using *saw, seen,* and *went, gone* correctly

One-Minute Warm-Up Have volunteers write their sentences on the chalkboard. Ask them to tell if their sentences tell about the past or now.

Focus on Instruction

Review that not all verbs that tell about the past need helping verbs. Also explain that not all verbs that tell about the past end in *ed.*

Try It Out

VIEWING Have children refer to the illustration to write questions and answers using the words *has, have, seen, saw, gone* and *went*. Record children's ideas in a chart. (Sample responses are shown.)

Questions	Answers
What has Jen seen?	Jen has seen deer at the lake.
Where have the two deer gone?	The two deer have gone away.

Meeting Individual Needs

RETEACHING
ALTERNATIVE STRATEGY

- Create two teams to play Build-a-Person. Each team will try to draw a complete person on the chalkboard by giving correct answers.
- Write sentences on the chalkboard using *saw, has seen, have seen, went, has gone, have gone.* Write two forms of the verb in each sentence. For example: Mother (*went, gone*) to the lake. Have team members take turns circling the correct verb.
- For each correct answer, children may add a body part to the team's person.

CHALLENGE

Partners can play tic-tac-toe with word cards for *see, saw, seen, go, went, gone.* Players take turns choosing word cards and using the words in sentences. For each correct sentence, a player can mark a square on the puzzle. Three marks in a row wins.

FOR STUDENTS ACQUIRING ENGLISH

Make sure children know see and go in the present before proceeding. Say, for example, *I see a boy with a red sweater. Show me the boy.* Then give directions with go. For example, Go to the chalkboard.

FOR STUDENTS ACQUIRING ENGLISH

- Have children listen to the Try It Out sentences on the audiotape. Distribute the SAE Practice page for Unit 5, Lesson 6.
- Help children suggest sentences about the photo in the book and the art on the Practice page. Say, *What is this animal called? I saw a deer last week. Have you ever seen a deer?* Next, write *saw, has seen, have seen* and *went, has gone, have gone*. Begin to differentiate between the past and the present perfect as one single event compared to something occurring over time. Children listen and say the correct verb. Then they write the sentence.
Example: Jane and I (saw, seen) two deer.

Summing Up Help children summarize these key points about the lesson:

The **helping verbs** *has* and *have* are used with *seen* and *gone*. They are not used with *saw* and *went*. These verbs already tell about the **past**.

You may want to have children complete the parts related to this lesson on Blackline Master 5-2.

On Your Own

Suggest that children test each sentence by saying it aloud with each verb choice.

FOR STUDENTS ACQUIRING ENGLISH

Distribute the SAE Practice page for Unit 5, Lesson 6. Help children suggest sentences for the art. You may want to dictate labels for the art. Children underline the correct verb and then write the sentence.

1. My family (gone, went) to the lake.
2. We have (gone, went) there for many years.

Writing Wrap-Up

Writing Tip: Have children draw the place and things they saw there to get ideas for their letters. See Blackline Master 5-5 for a sample letter.

SCHOOL-HOME CONNECTION

Children may wish to write a similar letter to a family member and ask for a letter in response. Have children circle *went*, *gone*, *have*, *has*, *saw*, and *seen* any time they appear in the family member's letter.

On Your Own

Write each sentence, using the correct verb.

Example We (went, gone) for a walk.
We went for a walk.

1. We (saw, seen) a skunk by a bush. saw
2. We have (seen, saw) skunks before. seen

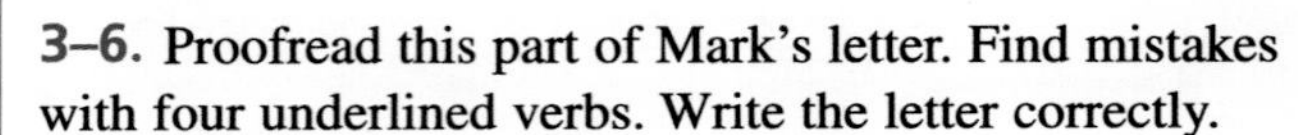

3–6. Proofread this part of Mark's letter. Find mistakes with four underlined verbs. Write the letter correctly.

Example Dad seen beavers by the pond.
Dad saw beavers by the pond.

Proofreading

Dear Grandpa,

Dad and I have ~~went~~ gone to the pond many times. We have ~~saw~~ seen many birds there. Yesterday Dad ~~seen~~ saw two eagles. We went fishing and caught five fish. I ~~goed~~ went right to bed when we got home!

Writing Wrap-Up WRITING • THINKING • LISTENING • SPEAKING

DESCRIBING

Write a Letter

Write about a place you went and what you saw. Use went or have gone and saw or have seen. Read your letter aloud. Have a classmate listen to check that you have used verbs correctly.

Letters will vary.

176 saw, seen and went, gone For Extra Practice, see page 201.

Meeting Individual Needs

● RETEACHING WORKBOOK, page 44

6 saw, seen and went, gone

Has and have are helping words.
Use helping words with seen and gone.
Do not use helping words with saw and went.
We **went** to Mom's office.
I **have gone** there before.
Julie **saw** the computers.
She **has seen** them before.

Write the correct verb to finish each sentence.

Example Julie and I ____ to Dad's office. (went, gone)
Julie and I went to Dad's office.

1. Julie has gone to Dad's office before. **(went, gone)**
2. We saw many tall tables. **(saw, seen)**
3. Julie has seen Dad's drawing tools often. **(saw, seen)**
4. I went home with a drawing. **(went, gone)**

▲■ WORKBOOK PLUS, pages 68–69

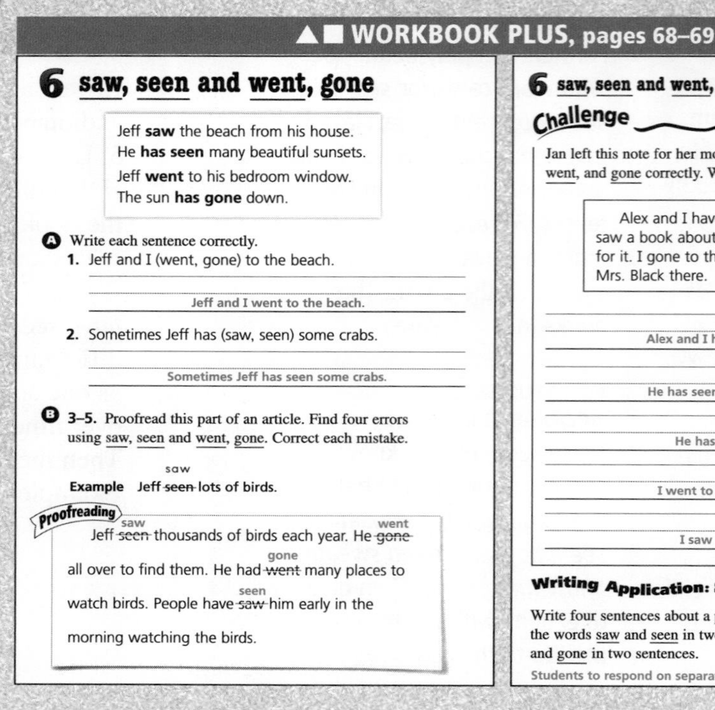

6 saw, seen and went, gone

Jeff **saw** the beach from his house.
He **has seen** many beautiful sunsets.
Jeff **went** to his bedroom window.
The sun **has gone** down.

A Write each sentence correctly.

1. Jeff and I (went, gone) to the beach.
Jeff and I went to the beach.
2. Sometimes Jeff has (saw, seen) some crabs.
Sometimes Jeff has seen some crabs.

B 3–5. Proofread this part of an article. Find four errors using saw, seen and went, gone. Correct each mistake.

Example Jeff ~~seen~~ saw lots of birds.

Proofreading

Jeff ~~seen~~ saw thousands of birds each year. He ~~gone~~ went all over to find them. He had ~~went~~ gone many places to watch birds. People have ~~saw~~ seen him early in the morning watching the birds.

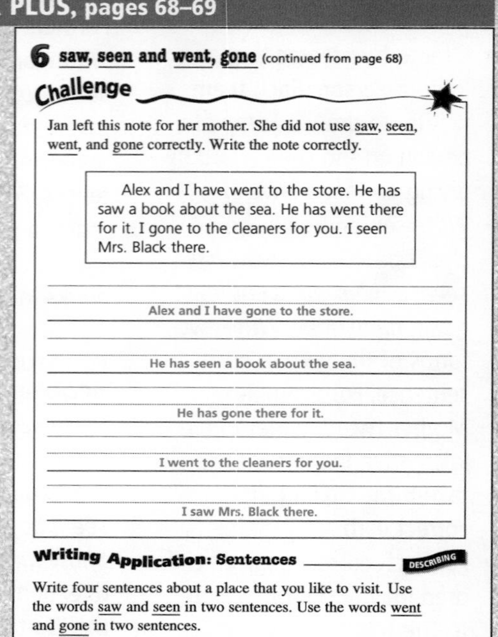

6 saw, seen and went, gone (continued from page 68)

Challenge

Jan left this note for her mother. She did not use saw, seen, went, and gone correctly. Write the note correctly.

Alex and I have went to the store. He has saw a book about the sea. He has went there for it. I gone to the cleaners for you. I seen Mrs. Black there.

Alex and I have gone to the store.
He has seen a book about the sea.
He has gone there for it.
I went to the cleaners for you.
I saw Mrs. Black there.

Writing Application: Sentences DESCRIBING

Write four sentences about a place that you like to visit. Use the words saw and seen in two sentences. Use the words went and gone in two sentences.

Students to respond on separate paper. Answers will vary.

Grammar / Usage

7 did, done and gave, given

One-Minute Warm-Up

What is wrong with this sentence? How can you fix it?

I done this puzzle by myself. The verb is incorrect; use did or have done.

The **helping verbs** has and have are used with done and given to tell about the past. Has and have are not used with did and gave. These **verbs** already tell about the past.

My grandmother **gave** us a puzzle.

She **has given** us many puzzles.

Matt and I **did** the puzzle.

We **have done** all of them.

Try It Out

Speak Up Say each sentence, using the correct verb.

1. A clown (did, done) a trick with balloons.
2. He has (did, done) the trick before.
3. He (gave, given) me two balloons.
4. I have (gave, given) one balloon away.

Write It Now write the sentences correctly.

Example A clown (did, done) a funny trick.
A clown did a funny trick. **did, done, gave, given**

Meeting Individual Needs

RETEACHING
ALTERNATIVE STRATEGY

- On the chalkboard write:
  do did done
  give gave given
- Explain that *do* and *give* tell about actions in the present, *did* and *gave* tell about actions in the past, and *done* and *given* tell about actions in the past and need helping verbs.
- Ask children to use verbs that tell about present action in sentences and write them on the chalkboard. Repeat the procedure for the other two categories of verbs.

CHALLENGE

Two teams can play this game, using a spelling bee format. Read aloud a cloze sentence in which a player must insert *did/done, gave/given, saw/seen, went/gone, came/come, or ran/run.* For example: *I have ___ my work.* Award one point for each correct answer.

FOR STUDENTS ACQUIRING ENGLISH

Make sure children know *give* in the present by saying, for example, *Give me a piece of chalk, please. Give ______ a pencil.* Make sure children know that *do* is sometimes a main verb and sometimes a helping verb.

did, done and gave, given

Lesson Objectives

Children will:

- use the verbs *did, done* and *gave, given* correctly in sentences in a story
- proofread for correct usage of *did, done, gave,* and *given*
- write a descriptive paragraph using *did, done, gave, given* and *has, have*

One-Minute Warm-Up Write the sentence on the chalkboard. Have volunteers write a verb to make the sentence correct. Ask why they chose those verbs.

Focus on Instruction

Remind children that verbs such as *ran*, *came*, *saw*, and *went* do not use *ed* to show past action.

Try It Out

LISTENING AND SPEAKING Have a volunteer read one sentence aloud. Ask another volunteer to change the sentence so the alternate verb choice is correct. For example, *A clown has done a trick with balloons.*

MEETING INDIVIDUAL NEEDS

FOR STUDENTS ACQUIRING ENGLISH

- Have children listen to the Try It Out sentences on the audiotape. Distribute the SAE Practice page for Unit 5, Lesson 7. 
- Help children suggest sentences about the photo in the book and the art on the Practice page. Children will likely experience interference from the first language with *make* and *do*, so plan to present phrases such as *do homework*, *do the dishes*, *do a puzzle*, *do a trick* but *make the bed*, *make a cake*, *make noise*. Say that in questions and negatives in the present and past, *do*, *does*, *did* are helping verbs. Write *gave*, *has given*, *have given* and *did*, *has done*, *have done*. Children listen and say the correct verb. Then they write the sentence.
  Example: The clown has (did, done) a trick.

Summing Up Help children summarize these key points about the lesson:

The **helping verbs** *has* and *have* are used with *done* and *given*. They are not used with *did* and *gave*. These **verbs** already tell about the **past**.

You may want to have children complete the parts related to this lesson on Blackline Master 5-2.

On Your Own

Suggest that children test each sentence by saying it aloud with and without a helping verb.

FOR STUDENTS ACQUIRING ENGLISH

Distribute the SAE Practice page for Unit 5, Lesson 7. Discuss the art; tell children that all the verbs in the art are *do* or *give*. Children underline the correct verb and then write the sentence.

1. Father has (did, done) the dishes.
2. Mona (gave, given) me a birthday present.

Writing Wrap-Up

Writing Tip: Suggest that children brainstorm lists of jobs before they begin writing. They can then choose the job they like best. See Blackline Master 5-5 for a sample description.

TECHNOLOGY CONNECTION

Children may wish to use a different type color when writing *gave, did, has, have, given,* or *done* in their paragraphs.

On Your Own

Write each sentence, using the correct verb.

Example Inez (did, done) a painting. Inez did a painting.

1. Ted has (gave, given) a speech. given
2. Julia and Pat (did, done) a play. did

3–5. Proofread Ling's news article. Find mistakes with three underlined verbs. Write the article correctly.

Example Teachers given each class a job.
Teachers gave each class a job.

Proofreading

School Clean Up

Mrs. Lee's class ~~done~~ did/has done posters about the clean up. A woman gave flowers to Mr. Johnson's class. The class planted a school garden. The children have ~~did~~ done a good job. They have ~~gave~~ given our school a wonderful gift.

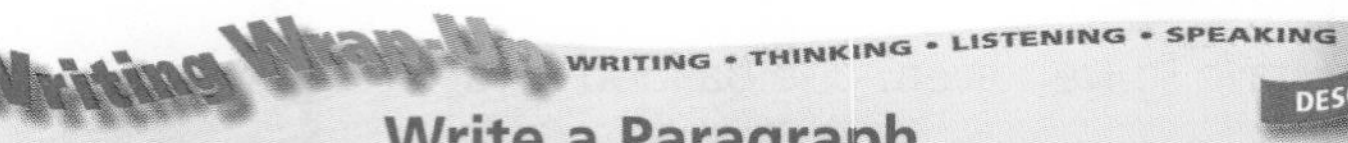

DESCRIBING

Write a Paragraph

Write about a job you have done. Use the verbs gave and did. Use has or have with given and done. Listen for these and other verbs when classmates read their paragraphs.

178 did, done and gave, given For Extra Practice, see page 202.

Meeting Individual Needs

● RETEACHING WORKBOOK, page 45

7 did, done and gave, given

Has and have are helping words.
Use helping words with done and given.
Do not use helping words with did and gave.
We **did** jobs. We **have done** them before.
Dad **gave** us directions. He **has given** us his help.

Write the correct verb to finish each sentence.

Example Frank ____ the breakfast dishes. (did, done)
Frank did the breakfast dishes.

1. I have given the dog her breakfast. (gave, given)
2. I gave the baby her bath. (gave, given)
3. Mom has given us more jobs. (gave, given)
4. Frank and I have done a lot of work. (did, done)

▲■ WORKBOOK PLUS, pages 70-71

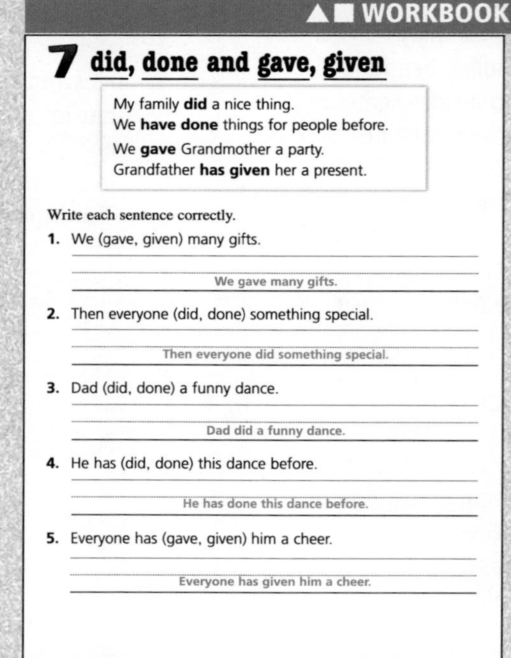

7 did, done and gave, given

My family **did** a nice thing.
We **have done** things for people before.
We **gave** Grandmother a party.
Grandfather **has given** her a present.

Write each sentence correctly.

1. We (gave, given) many gifts.
We gave many gifts.
2. Then everyone (did, done) something special.
Then everyone did something special.
3. Dad (did, done) a funny dance.
Dad did a funny dance.
4. He has (did, done) this dance before.
He has done this dance before.
5. Everyone has (gave, given) him a cheer.
Everyone has given him a cheer.

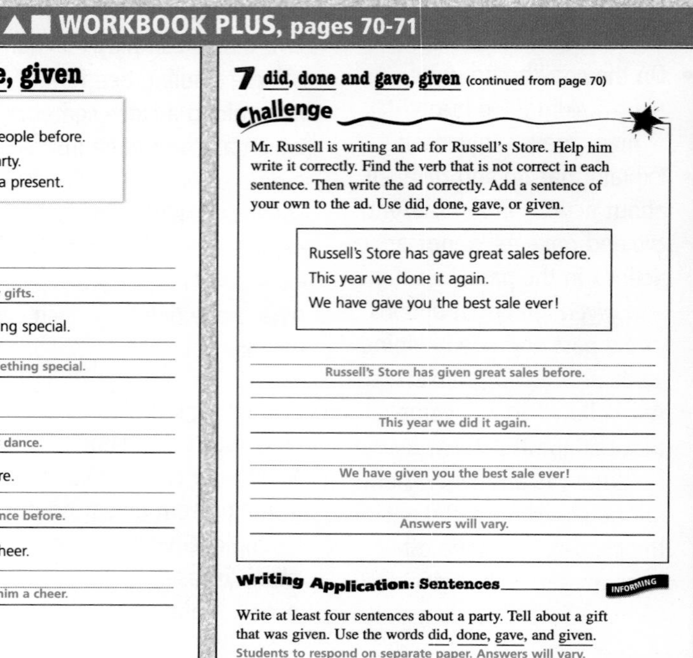

7 did, done and gave, given (continued from page 70)

Challenge

Mr. Russell is writing an ad for Russell's Store. Help him write it correctly. Find the verb that is not correct in each sentence. Then write the ad correctly. Add a sentence of your own to the ad. Use did, done, gave, or given.

Russell's Store has gave great sales before.
This year we done it again.
We have gave you the best sale ever!

Russell's Store has given great sales before.
This year we did it again.
We have given you the best sale ever!
Answers will vary.

Writing Application: Sentences INFORMING

Write at least four sentences about a party. Tell about a gift that was given. Use the words did, done, gave, and given.
Students to respond on separate paper. Answers will vary.

Grammar/Usage

8 is and are

The bear, the lion, and the monkey are in line. The bear is first. The lion is next. The monkey is last.

One-Minute Warm-Up

Answer these questions in complete sentences.

What animals are in line? Who is first in line? Who is next? Who is last?

The verbs is and are tell about something that is happening now. Use is if the sentence tells about **one** person, animal, place, or thing. Use are with nouns that name **more than one**. Read the sentences. Which tells about one? Which tells about more than one?

Jack is in the race.

Marti and Bill are also in the race.

Try It Out

Speak Up Say each sentence, using the correct verb.

1. The race (is, are) exciting.
2. Jack and Marti (is, are) fast.
3. People (is, are) cheering.
4. Jack (is, are) the winner.

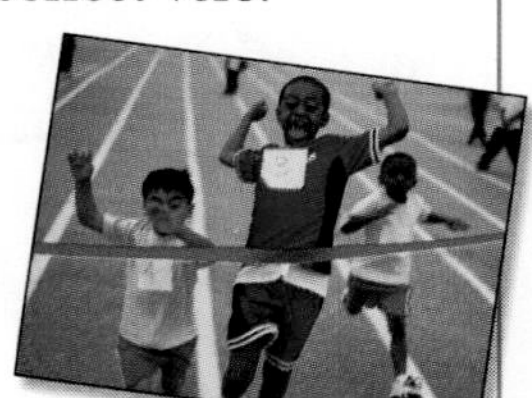

Write It Now write the sentences correctly.

Example The children (is, are) ready to race.
The children are ready to race. **is, are, are, is**

Meeting Individual Needs

RETEACHING
ALTERNATIVE STRATEGY

- Draw a winding road on oaktag and divide it into squares as a game board. Write twelve sentence cards, using *is* and *are* correctly and incorrectly. On the back of each write "right" or "wrong." If wrong, write the correct answer.
- Give each child a marker and place cards sentence-side-up. Children take turns reading cards and deciding if sentences are correct. If wrong, the child says the correct answer and checks the response. If correct, children move markers forward one space.

CHALLENGE

Have one child act as a TV anchorperson. Others can be reporters covering events. The anchorperson can call on each reporter to tell what is happening at that very moment. Reporters should use the verbs *is* and *are.*

is and are

Lesson Objectives

Children will:

- use *is* and *are* correctly with singular and plural nouns
- proofread for correct usage of *is* and *are*
- write definitions of nouns using *is* and *are*

One-Minute Warm-Up Write *bear*, *lion*, and *monkey* on separate cards and give to three volunteers. Have them read their cards aloud and stand in a line. Have others answer in complete sentences as you ask them who is in line.

Focus on Instruction

Remind children how verbs change to tell about either one or more than one. (Add *s* or *es* with one, and take away *s* or *es* for more than one.) Tell them that some words change completely when talking about one or more than one.

Try It Out

VIEWING Have children write questions about the photograph. Ask them to use *is* and *are*. Record their responses in a chart. (Sample responses are shown.)

Is	Are
What is the first boy doing?	What are the children doing?
What is the last boy doing?	Where are the children racing?

FOR STUDENTS ACQUIRING ENGLISH

- Have children listen to the Try It Out sentences on the audiotape. Distribute the SAE Practice page for Unit 5, Lesson 8.
- Help children suggest sentences about the photo in the book. Encourage the use of *is* and *are* with questions such as *What is this? Who is winning the race? How many are boys?* How many are girls? You may want to call attention to *is* and *are* as main verbs with pairs of sentences such as *My dog is Spot.*

Summing Up Help children summarize these key points about the lesson:

The verbs *is* and *are* tell about something that is happening now. Use *is* if the sentence tells about **one** person, place, animal, or thing. Use *are* with **more than one**.

You may want to have children complete the parts related to this lesson on Blackline Master 5-3.

On Your Own

Before children choose verbs, have them count how many people, places, animals, or things the sentence is about.

FOR STUDENTS ACQUIRING ENGLISH

Distribute the SAE Practice page for Unit 5, Lesson 8. Help children describe the art; make sure they know the names of all the animals. Children write *is* or *are* to complete each sentence.

1. Spot _____ a dog. (is)
2. His ears _____ long. (are)

Writing Wrap-Up

Writing Tip: Have children brainstorm nouns before they begin writing. See Blackline Master 5-5 for sample definitions.

SCHOOL-HOME CONNECTION
Children can work with a family member to make a picture dictionary about nouns found in the home.

On Your Own

Write each sentence, using is or are.

Example My pet _____ a rabbit. My pet is a rabbit.

1. Her ears __are__ long.
2. She __is__ friendly.

3–6. Proofread these sentences from Dana's picture dictionary. Find four mistakes in using is and are. Write each sentence correctly and draw a picture.

Example S The sun are in the sky.
The sun is in the sky.

Proofreading

Ants are small and black.
An apple ~~are~~ is good to eat.

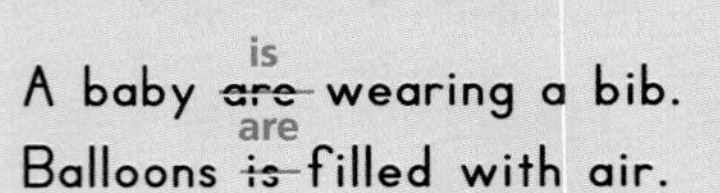

A baby ~~are~~ is wearing a bib.
Balloons ~~is~~ are filled with air.

Cats ~~is~~ are good pets.
A clock is used to tell time.

Writing Wrap-Up WRITING • THINKING • LISTENING • SPEAKING

CREATING

Write Picture Dictionary Sentences

Think of four nouns that begin with the same letter. Write sentences about the nouns, using is and are. Listen for the correct use of is and are as classmates read their sentences.

Sentences will vary.

180 is and are For Extra Practice, see page 203.

Meeting Individual Needs

● RETEACHING WORKBOOK, page 46

8 is and are

Use is with one.
Use are with more than one.
This pool **is** long.
Many people **are** here.

Read each pair of sentences. Write the correct sentence.

Example Jim are in the pool. Jim is in the pool.
Jim is in the pool.

1. His crutches are here. His crutches is here.
   His crutches are here.
2. Jim's parents is proud. Jim's parents are proud.
   Jim's parents are proud.
3. A smile is on Jim's face. A smile are on Jim's face.
   A smile is on Jim's face.
4. Jim are a great swimmer. Jim is a great swimmer.
   Jim is a great swimmer.

▲■ WORKBOOK PLUS, pages 72-73

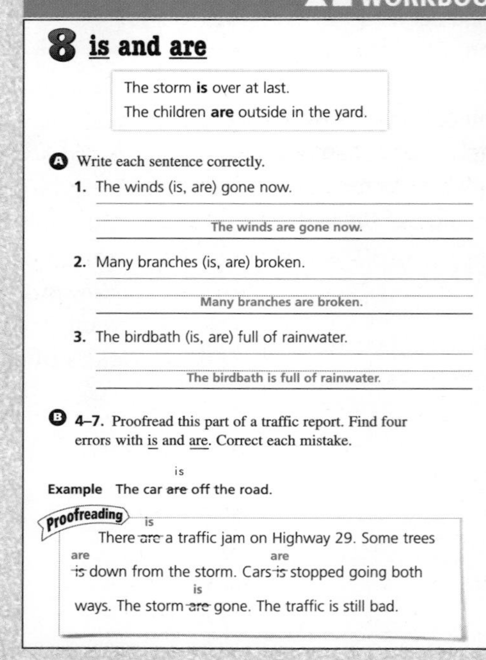

8 is and are

The storm **is** over at last.
The children **are** outside in the yard.

A Write each sentence correctly.

1. The winds (is, are) gone now.
   The winds are gone now.
2. Many branches (is, are) broken.
   Many branches are broken.
3. The birdbath (is, are) full of rainwater.
   The birdbath is full of rainwater.

B 4–7. Proofread this part of a traffic report. Find four errors with is and are. Correct each mistake.

Example The car ~~are~~ is off the road.

Proofreading
There ~~are~~ is a traffic jam on Highway 29. Some trees ~~is~~ are down from the storm. Cars ~~is~~ are stopped going both ways. The storm ~~are~~ is gone. The traffic is still bad.

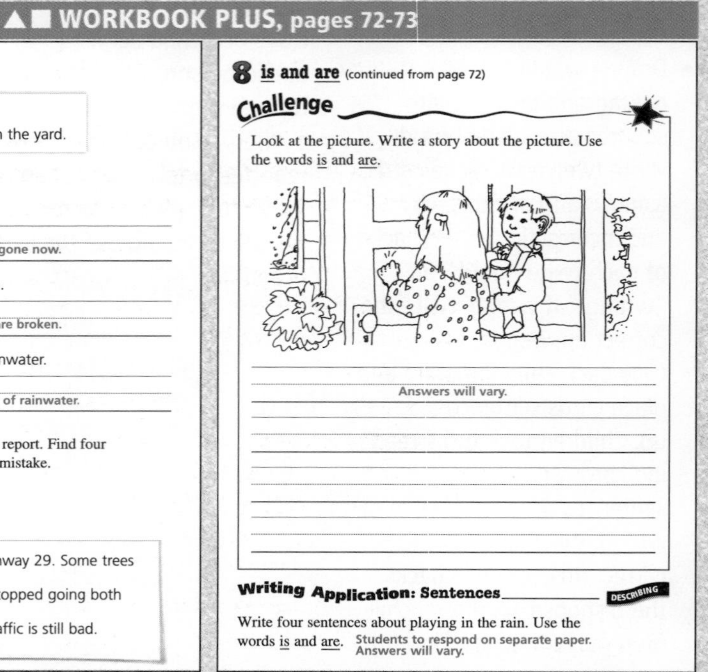

8 is and are (continued from page 72)

Challenge

Look at the picture. Write a story about the picture. Use the words is and are.

Answers will vary.

Writing Application: Sentences DESCRIBING

Write four sentences about playing in the rain. Use the words is and are. Students to respond on separate paper. Answers will vary.

Grammar / Usage

9 was and were

Read the sentence. Read it again using Danny and his friend as the naming part. How does the sentence change?

Danny was in a hurry. **The verb changes from was to were.**
—from Happy Birthday, Danny and the Dinosaur!, by Syd Hoff

The verbs was and were tell about something that happened in the past. Use was if the sentence tells about **one** person, animal, place, or thing. Use were with nouns that name **more than one**. Which sentence tells about one? Which tells about more than one?

Paco's **birthday** was yesterday.

The **gifts** were a surprise!

Try It Out

Speak Up Say each sentence, using the correct verb.

1. The birthday party (was, were) at Paco's house.
2. Paco's friends (was, were) there.
3. The gifts (was, were) just what Paco wanted.

Write It Now write the sentences correctly.

Example The cake (was, were) good.
The cake was good.

was, were, were

Meeting Individual Needs

RETEACHING
ALTERNATIVE STRATEGY

- Put an object in a box, and allow children to shake the box. Have them close their eyes while you remove the object from the box. Ask children to use a complete sentence to tell you what was in the box. Record their responses on the chalkboard.
- Place two objects in the box and repeat the process using the verb *were*. Close by asking children when to use *was* (with one) and when to use *were* (with more than one).

CHALLENGE

Have children write a story about a party or other special occasion that happened a while ago. Ask them to see how many times they can use *was* and *were*.

FOR STUDENTS ACQUIRING ENGLISH

Tell children that *was* and *were* are for things in the past. Ask which words we use to talk about things happening now. (*is* and *are*) Ask questions about actual events such as *Was the party fun? Were the cookies good?*

was and were

Lesson Objectives

Children will:
- use *was* and *were* correctly with singular and plural nouns
- proofread for correct usage of *was* and *were*
- write an expressive note using *was* and *were*

One-Minute Warm-Up Have one child be Danny and one child be his friend. Ask "Danny" to say aloud his sentence (Danny was in a hurry), and the two children to say aloud their sentence (Danny and his friend were in a hurry.). Discuss the change in the sentence.

Focus on Instruction

Help children see that *was* and *were* follow the same usage pattern as *is* and *are*, but are instead used to tell about the past.

Try It Out

LISTENING AND SPEAKING Have half the class say the sentences aloud. The others can raise one hand when the sentence is about one, and wave both hands when the sentence is about more than one. Then have them switch roles.

FOR STUDENTS ACQUIRING ENGLISH

- Have children listen to the Try It Out sentences on the audiotape. Distribute the SAE Practice page for Unit 5, Lesson 9. 
- Tell the children to look carefully at the drawing; allow them approximately five minutes. Then ask questions such as *How many packages were there? What color was the smallest package? What do you think was in the packages?* Encourage responses with *was* and *were*, whether short or long answers. Next, help children describe the art on the Practice page. Children listen and say the correct verb. Then they write the sentence.
  1. Aisha's party (was, were) Saturday.
  2. We (was, were) all invited.

Summing Up Help children summarize these key points about the lesson:

Use *was* if the sentence tells about **one** person, place, animal, or thing. Use *were* with **more than one**.

You may want to have children complete the parts related to this lesson on Blackline Master 5-3.

On Your Own

Before children choose verbs, have them count how many people, places, animals, or things the sentence is about and then test each sentence.

FOR STUDENTS ACQUIRING ENGLISH

Distribute the SAE Practice page for Unit 5, Lesson 9. Help children describe the art. Make sure children understand that *was* and *were* are the past of *is* and *are*. Children write *was* or *were* to complete each sentence.

1. The party _____ very nice!
2. The cookies and cake _____ delicious!

Writing Wrap-Up

Writing Tip: Suggest that children first choose something for which they are thankful. Then have them write their feelings or reasons. See Blackline Master 5-6 for a sample note.

TECHNOLOGY CONNECTION

Children may want to scan in photos or pictures to illustrate their thank-you notes.

On Your Own

Write each sentence, using was or were.

Example One gift _____ from Alma.
One gift was from Alma.

1. Two books <u>were</u> in a red box.
2. A new game <u>was</u> from Mother.

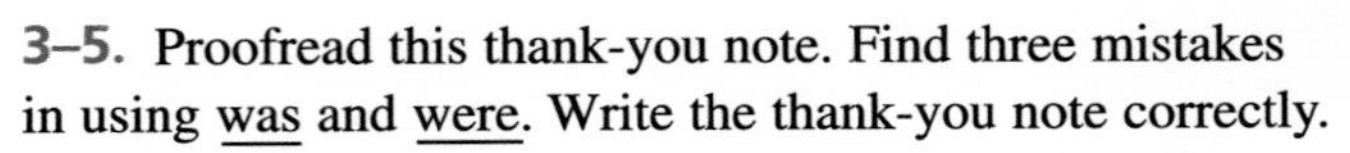

3–5. Proofread this thank-you note. Find three mistakes in using was and were. Write the thank-you note correctly.

Example My birthday were fun.
My birthday was fun.

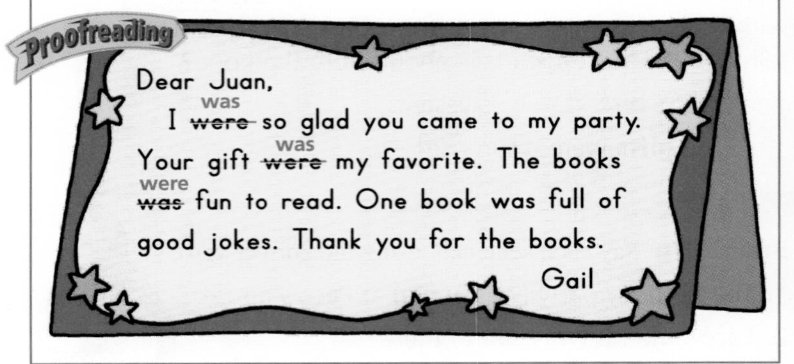

Writing Wrap-Up

WRITING • THINKING • LISTENING • SPEAKING

EXPRESSING

Write a Thank-You Note

Write a note thanking someone who gave you a gift or did something for you. Use was or were. Read your note aloud as classmates listen for the correct use of was and were.

Responses will vary.

182 was and were

For Extra Practice, see page 204.

Meeting Individual Needs

● RETEACHING WORKBOOK, page 47

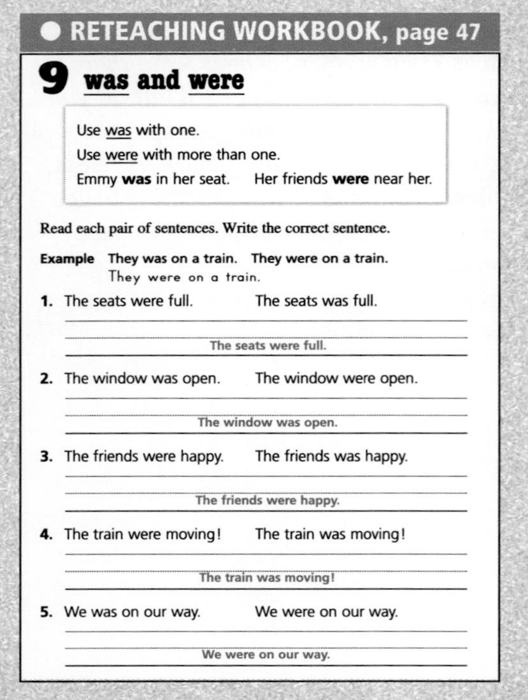

9 was and were

Use was with one.
Use were with more than one.
Emmy **was** in her seat. Her friends **were** near her.

Read each pair of sentences. Write the correct sentence.

Example They was on a train. They were on a train.
They were on a train.

1. The seats were full. The seats was full.
The seats were full.
2. The window was open. The window were open.
The window was open.
3. The friends were happy. The friends was happy.
The friends were happy.
4. The train were moving! The train was moving!
The train was moving!
5. We was on our way. We were on our way.
We were on our way.

▲■ WORKBOOK PLUS, pages 74-75

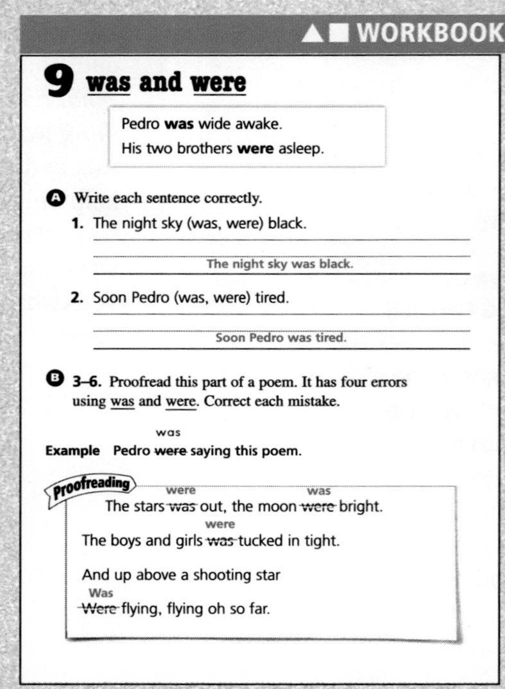

9 was and were

Pedro **was** wide awake.
His two brothers **were** asleep.

A Write each sentence correctly.

1. The night sky (was, were) black.
The night sky was black.
2. Soon Pedro (was, were) tired.
Soon Pedro was tired.

B 3–6. Proofread this part of a poem. It has four errors using was and were. Correct each mistake.

Example Pedro ~~were~~ was saying this poem.

Proofreading
The stars ~~was~~ were out, the moon ~~were~~ was bright.
The boys and girls ~~was~~ were tucked in tight.
And up above a shooting star
~~Were~~ Was flying, flying oh so far.

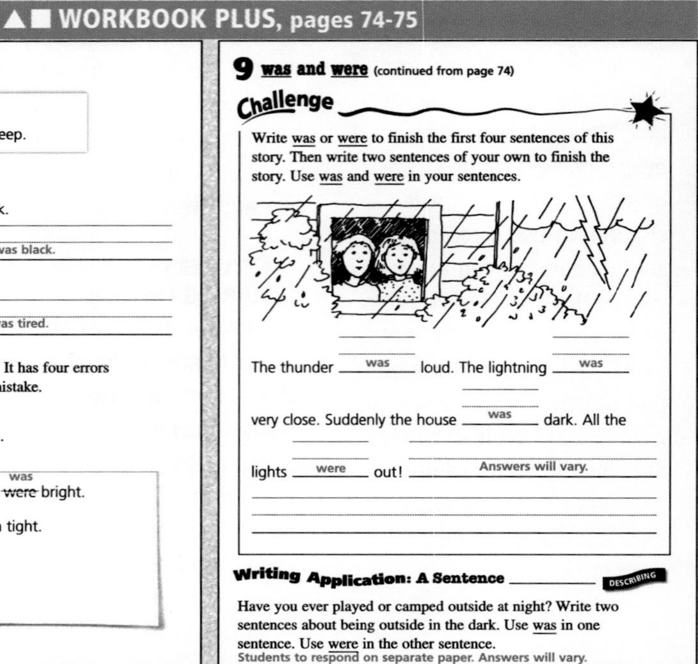

9 was and were (continued from page 74)

Challenge

Write was or were to finish the first four sentences of this story. Then write two sentences of your own to finish the story. Use was and were in your sentences.

The thunder <u>was</u> loud. The lightning <u>was</u> very close. Suddenly the house <u>was</u> dark. All the lights <u>were</u> out! Answers will vary.

Writing Application: A Sentence DESCRIBING

Have you ever played or camped outside at night? Write two sentences about being outside in the dark. Use was in one sentence. Use were in the other sentence.
Students to respond on separate paper. Answers will vary.

Grammar / Mechanics

10 Contractions

Some words are different; one sentence is longer; one sentence has contractions; the sentences mean the same.

One-Minute Warm-Up

Say these two sentences. How are they different? How are they the same?

If it does not stop raining, we cannot go camping.

If it doesn't stop raining, we can't go camping.

A **contraction** is a short way of writing two words. An **apostrophe** (') shows where letters were left out.

do not	don't
does not	doesn't
is not	isn't
cannot	can't

Try It Out

Speak Up Say the contractions for these words. Use each contraction in a sentence.

1. does not *doesn't*
2. cannot *can't*
3. is not *isn't*
4. do not *don't*

Write It Write the sentences, using a contraction for the underlined words.

Example This bird <u>is</u> <u>not</u> a pet. This bird isn't a pet.

5. Some birds <u>do</u> <u>not</u> fly south in winter. **don't**
6. An ostrich is a bird that <u>cannot</u> fly. **can't**

Contractions

Lesson Objectives

Children will:

- form the contractions *don't, doesn't, isn't,* and *can't*
- proofread for correct usage of contractions
- write a narrative using contractions

One-Minute Warm-Up Have a volunteer write the sentences on the chalkboard. Ask them to circle the words that are different in the two sentences.

Focus on Instruction

Point out that *cannot* is written as one word. Note that other words joined as contractions are written as two words.

Try It Out

VIEWING Have children write dialogue that may occur between the two birds. Ask them to use contractions in each line of dialogue. Use a cluster to generate ideas for each contraction. (Sample responses are shown.)

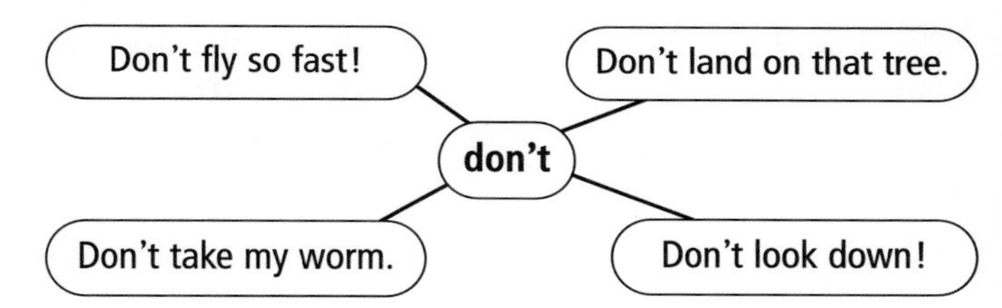

Meeting Individual Needs

RETEACHING
ALTERNATIVE STRATEGY

- Write the contractions from the lesson and the word or words that comprise each on separate index cards. Mix them up and place them face down for children to play a Concentration game.
- As each child turns over two cards, they must match the contraction to the two words that comprise it. To win the point, the child must say a sentence that uses the word or words and then repeat it using the contraction.

CHALLENGE

Ask children to create an answer for this riddle: A monkey does, but a whale doesn't. (climb a tree). Invite children to make up riddles using the contractions from the lesson. Use this prompt: A frog can, but _____.

FOR STUDENTS ACQUIRING ENGLISH

Write *is not* and *does not.* Ask if children have heard *isn't* and *doesn't* used. Explain what a contraction is; show children how to make the apostrophe. Continue with other contractions.

FOR STUDENTS ACQUIRING ENGLISH

- Have children listen to the Try It Out sentences on the audiotape. Distribute the SAE Practice page for Unit 5, Lesson 10.
- Write all the contractions for this lesson on the board, minus the apostrophe. Call on children to add the apostrophe. Check to be sure that each apostrophe is in the correct position and shaped properly. With children, practice saying the contractions. Make sure children understand that contractions represent spoken forms. Help children describe the art on the Practice page. Children listen and say the contractions. Then they give the contractions for the underlined word or words.
  1. <u>is not</u> (isn't)
  2. An ostrich <u>cannot</u> fly. (can't)

Summing Up Help children summarize these key points about the lesson:

A **contraction** is a short way of writing words. An **apostrophe** shows where letters were left out.

On Your Own

Suggest that children test their answers by comparing the letters in the original words and in the contractions.

FOR STUDENTS ACQUIRING ENGLISH

Distribute the SAE Practice page for Unit 5, Lesson 10. Briefly review the contractions in this lesson and make sure children know how to make apostrophes. Then children add apostrophes to the contractions in a paragraph.

Writing Wrap-Up

Writing Tip: Have children use a Venn diagram to list things that Mr. and Mrs. Nobody can't or won't do. Help them to use the outer areas as well as the shared center area of the diagram to organize their ideas. See Blackline Master 5-6 for sample story.

SCHOOL-HOME CONNECTION

Children can work with a family member to write a new chapter for their story about Mr. and Mrs. Nobody that tells about all the places they can't or won't go.

On Your Own

Write these sentences, using contractions for the underlined words.

Example Do not hike by yourself.
Don't hike by yourself.

1. Lindsay does not like camping. doesn't
2. Her tent is not new. isn't

3–5. Proofread Sarika's story. Find three mistakes with contractions. Copy the story and write the contractions correctly.

Example Dont give up, Mrs. Small. Don't give up, Mrs. Small.

Mrs. Small ~~cant~~ can't find her new hat. She looks inside. She ~~doesnt~~ doesn't find her hat. She looks outside. Her hat is in a bird's nest! Mrs. Small ~~isnt~~ isn't tall enough to reach it. She doesn't have a ladder. What will she do?

Writing Wrap-Up

WRITING • THINKING • LISTENING • SPEAKING

NARRATING

Write a Story

Write about Mr. and Mrs. Nobody who are not willing or able to do things. Use don't, doesn't, can't, and isn't. Read your story. Have classmates name and spell the contractions.

Stories will vary.

184 Contractions For Extra Practice, see page 205.

Meeting Individual Needs

● RETEACHING WORKBOOK, page 48

10 Contractions

A **contraction** is a short way of writing words. An **apostrophe** ' shows where letters have been left out.

do not	**don't**
does not	**doesn't**
is not	**isn't**
cannot	**can't**

Write each sentence. Use the contraction.

Example Kate (cannot, can't) find a shoe.
Kate can't find her shoe.

1. Her shoe (isn't, is not) in her closet.
Her shoe isn't in her closet.
2. It (cannot, can't) be in the washing machine.
It can't be in the washing machine.
3. Kate (does not, doesn't) know where to look now.
Kate doesn't know where to look now.
4. Shoes (do not, don't) walk by themselves.
Shoes don't walk by themselves.

▲■ WORKBOOK PLUS, pages 76-77

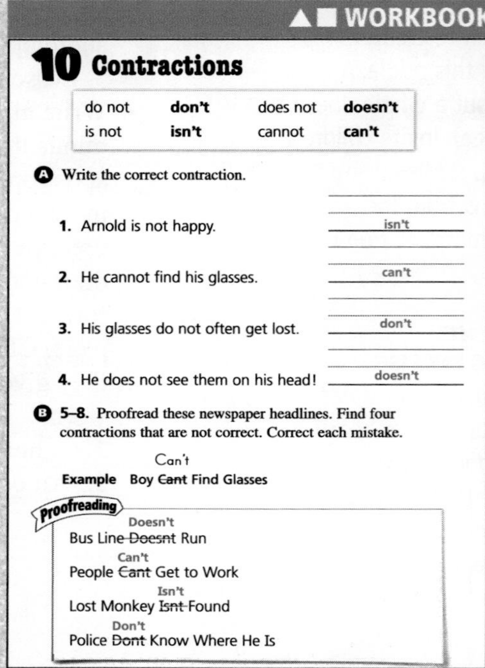

10 Contractions

do not	**don't**	does not	**doesn't**
is not	**isn't**	cannot	**can't**

A Write the correct contraction.

1. Arnold is not happy. isn't
2. He cannot find his glasses. can't
3. His glasses do not often get lost. don't
4. He does not see them on his head! doesn't

B **5–8.** Proofread these newspaper headlines. Find four contractions that are not correct. Correct each mistake.

Example Boy ~~Cant~~ Can't Find Glasses

Proofreading

Bus Line ~~Doesnt~~ Doesn't Run
People ~~Cant~~ Can't Get to Work
Lost Monkey ~~Isnt~~ Isn't Found
Police ~~Dont~~ Don't Know Where He Is

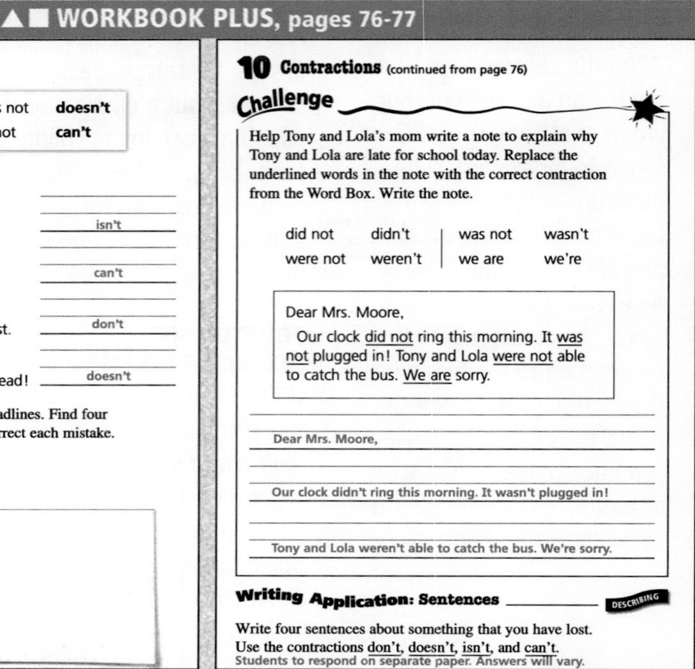

10 Contractions (continued from page 76)

Challenge

Help Tony and Lola's mom write a note to explain why Tony and Lola are late for school today. Replace the underlined words in the note with the correct contraction from the Word Box. Write the note.

did not	didn't	was not	wasn't
were not	weren't	we are	we're

Dear Mrs. Moore,
Our clock did not ring this morning. It was not plugged in! Tony and Lola were not able to catch the bus. We are sorry.

Dear Mrs. Moore,
Our clock didn't ring this morning. It wasn't plugged in!
Tony and Lola weren't able to catch the bus. We're sorry.

Writing Application: Sentences DESCRIBING

Write four sentences about something that you have lost. Use the contractions don't, doesn't, isn't, and can't.
Students to respond on separate paper. Answers will vary.

Revising Strategies — Vocabulary

Exact Verbs

Verbs are action words. When you write, use **exact verbs**. They make sentences come alive and tell your reader exactly what is happening.

The dogs jump for the ball.

The dogs **leap** for the ball.

Apply It

Writing Exact Verbs 1–5. Read this part of a science log. Copy the sentences and write an exact verb in place of each underlined verb. Use My First Thesaurus on page H45.

Example I made a cage for my hamster.
I built a cage for my hamster.

Our class has two new hamsters named Fluffy and Muffy. They eat the seeds we leave in their cage.

Fluffy finds a tube to run through. Muffy jumps on the wheel and makes it turn. Fluffy hides behind Muffy and looks at us. The hamsters make us laugh.

gobble up, munch; discovers, spots, locates
hops, leaps; gazes, peeks, stares; chuckle, giggle, howl

Exact Verbs

Lesson Objective

Children will:

- replace weak verbs with exact ones
- use a thesaurus

Focus on Instruction

- Discuss with children what information the verb *race* gives that *run* does not. (*Race* indicates that the dogs are running as fast as they can, each one trying to get to the ball first.) Have children close their eyes and picture each sentence. Ask: How are the images different?
- Have children give other examples of general and exact verbs. Then have them make up sentences that use these words. Write on the chalkboard: *The cat* jumped *into the air. The cat* leaped *into the air.*

Apply It

- Review with children the use of My First Thesaurus in the Tools and Tips section at the back of the student book.
- Read the example with the class. Point out that there will be more than one possible answer for each of these exercises. Ask children to tell how *built* improves the sentence. (It gives a clearer picture of what happened.)
- Have children complete the activity independently and discuss their verb choices.

Have children who need more support work with partners.

Ask children to find places in their own writing in progress where they can use exact verbs. Remind them to use an online thesaurus if they are working on a computer.

FOR STUDENTS ACQUIRING ENGLISH

This is a great opportunity for a mini - lesson on using a thesaurus. Children may not know any synonyms for *eat*, but they can learn to look them up. If possible, provide small groups of children with a thesaurus. Ask groups to find synonyms for the verbs from the section *Apply It*. Make a contest for most, best, and funniest.

Meeting Individual Needs

● RETEACHING WORKBOOK, page 49

Exact Verbs

Exact verbs tell your reader what is happening.
We laugh (giggle) as we go (skip) down the street.

Revising Change each underlined verb to a more exact verb. Choose words from the word box. Write the new sentence.

shouts	staring	spot	hopping	races

1. Then we see our friends.
   Then we spot our friends.
2. Luís comes over to us.
   Luís races over to us.
3. He calls to the rest of our friends.
   He shouts to the rest of our friends.
4. We are all looking at them.
   We are all staring at them.
5. They are all jumping at once!
   They are all hopping at once!

▲■ WORKBOOK PLUS, page 78

Exact Verbs

We went (raced) to the gate and gave (handed) the man our tickets.

Revising 1-5. Change each underlined verb to a more exact verb. Use words from the word box. Cross out the weak verb and write the exact verb over it. Sample answers

cracked	strolled	stared	caught	saw
dashed	hurled	slept	creep	tossed

Revising

The Sports Fair was about to begin. We were excited. First, we ~~looked~~ stared as a skater did flips. Then we ~~went~~ dashed over to the baseball area. I ~~threw~~ hurled the ball very fast! Next, I ~~walked~~ strolled to the basketball court. I tried to make some baskets, but then I just put ~~the~~ tossed ball aside. We really like going to Sports Fair and trying new things.

Enrichment

Objectives

Children will:

- match contractions with the words that make them by playing a card game
- use the verbs *is* and *are* in sentences about the United States' flag

Using the Activities

The Enrichment page provides fun, creative activities that reinforce children's understanding and use of sentences. The activities are designed to be enjoyed by all children. Here are some ideas for using the activities.

- Pair children who need extra support with more capable classmates.
- Children can work with these activities in class after they have completed other assignments.
- Activities that can be completed individually can be assigned as homework.

Notes on the Activities

CONTRACTION MATCH

This is a good activity to put in a learning center.

- You can make cards in advance. Store the game materials in a place where children can play independently.
- Go over the example with children. Remind them that a contraction is a short way of writing words and that an apostrophe shows where letters have been left out.
- When children finish, have them write a sentence for each contraction they matched.

FLAG FACTS

- When children have written their sentences, ask them to read them aloud to a partner or the class. Discuss the different things that children have written.
- As an alternative, have children do this activity with flags from other countries.

CHALLENGE Have children think about their school name and other things about the school they could include in a flag design. For example, does the school have an animal that represents it? Is the school near the ocean or a mountain?

FOR STUDENTS ACQUIRING ENGLISH

Before playing *Contraction Match* in pairs, play in two teams. Ask each team to make a set of cards. You hold up a contraction and the team chooses from their pile the correct verb card. For *Flag Facts*, challenge children to draw the flag from their native country and write sentences about it.

Enrichment

Verbs!

Contraction Match

Players	2
You Need	8 blank cards
Get Ready	Write don't, doesn't, isn't, and can't on four cards. Write the word or words that make each contraction on the other cards.

How to Play

Mix the cards. Put them face down in rows. Turn over two cards on each turn. Try to match a contraction with the word or words that make that contraction. For example, don't and do not are a match. If the cards match, keep them. If they do not match, turn them face down. The player with the most cards wins.

Flag Facts

- Draw and color the United States flag.
- Write two sentences about the flag. Use is, are, and verbs that show action.

Challenge Draw a school flag. Write sentences about it. Use is, are, and action verbs.

Checkup: Unit 5

Verbs (page 163)

Write the sentences and draw a line under each verb.

1. The leaves fall from the trees. **fall**
2. Children jump in the leaves. **jump**

Verbs That Tell About Now (page 165)

Write each sentence, using the correct verb.

3. Children (play, plays) baseball.
4. Anna (throw, throws) the ball.
5. Jeff (swings, swing) the bat.

Pronouns and Verbs (page 167)

Write each sentence, using the correct verb.

6. I (hit, hits) the ball and run to first base.
7. He (catch, catches) the ball.

Verbs with ed (page 169)

Write each sentence, using the verb that tells about the past.

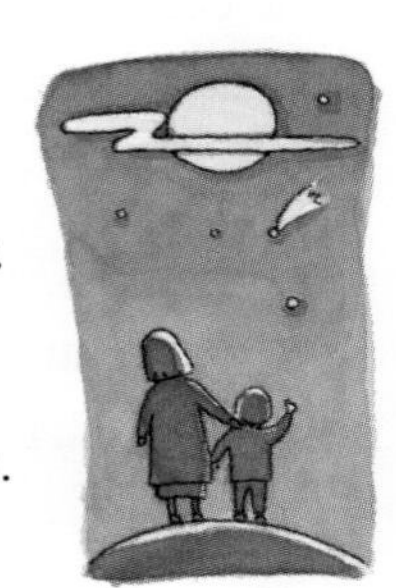

8. Last night we (watch, watched) the sky.
9. We (looked, look) for falling stars.
10. Some clouds (cover, covered) the moon.

Checkup

Objectives

Children will:

- identify verbs in sentences
- choose verbs that agree with singular and plural subjects
- identify verbs that agree with pronouns
- choose verbs that tell about the past

Using the Checkup

Use the Checkup exercises as assessment, as review for the unit test, as extra practice, or as a diagnostic aid to help determine those children who need reteaching.

INTERNET CONNECTION
Children can take an interactive quiz for this unit at www.eduplace.com /kids/hme/ and then get immediate feedback.

Objectives

Children will:
- choose correct verbs in sentences
- use *was, were, is,* and *are* correctly
- write contractions

Special Verbs (pages 173, 175, 177)

Write each sentence, using the correct verb.

11. Jan (ran, run) home.
12. She has (came, come) from the fair.
13. She (saw, seen) the horses.
14. Tom (did, done) a trick with his pony.
15. They (gave, given) his pony a prize.
16. Jan has (saw, seen) Tom ride before.

is and are (page 179)

Write each sentence correctly.
Use is or are.

17. Grapes ___are___ green.
18. A banana ___is___ soft.

was and were (page 181)

Write each sentence correctly.
Use was or were.

19. The bike ___is___ old.
20. The tires ___are___ flat.

Contractions (page 183)

Write the contractions for these words.

21. is not **isn't**
22. does not **doesn't**

Mixed Review

23–28. Proofread this letter. Find five mistakes with verbs and one mistake with a contraction. Write the letter correctly.

Proofreading Checklist

- ✔ Are came, went, and verbs that end in ed used to tell about the past?
- ✔ Is has/have used with given/done?
- ✔ Are was and were used correctly?
- ✔ Are contractions written correctly?
- ✔ Do verbs that tell about now and about one noun end with s?

Example The snails was moving slowly.
The snails were moving slowly.

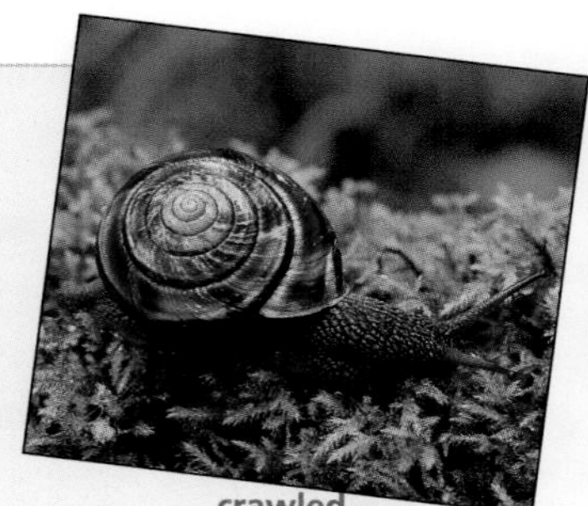

Dear Kevin,

Uncle Max gave me a pet snail. I named it Speedy. Speedy ~~live~~ lives in a glass bowl. He doesn't move around much. Uncle Max owns a snail too!

Last night the two snails raced. They ~~crawls~~ crawled on our racetrack. The race ~~were~~ was very slow! Uncle Max's snail went only ten inches in one hour. Speedy ~~done~~ did better. He crawled twenty inches. We have ~~gave~~ given Speedy a little blue ribbon. I ~~cant~~ can't wait until the next race!

Becky

See www.eduplace.com/kids/hme/ for an online quiz.

Objective

Children will:

- proofread a letter and correct errors in verbs and a contraction

Test Practice

Objective

Children will:

- practice completing a test format that requires them to choose the correct item among three

Using the Test Practice

- These Test Practice pages provide practice with common formats used in standardized or multiple-choice tests.
- The first page works with skills taught in the basic lessons in Unit 5. The second page works with skills taught in the lessons in Units 1, 3, and 5.

Notes on the Test Format

- Have a volunteer read the directions aloud to the class. Point out that there are three possible answers, only one of which is correct.
- Have children read the sentence in Item 1 aloud with each of the possible answers. Ask them to listen for the verb that sounds best. Then have children identify the two incorrect answers before marking the correct one.

FOR STUDENTS ACQUIRING ENGLISH

Review verb tenses, subject–verb agreement, and contractions. Review time words and phrases such as last week or yesterday that will help children determine the tense to use. Distribute the SAE Test Practice pages for Unit 5. Read the directions aloud for each section. Explain that in the first section children are to circle the correct verb to complete the sentence. In the second section they are to circle the sentence that does not have a mistake. Remind children to look for time words and phrases.

Assessment Link

Test Practice

Number a sheet of paper from 1 to 8. Read each sentence. The verb is missing. Choose the correct verb to put in the blank. Write the letter for that answer.

1 Last week Pedro ____.
- (A) painted
- B paint
- C paints

2 Matt has ____ the dishes.
- A does
- B did
- (C) done

3 Last night Pat ____ sad.
- A are
- (B) was
- C were

4 The cats ____ cute.
- A is
- (B) are
- C was

5 Dad has ____ me coins.
- A gave
- (B) given
- C give

6 Last month Scott ____ a TV show about whales.
- (A) saw
- B seen
- C see

7 They have ____ home.
- A go
- B went
- (C) gone

8 He ____ to the tree.
- A run
- (B) runs

190 Test Practice

Test Practice continued

Now write the numbers 9 to 14 on your paper. Read the four sentences by each number. Find the sentence that does not have any mistakes. Write the letter for that sentence.

9 **A** The rabbits hops.
B Two childs watch the rabbits.
(C) What do rabbits eat?
D Toms rabbit is brown.

10 **A** Where is the parade.
(B) The parade starts on Main Street.
C Last year the parade start late.
D Mom doesnt like parades.

11 **A** My brown puppy is named joe.
B I cant find my puppy.
C Joe hide in the bushes.
(D) Last night the puppy chased a boy.

12 **(A)** It is hot today!
B Marc make a paper fan.
C Beth eats peachs.
D I swims in the lake.

13 **(A)** The women in the picture are twins.
B The twins looks alike.
C Last week the twins plays a trick on me.
D do you know any twins

14 **A** Jack gone fishing with his friend.
B I and Jack saw a frog hidden in the mud.
C the frog jumped into the pond.
(D) The water isn't warm.

Objective

Children will:
- practice completing a test format that requires them to choose the correct item from among four

Notes on the Test Format

- Have a child read the directions aloud. Discuss what they mean, pointing out that children have taken this type of test before.
- Direct children's attention to Item 9. Point out that the sentences in this item include different types of errors: capitalization, punctuation, usage, or spelling errors. Explain to children that they will find a variety of errors in the other items as well.
- Have children carefully read each sentence. Explain that sometimes it is a good idea to read each sentence two or three times until they find an error. Have them locate errors in three sentences before deciding which one is correct.

Cumulative Review

Objectives

Children will:
- make complete sentences
- complete sentences by writing a naming or action part
- identify complete sentences and types of sentences

Using the Cumulative Review

This Cumulative Review provides cumulative practice with basic grammar, usage, and mechanics skills taught in Units 1, 3, and 5. You can use these pages for assessment, as a review for a test, as extra practice, or as a diagnostic aid to determine those students who may need reteaching.

Unit 1: The Sentence

What Is a Sentence? (pages 27–28)

Make sentences by matching the words in Box **A** with the words in Box **B**. Write the sentences.

A	B
1. The sun	eats a leaf.
2. The bug	sing in a tree.
3. Dad	shines brightly.
4. The birds	waters the garden.

Naming Part and Action Part (pages 29–32)

Write each sentence. Add your own naming part or action part to finish each one.

5. The girl ____. Answers will vary.
6. ____ tastes good. Answers will vary.

Is It a Sentence? (pages 33–34)

Write the complete sentence in each pair.

7. The letter was a surprise!
   A letter from Jill.
8. Fun to read.
   I answered it.

Which Kind of Sentence? (pages 37–46)

Write each sentence. Add the correct end mark. Tell if it is a telling sentence, question, command, or exclamation.

9. Do you like a circus ? question
10. Please be quiet . command
11. I see the clowns . telling sentence
12. This is exciting ! exclamation

Unit 3: Nouns and Pronouns

Nouns (pages 93–96)

Write the sentences. Draw a line under each noun.

13. Was the lake warm? **14.** A fly buzzed.

One and More Than One (pages 97–98, 101–104)

Write each noun to name more than one.

15. inch inches

16. woman women

17. child children

18. dog dogs

Special Nouns (pages 105–106)

Write each sentence correctly. Use capital letters for special nouns.

19. I miss my friend doug. Doug

20. He moved to denver. Denver

Pronouns (pages 107–108)

Write each sentence, using a pronoun in place of the underlined word or words. Use he, she, it, or they.

21. Carlos hit the ball. He hit the ball.

22. The ball went far. It went far.

Objective

Children will:

- use nouns, plural nouns, pronouns, and special nouns correctly

Objectives

Children will:

- use pronouns and possessive nouns correctly
- use verbs correctly

Naming Yourself Last (pages 111–112)

Write the sentences correctly.

23. (James and I, I and James) ride bikes.
24. (Alma and me, Alma and I) play ball.

Nouns Ending with 's and s' (pages 113–116)

Write each word group. Does the first noun name one or more than one? Make this noun show ownership.

25. two birds nests
    two birds' nests
26. cat dish
    cat's dish

Unit 5: Verbs

Verbs (pages 163–164)

Write the sentences. Draw a line under each verb.

27. Darlene hides.
28. Jason finds her.

Verbs: Now and in the Past (pages 165–166, 169–170)

Write each sentence. Use the correct verb.

29. Ron (help, helps) clean the house.
30. Yesterday I (mow, mowed) the lawn.

Pronouns and Verbs (pages 167–168)

Write each sentence. Use the correct verb.

31. He (fixes, fix) the bike.
32. They (make, makes) lunch.

Special Verbs (pages 173–178)

Write each sentence. Use the correct verb.

33. Kim (ran, run) in the race yesterday.

34. Her family (come, came) to watch.

35. Juan has (gone, went) to a movie.

36. I have (saw, seen) many movies.

37. I (did, done) the jigsaw puzzle.

38. I have (gave, given) it to Cam.

is and are, was and were

(pages 179–182)

Write each sentence. Use the correct verb.

39. The circus (was, were) great.

40. The clowns (was, were) the best part.

41. The clowns (is, are) always funny.

42. My favorite clown (is, are) very tall.

Contractions (pages 183–184)

Write the sentences. Use a contraction for the underlined words.

43. He is not tall. He isn't tall.

44. He cannot reach. He can't reach.

45. Do not fall. Don't fall.

Objectives

Children will:

- use special verbs correctly
- use *is* and *are*, *was* and *were* correctly
- write contractions

Verbs

Objective

Children will:
- identify and write verbs

Using the Extra Practice

The Extra Practice activities provide two levels of additional practice for the basic lesson: Easy/Average (●▲), and Challenging (■).

The Extra Practice activities can be used in the following ways.

- Assign activities according to children's needs and abilities as homework after children have completed the basic lesson.
- Assign the Easy/Average activities after using the lesson Reteaching instruction.
- Assign the Challenging exercises as a Bonus activity.
- Assign the Easy/Average activities to prepare children for the Checkup.
- Assign the Easy/Average activities to children who had difficulty with specific lessons on the Checkup.

(pages 163–164)

1 Verbs
- A verb names an action that someone or something does or did.

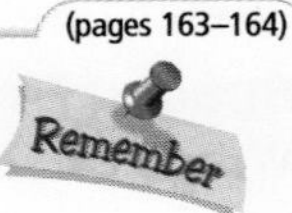

●▲ Choose the verb from the Word Box that belongs in each sentence. Write the sentences.

claps	toot	sings	plays

Example The band _____ music.
The band plays music.

1. A girl sings a song.
2. Two boys toot horns.
3. The crowd claps loudly.

■ **4–12.** Copy the box. Around the box, write each verb.

Example cut sheep [Verbs] cut

	Verbs	
chews		catch
dig		learn
sister		skips
read		first
run		crawl
swim		happy
teacher		sunny

Meeting Individual Needs — More Practice for Lesson 1

● EASY ▲ AVERAGE

Draw a line under each word that names an action. Write the word.

1. People see the circus.
2. The man plays a drum.
3. The clown rides a bike.
4. The girl pets a tiger.
5. A woman sells popcorn.
6. Two boys take tickets.
7. Three dogs jump through fire.
8. A person laughs loudly.
9. That baby likes the show.
10. The crowd goes home.

■ CHALLENGING

Write a verb to finish each sentence. (Answers will vary.)

1. The boy _____.
2. That woman ______.
3. The dog ________.
4. The two monkeys ________.
5. One bear ________.
6. Those men ________.
7. A lady ________.
8. The girls ________.
9. My dog ________.
10. Your cat ________.

Extra Practice

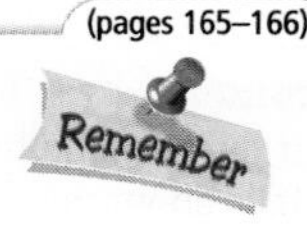

(pages 165–166)

2 Verbs That Tell About Now

- Add s to a verb that tells about one when the action is happening now.

Remember

●▲ Write the correct verb for each sentence.

Example Josh (swim, swims). swims

1. Janet and Rachel (talk, talks).
2. Pedro (play, plays) baseball.
3. Chris (feed, feeds) his pet.
4. Doug and Dan (read, reads).
5. Kelsey (kick, kicks) a soccer ball.

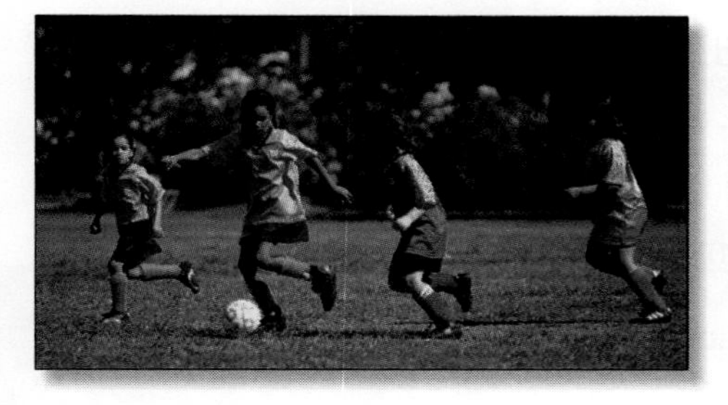

■ Write each sentence. Use the correct verb.

Example Mom (make, makes) birdhouses.
Mom makes birdhouses.

6. Amy and Susie (help, helps) her.
   Amy and Susie help her.
7. Susie (paint, paints) the houses.
   Susie paints the houses.
8. Amy (fill, fills) them with seeds.
   Amy fills them with seeds.

Verbs That Tell About Now

Objective

Children will:

- correctly add *s* to verbs that tell about one when the action is happening now

Meeting Individual Needs — More Practice for Lesson 2

● **EASY** ▲ **AVERAGE**

Draw a line under each correct verb.

1. The boys (walks, walk).
2. Mary Beth (sing, sings).
3. My father (drive, drives).
4. The two fish (swims, swim).
5. Jenna and Matthew (sleep, sleeps).
6. Jake (paints, paint).
7. The three mothers (works, work).
8. The teacher (write, writes).
9. The four mice (runs, run).
10. That squirrel (eats, eat).

■ **CHALLENGING**

Write each sentence. Use the correct verb.

1. Dad (cook, cooks) dinner.
   Dad cooks dinner.
2. Grandpa (bakes, bake) bread.
   Grandpa bakes bread.
3. Mom and I (cleans, clean) up.
   Mom and I clean up.
4. Jerry (serves, serve) dessert.
   Jerry serves dessert.
5. We all (likes, like) the pie.
   We all like the pie.
6. After, we all (read, reads) a story.
   After, we all read a story.
7. The clock (strike, strikes) nine.
   The clock strikes nine.
8. The whole family (sleep, sleeps).
   The whole family sleeps.
9. I (dreams, dream) about dogs.
   I dream about fun dogs.
10. The dogs (plays, play) with me.
    The dogs play with me.

Pronouns and Verbs

Objective

Children will:

- correctly identify and write verbs to go with pronouns *he, she, it, I, you, we,* and *they*

Extra Practice

(pages 167–168)

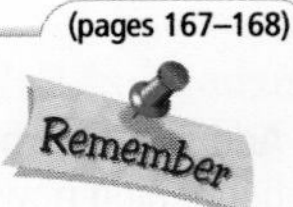

3 Pronouns and Verbs

- If the pronoun he, she, or it comes before a verb that tells about now, add s or es to the verb.

●▲ Write the correct sentence in each pair.

Example She like fruit. She likes fruit.
She likes fruit.

1. We shops for food.
   We shop for food.
2. He looks at the bread.
   He look at the bread.
3. It smells good.
   It smell good.
4. I wants some milk.
   I want some milk.

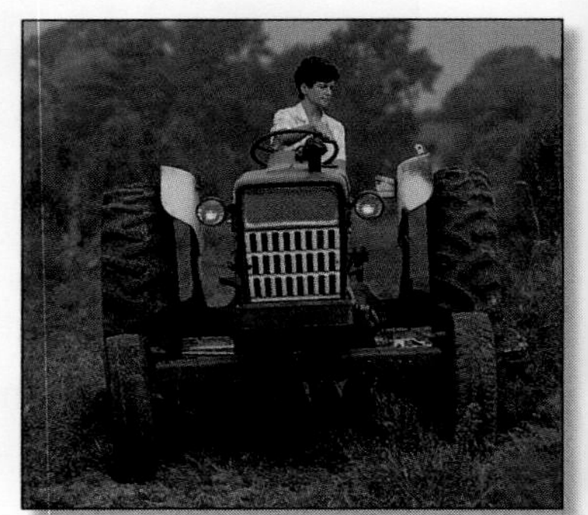

■ Write each sentence.
Use the correct verb.

Example She (drive, drives) a tractor.
She drives a tractor.

5. He (fix, fixes) the fence. He fixes the fence.
6. They (grow, grows) corn. They grow corn.
7. We (help, helps) pick corn. We help pick corn.

Meeting Individual Needs — More Practice for Lesson 3

● **EASY** ▲ **AVERAGE**

Draw a line under the correct sentence in each pair.

1. He work at home. He works at home.
2. It come to me. It comes to me.
3. I race my brothers. I races my brothers.
4. She mails a letter. She mail a letter.
5. We walks to town. We walk to town.
6. They sees a movie. They see a movie.
7. You buy a dress. You buys a dress.
8. He drops the ball. He drop the ball.
9. We needs to eat. We need to eat.
10. I sit in the chair. I sits in the chair.

■ **CHALLENGING**

Write each sentence. Use the correct verb.

1. They (buy, buys) a radio.
   They buy a radio.
2. It (work, works) fine. It works fine.
3. He (talks, talk) on the radio.
   He talks on the radio.
4. She (sing, sings) on the radio.
   She sings on the radio.
5. We (listen, listens) to the songs.
   We listen to the songs.
6. You (breaks, break) the radio.
   You break the radio.
7. He (gets, get) us a new one.
   He gets us a new one.
8. It (look, looks) pretty. It looks pretty.
9. She (hear, hears) a nice song.
   She hears a nice song.
10. The radio (play, plays) our favorite music.
    The radio plays our favorite music.

Extra Practice

(pages 169–170)

4 Verbs with ed

- Add ed to most verbs to show that the action happened in the past.

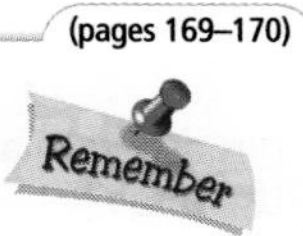

●▲ Write the sentences, using verbs that tell about the past.

Example Mother (starts, started) the car.
Mother started the car.

1. The car (turned, turns) left.
2. We (pass, passed) the school.
3. A school bus (honked, honks) at us.

■ Change each verb in ( ) so that the sentence tells about the past. Write the sentences correctly.

Example We ____ the car. (wash) We washed the car.

4. Dad turned on the water. (turn)
5. John filled the bucket. (fill)
6. Annie added some soap. (add)
7. I cleaned the windows. (clean)
8. The car looked great. (look)

Verbs with ed

Objective

Children will:

- correctly add *ed* to a verb to show that something happened in the past

Meeting Individual Needs

More Practice for Lesson 4

● **EASY** ▲ **AVERAGE**

Draw a line under each verb that tells about the past.

1. They (paint, painted) the house yellow.
2. The girls (lived, live) in the house.
3. Grandma (washes, washed) the clothes.
4. Grandpa (sews, sewed) a quilt.
5. Dad (played, plays) with the baby.
6. Mom (watches, watched) television.
7. Salina (starts, started) to cook.
8. James (bakes, baked) muffins.
9. Hank (talked, talks) on the phone.
10. Gigi (cooked, cooks) soup.

■ **CHALLENGING**

Rewrite each verb in ( ) so that the sentences tell about the past.

1. The party (starts). started
2. Chad (picks) up the gifts. picked
3. Jenny (tricks) her guests. tricked
4. Martha (turns) the chairs around. turned
5. We (open) the window. opened
6. The room (fills) up. filled
7. Dad (lifts) Jenny in the air. lifted
8. Everyone (jokes) about the silly dog. joked
9. The dog (jumps) onto the cake. jumped
10. Mother (wipes) up the mess. wiped

ran, run and came, come

Objective

Children will:

- identify when to use helping verbs *have* and *has* in sentences with the verbs *ran, run, come,* and *came*

Extra Practice

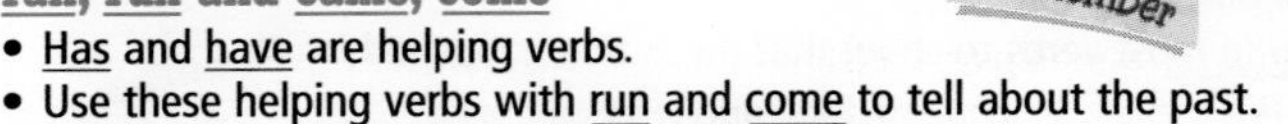

5 ran, run and came, come (pages 173–174) Remember

- Has and have are helping verbs.
- Use these helping verbs with run and come to tell about the past.
- Do not use these helping verbs with ran and came.

●▲ Write each sentence. Use the correct verb.

Example They have (come, came) for the party.
They have come for the party.

1. Jesse (run, ran) all the way.
2. Evan (came, come) an hour ago.
3. Now Julie has (run, ran) to the door.
4. Ira has (came, come) with a big present.

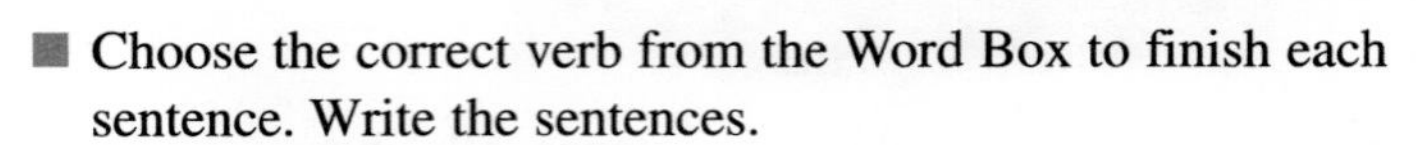

■ Choose the correct verb from the Word Box to finish each sentence. Write the sentences.

ran	run	came	come

Example The team _____ on a bus.
The team came on a bus.

5. Maria's friend has _come_ to the track meet.
6. Maria _ran_ in the relay race yesterday.
7. She has _run_ in every race so far.

Meeting Individual Needs — More Practice for Lesson 5

● EASY ▲ AVERAGE

Draw a line under the correct verb.

1. Fran (ran, run) home.
2. At last they have (came, come) to school.
3. Herbie has (ran, run) the race.
4. Andrea (came, come) to the window.
5. We (run, ran) around.
6. You have (came, come) to meet me.
7. She has (ran, run) so far.
8. They (come, came) over yesterday.
9. Lucas has (came, come) to dance.
10. Petra (run, ran) away.

■ CHALLENGING

Choose one of these words to finish each sentence: ran, run, came, come

1. Len has _____ to the party. come *or* run
2. Julia ____ in the relay race. ran
3. My car has _____ over a stick. run
4. They have _____ in every race this year. run
5. My friends _____ to my house. came *or* ran
6. Vince ____ around the block. ran *or* came
7. Ned has ____ to see the dog. come
8. Brenda and Dave have ____ up the road very fast. run
9. The cat ____ after the mouse. ran *or* came
10. The rabbit has ____ away. run

Extra Practice

(pages 175–176)

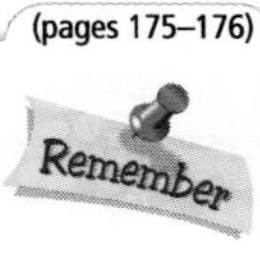

6 saw, seen and went, gone

- Has and have are helping verbs.
- Use these helping verbs with seen and gone to tell about the past.
- Do not use these helping verbs with saw and went.

●▲ Write each sentence. Use the correct verb.

Example Nick (saw, seen) many frogs at the pond.
Nick saw many frogs at the pond.

1. He has (saw, seen) them there all summer.
2. Now summer has (went, gone).
3. Nick (went, gone) back to the pond today.
4. He (saw, seen) only a few frogs.

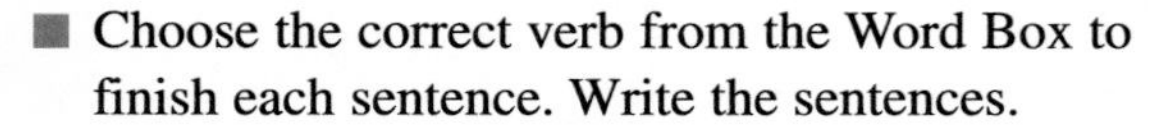

■ Choose the correct verb from the Word Box to finish each sentence. Write the sentences.

saw
seen
went
gone

Example Aunt Kim and I _____ on a whale watch.
Aunt Kim and I went on a whale watch.

5. Aunt Kim has gone on one before.
6. She has seen huge whales.
7. First we saw a whale's tail.
8. Then the whale went under the ship.

saw, seen and went, gone

Objective

Children will:

- identify when to use helping verbs *have* and *has* in sentences with the verbs *saw, seen, went,* and *gone*

Meeting Individual Needs

More Practice for Lesson 6

● **EASY** ▲ **AVERAGE**

Draw a line under each correct verb.

1. Tina (seen, saw) a lot of deer.
2. She has (saw, seen) them in the meadow before.
3. Rick (gone, went) to see them, too.
4. They have (saw, seen) raccoons, also.
5. Now the raccoons have (went, gone) away.
6. They (went, gone) to find food.
7. All the deer (saw, seen) where they went.
8. Rick has (went, gone) after them.
9. Tina (saw, seen) where Rick went.
10. They have (went, gone) to find the animals.

■ **CHALLENGING**

Choose one of these words to finish each sentence: saw, seen, went, gone

1. I have _____ my friend. seen
2. She has ____ down the street. gone
3. Kim ____ her, too. saw
4. We _____ to talk to her. went
5. Now we all have _____ to the movies. gone
6. We _____ a good movie. saw
7. I have ____ it before. seen
8. I _____ to see it last year. went
9. My brother has ____ to see it twice before. gone
10. Our family _____ to see it together. went

did, done, and gave, given

Objective

Children will:

- identify when to use helping verbs *have* and *has* in sentences with the verbs *did, done, gave* and *given*

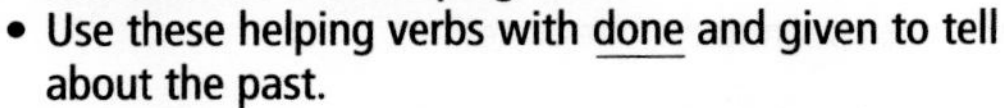
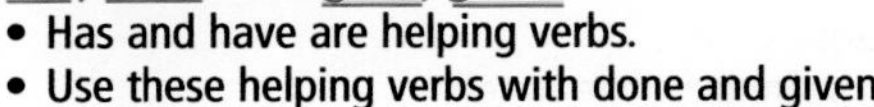

(pages 177–178)

7 did, done and gave, given

- Has and have are helping verbs.
- Use these helping verbs with done and given to tell about the past.
- Do not use these helping verbs with did and gave.

●▲ Write each sentence. Use the correct verb.

Example Carlos (gave, given) Rosa a book on birds.
Carlos gave Rosa a book on birds.

1. Rosa has (did, done) a report on birds.
2. She (gave, given) the report to her teacher.
3. Rosa has (did, done) a good job.
4. She (gave, given) the book to Sam.

■ Choose the correct verb from the Word Box to finish each sentence. Write the sentences.

did	done	gave	given

Example Dana _____ the prize to David.
Dana gave the prize to David.

5. Mother has given us apples.
6. Lisa has done a math project.
7. Fran and I did cartwheels.

Meeting Individual Needs — More Practice for Lesson 7

● **EASY** ▲ **AVERAGE**

Draw a line under each correct verb.

1. Bert (done, did) something nice.
2. He (gave, given) Wendy a dog.
3. He has (gave, given) her a cat, too.
4. Wendy has (done, did) a favor for Bert.
5. They have (gave, given) each other help.
6. The dog (done, did) tricks.
7. The cat has (done, did) tricks, too.
8. The dog (given, gave) the cat a kiss.
9. The cat (gave, given) the dog a scratch.
10. Then the dog (done, did) something else.

■ **CHALLENGING**

Choose one of these verbs to finish each sentence: did, done, gave, given

1. Joe has _____ a speech. given
2. He _____ everyone a piece of paper. gave
3. They all _____ what they were told. did
4. They have _____ it before. done *or* given
5. Shelly _____ me a peach. gave
6. I _____ it right. did
7. Janie has _____ everything wrong. done
8. She ___ not want to do it. did
9. We have _____ all our toys away. given
10. Someone _____ me a surprise. gave

Extra Practice

(pages 179–180)

8 is and are
- Is and are tell about something that is happening now.
- Use is to tell about one person, animal, place, or thing.
- Use are to tell about more than one.

●▲ Write each sentence. Use the correct verb.

Example The day (is, are) sunny.
The day is sunny.

1. The birds (is, are) singing.
2. Mother (are, is) picking flowers.
3. Dad (are, is) mowing the grass.
4. Rob and I (are, is) glad it is summer.

■ Use is or are to finish each sentence. Write the sentences correctly.

Example The zoo ____ full of animals.
The zoo is full of animals.

5. The baby elephant __is__ wobbly.
6. The monkeys __are__ funny.
7. The baby bears __are__ cute.
8. The giraffe __is__ tall.
9. The zookeeper __is__ busy.

is and are

Objective

Children will:
- correctly use *is* and *are* in sentences

Meeting Individual Needs — More Practice for Lesson 8

● **EASY** ▲ **AVERAGE**

Draw a line under each correct verb.

1. We (is, are) laughing.
2. They (are, is) running.
3. She (are, is) here.
4. The birds (is, are) flying.
5. That dog (are, is) happy.
6. The picnic (is, are) fun.
7. This summer (are, is) hot.
8. The clouds (are, is) pretty.
9. One fish (is, are) jumping.
10. Now we (is, are) going home.

■ **CHALLENGING**

Write *is* or *are* to finish each sentence correctly.

1. The zoo ___ close to my house. is
2. We ___ going there today. are
3. The lion __ roaring. is
4. The zoo keepers ___ feeding him. are
5. The seals _____ playing. are
6. The gorilla ___ alone. is
7. He ___ eating fruit. is
8. We ___ watching him. are
9. It ___ fun here. is
10. This day ___ great. is

was and were

Objective

Children will:
- correctly use *was* and *were* in sentences

Extra Practice

(pages 181–182)

9 was and were

- Was and were tell about something that happened in the past.
- Use was to tell about one person, animal, place, or thing.
- Use were to tell about more than one.

●▲ Write the correct verb for each sentence.

Example The boat (was, were) big. was

1. The sails (was, were) full of wind.
2. The wind (was, were) very strong.
3. White clouds (was, were) in the sky.
4. The sunshine (was, were) bright.
5. The waves (was, were) small.

■ Use was or were to finish each sentence. Write the sentences correctly.

Example Our hike _____ fun.
Our hike was fun.

6. The path _____ narrow. The path was narrow.
7. We _____ very high up. We were very high up.
8. Some hikers _____ tired. Some hikers were tired.

204 Extra Practice

Meeting Individual Needs — More Practice for Lesson 9

● **EASY** ▲ **AVERAGE**

Draw a line under each correct verb.

1. The ocean (were, was) blue.
2. Waves (was, were) hitting the beach.
3. People (were, was) swimming.
4. Children (was, were) making sand castles.
5. The beach (was, were) hot.
6. The sun (were, was) strong.
7. Then winds (were, was) coming.
8. Umbrellas (was, were) blowing away.
9. Women (was, were) running after them.
10. Men (were, was) packing up their bags.

■ **CHALLENGING**

Use *was* or *were* to write the sentences correctly.

1. Our trip ____ fun. was
2. We _____ excited to go. were
3. Lance ____ bringing the food. was
4. Carina _____ packing the car. was
5. My brother _____ not going. was
6. My sisters _____ going to meet us there. were
7. They _____ driving their own car. were
8. Our car ____ too small. was
9. Many people _____ going on the trip. were
10. I _____ not happy to come home. was

Extra Practice

(pages 183–184)

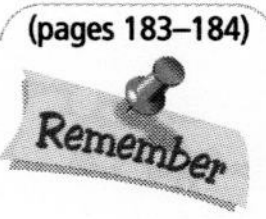

10 Contractions
- A contraction is a short way of writing two words.
- An apostrophe (') shows where letters were left out.

●▲ Write each sentence, using a contraction for the underlined word or words.

Example Dad cannot start the car.
Dad can't start the car.

1. It does not have any gas. doesn't
2. We cannot drive to school. can't
3. Buses do not come here. don't
4. It is not too far to walk. isn't

■ Write each sentence, using the word or words that make up the underlined contraction.

Example Ross can't go to school today.
Ross cannot go to school today.

5. Ross doesn't feel well. does not
6. He isn't getting out of bed. is not
7. I don't have any juice for him. do not

Contractions

Objective

Children will:
- correctly write contractions and the words that make up contractions

Meeting Individual Needs

More Practice for Lesson 10

● **EASY** ▲ **AVERAGE**

Write the contraction for each underlined word or group of words.

1. We do not want to leave. don't
2. She does not want to stay. doesn't
3. He is not here. isn't
4. They cannot come. can't
5. Please do not touch those. don't
6. I cannot look at them. can't
7. It is not too far. isn't
8. Connie does not live near. doesn't
9. They cannot walk to her house. can't
10. She is not at home. isn't

■ **CHALLENGING**

Write the word or words that make up each contraction.

1. Marta isn't at the party. is not
2. She can't find the house. cannot
3. We don't know what to do. do not
4. Peter doesn't want to look for her. does not
5. Mom isn't here yet. is not
6. Marta can't be with Mom. cannot
7. Mom doesn't know Marta. does not
8. They don't know each other. do not
9. There isn't anything we can do. is not
10. We can't start the party yet. cannot

Unit 6 Planning Guide

Writing Instructions

Writing Instructions: *2 weeks*
Special Focus and Communication Links: *1 week (optional)*

	Blackline Masters (TE)	Workbook Plus	Reteaching Workbook
A Published Model "Let's Make Rain" From the writers of *Your Big Backyard (207)*			
What Makes Great Instructions? *(209)*			
Student Model Working Draft *(210)* Final Copy *(211)*	6–1		
The Writing Process Write Instructions			
Prewriting Explore Your Topic *(213)*	6–2		
Focus Skill: Using Order Words *(214)*	6–3	79	50
Drafting Focus Skill: Topic Sentence *(215)*		80	51
Revising How Good Are Your Instructions? [rubric] *(217)*	6–4	81	52
Writing Conference *(218)*	6–5		
Revising Strategies *(220)*		82	53
Proofreading *(221)*			
Publishing and Reflecting *(222)*			
Writing Prompts and Test Practice *(224–225)*			
SPECIAL FOCUS ON INFORMING **Writing a Research Report** *(226–233)*			
COMMUNICATION LINKS **Listening/Speaking: Giving and Following Instructions** *(234–235)* **Viewing: Following Picture Directions** *(236–237)*			

Unit 6

Tools and Tips

- **Using the Dictionary,** *pp. H3–H12*
- **Using Technology,** *pp. H21–H30*
- **Writer's Tools,** *pp. H31–H34*
- **Spelling Guide,** *pp. H40–H44*
- **My First Thesaurus,** *pp. H45–H56*

School-Home Connection

Suggestions for informing or involving family members in classroom activities and learning related to this unit are included in the Teacher's Edition throughout the unit.

Meeting Individual Needs

- **FOR SPECIAL NEEDS/INCLUSION:** *Houghton Mifflin English* Audiotape
- **FOR STUDENTS ACQUIRING ENGLISH:**
  - Notes and activities are included in this Teacher's Edition throughout the unit to help you adapt or use pupil book activities with students acquiring English.
  - Students can listen to the published and student models on audiotape.
- **ENRICHMENT:** See *Teacher's Resource Book.*

All audiotape recordings are also available on CD.

Daily Language Practice

Each sentence or group of words includes two capitalization, punctuation, usage, or spelling errors based on skills presented in the Grammar and Spelling Connections in this unit or from Grammar Units 1, 3, and 5. Each day write one sentence on the chalkboard. Have children find the errors and write the sentence correctly on a sheet of paper. To make the activity easier, identify the kinds of errors.

1. The puppy drink water from a pink bowl The puppy drinks water from a pink bowl. (verbs in the present; end punctuation/statements)
2. Last nyt, Jess fix the lock on the back door. Last night, Jess fixed the lock on the back door. (spelling/long *i* sound; past tense/verbs)
3. Every day she get the mail out of the two boxs. Every day she gets the mail out of the two boxes. (pronouns and verbs; plural nouns with *es*)
4. Two man have came to put a new roof on the garage. Two men have come to put a new roof on the garage. (irregular plural nouns; irregular verbs)
5. Ingrid has ran to the store on spring Street. Ingrid has run to the store on Spring Street. (irregular verbs; capitalizing/proper nouns)
6. Dont throw papers in the pool? Don't throw papers in the pool. (contractions with *not*; end punctuation/commands)
7. Miss Lane wrytes the names of all the helper on the chart. Miss Lane writes the names of all the helpers on the chart. (spelling/long *i* sound; plural nouns with *s*)
8. I and Joel was in a hurry to get to the game. Joel and I were in a hurry to get to the game. (naming yourself last; verbs *was* and *were*)
9. Mi brother couldnt come to the school picnic. My brother couldn't come to the school picnic. (spelling/long *i* sound; contractions with *not*)
10. The dinner are going to be ready soon? The dinner is going to be ready soon. (verbs *is* and *are*; end punctuation/statements)

Additional Resources

Workbook Plus, Unit 6
Reteaching Workbook, Unit 6
Teacher's Resource Book
Audiotapes
Transparencies, Unit 6
Posters, Unit 6

Technology Tools

TEACHER'S RESOURCE DISK (for handwriting support)

CD-ROM: *Sunbuddy® Writer
Paint, Write & Play! (published by The Learning Company)
*Type to Learn Jr.™

INTERNET: http://www.eduplace.com/kids/hme/ or http://www.eduplace.com/rdg/hme/

Visit Education Place for these additional support materials and activities:

- author biographies
- student writing models
- graphic organizers
- an interactive rubric
- writing prompts

Assessment

Test Booklet, Unit 6

Keeping a Journal

Discuss with children the value of keeping a journal as a way of promoting self-expression and fluency. Encourage children to record their thoughts and ideas in a notebook. Inform students whether the journal will be private or will be reviewed periodically as a way of assisting growth. The following prompts may be useful for generating writing ideas.

Journal Prompts

- Where is the farthest away from home you have ever been? How did you get there?
- Tell about something that someone recently showed you how to do.
- What kinds of puzzles do you know how to do? What makes them easy or hard to do?

Introducing the Unit

Using the Photograph

- Have children look at the photograph, and ask a volunteer to read the caption aloud. Call on volunteers to tell about their experiences blowing soap bubbles. Have they ever been in a bubble-blowing contest?
- Ask children whether they think blowing soap bubbles like the boy is doing in the photograph would be easy. Why might instructions be helpful? (They could help someone blow big bubbles or direct the path of the bubbles.)
- Have children suggest steps for instructions for blowing bubbles for a younger child who has never done this activity.
- Tell children that they will learn about writing clear and easy-to-follow **instructions**.

Independent Writing

Children can benefit by having time each day or several times a week to write in their journals or do self-selected writing activities. Remind children to think about purpose and audience and choose an appropriate format for both.

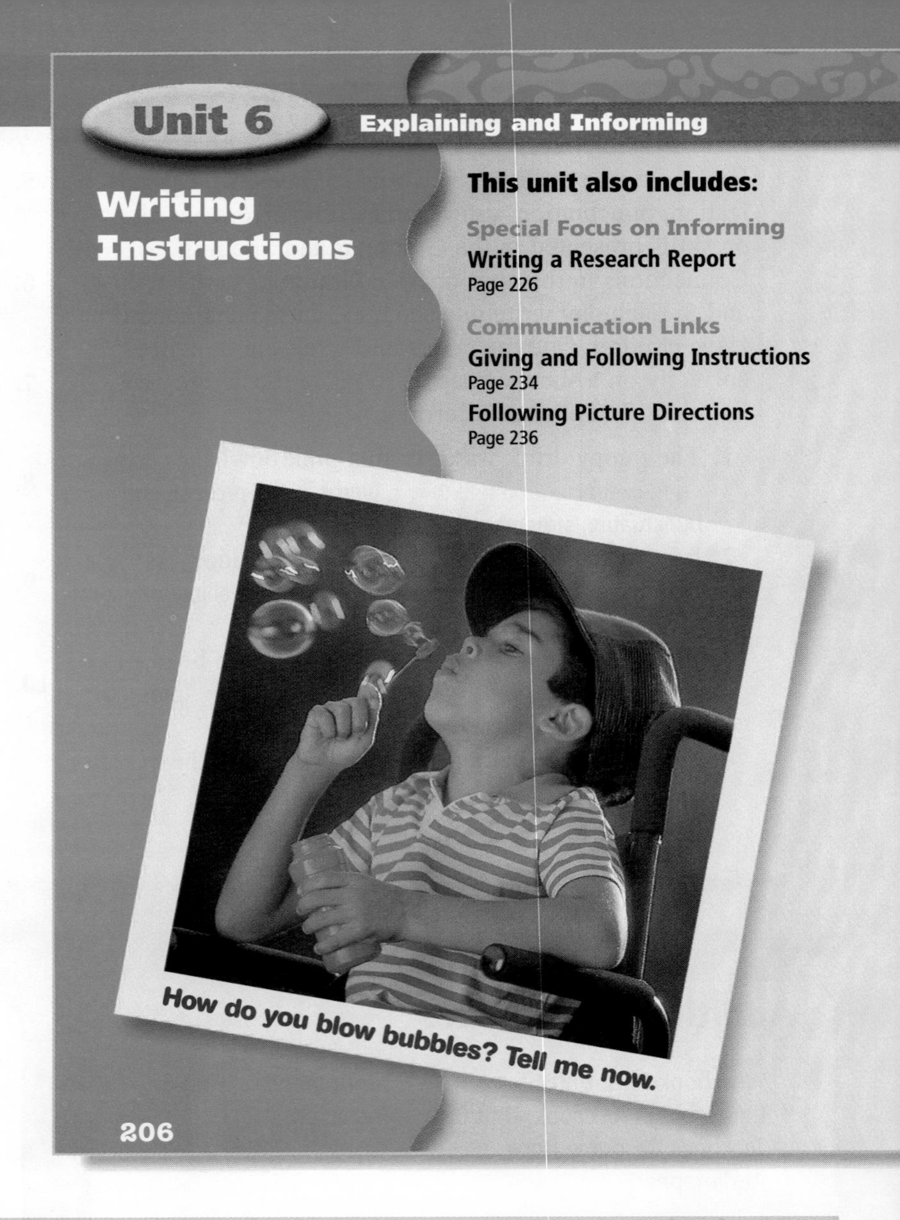

Shared Writing Activity

Work with children to develop clear and easy-to-follow instructions.

1. Have children work with partners to brainstorm topics for instructions. Have partners share their ideas with the class and then decide on one topic to develop as a class.
2. Ask volunteers to think of materials that might be needed. Write their suggestions on the board. Then continue with other volunteers suggesting steps in the process. Write each step on the board or on an overhead transparency.
3. Work as a class to check the order of the steps. Have children tell you in which order things should happen, and ask them to help you number the steps correctly.
   - At this time you may introduce order words, such as *first, next, then, now,* and so on.
4. Have volunteers read the list of steps in order, by number. Ask another volunteer to act out the steps as they are being read.
5. Discuss the accuracy of the information, the order of the steps, and any other observations the children may have about the instructions.

A Published Model

Listening to Instructions

"Let's Make Rain" gives instructions for making rain in a plastic bag. What are the main steps?

Let's Make Rain

from the writers of Your Big Backyard

topic sentence

How would you like to make it rain? You'll need a sealable plastic bag, soil, grass, a spoon, water, a straw, and tape.

First, put a few spoonsful of soil in the bottom of the bag. Add a handful of grass. Pour a spoonful of water over the grass.

order words

Next, place a straw at one end of the bag. Close the bag around the straw. Puff up the bag by blowing in the straw. Then have someone pull out the straw while you seal the bag.

Finally, tape the bag to a sunny window. After a while, you may see drops of water forming inside. When the drops get big enough they will roll down the sides. You've made rain in a bag!

Main Steps: put some grass, dirt, and water in the plastic bag; puff up and seal the bag; tape the bag in a sunny place.

Unit 6: Instructions 207

Bibliography

Here are other books that model this type of writing that children may enjoy reading.

- ***Loo-Loo Boo, and Art You Can Do*** by Denis Roche
- ***Play and Find Out About Nature*** by Janice VanCleave
- ***How a Seed Grows*** by Helene J. Jordan

"Let's Make Rain"

Lesson Objectives

Children will:
- read a published model of instructions
- identify characteristics of instructions
- understand sequence of instructions
- use visuals to enhance meaning
- write personal and critical responses

Focus on the Model

Building Background

Ask children to discuss experiments they have taken part in. What did they do? What did they find out? Tell children that they will read instructions that tell about that kind of experience.

Introducing Vocabulary

Introduce key vocabulary words by writing these sentences on the board.

The water could not leak out of the **sealable** bag.

She filled her spoon with flour because the recipe called for a **spoonful** of flour.

Reading the Selection

- Discuss the general purpose for listening to or reading instructions. Explain that instructions tell us how to make or do something.
- Read aloud the introduction to the selection and the purpose-setting question, which focuses on a characteristic of instructions. Tell children to read or listen for the answer to the question.
- Read aloud or have volunteers read aloud the selection if you wish to reinforce listening skills or if children need extra support.
- Explain that the experiment works because moisture is introduced into the bag. Heat from the sun interacts with the moisture to cause condensation. The air in the bag provides an area for the condensation to form.

  Alternatively, children can listen to the selection on audiotape.
- The call outs highlight characteristics of instructions that are addressed in the Think About the Instructions questions at the end of this selection.

FOR STUDENTS ACQUIRING ENGLISH

Before reading the model, look at the pictures and write the words sealable, soil, spoonful and handful on the board. Pair the children learning English with students who are fluent in English to follow the instructions together.

Focus on Instruction

Ask volunteers to retell the selection. Write their responses on the board or on an overhead transparency and help them develop a summary of the selection.

Answers to Reading As a Writer

The Think About the Instructions questions highlight criteria listed on the "What Makes Great Instructions?" and "How Good Are Your Instructions?" pages in the pupil book.

Think About the Instructions

- First, fill the bag with soil, grass, and water. Then, using a straw, puff up the bag and seal it. Finally, tape the bag to a sunny window.
- The writer used the words first, next, then, and finally.
- The first sentence, *How would you like to make it rain?* tells the topic of the instructions.

Think About Writer's Craft

- The writer wanted to separate the related steps into paragraphs.

Think About the Picture

- Taping the bag to a sunny window.

More About Writer's Craft

- Other Writer's Craft techniques or grammar elements that you can point out in "Let's Make Rain" include the use of interrogative and declarative sentences.

Notes on Responding

Ask volunteers to share personal responses. Remind children that although instructions must be followed in the correct order, children's responses don't have to be exactly the same.

Personal Response

Have children share their responses and relate any experiences they have had with science experiments.

Critical Thinking

Ask children to name another container that might work as well as a plastic bag. Why? (Sample answer: A jar with a lid because it holds moisture.)

A Published Model

Reading As a Writer See TE margin for answers.

Think About the Instructions

- What are the main steps in making a bag of rain?
- What order words did the writer use?
- Which sentence first tells the topic of the instructions?

Think About Writer's Craft

- Why do you think the writer put the instructions in four paragraphs?

Think About the Picture

- Which step of the instructions does the picture above help you understand?

Responding See TE margin for answers.

Write an answer to this question.

- **Personal Response** Would you enjoy making a bag of rain? Why or why not?

208 A Published Model

Mapping the Selection

Mapping helps children to visualize the structure of a piece of writing. After children have read the instructions, draw the following Order Chart on the chalkboard. Have children fill in the Order Chart by filling in each order word and step.

Let's Make Rain

Order Word	Step
First	
Next	
Finally	

What Makes Great Instructions?

Instructions tell how to do something. Remember to do these things when you write instructions.

- Write about something that you know how to do well and can explain clearly.
- Begin with an interesting topic sentence.
- Write all of the steps in order.
- Make each step clear and complete.
- Use order words, such as first, next, then, and finally.
- Write an ending that will make your readers want to follow the instructions.

GRAMMAR CHECK

Be sure that there is a verb in each sentence that you write.

What Makes Great Instructions?

Lesson Objective

Children will:
- discuss the characteristics of well-written instructions

Focus on Instruction

- Explain that "Let's Make Rain" was a great example of well-written instructions. Ask volunteers to read aloud the definition as well as the characteristics of instructions. Review which characteristics were used in "Let's Make Rain." (interesting topic sentence, instructions explained clearly; steps are in order; used words *first*, *next*, *then*, and *finally*; interesting ending will make readers want to follow instructions.)
- Have children read the Grammar Check on the page. Tell them that the Grammar Check is a reminder that great instructions must also be written correctly. Explain that they will check their papers for correct verbs in the proofreading stage.

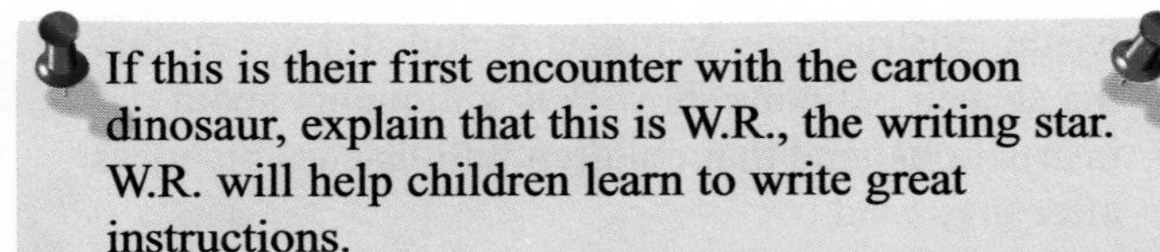

If this is their first encounter with the cartoon dinosaur, explain that this is W.R., the writing star. W.R. will help children learn to write great instructions.

Connecting to the Rubric

- These criteria are tied to the rubric on page 217.
- Explain to children that they will be writing their own instructions and that they will learn how to include the characteristics you've just discussed. Let children know that after they write their instructions, they will use these characteristics to help them evaluate their writing.

 This page is available as a poster.

Looking Ahead Tell children that they will next see how the characteristics listed on this page are applied in one child's working draft and final copy of instructions.

FOR STUDENTS ACQUIRING ENGLISH

Read aloud the first point about great instructions and caution children to choose an interesting, yet simple topic. Make a game of finding the parts of the rubric in the model. Children can work in small groups to find examples of a topic sentence, steps in order, order words, and an ending.

A Student Model: Working Draft

Lesson Objectives

Children will:
- read a working draft of student-written instructions
- discuss the ways the model meets the criteria for well-written instructions and ways that it could be improved

Focus on the Model

- Tell children that they will read a working draft of instructions written by a real student, Matthew Hodges. Remind children that a working draft is a work in progress. This means that the writer writes without making revisions, knowing that these will be made later.
- Have volunteers read the model aloud.

  Alternatively, children can listen to it read by another child (although not the student writer) on audiotape.
- Tell children to note which characteristics of well-written instructions Matthew included. Explain that the speech balloons show W.R.'s thoughts about the instructions and that children will discuss his ideas after they read.

> - Reading the draft aloud gives children practice listening and responding to a writer's work in progress and provides practice for peer conferences.
> - This working draft does not include any usage, capitalization, or punctuation mistakes so that children can focus on the content of the piece.

Answers to Reading As a Writer

- The first sentence should capture the interest of readers. The last sentence should tell what happens as the flower begins to grow.
- You can gather everything you need before you begin planting.
- It helped him to tell the steps in order.

Student Model

WORKING DRAFT

Matthew Hodges

Read Matthew's instructions and what W.R. said.

Here's how to grow a beautiful sunflower. You'll need a small shovel, a sunflower seed, and a sunny spot to plant it. First, ~~make~~ dig a hole that is two inches deep. Keep the dirt in one big pile to use later. Next, ~~cover the seed with dirt~~ drop the seed in the hole. Bury the seed with the dirt pile.

Each morning when you wake up, water the place where you planted the sunflower seed. Finally, you will wake up and see a beautiful sunflower.

Reading As a Writer See TE margin for answers.

- What changes might Matthew want to make?
- Why is it important to know what you need before you start to plant?
- Why did Matthew use first, next, and finally?

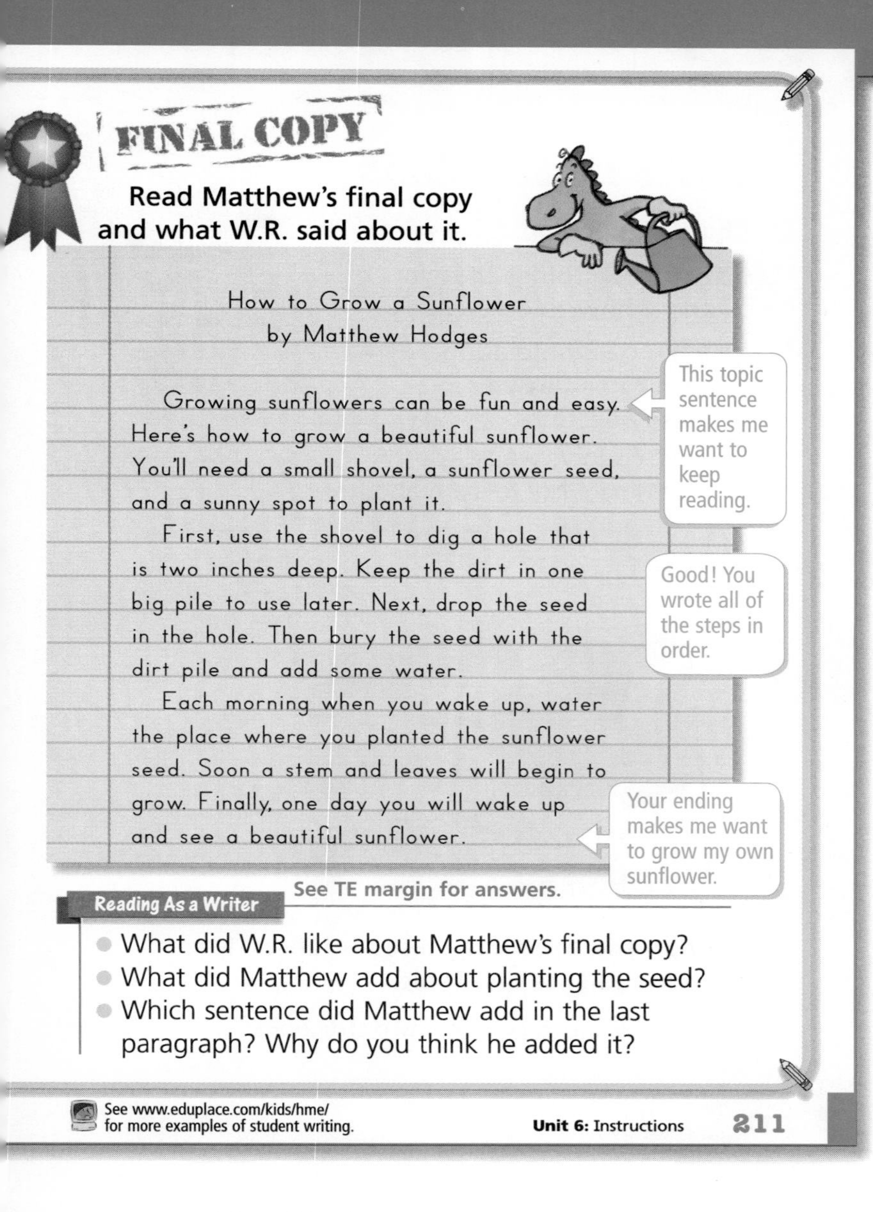

FINAL COPY

Read Matthew's final copy and what W.R. said about it.

How to Grow a Sunflower
by Matthew Hodges

Growing sunflowers can be fun and easy. Here's how to grow a beautiful sunflower. You'll need a small shovel, a sunflower seed, and a sunny spot to plant it.

First, use the shovel to dig a hole that is two inches deep. Keep the dirt in one big pile to use later. Next, drop the seed in the hole. Then bury the seed with the dirt pile and add some water.

Each morning when you wake up, water the place where you planted the sunflower seed. Soon a stem and leaves will begin to grow. Finally, one day you will wake up and see a beautiful sunflower.

Reading As a Writer See TE margin for answers.

- What did W.R. like about Matthew's final copy?
- What did Matthew add about planting the seed?
- Which sentence did Matthew add in the last paragraph? Why do you think he added it?

See www.eduplace.com/kids/hme/ for more examples of student writing.

A Student Model: Final Copy

Lesson Objectives

Children will:

- read a well-written final copy of a student's instructions
- note and compare the revisions that improved the first draft

Focus on the Model

SUMMARY OF REVISIONS In the final copy, Matthew included an attention-grabbing topic sentence, used order words, and reworked the ending to make it more interesting to readers. Blackline Master 6-1 provides a copy of the student's working draft, showing the revisions that were made.

Have volunteers read the model aloud. Alternatively, children can listen to it read by another student (although not the student writer) on audiotape.

Answers to Reading As a Writer

- W.R. liked the topic sentence, that the steps were in order, and the ending.
- He added the words *add some water.*
- Soon a stem and leaves will begin to grow. He added it to tell what happens before a sunflower grows.

More About Writer's Craft

Point out some descriptive words, such as *beautiful* and *sunny.* Tell children that these words help the reader see what the writer means.

Connecting to the Rubric

- Have children look again at the list of characteristics on page 209 and review with them how Matthew's final copy addressed each one.
- Reinforce the Grammar Check by having children check that Matthew included a verb in each sentence.

Looking Ahead Tell children that they will next write their own instructions, using the writing process. As they go along, they will learn how to include well-thought out steps for their instructions.

FOR STUDENTS ACQUIRING ENGLISH

Model following the working draft of Matthew's instructions on the board. Ask questions at the same points W.R. did. Ask children how Matthew can make those points of the working draft clearer. Write their ideas into Matthew's work on the board and compare them to his final draft. Highlight his use of paragraphing to show spacing.

INTERNET CONNECTION Send children to www.eduplace.com/kids/hme/ to see more models of student writing. You can also find and print these models at www.eduplace.com/rdg/hme/.

Write Instructions

Lesson Objectives

Children will:
- list their ideas for audience, purpose, and publishing/ sharing formats
- list ideas for writing instructions
- discuss their ideas with a partner
- choose an appropriate topic to write about

Start Thinking

Focus on Instruction

- Ask how writing instructions to young children might be different from writing instructions to older students. (might need to use fewer words and easier language)
- Ask what might be the purpose for writing instructions to find a place. (to give helpful information) to play a game? (to do something fun)
- Ask how writing instructions as a poster might be different from writing it as a letter. (Writing it as a poster would make it available for more people.)

Choose a Topic

Focus on Instruction

- Encourage children to write about something they know and understand very well. Children can turn to the Writing Prompts on page 224 for some more ideas.
- Suggest to children that they choose two topics so that if one does not work out, they can use the other.
- Review their final choices. If a topic seems too difficult to break into steps, have children go over their list with you for an alternative.

Have each child make a writing folder and title it *My Instructions*. Explain that they will keep notes, organizers, and drafts in this folder. Have children put their documents with their thoughts about audience, purpose, and publishing format in their writing folder.

SCHOOL-HOME CONNECTION Suggest that children discuss with a family member possible topics for writing instructions.

Write Instructions

Choose Your Topic

1. **List** three things that you know how to do well.
2. **Tell** a classmate about each topic. Answer these questions.
   - Which topic would your classmate like to learn about?
   - Which topic can you explain best?

Stuck for an Idea?

How about these?
- something you have made
- a game you play well
- a special thing you can do
- something you do just for fun

See page 224 for more ideas.

3. **Copy and complete** these sentences. Name your audience and topic.

_____ will read or hear my instructions.

I will write about how to _____.

Help with Choosing a Topic

MORE TOPIC IDEAS

Suggest that children:
- think of an activity or game they have been taught to do.
- brainstorm games and other activities that involve several steps.
- think of some things they really like to make or build.
- list their favorite place to go on a weekend. Have them think about how they get there.

TECH TIP

Children can refer to Using a Computer on page H23.

PREWRITING DRAFTING REVISING PROOFREADING PUBLISHING

Explore Your Topic

Sample answer: a plant beginning to grow a stem and leaves

1. **Look** at the pictures Matthew drew before he wrote. What other step could he have drawn?

1. 
2. 
3. 
4. 

2. **Think** about your instructions.
3. **Draw** each step.
4. **Talk** with a classmate about your drawings. Explain each step. Is each step clear? Did you draw every step?
5. **Think** about your classmate's ideas. Change your drawings to make the steps clearer. Add drawings for any steps that you left out.

Help with Exploring the Topic

IDEAS FOR EXPLORING

You can suggest these ideas to children as alternatives for exploring their topics.

- Make a cluster or chart to show their steps.
- Draw a comic strip to show the steps of their instructions.
- Review their steps with the person who taught them how to do the activity.

TECH TIP

Children can use the drawing feature of their word processing program to draw the steps of their instructions.

Lesson Objectives

Children will:

- suggest other steps student writer could have drawn
- draw each step of their instructions
- talk with a classmate about their drawings
- change drawings to make steps clearer

Explore Your Topic

Focus on Instruction

- Discuss with children the ideas in the Help Box on page 212. Explain that sometimes a topic that seemed like a good idea doesn't work out when one tries to develop it and that it is better to choose another topic than to continue with one that won't work.
- Review each child's drawings. Make sure that children have included a drawing for each step of their instructions and their changes make the steps clearer.
- Use Blackline Master 6-2 to help children explore their topics. Direct children to other appropriate organizers on page H17.

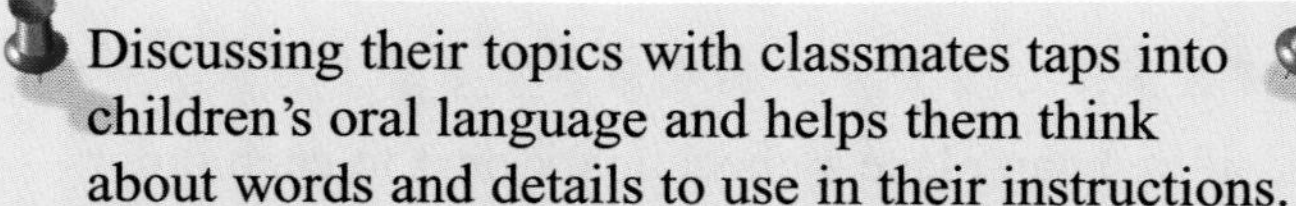

Discussing their topics with classmates taps into children's oral language and helps them think about words and details to use in their instructions.

INTERNET CONNECTION Send children to www.eduplace.com/kids/hme/ for graphic organizers. You can also find and print these organizers at www.eduplace.com/rdg/hme/.

MEETING INDIVIDUAL NEEDS

FOR STUDENTS ACQUIRING ENGLISH

Instead of having children think and then draw their steps, have them say them aloud to a partner, take notes and then draw. Vocalization is often the first language skill acquired by learners of any language. You may want to provide template squares for the drawings so children can cut and paste to order their steps.

Using Order Words

Lesson Objectives

Children will:
- write order words on their drawings
- complete an Order Chart

Focus on Instruction

- Write the order words from the lesson on the board.
- Work with children to write the words in time order. Remind children that some of the words have similar meanings.
- Ask children to create sentences beginning with the order words. Ask children if there are any sentences that seem in the wrong order.

Try It Together

Have small groups discuss an indoor activity that the class plays often. Ask children to explain why they used a specific order word with each step.

Think About Your Topic

- Children can place a check mark next to each order word as they include it in their Order Chart.
- Check that children wrote the correct order word next to each step.
- A copy of the organizer appears on Blackline Master 6-3. You can find other graphic organizers in the Tools and Tips section of the pupil book.

INTERNET CONNECTION Send your students to www.eduplace.com /kids/hme/ for graphic organizers. You can also find and print these organizers at www.eduplace.com/rdg/hme/.

FOR STUDENTS ACQUIRING ENGLISH

To demonstrate the use of order words, you may want to discuss a school game as a class in order to avoid confusion with the children's individual instructions. Ask volunteers to draw pictures of the game on the board. Then ask others to come and write an order word below each step.

Focus Skill

Using Order Words

Order words make your instructions clear. Use order words like those in the box.

Order Words	
first	second
next	third
last	finally
then	now

Try It Together Answers will vary.

Talk with your class about a game you play at school. Use order words to tell how to play.

Think About Your Topic

1. **Look** at your drawings. Think about the order of the steps. Write an order word on each drawing.
2. **Make** an Order Chart like the one below. Write the order word from each drawing. Then write what the drawing shows.

Order Chart	
Order Word	**Step**

See www.eduplace.com/kids/hme/ for graphic organizers.

Meeting Individual Needs

● RETEACHING WORKBOOK, page 50

Using Order Words

Order words help readers follow your instructions.
First, pour the milk into the glass.
Then add one spoonful of chocolate syrup.
Finally, mix the milk and chocolate with a spoon.

Read these instructions. Draw a line under the order word in each sentence. Then number the sentences in order.

2 Next, put a thin line of toothpaste on your toothbrush.

1 First, wet your toothbrush with a little cold water.

4 Finally, rinse off your toothpaste and rinse your mouth.

3 Then put your toothbrush in your mouth and carefully brush all your teeth.

▲■ WORKBOOK PLUS, page 79

Using Order Words

Order Words			
first	second	third	last
next	finally	then	now

Look at the pictures. Choose an order word for each step. Write the order word and the step in the chart. Sample answers

Order Word	Step
first,	get a scoop, a cone, and some ice cream
next,	scoop out some ice cream
last,	carefully put the ice cream on the cone

PREWRITING DRAFTING REVISING PROOFREADING PUBLISHING

Focus Skill

Topic Sentence

A **topic sentence** tells the main idea of your instructions. Begin your instructions with a strong topic sentence.

Weak Topic Sentence	Strong Topic Sentence
Here's how to grow a beautiful sunflower.	Growing sunflowers can be fun and easy.
I like to draw.	Drawing animals is one of my favorite things.

Try It Together Answers will vary.

Talk with your class about how to wash a dog. Together, write some good topic sentences.

Plan Your Instructions

1. **Write** two strong topic sentences for your instructions.
2. **Mark** the one you like better.

Topic Sentence

Lesson Objective

Children will:

- write topic sentences for instructions

Focus on Instruction

- Ask children: If a writer were writing instructions about how to make a snowflake, should she begin with a sentence, such as *I am going to tell you how to make snowflakes*? (No, it's too weak.) Ask volunteers to tell what a strong topic sentence might be.
- Write the following sentence on the board: *Mixing paint to get bright colors is fun and easy*. Then ask: Would the sentence make a good topic sentence for instructions? Why or why not? (Yes, it uses exciting words and an interesting idea to grab the attention of the reader.)

Try It Together

- Have small groups write two topic sentences for washing a dog.
- After groups decide on their two topic sentences, have a volunteer read aloud both.
- Ask children to discuss which is the strongest topic and why.

Plan Your Instructions

- Ask children to explain why they like one topic sentence more than the other.
- Children can work with partners to make their topic sentences stronger. Remind children to check if the writer's voice is clear. Have them ask: *Does the topic sentence sound like talking?*

Meeting Individual Needs

● RETEACHING WORKBOOK, page 51

Topic Sentence

A **topic sentence** tells the main idea of your instructions.

Weak Topic Sentence
Here's how to wash a dog.

Strong Topic Sentence
Giving the dog a bath can be wet and wonderful!

Draw a line under the weak topic sentence in these instructions. Then write a strong topic sentence.

Organizing your stuffed animals is not hard. First, put all the small animals in one group. Then put the medium-sized animals and the large animals in two different groups. Next, put the large animals in a row on your bed. Then put the medium-sized animals in front of them. Last, put the small animals in the front row. Now your stuffed friends are neat and easy to find.

Sample sentence: It's easy to organize all your stuffed animal friends so your room looks neat.

▲■ WORKBOOK PLUS, page 80

Topic Sentence

Weak Topic Sentence	Strong Topic Sentence
Here's how to break an egg.	Sometimes you have to break an egg. Here's how to do it right.

Write a strong topic sentence for these instructions. Sample answer

You can grow a carrot plant in a glass of water!

First, have a grown-up help you cut off the top of a carrot. Next, take three toothpicks and stick them into the side of the carrot top. Then, fill a plastic cup with water. Now, put the carrot top into the cup so the toothpicks rest on the edges and the carrot piece sticks into the water. Wait a few days and you will see roots start to grow. Last, green leaves will grow out of the top.

FOR STUDENTS ACQUIRING ENGLISH

Ask the class to break down the phrase topic sentence in order to define it. Remind children of voice in writing; how a writer's unique personality comes through. Present only the weak examples from the text and as a class write strong revisions, showing strong examples of voice.

Lesson Objective

Children will:

- use their topic sentence and their Order Chart to write instructions

Write Your Instructions

Focus on Instruction

- Point out how Matthew used his Order Chart to help him write his instructions. Have a volunteer tell which detail Matthew added to make the step in the lesson complete. (two inches deep)
- Display Matthew's final copy.

Drafting Reminders

- Tell children to focus their energy on writing down ideas, not fixing mistakes.
- Have them skip every other line as they write their drafts.
- Remind them to spell words as best they can and move on. They will have time to check for correct spelling in the revision stage.
- Tell children to cross out parts they decide they no longer want rather than starting over or erasing.

FOR STUDENTS ACQUIRING ENGLISH

Beginners can use their pictures and Order Chart as final instructions, drawing and writing phrases correctly and clearly. Intermediate and advanced children should practice sentence writing. Command forms are often different in other languages. Give a command mini-lesson.

Write Your Instructions

Matthew used his Order Chart to help him write his instructions.

Order Chart	
Order Word	**Step**
first	Make a hole.

First, ~~make~~ dig a hole that is two inches deep.

1. **Copy** the topic sentence you marked onto another sheet of paper.
2. **Write** your instructions, using your Order Chart. Include details to make each step clear and complete.
3. **Write** an ending that will make your readers want to try your instructions.

In your instructions, use a comma after all order words except <u>then</u> and <u>now</u>.

Help with Writing Your Instructions

MANAGEMENT TIP

Children can place a check mark next to each item in their Order Chart as they include it in their instructions.

TECH TIP

As children write their instructions on the computer, suggest they highlight in another color any words or ideas they may want to change later.

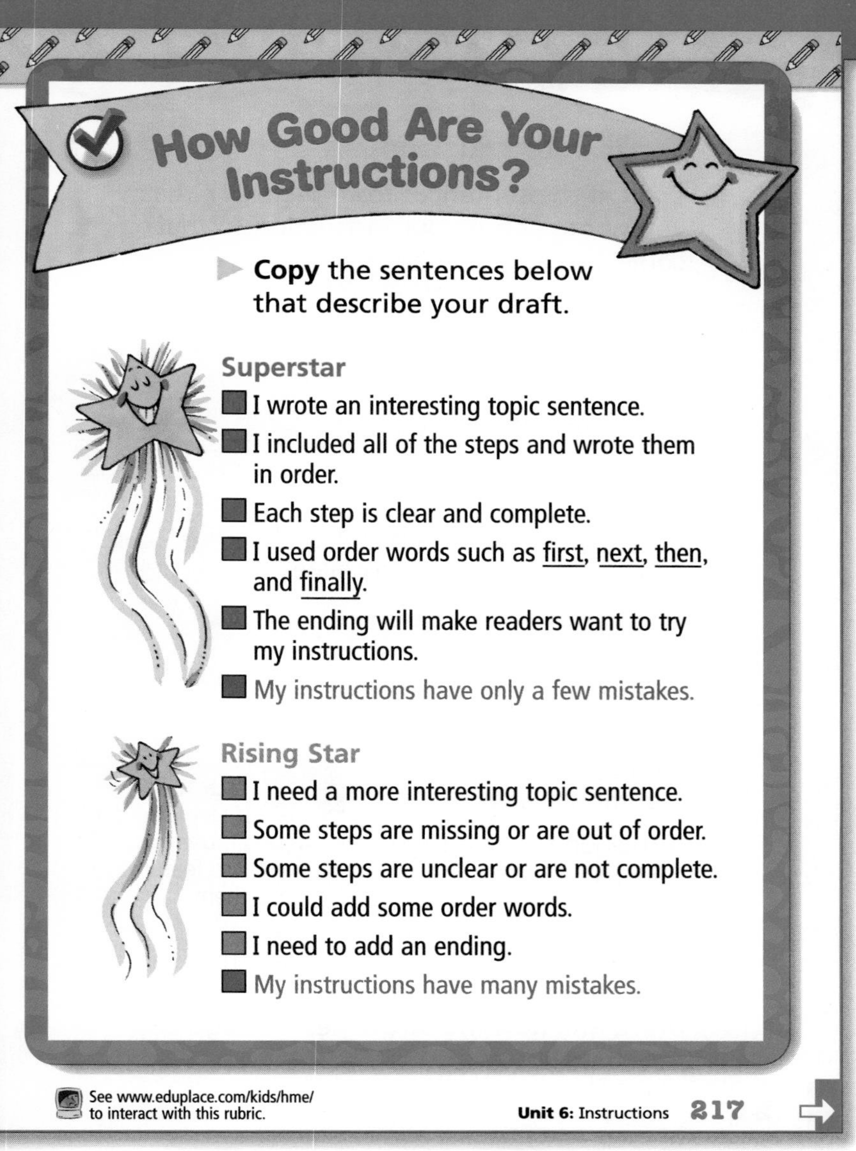

How Good Are Your Instructions?

▶ **Copy** the sentences below that describe your draft.

Superstar

- ■ I wrote an interesting topic sentence.
- ■ I included all of the steps and wrote them in order.
- ■ Each step is clear and complete.
- ■ I used order words such as first, next, then, and finally.
- ■ The ending will make readers want to try my instructions.
- ■ My instructions have only a few mistakes.

Rising Star

- ■ I need a more interesting topic sentence.
- ■ Some steps are missing or are out of order.
- ■ Some steps are unclear or are not complete.
- ■ I could add some order words.
- ■ I need to add an ending.
- ■ My instructions have many mistakes.

See www.eduplace.com/kids/hme/ to interact with this rubric.

How Good Are Your Instructions?

Lesson Objective:

Children will:

- evaluate their instructions, using a rubric

Connecting to the Criteria

Have children reread the characteristics of instructions listed on page 209. Then explain that the rubric refers to those characteristics. Tell them that the rubric will help them decide which parts of their instructions meet the standards of great instructions, and which parts they think still need more work.

Focus on Instruction

- Review the rubric with children. Have volunteers read aloud pairs of related characteristics. Discuss with children the differences between the sentences in each pair.
- Blackline Master 6-4 provides a copy of the rubric as a checklist for children using the hardbound editions. Alternatively, they can write the sentences that describe their instructions.
- See the Teacher's Resource Book for scoring rubrics.

INTERNET CONNECTION Have children go to www.eduplace.com/kids/hme/ to use an interactive version of the rubric shown in the pupil book. Children will get feedback and support depending on how they mark the rubric items.

This page is also available as a poster.

Meeting Individual Needs

● RETEACHING WORKBOOK, page 52

Revising Instructions

Have I	yes
• written an interesting topic sentence?	☐
• included all the steps and written them in order?	☐
• used order words such as first, next, then and finally?	☐

Revise these instructions. Check off each box when you have finished your changes. Write your changes in the spaces above each line, on the sides, and below the paragraph. Sample answers

Does your dog need a bath? Try this.
~~Here's how to wash your dog.~~ Get a lot of towels and put on some old clothes. Then fill the bathtub halfway with warm water and dog shampoo. Next, play with your dog a little so he gets kind of tired. Then ~~C~~carry him into the bathroom, put him in the tub, and rub him with the bubbles. [Finally, take him out of the tub and dry him off with the towels.] You will probably have to use a towel yourself, but you both will be nice and clean!

▲■ WORKBOOK PLUS, page 81

Revising Instructions

Have I	yes
• written an interesting topic sentence?	☐
• included all the steps and written them in order?	☐
• used order words such as first, next, then and finally?	☐

Revise these instructions. Check off each box when you have finished your changes. Write your changes in the spaces above each line, on the sides, and below the paragraph. Sample answers

A picture postcard is a fun way to say Hi!
~~You can make a picture postcard for a friend.~~ First, take a regular index card. Then, cut out a pretty magazine picture. [Next, glue the picture to the plain side of the index card.] Now, write a message on the left half of the lined side. Write your friend's address on the other half. Last, ~~S~~stamp your postcard and drop it in the mailbox.

FOR STUDENTS ACQUIRING ENGLISH

The day before evaluating, assign children the job of bringing in materials for the completion of the instructions that they wrote. If this is impossible, then ask children to bring in a few props to help pantomime the instructions. On evaluation day, ask children to test their instructions by first attempting to follow them themselves. Then ask them to exchange materials and instructions with a partner and to watch and take notes as the partner attempts the instructions. This exercise will certainly show the weak points of the instructions, but also the usefulness of writing clearly.

Lesson Objective

Children will:
- revise their working drafts, based on their evaluations

Revise Your Instructions

Focus on Instruction

Revising Reminders

Remind children that revising focuses on making their instructions clearer and more interesting. They should not worry about correcting mistakes at this stage.

- Review each child's evaluation of his or her instructions and discuss what revisions the child could make to improve it. As they revise each part, have them check off the appropriate sentence from the rubric. When they are finished revising, ask them to read their instructions again to be sure the papers are clear.

FOR STUDENTS ACQUIRING ENGLISH

Ask children who still have difficulty revising to try new topic sentences or try adding details. They can always go back and cut the new parts out, but they'll never know whether they want changes if they don't try them. A similar rule applies for conferencing. Ask children to find two good points to make and two questions to ask about their partners' work. If children don't, they won't learn how helpful conferences are.

Revise Your Instructions

1 Look at the sentences from page 217 that you wrote about your instructions. What could you add or change to make your instructions better?

2 Have a writing conference.

When You're the Writer
- Write a question about part of your instructions that you want help with.
- Share your instructions and your question with a classmate.

When You're the Listener
- Tell two things that you like about the instructions.
- Act out the steps. Ask questions about unclear or missing steps.
- Look on the next page for more ideas.

Tech Tip
If steps are out of order, use the Cut and Paste features to move them.

3 Revise your instructions.
Think about what you talked about with your classmate. Make changes to your draft. The Revising Strategies on page 220 may help you.

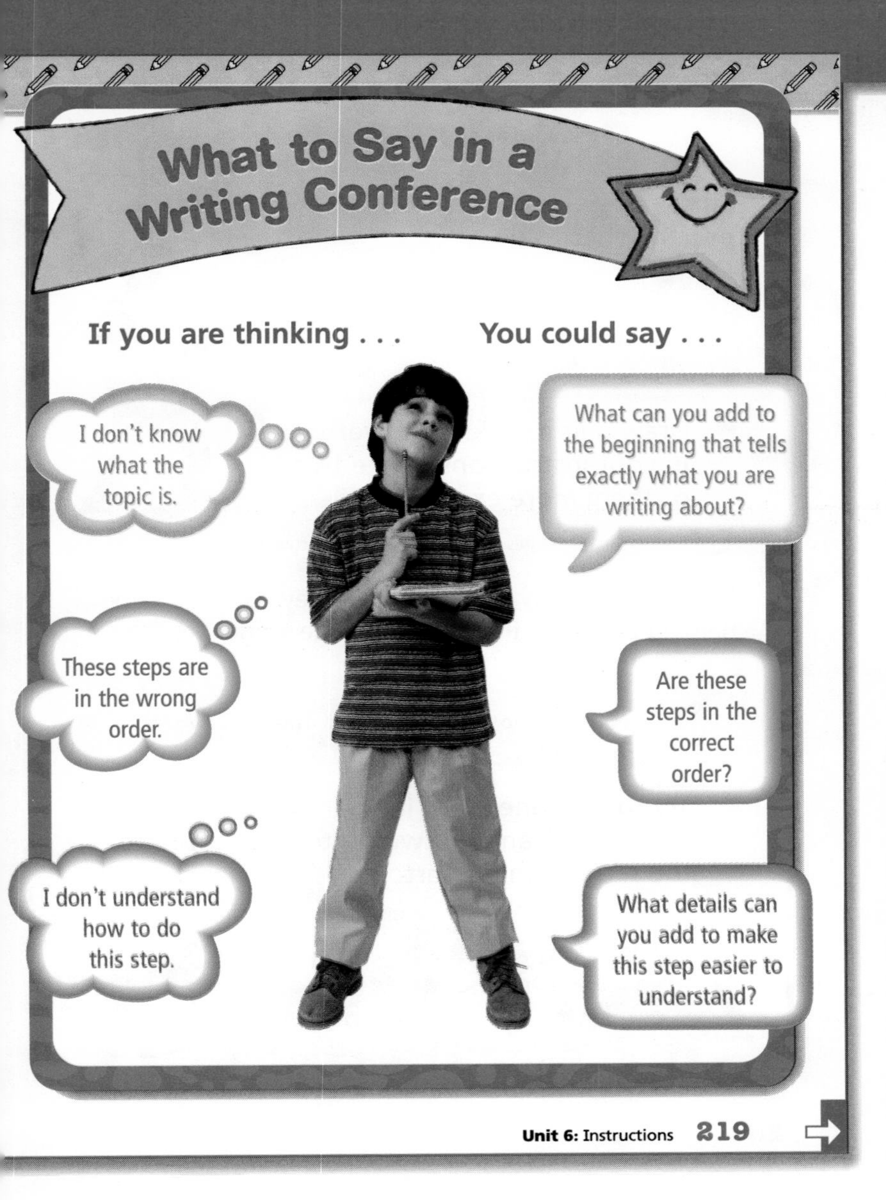

Help with Conferencing

ADDITIONAL CONFERENCING QUESTIONS

These questions may be useful during teacher-student conferences.

- Explain why you chose the topic. Can you add those reasons in your introduction?
- What happened *first*, *next*, *then*, and *finally*? How will adding order words make your instructions clearer for your audience?
- Tell about how useful the instructions are. Can you include these ideas in your ending?

EVALUATION TIP

Listen to make sure that children are covering relevant topics listed on the conferencing Blackline Master.

What to Say in a Writing Conference

Lesson Objectives

Children will:

- have a writing conference
- retell a spoken message by summarizing or clarifying

Read aloud and discuss with children the text in the thought and speech balloons. Explain that the thought balloons show what a listener might think while listening to instructions. The speech balloons show what the listener could ask to help the writer know what parts might not be clear or could be revised.

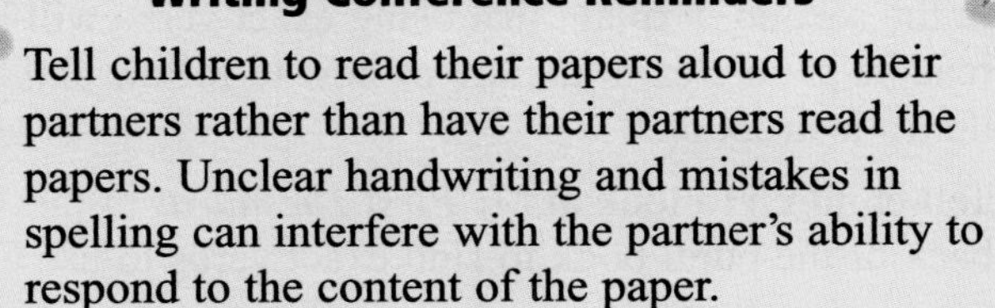

Writing Conference Reminders

- Tell children to read their papers aloud to their partners rather than have their partners read the papers. Unclear handwriting and mistakes in spelling can interfere with the partner's ability to respond to the content of the paper.
- Tell children to do these things when they are the listeners:

  Begin comments by giving positive feedback of a feature of the reader's instructions. Share the following possible compliments:

- You have a strong beginning sentence.
- I see that you wrote clear steps for your instructions.
- Your ending makes me want to follow your instructions.

  Retell what they have heard after listening to their partner's paper. They should tell the topic of the instructions and the important steps.

- Remind children to choose their words carefully. They want to be helpful, not make the writers feel bad.
- Direct children to speak slowly and clearly when they read their papers. They should speak softly if reading to a partner and louder if reading to a larger group.
- Tell children that they don't have to take all of their partner's suggestions, but they should think about them.

 This page is also available as a poster.

- Children can use Blackline Master 6-5 during their writing conferences.

Revising Strategies

Lesson Objectives

Children will:

- use exact verbs to make their instructions clearer
- combine short sentences to make one long sentence

Focus on Instruction

Word Choice

- Write this sentence pair on the board:

  The girl went down the street.

  The girl hopped down the street.

- Discuss with children the images that are evoked by the weak verb in the first example, and the exact verb in the second. Explain that using exact verbs will help readers get a clearer picture of how to follow children's instructions.
- Tell children to look at *My First Thesaurus* at the back of the pupil book to find exact verbs to use in their instructions.

Sentence Fluency

- Write the following sentences on the board:

  Jared toasts the bread.

  Jared cooks the eggs.

- Ask volunteers to suggest ways to make one long sentence from the two shorter ones. (Jared toasts the bread and cooks the eggs.)

Revising Strategies

Word Choice Choose verbs that tell your readers exactly what to do.

Then ~~make~~ draw a house.

▶ Draw a line under each verb in your instructions. Make two of them more exact.

Use My First Thesaurus on page H45 to find exact verbs.

Sentence Fluency Two sentences may have the same naming part. Join them to make one longer sentence.

You pick the flowers~~.~~ and ~~You~~ put them in water.

▶ Try to find one place in your instructions where you can join two sentences that have the same naming part.

FOR STUDENTS ACQUIRING ENGLISH

To learn how to use strong verbs, help children brainstorm a list of weak verbs (put, move, make, etc.) and strong replacements (attach, turn, form/mold, etc.). Children learning English may not readily use conjunctions in writing instructions. Show them how to include them in their instructions for reinforcement.

Meeting Individual Needs

● RETEACHING WORKBOOK, page 53

Revising Strategies: Word Choice

Exact verbs help your readers see what they are supposed to do in each step.
~~Put~~ Sprinkle the food in the fish tank.

Read each sentence. Choose an exact verb to replace each underlined verb. Write the new sentence. Sample answers

stir	drop	grab	slide	beat

1. Mix the eggs and the sugar together.
   Beat the eggs and the sugar together.
2. Add in the flour.
   Stir in the flour.
3. Put the cookie dough onto the cookie sheet.
   Drop the cookie dough onto the cookie sheet.
4. Take a potholder before you touch the oven.
   Grab a potholder before you touch the oven.
5. Put the cookie sheet into the oven.
   Slide the cookie sheet into the oven.

▲■ WORKBOOK PLUS, page 82

Revising Strategies: Word Choice

We ~~went~~ skipped across the field in the warm sun.

Read each sentence. Then choose an exact verb to replace each underlined verb. Write the new sentence. Answers will vary.

1. First, make some strips of colored paper.
2. Next, make one into a circle and tape the ends together.
3. Then, put another strip through the first circle and tape those ends together.
4. After all the strips are used, put the ends together to make a pretty wreath.

PREWRITING DRAFTING REVISING PROOFREADING PUBLISHING

Proofread Your Instructions

1. **Proofread** your draft. Use the Proofreading Checklist and the Proofreading Marks.
2. **Use** a class dictionary to check spellings.

Proofreading Checklist

- Each sentence has an action part.
- Each sentence begins with a capital letter.
- Each paragraph is indented.
- Each word is spelled correctly.

Proofreading Marks	
∧ Add	≡ Capital letter
Delete	/ Small letter
¶ Indent for new paragraph	

Using the Proofreading Marks

put cereal in a Bowl. Add some sum milk.

3. **Review** these rules before you proofread.

Grammar and Spelling Connections

Complete Sentences Be sure each sentence has a verb.

First, find a yellow crayon.

Then draw a sun.

Long Vowel Sounds The long **i** sound may be spelled **y**, **igh**, or **i**-consonant-**e**.

try might like

See the Spelling Guide on page H40.

See www.eduplace.com/kids/hme/ for proofreading practice.

Lesson Objective

Children will:
- proofread their instructions

Proofread Your Instructions

Focus on Instruction

Proofreading Reminders

- Remind children that the proofreading stage is when they should correct capitalization, usage, punctuation, and spelling.
- Review how and when to use the proofreading marks.
- Review with children the Proofreading Checklist in the pupil book. Review and clarify each item in the checklist, using any related Grammar and Spelling Connections. If children need extra support, review the related grammar lesson on page 163 with them.
- Provide dictionaries for children to check spellings. Tell them to circle any words they think are misspelled and check them in a dictionary after they have finished circling.
- For proofreading practice, see the usage and mechanics lessons in the Grammar units and the Mixed Review practice in each Grammar unit Checkup.

Help with Proofreading

MANAGEMENT TIPS

Have each child keep a checklist of what he or she needs to proofread for. Staple the list to the child's folder.

- Children can work with partners for extra help proofreading their instructions.

TECH TIP

Children can highlight words they are unsure of in a different color. This color can be removed after they have checked the spelling of the word.

MEETING INDIVIDUAL NEEDS **FOR STUDENTS ACQUIRING ENGLISH**

Ask children to reread their instructions, guessing which words are spelled wrong and circling them. Have them dictate these words to you, asking them to spell them out as you write them on the board and guide them to make corrections as necessary. Ask children to use the correct spellings to look up the words in the dictionary. For reinforcement, have them practice writing the words correctly at least three times.

Lesson Objectives

Children will:

- make neat final copies of their instructions
- choose a way to publish or share their instructions
- reflect on their writing experience
- evaluate the writing in comparison to others in their writing portfolio

Publish Your Instructions

Focus on Instruction

- Have children decide how they will share their writing, as it may affect the form of their final copy.
- Instruct children to make neat corrections on their final copies, rather than recopy their papers.
- Observe the way children hold their pencils and position their papers when they make their final copies. Check that they are gaining handwriting proficiency. Remind children to use word and letter spacing and margins to make their papers readable.
- For handwriting instruction and practice, see the Teacher's Resource Disk for printable blackline masters.

Keeping a Writing Portfolio

A writing portfolio is where students can keep samples of their writing. Here are suggestions for creating and using writing portfolios.

- **Selection** A paper might be selected because it is
  - ✓ generally noteworthy
  - ✓ a good example of a particular criterion
  - ✓ an example of a certain kind of writing
  - ✓ from a certain time in the school year
  - ✓ a typical example of the student's work
- **Labeling:** For every paper, have students complete a cover sheet giving the title, date of completion, and reason for inclusion.
- **Review:** Have students remove papers that no longer reflect their best work or aren't needed as baselines.
- **Evaluation:** Review students' portfolios with them to discuss growth and areas that need improvement.

SCHOOL-HOME CONNECTION Have children share their instructions with family members. Have them discuss if each step is clear.

The Writing Process: PREWRITING · DRAFTING · REVISING · PROOFREADING · PUBLISHING

Publish Your Instructions

1. **Make** a neat final copy of your instructions.
2. **Write** an interesting title. Use words that tell exactly what you are writing about.
3. **Look** at Ideas for Sharing on the next page.
4. **Publish** or share your instructions in a way that works for your audience.

- Be sure you wrote all letters correctly and used good spacing. Check that you fixed every mistake.
- Begin the first, last, and each important word in your title with a capital letter.

Reflect

Answer these questions about your instructions.

- What do you like most about your instructions?
- What do you like least about your instructions?
- What did you learn from writing your instructions?
-  Do you like your instructions better than other papers you have written? Why or why not?

Tech Tip If you wrote your instructions on a computer, fix all mistakes. Then print out a final copy.

222 Publishing

Ideas for Sharing

Write It

- Write each step on an index card. Put the cards in order and number them.
- Bind your instructions with others written by your classmates to make a class book.

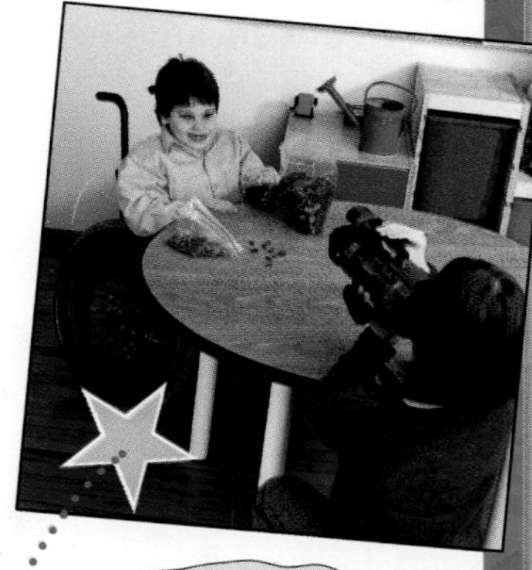

Say It

- Record your instructions so others can listen to the steps.
- Tell the steps in order while a friend tries to do them.

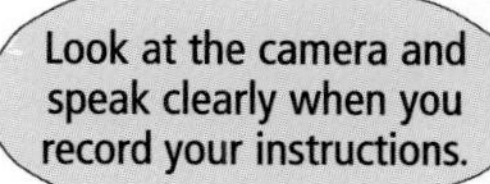

Show It

★ Explain and demonstrate your instructions on videotape.

- Draw a poster to show the steps.

Tech Tip Use the shift key to make a capital letter for the first, last, and each important word in your title.

Ideas for Sharing

- **Index Cards** Children can use a different color index card for each step.
- **Class Book:** Make various art supplies available to children.

TECH TIP Before children bind their book, help them scan the individual pages so they can be posted on the school's website.

- **Tape Recording:** Suggest that children practice reading aloud their instructions to a partner before they tape record their voices. Remind them to adjust their volume, rate, and expression.
- **Tell Order:** Provide children with appropriate props so that they can carry out the steps.
- **Poster:** Encourage children to decorate their posters with appropriate art.
- **Videotape:** Select small groups to act as video production crew: camera person, script prompter, director, etc. Help them decide on appropriate props to clarify and support their presentations.

This page is also available as a poster.

Writing Prompts

Objective

Children will:
- review prompts for choosing a topic or to practice for a writing test

Using the Prompts

You can use the prompts on this page in several ways.

- Ask children to review the prompts to help inspire them as they are choosing their topics for their instructions. Suggest that children use prompts that interest them, which they can then use to brainstorm ideas for their topics.
- Choose a prompt to provide practice for a writing test. Use it with the Test Practice on the next page.
- Choose a prompt that fits with a related topic in another subject to integrate writing instructions across the curriculum.

INTERNET CONNECTION Send your students to www.eduplace.com/kids/hme for more writing ideas. You can also find and print these prompts at www.eduplace.com/rdg/hme/.

FOR STUDENTS ACQUIRING ENGLISH

Prompts that are useful for children acquiring English are: Describe a science experiment you've done. Describe how to get ready for school in your native country. Is there an activity from your native country that isn't done here in the United States? Describe how to do it. (For example, you might ask children to dictate instructions about preparing something to eat, or about preparing for a special ceremony.)

Assessment Link

Writing Prompts

Use these prompts for ideas or to practice for a test. Write instructions that are easy to understand and follow. Include every step.

1 What are the steps in making a telephone call? Write instructions explaining each step.

2 How do you brush your teeth? Write instructions telling friends how to brush their teeth.

Writing Across the Curriculum

3 **SOCIAL STUDIES** Write instructions that explain how to do one of your chores. Tell how to do each step.

4 **ART** Write instructions that tell how to draw a house. Tell what you need and what you do first, next, and last.

5 **PHYSICAL EDUCATION** Write instructions telling how to throw a basketball through a hoop. Tell where to stand and what to do with the ball.

6 **MATH** Write instructions telling how to make a graph of the number of boys and girls in your class. Write the steps in order.

See www.eduplace.com/kids/hme/ for more prompts.

Test Practice

On a test, you may be asked to write about a picture prompt. Read this prompt and look at the pictures.

Write instructions to go with the pictures below. Explain how to make a peanut butter sandwich.

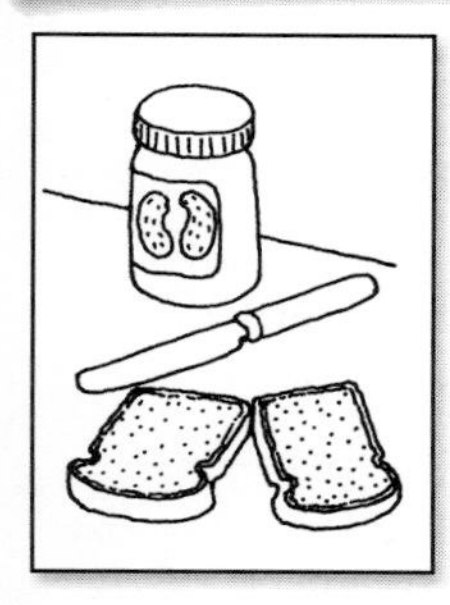

Follow these steps for writing to a picture prompt.

1. **Look** at each picture and answer these questions.
   - What materials and steps are shown?
   - How many steps are there?
   - In what order are they shown?
2. **Plan** your writing. Use an Order Chart like the one on page 214.
3. **Look** at page 217. What makes a Superstar?
4. **Write** your instructions.

See www.eduplace.com/kids/hme/ for graphic organizers.

Test Practice

Objective

Children will:

- learn strategies for evaluating a writing prompt and writing instructions for a test

Using the Test Practice

- Read through the page with children, discussing the strategies for evaluating and responding to a picture prompt to make a peanut butter sandwich.
- Have children write instructions in response to the picture prompt on this page. Ask children to use the Order Chart to plan their writing. Impose time limitations or other qualifications specific to the testing requirements of your school.
- Before they write their practice test, review the rubric on page 217 with children.

FOR STUDENTS ACQUIRING ENGLISH

Children at the early stages of acquiring English can supply phrases or words; children at the intermediate and advanced levels can write sentences. Act out the step shown in each picture with either real materials or props. Invite volunteers to join you. This enactment is important, as most children will not have made the sandwich before. Finally, have children list words that show order in the instructions that they wrote.

Writing a Research Report

Lesson Objective

Children will:
- read a model of a research report and identify its parts

Focus on the Model

- Discuss with children the purpose of a research report. Explain that we write research reports to present information about an interesting topic by bringing together facts from different sources. Point out that a research report is called "informative" writing because it gives readers information about a specific topic.
- Tell the class that they will read Candice's research report about giant pandas. Before children read the model, discuss the following words and their definitions:

  mammals warm-blooded animals that produce milk, have some hair on their bodies, and give birth to live babies rather than hatching them from eggs

  bamboo tall grass with hollow woody stems

  endangered in danger of extinction (no longer existing or living)

  reserve land set aside for a special reason
- Point out the blue call outs. Explain that they highlight the different parts of a research report. Tell the class that they will learn about these parts as they read the research report.
- Ask volunteers to read the research report aloud. Each volunteer can read one paragraph.

 Alternatively, children can listen to the model on audiotape.

FOR STUDENTS ACQUIRING ENGLISH

Show a photo of a panda, and ask children what this animal is called in English. Find out if anyone knows where pandas live, what they eat, and how big they are. Has anyone ever seen a panda? Help children locate China on a world map or globe. Ask if there are a lot of pandas in the world or only a few.

Special Focus on Informing

Writing a Research Report

A **research report** gives facts about a topic. Read Candice's research report about giant pandas and what W.R. said about it.

Giant Pandas

Giant pandas are mammals, just like dogs, cats, and people.

Giant pandas look like teddy bears. They are black and white. Some can be about five feet long, and they can weigh over two hundred pounds! Newborn giant pandas don't look special because they do not have black and white marks yet.

Giant pandas live in the mountain forests in China where there is bamboo for them to eat. Some giant pandas eat a huge amount of bamboo. Giant pandas will also eat plants, flowers, and even small animals. They can eat about thirty pounds of food in one day!

Giant pandas are endangered animals. Farmers cut down bamboo trees because they wanted to make room for farms. Many giant pandas died because they did not have bamboo to eat. Now people are

This is a good **opening**.

You give many **details** to support the **main ideas**.

226 A Research Report

Help with Writing a Research Report

MANAGEMENT TIP

If children are having difficulty visualizing giant pandas from the description in the research report, display pictures of these animals.

trying to help the giant pandas survive. There are places called reserves where people are planting more bamboo for them. These are safe places for giant pandas.

Giant pandas look like black and white teddy bears. They live in the forests, but people in China are also making reserves where these endangered animals can eat bamboo and live safely.

You summed up the main ideas in the **closing**. Great!

Sources

Schlein, Miriam. Jane Goodall's Animal World: Pandas. New York: Atheneum, 1989.

Snyder, Gregory K. "Panda." World Book Multimedia Encyclopedia. 1998 ed. CD-ROM. Chicago: World Book, Inc., 1998.

Reading As a Writer See TE margin for answers.

- What interesting fact about giant pandas did Candice put in her **opening**?
- What is the **main idea** of Candice's third paragraph? What **details** support her main idea?
- What facts did Candice sum up in her **closing**?

Lesson Objective

Children will:
- read a model of a research report and identify its parts

Focus on Instruction

- Discuss with the class the explanations of the call outs given in the Reading As a Writer section. Explain that Candice's opening is effective because instead of just naming the topic, it also includes an interesting fact and makes a comparison to other mammals.
- Point out that each of the three paragraphs begins with a topic sentence that states the main idea. Candice also includes several sentences that explain and support the main ideas.
- Show children how Candice sums up, or briefly explains, all the important points in her report.
- Have volunteers answer each of the questions.

Answers to Reading As a Writer

- Candice's interesting fact identifies giant pandas as mammals and compares them to other mammals, such as dogs, cats, and people.
- The main idea of the third paragraph is that giant pandas live in the mountain forests of China where they have bamboo to eat. Candice includes details about how much bamboo giant pandas eat and that they also eat plants, flowers, and small animals. Another detail tells that they can eat about thirty pounds of food a day.
- Giant pandas are black and white and look like teddy bears. They live in the forests in China. People are making reserves for giant pandas, places that give the giant pandas a safe home and plenty of bamboo to eat.

FOR STUDENTS ACQUIRING ENGLISH

Have children find the third paragraph in the report; teach ordinal numbers if needed. Then compare the facts in Candice's report with the class discussion you had about pandas. Demonstrate what it means to support something by, for example, pointing to the legs that hold up a table. Explain the meaning of sum up.

Lesson Objective

Children will:
- choose a topic for a research report

How to Write a Research Report

Focus on Instruction

- Discuss why people write research reports. Talk about who might read a research report, such as other children who want to learn about a topic. Help children understand that, while they use their own words in their reports, they would choose words that sound more like an article rather than the kinds of words they would use in a friendly letter.
- Stress the importance of coming up with topics that the writer finds interesting. Point out that these should be topics the writer wants to learn more about.
- Guide children to list topics that are manageable. Help them understand why it would be easier to write about a narrower topic such as *alligators* than a broad topic such as *animals*. If children generate large subjects instead of narrow topics, help them use inverted triangle organizers to narrow them.
- Have children talk with classmates about their topics. Suggest that they discuss how interesting the topic would be and how easy or difficult it might be to find information and facts about the topic.

How to Write a Research Report

1. **List** three topics that you would like to learn more about. Talk with a classmate about each topic. Answer these questions.
   - Is this topic interesting enough?
   - Can I find facts about this topic?

Stuck for a Topic?

How about these?
- an animal
- a famous person
- a famous place
- a sea creature
- a sport

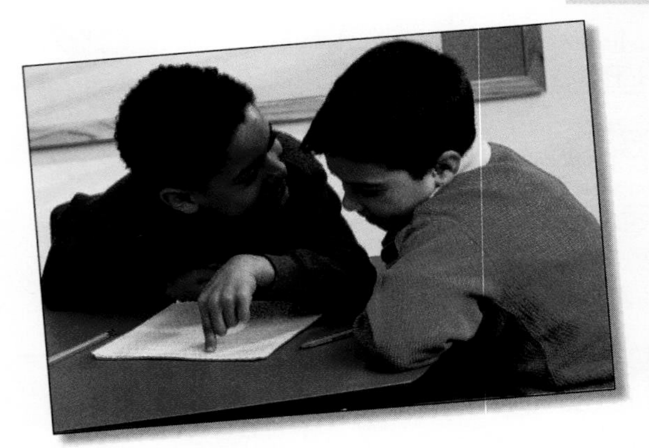

2. **Copy and complete** this sentence. Name your topic.

   I will write about ____.

Help with Writing a Research Report

MORE TOPIC IDEAS

Suggest these possibilities:
- an important event in the history of the town or community
- a famous national or state landmark
- an invention or its inventor
- a tradition, custom, or celebration

MANAGEMENT TIP

If children are having difficulty coming up with a suitable topic, suggest they look up the call number of an interesting nonfiction book in the school library catalogue reference. They can then go to that section of the library and look at that and other books on the same or related topics.

3 **Think** of your report as a puzzle. Facts and details in a report are like the pieces that complete the puzzle. Look at the chart Candice used to help her explore facts and details about giant pandas.

Topic: Giant pandas		
What I Know	**What I Want to Learn**	**Where to Find Answers**
Giant pandas eat bamboo.	What else do they eat?	books about giant pandas, encyclopedia

Now make a chart like the one Candice used. Write what you know about your topic. Then write two questions you want to answer.

4 **Talk** with your class about where you might find facts to answer your questions.

See www.eduplace.com/kids/hme/ for graphic organizers.

Lesson Objective

Children will:

- list facts and details about a topic

Focus on Instruction

- Have children write any facts and details they already know about the topic. Remind them that it is not necessary that they know a great deal about their topics at this point, since later they will fill in necessary information with research.
- Suggest that children write several questions they would like to answer, and then choose two of them to begin their research.
- Point out that children may think of new questions sparked by their own research. Explain that these questions can be added to their charts.

FOR STUDENTS ACQUIRING ENGLISH

Talk about the chart that Candice used. Have children work in groups to brainstorm possible topics for a report. Assist with vocabulary as needed. Then have children work with partners to write questions for their charts. Circulate and provide help as needed.

Help with Writing a Research Report

TECH TIP

Children can use the table feature of a word processing program to create a chart similar to the one in the lesson. They may input their information directly on the chart, or they may prefer to print out the chart and write the information by hand.

How to Write a Research Report *continued*

Lesson Objectives

Children will:
- identify reference sources for a topic
- distinguish between facts and opinions in reference sources

Focus on Instruction

- As children share resource information with one another, stress that they write the names of the sources recommended by classmates. Suggest that, with permission, children bring in any reference resources from home that others may find helpful for their topics.
- Help children identify key words to locate information about their topics. Point out that the key words that work best are the same in the library and an Internet search.
- Discuss with children the difference between facts and opinions and provide examples such as *I think that carrots are the best vegetable because of their bright color* and *The part of the carrot that we eat grows under the ground*. Have volunteers provide additional examples of facts and opinions. Point out that opinions often contain clue words such as *I think* or *I believe* and words such as *good*, *best*, and *worst*.
- Remind children to include only facts, not opinions, in their research reports. Point out that they should also keep a list of the reference sources they use.

Beside each question in your chart, write two sources you will try. See Using the Library on pages H15–H16 for more tips.

Tech Tip
Before you use an Internet source, check with your teacher.

Include facts in a research report. Do not include opinions.
- A **fact** is something that is true or real. Giant pandas are animals.
- An **opinion** tells what someone believes or feels. Giant pandas are cute.

5 **Write** each question from your chart on a separate sheet of paper. Then read to find facts that answer your questions.

Help with Writing a Research Report

MANAGEMENT TIP
Have each child make a folder for storing all notes, graphic organizers, and drafts for this assignment.

TECH TIP
You can set up a "Favorite Places" list by presetting approved sites for research papers. Excellent lists of Internet web sites are included in both the *World Almanac* and the *Information, Please Almanac*. If children use Internet sources at home, remind them to print out the address so you can check the source for reliability and suitability.

6 Take notes to remember the facts you find. Write only enough words to remember the information. Do not copy.

Read how one child took notes to answer this question. Where do toucans live? First, he found and read this information.

If you cannot find the facts you need in one source, use another one.

> Toucans are birds found in the rain forests of Central and South America. They make their nests and sleep inside tree trunks.

Then he took these notes.

Where do toucans live?
rain forests
Central and South America
nest and sleep inside
tree trunks

7 Order your notes. Number the questions from your chart in the order you will use them in your report.

Tech Tip
You can use a computer to record and organize your notes. See page H26.

Lesson Objective

Children will:
- take notes about their topic

Focus on Instruction

- Review the clue words that identify opinions. Remind children that opinions should not be included in their notes.
- Emphasize the importance of using notes to help writers frame the information in their own words. This can help prevent copying.
- Explain that this is only one way to organize notes for a topic. Discuss and suggest some other techniques, such as using one large index card for each question and the information found, or keeping a small notebook with four or five pages for each question and information.

How to Write a Research Report *continued*

Lesson Objectives

Children will:
- write the first draft of a research report
- revise a research report, using the Revising Checklist

Focus on Instruction

- Suggest that children use a colored marker to number their notes. This will make the numbering more readable.
- Explain to children that a *topic sentence* for a paragraph can be a question or a statement. Demonstrate how to turn a statement into a question. For example:

  Statement: It is the largest park in the state.

  Question: What is the largest park in the state?
- Stress that opening with a question helps draw readers into the report. This can make the opening more interesting.
- Have a volunteer read the directions for drafting the report. Be sure children understand the order in which they should write each section.
- Explain that the closing paragraph of a research report sums up or restates all the important points in the report.
- Children should make sure that every detail relates to the topic sentence and there are sufficient details to explain the point.

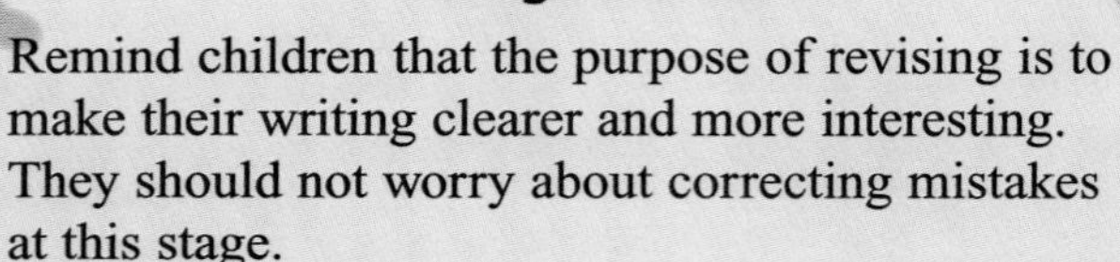

Revising Reminder

Remind children that the purpose of revising is to make their writing clearer and more interesting. They should not worry about correcting mistakes at this stage.

Connecting to the Criteria

Have children review the characteristics of a good research report described in the Reading As a Writer section of this lesson. Explain that the Revising Checklist on this page will help them evaluate their research reports in relation to those characteristics.

FOR STUDENTS ACQUIRING ENGLISH

Children may need guidance in providing feedback in English. You may find it useful to have them practice asking polite questions such as those in the book and providing polite criticism. Model and discuss correct intonation in information and yes-no questions as well as appropriate body language.

8 **Draft** your report.
- Write an opening paragraph that names your topic in an interesting way.
- Next, write one paragraph to answer each of your questions. Rewrite each of your questions as a topic sentence. Use your notes to write the details. Use your own words.
- Then write a closing paragraph that sums up the main ideas.

9 **Look** at the checklist. What can you do to make your research report better?

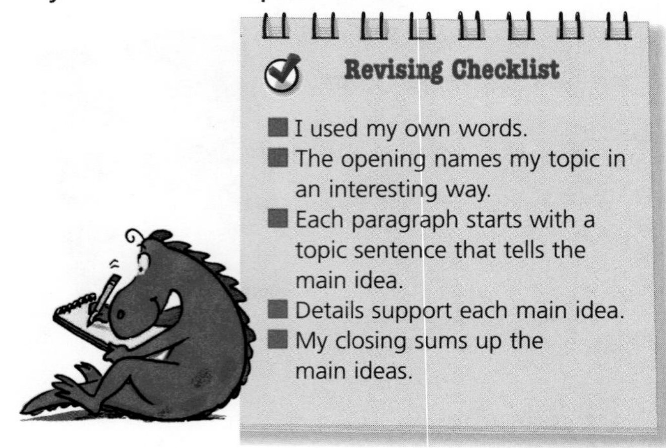

Revising Checklist
- I used my own words.
- The opening names my topic in an interesting way.
- Each paragraph starts with a topic sentence that tells the main idea.
- Details support each main idea.
- My closing sums up the main ideas.

10 **Have** a writing conference. Take notes to remember your classmate's ideas.

Help with Writing a Research Report

TECH TIP

Children can highlight their topic sentences in boldface and then check to see if all the other sentences in the paragraph support the topic sentence.

What to Say in a Writing Conference

If you are thinking . . . **You could say . . .**

11. **Revise** your report.
12. **Proofread** your report. Use the Proofreading Checklist on page 221. Use a class dictionary to check your spelling.
13. **Publish or share** your report.

    Make a neat final copy, using your best handwriting.
    Write a title for your report.
    Include any pictures, maps, or charts.

    - Read your report aloud or talk about it with a group. Show and explain your pictures.
    - ★ Draw a report cover. Put your report in a classroom library for others to read.

Help with Writing a Research Report

MORE CONFERENCING QUESTIONS
You may wish to use these questions as you conference with children:
- Would you like to use a question to make the opening more interesting?
- Where is each topic sentence?
- Which details help support your topic sentence in this paragraph? Which details don't?
- How does your closing sum up the main ideas?

TECH TIP
Children may use available hardware and software to scan charts, illustrations, or other visuals into their reports.

Lesson Objectives

Children will:
- discuss their research reports in a writing conference
- proofread their research reports
- publish and share their final copies

Revising Reminders

Remind children
- to read their papers aloud to their partners during the writing conference;
- to summarize the main points of the research report when they are the listeners so that the writer knows whether the research report was clear and which parts, if any, were not; and
- that questions or comments from their classmates are only suggestions and that the writers should decide what changes they want to make.

Proofreading Reminders

- Tell children to circle any words they think are misspelled and check them in a dictionary.
- Remind children to refer to the Capitalization, Punctuation, and Usage Guide and to the Spelling Guidelines in the back of their books.
- Check children's proofread research reports before they make their final copies.
- Review with children the Proofreading Checklist on page 221 and the use of proofreading marks.

Publishing Reminders

- Review children's publishing plans with them to help them address any special requirements.
- Explain that if children find any errors after they make their final copies, they can make the corrections neatly on the final copy.

SCHOOL-HOME CONNECTION Have children read their reports at home. Suggest that they and their family members share the most interesting thing or a new fact they learned from the report.

Discuss with each student whether this paper should go into the portfolio. Consider these possible reasons: (1) It is an especially good piece of writing; (2) it reflects a particular aspect of writing that the student did well; (3) it shows an aspect of writing that needs more work and could be used as a baseline for measuring growth.

Giving and Following Instructions

Lesson Objectives

Children will:
- give and follow instructions
- choose language, volume, and speaking rate appropriate to audience, purpose, and task

Giving Instructions

Focus on Instruction

- Have volunteers share their experiences telling someone how to do or make something. Ask if they enjoyed giving instructions or found it difficult.
- Point out the order words and talk about other times when children have used these words in their writing. Ask children to tell why they were used and how they were helpful.
- Ask volunteers to read the tips aloud. Following the tips, demonstrate a simple activity, such as taking a pencil out of your drawer, or opening the door. Ask children to identify any order words you used in your instructions.

Apply It

- On the chalkboard write the following groups of words: move/kick (the ball) ; go/walk (outside). Ask children which verb in each pair tells better directions and why. (kick, because it tells exactly how to move the ball; walk, because it tells exactly how to go outside.) Tell children to choose exact verbs when they plan their instructions. The right verbs will make their instructions easier to understand.
- Tell groups to practice telling and following their own instructions before sharing them with the class. Have them check to be sure the instructions are clear and there are no steps missing. Then have groups present their instructions for other groups to follow.
- Stress that children should adjust the volume of their voices as well as how quickly or slowly they speak. Remind them also that grammar is important when speaking, such as using subject-verb agreement, complete sentences, and correct tense.

FOR STUDENTS ACQUIRING ENGLISH

Suggest children teach a simple skill or give directions to a part of the classroom before trying the Apply It activity. Recommend they list the steps, order them, practice them, then give them. The listener can then practice taking notes, asking questions and following the steps.

Giving and Following Instructions

Giving Instructions

Have you ever told a friend or a younger child how to play a game or go from one place to another? If so, was it hard to do? Use these tips to give clear, easy-to-follow instructions.

Tips for Giving Instructions

- Tell what your instructions are about.
- Tell all of the important steps.
- Say the steps in the correct order.
- Use hand motions or other body movements.

Use Order Words
- First
- Next
- Then
- Finally

Apply It

Work with two classmates to plan instructions. Use order words and hand motions to explain how to walk from your classroom to another part of the school.

Listening to Instructions

Have you ever listened to instructions and then had to ask questions like these? Where do I put it? Which comes first? Use these tips to help you remember instructions and follow them correctly.

Tips for Listening to Instructions

- Give the speaker your full attention.
- Listen for details.
- Listen for order words.
- Watch for hand motions and other body movements.
- Retell the instructions.

Apply It

Listen to the instructions that your teacher will say. Use the tips above to help you remember them. Then follow the instructions.

Focus on Instruction

- Ask children to tell when and where they have listened to instructions recently and what they learned. (Answers will vary.)
- Ask a volunteer to read aloud the Tips for Listening to Instructions. Then focus your discussion on the practice of attentive listening. Ask children what they think it means to listen with all of their attention. (to watch the speaker and to listen without thinking of anything else or doing anything else) Ask why this is an important guideline. (If you don't listen well, you will miss something. You will have to ask questions or will make mistakes.)
- Discuss the illustration and ask why the student is repeating the instructions. (this is the best way to be sure he heard the all the information and heard it correctly) Remind children that retelling information is also a good way to remember it better.

Apply It

- Before reading aloud the first set of instructions, provide art materials for each child: a pencil, a blue crayon, a yellow crayon, and a piece of paper. Tell children to listen to all of the instructions before they begin the activity. Inform them that they will be drawing and coloring shapes.
- The second activity is more challenging. Give the instructions once. Then demonstrate the activity while repeating the instructions. Children should stand in line, side by side. Stand in front of children with your back to them while you demonstrate and repeat the instructions.

Drawing and Coloring Shapes

First, draw a large triangle in the center of your paper.

Next, draw a small square inside the triangle.

Then color the square yellow.

Finally, color the rest of the triangle blue.

Dance the Grapevine Step

First, take a step with your right foot.

Second, cross your left foot behind your right foot.

Next, take another step to the right with your right foot.

Then cross your left foot in front of right foot.

Finally, take another step to the right with your right foot.

Following Picture Directions

Lesson Objective

Children will:

- use pictures to obtain information

Focus on Instruction

- Discuss why people sometimes use pictures instead of words to give directions. (Picture directions use less space and are not as likely to be misunderstood. Some picture directions, such as a red circle with a line through it to signify "no," are recognized and understood by people all over the world, even though they speak many different languages.)
- Explain that some picture directions are learned symbols, such as a stop sign. Other picture directions, such as those for origami or assembling toys, may use a series of photographs or realistic drawings to explain how to do something.
- When discussing the images on page 236, have children tell when they have used signs to get information or follow directions.

Try it Together

- Provide partners with sheets of newsprint and ask them to complete the activity. If children have difficulty, have them start from the beginning and repeat the steps.

FOR STUDENTS ACQUIRING ENGLISH

For the Try It Together activity, have a think aloud: (*Let me read all the directions first so I know what I'll need and about how long this will take. I need a piece of paper, I wonder what else...*) Students should be experts at following visual clues; allow them to be peer leaders.

Following Picture Directions

Sometimes words are not needed to give directions. A picture or symbol can let you know what to do. Colors can also be used. Look at these examples. What does each picture mean?

Walk

No Biking

Handicapped Accessible

A set of pictures can show you how to do or make something. Each picture shows you one step.

Try It Together

Talk about these picture directions with your class. What do they show you how to make? What do you need to make it? What details do you notice in each picture? Work with a classmate to follow the directions.

a paper hat; one sheet of paper; fold in half, fold down corners, fold up bottom, fold up on other side

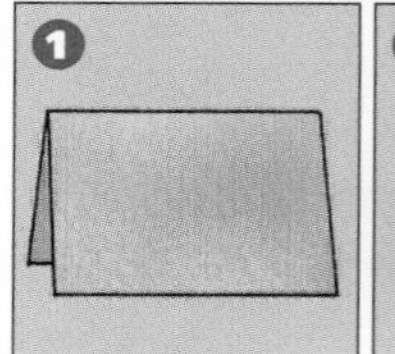

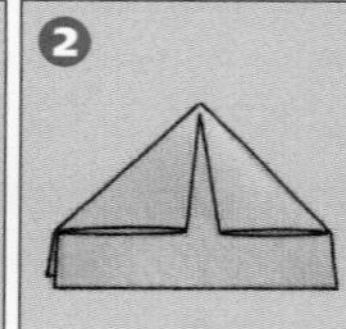

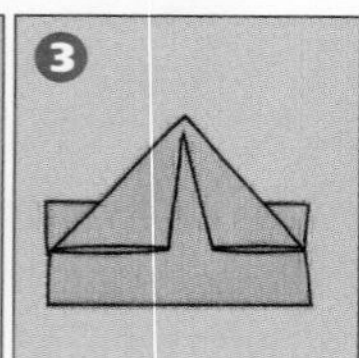

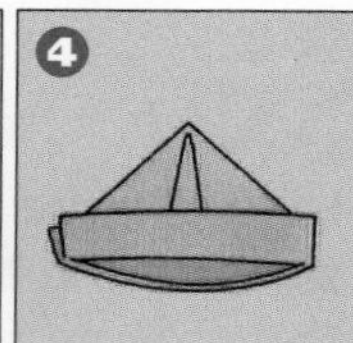

Tips for Following Picture Directions

- First, look over all the pictures.
- Then look for details in each one.
- Follow the steps in order.
- Finish the steps one at a time.
- Work slowly and carefully.

Apply It

Follow these picture directions.

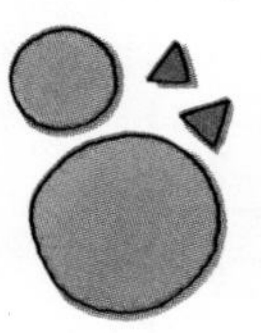

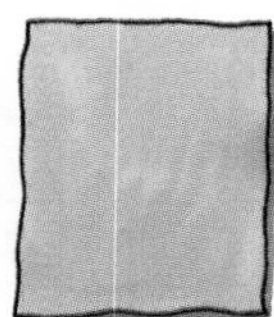

2

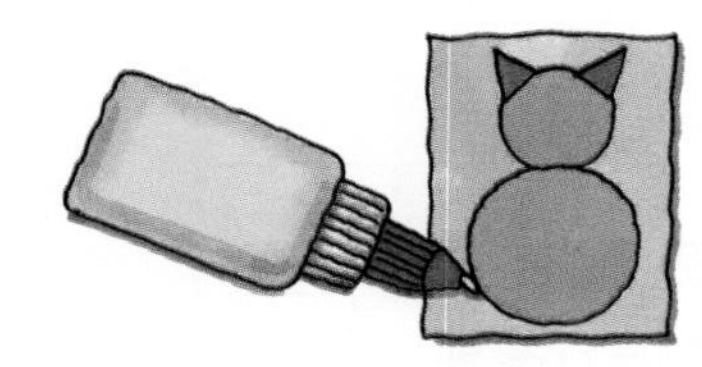

3

Focus on Instruction

- Have a volunteer read aloud the Tips for Following Picture Directions. As you discuss the points, have children relate the guidelines to their own experiences assembling toys or making something. Ask how pictures can help us figure something out. (You can study a picture and compare it to the toy or project until you are sure you have done it right.)
- Ask why it is important to follow the steps in order. (Sample answer: Most directions will not work unless you follow the steps in order.) Ask what might happen if you don't work slowly and carefully. (Sample answer: You might make a mistake and have to start over from the beginning.)

Apply It

- Provide each student with 8 1/2 x 11 inch white paper, cut-out shapes, glue, and pencils.
- Tell children to pay careful attention to the relative sizes of items in the pictures, as well as their shapes.
- Pair up any children who might have difficulty. Have partners take turns explaining the steps in the directions before beginning to work. Then each partner can complete his or her own picture.

Unit 7 Planning Guide

Adjectives

1 1/2 weeks

		Checkup (PE)	Extra Practice (PE)	Graphic Organizer (BLM)	Writing Wrap-Up (BLM)	More Practice (TE)	Workbook Plus	Reteaching Workbook	Students Acquiring English Practice Book
1	Adjectives: How Things Look *(239–240)*	255	261	7–1	7–4	261	83–84	54	65–66
2	Adjectives: Taste and Smell *(241–242)*	255	262	7–1	7–4	262	85–86	55	67–68
3	Adjectives: Sound and Texture *(243–244)*	256	263	7–1	7–4	263	87–88	56	69–70
	Revising Strategies: Sentence Fluency Expanding Sentences: Adjectives *(245–246)*						89–90	57–58	
4	Using *a* and *an* *(247–248)*	256	264	7–2	7–4	264	91–92	59	71–72
5	Adjectives with *er* and *est* *(249–250)*	256	265	7–3	7–5	265	93–94	60	73–74
	Revising Strategies: Sentence Fluency Combining Sentences (*251–252)*						95–96	61–62	
	Revising Strategies: Vocabulary Antonyms (*253)*						97	63	
	Enrichment *(254)*								
	Test Practice *(258–260)*								75–76

Unit 7

Tools and Tips

► **Grammar Glossary,** *pp. H35–H39*

School-Home Connection

Suggestions for informing or involving family members in classroom activities and learning related to this unit are included in the Teacher's Edition throughout the unit.

Meeting Individual Needs

► **FOR SPECIAL NEEDS/INCLUSION:** *Houghton Mifflin English* Audiotape See also Reteaching.

► **FOR STUDENTS ACQUIRING ENGLISH:**
- Notes and activities are included in this Teacher's Edition throughout the unit to help you adapt or use pupil book activities with students acquiring English.
- Additional support is available for students at various stages of English proficiency: **Beginning/Preproduction, Early Production/Speech Emergence,** and **Intermediate/ Advanced**. See Students Acquiring English Practice Book.
- Students can listen to the Try It Out activities on audiotape.

► **ENRICHMENT:** *PE p. 254*

All audiotape recordings are also available on CD.

Daily Language Practice

Each sentence or group of words includes two errors based on skills taught in this or previous Grammar units. Each day write one sentence on the chalkboard. Have children find the errors and write the sentence correctly on a sheet of paper. To make the activity easier, identify the kinds of errors.

1. Today Debbie seen a browner coat in the store window. Today Debbie saw a brown coat in the store window. (irregular verbs/comparing with/ adjectives)
2. Kris eat the juicy pear with an spoon. Kris eats the juicy pear with a spoon. (verbs in the present; using *a* and *an*)
3. Did You hear that loud growl outside. Did you hear that loud growl outside? (capitalization; end punctuation/ questions)
4. I and Lupe saw a airplane fly low over the trees. Lupe and I saw an airplane fly low over the trees. (naming yourself last; using *a* and *an*)
5. Ana's fish is two inch longest than Katy's fish. Ana's fish is two inches longer than Katy's fish. (plural nouns with *es*; comparing with adjectives)
6. This morning Tracy found the pinker Shell of all. This morning Tracy found the pinkest shell of all. (comparing with adjectives; capitalizing proper nouns)
7. What a softest pillow this is? What a soft pillow this is! (adjectives; end punctuation/exclamations)
8. This pumpkin are the rounder one of all. This pumpkin is the roundest one of all. (verbs *is* and *are*; comparing with adjectives)
9. Freddie come back from his aunts house. Freddie came back from his aunt's house. (irregular verbs; possessive nouns ending with *'s*)
10. Trish didnt like the littlest kitten of the two at the pet store. Trish didn't like the littler kitten of the two at the pet store. (contractions with *not*; comparing with adjectives)

Additional Resources

Workbook Plus, Unit 7
Reteaching Workbook, Unit 7
Students Acquiring English Practice Book, Unit 7
Teacher's Resource Book
Audiotapes

Technology Tools

TEACHER'S RESOURCE DISK (for handwriting support)
INTERNET: http://www.eduplace.com/kids/hme/ or http://www.eduplace.com/rdg/hme/
Visit Education Place for an interactive quiz.

Assessment

Test Booklet, Unit 7

Keeping a Journal

Discuss with children the value of keeping a journal as a way of promoting self-expression and fluency. Encourage children to record their thoughts and ideas in a notebook. Inform students whether the journal will be private or will be reviewed periodically as a way of assisting growth. The following prompts may be useful for generating writing ideas.

Journal Prompts

- Tell what you think it would be like to walk around in a big cave.
- Describe what you like best about school.
- What is your favorite song? Do you like to sing it, or do you just like to hear it?

Introducing the Unit

Using the Photograph

- Have children look at the photograph, and ask a volunteer to read the caption aloud. What words tell about the tiger? (*big*, *furry*, *wet*)
- Write *big*, *furry*, *wet tiger* on the chalkboard. Point out that the words *big*, *furry*, and *wet* tell how the tiger looks. Words that describe or tell how something looks are called **adjectives**. Adjectives can tell size, shape, color, and how many. Comment that adjectives help make sentences interesting and their meaning clear.
- Tell children that they will write sentences using adjectives that tell size, shape, color, and how many.

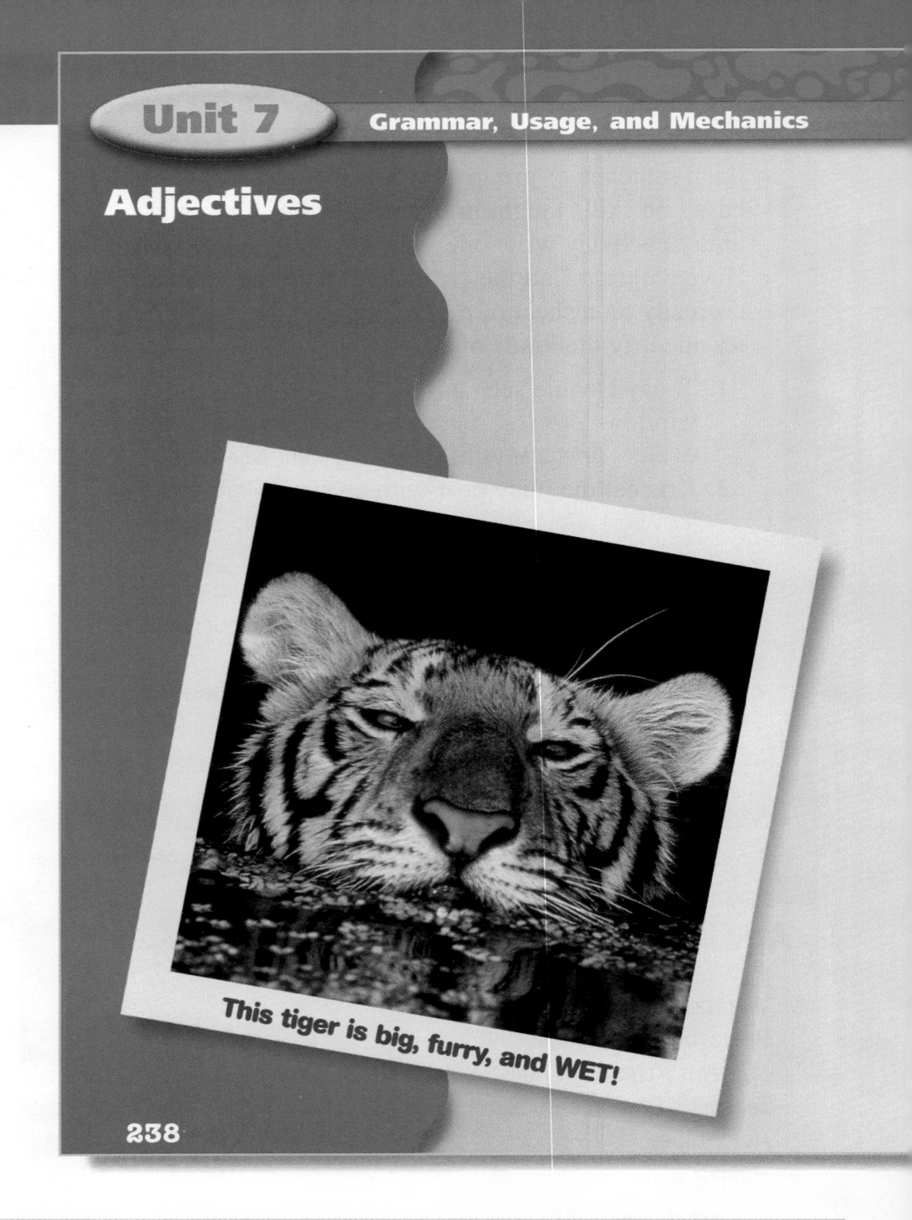

This tiger is big, furry, and WET!

Grammar Song

See Blackline Master G-2 for a song to help children remember concepts and rules taught in this unit.

Independent Writing

Children can benefit by having time each day or several times a week to write in their journals or do self-selected writing activities. Remind children to think about purpose and audience and choose an appropriate format for both.

Shared Writing Activity

Work with children to write sentences using adjectives that describe the nature setting in the photograph or another outdoor setting.

1. Write these column headings on the chalkboard: *Size*, *Shape*, *Color*, and *How Many.* Have children name adjectives that describe something in the photograph. Write the adjectives in the appropriate columns.
2. Have children then name other adjectives they know that fit the column headings. Write the adjectives in the appropriate columns.
3. Work with children to use adjectives from the lists to write sentences that describe the nature setting shown in the photograph or another familiar outdoor setting, such as a neighborhood park. Write the sentences on the chalkboard or on an overhead transparency.
4. Have volunteers read a sentence, name the adjective, and say whether it tells size, shape, color, or how many. Also suggest that they check the sentences for correct capitalization and end punctuation.
5. Have children organize the sentences into a paragraph and write a topic sentence that tells the main idea.

Grammar

1 Adjectives: How Things Look

Play I Spy. Think of a classroom object. Tell how it looks. Have classmates guess the object.

I spy something that is round and small.

A word that describes or tells how something looks is an adjective. **Adjectives** can tell size, color, shape, and how many. Say sentences, using the adjectives below.

Size	Color	Shape	How Many
big	red	round	three
small	gray	square	ten

Try It Out

Speak Up Say each sentence, using the correct adjective from the chart above.

1. Ben has three kittens. **(how many)**
2. He likes the gray one best. **(color)**
3. Button is very small. **(size)**

Write It Write the sentences correctly.

Example Button has a _____ face. **(shape)** three, gray, small
Button has a round face.

Meeting Individual Needs

RETEACHING
ALTERNATIVE STRATEGY

- Hold up a large ball. Ask children to tell its size shape, color, and how many they see. Write the describing words on the board, for example, *big*.
- Ask which word describes size, which describes shape, which describes color, and which tells how many. Explain that all the words are adjectives because they tell how something looks.

CHALLENGE

Write adjectives that tell size, shape, color, and how many on slips of paper and put them in separate piles. Ask children to draw a slip from two of the piles and write a sentence using the adjectives they chose.

FOR STUDENTS ACQUIRING ENGLISH

Show children how to play "I Spy." Say, for example, "I spy something red." Point at your eye to indicate that spy is similar to *see*. Ask a couple of questions, *Is it a ball? No, it isn't. Is it an apple? Yes, it is.* Continue.

Adjectives: How Things Look

Lesson Objectives

Children will:

- use describing words that tell size, shape, color, and how many
- write sentences using adjectives
- write a poem, using adjectives that tell size, shape, color, and how many

One-Minute Warm-Up Write the children's responses on the board. Have volunteers identify words that tell more about the naming words (nouns).

Focus on Instruction

Point out that an adjective usually comes before the word it describes, as in *A little dog runs,* but it may come after, as in *The dog is brown.*

Try It Out

LISTENING AND SPEAKING Write these questions on the board, saying each aloud:

How many kittens does Ben have? *(Ben has three kittens.)*

Which color kitten does he like best? *(He likes the gray best.)*

How big is Button? *(Button is very small.)*

Have a volunteer read a question. Have another child answer it, using one of the Try It Out sentences.

FOR STUDENTS ACQUIRING ENGLISH

- Have children listen to the Try It Out sentences on the audiotape. Distribute the SAE Practice page for Unit 7, Lesson 1.
- Help children describe the art in the book. As children describe the art, list their ideas. Write *adjective* on the board. Explain that an adjective tells what something looks like. Make a check mark next to the adjectives on the list. Ask for other words that tell what something looks like; add them to the list. Then help the children describe the art on the Practice page. Assist with vocabulary. Children listen and say the adjective that fits the sentence. Then they write the adjectives.
  1. We have _____ puppies. (four) **(how many)**
  2. The puppies are _____. (little) **(size)**

Summing Up Help children summarize these key points about the lesson: A word that describes or tells how something looks is an **adjective**. Adjectives can tell size, shape, color, and how many.

You may want to have children complete the parts related to this lesson on Blackline Master 7-1.

On Your Own

Have children test each adjective they select by asking:

Does this word tell how something looks?

FOR STUDENTS ACQUIRING ENGLISH

Distribute the SAE Practice page for Unit 7, Lesson 1. Brainstorm words for colors, size, and shape. Remind children that numbers are also adjectives. Children write a word from the box to complete each sentence, and they underline adjectives in sentences.

Example: A carrot is_____. (orange)
(color)

Writing Wrap-Up

Writing Tip: Suggest that children first use a web, writing the subject of their poem in a circle. Have them connect to the circle words or phrases that describe the subject. See Blackline Master 7-4 for a sample poem.

SCHOOL-HOME CONNECTION

Suggest children read only the adjectives in their poems. The family members should guess the subject.

On Your Own

Finish each sentence with an adjective from the berry. Write the sentences.

round
big
blue

Example The berry is _____. **(color)**
The berry is blue.

1. The berry is very big. **(size)**
2. The berry is round. **(shape)**

3–6. Copy Sid's poem. Draw lines under four adjectives.

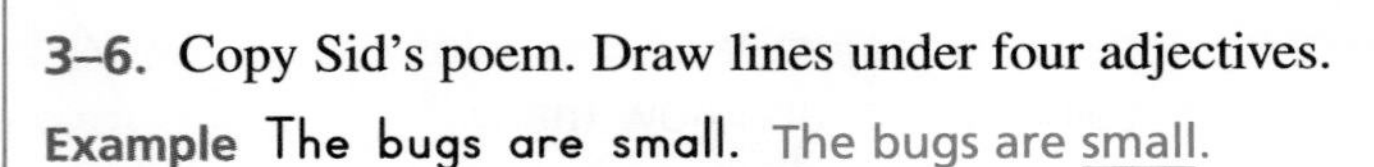

Example The bugs are small. The bugs are small.

Ladybugs

Two bugs are on the sack.
The bugs are red and black.
The bugs are round with spots.
I like the bugs a lot!

two
red
black
round

WRITING • THINKING • LISTENING • SPEAKING

CREATING

Write a Poem

Write a poem. Use adjectives that tell size, shape, color, and how many. Try to make some lines rhyme. Read your poem. Have a classmate say the adjectives. Poems will vary.

 For Extra Practice, see page 261.

Meeting Individual Needs

● RETEACHING WORKBOOK, page 54

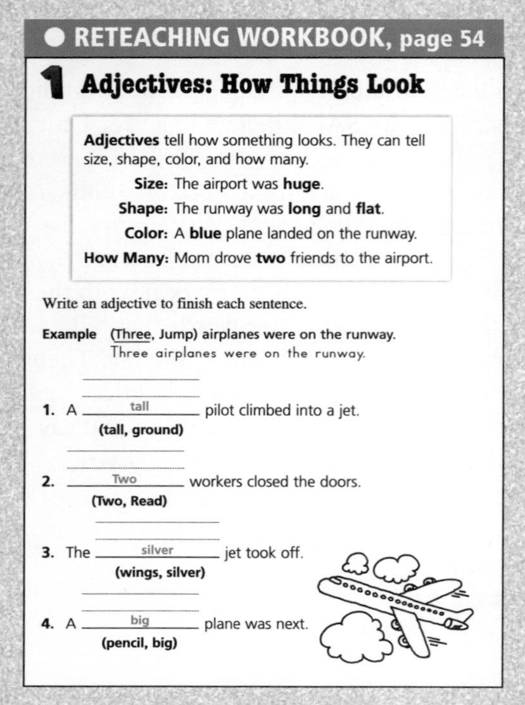

1 Adjectives: How Things Look

Adjectives tell how something looks. They can tell size, shape, color, and how many.

Size: The airport was **huge**.
Shape: The runway was **long** and **flat**.
Color: A **blue** plane landed on the runway.
How Many: Mom drove **two** friends to the airport.

Write an adjective to finish each sentence.

Example (Three, Jump) airplanes were on the runway.
Three airplanes were on the runway.

1. A tall pilot climbed into a jet. **(tall, ground)**
2. Two workers closed the doors. **(Two, Read)**
3. The silver jet took off. **(wings, silver)**
4. A big plane was next. **(pencil, big)**

▲■ WORKBOOK PLUS, pages 83-84

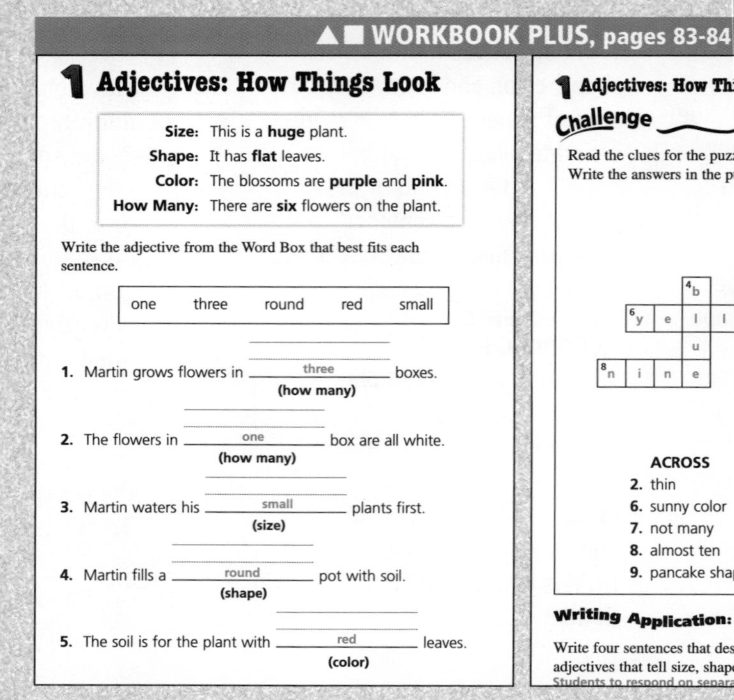

1 Adjectives: How Things Look

Size: This is a **huge** plant.
Shape: It has **flat** leaves.
Color: The blossoms are **purple** and **pink**.
How Many: There are **six** flowers on the plant.

Write the adjective from the Word Box that best fits each sentence.

one	three	round	red	small

1. Martin grows flowers in three boxes. **(how many)**
2. The flowers in one box are all white. **(how many)**
3. Martin waters his small plants first. **(size)**
4. Martin fills a round pot with soil. **(shape)**
5. The soil is for the plant with red leaves. **(color)**

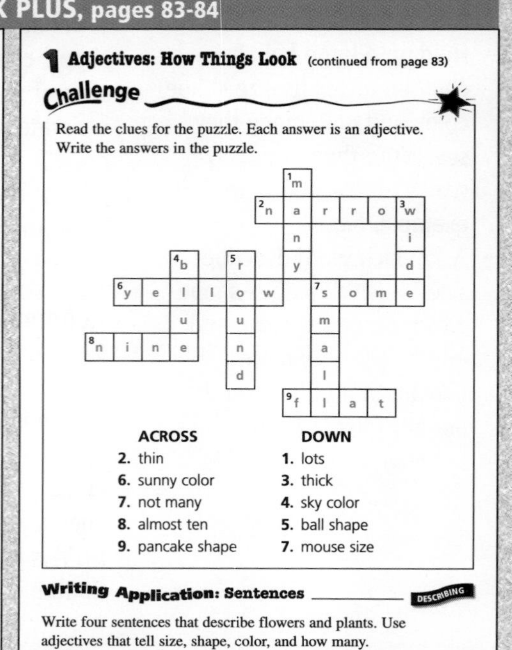

1 Adjectives: How Things Look (continued from page 83)

Challenge

Read the clues for the puzzle. Each answer is an adjective. Write the answers in the puzzle.

ACROSS
2. thin
6. sunny color
7. not many
8. almost ten
9. pancake shape

DOWN
1. lots
3. thick
4. sky color
5. ball shape
7. mouse size

Writing Application: Sentences DESCRIBING

Write four sentences that describe flowers and plants. Use adjectives that tell size, shape, color, and how many.
Students to respond on separate paper. Answers will vary.

Grammar

2 Adjectives: Taste and Smell

One-Minute Warm-Up

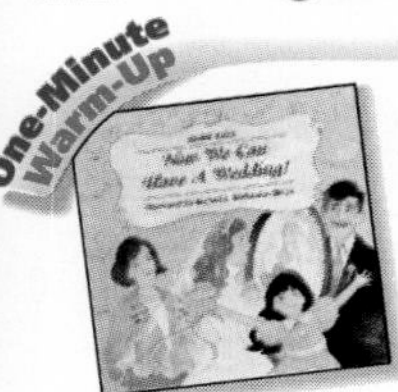

Read the sentence. Which word tells about kitchen smells?

Soon the kitchen fills with spicy smells. spicy

—from Now We Can Have a Wedding! by Judy Cox

What other kind of smells might come from a kitchen?
Answers will vary

Adjectives describe or tell how something looks. Adjectives also tell how something tastes and smells.

Taste		Smell
juicy →		← sweet
sour →		← fresh

Try It Out

Speak Up Say each sentence, using the correct adjective from the Word Box below.

1. The corn tastes sweet.
2. The toast smells burnt.
3. The pickle tastes sour.

spicy	sour
sweet	burnt

Write It Now write the sentences correctly.

Example The stew smells ____. The stew smells spicy.

Meeting Individual Needs

RETEACHING
ALTERNATIVE STRATEGY

- Hold up a ripe apple. Ask children how an apple tastes, for example, *juicy, sweet, sour.* Write responses on the board under the heading *Taste.*
- Ask children how an apple smells, for example, *sweet, ripe, fresh.* Write responses under the heading *Smell.*
- Review that words that tell how something tastes and smells are adjectives.

CHALLENGE

Have children pretend they are in a supermarket. Have them write sentences to describe the foods in different parts of the store. Ask them to use words that tell how the different foods taste and smell.

FOR STUDENTS ACQUIRING ENGLISH

Write the words *Taste* and *Smell* on the board. Say, *How do you smell things? Point to your nose. How do you taste things? Point to your tongue.* If possible, bring in a sliced orange, a sliced lemon, and some salt for children to experience different tastes and smells.

Adjectives: Taste and Smell

Lesson Objectives

Children will:
- use describing words that tell how something tastes and smells
- write sentences using adjectives that describe taste and smell
- write a journal entry about foods, using adjectives that describe taste and smell

One-Minute Warm-Up Write the children's responses on the board. Have them use the words in sentences and then discuss how the adjectives tell about smells.

Focus on Instruction

Explain that adjectives, by telling how something tastes and smells, add meaning to sentences.

Try It Out

VIEWING Have children say adjectives that tell how the corn in the picture might taste and smell and then use the adjectives in sentences. Record the sentences in a chart. Call on volunteers to read a sentence, underline the adjective, and write *taste* or *smell* to tell what the adjective describes. (Sample responses are shown.)

Adjective	What It Describes
I like sweet corn.	taste
You can smell the melted butter.	smell

Meeting Individual Needs

FOR STUDENTS ACQUIRING ENGLISH

- Have children listen to the Try It Out sentences on the audiotape. Distribute the SAE Practice page for Unit 7, Lesson 2.
- Help children suggest sentences about the photo in the book. Then ask children to think of words to describe the foods on the Practice page. Ask for examples of words to describe foods such as *juicy, sour, sweet, salty, bitter*. List them on the board under *Taste*. Do the same with *Smell*, but keep in mind that smells are more difficult to describe. You may want to discuss this aspect of smell. Mention that the words *taste* and *smell* are both nouns and verbs. Children listen. Then they say each sentence using the adjective from the box that fits.
Example: This lemon is ____. (sour)

Summing Up Help children summarize these key points about the lesson:

Adjectives describe or tell how something looks. Adjectives also tell how something tastes and smells.

You may want to have children complete the parts related to this lesson on Blackline Master 7-1.

On Your Own

Have children test each adjective they select by asking:

Does this word tell how something tastes or smells?

FOR STUDENTS ACQUIRING ENGLISH

Distribute the SAE Practice page for Unit 7, Lesson 2. Help children understand words for smells, including *piney, fishy, smoky* by asking them to think about the smell of a pine tree, a fish, and smoke. Children choose a word from the box to complete each sentence.

Example: The room smells _____ from the burnt toast. (smoky)

Writing Wrap-Up

Writing Tip: Suggest that children first create a chart of foods they like and foods they do not like. Tell them to then list adjectives that tell how the foods taste and smell, for example, *chili—hot, spicy, peppery.* See Blackline Master 7-4 for a sample journal entry.

TECHNOLOGY CONNECTION

Children may want to illustrate the foods described in their journal entries with clip art.

On Your Own

Write each sentence, using the correct adjective from the Word Box.

Example The forest smells ____.
The forest smells piney.

1. The peach tastes sweet.
2. The fire smells smoky.

smoky	sweet	piney

3–6. Read Carlota's journal entry. Copy the sentences. Circle the adjective that describes the underlined noun in each sentence.

Example I don't like sour milk. I don't like (sour) milk.

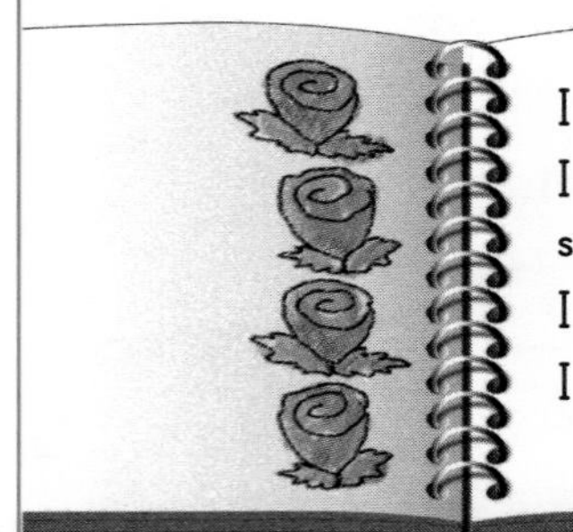

I like roses that smell sweet. (sweet)
I don't like a boat that smells fishy. (fishy)
I like to eat juicy plums. (juicy)
I don't like burnt toast. (burnt)

Writing Wrap-Up

WRITING • THINKING • LISTENING • SPEAKING

DESCRIBING

Write a Journal Entry

Describe foods you like and don't like. Use some adjectives that tell how each one tastes and smells. Read your entry. Have classmates name the adjectives you used.

Responses will vary.

242 Adjectives: Taste and Smell For Extra Practice, see page 262.

Meeting Individual Needs

● RETEACHING WORKBOOK, page 55

2 Adjectives: Taste and Smell

Adjectives tell how something tastes and smells.
Taste: Lois tastes the **fresh** fish.
Smell: There is a **sweet** smell in the kitchen.

Fresh Fish!

Draw a line under each adjective that tells how something tastes or smells. Then write the sentences.

Example Li's fish tastes (slow, salty).
Li's fish tastes salty.

1. She adds a taste of (soft, sour) lemon.
She adds a taste of sour lemon.
2. Lois likes the potatoes' (peppery, green) taste.
Lois likes the potatoes' peppery taste.
3. Li and Lois smell something (tall, fruity).
Li and Lois smell something fruity.
4. They smell (spicy, round) baked apples.
They smell spicy baked apples.

▲■ WORKBOOK PLUS, pages 85-86

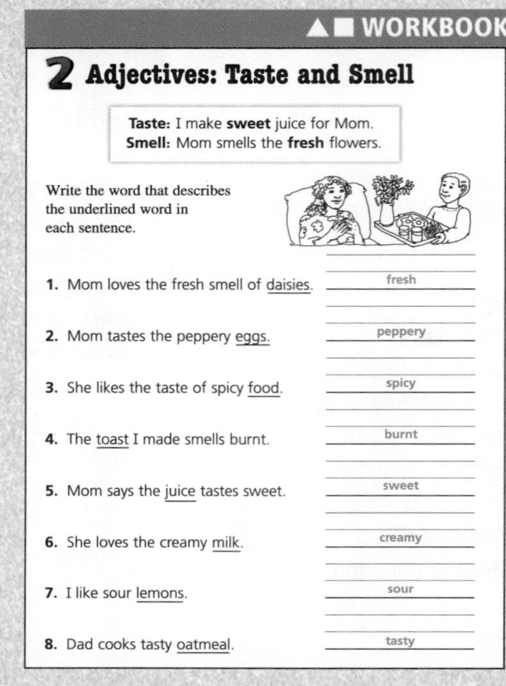

2 Adjectives: Taste and Smell

Taste: I make **sweet** juice for Mom.
Smell: Mom smells the **fresh** flowers.

Write the word that describes the underlined word in each sentence.

1. Mom loves the fresh smell of daisies. fresh
2. Mom tastes the peppery eggs. peppery
3. She likes the taste of spicy food. spicy
4. The toast I made smells burnt. burnt
5. Mom says the juice tastes sweet. sweet
6. She loves the creamy milk. creamy
7. I like sour lemons. sour
8. Dad cooks tasty oatmeal. tasty

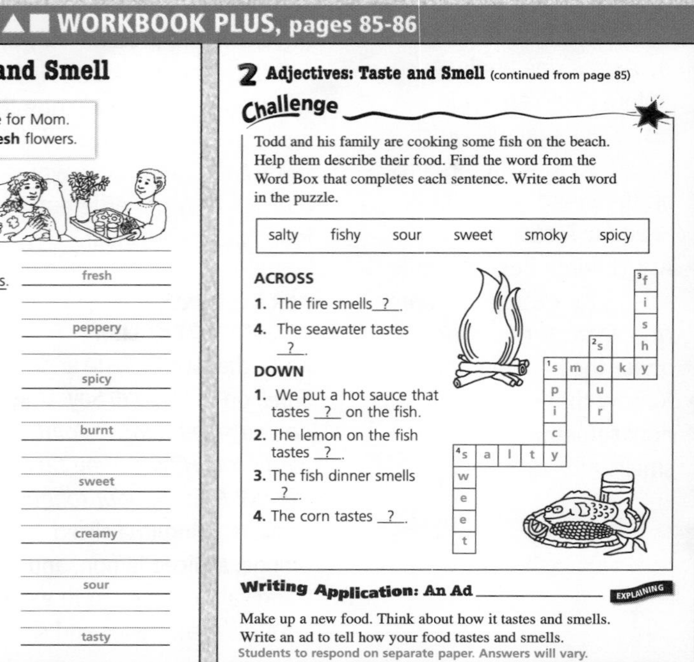

2 Adjectives: Taste and Smell (continued from page 85)

Challenge

Todd and his family are cooking some fish on the beach. Help them describe their food. Find the word from the Word Box that completes each sentence. Write each word in the puzzle.

salty	fishy	sour	sweet	smoky	spicy

ACROSS
1. The fire smells _?_. (smoky)
4. The seawater tastes _?_. (salty)

DOWN
1. We put a hot sauce that tastes _?_ on the fish. (spicy)
2. The lemon on the fish tastes _?_. (sour)
3. The fish dinner smells _?_. (fishy)
4. The corn tastes _?_. (sweet)

Writing Application: An Ad EXPLAINING

Make up a new food. Think about how it tastes and smells. Write an ad to tell how your food tastes and smells.
Students to respond on separate paper. Answers will vary.

3 Adjectives: Sound and Texture

Make a clapping sound and a clicking sound. What other kinds of sounds can you make? Now touch an object in your desk. How does it feel?
Responses will vary.

Adjectives describe how something looks, tastes, and smells. They also tell how something sounds and how it feels if you touch it.

The man has a **loud** voice. The cat's fur is **soft**.

Try It Out

Speak Up Say each sentence, using the best adjective from the Word Box.

barking	hard	crunching	wet

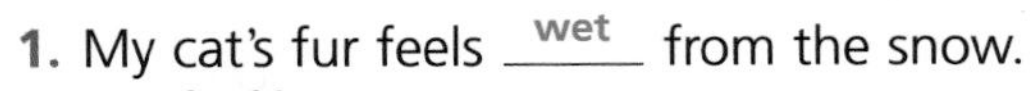

1. My cat's fur feels ___wet___ from the snow.
2. The ___barking___ dog slides on the ice.
3. This rock feels ___hard___.

Write It Now write the sentences correctly.

Example I hear a _____ sound in the snow.
I hear a crunching sound in the snow.

Adjectives: Sound and Texture

Lesson Objectives

Children will:

- use describing words that tell how something sounds and feels
- write sentences using adjectives that describe sound and touch
- write answers to riddles
- write a riddle, using adjectives that tell how something sounds or feels

One-Minute Warm-Up Write children's responses on the board. Then have children suggest words that describe the sounds they make, and write those on the board. Discuss how these words tell more about something.

Focus on Instruction

Review with children that an adjective can come after the thing it describes.

Try It Out

VIEWING Have children suggest sentences about the illustration, using adjectives from the Word Box. Record the sentences in a chart. Call on volunteers to read a sentence, underline the adjective, and write what the adjective describes. (Sample responses are shown.)

Adjective	What It Describes
The ice on the pond is hard.	how it feels
The cat hears the barking dog.	how it sounds
This wet cat sits on a rock.	how it feels

FOR STUDENTS ACQUIRING ENGLISH

- Have children listen to the Try It Out sentences on the audiotape. Distribute the SAE Practice page for Unit 7, Lesson 3.
- Help children suggest sentences about the photo in the book and the art on the Practice page. Write *Hearing* and *Touch* on the board. Say that we hear sounds and with touch we describe how something feels. Ask children for words to describe sounds and words to describe how something feels. Examples for sounds might include *loud, soft, noisy* and for touch *hard, soft, wet, cold*. Call attention to *soft* for both sounds and touch. Children listen and choose the correct adjective.
  1. The rabbit's fur feels _____. (soft)
  2. The ice feels _____. (cold)

Meeting Individual Needs

RETEACHING
ALTERNATIVE STRATEGY

- Drop a cotton ball on a desk and ask children how it sounds when it falls, for example, *quiet*. Write responses on the board under the heading *Sound*.
- Pass around the cotton ball and have children tell how it feels. Write responses under the heading *Feels*.
- Explain that words that tell how something sounds or feels are adjectives.

CHALLENGE

Have children write sentences about a favorite place, telling what sounds they hear and how things feel when they are there. For example, *I can hear sea gulls squawking, I can feel the warm sand.*

FOR STUDENTS ACQUIRING ENGLISH

Write the words *Hearing* and *Touch* on the board. Say, *How do you hear things? Point to your ears. How do you touch things? Show me your fingers.* With children, talk about all five senses.

Summing Up Help children summarize these key points about the lesson: **Adjectives** describe how something looks, tastes, smells, sounds and feels.

You may want to have children complete the parts related to this lesson on Blackline Master 7-1.

On Your Own

Have children test each adjective they select by asking:

> Does the word tell how something sounds or how it feels if you touch it?

FOR STUDENTS ACQUIRING ENGLISH

Distribute the SAE Practice page for Unit 7, Lesson 3. Help children acquire new vocabulary by presenting adjectives such as *hot, wet* with their opposites *cold, dry*. Then children draw a line under the adjective.

1. A _____ makes a ringing sound.
2. A _____ is sharp.

Writing Wrap-Up

Writing Tip: Suggest that children first make a list of things that have a certain sound and a certain feeling when you touch them, as possible subjects for their riddles. See Blackline Master 7-4 for a sample riddle.

SCHOOL-HOME CONNECTION

Have children ask family members to try to solve their riddles. Then suggest that they work together to write new riddles for other family members to solve.

On Your Own

Write each sentence, using the correct adjective from the Word Box.

loud
hot
fuzzy

Example The sun feels _____.
The sun feels hot.

1. We hear a loud meow.
2. I pet the kitten's fuzzy fur.

3–5. Copy Lisa's riddles. Draw a line under the adjective in each sentence that tells how something sounds or feels. Then write the answer to each riddle.

Example What animal makes a squeaking noise? a mouse

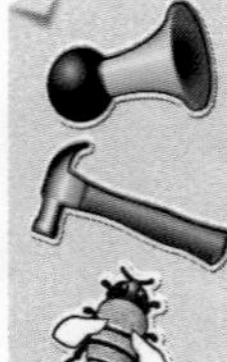

3. What has wheels and makes a honking sound? a car, bus, bike
4. What feels sharp and is used with a hammer? a nail
5. What feels sticky and bees make it? honey

honking, sharp, sticky

Writing Wrap-Up

WRITING • THINKING • LISTENING • SPEAKING

CREATING

Write a Riddle

Write a riddle that describes something. Include how it sounds or feels. Read your riddle aloud. Have classmates name the adjectives and guess the answer.

Riddles will vary.

 For Extra Practice, see page 263.

Meeting Individual Needs

● RETEACHING WORKBOOK, page 56

3 Adjectives: Sound and Texture

Adjectives tell how something sounds and feels.
Sound: Those trucks are making a **honking** noise.
Feel: They are driving on a **smooth** road.

Bumpy Road Ahead

Write the adjectives that tell how something sounds or feels.

Example Our road was very _____ (pink, bumpy).
Our road was very bumpy.

1. Cars made loud noises on it. **(loud, cold)**
2. People worked in the hot sun. **(big, hot)**
3. Tools made clicking sounds. **(many, clicking)**
4. The noisy machines came close to our house. **(noisy, new)**

▲■ WORKBOOK PLUS, pages 87-88

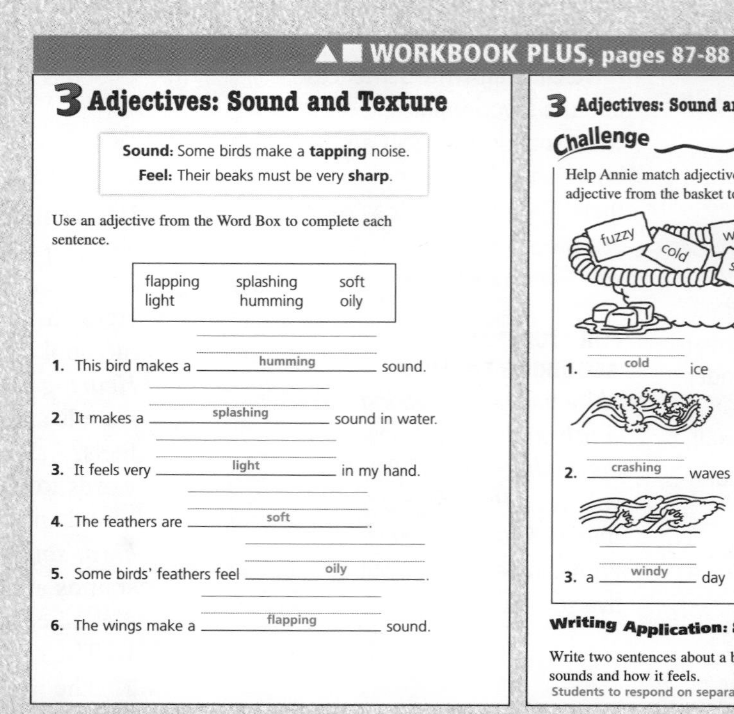

3 Adjectives: Sound and Texture

Sound: Some birds make a **tapping** noise.
Feel: Their beaks must be very **sharp**.

Use an adjective from the Word Box to complete each sentence.

flapping	splashing	soft
light	humming	oily

1. This bird makes a humming sound.
2. It makes a splashing sound in water.
3. It feels very light in my hand.
4. The feathers are soft.
5. Some birds' feathers feel oily.
6. The wings make a flapping sound.

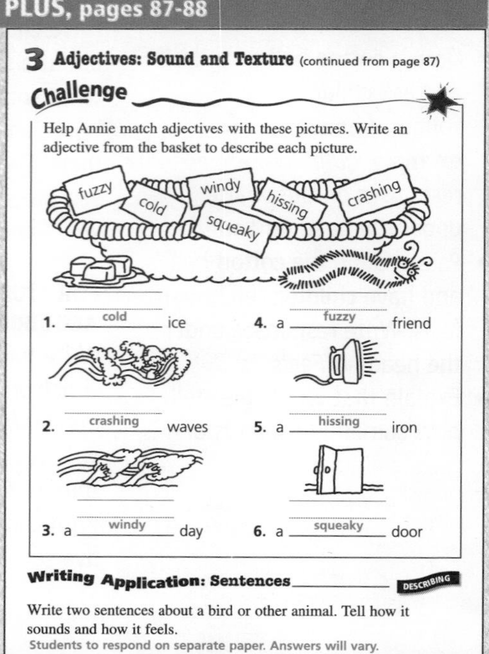

3 Adjectives: Sound and Texture (continued from page 87)

Challenge

Help Annie match adjectives with these pictures. Write an adjective from the basket to describe each picture.

1. cold ice
2. crashing waves
3. a windy day
4. a fuzzy friend
5. a hissing iron
6. a squeaky door

Writing Application: Sentences DESCRIBING

Write two sentences about a bird or other animal. Tell how it sounds and how it feels.
Students to respond on separate paper. Answers will vary.

Revising Strategies — Sentence Fluency

Expanding Sentences: Adjectives

Using Adjectives to Tell More You may use adjectives to tell more about the nouns in your sentences. Use adjectives in your writing to make your sentences clearer and more interesting.

Hold my turtle. Hold my **spotted** turtle.

Try It Out

Speak Up Read the sentences under the pictures. Use an adjective from the Word Box to tell more about each animal. Say the new sentences.

huge	silver
orange	colorful

1. 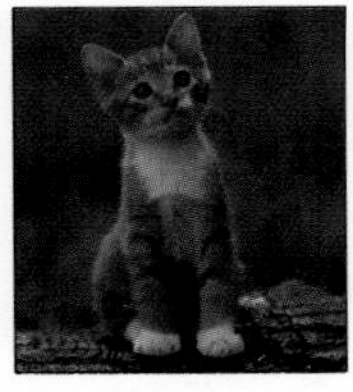

This orange kitty needs a hug!

2. 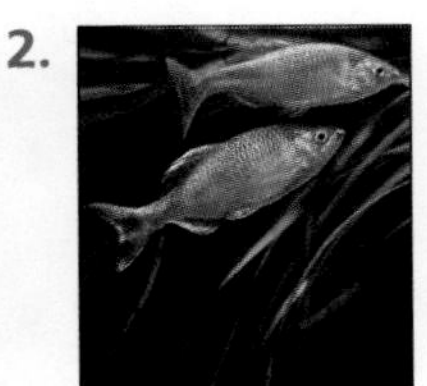

The silver fish swim fast!

3. 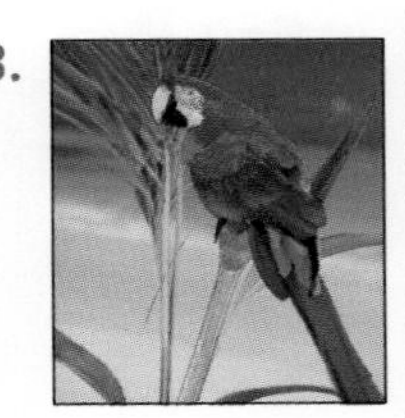

This colorful parrot talks.

Write It 1–3. Now write the new sentences. Draw a line under each adjective.

Example The ____ lizard eats bugs.

The huge lizard eats bugs.

Expanding Sentences: Adjectives

Lesson Objective

Children will:
- use adjectives to tell more about nouns

Focus on Instruction

- Remind children that adjectives include words that tell size, shape, color, and how many. Point out that adjectives also include words that tell how something tastes, smells, sounds, and feels. Invite children to name adjectives for each of these categories.
- Go over the example. Ask children to compare the two sentences and tell how the second is clearer than the first. (The second sentence states the way the turtle looks - that it is spotted)

Try It Out

SPEAK UP Direct children's attention to the word box. Explain that they will use these adjectives to complete the sentences in Exercises 1-3.

- Be sure children understand that they will find clues in the photos to tell them which adjective will best complete each sentence.

WRITE IT Go over the example with children.

- Have children double-check the spelling for each adjective they write.

Meeting Individual Needs

● RETEACHING WORKBOOK, page 57

Expanding Sentences: Adjectives

Adjectives tell more about the nouns in your sentences.
Without adjectives: I like grapes.
With adjectives: I like **green** grapes.

Using Adjectives to Tell More Use the adjective in ( ) to tell more about the underlined noun. Write the new sentence.

Example The bowl has fruit in it. (colorful)
The bowl has colorful fruit in it.

1. I save the peels for the birds. **(orange)**
   I save the orange peels for the birds.
2. The birds like the peels. **(little)**
   The little birds like the peels.
3. Joe saves bread for the birds. **(crusty)**
   Joe saves crusty bread for the birds.
4. The ducks like the bread too. **(brown)**
   The brown ducks like the bread too.
5. Their quacks make me laugh. **(noisy)**
   Their noisy quacks make me laugh.

▲■ WORKBOOK PLUS, page 89

Expanding Sentences: Adjectives

Without adjectives: This is my coat.
With adjectives: This is my **gray** coat.

Using Adjectives to Tell More 1-5. Read each underlined sentence. Use the adjective in ( ) to tell more. Write the new paragraph.

My mom and I went shopping. We both bought clothes. (new) Mom found a scarf. (purple) I got slippers. (fuzzy) Then we stopped for some soup. (tasty) Mom and I enjoyed our day. (great) It was lots of fun.

My mom and I went shopping. We both bought new clothes. Mom found a purple scarf. I got fuzzy slippers. Then we stopped for some tasty soup. Mom and I enjoyed our great day. It was lots of fun.

Expanding Sentences: Adjectives

Apply It

- Read the example with children. Have them read the sentence and then look at the adjectives in the word box. Ask them to try each adjective and then choose the best one for *frog*. Point out that *young* and *noisy* could work, but that *green* is the best choice.
- Have children complete the revising activity independently. Remind them that they should choose an adjective for each underlined noun.

Have children find places in their own writing in progress where they can add adjectives to make their writing clearer and more interesting.

FOR STUDENTS ACQUIRING ENGLISH

Have volunteers read the old sentences, then ask children to work alone to combine the adjectives. Children have practiced using *and*, so they will be confident. Ask volunteers to read the new sentence. For extra practice, ask children to write more double adjective sentences about the pictures on page 245.

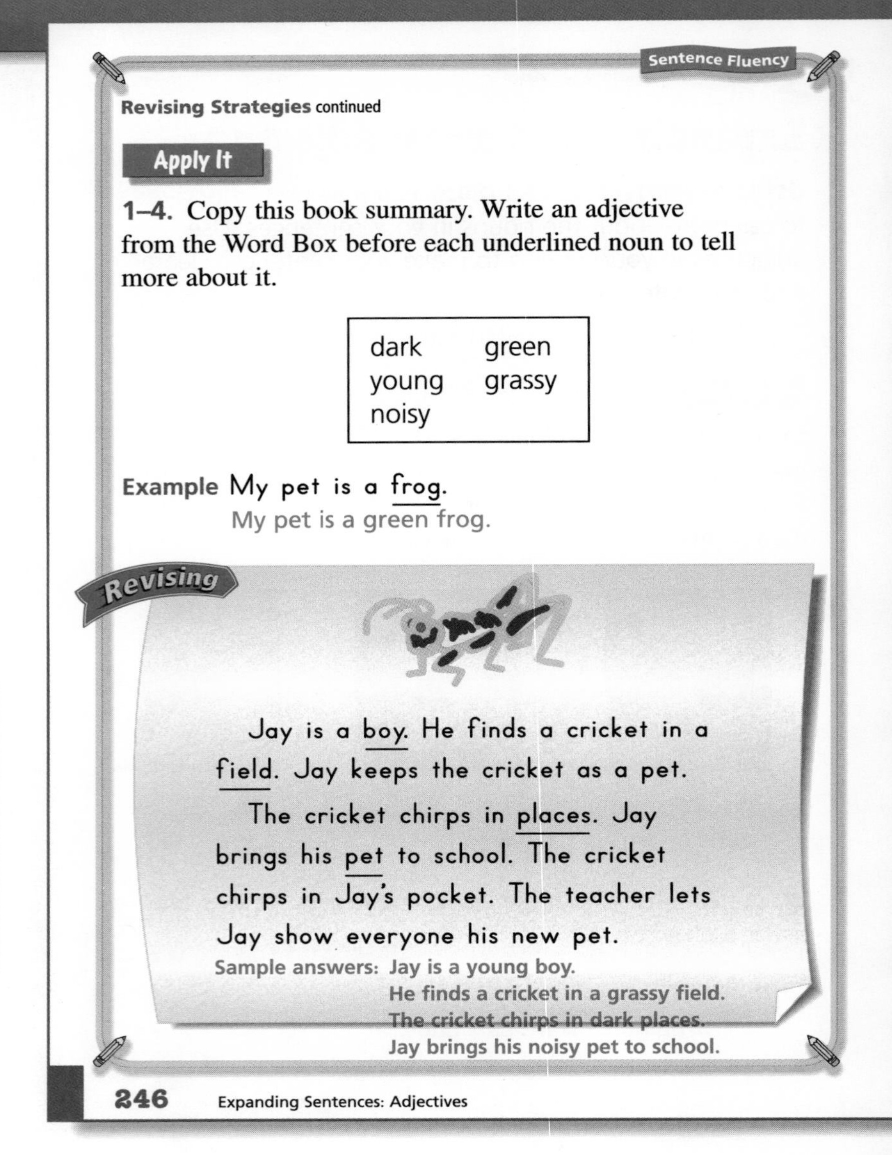

Sentence Fluency

Revising Strategies continued

Apply It

1–4. Copy this book summary. Write an adjective from the Word Box before each underlined noun to tell more about it.

dark	green
young	grassy
noisy	

Example My pet is a frog.
My pet is a green frog.

Revising

Jay is a boy. He finds a cricket in a field. Jay keeps the cricket as a pet.
The cricket chirps in places. Jay brings his pet to school. The cricket chirps in Jay's pocket. The teacher lets Jay show everyone his new pet.

Sample answers: Jay is a young boy.
He finds a cricket in a grassy field.
The cricket chirps in dark places.
Jay brings his noisy pet to school.

246 Expanding Sentences: Adjectives

Meeting Individual Needs

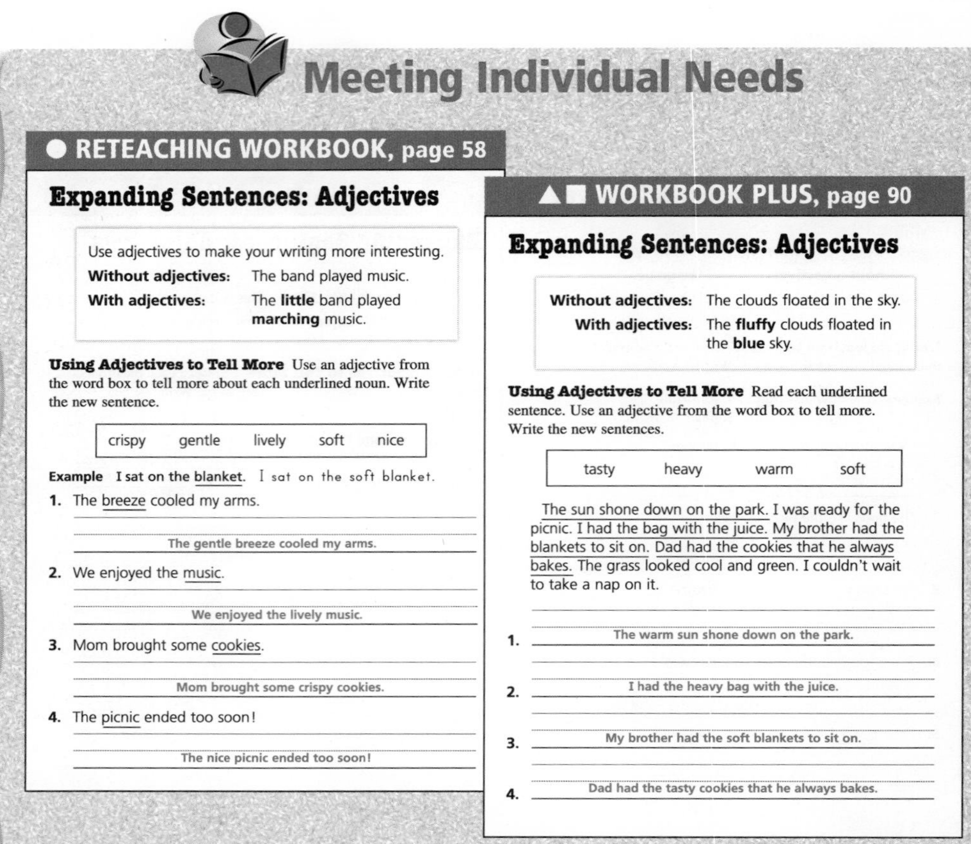

● RETEACHING WORKBOOK, page 58

Expanding Sentences: Adjectives

Use adjectives to make your writing more interesting.
Without adjectives: The band played music.
With adjectives: The **little** band played **marching** music.

Using Adjectives to Tell More Use an adjective from the word box to tell more about each underlined noun. Write the new sentence.

crispy	gentle	lively	soft	nice

Example I sat on the blanket. I sat on the soft blanket.

1. The breeze cooled my arms.
The gentle breeze cooled my arms.
2. We enjoyed the music.
We enjoyed the lively music.
3. Mom brought some cookies.
Mom brought some crispy cookies.
4. The picnic ended too soon!
The nice picnic ended too soon!

▲■ WORKBOOK PLUS, page 90

Expanding Sentences: Adjectives

Without adjectives: The clouds floated in the sky.
With adjectives: The **fluffy** clouds floated in the **blue** sky.

Using Adjectives to Tell More Read each underlined sentence. Use an adjective from the word box to tell more. Write the new sentences.

tasty	heavy	warm	soft

The sun shone down on the park. I was ready for the picnic. I had the bag with the juice. My brother had the blankets to sit on. Dad had the cookies that he always bakes. The grass looked cool and green. I couldn't wait to take a nap on it.

1. The warm sun shone down on the park.
2. I had the heavy bag with the juice.
3. My brother had the soft blankets to sit on.
4. Dad had the tasty cookies that he always bakes.

Grammar / Usage

4 Using a and an

Words will vary, but *a* should be used before nouns that begin with a consonant and *an* before nouns that begin with a vowel.

What might you find in your attic? With a classmate, take turns saying sentences like those on the chart. Use words that name one and say them in ABC order.

In my attic, I found an **anchor**.
In my attic, I found a **basket**.

The words **a** and **an** are **special adjectives**. Use these special adjectives before nouns that name one.

Use **a** before a noun that begins with a consonant sound. He had **a** job.	Use **an** before a noun that begins with a vowel sound. He cleaned out **an** attic.

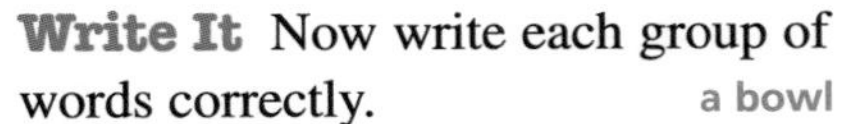

Speak Up Say each group of words, using the correct word in ( ).

1. (a, an) bowl — a bowl
2. (a, an) apron — an apron
3. (a, an) apple — an apple
4. (a, an) pie — a pie

Write It Now write each group of words correctly.

Example (a, an) table a table

a bowl
an apron
an apple
a pie

Using a and an

Lesson Objectives

Children will:

- identify *a* and *an* as special adjectives
- use *a* and *an* with nouns that name one
- write *a* and *an* in sentences
- proofread for correct use of *a* and *an*
- write informative sentences for a poster, using *a* and *an*

One-Minute Warm-Up Write on the board some of the nouns, preceded by *a* and *an*, that children use in sentences like those in the chart. Have volunteers say other sentences using the nouns and tell why they chose *a* or *an* to use before the nouns.

Focus on Instruction

Tell children that the word *the* used before nouns is also a special adjective.

Try It Out

LISTENING AND SPEAKING Provide each child with a word card with *a* lettered on one side and *an* on the other. Then say a noun from the lesson that names one. Ask children to hold up their card with *a* or *an* to show which word is used before the noun you say. Have a volunteer say the article and the noun.

FOR STUDENTS ACQUIRING ENGLISH

- Have children listen to the Try It Out sentences on the audiotape. Distribute the SAE Practice page for Unit 7, Lesson 4.
- Help children suggest sentences about the art on the Practice page. Help children use articles as they describe the art. Say that *a* is used before words that begin with the sound of a consonant; *an* is used before words that begin with the sound of a vowel. Ask for examples of consonant and vowel sounds. You may want to say that it is always the sound that they need to listen for, not the letter the word is written with as in *a horse* and *an hour*. Children listen and choose the correct article. Then they say the phrase.
Example: (a, an) orange

Meeting Individual Needs

RETEACHING
ALTERNATIVE STRATEGY

- Have children name single items in a grocery produce department, for example, *a beet, an orange.*
- List on the board items that children name. Place those preceded by *a* in one column and those preceded by *an* in another column.
- Point out that you use *a* before words beginning with a consonant sound and *an* before words beginning with a vowel sound.

CHALLENGE
Have children write three sentences about a book they have read, using *a* or *an* in each sentence. Have another child read their sentences and tell why *a* and *an* were used correctly or incorrectly.

FOR STUDENTS ACQUIRING ENGLISH
Indefinite and definite articles are challenging for students acquiring English. Help children make labels with articles for classroom objects.

Summing Up Help children summarize these key points about the lesson:

> *A* and *an* are special adjectives. Use *a* and *an* with nouns that name one. Use ***a* before** nouns that begin with a **consonant sound**. Use ***an* before** nouns that begin with a **vowel sound**.

You may want to have children complete the parts related to this lesson on Blackline Master 7-2.

On Your Own

Have children test each special adjective by looking at a list of vowels. Tell them to compare the list to the first letter of the word in each sentence.

FOR STUDENTS ACQUIRING ENGLISH

Distribute the SAE Practice page for Unit 7, Lesson 4. Discuss the art on the Practice page. Children underline the article that fits each sentence. Then they write the sentence again.

1. Mary wants (a, an) doll.
2. I need (a, an) umbrella.

Writing Wrap-Up

Writing Tip: Suggest that children first list details about the event or sale, including time and place. See Blackline Master 7-4 for a sample poster.

TECHNOLOGY CONNECTION

Children may wish to use a computer to use bold type or special print for words on their posters.

On Your Own

Write the sentences, using a or an correctly.

Example (A, An) toy store has a sale.
A toy store has a sale.

1. Nate buys (a, an) airplane.
   Nate buys an airplane.
2. Kim wants (a, an) teddy bear.
   Kim wants a teddy bear.

3–6. Proofread Jake's poster. Find four mistakes in using a and an. Write the poster correctly.

Example Jake made an poster for the yard sale.
Jake made a poster for the yard sale.

Proofreading

Come to a Yard Sale Today!

We have ~~a~~ an umbrella and a bike.

Choose ~~an~~ a toy to take home.

Get ~~an~~ a glass of juice and ~~a~~ an apple.

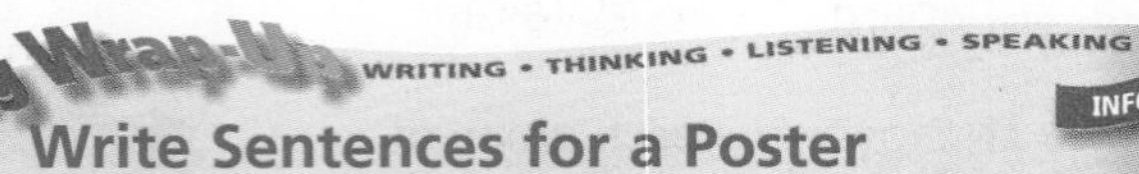

INFORMING

Write Sentences for a Poster

Write three sentences for a poster that tells about an event or a sale. Use a and an. Show and read all of the posters. Together, make a class list of words used with a and an.

Posters will vary.

 For Extra Practice, see page 264.

Meeting Individual Needs

● RETEACHING WORKBOOK, page 59

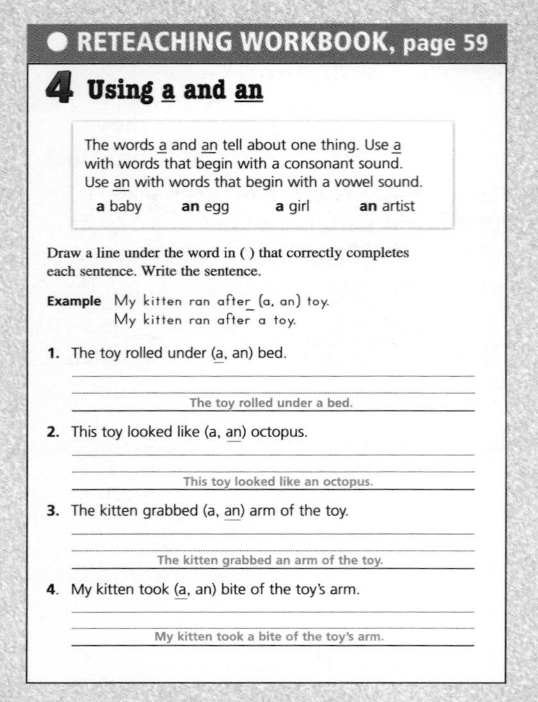

4 Using a and an

The words a and an tell about one thing. Use a with words that begin with a consonant sound. Use an with words that begin with a vowel sound.
a baby **an** egg **a** girl **an** artist

Draw a line under the word in ( ) that correctly completes each sentence. Write the sentence.

Example My kitten ran after (a, an) toy.
My kitten ran after a toy.

1. The toy rolled under (a, an) bed.
   The toy rolled under a bed.
2. This toy looked like (a, an) octopus.
   This toy looked like an octopus.
3. The kitten grabbed (a, an) arm of the toy.
   The kitten grabbed an arm of the toy.
4. My kitten took (a, an) bite of the toy's arm.
   My kitten took a bite of the toy's arm.

▲■ WORKBOOK PLUS, pages 91-92

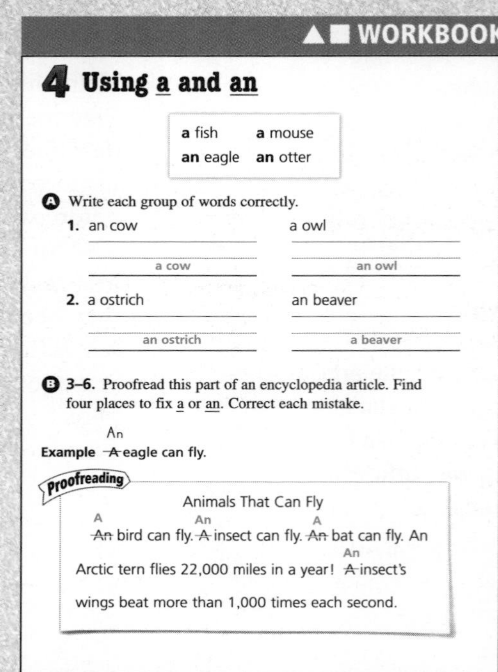

4 Using a and an

a fish **a** mouse
an eagle **an** otter

A Write each group of words correctly.

1. an cow — a cow; a owl — an owl
2. a ostrich — an ostrich; an beaver — a beaver

B **3–6.** Proofread this part of an encyclopedia article. Find four places to fix a or an. Correct each mistake.

Example ~~A~~ An eagle can fly.

Proofreading

Animals That Can Fly

~~An~~ A bird can fly. ~~A~~ An insect can fly. ~~An~~ A bat can fly. An Arctic tern flies 22,000 miles in a year! ~~A~~ An insect's wings beat more than 1,000 times each second.

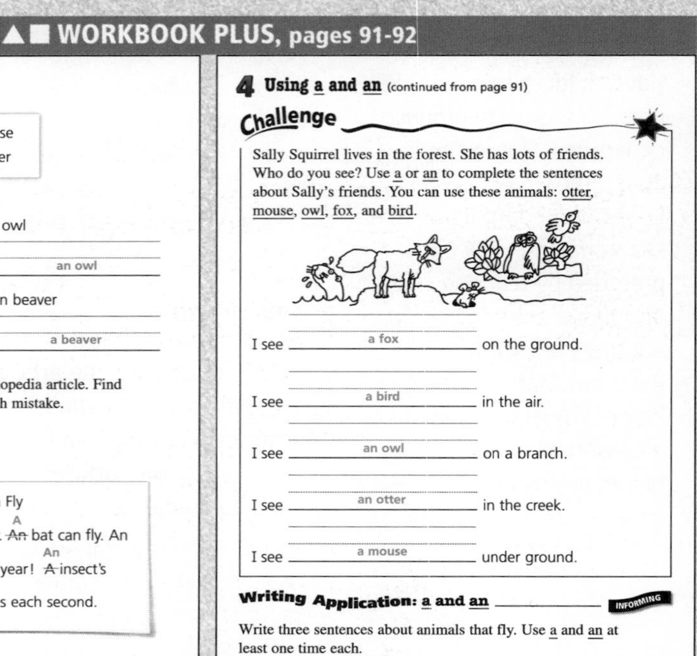

4 Using a and an (continued from page 91)

Challenge

Sally Squirrel lives in the forest. She has lots of friends. Who do you see? Use a or an to complete the sentences about Sally's friends. You can use these animals: otter, mouse, owl, fox, and bird.

I see a fox on the ground.
I see a bird in the air.
I see an owl on a branch.
I see an otter in the creek.
I see a mouse under ground.

Writing Application: a and an INFORMING

Write three sentences about animals that fly. Use a and an at least one time each.
Students to respond on separate paper. Answers will vary.

Grammar / Usage

Sample answer: The orange caterpillar is the longest. The green caterpillar is longer than the yellow caterpillar.

5 Adjectives with er and est

Look at the caterpillars. Say sentences that tell about their lengths.

Add **er** to adjectives to **compare two** people, animals, places, or things. Add **est** to **compare more than two** people, animals, places, or things.

short 

short**er** 

short**est** 

Try It Out

Speak Up Say each sentence, using the correct adjective.

1. Beth is (taller, tallest) than Jan.
   Beth is taller than Jan.
2. Nina is the (taller, tallest) girl of all.
   Nina is the tallest girl of all.

Write It Write the sentences correctly.

Example Nina is (taller, tallest) than Beth.
Nina is taller than Beth.

Beth is taller than Jan.

Nina is the tallest girl of all.

Adjectives with er and est

Lesson Objectives

Children will:

- form comparative and superlative forms correctly
- write sentences using comparative and superlative adjectives
- proofread for comparative and superlative adjectives using *er* and *est*
- write sentences that compare and contrast animals, using comparative and superlative adjectives

One-Minute Warm-Up Have volunteers ask questions about the lengths of the caterpillars for others to answer, for example, *Which caterpillar is longer than the yellow caterpillar?* (The green caterpillar is longer than the yellow caterpillar.) *Which caterpillar is the shortest?* (The yellow caterpillar is the shortest.)

Focus on Instruction

Make sure children understand that *compare* means to find out how things are alike or how they are different.

Try It Out

LISTENING AND SPEAKING Have children listen as you say sentences from the lesson. Ask children how many people are compared in a sentence (two *or* more than two) and what is added to the adjective (er *or* est). Then have a child say the sentence.

FOR STUDENTS ACQUIRING ENGLISH

- Have children listen to the Try It Out sentences on the audiotape. Distribute the SAE Practice page for Unit 7, Lesson 5.
- Help children suggest sentences about the art on the Practice page. Guide the discussion with questions such as, *What is the name of the boy in the middle? What is the name of the boy on the left?* For extra practice, children can ask the questions. Tell children to listen for *than* as a clue for comparing two people or things and *the* as a clue for comparing three or more. Children listen. Then they say each sentence, using the correct adjective.
  1. Bill is (taller, tallest) than Ryan.
  2. Tom is the (taller, tallest) boy.

Meeting Individual Needs

RETEACHING
ALTERNATIVE STRATEGY

- Line up five books by height. Choose two books from the group and ask which is taller? Have volunteers answer the question in a complete sentence that uses the word *taller*.
- Ask someone to tell, in a complete sentence, which is the tallest of the five books.
- Tell children that when two things are compared, *er* is added to the adjective, and that when more than two are compared, *est* is added.

CHALLENGE

Write these adjectives on the board: *small, strong, green, high, cold.* Have children write sentences comparing two or more people, animals, places, or things, using each adjective and adding *er* or *est.*

FOR STUDENTS ACQUIRING ENGLISH

Find out what children know about words for comparing. For example, arrange three pencils and ask, *Is the blue pencil longer than the yellow pencil? Which is the longest pencil?* Continue with other comparisons.

Summing Up Help children summarize these key points about the lesson: Add **er** to adjectives to **compare two** people, animals, places, or things. Add **est** to **compare more than two**.

You may want to have children complete the parts related to this lesson on Blackline Master 7-3.

On Your Own

Have children test each comparative or superlative adjective by asking: Is this comparing two things? Is this comparing more than two things?

FOR STUDENTS ACQUIRING ENGLISH

Distribute the SAE Practice page for Unit 7, Lesson 5. Say, *What are the names of these animals? Compare two animals.* Children write the correct adjective for each sentence.

1. The elephant is the (bigger, biggest) animal.
2. The rabbit runs (faster, fastest) than the turtle.
3. The turtle is the (slower, slowest) of these animals.

Writing Wrap-Up

Writing Tip: Suggest that children first list ways the animals are alike and ways they are different. See Blackline Master 7-5 for sample sentences.

TECHNOLOGY CONNECTION

Children may wish to use a computer to make a Venn diagram that compares the animals.

On Your Own

Write each sentence, using the correct adjective.

Example A rabbit has (longer, longest) ears than a cat.
A rabbit has longer ears than a cat.

1. A horse is (faster, fastest) than a dog. faster
2. The blue whale is the (larger, largest) animal of all. largest

3–5. Proofread Miguel's notes. Find three mistakes in using er and est. Write each animal fact correctly.

Example A duck is smallest than a turkey.
A duck is smaller than a turkey.

Proofreading

Animal Facts

For short distances, a cheetah is the ~~faster~~ fastest animal of all.
A camel is ~~tallest~~ taller than a dog.
A swordfish is faster than a blue shark.
A giraffe is the ~~taller~~ tallest animal.

Writing Wrap-Up

WRITING • THINKING • LISTENING • SPEAKING

COMPARING & CONTRASTING

Write Animal Facts

Compare three animals. Use some adjectives that end in er and est. Read your sentences. Have a classmate name the adjectives you used. Draw pictures to go with your facts.

250 Adjectives with er and est

For Extra Practice, see page 265.

Meeting Individual Needs

● RETEACHING WORKBOOK, page 60

5 Adjectives with er and est

Add er to compare two people or things.
Add est to compare more than two people or things.

tall taller tallest

Write the correct word for each sentence.

Example The woods are ______ than the street. (quieter, quietest)
The woods are quieter than the street.

1. The woods are the quietest place of all. (quieter, quietest)
2. This tree is older than that one. (older, oldest)
3. That tree is the oldest tree of all. (older, oldest)
4. It is the tallest tree of these three. (taller, tallest)

▲■ WORKBOOK PLUS, pages 93-94

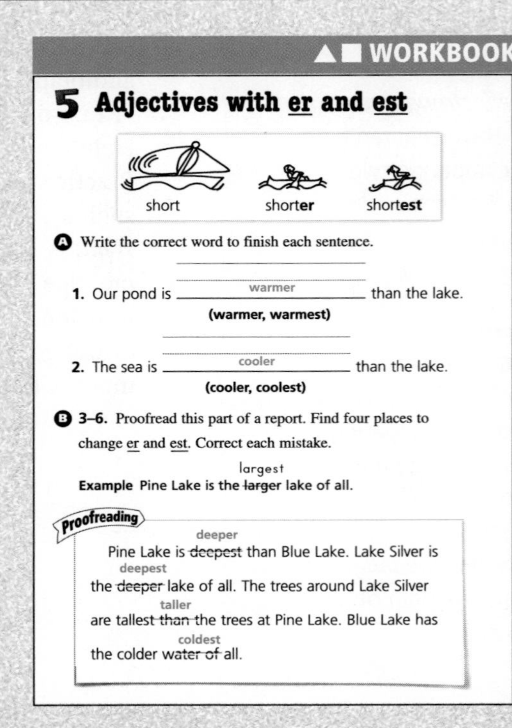

5 Adjectives with er and est

short shorter shortest

A Write the correct word to finish each sentence.

1. Our pond is warmer than the lake. (warmer, warmest)
2. The sea is cooler than the lake. (cooler, coolest)

B 3–6. Proofread this part of a report. Find four places to change er and est. Correct each mistake.

Example Pine Lake is the ~~larger~~ largest lake of all.

Proofreading

Pine Lake is ~~deepest~~ deeper than Blue Lake. Lake Silver is the ~~deeper~~ deepest lake of all. The trees around Lake Silver are ~~tallest than~~ taller the trees at Pine Lake. Blue Lake has the ~~colder water of~~ coldest all.

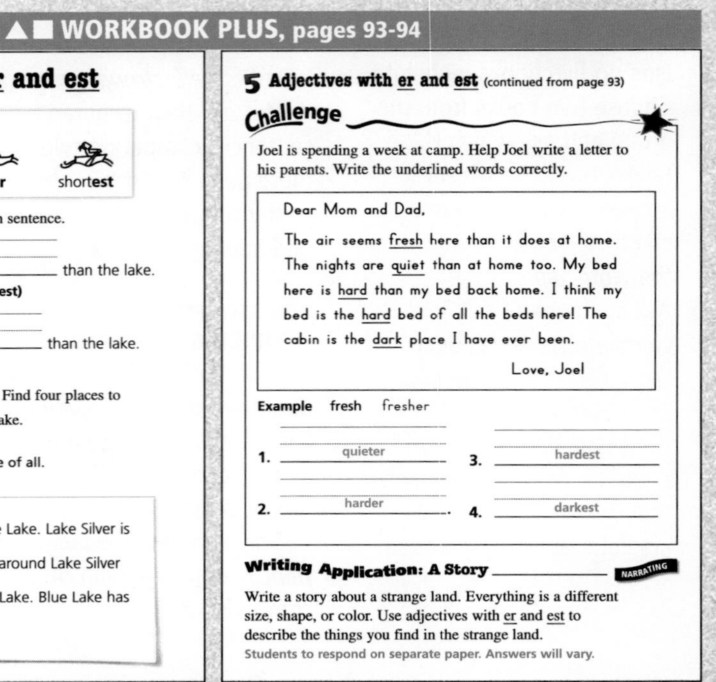

5 Adjectives with er and est (continued from page 93)

Challenge

Joel is spending a week at camp. Help Joel write a letter to his parents. Write the underlined words correctly.

Dear Mom and Dad,
The air seems fresh here than it does at home. The nights are quiet than at home too. My bed here is hard than my bed back home. I think my bed is the hard bed of all the beds here! The cabin is the dark place I have ever been.
Love, Joel

Example fresh fresher

1. quieter
2. harder
3. hardest
4. darkest

Writing Application: A Story NARRATING

Write a story about a strange land. Everything is a different size, shape, or color. Use adjectives with er and est to describe the things you find in the strange land.
Students to respond on separate paper. Answers will vary.

Revising Strategies | Sentence Fluency

Combining Sentences: Adjectives

Joining Sentences with Adjectives You may write two sentences with **adjectives** that tell about the same noun. Join the two sentences, using and between the two adjectives. This will make your writing better.

The lizard is **large.**

The lizard is **scaly.**

The lizard is **large** and **scaly.**

Try It Out

Speak Up/Write It Read the two sentences under each picture. Join the sentences, using and between the two adjectives. Say and write each new sentence.

Example A bat is small. A bat is furry.
A bat is small and furry.

1.

A turtle's shell is large.
A turtle's shell is hard.
A turtle's shell is large and hard.

2.

A manatee is big.
A manatee is friendly.
A manatee is big and friendly.

Combining Sentences: Adjectives

Lesson Objective

Children will:

- join sentences by using *and* between adjectives that describe the same noun

Focus on Instruction

- Remind children that adjectives tell something about a person, place, or thing.
- Point out that children already know how to join naming parts and action parts with *and*. Explain that now they will form new sentences by joining adjectives.
- Go over the example. Help children identify the adjective in each sentence. (large; scaly) Point out that both adjectives tell about the noun, *lizard*.

Try It Out

SPEAK UP/WRITE IT Have children identify the adjectives in the example. (small; furry) Ask them to name the noun the adjectives describe. (bat) Then read the answer, pointing out that they should do the same process for the exercises.

- When children write each sentence, be sure they use correct capitalization and punctuation.

Meeting Individual Needs

● RETEACHING WORKBOOK, page 61

Combining Sentences: Adjectives

You can join two sentences with adjectives that tell about the same noun. Use and between the two adjectives

Two sentences: Our yard is grassy. Our yard is shady.
One sentence: Our yard is grassy and shady.

Joining Sentences with Adjectives Read the sentence pairs. Use and to join the underlined adjectives in each sentence pair. Complete the new sentence.

Example: The trees are tall. The trees are leafy.
The trees are tall and leafy.

1. Our games are fun. Our games are noisy.
Our games are fun and noisy
2. Now the yard is wet. Now the yard is muddy.
Now the yard is wet and muddy
3. We get dirty. We get mushy.
We get dirty and mushy
4. The wet yard makes us muddy. The wet yard makes us happy.
The wet yard makes us muddy and happy

▲■ WORKBOOK PLUS, page 95

Combining Sentences: Adjectives

Two sentences: This fish is **small**. This fish is **shiny**.
One sentence: This fish is **small** and **shiny**.

Joining Sentences with Adjectives 1-4. Read the underlined sentence pairs. Join the sentences using and between the adjectives. Write the new paragraph.

I have a fish tank with lots of fish. The tank is big. The tank is heavy. The fish food is soft. The fish food is flaky. I keep the water clear. I keep the water warm. These fish dash. These fish dart. They are very lively to watch.

I have a fish tank with lots of fish. The tank is big and heavy. The fish food is soft and flaky. I keep the water clear and warm. These fish dash and dart. They are very lively to watch.

Combining Sentences: Adjectives

Apply It

- Read the example with children. Ask volunteers to name the adjectives. (large; scary) Then, have them identify the words that are the same in each sentence. (We saw animals that were) Finally, ask children to read the answer aloud.
- Have children complete the revising activity independently. Point out that they need to first find the sentences that can be joined. Then, they should identify the adjectives and join them with *and* to form a new sentence.

Have children find places in their own writing in progress where they can combine two sentences by joining adjectives with *and.*

FOR STUDENTS ACQUIRING ENGLISH

Although the adjectives lend themselves to specific nouns, ask children to have fun with them. If the sentences they make are silly, ask them to draw pictures to match, for example, a scaly parrot and a green boy. This will demonstrate the power of effective adjectives. Then have them draw pictures that show appropriate or more likely combinations of adjectives with nouns (scaly fish, green pond, etc.).

Sentence Fluency

Revising Strategies continued

Apply It

1–3. Read this part of a class report about a zoo trip. Copy the underlined sentences and circle the two adjectives. Join the two sentences, using and between the two adjectives. Then write the new sentence.

Example We saw animals that were large.
We saw animals that were scary.
We saw animals that were large and scary.

Revising

We saw a lion that was beautiful and proud.

We saw a lion that was beautiful. We saw a lion that was proud. The lion was with her cub.

4–6. Now read the rest of the report. Copy the underlined sentences and circle the two adjectives. Join the two sentences, using and between the two adjectives. Then write the new sentence.

Revising

The cub let out a roar that was loud and fierce.

The lion walked through the tall grass. The cub let out a roar that was loud. The cub let out a roar that was fierce. Then the lion went back to her cub.

252 Combining Sentences: Adjectives

Meeting Individual Needs

● RETEACHING WORKBOOK, page 62

Combining Sentences: Adjectives

Use and to join two adjectives that tell about the same noun. This will make your writing clearer.

Two sentences: That balloon is **round**. That balloon is **blue**.
One sentence: That balloon is **round** and **blue**.

Joining Sentences with Adjectives Read each sentence pair. Join the sentences by using and between the adjectives. Write the new sentence.

Example: His hat is big. His hat is colorful.
His hat is big and colorful.

1. The clown is tall. The clown is funny.
   The clown is tall and funny.
2. The clown car is small. The clown car is yellow.
   The clown car is small and yellow.
3. Those ponies are cute. Those ponies are smart.
   Those ponies are cute and smart.
4. The circus is loud. The circus is exciting.
   The circus is loud and exciting.

▲■ WORKBOOK PLUS, page 96

Combining Sentences: Adjectives

Two sentences: My piggy bank is **big**. My piggy bank is **pink**.
One sentence: My piggy bank is **big** and **pink**.

Joining Sentences with Adjectives Read the underlined sentence pairs. Join the sentences using and between the adjectives. Write the new sentences.

The money in my bank is shiny. The money in my bank is jingly. I will buy something big. I will buy something soft. The toy I buy will be brown. The toy I buy will be white. The toy I buy will have shoes. The toy I buy will have a hat. The toy I buy will keep me company at night. It is a teddy bear!

1. The money in my bank is shiny and jingly.
2. I will buy something big and soft.
3. The toy I buy will be brown and white.
4. The toy I buy will have shoes and a hat.

Revising Strategies — Vocabulary

Antonyms

Words whose meanings are as different as they can be are called **antonyms** or **opposites**. Look at the pictures and read the sentence.

I can see that the **sad** girl is **happy** again.

Apply It

Writing Antonyms 1–3. Read and copy this journal entry. Finish each sentence with an antonym from the box that is the opposite of each underlined adjective.

Adjectives	Antonyms
shortest	tallest, longest
large	small, little
smooth	uneven, rough
light	heavy, dark

Example Ben has smooth stones, and Callie has ____ stones.
Ben has smooth stones, and Callie has rough stones.

Today we went hiking. We saw a large oak tree with a ____ pine tree at its base. Beth carried a light box of leaves, and Alex filled a box with ____ rocks for our campfire. Some of us took the shortest trail, but others took the ____ trail.

small or little
heavy
longest

Antonyms

Lesson Objective

Children will:
- choose antonyms for adjectives

Focus on Instruction

- Review the definition of antonyms. Ask volunteers to give examples and write them on the chalkboard. These could include: *up/down; hot/cold; fast/slow; thick/thin; wet/dry.*
- Go over the example with children. Direct their attention to the girl's expression in each of the photos. Then have them name the antonym for *sad*.

Apply It

- Read the example aloud. Explain that while both *uneven* and *rough* are antonyms for *smooth*, *rough* works better in this sentence.
- Have children complete the activity independently. Tell them that in some cases either word will work well, but that in others they will have to choose the word that best fits the meaning of the sentence. When they are done, ask children to talk about their choices.

Have children who need more support work with partners.

Have children find places in their own writing in progress where they can use antonyms. Remind them to use an online thesaurus or dictionary if they are working on a computer.

Meeting Individual Needs

● RETEACHING WORKBOOK, page 63

Antonyms

An **antonym** is a word whose meaning is the opposite of another word.
My **big** dog Pongo sleeps in a **little** bed.

Revising Change each underlined word to an antonym. Use words from the word box. Write the new sentence.

soft wet straight cool quiet

Example: Pongo's bed is hard.
Pongo's bed is soft.

1. Pongo's crooked tail wags quickly.
Pongo's straight tail wags quickly.
2. He has a very loud bark.
He has a very quiet bark.
3. I like Pongo's dry nose.
I like Pongo's wet nose.
4. It is always very warm.
It is always very cool.

▲■ WORKBOOK PLUS, page 97

Antonyms

See the **bright** moon in the **dark** sky.

Revising 1-4. Change each underlined word to an antonym. Use words from the word box. Cross out the word and write the antonym over it.

larger green fast bigger
warm wet soft yellow

Revising

The night was ~~cool~~ warm and clear. We sat on the ~~hard~~ soft ground and watched the stars. There was a ~~small~~ large star next to the moon. I thought it was a planet. Then it seemed to get ~~tinier~~ larger. It wasn't a planet. It was the lights of a plane!

FOR STUDENTS ACQUIRING ENGLISH

Children may not know the antonyms of the words. Remind them of how they practiced using a thesaurus to find synonyms. Show that antonyms are also in the thesaurus. However, ask children to guess some possible antonyms based on context before using the thesaurus. Finally, model both guessing and thesaurus use.

Enrichment

Objectives

Children will:
- generate adjectives to use in a poem that describes something
- generate adjectives for a riddle about an animal or a thing

Using the Activities

The Enrichment page provides fun, creative activities that reinforce children's understanding and use of sentences. The activities are designed to be enjoyed by all children. Here are some ideas for using the activities.

- Pair children who need extra support with more capable classmates.
- Children can work with these activities in class after they have completed other assignments.
- Activities that can be completed individually can be assigned as homework.

Notes on the Activities

PET POEMS

- Have children read the example. Ask them to identify the adjectives in the poem. (long, brown, spotted, small) Then have them suggest nouns other than *dogs* that they could use in a poem.
- Ask children to read their poems aloud.
- Some children may enjoy turning their poems into songs and singing them with a partner or group.

CHALLENGE Ask children to choose a topic they know well or like. Before they begin, have them write down several ideas for poems.

RIDDLE ROUNDUP

- Go over the example with the class. Point out that the drawing is showing two sides of a single sheet of paper. Explain that the riddle uses three adjectives and that the answer to the riddle is drawn on the back side of the page.
- Children can do this activity independently in the classroom or at home.

FOR STUDENTS ACQUIRING ENGLISH

Ask children to write poems in pairs. Poems written by children acquiring English can be very beautiful. Remind children that poetry can have one word or many words on each line. Challenge children who have an intermediate or advanced level of English to try to use comparisons and to include sounds in their poems.

Enrichment

Pet Poems

- Read this poem. What adjectives describe the noun <u>dogs</u>?
- Write your own poem about another pet, using this one as a model.
- Change the kind of pet and the adjectives.
- Draw a picture of your poem.

Challenge Make a book of poems describing other animals.

I like dogs.
Long dogs,
Brown dogs,
Spotted dogs,
Small dogs,
I like dogs.

Riddle Roundup

- Write a riddle about an animal or thing. Use three adjectives to describe it. Draw the answer on the back.
- Trade riddles with classmates. Guess the answers.

254 Enrichment

Adjectives: How Things Look (page 239)
Choose the correct adjective from the Word Box to finish each sentence. Use the words in ( ) to help you.
Write the sentences.

round
yellow
four
tiny

1. There are four baby birds. **(how many)**
2. They live in a round nest. **(shape)**
3. They are tiny birds. **(size)**
4. They have yellow feathers. **(color)**

Adjectives: Taste and Smell (page 241)
Write the sentences. Circle the adjective that describes each underlined noun.

5. The soap smells flowery.
6. The cheese tastes creamy.
7. I like spicy chili.
8. I threw away the sour milk.
9. The clams taste fishy.
10. The room smells smoky.

Checkup

Objectives

Children will:
- choose correct adjectives
- identify adjectives in sentences

Using the Checkup

Use the Checkup exercises as assessment, as review for the unit test, as extra practice, or as a diagnostic aid to help determine those children who need reteaching.

INTERNET CONNECTION
Children can take an interactive quiz for this unit at www.eduplace.com /kids/hme/ and then get immediate feedback.

Objectives

Children will:
- write correct adjectives
- use *a* and *an* correctly in sentences
- choose correct adjectives that compare

Adjectives: Sound and Texture (page 243)

Write each sentence, using the correct adjective from the Word Box.

creaky
noisy
sticky
smooth

11. Glue is sticky to touch.
12. The playground sounds noisy.
13. The old door is creaky.
14. The egg feels smooth.

Using a and an (page 247)

Write each group of words, using a or an correctly.

15. (a, an) girl
16. (a, an) ox
17. (a, an) clown
18. (a, an) eel
19. (a, an) man
20. (a, an) insect

Adjectives with er and est (page 249)

Write each sentence. Use the correct adjective.

21. Terry is (older, oldest) than John.
22. Which of the three girls has the (longer, longest) hair?
23. John's hair is (darker, darkest) than my hair.
24. Ann is (shorter, shortest) than Amy.

Proofreading Checklist

- ✔ Is a used before a noun that begins with a consonant sound?
- ✔ Is an used before a noun that begins with a vowel sound?
- ✔ Are adjectives ending with er used to compare two people, animals, places, or things?
- ✔ Are adjectives ending with est used to compare more than two people, animals, places, or things?

Mixed Review

25–30. Proofread this riddle. Find three mistakes with a and an and three mistakes with adjectives that compare. Write the riddle correctly.

Example Here is an riddle for you to solve.
Here is a riddle for you to solve.

I am an animal.
I am the ~~bigger~~ biggest animal on earth!
I weigh more than an elephant.
I am ~~longest~~ longer than a school bus.
I live in ~~a~~ an ocean, but I am not a fish.
I breathe through ~~an~~ a hole on top of my head.
I eat tiny sea creatures called krill.
Krill are ~~smallest~~ smaller than your finger.
I can eat thirty million krill in ~~an~~ a day!
What am I?

Answer: I am a blue whale!

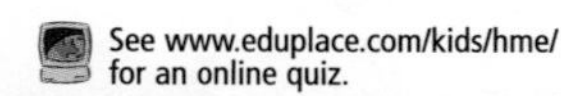

See www.eduplace.com/kids/hme/ for an online quiz.

Objective

Children will:

- proofread a riddle and correct mistakes with *a* and *an* and with adjectives that compare

Test Practice

Objective

Children will:

- practice completing a test format that requires them to choose the correct item among two or three

Using the Test Practice

- These Test Practice pages provide practice with common formats used in standardized or multiple-choice tests.
- The first page works with skills taught in the basic lessons in Unit 7. The second page works with skills taught in the lessons in Units 1, 3, 5 and 7.

Notes on the Test Format

- Go over the directions with children. Have children explain what the directions ask them to do. Point out that they have done this type of test question before so it should be familiar. Explain that there will be either two or three possible answers for each item.
- Have children read Item 1 with each of the possible answers. Be sure they understand that the correct answer must fit best in the blank. Then have children identify the two incorrect answers before marking the bubble next to the correct one.

FOR STUDENTS ACQUIRING ENGLISH

Review definite and indefinite articles. Then review what an adjective does as well as the comparative and superlative forms of adjectives. Distribute the SAE Test Practice pages for Unit 7. Read the directions aloud. Explain that in the first section children are to circle the correct adjective. In the second section, children are to circle the sentence that does not have a mistake. Remind children to look for *than* and *the* as clues for comparing.

Test Practice

Number a sheet of paper from 1 to 8. Read each sentence. An adjective is missing. Choose the correct adjective to go in the blank. Write the letter for that answer.

1 Julia is _____ than Laura.

- **A** tallest
- Ⓑ taller
- **C** tall

2 Spot is the _____ of the six puppies.

- **A** small
- **B** smaller
- Ⓒ smallest

3 Rosa sat in _____ chair.

- Ⓐ a
- **B** an

4 Jody ate _____ apple for a snack.

- **A** a
- Ⓑ an

5 Pablo is the _____ runner in our whole school.

- **A** faster
- **B** fast
- Ⓒ fastest

6 We heard _____ owl last night.

- **A** a
- Ⓑ an

7 The pink rose is _____ than the yellow rose.

- **A** bright
- Ⓑ brighter
- **C** brightest

8 The dog pushed over _____ trash can.

- Ⓐ a
- **B** an

Test Practice continued

Now write the numbers 9 to 14 on your paper. Read the four sentences by each number. Find the sentence that does not have any mistakes. Write the letter for that sentence.

9
- **A** we love camping!
- **B** I have went camping before.
- **C** We sleep in an tent.
- Ⓓ Pack some food.

10
- **A** This clock is loudest than that clock.
- **B** Dans clock is in the shape of a train.
- Ⓒ Did the clock stop?
- **D** I and Mandy looked at the clock.

11
- **A** These tigers lives in zoos.
- **B** One tiger is named stripes.
- **C** The tigers tail is long.
- Ⓓ Stripes is the biggest of five tigers.

12
- Ⓐ It is Ted's birthday.
- **B** Make some wishs.
- **C** Balloons is all over the room.
- **D** Do you want cake.

13
- **A** Yesterday the class gone to the park.
- Ⓑ This slide is bigger than that slide.
- **C** The park is on Main street.
- **D** John has gave me a push on the swing.

14
- **A** Your hair is longer than my hair
- Ⓑ Did you get your bangs cut?
- **C** Jenna wear a bow.
- **D** Jasmin and me braided our hair.

Objective

Children will:
- practice completing a test format that requires them to choose the correct sentence from among four

Notes on the Test Format

- Ask a volunteer to read the directions to the class. Be sure that children clearly understand what to do.
- Have children carefully read and evaluate each sentence in Item 9. Point out that the sentences in this item include different types of errors. Explain to children that they should expect to see a variety of errors in the other items as well.
- Have children locate errors in three sentences before deciding which one is correct.

Test Practice *continued*

Objective

Children will:

- practice completing a test format that requires them to choose the correct sentence from among four

Notes on the Test Format

The test format on this page is the same as the format on the preceding page.

Test Practice continued

Now write the numbers 15 to 20 on your paper. Read the four sentences by each number. Find the sentence that does not have any mistakes. Write the letter for that sentence.

15 **A** She put her books in two boxs.
B Maria and alma played with buttons.
(C) The old doll is softer than the new doll.
D The wheels have came off the toy car.

16 **A** My shoes is black.
(B) The hats are on the top shelf.
C Joe put on an shirt.
D Do the shoes fit.

17 **(A)** The TV doesn't work.
B Nana given us her old toaster.
C Last week the man paints the house.
D The childs have two broken toys.

18 **A** Today is the longer day of the summer.
B In spring I saw an nest with baby birds.
(C) Do you like winter?
D Kelly and I cant wait.

19 **A** We camps in the woods every summer.
B The red tent is biggest than the blue tent.
(C) This is fun!
D The campers cooked over a fire?

20 **A** The farmers house is big and white.
B Jane's house has two porchs.
C How many rooms is in your house?
(D) Jack lives in a cabin.

260 Test Practice

Extra Practice

(pages 239–240)

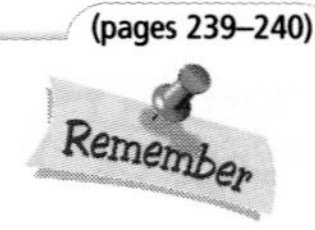

1 Adjectives: How Things Look
- A word that describes how something looks is an adjective.
- Adjectives can tell size, color, shape, and how many.

●▲ Write each sentence, using an adjective from the Word Box. Look at the word in ( ) for help.

large	green
round	one

Example The store sold _____ beach ball today. **(how many)**
The store sold one beach ball today.

1. The beach balls are round. **(shape)**
2. This one is very large. **(size)**
3. It has big green dots. **(color)**

■ Write the sentences. Draw a line under each adjective.

Example The toys are small. **(size)**
The toys are small.

4. I have three cars. **(how many)**
5. I like the blue car best. **(color)**
6. The tires are big. **(size)**
7. The windows are square. **(shape)**
8. It has four doors. **(how many)**
9. The red car has a stripe on it. **(color)**
10. The stripe is thin. **(size)**

Adjectives: How Things Look

Objective

Children will:
- identify and write adjectives that tell how things look

Using the Extra Practice

The Extra Practice activities provide two levels of additional practice for the basic lesson: Easy/Average (●▲), and Challenging (■).

The Extra Practice activities can be used in the following ways.

- Assign activities according to children's needs and abilities as homework after children have completed the basic lesson.
- Assign the Easy/Average activities after using the lesson Reteaching instruction.
- Assign the Challenging exercises as a Bonus activity.
- Assign the Easy/Average activities to prepare children for the Checkup.
- Assign the Easy/Average activities to children who had difficulty with specific lessons on the Checkup.

Meeting Individual Needs — More Practice for Lesson 1

● **EASY** ▲ **AVERAGE**

Look at the word in ( ) for help, then choose one of these adjectives to finish each sentence: two, red, blue, small, big, five, square, round, green, yellow

1. The apples are _____. (color) red
2. The trees are _____. (size) big
3. The sky is _______. (color) blue
4. The children had _____ apples. (how many) two *or* five
5. The books are _____. (shape) square
6. The grass is _______. (color) green
7. The apples are _______. (shape) round
8. The mouse is _______. (size) small
9. The mouse ate _______ bites. (how many) two *or* five
10. The lemons are _____. (color) yellow

■ **CHALLENGING**

Draw a line under each adjective.

1. My house has ten windows. (how many)
2. I have three cats. (how many)
3. The pillow is square. (shape)
4. That ball is round. (shape)
5. I like the red chair. (color)
6. It is a large chair. (size)
7. I put a round pillow on the chair. (shape)
8. The cats are all black. (color)
9. Did you see the yellow cat? (color)
10. She has a long tail. (size)

Adjectives: Taste and Smell

Objective

Children will:
- identify and write adjectives that tell how things taste and smell

Extra Practice

(pages 241–242)

2 Adjectives: Taste and Smell
- Adjectives can tell how something tastes and smells.

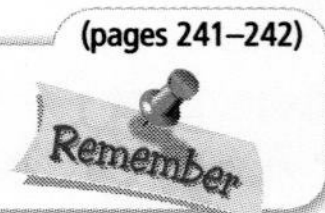

●▲ Choose an adjective from the Word Box to finish each sentence. Write the sentences.

sweet	spicy	stale	smoky

Example The perfume smells ____.
The perfume smells sweet.

1. The old crackers taste stale.
2. Our campfire smells smoky.
3. Many Mexican foods taste spicy.

■ Write the sentences. In each sentence, circle the adjective that describes the underlined word.

Example The stew tastes peppery. The stew tastes (peppery.)

4. The wash smells (soapy.)
5. The milk tastes (sour.)
6. The ice cream tastes (minty.)
7. The woods smell (piney.)
8. The roses smell (sweet.)

262 Extra Practice

Meeting Individual Needs

More Practice for Lesson 2

● **EASY** ▲ **AVERAGE**

Choose one of these adjectives to finish each sentence: sweet, sour, nutty, stale, spicy, smoky, tart, bitter, mild, sharp (Possible answers shown.)

1. That old bread smells ____. stale
2. This white cheese tastes ____. mild
3. The yellow cheese tastes ____. sharp
4. The candy tastes ____. sweet
5. The peanut butter smells ____. nutty
6. My apples taste ____. tart
7. Some medicines smell ____. bitter
8. Our barbeque smells ____. smoky
9. Some chili is ____. spicy
10. That lemon is so ____! sour

■ **CHALLENGING**

Draw a line under the adjective that describes the underlined word in each sentence.

1. The perfume smells flowery.
2. The fruit smells fresh.
3. That cream tastes sour.
4. This tea tastes hot.
5. My rice tastes spicy.
6. Mom's bath smells soapy.
7. Those walnuts smell nutty.
8. Your cake tastes sweet.
9. This paint smells sharp.
10. The fire smells smoky.

Extra Practice

3 Adjectives: Sound and Texture

(pages 243–244)

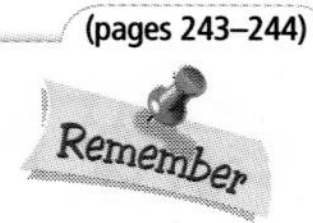

- Adjectives can tell how something sounds and how it feels when you touch it.

●▲ Choose an adjective from the Word Box to finish each sentence. Write the sentences.

cool	hot	loud	soft

Example The sun feels ____.
The sun feels hot.

1. A whisper sounds soft.
2. The shade feels cool.
3. The horn sounds loud.

■ Write the sentences.
Draw a line under each adjective.

Example The grass feels wet.
The grass feels wet.

4. The band plays loud music.
5. I sit on the soft blanket.
6. The breeze feels cool on my face.
7. I am wearing a silky dress.
8. I hear a buzzing bee.

Adjectives: Sound and Texture

Objective

Children will:

- identify and write adjectives that tell how something sounds and feels

Meeting Individual Needs

More Practice for Lesson 3

● EASY ▲ AVERAGE

Choose one of these adjectives to finish each sentence: soft, bumpy, thorny, smooth, loud, chirping, croaking, mooing, barking, hot

1. I hear a ______ frog. croaking
2. Listen to the ______ birds. chirping
3. A teddy bear feels ______. soft
4. This road feels too ______. bumpy
5. Do you hear the ______ cows? mooing
6. Stop those ______ dogs! barking
7. The roses feel ______. thorny
8. This silk feels so ______. smooth
9. A crash sounds ______. loud
10. The sun feels ______. hot

■ CHALLENGING

Draw a line under the adjective in each sentence.

1. The ocean feels wet.
2. The hot sand makes my feet burn.
3. The breeze sounds soft.
4. The loud children play in the sand.
5. My bathing suit feels silky.
6. The sand feels grainy.
7. I hear a crying seagull.
8. Your splashes feel so cold!
9. I drink the cool juice.
10. The warm sun is above us.

Using a and an

Objective

Children will:

- correctly use *a* and *an* before words that name one, words that begin with a consonant sound, and words that begin with a vowel sound

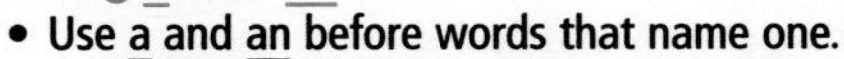
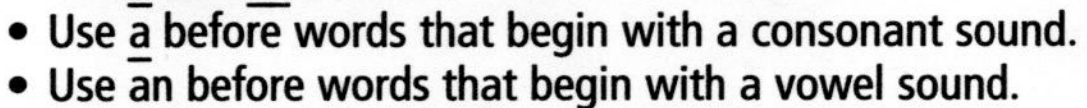

Extra Practice

(pages 247–248)

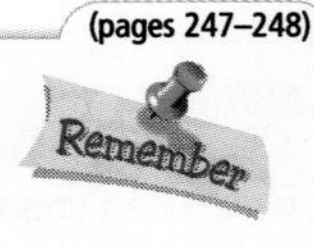

4 Using a and an

- Use a and an before words that name one.
- Use a before words that begin with a consonant sound.
- Use an before words that begin with a vowel sound.

●▲ Choose the correct word in ( ). Write each group of words.

Example (a, an) ox an ox

1. (a, an) cookie
2. (a, an) egg
3. (a, an) apple
4. (a, an) pear
5. (a, an) frog
6. (a, an) otter
7. (a, an) hen
8. (a, an) elephant

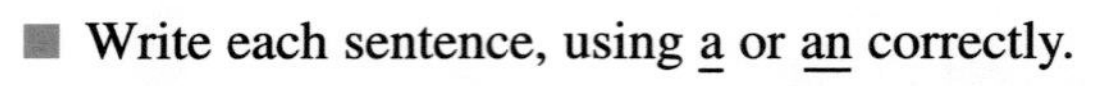

■ Write each sentence, using a or an correctly.

Example I can ride ____ horse.
I can ride a horse.

9. Can you find __an__ ant on the flower?
10. That animal covered with mud is __a__ pig!
11. I see __an__ inchworm on a leaf.
12. Where does __a__ bear live?

Meeting Individual Needs

More Practice for Lesson 4

● EASY ▲ AVERAGE

Draw a line under the correct word in ( ) for each group of words.

1. (a, an) apple
2. (a, an) box
3. (a, an) cat
4. (a, an) umbrella
5. (a, an) eggshell
6. (a, an) toy
7. (a, an) foot
8. (a, an) inch
9. (a, an) chair
10. (a, an) boat

■ CHALLENGING

Write *a* or *an* in each sentence.

1. Did you see __ ant? an
2. I saw ___ octopus! an
3. There is ____ bear. a
4. Next to him is ___ lion. a
5. He is carrying ___ umbrella. an
6. They are riding in __ boat. a
7. Did he eat ___ apple? an
8. I think he ate ___ orange. an
9. She said he ate ____ egg. an
10. He really ate ___ cookie. a

Extra Practice

5 Adjectives with er and est

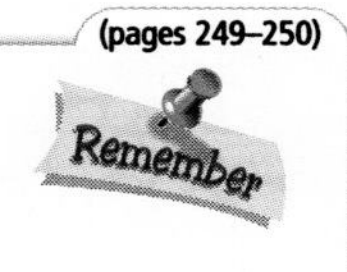

(pages 249–250)

- Add er to adjectives to compare two people, animals, places, or things.
- Add est to adjectives to compare more than two.

●▲ Choose the correct adjective for each sentence. Write the sentences.

Example Is my room (smallest, smaller) than your room?
Is my room smaller than your room?

1. The bookcase is (taller, tallest) than the door.
2. This is the (stronger, strongest) chair of all.
3. Which is the (shorter, shortest) book of the four?
4. The wall is (cleanest, cleaner) than the floor.

■ Add er or est to each adjective in ( ). Write the sentences correctly.

Example Jim is (short) than Sue.
Jim is shorter than Sue.

5. Spot is the (old) pet of the four. Spot is the oldest pet of the four.
6. Inez has (long) hair than Anna. Inez has longer hair than Anna.
7. Lee is (young) than Tom. Lee is younger than Tom.

Adjectives with er and est

Objective

Children will:
- identify when to use adjectives with *er* and *est*

Meeting Individual Needs — More Practice for Lesson 5

● EASY ▲ AVERAGE

Draw a line under the correct adjective.

1. That cat has the (longer, longest) tail of all the cats.
2. This dog is (meaner, meanest) than that dog.
3. The bear is (louder, loudest) than the frog.
4. Which frog is the (greener, greenest) of all?
5. Who is the (smarter, smartest) of all the animals?
6. The rabbit is (nicer, nicest) than the shark.
7. This snake is the (smoother, smoothest) of all the snakes.
8. This apple is (rounder, roundest) than that apple.

■ CHALLENGING

Add *er* or *est* to each adjective in ( ). Write the sentences correctly.

1. Mom is (tall) than I am.
   Mom is taller than I am.
2. Eva is (short) than Mom.
   Eva is shorter than Mom.
3. Bruce is the (short) of all.
   Bruce is the shortest of all.
4. My room is (clean) than yours.
   My room is cleaner than yours.
5. Your room is (neat) than mine.
   Your room is neater than mine.
6. Ken's room is (neat) of all.
   Ken's room is neatest of all.
7. This drink is (sweet) than that one.
   This drink is sweeter than that one.
8. The cake is the (sweet) thing on the whole table. The cake is the sweetest thing on the whole table.
9. Who can find the (small) shell?
   Who can find the smallest shell?
10. She is the (smart) girl in our class.
    She is the smartest girl in our class.

Unit 8 Planning Guide

Writing a Description

Writing a Description: *2 weeks*
Special Focus and Communication Link: *1 week (optional)*

	Blackline Masters (TE)	Workbook Plus	Reteaching Workbook
A PUBLISHED MODEL "The Fog Rolls In" by Alvin Tresselt *(267–269)*			
What Makes a Great Description? *(271)*			
STUDENT MODEL Working Draft *(272)* Final Copy *(273)*	*8–1*		
The Writing Process Write a Description			
Prewriting Focus Skill: Using Your Senses *(275)* Plan Your Description *(276)*	8–2 8–3	98	64
Drafting Focus Skill: Writing Similes *(277)* Focus Skill: Topic Sentence *(278)*		99 100	65 66
Revising How Good Is Your Description? [rubric] *(279)* **Writing Conference** *(280)* **Revising Strategies** *(282)*	8–4 8–5	101 102	67 68
Proofreading *(283)*			
Publishing and Reflecting *(284)*			
Writing Prompts and Test Practice *(286–287)*			
SPECIAL FOCUS ON EXPRESSING Writing a Poem *(288–293)*			
COMMUNICATION LINK Speaking/Viewing: Giving a Talk *(294–295)*			

Tools and Tips

- **Using the Dictionary,** *pp. H3–H12*
- **Using Technology,** *pp. H21–H30*
- **Writer's Tools,** *pp. H31–H34*
- **Spelling Guide,** *pp. H40–H44*
- **My First Thesaurus,** *pp. H45–H56*

School-Home Connection

Suggestions for informing or involving family members in classroom activities and learning related to this unit are included in the Teacher's Edition throughout the unit.

Meeting Individual Needs

- **FOR SPECIAL NEEDS/INCLUSION:** *Houghton Mifflin English* Audiotape
- **FOR STUDENTS ACQUIRING ENGLISH:**
  - Notes and activities are included in this Teacher's Edition throughout the unit to help you adapt or use pupil book activities with students acquiring English.
  - Students can listen to the published and student models on audiotape.
- **ENRICHMENT:** See *Teacher's Resource Book.*

All audiotape recordings are also available on CD.

Daily Language Practice

Each sentence or group of words includes two capitalization, punctuation, usage, or spelling errors based on skills presented in the Grammar and Spelling Connections in this unit or from Grammar Units 1, 3, 5, and 7. Each day write one item on the chalkboard. Have children find the errors and write the sentence correctly on a sheet of paper. To make the activity easier, identify the kinds of errors.

1. The corn plant were tallest than the fence. The corn plant was taller than the fence. (verbs *was* and *were*; comparing with adjectives)
2. I will chuse the smaller of the five kittens. I will choose the smallest of the five kittens. (spelling words with |o͞o| sound; comparing with adjectives)
3. I and Margie are going skating at nune. Margie and I are going skating at noon. (naming yourself last; spelling words with |o͞o| sound)
4. What a loudest noise the fire engine makes? What a loud noise the fire engine makes! (adjectives; end punctuation/exclamations)
5. Lori rode on a airplane to visit her grandmother in baytown. Lori rode on an airplane to visit her grandmother in Baytown. (using *a* and *an*; capitalizing proper nouns)
6. Wouldnt you like to have this ripe peach. Wouldn't you like to have this ripe peach? (contractions with *not*; end punctuation/questions)
7. The brighter star of all. Twinkled above the trees. The brightest star of all twinkled above the trees. (comparing with adjectives; complete sentences)
8. she come to every track meet. She comes to every track. (beginning capitalization; pronouns and verbs)
9. Yesterday the teacher show Chucks class some slides. Yesterday the teacher showed Chuck's class some slides. (verbs in the past with *ed*; possessive nouns ending with *'s*)
10. Stacey is two years youngest than her brother russ. Stacey is two years younger than her brother Russ. (comparing with adjectives; capitalizing proper nouns)

Additional Resources

Workbook Plus, Unit 8
Reteaching Workbook, Unit 8
Teacher's Resource Book
Transparencies, Unit 8
Posters, Unit 8
Audiotapes

Technology Tools

TEACHER'S RESOURCE DISK (for handwriting support)

CD-ROM: *Sunbuddy® Writer
Paint, Write & Play! (published by The Learning Company)
*Type to Learn Jr.™

INTERNET: http://www.eduplace.com/kids/hme/ or http://www.eduplace.com/rdg/hme/

Visit Education Place for these additional support materials and activities:
- author biographies
- student writing models
- graphic organizers
- an interactive rubric
- writing prompts

Assessment

Test Booklet, Unit 8

Keeping a Journal

Discuss with children the value of keeping a journal as a way of promoting self-expression and fluency. Encourage children to record their thoughts and ideas in a notebook. Inform students whether the journal will be private or will be reviewed periodically as a way of assisting growth. The following prompts may be useful for generating writing ideas.

Journal Prompts

- What do the shapes of different clouds make you think of?
- Tell about a picnic that you went to.
- What snapshot of yourself do you like? Where and when was it taken?

Introducing the Unit

Using the Photograph

- Discuss with children the five senses and how they help people know the world around them. Tell children that describing words can also make a person see, hear, smell, taste, and feel what writers are writing about.
- Explain that word pictures that tell how things look, sound, smell, taste, and feel are called **descriptions**.
- Have children look at the photograph, and ask a volunteer to read the caption. Call on volunteers to suggest sense words to describe the sunflower, the sky, and other images in the photograph. Ask what they might hear, smell, or feel if they were standing next to the sunflower. List their ideas under the heading *See*, *Hear*, *Smell*, and *Feel* on the chalkboard or an overhead transparency.

Independent Writing

Children can benefit by having time each day or several times a week to write in their journals or do self-selected writing activities. Remind children to think about purpose and audience and choose an appropriate format for both.

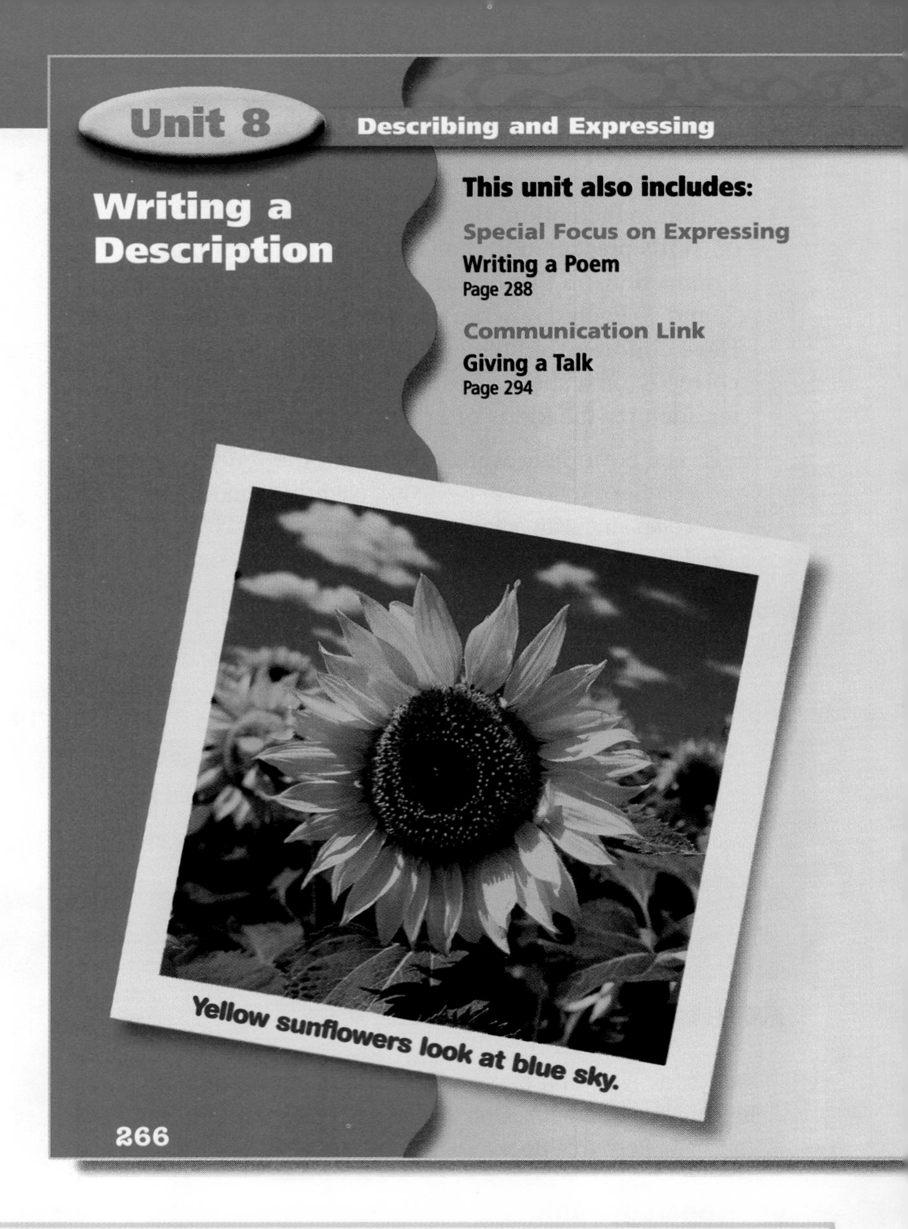

Shared Writing Activity

Work with children to write a descriptive paragraph.

1. Together, read the words or phrases in each column listed on the board.
2. Remind children that these words all tell more about the sunflower in the picture. Then ask volunteers to use the words or phrases in sentences about the sunflower. Write each of the sentences on the board.
3. Work as a class to develop a topic sentence for a paragraph about the sunflower. Write this sentence on the board or at the top of an overhead transparency.
4. Work together to choose detail sentences from those already generated to include in the paragraph. As you write the sentence in paragraph form (either on the board or on the transparency), place them in a logical order. Discuss the placement with the class.
5. Read the paragraph with the class. Ask volunteers if there are any nouns or verbs that they would like to change to more exact words. Show any changes on the board.

A Published Model

Listening to a Description

"The Fog Rolls In" describes what people do as the weather changes in a beach town. What sensory words does the writer use to help you feel and see what is happening?

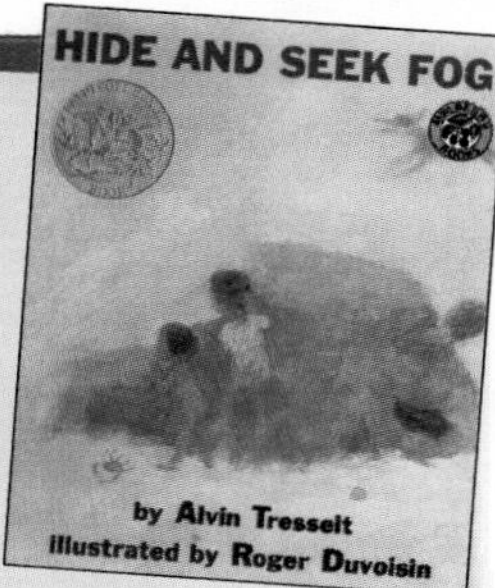

The Fog Rolls In

from Hide and Seek Fog, by Alvin Tresselt

sensory word — On the beach, the sand was suddenly cold and sticky. The mothers and fathers gathered up blankets and picnic baskets. They called — "Cathy! John! Come out of the water! We're going now!"

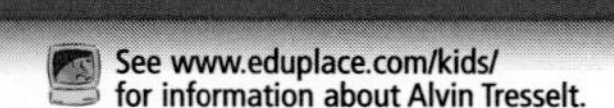

See www.eduplace.com/kids/ for information about Alvin Tresselt.

About the Author

INTERNET CONNECTION Send children to www.eduplace.com/kids/ for information about Alvin Tresselt.

Resources

Both fiction and nonfiction texts include excellent descriptions of characters, animals, scenes, and events. Ask children to look for strong descriptive passages that appeal to the senses when they read and to share some of these passages with the class.

FOR STUDENTS ACQUIRING ENGLISH

Review the five senses using the technique of total physical response (TPR). When you say "see," have students imitate you as you point to the eyes, the body part that sees. As you read the model, students point similarly for each sense that is being used.

"The Fog Rolls In"

Lesson Objectives

Children will:

- read a published model of a description
- identify characteristics of descriptions
- identify examples of dialogue
- evaluate the relationship between illustration and text
- write personal and critical responses

Focus on the Model

Building Background

- Ask children if they have ever been outdoors when a sudden storm came up. Have them compare how they felt when the sun was shining and when it disappeared behind clouds.
- Tell children they are going to read a description of how people reacted when thick, damp fog rolled in over a beach and town.

Introducing Vocabulary

Introduce key vocabulary words by writing them in context sentences on the board.

It was hard to walk in the mud, so we **trudged** slowly along the path.

The piece of **driftwood** had floated for two days, and then the branch finally washed up on shore to dry.

Reading the Selection

- Read the selection aloud to children if you wish to reinforce listening skills or if children need extra support.

Alternatively, children can listen to the selection on audiotape.

- Remind children that they may read or listen to a selection for pleasure or for information. Point out that they can read or listen to a description to find out how something looks, feels, tastes, smells, sounds, or acts, and they can also listen to a description just for enjoyment.
- Read aloud the introduction to the selection and the purpose-setting question, which focuses on what senses the writer selects to help the listener feel and see what is going on. Tell children to listen for sensory descriptions.
- Read aloud or have volunteers read aloud the selection.
- The call outs highlight key characteristics of a description that are addressed in the Thinking About the Description questions at the end of this selection.

A Published Model

sensory word

The children ran in and out one more time, blue-lipped and shivering. They scurried about looking for lost pails and shovels. They scooped up one more pretty shell and a gray seagull feather. Then everyone trudged across the chilly sand and cold rocks back to cars and cottages.

The lobsterman delivered his lobsters to the fishing wharf. He hurried home through winding streets, just as the fog began to hide the town.

268 A Published Model

omparison–The sailboats bobbled like corks on the dull gray water of the cove. Their sails were wrapped for the night, and the sailors rowed through the misty fog back to land.

But indoors in the seaside cottages the children toasted marshmallows over a driftwood fire, while the fog tip-toed past the windows and across the porch.

"The Fog Rolls In"

Focus on Instruction

After the selection has been read but before discussing the Reading As a Writer questions, ask children to retell and summarize the selection. As volunteers offer suggestions, write their ideas on the chalkboard or on an overhead transparency. Work with the ideas to generate a model summary of the selection.

Answers to Reading As a Writer

The Think About the Description questions highlight criteria listed on the "What Makes a Great Description?" and "How Good Is Your Description?" pages in the pupil book.

Think About the Description

- Some of the sense words that the writer uses are: **adjectives**: cold, sticky, shivering, chilly, blue-lipped, pretty, gray, winding, dull, misty; **verbs**: gathered up, scurried, scooped up, trudged, delivered, hurried, bobbled, rowed, toasted, tip-toed.
- Page 269 says that the "fog tip-toed past the windows and across the porch."

Think About Writer's Craft

- Alvin Tresselt compares the sailboats to corks. They are alike because they both float or bobble in the water.

Think about the Picture

- The picture on page 269 shows the fog. The artist painted a light gray color over the picture to make it look foggy.

More About Writer's Craft

- The writer uses different kinds of sentences and different kinds of punctuation. Point out that the writer's use of exclamation marks showed that the parents wanted their children to get off the beach quickly.
- Other grammar elements besides quotation marks and exclamation marks include capitalizing proper nouns such as Cathy and John.

Notes on Responding

Personal Response

Answers will vary.

Critical Thinking

Does the writer create a different feeling at the end of the story than at the beginning? What is that feeling? (Sample answer: At the beginning of the story, everyone is rushing and trying to get out of the fog. At the end, it seems restful or peaceful with the children toasting marshmallows.)

A Published Model

See TE margin for answers.

Reading As a Writer

Think About the Description

- What sensory words does the writer use to help you feel and see what is happening?
- Which words on page 269 tell how the fog moved past the houses?

Think About Writer's Craft

- What does the writer compare the sailboats to? How are the two things alike?

Think About the Pictures

- Look at the pictures on pages 268 and 269. Which picture shows the fog? How do you know?

Responding

See TE margin for answers.

Write an answer to this question.

- **Personal Response** What part of the description did you enjoy most? Why?

270 A Published Model

Mapping the Selection

Draw the diagram on the chalkboard and tell children that mapping a piece of writing helps the writer visualize its structure and also helps them organize their own writing. Have children look at the published model and identify the topic and details.

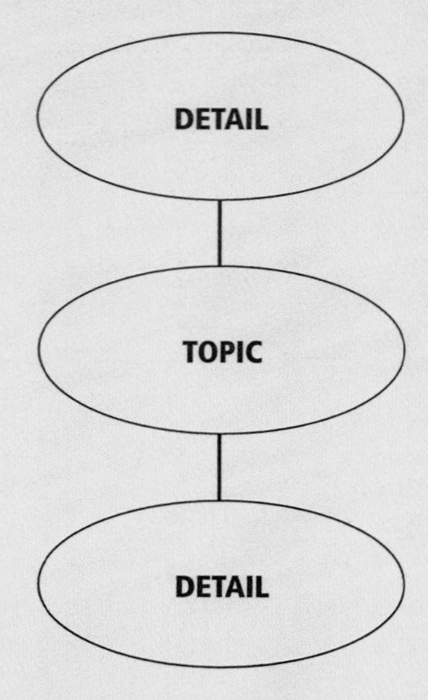

What Makes a Great Description?

A **description** helps your readers see, feel, hear, taste, and smell what you are writing about. When you write a description, remember to do these things.

- Describe one thing, place, or event.
- Begin with a clear and interesting topic sentence that tells what you will describe.
- Use your senses to get information about your topic. Use sensory words to write about it.
- Use exact words and details.
- Use words that compare or tell how your topic is like something else.

What Makes a Great Description?

Lesson Objective

Children will:
- discuss the characteristics of a well-written description

Focus on Instruction

- Point out that "The Fog Rolls In" is an example of a well-written description. Ask volunteers to read aloud the definition and characteristics of a description. Review the senses that were referred to in the published model.
- Have children read the Grammar Check. Explain that the Grammar Check reminds them to use the endings *er* and *est* correctly with adjectives. Tell them they will check their work to be sure they used adjectives correctly when they proofread it.

If this is children's first encounter with W.R., the Writing Star, point out that he will help them learn to write great descriptions.

Connecting to the Rubric

- These criteria are tied to the rubric on page 279.
- Tell children that they will be writing their own descriptions and they will learn how to refer to their own sensory experiences in their work. After they write their descriptions they will use the criteria to help them evaluate their work.

This page is available as a poster.

Looking Ahead Tell children that they will see how the characteristics listed on this page are applied in one child's working draft and final copy of a description.

FOR STUDENTS ACQUIRING ENGLISH

Before children can determine what makes the given model great, they must know some vocabulary. Based on the context of the excerpt, help children define *fog*, *beach*, *scooped*, *trudged*, *bobbled*, and *tip-toed*. Then reread the model, comparing it to the rubric. Act out the sensory sentences to help children see their use.

A Student Model: Working Draft

Lesson Objectives

Children will:

- read a working draft of a student-written description
- discuss the ways the model meets the criteria for a well-written description and ways that it could be improved

Focus on the Model

- Tell children they will read a working draft of a description written by a real student, Christine Guzman. Explain that a working draft is a work in progress. The writer is just trying to get ideas on paper, knowing he or she can make revisions later.
- Have volunteers read the model aloud.

Alternatively, children can listen to the draft read by a student, although the student writer is not reading on the audiotape.

- Tell children to think about whether or not Christine included the important characteristics of a description. Point out that W.R.'s thoughts about the description are shown in thought balloons and they will discuss his ideas after they read.

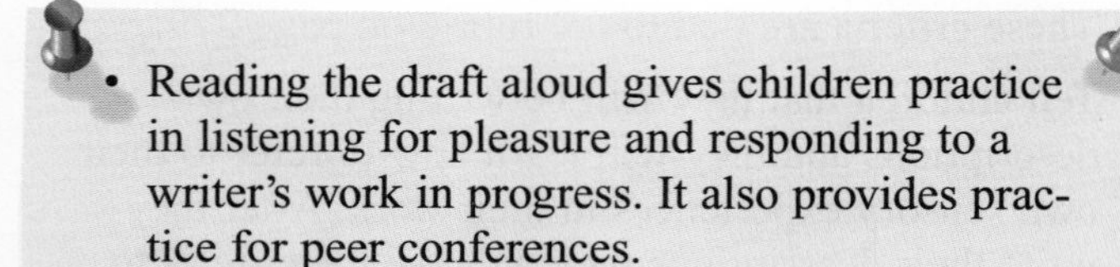

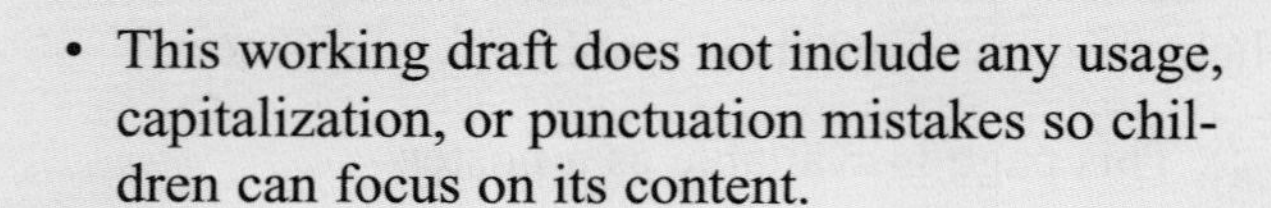

- Reading the draft aloud gives children practice in listening for pleasure and responding to a writer's work in progress. It also provides practice for peer conferences.
- This working draft does not include any usage, capitalization, or punctuation mistakes so children can focus on its content.

Answers to Reading As a Writer

- She described her grandmother's new swimming pool.
- Sample answer: She can add words to tell what the splash sounded like.

Student Model

WORKING DRAFT

Read Christine's description and what W.R. said about it.

Christine Guzman

I like my grandmother's new swimming pool. It is shaped like a fat peanut. The pool is built-in, and it is about ten feet deep. ~~My brother and I always~~ If you look inside it, you see that the bottom of the pool is light blue. The stairs are light blue too. The sides are white, and so is the diving board.

When you dive into the pool, it feels cold. You can put ~~cold~~ freezing water on your body first and then jump into the pool. Then the pool feels very, very warm. If you jump in the pool from the diving board, it makes a splashing sound. I wish I could swim there every day.

I like the way you tell how the pool is like a peanut.

What can you compare the cold water to?

Freezing is a good sensory word!

Reading As a Writer See TE margin for answers.

- What one thing did Christine describe?
- What can Christine add to help her readers hear the splashing sound?

272 Student Model

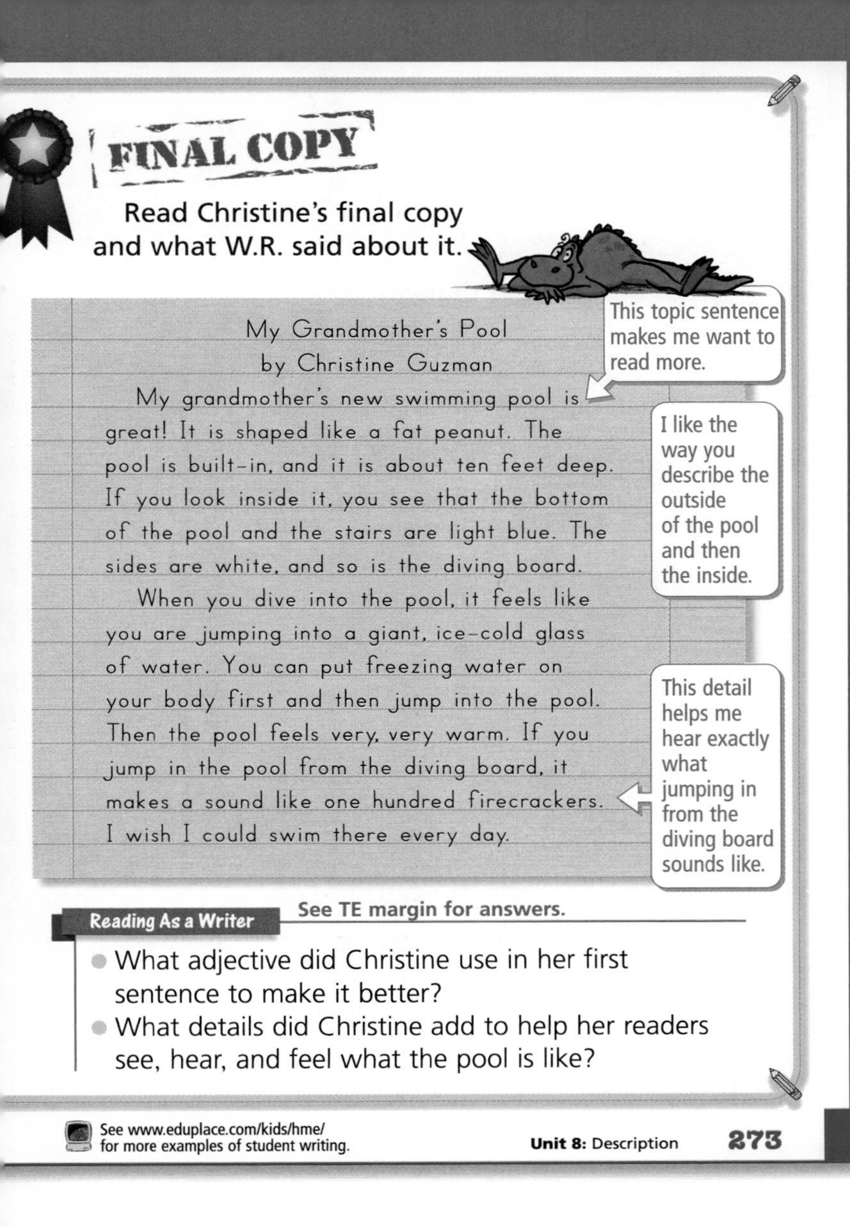

FINAL COPY

Read Christine's final copy and what W.R. said about it.

My Grandmother's Pool
by Christine Guzman

My grandmother's new swimming pool is great! It is shaped like a fat peanut. The pool is built-in, and it is about ten feet deep. If you look inside it, you see that the bottom of the pool and the stairs are light blue. The sides are white, and so is the diving board.

When you dive into the pool, it feels like you are jumping into a giant, ice-cold glass of water. You can put freezing water on your body first and then jump into the pool. Then the pool feels very, very warm. If you jump in the pool from the diving board, it makes a sound like one hundred firecrackers. I wish I could swim there every day.

This topic sentence makes me want to read more.

I like the way you describe the outside of the pool and then the inside.

This detail helps me hear exactly what jumping in from the diving board sounds like.

Reading As a Writer See TE margin for answers.

- What adjective did Christine use in her first sentence to make it better?
- What details did Christine add to help her readers see, hear, and feel what the pool is like?

See www.eduplace.com/kids/hme/ for more examples of student writing.

Unit 8: Description 273

A Student Model: Final Copy

Lesson Objectives

Children will:
- read a well-written final copy of a student's description
- note and compare the revisions that improved the first draft

Focus on the Model

SUMMARY OF REVISIONS In her final copy, Christine improved her topic sentence, combined sentences, added details, used sense words, and added words to compare jumping in the pool to something else. Blackline Master 8-1 provides a copy of the student's working draft, showing the revisions that were made.

Have volunteers read the model aloud. Alternatively, children can listen to it read by a student (although not the student writer) on audiotape.

Answers to Reading As a Writer

- She used the adjective *great*.
- Sample answer: Christine compared jumping in the pool to jumping into a glass of ice-cold water. She compared the sound to a hundred firecrackers.

Connecting to the Rubric

- Have children look at the list of characteristics on page 271 and review with them how Christine's final copy addressed them.

More About Writer's Craft

- Discuss why Christine did not have to change her paragraphs. (Each paragraph should cover a different subject. Christine's first paragraph tells what the pool looks like from the outside, her second paragraph tells how it feels when she is in it.) Ask why it is important to organize writing into paragraphs. (It helps the reader know when the writer is changing the subject.)

Looking Ahead Tell children they will be writing their own descriptions, using the writing process. As they go along they will learn how to use their senses, write similes, and write a topic sentence.

FOR STUDENTS ACQUIRING ENGLISH

While reading the student model, point to parts of your body to indicate which sense is being evoked in the description. Depending on children's proficiency in English, you may wish to have them show you which sense is being evoked: pause at each sense reference and ask them to point to the appropriate body part. Challenge children to compare cold water to at least three different things. Suggest first "ice."

INTERNET CONNECTION Send your children to www.eduplace.com/kids/hme/ to see more models of student writing. You can also find and print these models at www.eduplace.com/rdg/hme/.

Write a Description

Lesson Objectives

Children will:
- list their ideas for audience, purpose, and publishing/sharing formats
- list ideas for a description
- discuss their ideas with a partner
- choose a topic to write about

Start Thinking

Focus on Instruction

- Ask how a description written in a story might differ from a description in a letter. (A description in a story might include the reactions of characters in the story, it might have more details; a description in a letter might include only the letter-writer's reactions and what he or she wants the audience to know.)
- Discuss how descriptions in poems differ from descriptions in stories. (Descriptions in poems are usually condensed, not every detail is spelled out; descriptions in stories are often long and detailed.)

Choose Your Topic

Focus on Instruction

Point out the Help box for assistance in thinking of ideas. Draw children's attention to the Writing Prompts on page 286.

- Reassure children that an everyday experience or thing, such as describing a vegetable they love, can be just as good a topic as describing a vacation. Suggest that they choose two topics so that if one does not work well, they can use the other topic.
- Have children discuss their topic choices with a classmate. Remind them to try to think of narrow topics as they give one another feedback.
- Review children's final topic choices. Be sure each subject can actually be described in a short paragraph.

Have children start a writing folder titled *My Description*. Tell them to keep all notes, graphic organizers, and drafts of their descriptions in this folder, as well as notes with their thoughts about audience, purpose, and publishing format.

SCHOOL-HOME CONNECTION Suggest that children talk with a family member to get help recalling information or details about a possible topic choice.

Write a Description

Choose Your Topic

1. **List** three things that you could describe.

2. **Share** and talk about each of your ideas with a classmate. Answer these questions.
   - Which idea does your classmate think is the most interesting?
   - Which topic can you describe best?
3. **Copy and complete** these sentences. Name your audience and topic.

   _____ will read or hear my description.

   I will describe _____.

Help with Choosing a Topic

MORE TOPIC IDEAS
Suggest these subjects to prompt topic ideas:
- the worst present you ever received,
- the best party you ever went to,
- the first thing you remember about first grade.

TECH TIP

Children who are using a computer can refer to the Using the Computer in the Writing Process on page H23.

Focus Skill

Using Your Senses

You use your five senses to taste, smell, touch, hear, and see. Gather details about your topic, using your senses.

Try It Together Sample answers: *colorful, quiet, noisy, clean*

How does your classroom look, sound, and smell? With your class, make a list of adjectives that describe your classroom.

Explore Your Topic

1. **Think** about your topic.
2. **Make** a chart like the one below. Write details about your topic. Describe what you observe, using your senses. List details for at least three senses.

Five Senses Chart

My Topic:

See	Hear	Touch	Taste	Smell

See www.eduplace.com/kids/hme/ for graphic organizers.

Using Your Senses

Lesson Objective

Children will:
- create a chart of the five senses

Focus on Instruction

- Have volunteers select one of the senses and describe something using only that one sense.
- Have children describe something in the classroom by using one of the five senses. The class should guess what they are describing and what sense is being used. For example, the object is shaped like a rectangle, is gray with white dust on it, and it fits in your hand. (eraser, seeing)
- Discuss why using the senses in a description makes the description come alive.

Try It Together

Have children select one sense at a time and write as many adjectives, verbs, or adverbs they might use to describe the classroom with that one sense.

Explore Your Topic

- Help children understand that with this chart, as with their own topics, they may not be able to find appropriate details for each sense.
- Suggest that children make a quick sketch of their topic. This may help make the details more concrete as children generate information for the Five Senses Chart.
- See Blackline Master 8-2 for a graphic organizer children can use to explore their topics. Children can also refer to the graphic organizers in the Tools and Tips section of the pupil book.

INTERNET CONNECTION Send children to www.eduplace.com/kids/hme/ for graphic organizers. You can also find and print these at www.eduplace.com/rdg/hme/.

Meeting Individual Needs

● RETEACHING WORKBOOK, page 64

Using Your Senses

The five senses will help you describe interesting details.

Taste	Smell	Feel	Hear	See
sweet	rotten	scratchy	quiet	bright
lemony	fresh	soft	noisy	green

Use the pictures to choose a topic. Write the topic in the chart. Use your senses to think of details. Complete the chart. Answers will vary.

My Topic:

See:

Feel:

Hear:

Taste:

Smell:

▲■ WORKBOOK PLUS, page 98

Using Your Senses

Taste	Smell	See	Hear	Feel
sweet	burnt	bright	loud	sandy
salty	fresh	neat	quiet	fluffy
sour	flowery	yellow	crackling	smooth

Choose a topic from the list below. Write the topic in the chart. Complete the chart. List and describe what you observe using your senses. Topics and descriptions will vary.

an apple a playground a city street new pajamas

Five Senses Chart

My Topic:

See

Smell

Taste

Hear

Feel

FOR STUDENTS ACQUIRING ENGLISH

Instead of having children describe the classroom, ask them to write a list of sensory descriptions about their topic. You can model for them as you describe the classroom. Children of all levels should feel confident about listing sense words, especially if you model a possible list: *bright* (involves sight); *giggles* (involves sound), etc.

Lesson Objectives

Children will:
- think about a topic
- choose a way to organize details from the Five Senses Chart

Plan Your Description

Focus on Instruction

- Remind children that it is often better to choose another topic than to struggle with one that is not working out.
- Review each child's topic and list of details. Be sure each one has enough information about the thing or person they are planning to describe. Suggest that they note the wealth of details shown in the word web. A copy of the organizer appears on Blackline Master 8-3.
- Children may want to try other ways of organizing. Refer them to the graphic organizers in the Tools and Tips section of the pupil book.
- As children share their plans, suggest that they ask classmates if there is anything else about the topic they would like to know.

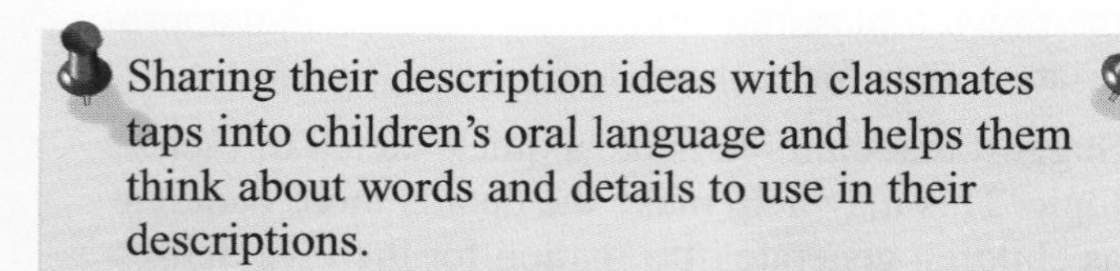

Sharing their description ideas with classmates taps into children's oral language and helps them think about words and details to use in their descriptions.

INTERNET CONNECTION Send your students to www.eduplace.com/kids/hme/ for graphic organizers. You can also find and print these organizers at www.eduplace.com/rdg/hme/.

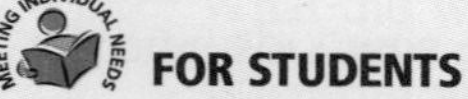

FOR STUDENTS ACQUIRING ENGLISH

Show children that they have already made their list of descriptors like Christine's; however, they now need to order them. Ask volunteers to suggest ways of ordering: by location (where each descriptor is), by importance (best descriptors first), by sense (all colors first), etc.

Plan Your Description

You can organize your details in many ways. Christine used a word web to organize the details from her Five Senses Chart. She wrote details telling what the pool is like from the outside and from the inside.

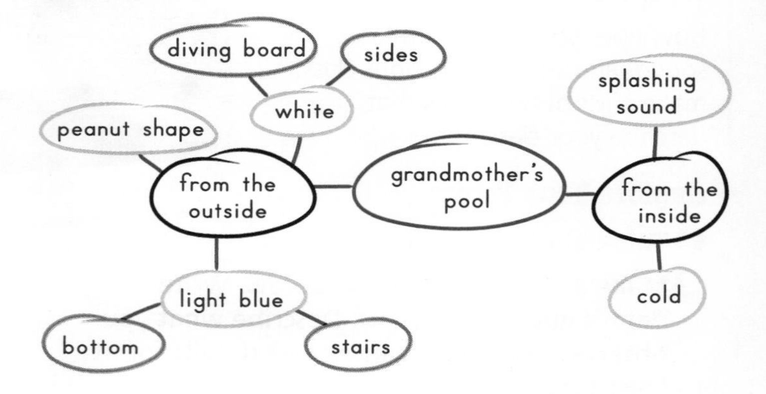

1. **Think** about your topic. Will you describe your topic from top to bottom, left to right, inside to outside, or in another way?
2. **Organize** the details from your Five Senses Chart in a word web.

See www.eduplace.com/kids/hme/ for graphic organizers.

Help with Planning a Description

MANAGEMENT TIP

Circulate as children discuss their topics and details with classmates. Remind children of the five senses and make sure they are staying focused on discussion of details.

PREWRITING DRAFTING REVISING PROOFREADING PUBLISHING

Focus Skill

Writing Similes

A **simile** uses the word as or like to compare two unlike things.

Similes

His cheeks were as red as strawberries.

The rain sounded like a beating drum.

Try It Together Answers will vary.

With your class, choose a classroom object. Think of other things that the object is like in some way. Work together to write a simile describing the classroom object.

Write Your Similes

1. **Look** at your Five Senses Chart and think about your topic.
2. **List** objects that are like your topic in some way.
3. **Write** two similes comparing your topic with two different objects. Similes will vary.

Writing Similes

Lesson Objectives

Children will:

- list objects that are like their topics
- learn to write similes

Focus on Instruction

- Read aloud the definition of a simile. Give a few examples such as *wrinkled as a piece of paper*; *smiled like a bright headlight*, *loud as a popping balloon*.
- Write *as* and *like* on the board. Then say words that include all five senses such as *hot*, *loud*, *smoky*, *blue*, *sweet*, and have children use them in similes. Indicate *as* or *like* each time they are used correctly in the responses.

Try It Together

Arrange children in five groups and assign one of the senses to each group. Have them generate details related to their sense for each of the listed classroom items. Then use the details from each group to generate the similes.

Write Your Similes

Have children make quick sketches of their topic, or refer to sketches they made earlier. Suggest that they look at the pictures and the details in their Five Senses Charts to help spark ideas for similes.

Meeting Individual Needs

● RETEACHING WORKBOOK, page 65

Writing Similes

A simile uses as or like to compare two unlike things.

His nose looked like a potato.

Her eyes were as round as a plate.

Use your five senses as you look at each picture. Then finish each simile. Remember to use as or like.
Sample answers

1. The apple is as crispy as crackers.
2. The chair is like a soft cloud.
3. The puppy is as funny as a clown.
4. The truck is like a noisy elephant.

▲■ WORKBOOK PLUS, page 99

Writing Similes

Her eyes twinkled like stars.

The grass was as green as emeralds.

Think about an object in your kitchen at home. Then write two sentences that compare the object to something else. Use your five senses to help you. Remember to use as or like in your sentences. Sample answers

1. The mixing bowl was as blue as the sky.
2. The mixing bowl was like a deep well.

MEETING INDIVIDUAL NEEDS — FOR STUDENTS ACQUIRING ENGLISH

Ask children to return to their list of descriptors and pick an interesting or weak one (any example that stands out). Ask each child to share samples with others. Then, as a class, write similes for some descriptors. Before dismissing similes that may seem odd, gently ask the child who created it and what it means.

Topic Sentence

Lesson Objectives

Children will:

- write two strong topic sentences
- choose the topic sentence they like better
- write their description

Focus on Instruction

- Read aloud the definition of a topic sentence.
- Discuss the sentences in the chart. Ask volunteers to tell why the examples are weak or strong. Point out that the strong topic sentence gave more details about the topic than the weak topic sentence did.

Try It Together

Discuss the topic sentences generated by the class. Have volunteers tell why they think each one is weak or strong. Work together to improve any weak topic sentences.

Write Your Description

Drafting Reminders

- Remind children that at this point they are just getting their ideas down on paper. They do not have to worry about making mistakes as they write.
- Tell children if they don't know how to spell a word, they should spell it as best they can and go on. They can fix the spelling later.
- Remind children to skip every other line to leave room for changes. Tell them just to cross out words they don't like if they change their minds. They should not start over.

FOR STUDENTS ACQUIRING ENGLISH

Write sample topic sentences on the board and ask children to tell whether the samples are weak or strong; have them explain why. Suggest children choose their favorite simile or descriptor and consider starting there. Ask volunteers to read and explain their choices.

The Writing Process: PREWRITING · DRAFTING · REVISING · PROOFREADING · PUBLISHING

Focus Skill

Topic Sentence

A **topic sentence** tells the main idea of a paragraph in an interesting way.

Weak Topic Sentence	Strong Topic Sentence
This is what the storm last week was like.	The storm last week was really wild and a little scary too!

Try It Together Answers will vary.

Work with your class to write some good topic sentences about your classroom or objects in it.

Write Your Description

1. **Write** two strong topic sentences for your description. Mark the one you like better.
2. **Write** your description, using your word web. Include your topic sentence and similes.

278 Drafting

Meeting Individual Needs

● RETEACHING WORKBOOK, page 66

Topic Sentence

A strong topic sentence will help readers stay interested in your writing.
Weak Topic Sentence: The new car was red.
Strong Topic Sentence: The new car was cherry red with soft white seats.

Draw a line under the weak topic sentence in the description below. Then write two strong topic sentences. Circle the one you like better. Sample answers

We like apple pie. Mom made it in a glass pie plate. It was too hot to eat right away. We just stood there, smelling the sugar and spice. The crust was perfect. We couldn't wait to dig in!

Topic Sentence 1 My mom's apple pie was the best in town.

Topic Sentence 2 We were very excited because the apple pie was almost ready.

▲■ WORKBOOK PLUS, page 100

Topic Sentence

Weak Topic Sentence: The toy was old.
Strong Topic Sentence: The toy was an old bear that played a drum.

Write two strong topic sentences for the description below. Circle the one you like better. Sample answers

The clock is painted with leaves and flowers. One flower is a blooming rose. Every hour, the chimes make bell sounds. They play a tune like a music box. Best of all, when the hands point to twelve o'clock, a little bird comes out of a door.

Topic Sentence 1 I love telling time with our special clock.

Topic Sentence 2 Our clock makes telling time fun.

How Good Is Your Description?

▶ **Read** your draft.

▶ **Copy** the sentences below that tell about your description.

Superstar

- I wrote about one thing, place, or event.
- My topic sentence is clear and interesting.
- I used lots of sensory words.
- I used exact adjectives and details to describe my topic.
- I used a simile to compare my topic to something else.
- My description has only a few mistakes.

Rising Star

- I described more than one thing, place, or event.
- I can make my topic sentence more interesting.
- I could use more sensory words.
- I need to add exact adjectives or details.
- I need to add a simile.
- My description has many mistakes.

See www.eduplace.com/kids/hme/ to interact with this rubric.

How Good Is Your Description?

Lesson Objective

Children will:
- evaluate their descriptions, using a rubric

Connecting to the Criteria

- Refer children back to the elements that make a great description on page 271. Explain that the rubric shown on this page refers to those characteristics. Tell them that the rubric will help them decide what parts of their descriptions meet the standards of a great description and what parts they think still need more work.

Focus on Instruction

- Review the rubric with children. Have volunteers read aloud points of related characteristics. Discuss with children the differences between sentences in each pair.
- Blackline Master 8-4 provides a copy of the rubric as a checklist for children using the hardbound edition. Alternatively they can write the sentences that describe their descriptions.
- See the Teacher's Resource Book for scoring rubrics.

INTERNET CONNECTION Have children go to www.eduplace.com/kids/hme/ to use an interactive version of the rubric shown in the pupil book. Children will get feedback and support depending on how they mark the rubric items.

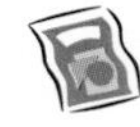

This page is available as a poster.

Meeting Individual Needs

● RETEACHING WORKBOOK, page 67

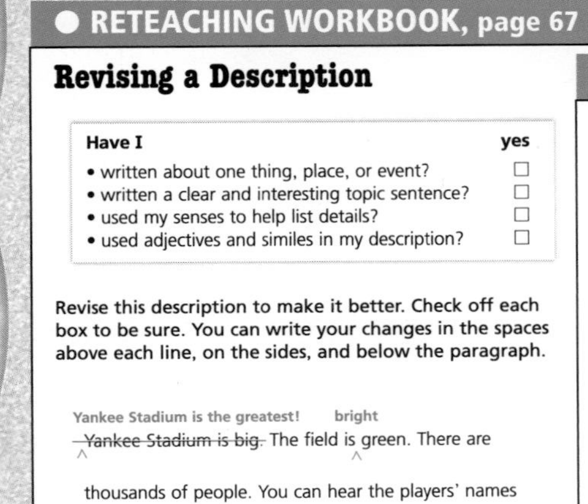

Revising a Description

Have I	yes
• written about one thing, place, or event?	☐
• written a clear and interesting topic sentence?	☐
• used my senses to help list details?	☐
• used adjectives and similes in my description?	☐

Revise this description to make it better. Check off each box to be sure. You can write your changes in the spaces above each line, on the sides, and below the paragraph.

Yankee Stadium is the greatest! bright
~~Yankee Stadium is big.~~ The field is green. There are thousands of people. You can hear the players' names when they run out on the field. Tim wants to be a ~~baseball player.~~ The air smells ~~good.~~ like hot dogs and peanuts The sun was warm as we watched the game. Yankee Stadium was fun.

▲■ WORKBOOK PLUS, page 101

Revising a Description

Have I	yes
• written about one thing, place, or event?	☐
• written a clear and interesting topic sentence?	☐
• used my senses to help list details?	☐
• used adjectives and similes in my description?	☐

Revise this description to make it better. Check off each box to be sure. You can write your changes in the spaces above each line, on the sides, and below the paragraph.

Sample answers

Yosemite Park is a great place to visit!
~~I like Yosemite Park.~~ There are trees and waterfalls. The waterfalls look ~~nice.~~ like clear curtains The air smells fresh and clean. Yosemite is a valley with huge rock walls. Thousands of people visit it every year. ~~Yellowstone is also nice.~~ In the summer, Yosemite is full of visitors taking pictures. There are a lot of beautiful sights.

FOR STUDENTS ACQUIRING ENGLISH

Help children become more conscious of their own abilities to evaluate. Have volunteers describe what they do and think as they evaluate by asking: "What do you do before you begin evaluating?"; "What do you usually have the most trouble with?" Children may be inclined to try to find one "right" way of evaluating, but explain that there are many appropriate ways. Because these pieces are short, ask children to read their pieces a few times, each time checking some new aspect of grammar and mechanics: punctuation, capitalization, etc.

Lesson Objective

Children will:

- revise their working drafts, based on their own evaluations

Revise Your Description

Focus on Instruction

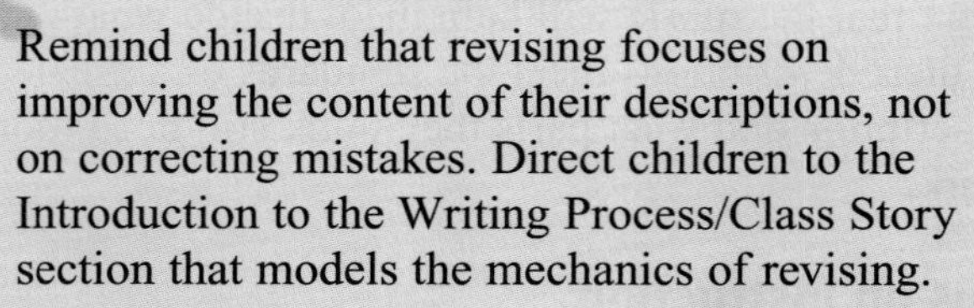

Revising Reminders

Remind children that revising focuses on improving the content of their descriptions, not on correcting mistakes. Direct children to the Introduction to the Writing Process/Class Story section that models the mechanics of revising.

- Review children's evaluations of their descriptions and discuss possible revisions that might improve their work. As they revise each part, have them check off the appropriate items from the rubric. When they are finished revising, encourage them to read their descriptions again to be sure that their work is clear.

Revise Your Description

- Change your topic sentence. Make it more interesting.
- Replace weak adjectives with strong ones.

1. **Look** at the sentences from page 279 that you wrote about your description. What can you do to make your description better?

2. **Have a writing conference.**

   When You're the Writer
   - Write one question about a part of your description that you want help with.
   - Share your description with a classmate. Ask your question.

   When You're the Listener
   - Tell two things you like about the description.
   - Ask questions about parts that aren't clear.
   - Look at the next page for more ideas.

3. **Revise** your description.

   Think about your talk with your classmate. Make changes to your draft. The Revising Strategies on page 282 may help you.

Use the Word Banks of sensory words in My First Thesaurus on page H45.

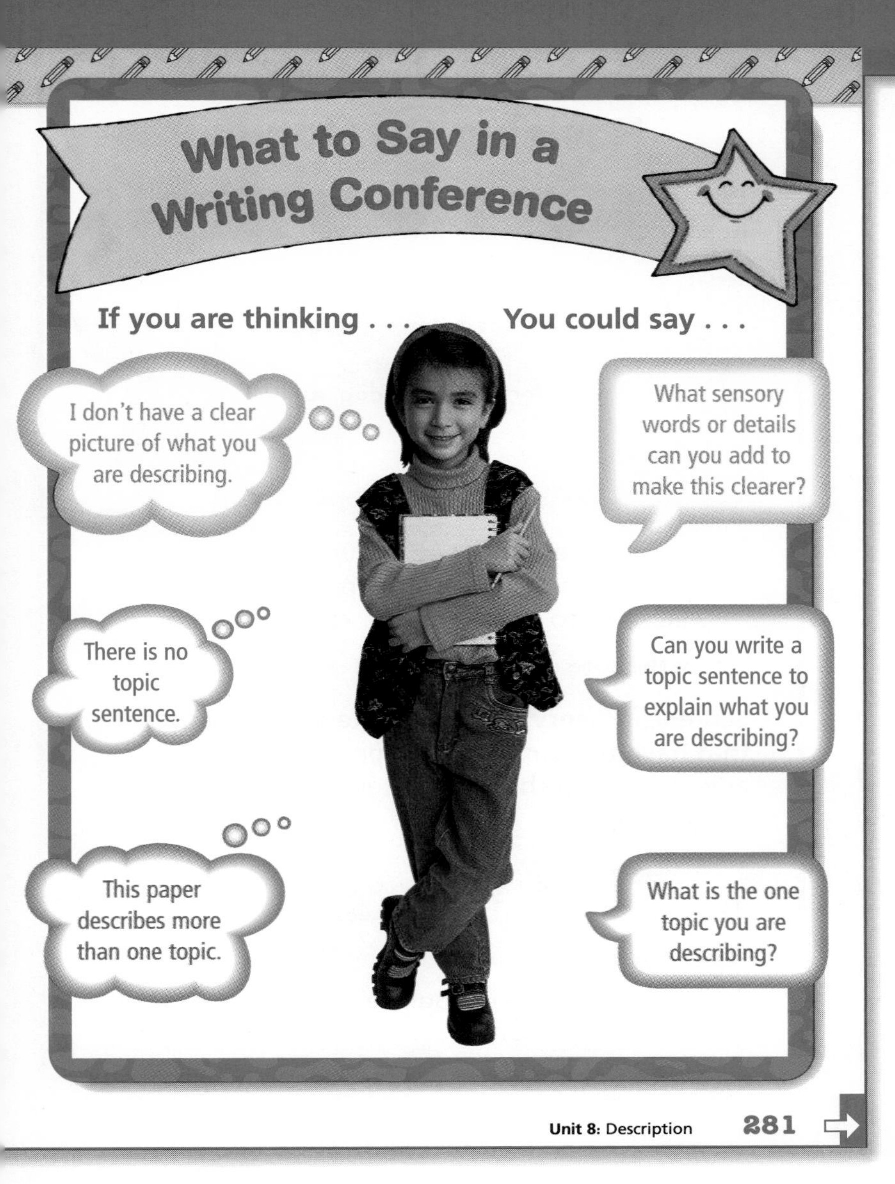

Help with Conferencing

ADDITIONAL CONFERENCING QUESTIONS

Here are other questions that might be helpful during the teacher-student writing conference.

- What did ________ smell (feel, sound, look) like?
- Could you give more details about ________ so I can picture it clearly?
- How did you feel when you saw (felt, heard, smelled, tasted) ________ ?

EVALUATION TIP

Listen to find out if children are asking questions about their partners' papers or trying to tell each other what to do. Remind children that they are only making suggestions to one another. Have them review the conferencing questions in the student book for ideas of what to ask.

What to Say in a Writing Conference

Lesson Objectives

Children will:

- have a writing conference
- retell a spoken message by summarizing or clarifying

Read aloud and discuss with children the text in the thought and speech balloons. Explain that the thought balloons show what a listener might think while listening to a description. The speech balloons show what the listener could ask to help the writer know what parts might not be clear or could be revised.

 This page is also available as a poster.

- Tell children they may use Blackline Master 8-5 during the writing conference.

Writing Conference Reminders

- Ask children to read their stories aloud. Mistakes in spelling and grammar or messy handwriting can interfere with their classmates ability to understand and respond. Remind children to read slowly and clearly and at an appropriate volume for the setting and audience.
- Tell children to do these things when they are the listeners:

  Always compliment the writer. Discuss some possibilities, such as the beginning makes me want to read more or your sensory words make your description clear.

  Retell what they have heard after listening to their partner's paper. They should tell what the story is about and include the important ideas and details.
- Suggest that children choose their words carefully. They don't want to hurt the writer's feelings.
- Explain to children that they don't have to use every one of their classmate's suggestions.

FOR STUDENTS ACQUIRING ENGLISH

Some other questions to consider in the conferences are: "Are there skimpy parts that need more details?" "Are there long parts that don't fit?" "Where can you add?' "Where should you delete?" Encourage children to listen for "skimpy" and "long" passages in their partners' work. When you confer with children and find something that doesn't seem to make sense, say, " I know this place is important to you. Can you tell me why? When did you first go there? With whom?"

Revising Strategies

Lesson Objectives

Children will:
- add adjectives to improve a description
- combine sentences that have the same subject with different adjectives

Focus on Instruction

Word Choice

- Write the words *bitter*, *green*, *screaming*, *smelly*, and *velvety* on the chalkboard. Have children tell which sense each adjective reflects and how each adjective might add to a description of a fruit, a child, an animal, and a pillow.
- Review children's evaluations of their work and discuss revisions they could make to improve their descriptions.
- Remind children that *My First Thesaurus* is a good resource for descriptive words. Draw their attention to the word banks for sensory words.

Sentence Fluency

- Review that the naming part of a sentence tells who or what the sentence is about.
- Have children look for repeated words in their sentences. This is often a clue that sentences can be combined. Tell them to join sentences that have the same naming part with different adjectives.

FOR STUDENTS ACQUIRING ENGLISH

Ask children what they will do with their descriptions once they're done. Tell them to make their own decisions, but use the suggestions from the book if they are having trouble. While revising, children may be more comfortable conferencing and editing in small groups.

Revising Strategies

Word Choice Adjectives help your readers see, hear, feel, taste, or smell what you are describing.

large, red
The ^ fire engine raced down the street.
screaming / spotted
The ^ siren was very loud. A ^ dog sat in the back.

▶ Draw a line under each noun in your description. Can you add an adjective before each one to make your description clearer?

Use My First Thesaurus on page H45 to find adjectives.

Sentence Fluency You may write two sentences that have the same naming part with different adjectives. Join the two sentences to make a longer one.

and yellow
The door was big ^. ~~The door was yellow.~~

▶ Look for places in your description where you can join two sentences.

282 Revising

Meeting Individual Needs

● RETEACHING WORKBOOK, page 68

Revising Strategies: Sentence Fluency

Use interesting adjectives to describe nouns in your sentences.

Kaleb read the ^ (scary) story. Mom bought ^ (yellow) flowers.

Choose an adjective to describe each underlined noun. Write the new sentence.

crispy	windy	fluffy	silly	sparkly

1. I ate a cookie.
   I ate a crispy cookie.
2. The storm finally stopped.
   The windy storm finally stopped.
3. The kitten played with a ball.
   The fluffy kitten played with a ball.
4. Tom and I saw a movie.
   Tom and I saw a silly movie.
5. Maria lost her ring. Maria lost her sparkly ring.

▲■ WORKBOOK PLUS, page 102

Revising Strategies: Sentence Fluency

My ^ (older) sister came down the ^ (slippery) stairs.

Add one or two adjectives to each sentence to describe the underlined nouns. Sample answers

1. The apple was on the table.
   The shiny apple was on the little table.
2. The campfire lit our faces.
   The warm campfire lit our sleepy faces.
3. A bird landed on the branch.
   A yellow bird landed on the strong branch.
4. The man saw a fox.
   The young man saw a fluffy fox.
5. The squirrel ate the nut.
   The gray squirrel ate the tasty nut.

PREWRITING DRAFTING REVISING PROOFREADING PUBLISHING

Proofread Your Description

1. **Proofread** your draft. Use the Proofreading Checklist and the Proofreading Marks.
2. **Use** a class dictionary to check spellings.

Proofreading Checklist

- Each sentence begins with a capital letter.
- Each sentence ends with the correct end mark.
- Each paragraph is indented.
- Each word is spelled correctly.

Proofreading Marks	
∧ Add	≡ Capital letter
Delete	/ Small letter
¶ Indent for new paragraph	

Using the Proofreading Marks

Jade park has tall ~~tres.~~ trees

One tree has a tire Swing.

3. **Review** these rules before you proofread.

Grammar and Spelling Connections

Adjectives Add er to most adjectives to compare two things. Add est to most adjectives to compare more than two things.

The new jacket was warmer than the sweater.

The colorful snowsuit was the warmest of all.

Vowel Sounds The vowel sound in cool may be spelled oo.

food pool soon

See the Spelling Guide on page H40.

See www.eduplace.com/kids/hme/ for proofreading practice.

Help with Proofreading

MANAGEMENT TIP

Have children keep personal checklists of skills they need to proofread for. Staple the list to each child's folder. Also have children keep a running of list of misspelled words they can practice and/or refer to.

EVALUATION TIP

Check children's proofread descriptions before they make their final copies.

TECH TIP

Remind children that computer spelling tools do not find words that are misspelled if they are other words.

Lesson Objective

Children will:

- proofread their description

Proofread Your Description

Focus on Instruction

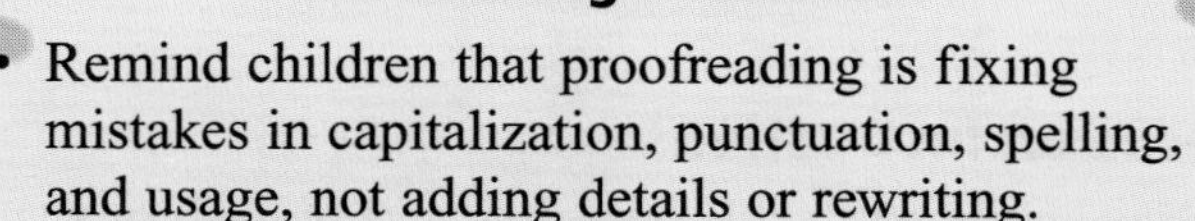

Proofreading Reminders

- Remind children that proofreading is fixing mistakes in capitalization, punctuation, spelling, and usage, not adding details or rewriting.
- Review with children how and when to use the proofreading marks.
- Have children use the Proofreading Checklist in the pupil book. Review and clarify each item in the checklist, using any related Grammar and Spelling Connections. If children need extra support, review the related grammar lesson on page 249 with them.
- Provide dictionaries for children to check spellings. Tell them to circle any words they think are misspelled and check them in a dictionary after they have finished circling.
- For proofreading practice, see the usage and mechanics lessons in the Grammar units and the Mixed Review practice in each Grammar unit Checkup.
- Make proofreading corrections with a pen or pencil that is different from the one used in writing the description.

FOR STUDENTS ACQUIRING ENGLISH

If you have trouble editing children's work, ask them to read and explain it to you. Solve the most persistent or most important error in a childs writing without interfering with content. Try to maintain individual goals for children, remembering that their writing is a piece of themselves, especially if it's a personal description.

Lesson Objectives

Children will:
- make neat, final copies of their descriptions
- choose a way to publish or share their descriptions
- reflect on their writing experience
- evaluate the writing in comparison to others in their writing portfolio

Publish Your Description

Focus on Instruction

- Have children decide how they will publish or share their writing.
- Have children make neat corrections on their final copies rather than recopy them.
- Check children's posture, the way they hold their pencils and the way they position their papers when they make their final copies. Check that they are gaining handwriting proficiency. Remind children to use word and letter spacing and margins to make their papers readable.
- For handwriting instruction and practice, see the Teacher's Resource Disk for printable blackline masters.

Keeping a Writing Portfolio

A writing portfolio is where children keep selected samples of their writing. Here are suggestions for writing portfolios.

Selection: Papers can be selected for the portfolio for various reasons. A paper might be selected because it is

✓ generally noteworthy
✓ a good example of a particular aspect of writing
✓ an example of a particular kind of writing
✓ a paper written at a particular point in the school year
✓ a typical example of the child's work

Labeling: For every paper selected for the portfolio, have children complete a cover sheet that gives the title, the date of completion, and the child's reason for selecting it.

Review: Periodically have children remove papers from their portfolios that no longer reflect their best work or that don't need to be kept as baselines.

Evaluation: Periodically review children's portfolios with them to identify aspects of their writing that show growth as well as areas that need more development.

Publish Your Description

1. **Make** a neat final copy of your description.
2. **Write** an interesting title.
3. **Look** at Ideas for Sharing on the next page.
4. **Publish** or share your description in a way that works for your audience.

- Be sure you wrote all letters correctly and used good spacing. Check that you fixed every mistake.
- Begin the first, last, and each important word in your title with a capital letter.

Reflect

Answer these questions about your description.

- What was easy about writing your description? What was hard?
- What do you like best about your description?
- Do you like your description better than other papers you have written? Why or why not?

Tech Tip If you wrote your description on a computer, fix all mistakes. Then print out a final copy.

SCHOOL-HOME CONNECTION Ask children to share their description with a family member. Suggest they point out the sensory details in the work.

Ideas for Sharing

Write It

- Write your description in a shape book.
- ★ Send your description in an e-mail to an aunt, uncle, cousin, or pen pal.

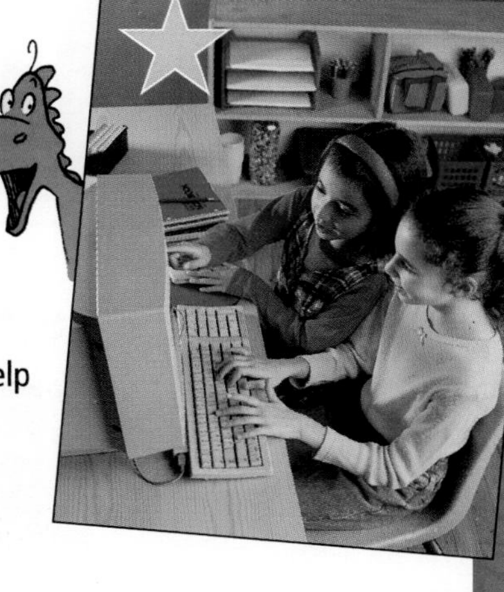

Always check for spelling mistakes before you send an e-mail.

Say It

- Recite all or part of your description. Use your body and your voice to help bring your description to life.
- Read it aloud in the Author's Chair.

Show It

- Draw pictures showing what you described.
- Add photos of your topic to your description.

Tech Tip You can use different styles of letters to make your writing look more interesting.

Ideas for Sharing

- **Shape Book** Explain that a shape book is literally shaped like the subject of the book, such as a cat or a baseball or a kite. Tell children that if, for example, they are describing a banana, they could cut their pages into the shape of a large banana and color the cover yellow.
- **E-mail** Have children look at the model of a friendly letter on page 84 and review the five parts.

TECH TIP Explain that it is not necessary to write a heading in an e-mail because the date and e-mail address are shown automatically.

- **Recite** Remind children to speak clearly and with appropriate volume when they read their descriptions and to emphasize important words. Encourage them to use gestures to emphasize words or phrases. Provide children with any appropriate props.
- **Author's Chair** After each child finishes in the Author's Chair, he or she might ask the audience if they would like to know anything more about the topic.
- **Draw Pictures** Tell children they might attach their written work to their pictures or paintings to make a larger display.
- **Add Photos** Suggest that children use magazine photos of the topic if personal photos are not available.

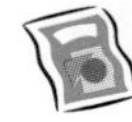

This page is also available as a poster.

Help with Publishing

TECH TIP

Children who send their descriptions via e-mail may wish to use available software or hardware to attach or scan in photographs, pictures, or clip art. Remind children to save any additions and to reread their e-mails before sending them.

Writing Prompts

Objectives

Children will:

- review prompts for choosing a topic or to practice for a writing test
- view critically a work of fine art and use it to write descriptions

Using the Prompts

You can use the prompts on this page in several ways.

- Have children review the prompts to help spark ideas when they are choosing their own topics for a description. Suggest that children choose one or two prompts that interest them and brainstorm ideas.
- Choose a prompt to provide practice for a writing test. Use it with the Test Practice on the next page.
- Choose a prompt that fits a related topic in another subject area to integrate writing a description across the curriculum.

Encourage children to think about the painting by discussing the following questions.

- What is the mood of the picture? How do the colors in the painting add to the mood? (Sample answer: They might be a little scary. The colors are strong, sharp colors; they are not gentle colors.)
- Does the tiger look like a real tiger? (Sample answer: It has stripes like a real tiger, but looks more frightening.)
- How does the artist show movement? (Sample answer: The leaves and grass look as if they are blowing.)

INTERNET CONNECTION Send your students to www.eduplace.com/kids/hme for more writing ideas. You can also find and print these prompts at www.eduplace.com/rdg/hme/.

FOR STUDENTS ACQUIRING ENGLISH

Ask children to consider the people, places, and things asssociated with their finished descriptions. "What other parts of this description can you write more about?" "Does this or another student's piece remind you of a topic?" "If you look back on all your other writing,what other topics do you find for a good description?"

Assessment Link

Use these prompts for ideas or to practice for a test. Use sensory words and similes to make your description clear to your readers.

1. Write a description of a bakery or market that you have visited. Try to use words that describe what you taste, smell, feel, see, and hear.

2. Write a description of your favorite fruit. How does it look and smell before it is ready to eat? What does it taste like?

Writing Across the Curriculum

3. **FINE ART**
What is happening in this painting? What is the tiger doing? Use your senses as you write a description of the painting.

Tiger in a Tropical Storm (Surprised!) 1891
(oil on canvas)

Henri J.F. Rousseau (Le Douanier) 1844-1910 National Gallery, London, UK/The Bridgeman Art Library

286 Writing Prompts

See www.eduplace.com/kids/hme/ for more prompts.

About the Artist

Henri Rousseau

Henri Rousseau, born in France in 1844, began painting as a hobby. He had been in the army and was working with the Paris Customs Office when he took early retirement in order to concentrate on his art.

Because Rousseau was untrained, his art is considered naïve or primitive. His figures and backgrounds are highly stylized, and often his works were greeted with ridicule.

Two years before Rousseau's death, Pablo Picasso brought him to the attention of the serious art world. Unfortunately, true appreciation and recognition of his work did not come until after his death in 1910.

Assessment Link

Test Practice

Read this writing prompt.

Write a description of your favorite fruit. How does it look and smell before it is ready to eat? What does it taste like?

Follow these steps for writing to a prompt.

1. **Look** for clues that tell you what to write about. Favorite fruit, look, smell, and taste are clues.
2. **Look** for questions in the prompt. Answer the questions as you write.
3. **Think** about your topic. Make and fill in a chart like the one on this page.

Answering a Writing Prompt		
My Topic: my favorite fruit		
Looks?	Tastes?	Smells?

4. **Plan** your writing. Use a word web.
5. **Look** at page 279. What makes a Superstar?
6. **Write** your description.

See www.eduplace.com/kids/hme/ for graphic organizers.

Test Practice

Objective

Children will:

- learn strategies for evaluating a writing prompt and writing a description for a test

Using the Test Practice

- Read through the page with children. Discuss the strategies for evaluating and responding to a prompt to write a description.
- Review the rubric on page 279 before children write their practice test.
- Have children select a prompt on this page or on the previous page and write a description. Follow the testing requirements in your school regarding time allotted and other qualifications or restrictions.

FOR STUDENTS ACQUIRING ENGLISH

Using the writing prompts mentioned here, encourage children to apply what they've learned from the finished description. Children may feel most comfortable working in small groups, sharing their ideas and work. Make it clear from the beginning of the test how you plan to grade the descriptions.

INTERNET CONNECTION Send children to www.eduplace.com/kids/hme/ for graphic organizers. You can also find and print these organizers at www.eduplace.com/rdg/hme/.

Writing a Poem

Lesson Objectives

Children will:
- read models of poems
- learn how sounds can make special effects in poems

Focus on the Models

- Discuss with the class the purpose of a poem. Guide children to see that poems express emotions, thoughts, and experiences in a special way. Explore how poems can describe everyday happenings by using vivid language and images. Ask volunteers to tell about some of their favorite poems. Have children discuss what they notice about the poems and what they particularly like.
- Tell children that they will read several poems. Explain that while each poem has some kind of rhyme, not all poems have to rhyme. Point out that these poems also have words that sound like the things or actions they describe and that this adds to the effects of the poems. These poems also have a set rhythm, or a pattern of beats.
- Ask different volunteers to read aloud the poems on these pages. As volunteers read, have the rest of the class follow along in their books.

 Alternatively, children can listen to the poems on audiotape.

- As the poems are read aloud, have children look for the feelings, ideas, and experiences the poet describes. Discuss each of these after each poem is read. Note some of the children's ideas on the board or on chart paper.

FOR STUDENTS ACQUIRING ENGLISH

Ask the children to read the titles and think about what each poem might be about. How would a wind song sound? Show a balsa glider. How does it fly? Has anyone seen fish in a pond in the evening? Why might someone write about commas? Show a photo of a crocus. Read the poems aloud as children listen.

Writing a Poem

The words in poems create pictures and make music. Some words sound like what they mean. Listen for sound words and rhyming words in these poems.

Wind Song

When the wind blows
the quiet things speak.
Some whisper, some clang,
Some creak.

Grasses swish.
Treetops sigh.
Flags slap
and snap at the sky.
Wires on poles
whistle and hum.
Ashcans roll.
Windows drum.

When the wind goes—
suddenly
then, the quiet things
are quiet again.

Lilian Moore

My Glider

My glider is graceful,
my glider is grand,
I launch it aloft
with a flick of my hand.
It smoothly ascends,
then it pauses and swoops,
it hovers in space
and turns intricate loops.

My glider is delicate,
nimble and rare,
it rises on gossamer
currents of air.
My glider is presently
useless to me—
my glider is stuck
in a very tall tree.

Jack Prelutsky

In these poems, listen for words that begin with the same sounds and for rhythm, or a pattern of beats.

Commas

Do commas have mommas
Who teach them to pause,
Who comfort and calm them,
And clean their sharp claws?
Who tell them short stories
Of uncommon commas
And send them to bed
In their comma pajamas?

Douglas Florian

Fishes' Evening Song

Flip flop,
Flip flap,
Slip slap,
Lip lap;
Water sounds,
Soothing sounds.
We fan our fins
As we lie
Resting here
Eye to eye.
Water falls
Drop by drop,
Plip plop,
Drip drop.
Plink plunk,
Splash splish;
Fish fins fan,
Fish tails swish,
Swush, swash, swish.
This we wish …
Water cold,
Water clear,
Water smooth,
Just to soothe
Sleepy fish.

Dahlov Ipcar

Lesson Objective

Children will:
- choose a topic for their poems

How to Write a Poem

Answers to Reading As a Writer
- The word *sigh* describes the sound of the treetops. The words *slap* and *snap* describe the sounds of the flags.
- The rhyming words are *grand* and *hand*; *swoops* and *loops*; *rare* and *air*; *me* and *tree*. The rhyming lines are 2 and 4, 6 and 8, 10 and 12, and 14 and 16.
- The beginning sound in the first two lines are *fl*; the beginning sounds in lines 15, 16, and 19 are *pl*, *spl*, and *sw*, respectively.
- There are two beats in each line.

Focus on Instruction

- Discuss the purposes for writing a poem. Explain that some poems tell a story, some describe a place or event, and others express the writer's feelings. Point out all poems contain some kind of vivid language to help the readers see what the poet is expressing. Work with children to select the type of poem that best suits their topic and writing style.
- If children are having difficulty choosing a topic, suggest they sketch a scene. This can give them an idea for a poem and help them establish a mood or feeling.
- Suggest that they play with the sound of words, such as *bark*, *shark*, and *park*. Playing with rhyme can help them decide how their poem will sound.

MEETING INDIVIDUAL NEEDS — FOR STUDENTS ACQUIRING ENGLISH

Ask for examples of sound words. Talk about the sound words in these poems. Call out a word such as *cat* and ask children to say as many rhyming words as they can think of. Show the children how to count the beats. Then have them count with you. Make sure they see that *rhythm* and *rhyme* are spelled differently.

Reading As a Writer See TE margin for answers.

- What word describes the sound the treetops make in "Wind Song"? What words describe the sounds the flags make?
- What are the rhyming words in "My Glider"? Which lines rhyme?
- What beginning sound repeats in the first two lines of "Fishes' Evening Song"? What sounds repeat in lines 15, 16, and 19?
- How many beats do you hear in each line of "Commas"?

How to Write a Poem

1. **Choose** a topic. You can write a poem about almost anything—nature, an event, a favorite place, or a person.

HELP ? Stuck for an Idea?

How about these?
- a color
- a kind of food
- a type of weather
- an animal
- a feeling

2 Explore your topic by making an idea tree .

- Write your topic below the tree.
- Write verbs and adjectives about your topic on the trunk.
- Think of words that rhyme with your verbs and adjectives. Write those words on one of the big limbs.
- Think of words with the same beginning sounds as words on your tree. Write those words on the other big limb.
- Write sound words for your topic on the smaller branches.

See www.eduplace.com/kids/hme/ for graphic organizers.

Help with Writing a Poem

MORE TOPIC IDEAS

Use these suggestions to spark topic ideas for poems.

- a favorite song
- a family celebration
- a special event
- a funny or exciting experience

TECH TIP

Children may use an online thesaurus to help them generate synonyms, antonyms, and images to use in their poems. For example, for the word *red*, children can find the synonyms *scarlet, ruby, cherry, pink.*

Lesson Objective

Children will:

- list and organize details on an idea tree

Focus on Instruction

- Guide children to make idea trees with their own ideas for poems. Model the process on the board, as children suggest subtopics and images.
- Before children begin to write, have them talk about their topics with classmates. Tell them to discuss the kinds of words and descriptive phrases they are planning to use, and to listen to any others that classmates might suggest.

Lesson Objectives

Children will:

- write a first draft of their poems
- revise their poems, using the Revising Checklist
- discuss their poems in a writing conference
- proofread their poems
- publish and share their final copies

Focus on Instruction

- Suggest that children mark off words and phrases on their idea trees. This will help them keep track of the entries they want to include.
- After children draft their first copies, remind them that the purpose of revising is to make their poems clearer and more interesting to help readers visualize the subject. Help children choose precise words rather than general ones.
- Review with children the Proofreading Checklist on page 283 and the use of proofreading marks.
- Check children's proofread poems before they make their final copies.
- Review with children their publishing plans to help them address any special requirements.
- Remind children that the way they use their voices and body movements helps the audience understand what the poem is expressing.

Connecting to the Criteria

As children revise, have them look again at their idea trees for sound words, words that rhyme, and other details.

SCHOOL-HOME CONNECTION Have children send their poems in greeting cards to family members.

Discuss whether this paper should go into the portfolio. Consider these reasons: (1) It is a good piece of writing; (2) it reflects an aspect of writing that the student did well; (3) it shows an aspect of writing that could be used as a baseline for measuring growth.

FOR STUDENTS ACQUIRING ENGLISH

Ask children to pick a topic for a poem and write down some words. Then have them think of rhyming words for those they have chosen. Explain that for rhyming it is the sound of the word that matters, not the spelling. Illustrate this with *box* and *socks*.

3. **Write** your poem. Use words from your idea tree. End lines where you want your readers to pause.

Which of these will you put in your poem?
- sound words
- rhyme
- repeated beginning sounds
- special rhythm

4. **Reread** your poem. Do your words paint a clear picture of your topic? Does your poem have interesting sounds?
5. **Read** your poem to a classmate. Think about your classmate's ideas.
6. **Revise** your poem if you want to make changes.
7. **Proofread** your poem. Use the Proofreading Checklist on page 283. Use a class dictionary to check spellings.
8. **Publish** or share your poem. Make a neat final copy, using your best handwriting.
   - ★ With a group, do a choral reading of your poem.
   - ● Act out your poem as a classmate reads it aloud.

Help with Writing a Poem

TECH TIP

Children can add clip art to illustrate their poems. They may also wish to add decorative borders, interesting type styles, and other embellishments.

EVALUATION TIP

Review children's use of punctuation in their poems. Check that they can articulate any purposeful use of nonstandard punctuation.

Writing a Shape Poem

A shape poem is a special kind of poem. Its shape helps readers see what the poem is about. Look at and listen to this shape poem.

How to Write a Shape Poem

1. **Choose** a topic that will be fun to write about and read about. You might choose a kite, a roller coaster, a seashell, an animal, or the moon.
2. **Think** about how you will use sound. Will you use rhyme or a special rhythm? Will you use sound words or repeat any beginning sounds?
3. **Write** your poem.
4. **Reread** your poem. Then read it to a classmate. Make any changes you want.
5. **Proofread** your poem.
6. **Publish** or share your poem. Draw your shape on a piece of paper. Write your poem inside it.

Help with Writing a Shape Poem

TOPIC IDEAS
Suggest these topic ideas that have strong shape possibilities:
- fruits, such as apples, bananas, bunches of grapes
- flowers, such as daisies and tulips
- buildings
- mountains

TECH TIP
Children may wish to draft their shape poems on a computer to help them line up the words within the shape.

Lesson Objectives

Children will:
- choose a topic
- write a shape poem
- discuss their poems with a classmate
- revise their shape poem
- proofread their shape poem
- publish their shape poem

Writing a Shape Poem

Focus on the Model

Have volunteers identify the shape of this poem. Write the poem on the board in three lines: Mushrooms are *umbrellas/for ladybugs/and their fellas*. Discuss how the shape helps the reader understand the writer's idea.

 Alternatively, children can listen to the poem on audiotape.

Focus on Instruction

- As children choose topics, tell them to sketch the shape of their poem to help them select concrete topics and words. Be sure children understand that the shape of the poem must match its subject.
- Have children discuss their poem topics and their shape ideas with classmates. Tell them to listen for suggestions and ideas that they may want to use as they draft their poems.
- As children revise their drafts, remind them to check for vivid images and precise words to help them get their ideas across.
- Review with children the Proofreading Checklist on page 283 and the use of proofreading marks.
- After children complete their final copies, they can cut out the shape and place it on a sheet of construction paper or other decorated paper.

Connecting to the Criteria

As children review and revise their poems, remind them to look for rhythm, rhyme, and sound words as well as imagery. Suggest also that they check to make sure their chosen shape is appropriate for their poem.

MEETING INDIVIDUAL NEEDS — FOR STUDENTS ACQUIRING ENGLISH

First, ask what the word *shape* means. Show several photos of mushrooms. Have children draw mushrooms; compare the poem to the shape of a mushroom. Then, help the children describe the shapes of some common objects such as a pencil, a ball, an egg, or a box. Ask the children to choose one for a group shape poem.

Giving a Talk

Lesson Objectives

Children will:
- discuss the important elements of giving a talk
- think about using props while giving a talk
- give a talk to practice establishing eye contact, using props, and speaking effectively and correctly

Focus on Instruction

- Ask a volunteer to share the definition of the word prop and have other children give examples of props. (A prop is an object that someone uses in a play or while giving a talk. A prop in a play might be a broom or a chair. A prop for a talk might be a picture, map, or an object that is being discussed.)

Think and Discuss

- Ask children how the girl's talk would be different if she did not have the guitar with her. (She would have to describe the guitar and ask her audience to visualize it. It would be harder to describe the pegs and explain what they do.)
- Discuss the bulleted questions with the class. When you discuss volume, ask children how speakers might make sure everyone can hear them. (Sample answer: speak slowly and loudly; take deep breaths to help project your voice; stop to ask if everyone can hear you and understand you.)
- Point out that it may sometimes be difficult to look at the audience, especially if a speaker has to look down at notes and find props. Discuss how the children in the photographs may have prepared ahead of time. (They might have memorized their talks and practiced speaking with the props.)

Giving a Talk

Giving a talk is a great way to share your work and your ideas. When you give a talk, show props such as pictures, objects, or charts to help explain what you mean.

Think and Discuss

- Why is everyone able to see the tiger picture? It is large enough.
- Is everyone able to see the guitar? Why or why not? Yes, she's holding it high enough.
- Which part of the guitar is the girl talking about? How do you know? the pegs; using her hands to show what she means
- Where are the speakers looking? Why? at the audience; to keep their attention
- What might they do differently if they were talking to the whole class? hold props higher, get closer, talk louder

Tips for Giving a Talk

- Begin speaking when your audience is ready to listen.
- Show pictures, objects, or charts.
- Be sure everyone can see you and your props.
- Look at your listeners and speak directly to them.
- Speak loudly enough for everyone to hear.
- Speak slowly and clearly.
- Use words that "fit" your listeners.

Apply It

Give a talk to your class or to a small group of classmates. Speak about a topic that you know and understand very well. Use the tips above to help you.

Stuck for a Topic?

How about these?
- a toy or model
- part of a collection
- how something works
- a favorite place

Focus on Instruction

- Have one or two volunteers read the Tips for Giving a Talk. Discuss with children that they have learned and practiced many of these speaking guidelines when telling stories, messages, and instructions. Ask children to explain how they followed these guidelines in the past.
- Explain that it is always a good idea to begin a talk by asking, "Can everyone see me and my prop?" and "Can everyone hear me?"

Apply It

- To focus children on their topics and audience, have them discuss their choices with a classmate. Have one child tell their topic choice and the other child ask questions about it. As children plan their talks, remind them to continue thinking what their classmates might like to learn from them.
- Point out that any props must be large enough for everyone to see. Work with individuals to help them choose an appropriate prop. For example, children who want to talk about a small toy or a family member might bring in drawings or photographs that are large enough for the entire class to see. They might also use the overhead projector to magnify small photographs.
- Remind children to remember and use the rules of grammar they have learned. Monitor children's use of the articles *a* and *an*. Remind them also to describe their topics by comparing and contrasting them to other things, using comparatives and antonyms to add interest.

FOR STUDENTS ACQUIRING ENGLISH

Children may have many cultural objects or skills they can share; suggest it but don't force them to do so. They may want to blend in by sharing an "American" object or skill. Help them prepare for their talk; ask: "Why is this important to you? Where did you get/learn it?"

Unit 9 Planning Guide

More Capitalization and Punctuation

3 weeks

	Lesson	Checkup (PE)	Extra Practice (PE)	Graphic Organizer (BLM)	Writing Wrap-Up (BLM)	More Practice (TE)	Workbook Plus	Reteaching Workbook	Students Acquiring English Practice Book
1	Days *(297–298)*	320	330	9–1	9–6	330	103–104	69	77–78
2	Holidays *(299–300)*	320	331	9–1	9–6	331	105–106	70	79–80
3	Months *(301–302)*	320	332	9–1	9–6	332	107–108	71	81–82
4	Titles for People *(303–304)*	320	333	9–2	9–6	333	109–110	72	83–84
5	Writing Book Titles *(305–306)*	320	334	9–2	9–7	334	111–112	73	85–86
6	Ending Sentences *(307–308)*	321	335	9–3	9–7	335	113–114	74	87–88
	Revising Strategies: Sentence Fluency Writing Correct Sentences *(309–310)*						115–116	75–76	
7	Commas in Dates *(311–312)*	321	336	9–4	9–7	336	117–118	77	89–90
8	Commas with Names of Places *(313–314)*	321	337	9–4	9–7	337	119–120	78	91–92
9	Quotation Marks *(315–316)*	321	338	9–5	9–8	338	121–122	79	93–94
10	More About Quotation Marks *(317–318)*	321	339	9–5	9–8	339	123–124	80	95–96
	Enrichment *(319)*								
	Cumulative Review *(326–329)*								
	Test Practice *(323–325)*								97–98

Unit 9

Tools and Tips

▶ **Grammar Glossary,** *pp. H35–H39*

School-Home Connection

Suggestions for informing or involving family members in classroom activities and learning related to this unit are included in the Teacher's Edition throughout the unit.

Meeting Individual Needs

▶ **FOR SPECIAL NEEDS/INCLUSION:** *Houghton Mifflin English* Audiotape See also Reteaching.

▶ **FOR STUDENTS ACQUIRING ENGLISH:**
- Notes and activities are included in this Teacher's Edition throughout the unit to help you adapt or use pupil book activities with students acquiring English.
- Additional support is available for students at various stages of English proficiency: **Beginning/Preproduction, Early Production/Speech Emergence,** and **Intermediate/ Advanced**. See Students Acquiring English Practice Book.
- Students can listen to the Try It Out activities on audiotape.

▶ **ENRICHMENT:** *PE p. 319*

All audiotape recordings are also available on CD.

Daily Language Practice

Each sentence or group of words includes two errors based on skills taught in this or previous Grammar units. Each day write one item on the chalkboard. Have children find the errors and write the sentence correctly on a sheet of paper. To make the activity easier, identify the kinds of errors.

1. Are you going to play practice on tuesday! Are you going to play practice on Tuesday? (capitalizing days; end punctuation/questions)
2. The family gone for a boat ride on labor day. The family went for a boat ride on Labor Day. (irregular verbs/capitalizing holidays)
3. The shorter month of the year is february. The shortest month of the year is February. (comparing with adjectives; capitalizing months)
4. The name of Lindas teacher is mrs. Brown. The name of Linda's teacher is Mrs. Brown. (possessive nouns with *'s*; titles for people)
5. Taylor finish reading the little black Puppy last night. Taylor finished reading The Little Black Puppy last night. (verbs in the past with *ed*; writing book titles)
6. Doesnt Erin know where the meeting is. Doesn't Erin know where the meeting is? (contractions with *not*; end punctuation/questions)
7. Something special happened to marty on July 9 2000. Something special happened to Marty on July 9, 2000. (proper nouns; commas in dates)
8. My family. Visited Asheville North Carolina. My family visited Asheville, North Carolina. (complete sentences; commas with names of places)
9. Ahmed asked, Is there a apple in my lunch box? Ahmed asked, "Is there an apple in my lunch box?" (quotation marks; using *a* and *an*)
10. Raul said "I mowed ms. Hay's yard today." Raul said, "I mowed Ms. Hay's yard today." (punctuating quotations; capitalizing titles for people)

Additional Resources

Workbook Plus, Unit 9
Reteaching Workbook, Unit 9
Students Acquiring English Practice Book, Unit 9
Teacher's Resource Book
Audiotapes

Technology Tools

TEACHER'S RESOURCE DISK (for handwriting support)
INTERNET: http://www.eduplace.com/kids/hme/ or http://www.eduplace.com/rdg/hme/
Visit Education Place for an interactive quiz.

Assessment

Test Booklet, Unit 9

Keeping a Journal

Discuss with children the value of keeping a journal as a way of promoting self-expression and fluency. Encourage children to record their thoughts and ideas in a notebook. Inform students whether the journal will be private or will be reviewed periodically as a way of assisting growth. The following prompts may be useful for generating writing ideas.

Journal Prompts

- What time of day do you like best? Why?
- What is the best outdoor place to play games?
- Do you think it would be fun to ride a pony in a circus? Why or why not?

Introducing the Unit

Using the Photograph

- Have children look at the photograph and ask a volunteer to read the caption aloud. Copy the caption on the board. Call on a volunteer to underline the name of the holiday. Using the underlined name of the holiday as an example, tell children that each important word in the name of a holiday begins with a capital letter.
- Remind children that some nouns name special people, animals, places, or things, and that these special nouns begin with capital letters. Explain to children that in this unit they will learn about other special words that begin with capital letters.
- Tell children that they will write sentences that use correct capitalization and punctuation.

Grammar Song

See Blackline Master G-2 for a song to help children remember concepts and rules taught in this unit.

Independent Writing

Children can benefit by having time each day or several times a week to write in their journals or do self-selected writing activities. Remind children to think about purpose and audience and choose an appropriate format for both.

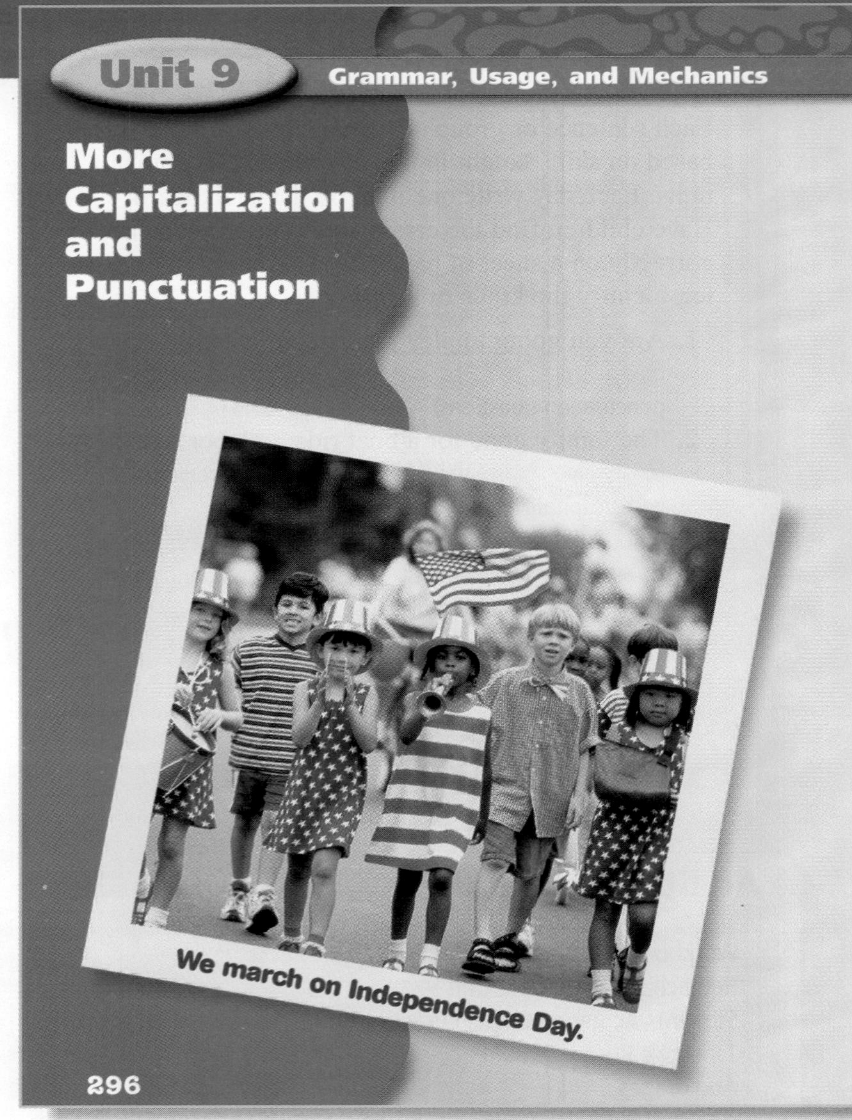

We march on Independence Day.

Shared Writing Activity

Work with children to write a paragraph about the photograph.

1. Ask children to look carefully at the photograph. Have them tell what colors, people, and things they see. List these details on the board.
2. Have volunteers tell what sounds and smells might be at this parade. What might the children say to one another? Add these suggestions to the details list on the board.
3. As a class, develop a topic sentence about this Independence Day parade. Write the sentence on the board or at the top of an overhead transparency.
4. Work together to use the generated details to create sentences for the paragraph about the parade.
5. Write the sentences in paragraph form. Ask children to establish a logical order for the sentences. Reinforce what children have learned about using capital letters and end marks.
6. Ask volunteers to read the completed paragraph.

Grammar / Mechanics

1 Days

It needs a capital letter; change *s* to *S*.

One-Minute Warm-Up

How can you fix the answer to this riddle?

Riddle: On which day does it never rain?

Answer: sunday

There are seven days in a week. The names of the **days** of the week begin with **capital letters**.

Sunday Monday Tuesday Wednesday
Thursday Friday Saturday

Try It Out

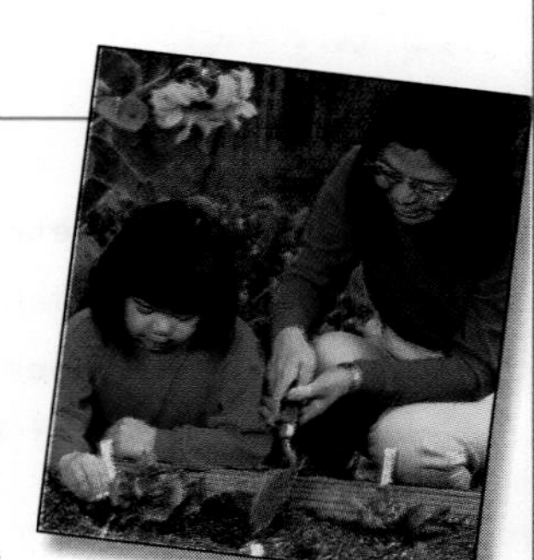

Speak Up Read the sentences. Tell which words need capital letters.

1. On tuesday I go food shopping. Tuesday
2. Lian has a piano lesson on friday. Friday
3. I have a meeting on wednesday. Wednesday
4. On thursday we will plant a garden. Thursday

Write It Now write each sentence. Begin the name of each day correctly.

Example I need to call Tom on monday.
I need to call Tom on Monday.

Tuesday, Friday, Wednesday, Thursday

Days

Lesson Objectives

Children will:

- capitalize the names of the days of the week
- proofread for capitalization of the names of the days of the week
- write an informative weather chart for the days of the week

One-Minute Warm-Up Have a volunteer read the day of the week. Ask children to tell how they knew which letter to change.

Focus on Instruction

Review with children that sentences begin with capital letters and end with a period, question mark, or exclamation point. Also review that nouns that name special persons, places, and things begin with capital letters. Tell children that the days of the week are other special naming words.

Try It Out

LISTENING AND SPEAKING Have children draw a calendar and write the names of the days of the week for one week. Ask a volunteer to read the sentences in numbered order. When children hear the name of a day of the week, they should write the number of the sentence it appeared in on their calendars.

FOR STUDENTS ACQUIRING ENGLISH

- Have children listen to the Try It Out sentences on the audiotape. Distribute SAE Practice page for Unit 9, Lesson 1 to support listening.
- Have a volunteer explain the riddle in the Warm-Up. Then help children suggest sentences about the photo and schedule in the book. Say that in English the days all begin with capital letters. (This is not true in languages such as Spanish.) List the days. Have children say the words with you. Pay special attention to *Wednesday* and to the initial syllable in *Thursday*. Ask children questions about what they and their families usually do on specific days. Children listen and say which words need capital letters. Then they write the days. Example: I have a swimming lesson on monday. (Monday)

Meeting Individual Needs

RETEACHING
ALTERNATIVE STRATEGY

- Write the days of the week on index cards and place them face down in a pile. List the days of the week in order on the chalkboard.
- Have children take turns choosing a card from the pile. Ask them to read the name of the day, and to use it in a sentence, telling something they do on that day.
- Refer children to the chalkboard list. Have them tell you what number day of the week their day is.
- Ask each child to write their day on the chalkboard under the appropriate day on your list. Check for capitalization.

CHALLENGE
Have each child design a colorful class calendar for one month. Ask them to list birthdays, tests, trips or other class activities that will occur that month. Provide a list of activities or a schedule on the chalkboard for children to use as reference.

FOR STUDENTS ACQUIRING ENGLISH
Make sure children know the days of the week. Use a calendar, noting the capital letters. Ask questions such as, *How many days are there in the week? What day is today? What day is tomorrow? What days do we go to school?*

Summing Up Help children summarize these key points about the lesson:

There are seven days in a week. The names of the **days** of the week begin with **capital letters**.

You may want to have children complete the parts related to this lesson on Blackline Master 9-1.

On Your Own

Tell children to read the sentences to themselves to find the day of the week. Have them use a calendar for reference as they work.

FOR STUDENTS ACQUIRING ENGLISH
Distribute SAE Practice page for Unit 9, Lesson 1. Review the days. Remind children that we consider Sunday the first day of the week. Children underline the word that needs a capital letter. Then they write the word correctly.
1. I went to a party on saturday. (Saturday)
2. We go to Grandma's house on sunday. (Sunday)

Writing Wrap-Up

Writing Tip: Have children brainstorm a list of weather words and phrases such as *rainy*, *sunny*, *cloudy*, and *snow* before they begin. See Blackline Master 9-6 for a sample weather chart.

TECHNOLOGY CONNECTION
Children may wish to use available software to add clip art to their weather charts.

On Your Own

Write the sentences. Use capital letters correctly.

Example John plays baseball on wednesday.
John plays baseball on Wednesday.

1. Clara's birthday is on saturday. Saturday
2. On monday I will clean the house. Monday

3–6. Proofread this list of jobs. Find four mistakes with capital letters. Write the list correctly.

Example Take out the trash on tuesday.
Take out the trash on Tuesday.

Proofreading

Weekly Chores

Clean the hamster's cage on ~~monday~~. Monday
Set the table on Wednesday and ~~friday~~. Friday
Clean my room on ~~saturday~~. Saturday
Rest on ~~sunday~~! Sunday

Writing Wrap-Up WRITING • THINKING • LISTENING • SPEAKING

INFORMING

Write a Weather Chart

List the days of the week. Write words and draw symbols to describe the weather each day. Discuss your chart with a classmate. Check for the correct use of capital letters.
Charts will vary.

 For Extra Practice, see page 330.

Meeting Individual Needs

● RETEACHING WORKBOOK, page 69

1 Days

Use capital letters to begin the names of the days of the week.

Sunday Tuesday Thursday Saturday
Monday Wednesday Friday

Ned will take his piano lesson on Tuesday.

Draw a line under the correct word. Then write the sentence correctly.

Example Ned cleans on (friday, Friday). Ned cleans on Friday.

1. Ned visits Gramps on (Sunday, sunday).
Ned visits Gramps on Sunday.
2. On (thursday, Thursday) Ned plays soccer.
On Thursday Ned plays soccer.
3. Ned studies on (Monday, monday).
Ned studies on Monday.
4. Ned has a picnic on (Saturday, saturday).
Ned has a picnic on Saturday.

▲■ WORKBOOK PLUS, pages 103-104

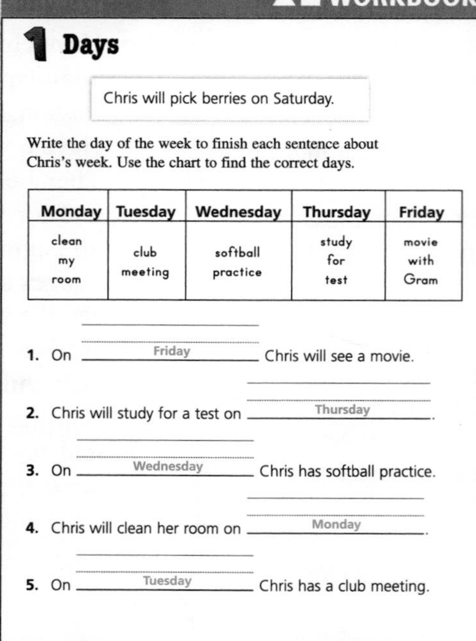

1 Days

Chris will pick berries on Saturday.

Write the day of the week to finish each sentence about Chris's week. Use the chart to find the correct days.

Monday	Tuesday	Wednesday	Thursday	Friday
clean my room	club meeting	softball practice	study for test	movie with Gram

1. On Friday Chris will see a movie.
2. Chris will study for a test on Thursday.
3. On Wednesday Chris has softball practice.
4. Chris will clean her room on Monday.
5. On Tuesday Chris has a club meeting.

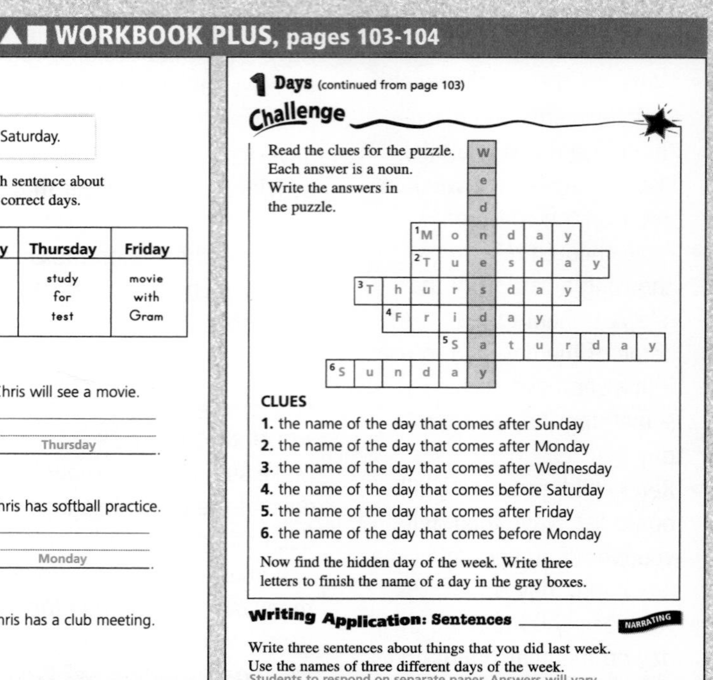

1 Days (continued from page 103)

Challenge

Read the clues for the puzzle. Each answer is a noun. Write the answers in the puzzle.

W e d n e s d a y (hidden word)
1 Monday
2 Tuesday
3 Thursday
4 Friday
5 Saturday
6 Sunday

CLUES
1. the name of the day that comes after Sunday
2. the name of the day that comes after Monday
3. the name of the day that comes after Wednesday
4. the name of the day that comes before Saturday
5. the name of the day that comes after Friday
6. the name of the day that comes before Monday

Now find the hidden day of the week. Write three letters to finish the name of a day in the gray boxes.

Writing Application: Sentences NARRATING

Write three sentences about things that you did last week. Use the names of three different days of the week.
Students to respond on separate paper. Answers will vary.

Grammar / Mechanics

2 Holidays

turkey: Thanksgiving Day; heart: Valentine's Day; American flag: Independence Day or Flag Day; answers to the second question will vary.

Which holidays do the pictures make you think of? What have you learned about holidays?

Holidays are special days. New Year's Day and Thanksgiving Day are holidays. Each important word in the name of a **holiday** begins with a **capital letter**.

There are parades on **L**abor **D**ay.

People play jokes on **A**pril **F**ools' **D**ay.

Try It Out

Speak Up Read each sentence. Say the words that need capital letters.

1. Some people plant trees on arbor day. Arbor Day
2. Did you remember mother's day? Mother's Day
3. On columbus day, school is closed. Columbus Day

Write It Now write each sentence. Use capital letters correctly.

Example When is earth day?
When is Earth Day?

Arbor Day, Mother's Day, Columbus Day

Meeting Individual Needs

RETEACHING
ALTERNATIVE STRATEGY

- Ask children to name some holidays. List their responses on the chalkboard and discuss what is celebrated on each occasion.
- Assign a holiday to each child. Remind children that every word in a holiday's name begins with a capital letter. Have them draw a picture of the holiday and write sentences about it.
- Display the pictures on a bulletin board under the caption "Names of Holidays Begin with a Capital Letter."

CHALLENGE
Have children write a short set of instructions for how to make something for their favorite holiday. Suggest that they write about a decoration, gift, or easy recipe.

FOR STUDENTS ACQUIRING ENGLISH
Find out how many U.S. holidays children can name. Write children's ideas on the board. Use a calendar to show when each is. Ask children what ideas they associate with each holiday.

Holidays

Lesson Objectives

Children will:
- capitalize the names of holidays
- proofread for capitalization of holidays
- write a paragraph comparing and contrasting holidays

One-Minute Warm-Up Have volunteers share the names and customs of holidays they celebrate. List the names of the holidays on the chalkboard.

Focus on Instruction

Remind children that holiday names may consist of more than one word, and that all words in the name begin with a capital letter. Explain to children what the different holidays mentioned in this lesson commemorate.

Try It Out

LISTENING AND SPEAKING Have a volunteer read aloud the sentences. Ask children to listen for the name of the holiday in each sentence. Then have volunteers tell the name of the holiday in a complete sentence. For example: The name of the holiday is Arbor Day.

FOR STUDENTS ACQUIRING ENGLISH

- Have children listen to the Try It Out sentences on the audiotape. Distribute SAE Practice page for Unit 9, Lesson 2 to support listening.
- With children's help, list major holidays and their dates. Add to the list as needed. Show children how to use the calendar to find the actual days and dates for each holiday. Then have partners or small groups work with calendars to locate each holiday you have listed on the board. You may want to say which are religious holidays. Ask children about important holidays in their cultures. Discuss which holidays are vacation days for many people and which are not. Children listen and say which words need capital letters. Then they write the words. Example: When is father's day? (Father's Day)

Summing Up Help children summarize these key points about the lesson:

Holidays are special days. Each important word in the name of a **holiday** begins with a **capital letter**.

You may want to have children complete the parts related to this lesson on Blackline Master 9-1.

On Your Own

Point out that the word *holiday* contains the small word *day*. Review the names of holidays with children and help them to see that the word *day* often occurs in the names of holidays.

FOR STUDENTS ACQUIRING ENGLISH

Distribute SAE Practice page for Unit 9, Lesson 2. Discuss the customs associated with some of the U.S. holidays. Then children write sentences adding capital letters where needed.

1. On valentine's day we give cards. (Valentine's Day)
2. People eat turkey on thanksgiving. (Thanksgiving)

Writing Wrap-Up

Writing Tip: Suggest that children use a Venn diagram to compare and contrast facts about the two holidays before they begin writing. See Blackline Master 9-6 for a sample paragraph.

SCHOOL-HOME CONNECTION

Have children ask family members about their favorite holidays. Ask them to compare and contrast the responses they receive.

On Your Own

Write the sentences. Use capital letters correctly.

Example June 14 is flag day. June 14 is Flag Day.

1. January 1 is new year's day. January 1 is New Year's Day.
2. May 1 is may day. May 1 is May Day.

3–6. Proofread a paragraph from Todd's journal. Find four mistakes with capital letters. Write the paragraph correctly.

Example I gave my dad a tie on father's day.
I gave my dad a tie on Father's Day.

I like holidays. We have a party at school on Valentine's Day. My family eats a big dinner on ~~thanksgiving day~~ Thanksgiving Day. On ~~memorial day~~ Memorial Day, we honor those who died in wars.

Writing Wrap-Up

WRITING • THINKING • LISTENING • SPEAKING

COMPARING & CONTRASTING

Write a Paragraph

Write about two holidays. Tell how they are alike and different. Read your paragraph to a classmate. Together, check for the correct use of capital letters in the names of holidays.

Paragraphs will vary.

 For Extra Practice, see page 331.

Meeting Individual Needs

● RETEACHING WORKBOOK, page 70

2 Holidays

Begin the names of holidays with capital letters.
Today is Father's Day.

Happy Father's Day!

Write the names of the underlined holidays correctly.

Example Does school begin before labor day? Labor Day

1. We have a picnic on flag day. Flag Day
2. Do you go to school on columbus day? Columbus Day
3. Grandma will be here on thanksgiving day. Thanksgiving Day
4. I gave Dad a card for valentine's day. Valentine's Day
5. On presidents' day we saw a parade. Presidents' Day

▲■ WORKBOOK PLUS, pages 105-106

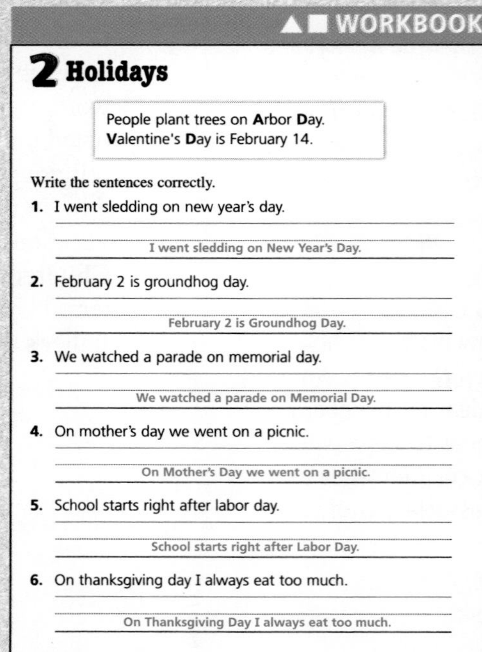

2 Holidays

People plant trees on Arbor Day.
Valentine's Day is February 14.

Write the sentences correctly.

1. I went sledding on new year's day. I went sledding on New Year's Day.
2. February 2 is groundhog day. February 2 is Groundhog Day.
3. We watched a parade on memorial day. We watched a parade on Memorial Day.
4. On mother's day we went on a picnic. On Mother's Day we went on a picnic.
5. School starts right after labor day. School starts right after Labor Day.
6. On thanksgiving day I always eat too much. On Thanksgiving Day I always eat too much.

2 Holidays (continued from page 105)

Challenge

Choose four months. Look at a calendar. Write the name of a holiday that takes place in each month.

Answers will vary.

Writing Application: A Description DESCRIBING

Make up a new holiday. Tell the name of your holiday. Describe what people do on your holiday. Students to respond on separate paper. Answers will vary.

Grammar / Mechanics

3 Months

August; it begins with a capital letter.

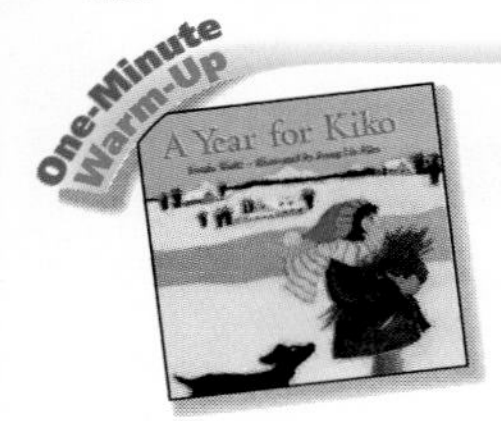

Read the sentences. Which word names a month? How does the word begin?

Kiko wears her bathing suit. She sits in her pool.
Now August feels cool.

—from A Year for Kiko, by Ferida Wolff

The names of the **months** begin with **capital letters**.

January	February	March	April
May	June	July	August
September	October	November	December

Try It Out

Speak Up Tell which words need capital letters.

1. In may we planted the seeds. May
2. In june the plants began to grow. June
3. Did the flowers bloom in july? July
4. Some of them bloomed in august. August

Write It Write each sentence correctly.

Example We planned the garden in march.
We planned the garden in March.

May, June, July, August

Meeting Individual Needs

RETEACHING
ALTERNATIVE STRATEGY

- Help children make month clocks. Tell them to draw a large circle and divide it into twelve sections. Write the names of the months on the chalkboard and circle the capital letters.
- Tell children to write the name of a month, beginning with a capital letter, in each section of the month clock. They may also draw a symbol for the month.
- Cut out a paper clock hand and help children attach it to the clock's center with a paper fastener. Have children turn the hand to the correct month as you ask questions about that month.

CHALLENGE
Have children write a description of their favorite month. Suggest that they tell what the weather feels like and what the flowers and trees look like. Have them tell what activities or foods are special that month.

FOR STUDENTS ACQUIRING ENGLISH
Make sure children know the months of the year. Use a calendar to practice, noting the capital letters. Ask questions such as, *How many months are there? When is your birthday? In what month do we start school?*

Months

Lesson Objectives

Children will:

- capitalize the names of the months of the year
- proofread for capitalization the names of the months of the year
- write a poem about months; have others identify months and the capital letter that begins each one

One-Minute Warm-Up Write the quoted sentences on the board. Then have volunteers identify the month and tell how they recognized the word.

Focus on Instruction

Explain that there are twelve months in a year, and that the names of the months always begin with a capital letter. Be sure children understand that the twelve months occur in the order shown on a calendar.

Try It Out

VIEWING Have children generate sentences about the girl and her garden. Tell them to use the name of a month in each sentence. Record their responses in chart. (Sample responses are shown.)

Months	Sentences
May	In May she digs in the soil.
June	June is when she pulls out weeds.
July	In July she picks some flowers.

MEETING INDIVIDUAL NEEDS — FOR STUDENTS ACQUIRING ENGLISH

- Have children listen to the Try It Out sentences on the audiotape. Distribute SAE Practice page for Unit 9, Lesson 3 to support listening.
- Help children suggest sentences about the photo in the book and on the Practice page. Remind children that in English the months of the year all have capital letters. Have children take turns saying and spelling aloud the months of the year; they can do it from memory or by looking at the chart in the book. Remind them to begin spelling with "Capital _____." Going through the months in order, ask children to name some things they associate with each month. Children listen and say which words need capital letters. Then children write the words. Example: Mother's Day is in may. (May)

Summing Up Help children summarize these key points about the lesson:

The names of the **months** begin with **capital letters**.

You may want to have children complete the parts related to this lesson on Blackline Master 9-1.

On Your Own

Remind children that the word *may* has two meanings: *might happen* or *the name of a month*. Suggest that they substitute the word *might* for *may* whenever they see it in a sentence and see if it makes sense. If not, the word *may* probably means *the name of a month*.

FOR STUDENTS ACQUIRING ENGLISH

Distribute SAE Practice page for Unit 9, Lesson 3. Ask children to name some things they associate with each month. Children write sentences adding capital letters where needed.

1. New Year's Day is january 1. (January)
2. The weather is hot in august. (August)

Writing Wrap-Up

Writing Tip: Suggest that children brainstorm a list of rhyming words related to each month. For example: *April*, *rain*, *train*; *May*, *flower*, *shower*. See Blackline Master 9-6 for a sample poem.

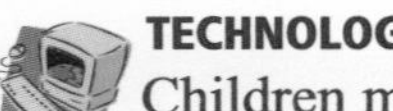

TECHNOLOGY CONNECTION

Children may want to use available software to create art to illustrate their poems.

On Your Own

Write the sentences. Use capital letters correctly.

Example We gave a concert in may.
We gave a concert in May.

1. School started in august. August
2. In november we had a field trip. November

3–6. Proofread Abby's poem. Find four mistakes with capital letters. Write the poem correctly.

Example In october leaves fall from the trees.
In October leaves fall from the trees.

Proofreading

In ~~january~~ January it may snow.
In ~~march~~ March the wind may blow.
In ~~june~~ June flowers grow.
In ~~august~~ August there is grass to mow.

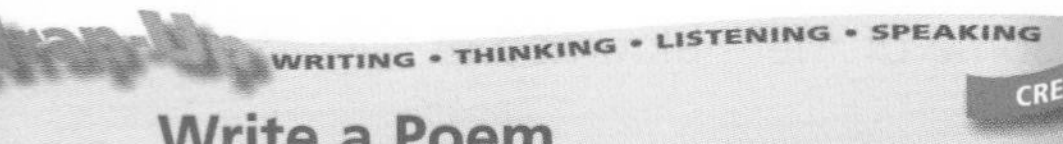

Write a Poem

Write a poem about one or more months. Try to make some lines rhyme. Read your poem to classmates. Have them name each month and the capital letter with which it begins.

Poems will vary.

 For Extra Practice, see page 332.

Meeting Individual Needs

● RETEACHING WORKBOOK, page 71

3 Months

Begin the names of the months with capital letters.

January	May	September
February	June	October
March	July	November
April	August	December

In January Mom ordered seeds for our garden.

Write the names of the underlined months correctly.

Example In march we planted peas. March

1. It rained for nine days in april. April
2. In may Dad planted corn. May
3. In june we picked peas. June
4. I weeded the garden in july. July
5. In september we ate a lot of corn. September

▲■ WORKBOOK PLUS, pages 107-108

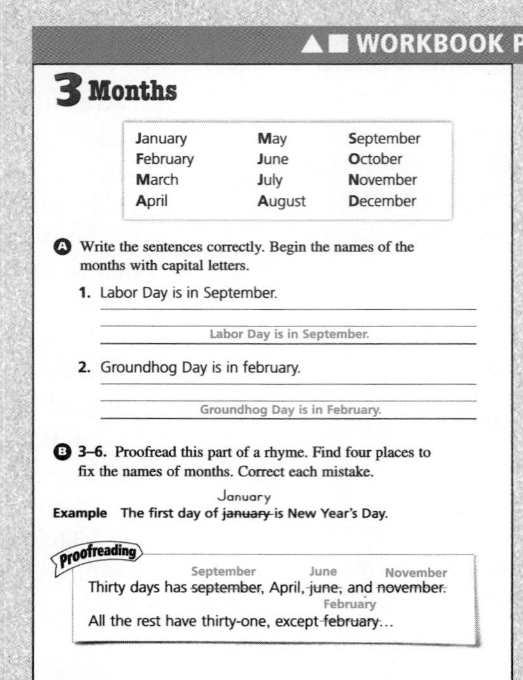

3 Months

January	May	September
February	June	October
March	July	November
April	August	December

A Write the sentences correctly. Begin the names of the months with capital letters.

1. Labor Day is in September.
Labor Day is in September.
2. Groundhog Day is in february.
Groundhog Day is in February.

B 3–6. Proofread this part of a rhyme. Find four places to fix the names of months. Correct each mistake.

Example The first day of ~~january~~ January is New Year's Day.

Proofreading

Thirty days has ~~september~~ September, April, ~~june~~ June, and ~~november~~ November.
All the rest have thirty-one, except ~~february~~ February...

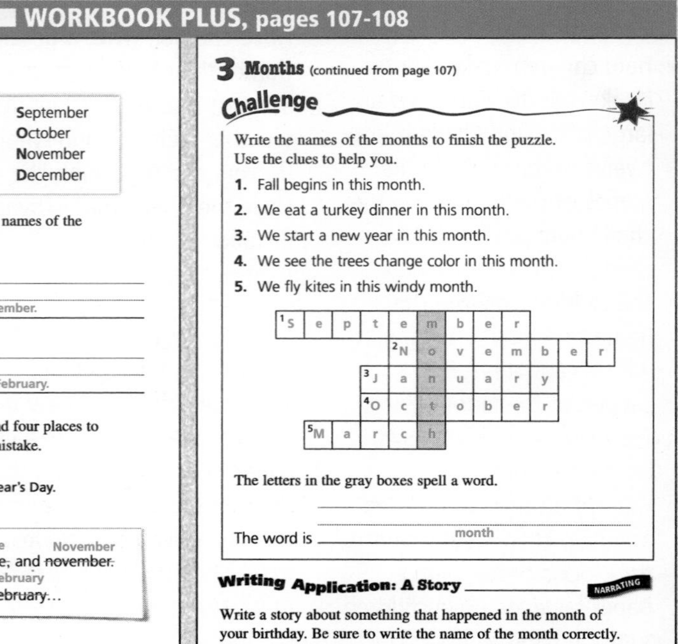

3 Months (continued from page 107)

Challenge

Write the names of the months to finish the puzzle. Use the clues to help you.

1. Fall begins in this month.
2. We eat a turkey dinner in this month.
3. We start a new year in this month.
4. We see the trees change color in this month.
5. We fly kites in this windy month.

1 September
2 November
3 January
4 October
5 March

The letters in the gray boxes spell a word.

The word is month.

Writing Application: A Story NARRATING

Write a story about something that happened in the month of your birthday. Be sure to write the name of the month correctly.

Students to respond on separate paper. Answers will vary.

Grammar / Mechanics

4 Titles for People

Miss; answers will vary.

One-Minute Warm-Up

Read the sentence. What title is used before a person's last name? What other titles for people do you know?

The next morning Miss Nelson did not come to school.

—from Miss Nelson Is Missing! by Harry Allard

A **title** may be used before a person's name. A title begins with a capital letter and usually ends with a period. Read each name. Say the title. Which title does not end with a period?

Mrs. Mann Mr. Chan Ms. Willis
Miss Gomez Dr. Rogers

Try It Out

Speak Up Read the names. Tell how to write each title correctly.

1. dr Lee (Dr.)
2. miss Santos (Miss)
3. mrs Lane (Mrs.)
4. ms Jackson (Ms.)

Write It Now write the titles and names correctly.

Example mr Smith Mr. Smith

Dr. Lee, Miss Santos, Mrs. Lane, Ms. Jackson

Titles for People

Lesson Objectives

Children will:
- capitalize titles before names
- put a period after the titles *Mrs.*, *Mr.*, *Ms.*, and *Dr.*
- proofread for capitalization and punctuation in titles
- write a narrative that includes people's names and titles

One-Minute Warm-Up Write the names and titles of people with whom children are familiar on the chalkboard. Have children read aloud the names and titles and identify any capital letters or punctuation marks.

Focus on Instruction

Explain that titles may tell if the person is a man or a woman. Titles may also tell if a woman is single or married. Other titles tell about the kind of job a person has.

Try It Out

LISTENING AND SPEAKING Have volunteers take turns reading aloud the names and titles. Ask the boys to stand when they hear the title of a man and the girls to stand when they hear the title of a woman. Have all children stand when the title could refer to either a man or a woman.

Meeting Individual Needs

RETEACHING
ALTERNATIVE STRATEGY
- Write the following on the chalkboard: Mr. Kline, Mrs. Fadden, Dr. Kramer, Ms. Johnson, Miss Parker. Point out that the title before each name begins with a capital letter and ends, except for *Miss*, with a period.
- Have children close their eyes. Erase a capital or a period in the title. Have a volunteer identify and add the missing mark.
- Write sentences containing a person's name, with a space before the name. Have a child add a title before the name and read each sentence aloud.

CHALLENGE
Have children write a story about Mr. and Mrs. Mix-up and one of their mixed-up days. Encourage children to include other characters with titles in their names. Ask volunteers to read their stories aloud.

FOR STUDENTS ACQUIRING ENGLISH
Ask children what they call adults in their lives, including you, the principal, the owner of the local store, the person they go to when they are sick, and the person who checks their teeth. Write the names, noting the titles.

FOR STUDENTS ACQUIRING ENGLISH
- Have children listen to the Try It Out sentences on the audiotape. Distribute SAE Practice page for Unit 9, Lesson 4 to support listening.
- Help children suggest sentences about the art on the Practice page. Ask children for all the titles they can think of in English. List on the board. Note the capital letters and periods. Discuss titles. Ask children how they know what to call people they meet for the first time or people they have known for a long time. Keep in mind that many languages use more titles and grammatical forms relating to a person's status than English does. Children listen and write the titles correctly.
  1. dr Garcia
  2. ms Peters

Summing Up Help children summarize these key points about the lesson:

A **title** may be used before a person's name. A title begins with a capital letter. Most titles end with a period.

You may want to have children complete the parts related to this lesson on Blackline Master 9-2.

On Your Own

Remind children that titles always come before a name. The word *doctor* means the same as the title *Dr.* but is not used as a title.

FOR STUDENTS ACQUIRING ENGLISH

Distribute SAE Practice page for Unit 9, Lesson 4. Review titles. Briefly discuss all the professions covered by the title *Dr.*, including that of a professor. Children find errors in titles and they write the titles correctly.

1. My doctor is Dr Crawford. (Dr.)
2. Our neighbors are mr and mrs Wiley. (Mr. Mrs.)

Writing Wrap-Up

Writing Tip: Suggest that children list all the names and titles of the characters in their stories before they begin writing. See Blackline Master 9-6 for a sample story.

SCHOOL-HOME CONNECTION

Invite children to work with a family member to create a family tree that includes the names and titles of all the family members they know.

On Your Own

Write the titles and names correctly.

Example mr. Li Mr. Li

1. miss Hill Miss Hill
2. Mrs Bok Mrs. Bok
3. Ms Vega Ms. Vega
4. dr Hale Dr. Hale

5–8. Proofread Hana's story. Find four mistakes with titles of people. Write the story correctly.

Example I bought my bike from mr Miller.
I bought my bike from Mr. Miller.

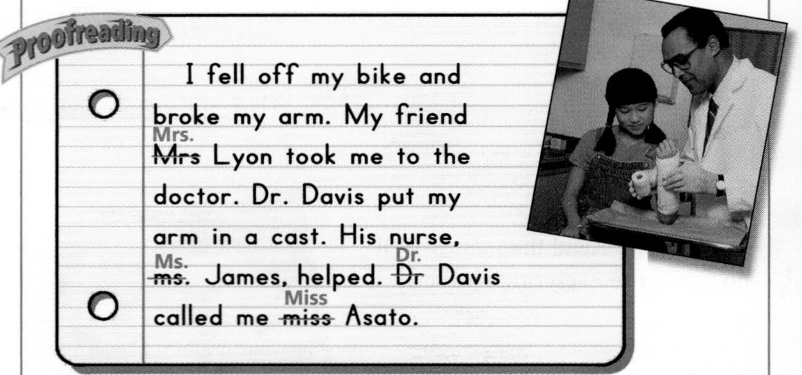

Proofreading

I fell off my bike and broke my arm. My friend ~~Mrs~~ Mrs. Lyon took me to the doctor. Dr. Davis put my arm in a cast. His nurse, ~~ms.~~ Ms. James, helped. ~~Dr~~ Dr. Davis called me ~~miss~~ Miss Asato.

Writing Wrap-Up

WRITING • THINKING • LISTENING • SPEAKING

NARRATING

Write a Story

Write about someone visiting a doctor or dentist. Use people's names and titles in your story. Read your story aloud. Have a classmate name and spell each title.

Stories will vary.

304 Titles for People For Extra Practice, see page 333.

Meeting Individual Needs

● RETEACHING WORKBOOK, page 72

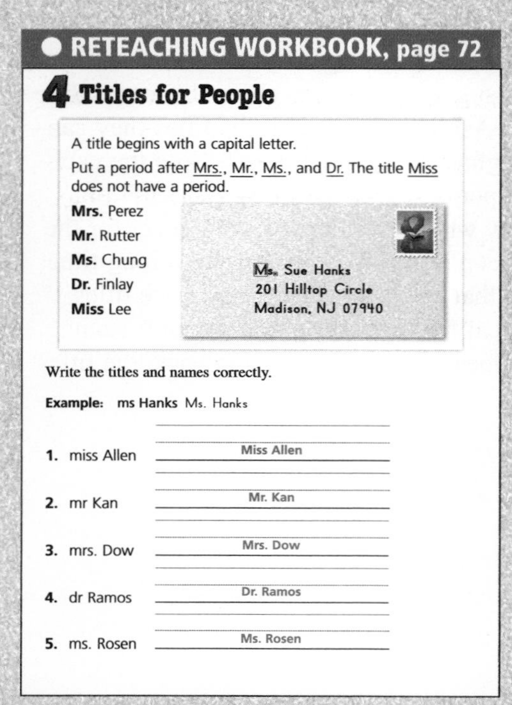

4 Titles for People

A title begins with a capital letter.

Put a period after Mrs., Mr., Ms., and Dr. The title Miss does not have a period.

Mrs. Perez
Mr. Rutter
Ms. Chung
Dr. Finlay
Miss Lee

Ms. Sue Hanks
201 Hilltop Circle
Madison, NJ 07940

Write the titles and names correctly.

Example: ms Hanks Ms. Hanks

1. miss Allen — Miss Allen
2. mr Kan — Mr. Kan
3. mrs. Dow — Mrs. Dow
4. dr Ramos — Dr. Ramos
5. ms. Rosen — Ms. Rosen

▲■ WORKBOOK PLUS, pages 109-110

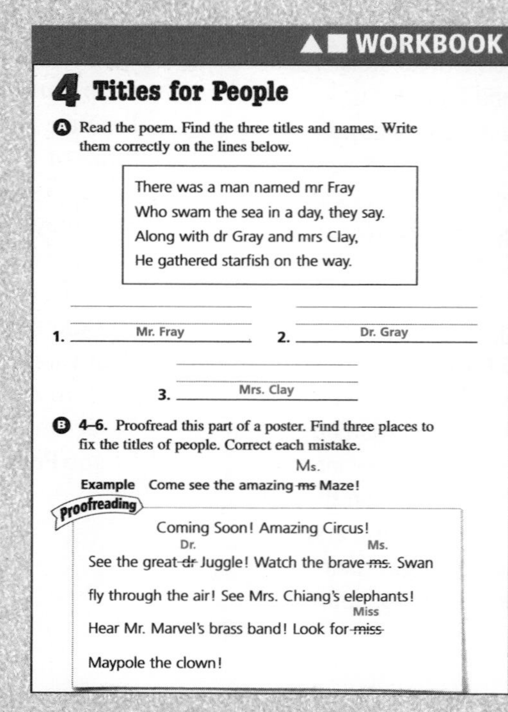

4 Titles for People

A Read the poem. Find the three titles and names. Write them correctly on the lines below.

There was a man named mr Fray
Who swam the sea in a day, they say.
Along with dr Gray and mrs Clay,
He gathered starfish on the way.

1. Mr. Fray
2. Dr. Gray
3. Mrs. Clay

B 4–6. Proofread this part of a poster. Find three places to fix the titles of people. Correct each mistake.

Example Come see the amazing ~~ms~~ Ms. Maze!

Proofreading

Coming Soon! Amazing Circus!
See the great ~~dr~~ Dr. Juggle! Watch the brave ~~ms.~~ Ms. Swan fly through the air! See Mrs. Chiang's elephants! Hear Mr. Marvel's brass band! Look for ~~miss~~ Miss Maypole the clown!

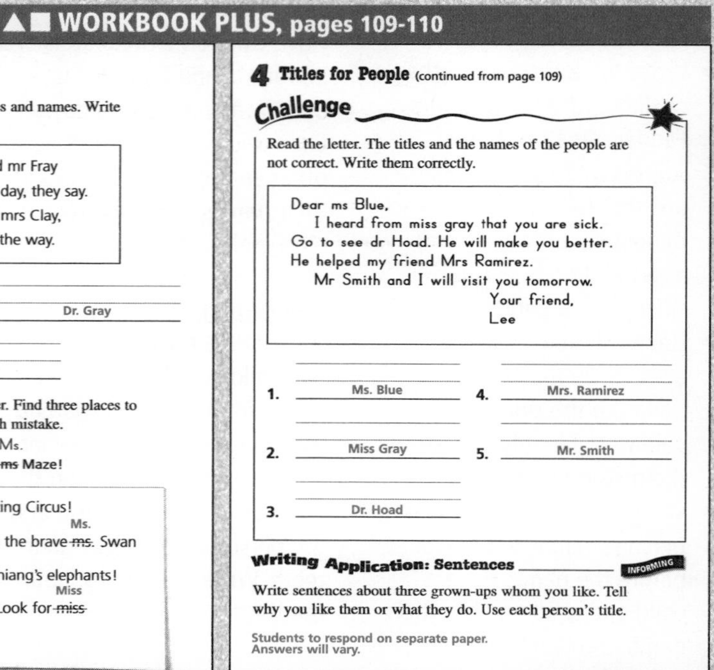

4 Titles for People (continued from page 109)

Challenge

Read the letter. The titles and the names of the people are not correct. Write them correctly.

Dear ms Blue,
I heard from miss gray that you are sick.
Go to see dr Hoad. He will make you better.
He helped my friend Mrs Ramirez.
Mr Smith and I will visit you tomorrow.
Your friend,
Lee

1. Ms. Blue
2. Miss Gray
3. Dr. Hoad
4. Mrs. Ramirez
5. Mr. Smith

Writing Application: Sentences INFORMING

Write sentences about three grown-ups whom you like. Tell why you like them or what they do. Use each person's title.

Students to respond on separate paper. Answers will vary.

Grammar / Mechanics

5 Writing Book Titles

Book lists will vary.

One-Minute Warm-Up

Make a list of your three favorite books. Compare your list with a classmate's list. Are any of the titles the same?

In a **book title**, the first word, the last word, and each important word begin with a **capital letter**. The title is **underlined**. Short words like a, an, and, the, in, for, and at do not begin with a capital letter unless they are the first word in the title.

The book The Cat in the Hat is funny.

I read A Birthday Basket for Tía yesterday.

Try It Out

Speak Up Tell how to make each title correct.

1. abuela
2. frog and toad
3. nate the great

Underline each book title; capitalize the first, last, and each important word in the title.

Write It Now write the book titles correctly.

Example the seashore book
The Seashore Book

Abuela, Frog and Toad, Nate the Great

Meeting Individual Needs

RETEACHING
ALTERNATIVE STRATEGY

- On the chalkboard write: The Tale of Peter Rabbit. Ask which words are capitalized and why. Point out that the entire title is underlined.
- On the chalkboard write: Alexander the Wind-Up Mouse
  goes for a walk
  finds a friend
- Have children choose a phrase to complete the book title. Then have each child design a book jacket using their title. Be sure they capitalize correctly.

CHALLENGE
Have children suppose that they are authors. Ask them to write a list of titles for books they would like to write. Ask them to include a one- or two-line summary for each book.

FOR STUDENTS ACQUIRING ENGLISH
Hold up several books. Call on children to point out the titles and say which words have capital letters.

Writing Book Titles

Lesson Objectives

Children will:

- capitalize the first word, last word, and each important word in a book title
- underline book titles
- proofread for correct capitalization and underlining in book titles
- write an expressive letter to the author of a book

One-Minute Warm-Up Provide books and have children read the titles aloud. Ask children to point out all the capital letters in the titles.

Focus on Instruction

Point out that words such as *and*, *at*, *a*, *for*, *to* and *the* are not capitalized unless they are the first word in a title. Also note that book titles are underlined in text but may not be underlined on the actual book cover.

Try It Out

VIEWING Ask children to suppose that the illustration is the cover of a book. Have them suggest titles for the book. Record their responses on a web. (Sample responses are shown.)

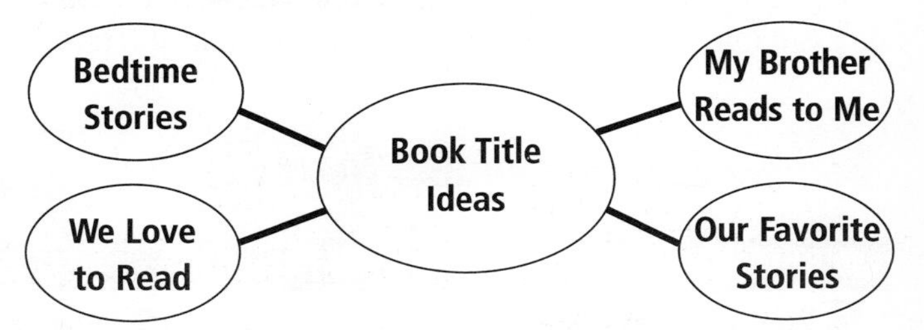

FOR STUDENTS ACQUIRING ENGLISH

- Have children listen to the Try It Out sentences on the audiotape. Distribute SAE Practice page for Unit 9, Lesson 5 to support listening.
- Display several books. Show children how to copy the titles. (Avoid books that have capitals added to prepositions for design reasons.) Say that only important words have capital letters in English titles. Keep in mind that rules for capital letters in titles vary in different languages. For example, Spanish capitalizes only the first word and proper names. Explain that we underline a book title when we write by hand. Show children how to underline the entire title. Children listen and add underlining and capital letters to titles. Example: green eggs and ham (Green Eggs and Ham)

Summing Up Help children summarize these key points about the lesson:

In a **book title** the first word, last word, and each important word begin with a **capital letter**. The title is **underlined**. Short words like *a, an, the, in, for and at* do not begin with a capital letter unless they are the first word in the title.

You may want to have children complete the parts related to this lesson on Blackline Master 9-2.

On Your Own

Children should test each title by reading it aloud and deciding which words are important.

FOR STUDENTS ACQUIRING ENGLISH

Distribute SAE Practice page for Unit 9, Lesson 5. Children find mistakes in book titles and correct them.

1. goldilocks and the three bears (Goldilocks and the Three Bears)
2. curious george (Curious George)

Writing Wrap-Up

Writing Tip: Suggest that children use webs to generate thoughts about the characters, plot, and settings of the books before they begin to write. See Blackline Master 9-7 for a sample letter.

TECHNOLOGY CONNECTION

Children may want to use a prepared letter format on available software to design and write their letters.

On Your Own

Write the correct book title in each pair.

Example My First American Friend My First American Friend
Danny and the dinosaur

1. My Pet Rabbit (circled)
   I'm Growing
2. The great Ball Game
   The Puddle Pail (circled)

3–6. Proofread Antonio's letter. Find four mistakes with book titles. Copy the letter and write the titles correctly.

Example Mr. Putter and Tabby Take the train
Mr. Putter and Tabby Take the Train

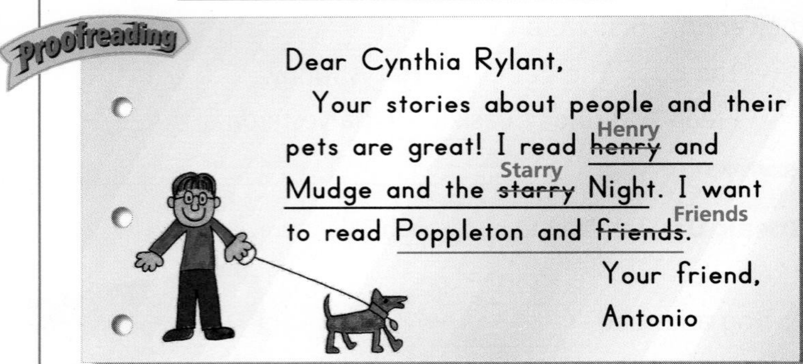
Proofreading

Dear Cynthia Rylant,

Your stories about people and their pets are great! I read ~~henry~~ Henry and Mudge and the ~~starry~~ Starry Night. I want to read Poppleton and ~~friends~~ Friends.

Your friend,
Antonio

Writing Wrap-Up

WRITING • THINKING • LISTENING • SPEAKING

EXPRESSING

Write a Letter

Write a letter to the author of a book you have read. Tell why you liked the book. Read your letter to a classmate. Work together to check that you wrote the book titles correctly.

Letters will vary.

For Extra Practice, see page 334.

Meeting Individual Needs

● RETEACHING WORKBOOK, page 73

5 Writing Book Titles

Begin the first word, the last word, and each important word in a book title with a capital letter. Draw a line under the title.

My favorite book is Make Way for Ducklings.

Write the correct book titles.

Example King of the cats King of the Cats
King of the Cats

1. One Morning in Maine one morning in Maine
   One Morning in Maine
2. Whistle for Willie Whistle for Willie
   Whistle for Willie
3. Green Eggs and ham Green Eggs and Ham
   Green Eggs and Ham
4. William's Doll William's Doll
   William's Doll

▲■ WORKBOOK PLUS, pages 111-112

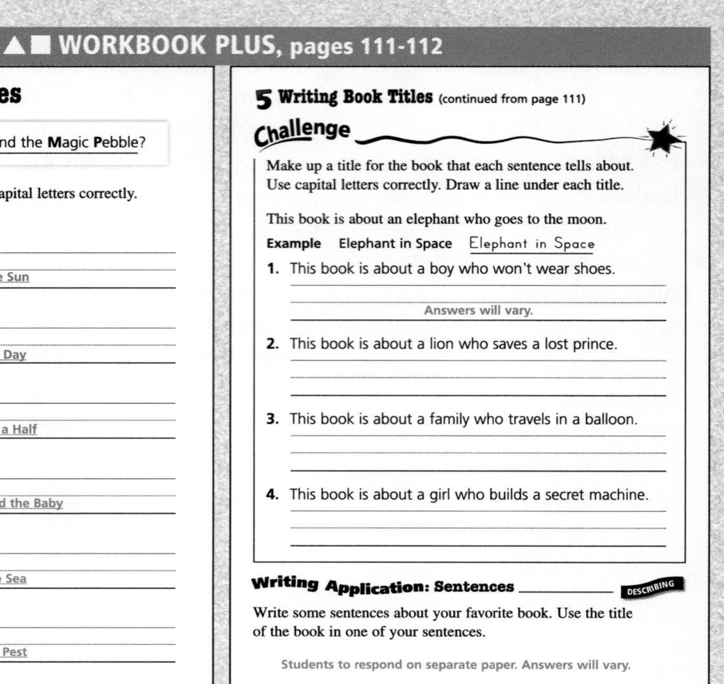

5 Writing Book Titles

Have you read Sylvester and the Magic Pebble?

Write these book titles correctly. Use capital letters correctly. Draw a line under each title.

1. arrow to the sun
   Arrow to the Sun
2. a three hat day
   A Three Hat Day
3. a giraffe and a half
   A Giraffe and a Half
4. amelia bedelia and the baby
   Amelia Bedelia and the Baby
5. three by the sea
   Three by the Sea
6. ramona the pest
   Ramona the Pest

5 Writing Book Titles (continued from page 111)

Challenge

Make up a title for the book that each sentence tells about. Use capital letters correctly. Draw a line under each title.

This book is about an elephant who goes to the moon.

Example Elephant in Space Elephant in Space

1. This book is about a boy who won't wear shoes.
   Answers will vary.
2. This book is about a lion who saves a lost prince.
3. This book is about a family who travels in a balloon.
4. This book is about a girl who builds a secret machine.

Writing Application: Sentences DESCRIBING

Write some sentences about your favorite book. Use the title of the book in one of your sentences.

Students to respond on separate paper. Answers will vary.

Grammar / Mechanics

6 Ending Sentences

Responses will vary.

Look at these end marks. Say a sentence that ends with each mark.

A question ends with a **question mark**. An exclamation ends with an **exclamation point**. A command and a telling sentence end with a **period**.

Can we go fishing? Clean your room first.

That is a great idea! I will make lunch.

Try It Out

Speak Up Tell what kind of sentence each group of words is. Name the end mark that should be used.

1. Line up the turtles (command, period)
2. My turtle is faster (telling sentence, period)
3. Will it win the race (question, question mark)
4. Hooray, my turtle won (exclamation, exclamation point)

Write It Write each sentence. Add the correct end mark.

Example I have a small turtle I have a small turtle.

5. Your turtle is huge Your turtle is huge!
6. What does it eat What does it eat?

Ending Sentences

Lesson Objectives

Children will:

- end telling sentences with periods
- end questions with question marks
- proofread for correct end marks of sentences
- write and identify different kinds of sentences

One-Minute Warm-Up Write children's responses on the board. Have volunteers locate and identify each end mark.

Focus on Instruction

Remind children that all sentences begin with a capital letter and that every sentence tells a complete thought.

Try It Out

VIEWING Refer children to the illustration. Have them suggest things the two turtles might say to one another. Record their responses in a chart. (Sample responses are shown.)

Turtle #5	Turtle #7
That is the biggest turtle I have ever seen!	I have seen a bigger turtle.
Is that your number?	This is my favorite number.

Meeting Individual Needs

RETEACHING
ALTERNATIVE STRATEGY

- Write one telling sentence and one question on the board. Ask which sentence is a question and why. (It asks something and ends with a question mark.) Ask why the other sentence is a telling sentence. (It tells something and ends with a period.)
- Draw turtles on the chalkboard and write a word in each such as, *What, turtle, it, ran, race, Where, Which* and *won.* Have children choose words to use in telling and asking sentences. Write the sentences on the chalkboard and have volunteers add end marks. Continue with commands and exclamations.

CHALLENGE
Have partners act like characters from their favorite book or movie. Ask them to write interview questions for each other. Have interviewees take turns writing their answers.

FOR STUDENTS ACQUIRING ENGLISH
Make a period, a question mark, and an exclamation point on the board. Ask what these are called and what they are used for. Ask volunteers for example sentences for each.

FOR STUDENTS ACQUIRING ENGLISH

- Have children listen to the Try It Out sentences on the audiotape. Distribute SAE Practice page for Unit 9, Lesson 6 to support listening. 
- Help children suggest sentences about the art in the book and on the Practice page. Ask, *What are these animals called? What are they doing? Who do you think will win?* Ask children what mark to use with a question. Then ask what to use with an exclamation such as *Ouch* or *Hi*. Finally, ask what to use at the end of other sentences. Make sure children know that we don't use these marks at the beginning, only at the end (in contrast to Spanish, for example). Children listen and tell what type of sentence each is and what end mark is needed. Example: Do you have a turtle (question, ?)

Summing Up Help children summarize these key points about the lesson:

A telling sentence and a command end with a **period**. A question ends with a **question mark**. An exclamation ends with an **exclamation point**.

You may want to have children complete the parts related to this lesson on Blackline Master 9-3.

On Your Own

Have children test each sentence by reading it quietly to themselves and listening to their inflection.

FOR STUDENTS ACQUIRING ENGLISH

Distribute SAE Practice page for Unit 9, Lesson 6. Explain what a tongue twister is. Write *She sells seashells by the seashore.* Have children read it along with you. Then children listen and write each sentence adding the end mark. Example: Tommy Turtle tripped Tammy Tomato twice (Tommy Turtle tripped Tammy Tomato twice!)

Writing Wrap-Up

Writing Tip: Suggest that children use a dictionary to get ideas for words with the same beginning letters. See Blackline Master 9-7 for sample tongue twisters.

SCHOOL-HOME CONNECTION
Have children work with a family member to write additional tongue twisters for each kind of sentence they have studied.

On Your Own

Write each sentence. Add the correct end mark.

Example I am so excited I am so excited!

1. We drive to the city
We drive to the city.
2. When will we get there
When will we get there?

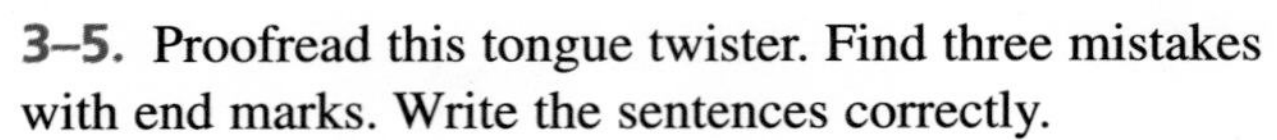

3–5. Proofread this tongue twister. Find three mistakes with end marks. Write the sentences correctly.

Example Sue sees some lights? Sue sees some lights.

Proofreading

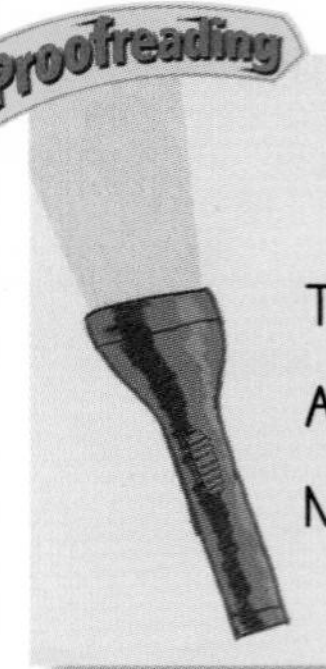

Mike likes nice bright lights?.
Turn on Mike's bright lights.
Are Mike's lights bright at night.?
Mike's lights are too bright!

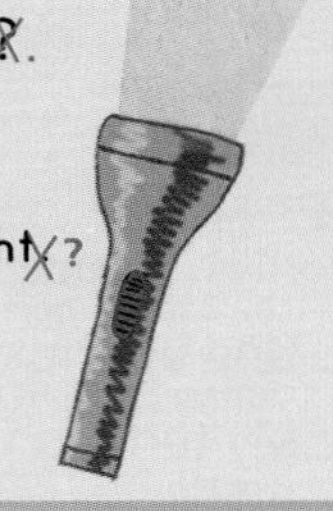

Writing Wrap-Up

WRITING • THINKING • LISTENING • SPEAKING

CREATING

Write Tongue Twisters

Write two kinds of sentences. Repeat letter sounds in the words you use. For example, Snakes slither slowly. Does Dan dance? Read your tongue twisters aloud. Have classmates say each one and tell what kind of sentence it is.

Tongue twisters will vary.

 For Extra Practice, see page 335.

Meeting Individual Needs

● RETEACHING WORKBOOK, page 74

6 Ending Sentences

A telling sentence ends with a period.
Those blue flowers are pretty.
A question ends with a question mark.
Did someone plant them there?

I planted them.

Write the correct end mark for each sentence. Write **Q** after each question. Write **T** after each telling sentence.

Example How do flowers make new plants? Q

1. Some flowers make seeds . T
2. Do the seeds fall to the ground ? Q
3. Rain and sun make the seeds grow . T
4. Do birds carry flower seeds ? Q
5. Birds drop the seeds in new places . T
6. Do other animals carry seeds ? Q

▲■ WORKBOOK PLUS, pages 113-114

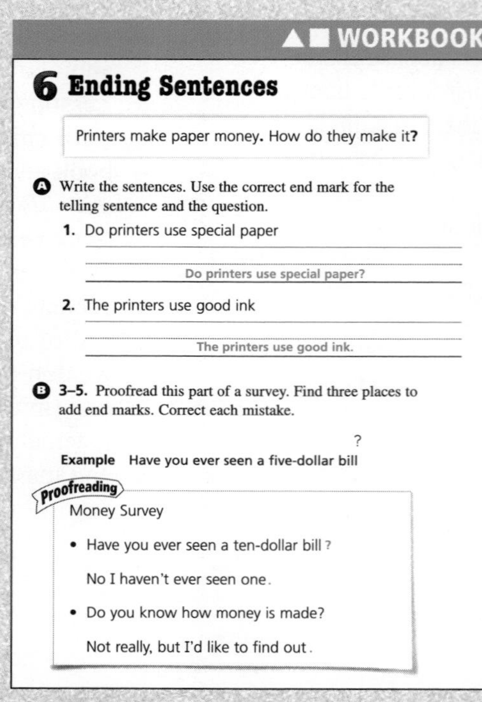

6 Ending Sentences

Printers make paper money. How do they make it?

A Write the sentences. Use the correct end mark for the telling sentence and the question.

1. Do printers use special paper
Do printers use special paper?
2. The printers use good ink
The printers use good ink.

B 3–5. Proofread this part of a survey. Find three places to add end marks. Correct each mistake.

Example Have you ever seen a five-dollar bill ?

Proofreading

Money Survey

- Have you ever seen a ten-dollar bill ?
No I haven't ever seen one.
- Do you know how money is made?
Not really, but I'd like to find out.

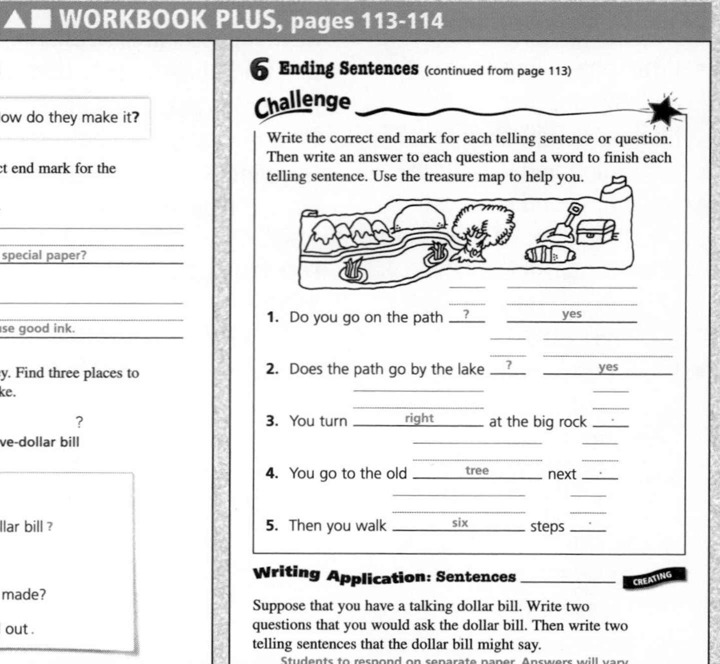

6 Ending Sentences (continued from page 113)

Challenge

Write the correct end mark for each telling sentence or question. Then write an answer to each question and a word to finish each telling sentence. Use the treasure map to help you.

1. Do you go on the path ? yes
2. Does the path go by the lake ? yes
3. You turn right at the big rock .
4. You go to the old tree next .
5. Then you walk six steps .

Writing Application: Sentences CREATING

Suppose that you have a talking dollar bill. Write two questions that you would ask the dollar bill. Then write two telling sentences that the dollar bill might say.

Students to respond on separate paper. Answers will vary.

Revising Strategies | Sentence Fluency

Writing Correct Sentences

Fixing Run-on Sentences A **run-on sentence** is really two sentences that should not be joined together. Turn a run-on sentence into two shorter sentences. Use **capital letters** and **end marks** correctly.

Wrong: Dad looks up he sees stars.

Right: Dad looks up. He sees stars.

Try It Out

Speak Up/Write It Read the run-on sentences. Turn each one into two shorter sentences. Say the two sentences. Then write them correctly.

Example Sam looks at the sky the stars make pictures.
Sam looks at the sky. The stars make pictures.

Seven stars make a picture. They look like a big spoon.
1–2. Seven stars make a picture they look like a big spoon.

Three stars shine brightly. They make a belt.
3–4. Three stars shine brightly they make a belt.

Writing Correct Sentences

Lesson Objective

Children will:
- fix run-on sentences

Focus on Instruction

- Begin by pointing out that good sentences make sense. Explain that long sentences can be confusing. Tell children that sometimes it is a good idea to break one long sentence into two shorter ones.
- Read the example aloud without pausing. Then read the next example, being sure to pause between sentences. Ask children to say which example is easier to understand.
- Ask children to provide a few examples of sentences that have too many naming and action parts.

Try It Out

SPEAK UP/WRITE IT Go over the example with the class. Ask volunteers to say how many naming parts and action parts are in the sentence and to identify them. (2 each)

- Have children say the sentences aloud, pausing where they think the first sentence should end.
- Be sure children use correct capital letters and end marks when they write their sentences.

Meeting Individual Needs

● RETEACHING WORKBOOK, page 75

Writing Correct Sentences

Use capital letters and end marks to fix run-on sentences.
Wrong: The dishes are dirty we will wash them.
Right: The dishes are dirty. We will wash them.

Fixing Run-on Sentences Draw a line under the sentences that are correct. Write the correct sentences.

Example We sweep we help Mom. We sweep. We help Mom.
We sweep. We help Mom.

1. Everyone helps clean those are the house rules.
Everyone helps clean. Those are the house rules.
Everyone helps clean. Those are the house rules.
2. Jay and I like to dust. We think it is fun.
Jay and I like to dust we think it is fun.
Jay and I like to dust. We think it is fun.
3. We sneeze a lot. It makes us laugh.
We sneeze a lot it makes us laugh.
We sneeze a lot. It makes us laugh.
4. Our house is clean we all work together.
Our house is clean. We all work together.
Our house is clean. We all work together.

▲■ WORKBOOK PLUS, page 115

Writing Correct Sentences

Wrong: Trees are important we need trees.
Right: Trees are important. We need trees.

Fixing Run-on Sentences 1-5. Find the run-on sentences. Turn them into shorter sentences. Write the new paragraph.

Trees do so many things for us. They give us shade they give us fruit to eat. Trees are homes for animals they are homes for birds. Trees also give us wood to build our homes the wood also keeps us warm. We should take care of our trees trees take care of us.

Trees do so many things for us. They give us shade. They give us fruit to eat. Trees are homes for animals. They are homes for birds. Trees give us wood to build our homes. The wood also keeps us warm. We should take care of our trees. Trees take care of us.

Writing Correct Sentences

Apply It

- Have children read the example. Talk about how the two sentences are easier to understand than the one longer sentence.
- Have children complete the revising activity independently. Remind them to capitalize the first word of each sentence and to use correct end marks.

Have children find places in their own writing in progress where they can make two sentences from one long sentence.

FOR STUDENTS ACQUIRING ENGLISH

As children learn to combine nouns, verbs, and adjectives, they may also combine sentences. Review the definition of a sentence, then practice sentence separation by asking children to draw each idea, making a new sentence for each new idea. Use the model and then your own run-on sentences for children to separate.

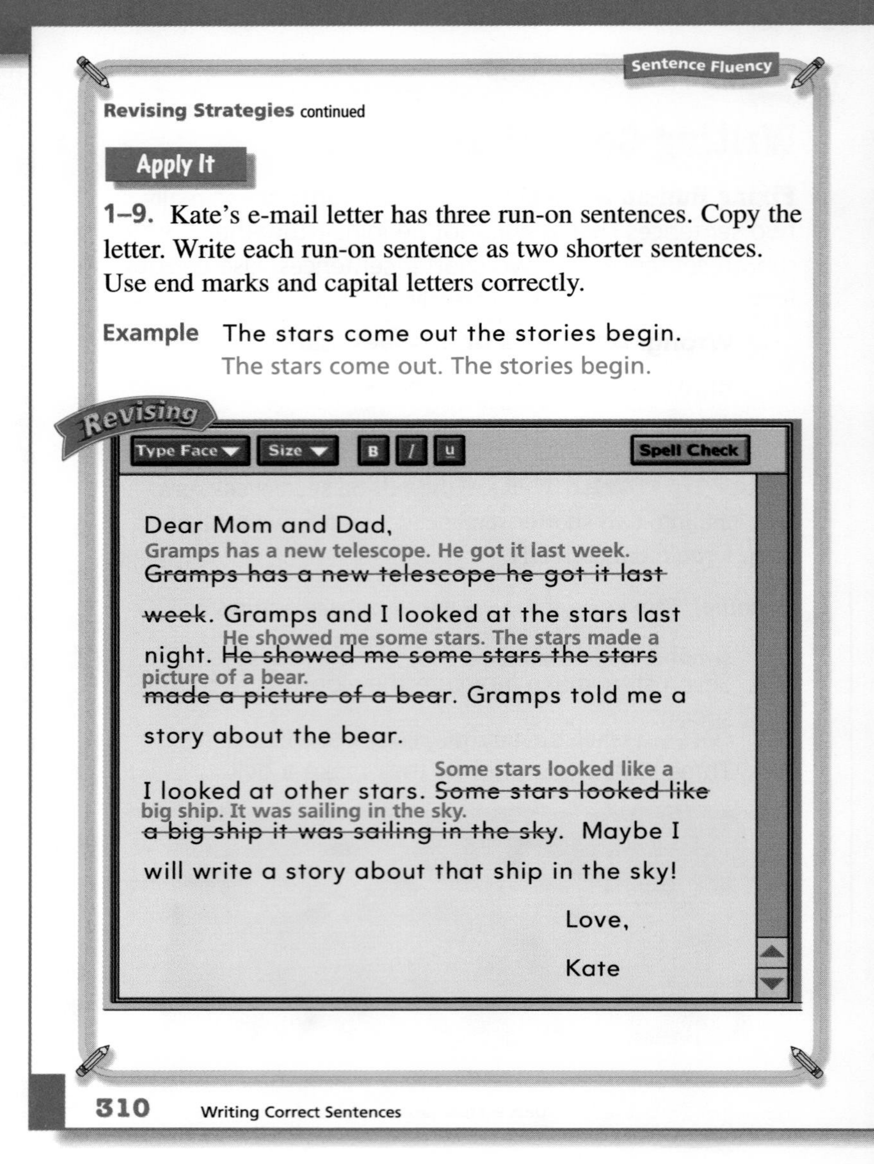

Sentence Fluency

Revising Strategies continued

Apply It

1–9. Kate's e-mail letter has three run-on sentences. Copy the letter. Write each run-on sentence as two shorter sentences. Use end marks and capital letters correctly.

Example The stars come out the stories begin.
The stars come out. The stories begin.

Revising

Type Face Size B I U Spell Check

Dear Mom and Dad,
Gramps has a new telescope. He got it last week.
~~Gramps has a new telescope he got it last week~~. Gramps and I looked at the stars last night. He showed me some stars. The stars made a picture of a bear.
~~He showed me some stars the stars made a picture of a bear~~. Gramps told me a story about the bear.

I looked at other stars. Some stars looked like a big ship. It was sailing in the sky.
~~Some stars looked like a big ship it was sailing in the sky~~. Maybe I will write a story about that ship in the sky!

Love,
Kate

310 Writing Correct Sentences

Meeting Individual Needs

● RETEACHING WORKBOOK, page 76

Writing Correct Sentences

To fix a run-on sentence, use capital letters and end marks correctly.

Wrong: The car trip was long it was five hours.
Right: The car trip was long. **I**t was five hours.

Fixing Run-on Sentences Read the run-on sentences. Decide where to put end marks and capital letters. Write the new sentences.

Example We were hot the car was stuffy.
We were hot. The car was stuffy.

1. The beach was far away we were bored.
   The beach was far away. We were bored.
2. Mom started to sing she said we could sing too.
   Mom started to sing. She said we could sing too.
3. We forgot about the hot car we had fun.
   We forgot about the hot car. We had fun.
4. We got to the beach we were still singing!
   We got to the beach. We were still singing!

▲■ WORKBOOK PLUS, page 116

Writing Correct Sentences

Wrong: Wanda swims every day she loves the water.
Right: Wanda swims every day. She loves the water.

Fixing Run-on Sentences Find the run-on sentences. Turn them into shorter sentences. Write the new sentences.

Wanda is always ready to jump in the pool. She likes to dive from the low board it is easier. Then she swims back and forth it is hard work. Once a week she takes lessons her teacher is very nice. Wanda will swim in a contest next week she will have a good time.

1. She likes to dive from the low board. It is easier.
2. Then she swims back and forth. It is hard work.
3. Once a week she takes lessons. Her teacher is very nice.
4. Wanda will swim in a contest next week. She will have a good time.

Grammar / Mechanics

7 Commas in Dates

One-Minute Warm-Up

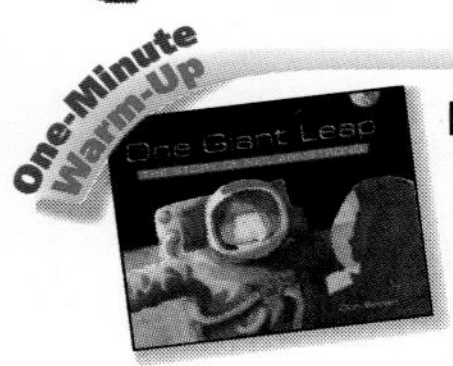

Neil Armstrong walked on the moon. When was he born?

Neil had been born in the living room of his grandparents' nearby farm on August 5, 1930.

—from One Giant Leap: The Story of Neil Armstrong, by Don Brown

August 5, 1930

Every day has a date. A **date** tells the month, the number of the day, and the year. A **comma** (,) is used between the number of the day and the year.

Ali was born February 21**,** 1995.

She started school on September 2**,** 2000.

Try It Out

Speak Up Read each date. Tell where a comma belongs.

1. May 5 2000 after 5
2. June 30 2001 after 30
3. March 24 2002 after 24
4. April 7 2004 after 7

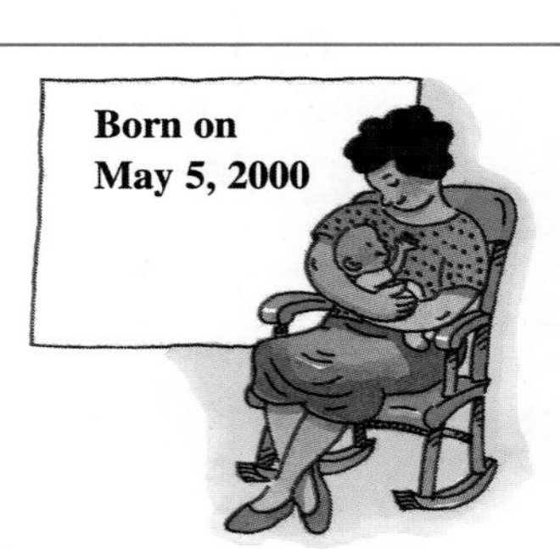

Write It Write the dates correctly.

Example November 23 1999 November 23, 1999

May 5, 2000, June 30, 2001, March 24, 2002, April 7, 2004

Meeting Individual Needs

RETEACHING
ALTERNATIVE STRATEGY

- Make cards with a month, a number from 1 to 30 followed by a comma, or a year written on them. Make one card for each child and put the cards in a bag.
- Write a date on the chalkboard, such as June 10, 2001. Point out the month, and the comma after the date, which separates the number from the year.
- Have each child choose a card. Tell them that they each have one part of a date and must find two classmates who have the other parts. When three parts of a date are found, have children arrange themselves in the correct order.

CHALLENGE
Help children calculate how old they will be in the year 2015. Ask them to write a story about what they would like to be doing on the date June 1, 2015. Tell them to include the date several times in their stories.

FOR STUDENTS ACQUIRING ENGLISH
Review the months of the year. Children can take turns naming and spelling the months in order; or ask questions such as *What is the first month of the year? In what month is Mother's Day?* Then have children dictate the months to each other.

Commas in Dates

Lesson Objectives

Children will:

- recognize that a date includes a day, month, and year
- use a comma in dates between the day and the year
- proofread for correct usage of commas in dates
- write informative sentences for a yearbook that includes dates

One-Minute Warm-Up Write the quoted sentence on the board. Have volunteers identify the date and tell the parts they recognize.

Focus on Instruction

Remind children that a comma appears only between the day and the year and not between the month and the day. Point out that the year is listed last in a date.

Try It Out

LISTENING AND SPEAKING Have children practice reading the dates. Model how to pause at the comma. Ask others to listen for the pause and then raise their hands when they hear the year.

MEETING INDIVIDUAL NEEDS

FOR STUDENTS ACQUIRING ENGLISH

- Have children listen to the Try It Out sentences on the audiotape. Distribute SAE Practice page for Unit 9, Lesson 7 to support listening.
- Help children suggest sentences about the art in the book. Write today's date. Call on children to mark the month, day, and year with different colors of chalk. Have another circle the comma. Note that the order of elements and the way dates are read differ in other languages. Model how to read dates in English, noting the days (which are ordinals) and years (which are read mainly in pairs). Practice saying dates with children. Next ask each child to write and say when he or she was born. Children listen and add commas to dates.
  Example: July 4 1776 (July 4, 1776)

Summing Up Help children summarize these key points about the lesson:

> Every day has a date. A **date** tells the month, the number of the day, and the year. A **comma** (,) is used between the number of the day and the year.

You may want to have children complete the parts related to this lesson on Blackline Master 9-4.

On Your Own

Have children test the items by looking for each component of each date: the month, day, and year.

FOR STUDENTS ACQUIRING ENGLISH

Distribute SAE Practice page for Unit 9, Lesson 7. Explain to children what a time line is. Then tell children to complete the sentences with dates from their own lives. Help children with actual dates where possible.

1. I was born on ______. (Answers will vary.)
2. School will end on ______. (Answers will vary.)

Writing Wrap-Up

Writing Tip: Suggest that children list class events. They can list the events in chronological sequence after they have written them all down. See Blackline Master 9-7 for a sample class events page.

TECHNOLOGY CONNECTION

Children may wish to use the cut and paste feature to organize their class events lists.

On Your Own

Write each sentence, using the correct date.

Example Tim was born on ______.
Tim was born on October 2, 1993.

1. I was born on ______. *Answers will vary.*
2. Today is ______. *Answers will vary.*

3–5. Proofread these events for Juanita's time line. Find three mistakes with commas in dates. Write each sentence and date correctly.

Example I lost my first tooth on May, 6 1998.
I lost my first tooth on May 6, 1998.

Proofreading

Time Line Events

I was born on June 22, 1992.
I moved to Austin on August,5, 1996.
I started school on August 28, 1997.
My first day at camp was July 13, 1998.

Writing Wrap-Up

WRITING • THINKING • LISTENING • SPEAKING

INFORMING

Write a Page for a Class Yearbook

Work with your class to make a chart of names and dates of class events this year. Then write a page about yourself. Include class events you enjoyed and their dates. Draw your picture. Have classmates check commas in dates.
Sentences will vary.

312 Commas in Dates For Extra Practice, see page 336.

Meeting Individual Needs

● RETEACHING WORKBOOK, page 77

7 Commas in Dates

A **date** tells a month, a day, and a year. Use a **comma (,)** between the day and the year in a date.
Eva was born February 2, 1982.

Write the correct date.

Example March 7, 1990 March 7 1990 *March 7, 1990*

1. September, 18 1955 September 18, 1955 — *September 18, 1955*
2. July 12, 1979 July 12 1979 — *July 12, 1979*
3. August 4, 1985 August, 4 1985 — *August 4, 1985*
4. June 28 1983 June 28, 1983 — *June 28, 1983*
5. January 21 2005 January 21, 2005 — *January 21, 2005*

▲■ WORKBOOK PLUS, pages 117-118

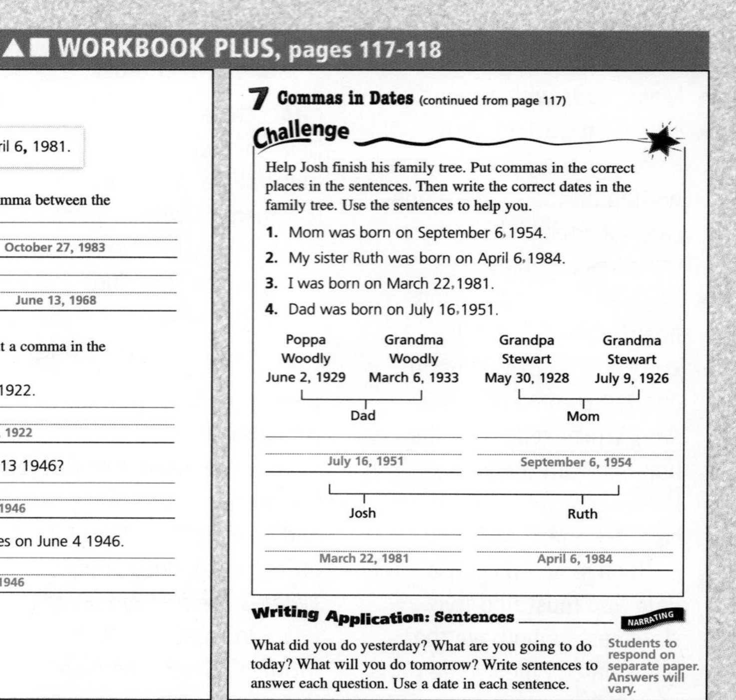

7 Commas in Dates

Louise was born April 6, 1981.

A Write each date correctly. Use a comma between the day and the year.

1. October 27 1983 — *October 27, 1983*
2. June 13 1968 — *June 13, 1968*

B Write the date in each sentence. Put a comma in the correct place.

3. Gram was born on August 2 1922. — *August 2, 1922*
4. Did she leave Greece on May 13 1946? — *May 13,1946*
5. She arrived in the United States on June 4 1946. — *June 4, 1946*

7 Commas in Dates (continued from page 117)

Challenge

Help Josh finish his family tree. Put commas in the correct places in the sentences. Then write the correct dates in the family tree. Use the sentences to help you.

1. Mom was born on September 6, 1954.
2. My sister Ruth was born on April 6, 1984.
3. I was born on March 22, 1981.
4. Dad was born on July 16, 1951.

Poppa Woodly June 2, 1929 — Grandma Woodly March 6, 1933 — Grandpa Stewart May 30, 1928 — Grandma Stewart July 9, 1926

Dad *July 16, 1951* — Mom *September 6, 1954*

Josh *March 22, 1981* — Ruth *April 6, 1984*

Writing Application: Sentences NARRATING

What did you do yesterday? What are you going to do today? What will you do tomorrow? Write sentences to answer each question. Use a date in each sentence.

Students to respond on separate paper. Answers will vary.

Grammar / Mechanics

8 Commas with Names of Places

List cities or towns and states that you know or would like to visit. Start with the name of the place where you live now. Can you find each place on a map?
Answers will vary.

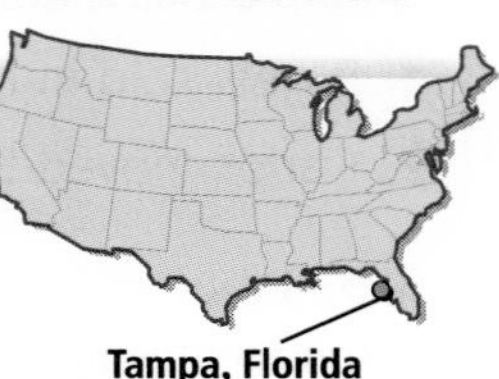

Use a **comma** (**,**) between the name of a **city** or **town** and the name of a **state**.

We watched fireworks in Miami**,** Florida.

We went to a fair in Tyler**,** Texas.

Try It Out

Speak Up Read each place name. Tell where a comma belongs.

1. Lima Ohio — between *Lima* and *Ohio*
2. Portland Maine — between *Portland* and *Maine*
3. Waco Texas — between *Waco* and *Texas*

Write It Now write the names of the cities and states correctly.

Example Logan Utah Logan, Utah

Lima, Ohio
Portland, Maine
Waco, Texas

Meeting Individual Needs

RETEACHING
ALTERNATIVE STRATEGY

- Write the name of your city and state on the chalkboard. Ask what mark always goes between the name of the city and state (a comma) and what words always begin with a capital (names and places such as cities and states).
- Have children choose a city they would like to visit and draw a picture postcard for that place. Help them to spell the name of the city and state correctly and ask them to write it on their postcard. Have them point out the commas on each postcard.

CHALLENGE
Give partners road maps of your state. Have children choose cities they would like to visit and write sentences telling what they think each place is like. Tell them to name the city and the state in each sentence.

FOR STUDENTS ACQUIRING ENGLISH
Ask children what city or town and what state you live in. Write the answer on the board. Note the comma between the city and state. Ask children for names of other places they have lived. List them on the board, again noting commas.

Commas with Names of Places

Lesson Objectives

Children will:

- use a comma between the names of a city and a state
- proofread for correct usage of commas in the names of places
- write a descriptive paragraph about a place using commas

One-Minute Warm-Up List children's responses on the chalkboard. Read them aloud in a rhythm that highlights the pause at the commas. Have volunteers circle all the commas.

Focus on Instruction

To reinforce the concept of city and state, have children identify the city and the state in each item.

Try It Out

VIEWING Have children write questions and answers about the place named on the sign in the illustration. Record their responses in a chart. (Sample responses are shown.)

Questions	Answers
What is the weather like in Houston, Texas?	The weather can be very warm in Houston, Texas.
How many miles from my house is Houston, Texas?	My house is 800 miles from Houston, Texas.

FOR STUDENTS ACQUIRING ENGLISH

- Have children listen to the Try It Out sentences on the audiotape. Distribute SAE Practice page for Unit 9, Lesson 8 to support listening.
- Help children suggest sentences about the art in the book and on the Practice page. Make sure children understand that a comma appears between the city and state or the city and country as in *Houston, Texas* or *Tokyo, Japan*. Be prepared to help children locate all the places in this lesson on a map of the United States. Also help children pronounce the names of the cities and states in this lesson. Children listen and read the place names, saying where the comma belongs.
  1. New York New York (New York, New York)
  2. San Antonio Texas (San Antonio, Texas)

Summing Up Help children summarize these key points about the lesson:

Use a **comma** (,) between the name of a **city** or **town** and the name of a **state**.

You may want to have children complete the parts related to this lesson on Blackline Master 9-4.

On Your Own

Explain that a comma helps to separate words. The comma between a city or town and its state helps readers know that two separate places are being named.

FOR STUDENTS ACQUIRING ENGLISH

Distribute SAE Practice page for Unit 9, Lesson 8. Children listen and add commas to place names in sentences.

1. Samantha was born in Eugene Oregon. (Eugene, Oregon)
2. Her family moved to Jonesboro Arkansas. (Jonesboro, Arkansas)

Writing Wrap-Up

Writing Tip: Suggest that children make clusters of describing words for the place they will write about. Have them list the name of the place in the center circle and describing words in the smaller circles. See Blackline Master 9-7 for a sample paragraph.

SCHOOL-HOME CONNECTION

Have children interview a family member about the city and state where that person was born or lived.

On Your Own

Write each sentence. Put a comma in the correct place.

Example Nell is from Mesa Arizona. Nell is from Mesa, Arizona.

1. It gets cold in Nome Alaska. **Nome, Alaska**
2. Carlos moved to Salem Oregon. **Salem, Oregon**

3–5. Proofread this road sign. Find three mistakes with commas in place names. Write the sign correctly.

Example Boise Idaho 1711 miles
Boise, Idaho 1711 miles

Proofreading

Miles from Chicago, Illinois

Detroit, Michigan	279 miles
San Antonio, Texas	1209 miles
Miami, Florida	1397 miles

Writing Wrap-Up

WRITING • THINKING • LISTENING • SPEAKING

DESCRIBING

Write a Paragraph

Write about where you live. Include the name of your town or city and state. Tell what you can see and do there. Read your paragraph to a classmate. Have the classmate check that you have used commas correctly with names of places.

Paragraphs will vary.

314 Commas with Names of Places For Extra Practice, see page 337.

Meeting Individual Needs

● RETEACHING WORKBOOK, page 78

8 Commas with Names of Places

Use a comma between the name of a city and the name of a state.

Daniel goes to camp in Camden, Maine.

Daniel Lee
Camp Windblown
Camden, Maine 04843

Write each underlined city and state correctly. Put a comma in the correct place.

Example Daniel lives in Detroit Michigan. Detroit, Michigan.

1. Joey comes to camp from Omaha Nebraska. Omaha, Nebraska
2. Joey travels through Chicago Illinois. Chicago, Illinois
3. Mary comes from Richmond Virginia. Richmond, Virginia
4. Mary rides on a train from Baltimore Maryland. Baltimore, Maryland

▲■ WORKBOOK PLUS, pages 119-120

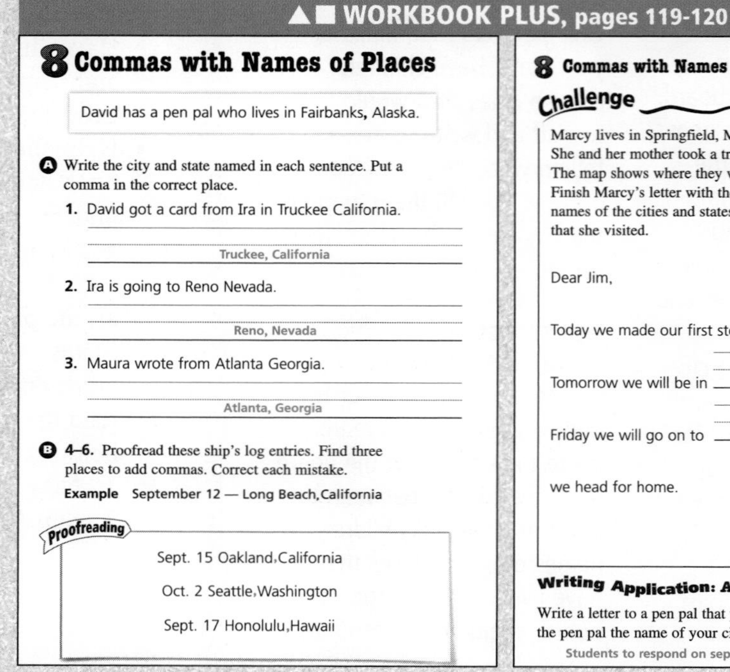

8 Commas with Names of Places

David has a pen pal who lives in Fairbanks, Alaska.

A Write the city and state named in each sentence. Put a comma in the correct place.

1. David got a card from Ira in Truckee California. Truckee, California
2. Ira is going to Reno Nevada. Reno, Nevada
3. Maura wrote from Atlanta Georgia. Atlanta, Georgia

B 4–6. Proofread these ship's log entries. Find three places to add commas. Correct each mistake.

Example September 12 — Long Beach, California

Proofreading

Sept. 15 Oakland, California
Oct. 2 Seattle, Washington
Sept. 17 Honolulu, Hawaii

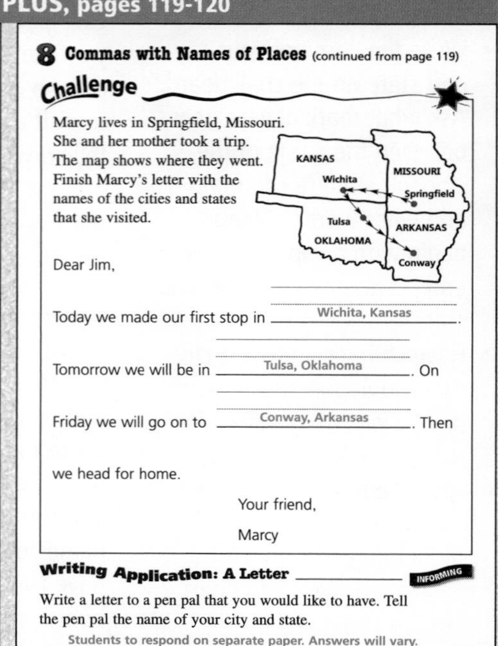

8 Commas with Names of Places (continued from page 119)

Challenge

Marcy lives in Springfield, Missouri. She and her mother took a trip. The map shows where they went. Finish Marcy's letter with the names of the cities and states that she visited.

Dear Jim,

Today we made our first stop in Wichita, Kansas. Tomorrow we will be in Tulsa, Oklahoma. On Friday we will go on to Conway, Arkansas. Then we head for home.

Your friend,
Marcy

Writing Application: A Letter INFORMING

Write a letter to a pen pal that you would like to have. Tell the pen pal the name of your city and state.

Students to respond on separate paper. Answers will vary.

Grammar / Mechanics

9 Quotation Marks

One-Minute Warm-Up

Look at the picture. Say something funny that the porcupine might say if it could talk.
Sample response: "Cactus, stick by me."

When you write, show what someone says by putting **quotation marks** (" ") at the beginning and end of the speaker's exact words.

Rosa said, "I know a joke."

Juan asked, "What is the joke about?"

Try It Out

Speak Up Read each person's exact words. Tell where quotation marks belong.

1. Rosa said, I like joke books. "I like joke books."
2. Juan asked, Where can I get one? "Where can I get one?"

Write It Now write the sentences correctly.

Example Juan said, That is a funny joke.
Juan said, "That is a funny joke."

Rosa said, "I like joke books."
Juan asked, "Where can I get one?"

Meeting Individual Needs

RETEACHING
ALTERNATIVE STRATEGY

- Use a familiar storybook to point out quotation marks. Have volunteers read aloud a paragraph or two that contains dialogue. Help them to see that tags such as *she said* help indicate words that belong in quotation marks.
- Point out that quotation marks help readers to know when someone is talking. Explain that in a story, speech gives information in a way that is different from narration.

CHALLENGE
Have partners hold a short conversation about something fun they have recently done. Partners can write down what each person says in quotation marks.

FOR STUDENTS ACQUIRING ENGLISH
Tell children that the animal shown in the Warm-Up is a porcupine. With the children, write possible lines of dialogue for this art. For example, *Mr. Porcupine said, "Don't touch me!"* Point out the quotation marks.

Quotation Marks

Lesson Objectives

Children will:

- use quotation marks
- proofread for correct usage of quotation marks
- write a dialogue using quotation marks

One-Minute Warm-Up Have volunteers suggest dialogue while you list their responses with quotation marks on the board.

Focus on Instruction

Point out that the placement of quotation marks is near the tops of letters, unlike the comma which comes near the bottom of letters.

Try It Out

LISTENING AND SPEAKING Have volunteers read aloud the sentences. Model how to make the 'in quotes' sign with their fingers. Have listeners make this sign as they repeat the words that belong in quotes in each sentence.

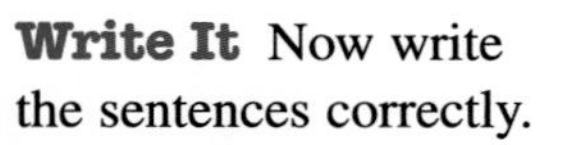

FOR STUDENTS ACQUIRING ENGLISH

- Have children listen to the Try It Out sentences on the audiotape. Distribute SAE Practice page for Unit 9, Lesson 9 to support listening. 
- Help children suggest sentences about the art in the book and on the Practice page. Explain to children that when they plan dialogues or conversations, they are writing what people will say. Point out that the verbs that are used most often in dialogues are *said* and *asked*. Ask which of the two would be used for questions. Children listen and say where to put the quotation marks. Later, have children read the lines in pairs.
  1. Nora asked, Do you like jokes? (Nora asked, "Do you like jokes?")
  2. Randy said, Yes, I do. (Randy said, "Yes, I do.")

Summing Up Help children summarize these key points about the lesson:

When you write, show what someone says by putting **quotation marks** at the beginning and end of their exact words.

You may want to have children complete the parts related to this lesson on Blackline Master 9-5.

On Your Own

Have children read the sentences quietly to themselves. Direct them to look for words that give clues as to who is speaking, such as *said* and *asked*.

FOR STUDENTS ACQUIRING ENGLISH

Distribute SAE Practice page for Unit 9, Lesson 9. Children write each sentence, adding quotation marks.

1. I asked, Where did you put my book? (I asked, "Where did you put my book?")
2. John said, I don't have your book. (John said, "I don't have your book.")

Writing Wrap-Up

Writing Tip: Suggest that children decide on a setting and a problem to be solved before they begin writing. See Blackline Master 9-8 for a sample conversation.

TECHNOLOGY CONNECTION
Children may want to use available hardware to scan in photos or pictures to illustrate their conversations.

On Your Own

Write each sentence. Put quotation marks around the speaker's exact words.

Example Joy said, Our class played a joke.
Joy said, "Our class played a joke."

1. Roy asked, What did you do?
   Roy asked, "What did you do?"
2. Joy said, We switched seats.
   Joy said, "We switched seats."

3–5. Proofread these jokes. Find three sentences with missing quotation marks. Write the sentences. Put quotation marks where they belong.

Example Lee asked, What has four wheels and flies?
Lee asked, "What has four wheels and flies?"

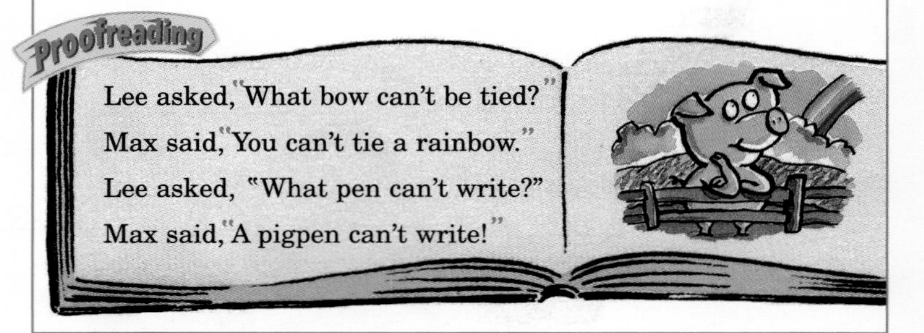

Writing Wrap-Up WRITING • THINKING • LISTENING • SPEAKING

NARRATING

Write a Conversation

Write what two people or animals say to each other. Name each speaker. Use quotation marks around each speaker's exact words. With a classmate, read aloud what each one says.

 For Extra Practice, see page 338.

Meeting Individual Needs

● RETEACHING WORKBOOK, page 79

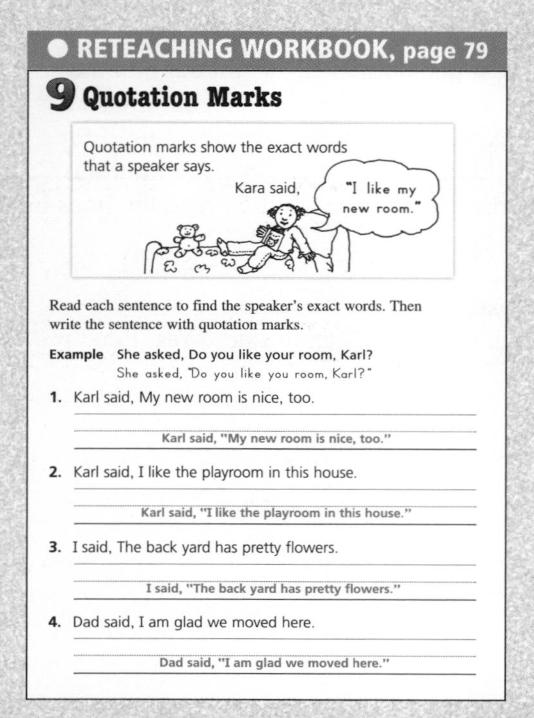

9 Quotation Marks

Quotation marks show the exact words that a speaker says.

Kara said, "I like my new room."

Read each sentence to find the speaker's exact words. Then write the sentence with quotation marks.

Example She asked, Do you like your room, Karl?
She asked, "Do you like your room, Karl?"

1. Karl said, My new room is nice, too.
   Karl said, "My new room is nice, too."
2. Karl said, I like the playroom in this house.
   Karl said, "I like the playroom in this house."
3. I said, The back yard has pretty flowers.
   I said, "The back yard has pretty flowers."
4. Dad said, I am glad we moved here.
   Dad said, "I am glad we moved here."

▲■ WORKBOOK PLUS, pages 121-122

9 Quotation Marks

José said, "I like to play the trumpet."

Write each sentence. Put quotation marks around exact words.

1. Leslie said, I like to play the drums
   Leslie said, "I like to play the drums."
2. Theo said, I like the drums also.
   Theo said, "I like the drums also."
3. Ray asked, Is it hard to play piano?
   Ray asked, "Is it hard to play piano?"
4. Mr. Ramos replied, Not really, you just have to practice.
   Mr. Ramos replied, "Not really, you just have to practice."
5. Jason said, I want to play the violin.
   Jason said, "I want to play the violin."
6. That's a good idea, said Rafael.
   "That's a good idea," said Rafael.

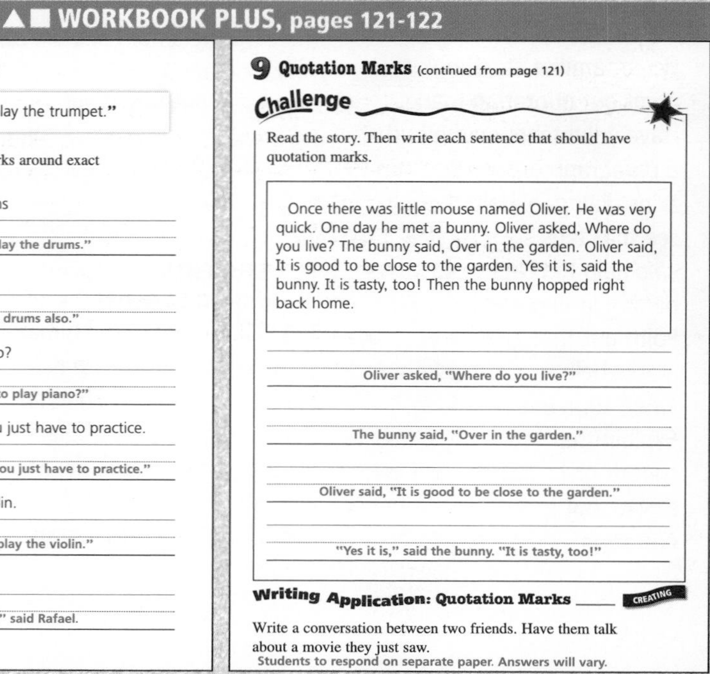

9 Quotation Marks (continued from page 121)

Challenge

Read the story. Then write each sentence that should have quotation marks.

Once there was little mouse named Oliver. He was very quick. One day he met a bunny. Oliver asked, Where do you live? The bunny said, Over in the garden. Oliver said, It is good to be close to the garden. Yes it is, said the bunny. It is tasty, too! Then the bunny hopped right back home.

Oliver asked, "Where do you live?"

The bunny said, "Over in the garden."

Oliver said, "It is good to be close to the garden."

"Yes it is," said the bunny. "It is tasty, too!"

Writing Application: Quotation Marks CREATING

Write a conversation between two friends. Have them talk about a movie they just saw.
Students to respond on separate paper. Answers will vary.

Grammar / Mechanics

10 More About Quotation Marks

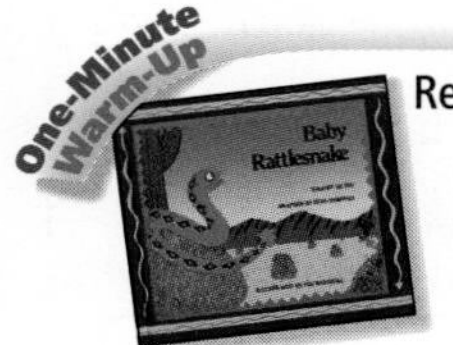

One-Minute Warm-Up

Read the exact words that Mother and Father said.

Mother and Father warned Baby Rattlesnake, "You must not use your rattle in such a way."

—from Baby Rattlesnake, told by Te Ata, adapted by Lynn Moroney

Follow these rules when you use quotation marks.

1. Put a **comma** after words such as said and asked.
2. Begin the first word inside the quotation marks with a **capital letter**.
3. Put the **end mark** inside the quotation marks.

Hoshi said, "My cat is lost."

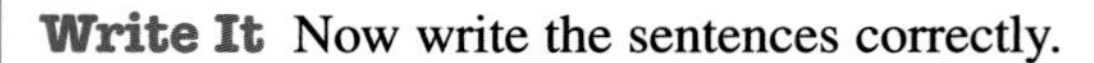

Try It Out

Speak Up Tell how to correct each sentence.

1. Leo said,"Mmine can change colors!"
2. Ruby asked,"What does it eat?"

Write It Now write the sentences correctly.

Example Ruby asked "what can a lizard do"
Ruby asked, "What can a lizard do?"

Leo said, "Mine can change colors."
Ruby asked, "What does it eat?"

More About Quotation Marks

Lesson Objectives

Children will:

- correctly use commas with quotation marks
- proofread for correct usage of commas, capital letters, and end marks in quotations
- write sentences correctly using commas and quotation marks

One-Minute Warm-Up Ask volunteers to read aloud the sentences. Have volunteers repeat the speaker's exact words.

Focus on Instruction

Point out that when words inside quotation marks are a complete sentence, they begin with a capital letter and finish with an end mark.

Try It Out

VIEWING Have children think of things to ask the lizard in the picture. They can then think of responses for the lizard. Record their responses in a chart.

Questions	Answers
Bob asked, "What color are you now?"	"Now I am pink," said the lizard.
Marie asked, "Why do you change colors?"	The lizard said, "I like to hide."

Meeting Individual Needs

RETEACHING
ALTERNATIVE STRATEGY

- Write beginning quotation marks, end quotation marks, a comma, period, question mark, and exclamation point on separate cards. Have children name each mark.
- Have children make up sentences. List their ideas on the chalkboard without any punctuation, leaving space for a punctuation card to be inserted. For example: *Matt said I like to ride my bicycle in the park*
- Ask each child to place the correct punctuation card on the appropriate spot in the sentence.

CHALLENGE

Ask children to write a short puppet play using the form: (Character) said, "(dialogue)." Have them make construction paper and stick puppets and act out their plays for the class.

FOR STUDENTS ACQUIRING ENGLISH

Review by having partners or small groups write their own two-line question and answer dialogues. Tell children to begin with the question. For example, *Mr. Bear asked, . . . , Mrs. Bear said, ...*

FOR STUDENTS ACQUIRING ENGLISH

- Have children listen to the Try It Out sentences on the audiotape. Distribute SAE Practice page for Unit 9, Lesson 10 to support listening.
- Help children suggest sentences about the photo in the book. Ask, *What is this animal called?* (a lizard or chameleon) *Have you ever seen one? Tell us about it. What do you call the group that includes lizards and snakes?* (reptiles) Help children name the reptiles on the Practice page. With the children, write a two-line question and answer dialogue about the art; mark the punctuation. Next, children listen and say how to correct punctuation in quotations. Then they write the sentences to correct them. Example: Dario asked "how big is your lizard" (Dario asked, "How big is your lizard?")

Summing Up Help children summarize these key points about the lesson:

Put a **comma** after words like *said* and *asked*.
Begin the first word inside **quotation marks** with a capital letter. Put the **end mark** inside quotation marks.

You may want to have children complete the parts related to this lesson on Blackline Master 9-5.

On Your Own

On the chalkboard write a list of the rules for quotations for children's reference as they do the activity.

FOR STUDENTS ACQUIRING ENGLISH

Distribute SAE Practice page for Unit 9, Lesson 10. Briefly review the punctuation in quotations, including the placement inside the quotes of the different types of end punctuation. Children underline the correct sentence in each pair.

Example: Aisha said, "I lost my snake!"
Aisha said "I lost my snake!

Writing Wrap-Up

Writing Tip: Tell children to speak slowly and repeat their answers so others can write down their exact words. See Blackline Master 9-8 for sample sentences.

SCHOOL-HOME CONNECTION

Ask children to interview family members about things they like. Have them use the same format as the Writing Wrap-Up to record their answers.

On Your Own

1–6. Proofread this interview. Find six mistakes with commas, capital letters, and end marks in quotations. Two sentences are correct. The others have one mistake each. Write the sentences correctly.

Example: Paco asked "who owns that snake"
Paco asked, "Who owns that snake?"

Proofreading

Paco asked, "~~what~~ What kind of snake is that?"
The woman said, "It is called a boa."
Paco asked, "How big is it?"
The woman said, "It is ten feet long!"
Paco asked, "Does a boa close its eyes?"
The woman said, "No, snakes have no eyelids."
Paco asked, "~~does~~ Does a boa shed its skin?"
The woman said, "Yes, all snakes shed their skins."

Writing Wrap-Up WRITING • THINKING • LISTENING • SPEAKING

EXPRESSING

Write an Interview

Ask three children this question. What animal do you like best? Use this sentence frame to record their exact words. (Name) said, "(Answer)." Read aloud your interview.

Responses will vary.

318 More About Quotation Marks For Extra Practice, see page 339.

Meeting Individual Needs

● RETEACHING WORKBOOK, page 80

10 More About Quotation Marks

Use a comma to separate the speaker's exact words from the rest of the sentence.
Begin a quotation with a capital letter.
Put the end mark before the last quotation mark.

Mom said, "I will make a sweater."

Draw a line under the sentence that is written correctly.

Example She said, "it won't take too long to make."
She said, "It won't take too long to make."

1. I said, "A new sweater would be nice."
   I said, "A new sweater would be nice"
2. Chaz asked, "What color will the sweater be?"
   Chaz asked, "what color will the sweater be?"
3. Dad said, "I would like a green sweater."
   Dad said "I would like a green sweater."
4. Mom answered, This sweater is for our dog Buggsy."
   Mom answered, "This sweater is for our dog Buggsy."

▲■ WORKBOOK PLUS, pages 123-124

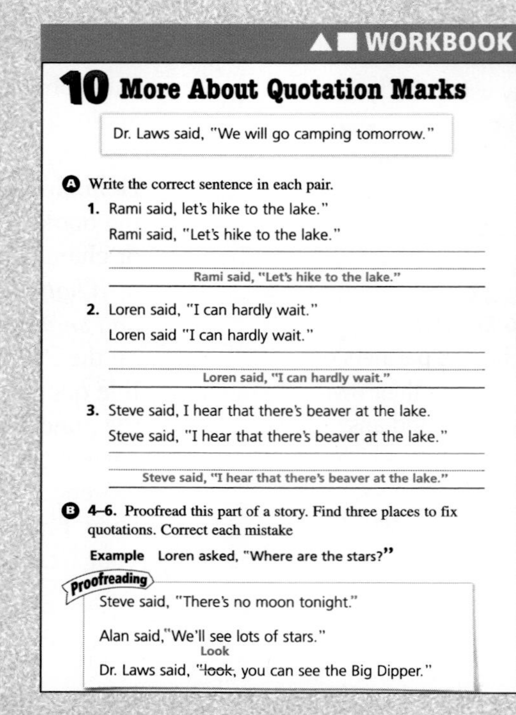

10 More About Quotation Marks

Dr. Laws said, "We will go camping tomorrow."

A Write the correct sentence in each pair.

1. Rami said, let's hike to the lake."
   Rami said, "Let's hike to the lake."
   Rami said, "Let's hike to the lake."
2. Loren said, "I can hardly wait."
   Loren said "I can hardly wait."
   Loren said, "I can hardly wait."
3. Steve said, I hear that there's beaver at the lake.
   Steve said, "I hear that there's beaver at the lake."
   Steve said, "I hear that there's beaver at the lake."

B 4–6. Proofread this part of a story. Find three places to fix quotations. Correct each mistake

Example Loren asked, "Where are the stars?"

Proofreading

Steve said, "There's no moon tonight."
Alan said,"We'll see lots of stars."
Dr. Laws said, "~~look~~ Look, you can see the Big Dipper."

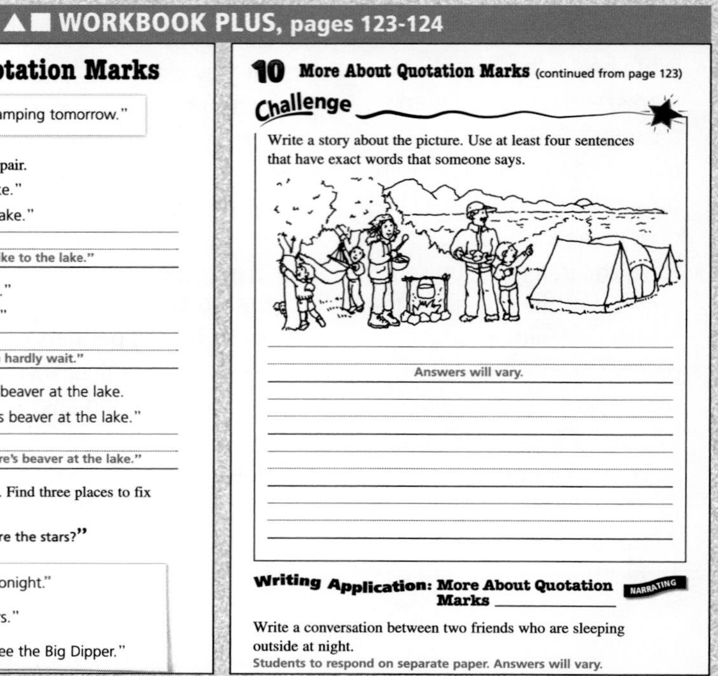

10 More About Quotation Marks (continued from page 123)

Challenge

Write a story about the picture. Use at least four sentences that have exact words that someone says.

Answers will vary.

Writing Application: More About Quotation Marks NARRATING

Write a conversation between two friends who are sleeping outside at night.
Students to respond on separate paper. Answers will vary.

Enrichment

My Journal

- Make a journal to use next week. Use one page for each day. On the top, write the day of the week. Under that write the month, the number of the day, and the year.
- On each page, write about something you did that day. Draw a picture of it.

Sentence Worms

- Write a question. Then write a sentence that answers the question.
- Cut out circles from colored paper. Write one word or end mark on each circle.
- Paste the circles in the correct order to make a question worm and an answer worm.

Challenge Mix up the circles for each sentence. Have a classmate make your two sentence worms.

Enrichment

Objectives

Children will:
- write capital letters and punctuation correctly for a journal entry
- write capital letters and punctuation correctly for a "sentence worm."

Using the Activities

The Enrichment page provides fun, creative activities that reinforce children's understanding and use of sentences. The activities are designed to be enjoyed by all children. Here are some ideas for using the activities.

- Pair children who need extra support with more capable classmates.
- Children can work with these activities in class after they have completed other assignments.
- Activities that can be completed individually can be assigned as homework.

Notes on the Activities

MY JOURNAL

- Have children look at the example. Point out that *Sunday* and *May* are capitalized and that there is a comma between *17* and *2001* in the date.
- Tell children to think of the most interesting or exciting thing they did for each day.

SENTENCE WORMS

- Children will need colored paper, scissors, paste, and markers for this activity.
- Have children look at the art for the example. Explain that each worm forms a complete sentence. The worm at the top asks a question, and the worm at the bottom answers it.
- Be sure children understand that they will cut out a circle for each word and each end mark.

CHALLENGE Children who are going to do this activity should not paste their circles. They should create new sentences and cut out the words and end marks to share with a partner.

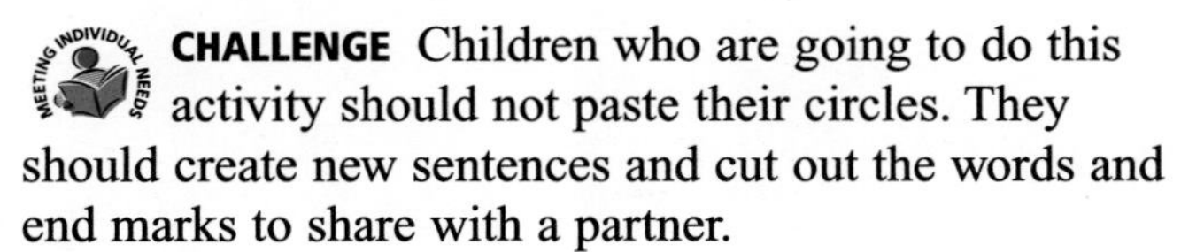

FOR STUDENTS ACQUIRING ENGLISH

Children may not be familiar with the open-ended personal writing that is needed for journals. Give specific topics (special traditional celebrations, friends from children's native countries, new friends they've made in the United States, greatest moment of the day, worst moment of the day, etc.

Checkup

Objectives

Children will:

- capitalize days, holidays, and months correctly
- capitalize titles of people and books correctly

Using the Checkup

Use the Checkup exercises as assessment, as review for the unit test, as extra practice, or as a diagnostic aid to help determine those children who need reteaching.

INTERNET CONNECTION
Children can take an interactive quiz for this unit at www.eduplace.com /kids/hme/ and then get immediate feedback.

Checkup: Unit 9

Days and Holidays (pages 297, 299)
Write the sentences. Add a capital letter to each word that needs one.

1. My birthday is on wednesday. **Wednesday**
2. We had a picnic on labor day. **Labor Day**

Months (page 301)
Write the sentences. Add a capital letter to each word that needs one.

3. Mark went to camp in august. **August**
4. In march Meg got a puppy. **March**

Titles for People (page 303)
Write each title and name correctly.

5. mr. Nye **Mr. Nye**
6. mrs Chan **Mrs. Chan**

Writing Book Titles (page 305)
Write the book title correctly.

7. letter to the lake **Letter to the Lake**

Ending Sentences (page 307)

Write each sentence. Add the correct end mark.

8. A dog barks at me .
9. Is the dog friendly ?
10. I am so afraid !
11. Don't run fast .

Commas in Dates (page 311)

Write each date. Use commas correctly.

12. March 2 2001
    March 2, 2001
13. May 15 2002
    May 15, 2002

Commas with Names of Places (page 313)

Write the city and state. Use commas correctly.

14. Orlando Florida
    Orlando, Florida
15. San Jose California
    San Jose, California

Quotation Marks (pages 315 and 317)

Write the sentences. Add quotation marks, an end mark, a comma, and a capital letter to each sentence.

16. Mom asked how are you
    Mom asked, "How are you?"
17. Carla said i am fine
    Carla said, "I am fine."

Objectives

Children will:

- write end marks correctly in sentences
- use commas correctly for dates, cities, and states
- write quotations correctly

Objective

Children will:

- proofread a journal entry for mistakes in capital letters and punctuation marks

Mixed Review

18–25. Proofread this journal entry. Find eight mistakes with capital letters and punctuation marks. Then write the journal entry correctly.

Proofreading Checklist

- ✔ Do days, holidays, months, and people's titles begin with capital letters?
- ✔ Are book titles written correctly?
- ✔ Are commas used correctly in dates and names of places?
- ✔ Does a quotation have quotation marks, capital letters, a comma, and an end mark?

Example our vacation has been fun.
Our vacation has been fun.

Austin, ~~texas~~ Texas
July 3, 2002

I am having a great time in Texas. Today we visited the Alamo~~?~~. I heard about all that happened there on ~~march~~ March 6, 1836. ~~mrs.~~ Mrs. Valero, our guide, asked, "~~did~~ Did you know that Jim Bowie fought here?" I was the only one in our group who knew that.

After our tour, we visited the gift shop. I bought a book called ~~heroes~~ Heroes of the Alamo. I will read it on our flight to Roswell, New Mexico. We will spend ~~independence~~ Independence Day there.

See www.eduplace.com/kids/hme/ for an online quiz.

Assessment Link

Test Practice

Number a sheet of paper from 1 to 8. Read each sentence. Find the part of the sentence that needs a capital letter. Write the letter for that part.

1 Did your sister / borrow Ira sleeps Over / from the library?
A (B) C

2 Andrew said, / "we have to catch the train / to Boston."
A (B) C

3 My mother / picks me up after school / on tuesday.
A B (C)

4 On thanksgiving Day, / the family / had turkey for dinner.
(A) B C

5 Anna asked, / "May I have some peanuts, / miss Rios?"
A B (C)

6 In july / Marshall will go / to the seashore.
(A) B C

7 Juan asked, / "is it time / to go to the movie?"
A (B) C

8 You can swim / in the ocean / at daytona Beach, Florida.
A B (C)

Test Practice

Objective

Children will:

- practice completing a test format that requires them to identify an error in one of three parts of a sentence

Using the Test Practice

These Test Practice pages provide practice with common formats used in standardized or multiple-choice tests.

The first page works with skills taught in the basic lessons in Unit 9. The second page works with skills taught in the lessons in Units 1, 3, 5, 7, and 9.

Notes on the Test Format

- Read the directions aloud. Then discuss them with the class. Point out that each item has a sentence that is broken into three parts. Two of the sentence parts contain no errors. One contains an error.
- Explain that the errors are different in each sentence and include mistakes in capitalization, punctuation, usage, and spelling.
- Have children read Item 1 and carefully evaluate each part of the sentence. Help them see that the book title is not correctly capitalized. Point out that it is easy to miss mistakes when reading an entire sentence. Suggest that they reread each part several times.

FOR STUDENTS ACQUIRING ENGLISH

First, review the days of the week and months of the year. Remind children that these words all begin with capital letters. Then talk about capital letters on holidays and titles such as *Mrs.* Then review commas in dates and places. Discuss which words in book titles have capital letters in English; remind children that book titles are underlined. Distribute the SAE Test Practice page for Unit 9. Read the directions aloud. Explain that in the first section children are to circle the part that needs a capital letter. In the second part, children are to circle the letter of the part that has a mistake.

Objective

Children will:

- practice completing a test format that requires them to identify an error in one of three parts of a sentence

Notes on the Test Format

The test format on this page is the same as the format on the preceding page.

Test Practice continued

Now write the numbers 9 to 16 on your paper. Read each sentence. Find the part of the sentence that has a mistake. Write the letter for that part.

9 Jake / made a silly card / for valentine's Day.
A B (C)

10 In may / our class / will go on a field trip.
(A) B C

11 Dad bought a new car / from Mr Bates / in March.
A (B) C

12 My little brother / is reading a book / called Little Bear.
A B (C)

13 We went / to Phoenix Arizona / to visit my grandmother.
A (B) C

14 Neil Armstrong / walked on the moon / on July, 20 1969.
A B (C)

15 Nora asked, / "What day / is the picnic"
A B (C)

16 Mom said / "The picnic is / on Saturday."
(A) B C

324 Test Practice

Test Practice continued

Now write the numbers 17 to 22 on your paper. Read the four sentences by each number. Find the sentence that does not have any mistakes. Write the letter for that sentence.

17 **A** There was a dog show in Wayne New Jersey.
B The dog show took place on july 4, 2000.
C Mrs. chang gave ribbons to the winners.
(D) Roy shouted, "My dog won first prize!"

18 **A** Can you see the moon.
(B) There will be a full moon on Friday.
C I have saw many stars.
D That is the brighter of all the stars in the sky.

19 **A** Inez pulled her friends wagon up the hill.
B Wagons is good for carrying things.
C I and Kevin smiled.
(D) I read The Little Red Wagon.

20 **A** Abby said, I want to hike up the hill.
B We climbed a hill near Boise Idaho.
(C) This hill is taller than that hill.
D We went hiking in may.

21 **(A)** My sister was born on October 13, 1998.
B I gave her an rattle.
C Grandma has came to help with the baby.
D Babies sleeps a lot.

22 **(A)** Nick said, "Watch this card trick."
B Miguel has saw the card trick.
C Amy played a card game with miss green.
D I have a book called Ten Great Card games.

Objective

Children will:

- practice completing a test format that requires them to choose the correct item among four

Notes on the Test Format

- Ask a volunteer to read the directions aloud. Point out that there will be only one correct answer.
- Then have children carefully read each sentence in Item 17. Explain that they should read all four possible answers before choosing the one that does not have any mistakes.

Unit 9 Cumulative Review

Units 1, 3, 5, 7 and 9

Cumulative Review

Objectives

Children will:

- identify naming and action parts of sentences
- identify different types of sentences
- identify singular nouns

Using the Cumulative Review

This Cumulative Review provides cumulative practice with basic grammar, usage, and mechanics skills taught in Units 1, 3, 5, 7, and 9. You can use these pages for assessment, as a review for a test, as extra practice, or as a diagnostic aid to determine those children who may need reteaching.

Unit 1: The Sentence

Naming Part and Action Part (pages 29–32)

Write each sentence. Circle the naming part. Draw a line under the action part.

1. Dad and I went to the zoo.
2. The huge lion roared.
3. The tall giraffe ate leaves.
4. The seal swam around.

Which Kind of Sentence? (pages 37–46)

Write each sentence correctly. Tell if it is a telling sentence, a question, a command, or an exclamation.

5. the gift is for Emma **telling sentence The gift is for Emma.**
6. what is it **question What is it?**
7. open it **command Open it.**
8. i love this hat **exclamation I love this hat!**

Unit 3: Nouns and Pronouns

Nouns (pages 93–96)

Write the sentences. Draw a line under each noun.

9. Is the girl cold? **girl**
10. The grass is wet. **grass**

One and More Than One (pages 97–98, 101–104)

Write each noun to name more than one.

11. box boxes **12.** cat cats **13.** man men

Pronouns (pages 107–108)

Write each sentence, using a pronoun in place of the underlined word or words. Use he, she, it, or they.

14. Donna got a bike. She got a bike.

15. The bike is red. It is red.

Nouns Ending with 's and s' (pages 113–116)

Write each sentence, using the correct noun.

16. My bike is much older than (Jims', Jim's) bike.

17. The two (dogs', dog's) leashes are the same color.

Unit 5: Verbs

Verbs That Tell About Now and About the Past

(pages 165–166, 169–170)

Write each sentence, using the correct verb.

18. Meg and Pat (dance, dances) well.

19. Meg (give, gives) dance lessons.

20. Last week Meg (plants, planted) her garden.

Objectives

Children will:

- write plural nouns
- use pronouns correctly
- write possessive nouns
- write present and past verbs correctly

Objectives

Children will:

- choose the correct special verb
- write contractions correctly
- choose adjectives to complete sentences

Special Verbs (pages 173–182)

Write each sentence, using the correct verb.

21. Paco's best friend (went, gone) to camp with him.
22. The camp (is, are) on a lake.
23. The boys and girls have (saw, seen) a rainbow.
24. The campers (was, were) tired after the hike.

Contractions (pages 183–184)

Write the contractions for these words.

25. do not **don't** 26. does not **doesn't**

Unit 7: Adjectives

How Something Looks, Tastes, Smells, Sounds, and Feels (pages 239–244)

Write sentences by matching each word group in Box **A** to an adjective in Box **B**.

A	B
27. The color of his hat is	loud.
28. The music sounds	cold.
29. The water feels	red.
30. The campfire smells	big.
31. The soup tastes	smoky.
32. The tent is	salty.

Special Adjectives (pages 247–250)

Write each sentence, using the correct word in ( ).

33. Are ants (smaller, smallest) than worms?

34. Does (a, an) octopus live in the ocean?

Unit 9: More Capitalization and Punctuation

Days, Holidays, and Months (pages 297–302)

Write the sentence correctly.

35. The first monday in september is labor day.
The first Monday in September is Labor Day.

Titles for People and Books (pages 303–306)

Write the titles correctly.

36. ms kent Ms.

37. dear zoo Dear Zoo

Commas: Dates, Place Names (pages 311–314)

Write the date and place name correctly.

38. August 17, 2001

39. Miami, Florida

Quotation Marks (pages 315–318)

Write the sentence correctly. Add quotation marks, a comma, an end mark, and a capital letter.

Sam asked, "Where do you swim?"
40. Sam asked where do you swim

Objectives

Children will:

- use comparative adjectives and *a* and *an* correctly
- use capital letters and end marks correctly with dates, titles, days, holidays, months, addresses
- write direct quotes correctly

Days

Objective

Children will:
- identify and write the days of the week

Using the Extra Practice

The Extra Practice activities provide two levels of additional practice for the basic lesson: Easy/Average (●▲), and Challenging (■).

The Extra Practice activities can be used in the following ways.

- Assign activities according to children's needs and abilities as homework after children have completed the basic lesson.
- Assign the Easy/Average activities after using the lesson Reteaching instruction.
- Assign the Challenging exercises as a Bonus activity.
- Assign the Easy/Average activities to prepare children for the Checkup.
- Assign the Easy/Average activities to children who had difficulty with specific lessons on the Checkup.

Extra Practice

(pages 297–298)

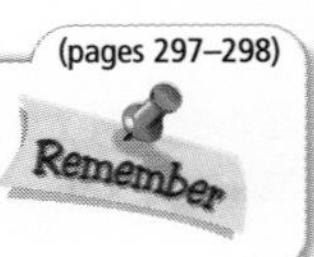

1 Days
- Begin the names of days of the week with capital letters.

●▲ Find the word in each sentence that needs a capital letter. Then write the sentences correctly.

Example On tuesday we gave a puppet show.
On Tuesday we gave a puppet show.

1. The spelling test is on wednesday. Wednesday
2. Our class is having a party on friday. Friday
3. On thursday our class has gym. Thursday

■ Answer each question with a sentence that names a different day of the week.

Example When is your favorite TV show on?
My favorite TV show is on Monday.

4. What is your favorite day? Answers will vary.
5. When don't you go to school? Answers will vary.
6. When do you go to school? Answers will vary.

330 Extra Practice

Meeting Individual Needs — More Practice for Lesson 1

● EASY ▲ AVERAGE

Draw a line under the words that need capital letters. Write the words correctly.

1. The queen came to my house on sunday. Sunday
2. On tuesday, the baker baked a hundred cookies. Tuesday
3. This saturday I am flying to Mesa. Saturday
4. My best friend is having a party on friday. Friday
5. School starts on monday. Monday
6. I ran a race on wednesday. Wednesday
7. thursday is my favorite day. Thursday
8. Would you like to meet on sunday? Sunday
9. She flew a kite on wednesday. Wednesday
10. They had fun on tuesday. Tuesday

■ CHALLENGING

Answer each question with a day of the week. Use all the days at least once. (Answers will vary.)

1. When do you eat lunch?
2. When do you go to sleep?
3. When do you go to school?
4. When do you play?
5. What is your favorite day to read a book?
6. What is your favorite day to sing a song?
7. When do you take a walk?
8. What is your favorite day to meet a friend?
9. When do you do your chores?
10. When do you help the teacher?

2 Holidays

(pages 299–300)

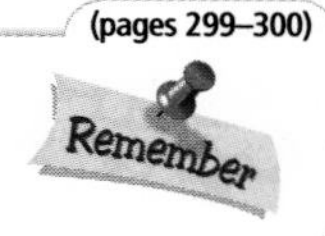

- Begin each important word in the name of a holiday with a capital letter.

●▲ Look at each pair of sentences. Write the sentence in which the holiday is written correctly.

Example We have a vacation on columbus Day.
We have a vacation on Columbus Day.
We have a vacation on Columbus Day.

1. February 14 is Valentine's Day.
   February 14 is valentine's day.
2. We ate turkey on Thanksgiving day.
   We ate turkey on Thanksgiving Day.
3. Dad made dinner on mother's Day.
   Dad made dinner on Mother's Day.

■ Find the words that need capital letters. Then write each sentence correctly.

Example When is flag day? When is Flag Day?

4. Friends visit on new year's day. New Year's Day
5. Did you forget father's day? Father's Day
6. What day is labor day? Labor Day
7. Why do we celebrate earth day? Earth Day

Holidays

Objective

Children will:

- identify and write the names of holidays

Meeting Individual Needs

More Practice for Lesson 2

● **EASY** ▲ **AVERAGE**

Write *yes* if the sentence is written correctly. Write *no* if the sentence is not written correctly.

1. I will go skiing during christmas vacation. no
2. Do you celebrate Kwaanza? yes
3. I like to wear green on st. patrick's day. no
4. We watch fireworks on independence day. no
5. I watch the parade on Chinese New Year. yes
6. What day is Martin Luther King Jr. Day? yes
7. School is closed on election day. no
8. Send me a card on Valentine's Day. yes
9. Plant a tree on arbor day. no
10. We eat turkey on Thanksgiving Day. yes

■ **CHALLENGING**

Write the words that need capital letters.

1. I stay up late on new year's eve. New Year's Eve
2. We have a picnic on independence day. Independence Day
3. She gave me a present for chanukah. Chanukah
4. My dad rests on labor day. Labor Day
5. Clean up the yard on earth day. Earth Day
6. Did you wave a flag on flag day? Flag Day
7. We sang songs on christmas day. Christmas Day
8. The whole family came to celebrate kwaanza. Kwaanza
9. She tricked me on april fool's day. April Fool's Day
10. I marched on memorial day. Memorial Day

Months

Objective

Children will:

- identify and write the names of the months

Extra Practice

(pages 301–302)

3 Months

- Begin the names of months with capital letters.

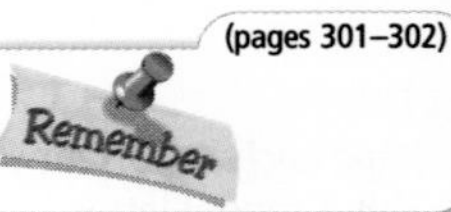

●▲ Find the word in each sentence that needs a capital letter. Write the sentences correctly.

Example Jason read four books in november.
Jason read four books in November.

1. It snowed in january. January
2. In april it rained a lot. April
3. It was hot in august. August
4. In october he saw pumpkins. October

■ **5–8.** Find the word in each sentence that needs a capital letter. Then write the story sentences correctly.

Example They sold their house in july.
They sold their house in July.

They moved to Florida in september. In february Rosa got a new puppy. In march her mother started a new job. They planted a big garden in may. September, February, March, May

332 Extra Practice

Meeting Individual Needs

More Practice for Lesson 3

● **EASY** ▲ **AVERAGE**

Write the word in each sentence that needs a capital letter.

1. We made a snow fort in december. December
2. I went sledding in february. February
3. My mother went on a trip in may. May
4. Sara started school in september. September
5. Our garden bloomed in june. June
6. We gathered the corn in august. August
7. I took a test in october. October
8. It was cloudy in november. November
9. My birthday is in march. March
10. In july it was very sunny. July

■ **CHALLENGING**

Draw a line under the names of the months in this story. Write the months correctly.

Sam moved here in december. It got colder in january. We went sledding in february. Then Sam got sick in march. In april he got better. We went to the circus in may. I slept at his house in june. He slept at mine in july. We became best friends in august. He gave me a puppy in september. I gave him a kitten in october. Our new pets became friends in november.

December, January, February, March, April, May, June, July, August, September, October, November

Extra Practice

4 Titles for People

(pages 303–304)

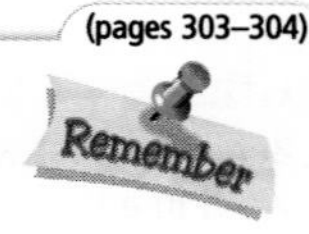

- Begin a title before a person's name with a capital letter.
- Put a period after Mrs., Mr., Ms., and Dr.
- The title Miss does not have a period.

●▲ Write the titles and special nouns correctly.

Example dr pang Dr. Pang

1. miss lee Miss Lee
2. mr vega Mr. Vega
3. ms kemp Ms. Kemp
4. mrs shaw Mrs. Shaw

■ 5–8. Copy this story. Write the four titles and last names correctly.

Example First, mr klein wiggled his ears.
First, Mr. Klein wiggled his ears.

The neighbors tried to make my baby sister smile. If mrs ito (Mrs. Ito) tickled Sally, would she smile? Sally didn't smile. Funny dr santos (Dr. Santos) flapped his arms like a bird. Sally didn't smile. ms stone (Ms. Stone) jumped up and down. Sally didn't smile. Then miss shaw (Miss Shaw) made a funny face. Sally didn't smile. Finally, they went home. Sally smiled!

Titles for People

Objective

Children will:

- identify and write the titles *Mrs.*, *Mr.*, *Ms.*, *Dr.*, and *Miss*

Meeting Individual Needs — More Practice for Lesson 4

● EASY ▲ AVERAGE

Write the titles and special nouns correctly.

1. dr white Dr. White
2. miss marks Miss Marks
3. mr biddle Mr. Biddle
4. mrs unger Mrs. Unger
5. ms green Ms. Green
6. dr disto Dr. Disto
7. mr google Mr. Google
8. ms french Ms. French
9. miss partman Miss Partman
10. mrs derado Mrs. Derado

■ CHALLENGING

Draw a line under the names with titles in the story. Write them correctly.

miss goody mailed a letter to mrs. bright. The address was wrong and the letter went to dr yan. He was friends with mr bright. dr yan would give the letter to mr bright to give to his wife. On the way, a wind came and blew the letter into the yard of ms gomez. She took it to her friend dr stein. He gave it to his mother, mrs stein. She saw dr yan and gave it to him. He gave it to mr bright. Finally, mrs bright got her letter!

Miss Goody, Mrs. Bright, Dr. Yan, Mr. Bright, Ms. Gomez, Dr. Stein, Mrs. Stein

Writing Book Titles

Objectives

Children will:
- correctly capitalize words in book titles
- draw lines under book titles

Extra Practice

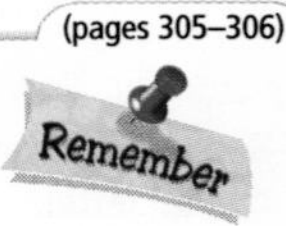

(pages 305–306)

5 Writing Book Titles
- Begin the first word, last word, and each important word in a book title with a capital letter.
- Draw a line under the title.

●▲ Write the book titles correctly.

Example brothers and sisters
Brothers and Sisters

1. dragon gets by **Dragon Gets By**
2. ben and me **Ben and Me**
3. too many tamales **Too Many Tamales**

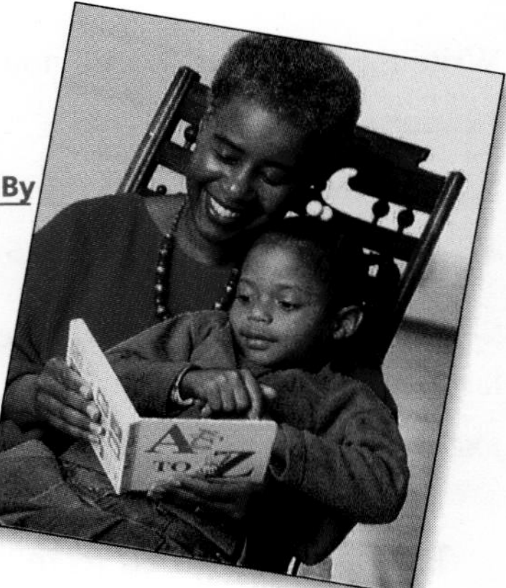

■ Write each sentence and its book title correctly.

Example I read ira sleeps over
I read Ira Sleeps Over.

4. Ron read mrs. brown went to town. **Ron read Mrs. Brown Went to Town.**
5. Jill read ramona the pest. **Jill read Ramona the Pest.**

Meeting Individual Needs — More Practice for Lesson 5

● **EASY** ▲ **AVERAGE**

Write the book titles correctly. Draw a line under each one.

1. my best friend My Best Friend
2. who stole the shoes? Who Stole the Shoes?
3. peter and the pumpkin Peter and the Pumpkin
4. the fastest train The Fastest Train
5. are you afraid? Are You Afraid?
6. a special girl A Special Girl
7. sally and sam Sally and Sam
8. this messy mouse This Messy Mouse
9. slim walks in Slim Walks In
10. how do you do? How Do You Do?

■ **CHALLENGING**

Write each sentence and its book title correctly.

1. Fred read green gophers go. Fred read Green Gophers Go.
2. Julie read burt keeps bees. Julie read Burt Keeps Bees.
3. Marat read wild woolly things. Marat read Wild Woolly Things.
4. Bob read sheldon and I. Bob read Sheldon and I.
5. Skippy read too much trouble. Skippy read Too Much Trouble.
6. Ivan read the adventures of baron foot. Ivan read The Adventures of Baron Foot.
7. Who will read emir and the ice queen? Who will read Emir and the Ice Queen?
8. The teacher read us up and down and all around. The teacher read us Up and Down and All Around.
9. Did you ever read safety first? Did you ever read Safety First?
10. I read the young boy and his dog. I read The Young Boy and His Dog.

Extra Practice

6 **Ending Sentences**

(pages 307–308)

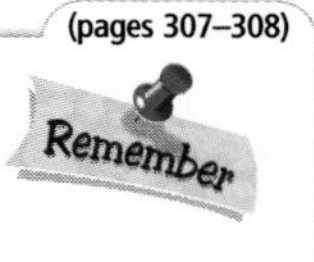

- A telling sentence and a command end with a period. (.)
- A question ends with a question mark. (?)
- An exclamation ends with an exclamation point. (!)

●▲ Write the correct sentence in each pair.

Example I am hungry. I am hungry.
When can I eat.

1. Do you like ice cream.
   This tastes great!
2. Do you want more?
   Wipe your mouth?

■ Write the sentences. Add the correct end marks.

Example It is my birthday
It is my birthday.

3. Will I get gifts
   Will I get gifts?
4. Look in the kitchen
   Look in the kitchen.
5. What a surprise
   What a surprise!
6. The kitten is for me
   The kitten is for me.

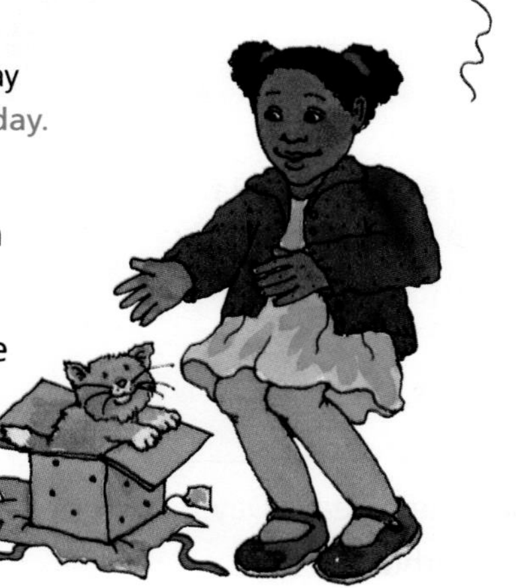

Ending Sentences

Objective

Children will:

- correctly identify and use periods, question marks, and exclamation marks at the ends of sentences

Meeting Individual Needs — More Practice for Lesson 6

● **EASY** ▲ **AVERAGE**

Draw a line under the sentence in each pair with the correct end mark.

1. Are you here? Is she there.
2. Don't go there? Watch out!
3. Do you like this? How are you.
4. Will you wait for me. This is great!
5. Tell me a story. Did you read it.
6. This is so exciting! I don't like this?
7. Can you come over. Have a nice day.
8. When will it end? When are they coming.
9. How many are there. I am falling!
10. Please take this bag. Are you sure.

■ **CHALLENGING**

Write the sentences. Add the correct end marks.

1. How big is the dog
   How big is the dog?
2. Look out for that bear
   Look out for that bear!
3. There are five cats There are five cats.
4. Be careful of that fire
   Be careful of that fire!
5. Is it raining Is it raining?
6. Do you have a coat
   Do you have a coat?
7. Today is a nice day Today is a nice day.
8. What time is it What time is it?
9. I am so scared I am so scared!
10. The grass is green The grass is green.

Commas in Dates

Objective

Children will:

- identify and correctly use a comma between the number of the day and the year when writing dates

(pages 311–312)

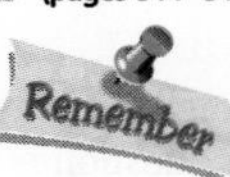

7 Commas in Dates

- A date tells the month, the number of the day, and the year.
- Use a comma (,) between the number of the day and the year.

●▲ Write each date. Use commas correctly.

Example July 4 1776
July 4, 1776

1. May 16 2001 — May 16, 2001
2. June 12 1990 — June 12, 1990
3. August 9 2004 — August 9, 2004

■ Write the sentences and finish each one with the correct date. Use commas correctly.

Example Joe was born on ____.
Joe was born on September 25, 1996.

4. Today is ____. Answers will vary.
5. School began on ____. Answers will vary.
6. Next New Year's Day is ____. Answers will vary.
7. My birthday is ____. Answers will vary.

336 Extra Practice

Meeting Individual Needs

More Practice for Lesson 7

● **EASY** ▲ **AVERAGE**

Write each date. Use commas correctly.

1. June 24 1999 — June 24, 1999
2. August 3 2005 — August 3, 2005
3. November 11 2009 — November 11, 2009
4. May 16 2001 — May 16, 2001
5. January 1 2002 — January 1, 2002
6. March 5 2003 — March 5, 2003
7. July 4 2006 — July 4, 2006
8. September 23 2007 — September 23, 2007
9. April 3 1998 — April 3, 1998
10. October 7 1963 — October 7, 1963

■ **CHALLENGING**

Finish each sentence with a date.
Use commas correctly. Answers will vary.

1. Maria was born on
2. Yesterday was
3. Tomorrow is
4. Next Independence Day is
5. My birthday is on
6. My best friend's birthday is on
7. Next Monday is
8. Vacation starts on
9. This year ends on
10. I will graduate from this grade on

Extra Practice

(pages 313–314)

8 Commas with Names of Places

- Use a comma (,) between the name of a city or town and the name of a state.

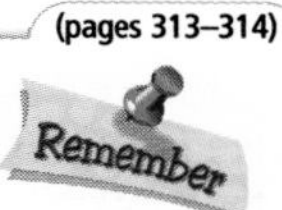

●▲ Write each city and state. Put commas in the correct places.

Example Niagara Falls New York
Niagara Falls, New York

1. Chico California Chico, California
2. Denton Texas Denton, Texas

■ Write the sentences. Put commas in the correct places.

Example My aunt lives in Stowe Vermont.
My aunt lives in Stowe, Vermont.

3. An airport is in Orlando Florida. Orlando, Florida
4. My family drove through Oxford Ohio. Oxford, Ohio
5. Brownsville Texas is near the Mexican border. Brownsville, Texas

Commas in Names of Places

Objective

Children will:

- correctly identify and use commas between the names of cities or towns and the names of states

Meeting Individual Needs

More Practice for Lesson 8

● **EASY** ▲ **AVERAGE**

Write each city and state. Put commas in the correct places.

1. Bakersfield California — Bakersfield, California
2. Elko Nevada — Elko, Nevada
3. Syracuse New York — Syracuse, New York
4. Atlanta Georgia — Atlanta, Georgia
5. Fort Lee New Jersey — Fort Lee, New Jersey
6. Providence Rhode Island — Providence, Rhode Island
7. Boise Idaho — Boise, Idaho
8. Houston Texas — Houston, Texas
9. Madison Wisconsin — Madison, Wisconsin
10. Ann Arbor Michigan — Ann Arbor, Michigan

■ **CHALLENGING**

Write the city and state named in each sentence. Put commas in the correct places.

1. My friend was born in Boston Massachusetts Boston, Massachusetts
2. I work in Peterborough New Hampshire. Peterborough, New Hampshire
3. We visited Ithaca New York. Ithaca, New York
4. She lives in Nashville Tennessee. Nashville, Tennessee
5. I took the train to Seattle Washington. Seattle, Washington
6. We drove to Oakland California. Oakland, California
7. I saw it in Orlando Florida. Orlando, Florida
8. The factory was in Allentown Pennsylvania. Allentown, Pennsylvania
9. They met in Portland Oregon. Portland, Oregon
10. He flew from Chicago Illinois. Chicago, Illinois

Quotation Marks

Objective

Children will:

- correctly identify and write quotation marks at the beginning and end of the exact words a person says

Extra Practice

(pages 315–316)

9 Quotation Marks

- Put quotation marks (" ") at the beginning and end of the speaker's exact words.

●▲ Write each sentence. Draw a line under the speaker's exact words.

Example Marta said, "We wrote our names backward."
Marta said, "We wrote our names backward."

1. Marta said, "Today was Backward Day."
2. Dad asked, "What is that?"
3. Marta said, "We put our clothes on backward."
4. Dad asked, "Did you walk backward too?"

■ Write each sentence correctly. Add quotation marks.

Example Jim asked, Do you have a pet?
Jim asked, "Do you have a pet?"

5. Sam said, I have a dog. Sam said, "I have a dog."
6. Jim asked, What is its name? Jim asked, "What is its name?"
7. Sam said, His name is Rex. Sam said, "His name is Rex."
8. Jim said, I like dogs. Jim said, "I like dogs."

338 Extra Practice

Meeting Individual Needs — More Practice for Lesson 9

● **EASY** ▲ **AVERAGE**

Draw a line under the exact words that a person says.

1. Jed said, "I want to have a party."
2. Fred asked, "Can I come?"
3. Chris said, "I will bring a cake."
4. John said, "I will bring some games."
5. Juan asked, "What shall I bring?"
6. Jed told them, "Just bring yourselves!"
7. Jed's mother said, "We will take care of everything."
8. Peter asked, "Will you have enough chairs?"
9. Jed's father said, "Yes, we will."
10. Rosa said, "I can't wait!"

■ **CHALLENGING**

Write each sentence correctly. Add quotation marks.

1. Nicky said, I am tall.
   Nicky said, "I am tall."
2. June said, I am short.
   June said, "I am short."
3. Brad said, I have red hair.
   Brad said, "I have red hair."
4. Tino asked, What color are his eyes?
   Tino asked, "What color are his eyes?"
5. Gloria said, His eyes are blue.
   Gloria said, "His eyes are blue."
6. Sven asked, How tall are you?
   Sven asked, "How tall are you?"
7. Mario said, I have ten toes.
   Mario said, "I have ten toes."
8. Felipe said, I have two hands.
   Felipe said, "I have two hands."
9. Ko said, My hair is black.
   Ko said, "My hair is black."
10. Alec asked, Who has brown eyes?
    Alec asked, "Who has brown eyes?"

Extra Practice

10 More About Quotation Marks (pages 317–318)

Remember

- Put a comma after words like said and asked.
- Begin the first word inside the quotation marks with a capital letter.
- Put the end mark inside the quotation marks.

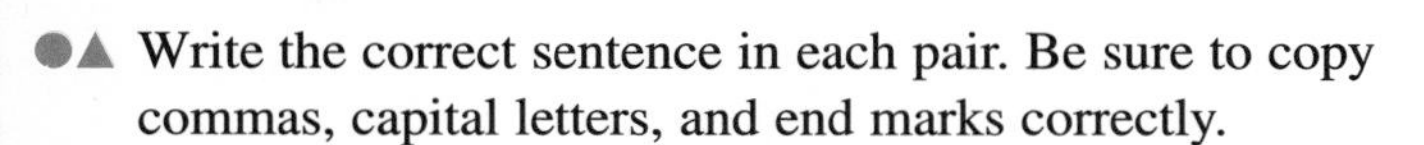

●▲ Write the correct sentence in each pair. Be sure to copy commas, capital letters, and end marks correctly.

Example Mom asked, "What animal is this?"
Mom asked, "What animal is this"
Mom asked, "What animal is this?"

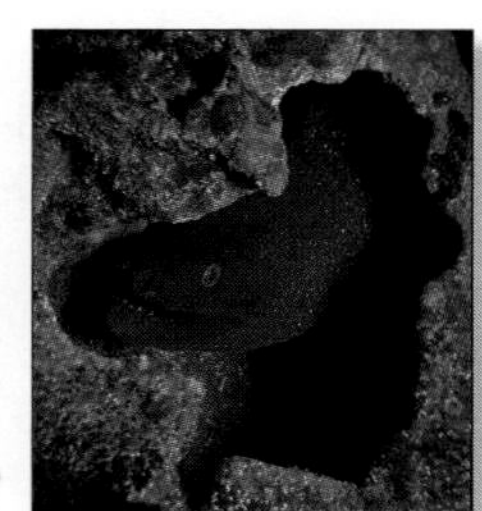

1. Nan said, "it looks like a snake."
   Nan said, "It looks like a snake."
2. Mom said "It is a fish called an eel"
   Mom said, "It is a fish called an eel."
3. Nan asked, "How does an eel swim?"
   Nan asked, "How does an eel swim"?

■ Write each sentence correctly. Add a comma, end mark, and capital letter.

Example Max asked "what is that"
Max asked, "What is that?"

4. Dad said "it is a starfish" Dad said, "It is a starfish."
5. Mom said "it has five arms" Mom said, "It has five arms."

More About Quotation Marks

Objectives

Children will:

- correctly identify and write commas after words such as *said* and *asked*
- correctly identify and write with a capital letter the first word a person says
- correctly identify and write end marks inside quotation marks

Meeting Individual Needs — More Practice for Lesson 10

● EASY ▲ AVERAGE

Write *yes* if the sentence is correct. Write *no* if the sentence is not correct.

1. Dani said, "I like to dance." yes
2. Coco said, "I like to sing." yes
3. Avram asked "what do you like to do?" no
4. Zoe said, "I like to swim in lakes." yes
5. Joan asked, "Who likes to climb trees"? no
6. Meghan said, I like to hike." no
7. Joyce asked, "Who likes to read? no
8. Katya said, "I like to sew." yes
9. Bruce said, "I love to do everything!" yes
10. Dario said "I don't like to do anything" no

■ CHALLENGING

Write each sentence correctly. Add a comma, end mark, and capital letter.

1. Dad asked "who wants to go fishing" Dad asked, "Who wants to go fishing?"
2. Ollie said "we are too tired" Ollie said, "We are too tired."
3. Mom said "we can go to the movies" Mom said, "We can go to the movies."
4. Janet asked "what will we see" Janet asked, "What will we see?"
5. Seth said "we can see a cartoon" Seth said, "We can see a cartoon."
6. Ida said "we all love cartoons" Ida said, "We all love cartoons!"
7. Jorge asked "may we have ice cream, too" Jorge asked, "May we have ice cream, too?"
8. Bilha said "we can go to the park" Bilha said, "We can go to the park."
9. Dad said "that's a good idea" Dad said, "That's a good idea."
10. Mom asked "who wants to feed the ducks" Mom asked, "Who wants to feed the ducks?"

Unit 10 Planning Guide

Writing to Express an Opinion

Writing to Express an Opinion: *2 weeks*
Special Focus and Communication Link: *1 week (optional)*

	Blackline Masters (TE)	Workbook Plus	Reteaching Workbook
A PUBLISHED MODEL "My Life in the Country" by Tomie de Paola *(341–343)*			
What Makes a Great Opinion Essay? *(345)*			
STUDENT MODEL Working Draft *(346)* Final Copy *(347)*	10–1		
The Writing Process Write an Opinion Essay			
Prewriting Explore Your Topic *(349)* Focus Skill: Using Examples to Explain *(350)*	10–2 10–3	 125	 81
Drafting Focus Skill: Openings and Closings *(351)* Focus Skill: Writing with Voice *(352)*		126 127	82 83
Revising How Good Is Your Opinion Essay? [rubric] *(353)* **Writing Conference** *(354)* **Revising Strategies** *(356)*	10–4 10–5 	128 129	84 85
Proofreading *(357)*			
Publishing and Reflecting *(358)*			
Writing Prompts and Test Practice *(360–361)*			
SPECIAL FOCUS ON INFLUENCING Writing to Persuade *(362–369)*			
COMMUNICATION LINK Listening/Viewing/Media: Comparing Media *(370–371)*			

Unit 10

Tools and Tips

- **Using the Dictionary,** *pp. H3–H12*
- **Using Technology,** *pp. H21–H30*
- **Writer's Tools,** *pp. H31–H34*
- **Spelling Guide,** *pp. H40–H44*
- **My First Thesaurus,** *pp. H45–H56*

School-Home Connection

Suggestions for informing or involving family members in classroom activities and learning related to this unit are included in the Teacher's Edition throughout the unit.

Meeting Individual Needs

- **FOR SPECIAL NEEDS/INCLUSION:** *Houghton Mifflin English* Audiotape
- **FOR STUDENTS ACQUIRING ENGLISH:**
  - Notes and activities are included in this Teacher's Edition throughout the unit to help you adapt or use pupil book activities with students acquiring English.
  - Students can listen to the published and student models on audiotape.
- **ENRICHMENT:** See *Teacher's Resource Book.*

All audiotape recordings are also available on CD.

Daily Language Practice

Each sentence or group of words includes two capitalization, punctuation, usage, or spelling errors based on skills presented in the Grammar and Spelling Connections in this unit or from Grammar Units 1, 3, 5, 7, and 9. Each day write one sentence on the chalkboard. Have children find the errors and write the sentence correctly on a sheet of paper. To make the activity easier, identify the kinds of errors.

1. Clint find a animal in the garage. Clint finds an animal in the garage. **(subject-verb agreement; using *a* and *an*)**
2. The four girls talks to miss Chin. The four girls talk to Miss Chin. **(subject-verb agreement; titles for people)**
3. Margo take home the book <u>pet parade</u>. Margo takes home the book <u>Pet Parade</u>. **(subject-verb agreement; writing book titles)**
4. The wind blow Joys kite into a tree. The wind blows Joy's kite into a tree. **(subject-verb agreement; possessive nouns with *'s*)**
5. Every sunday Mom and I has gone to Grandma's house. Every Sunday Mom and I have gone to Grandma's house. **(capitalizing days; subject-verb agreement)**
6. Paco said, Our bikes are in the hal. Paco said, "Our bikes are in the hall." **(quotation marks; spelling/double final consonants)**
7. Every memorial day we swims at the lake. Every Memorial Day we swim at the lake. **(capitalizing holidays; subject-verb agreement)**
8. Jamie moved to Tampa on June, 9 2000? Jamie moved to Tampa on June 9, 2000. **(commas in dates; end punctuation/telling sentences)**
9. Now Pete and his dad lives by a big lake in Chicago Illinois. Now Pete and his dad live by a big lake in Chicago, Illinois. **(subject-verb agreement; commas with names of places)**
10. Barbara asked, "What kind of baseball mit is that." Barbara asked, "What kind of baseball mitt is that?" **(spelling/double final consonants; end marks in quotations)**

Additional Resources

Workbook Plus, Unit 10
Reteaching Workbook, Unit 10
Teacher's Resource Book
Transparencies, Unit 10
Posters, Unit 10

Technology Tools

TEACHER'S RESOURCE DISK (for handwriting support)

CD-ROM: *Sunbuddy® Writer
Paint, Write & Play! (published by The Learning Company)
*Type to Learn Jr.™

INTERNET: http://www.eduplace.com/kids/hme/ or http://www.eduplace.com/rdg/hme/

Visit Education Place for these additional support materials and activities:

- author biographies
- student writing models
- graphic organizers
- an interactive rubric
- writing prompts

Assessment

Test Booklet, Unit 10

Keeping a Journal

Discuss with children the value of keeping a journal as a way of promoting self-expression and fluency. Encourage children to record their thoughts and ideas in a notebook. Inform students whether the journal will be private or will be reviewed periodically as a way of assisting growth. The following prompts may be useful for generating writing ideas.

Journal Prompts

- Name some sounds that you do not like. Why don't you like them?
- What is your favorite kind of music? Why?
- What would be fun about splashing in puddles after a rainstorm?

Introducing the Unit

Using the Photograph

- Have children look at the photograph. Ask a volunteer to read the caption aloud. Tell children that the caption states an **opinion**. It tells what someone believes or feels about a shark.
- Have children suggest other opinions about a shark, for example, "A shark is a beautiful fish" or "A shark is a frightening fish."
- Explain that because an **opinion** tells what someone believes or feels about something, it cannot be proven right or wrong. Tell children that they will learn about writing to express their opinion about something.
- Write this statement on the chalkboard and have children copy it: A shark's mouth is on the underside of its head. Point out that it is a statement of fact because it can be proven true. Work with children to create a statement of opinion about the mouth, such as "I think a shark's mouth is ugly." Ask volunteers to identify any clue words in the opinion statement. (I think.)

Independent Writing

Children can benefit by having time each day or several times a week to write in their journals or do self-selected writing activities. Remind children to think about purpose and audience and choose an appropriate format for both.

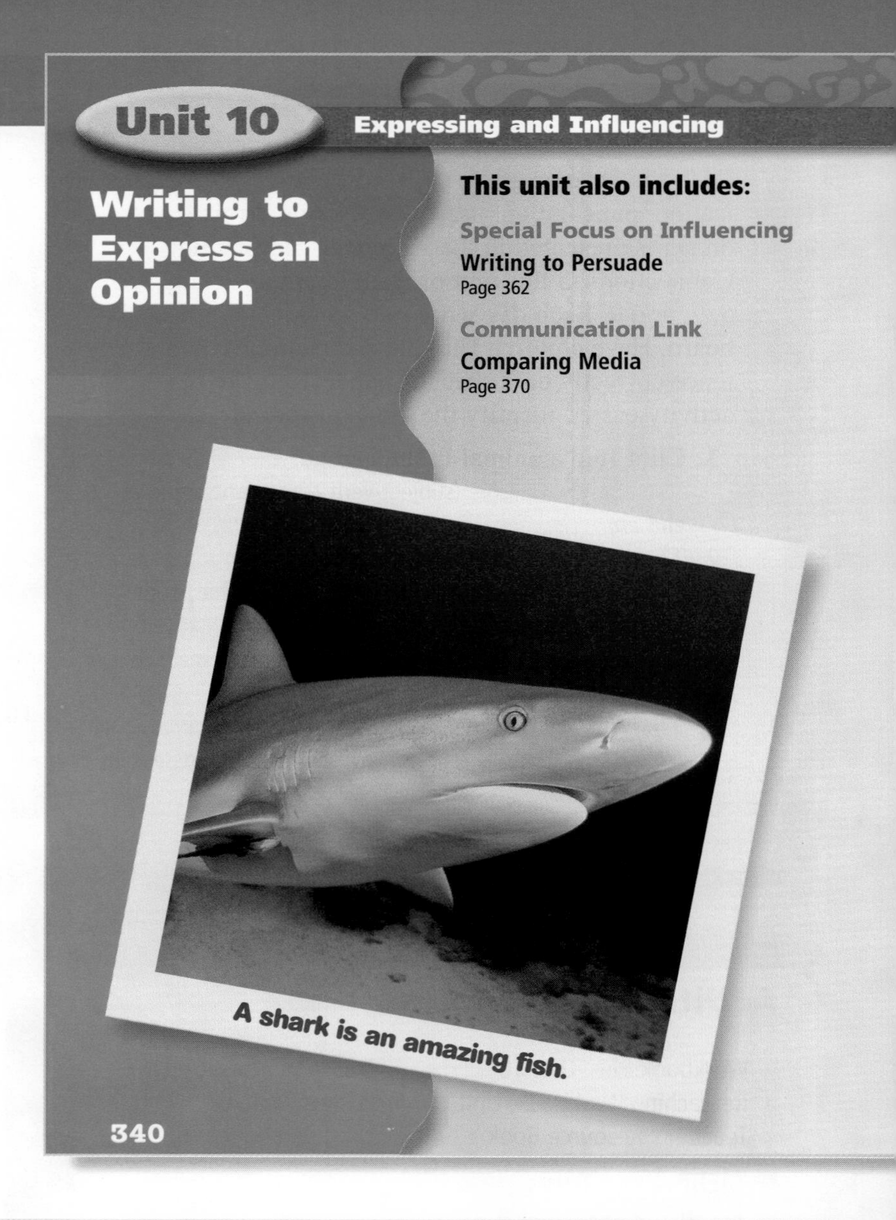

A shark is an amazing fish.

Shared Writing Activity

Work with children to write an opinion paragraph about sharks.

1. Work with children to generate an opinion statement about sharks, such as "Sharks are scary." Write this statement on the board.
2. Ask volunteers to tell reasons that they feel support this opinion. List the reasons on the board below the opinion statement.
3. Choose two reasons to include in the opinion paragraph.
4. Work together to develop fact and example sentences that support each reason. Remind children that a fact can be proven true. Write the sentences on the board.
5. Once the fact and example sentences have been established, write the final paragraph with the opinion statement.

Ask volunteers to read the paragraph and discuss how the facts and examples support the reasons.

A Published Model

Listening to an Opinion Essay

In "My Life in the Country," the writer gives his opinion, or tells how he feels, about living in the country. What is the writer's opinion? What are some of the reasons the writer gives to explain the way he feels?

My Life in the Country

by Tomie dePaola

opinion I live in the country and I love it. When I was young, I grew up in a small city that had a busy "downtown" with stores and restaurants, ice cream parlors, and movie theaters. One summer, my whole family went on a real go-away vacation to Vermont. We went through little towns, past red barns, farm houses, and big meadows. It was the very first time I had seen the real COUNTRY, and I fell in love with it. I remember saying to myself, "When I grow up, I'd like to live in the country, just like Vermont." New Hampshire, where I live now, is right next door to Vermont and just as much "country."

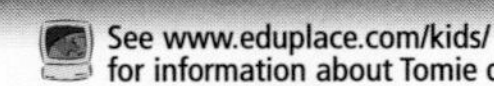

See www.eduplace.com/kids/ for information about Tomie dePaola.

About the Author

INTERNET CONNECTION Send children to www. eduplace.com/kids/ for information about Tomi dePaola.

Resources

Encourage children to look for opinions as they read nonfiction and fiction books, such as the author's expression of opinion about the subject of his or her book. Provide opportunities for children to share some of their finds with the class.

"My Life in the Country"

Lesson Objectives

Children will:

- read a published model of an opinion essay
- identify characteristics of opinion essays
- identify a writer's opinion on a topic
- use illustrations to enhance meaning of story
- write personal and critical responses

Focus on the Model

Building Background

Ask children to discuss places they have visited for the first time. What were they like? Did they like them right away? Tell children that they will read an opinion essay that tells about that kind of experience.

Introducing Vocabulary

Introduce key vocabulary words by writing these sentences on the board. Have a volunteer read each sentence aloud. Ask children to explain the meaning of the boldface words.

The **dew** drops on the flowers looked like rain drops.

The quiet **atmosphere** of the park was calmer than the noisy atmosphere of the classroom.

Reading the Selection

- Discuss with children the general purpose for listening or reading opinion essays. Explain that we read opinion essays to find out how writers feel about something.
- Read aloud the introduction to the selection and the purpose-setting question, which focuses on a characteristic of opinion essays. Tell children to read or listen for the answer to the question.
- Read aloud or have volunteers read aloud the selection if you wish to reinforce listening skills or if children need extra support.

Alternatively, children can listen to the selection on audiotape.

- The call outs highlight key characteristics of an opinion essay that are addressed in the Think About the Opinion Essay questions at the end of this selection.

FOR STUDENTS ACQUIRING ENGLISH

After reading the model, ask children to list words they remembered and liked. Discuss whether these are important reasons or facts for the essay and why or why not.

A Published Model

Why do I like living in the country? First of all, I like the peace and quiet. I like to hear the birds singing in the early morning. I like to see the fresh dew on the meadow first thing in the morning during the summer, and the frost in the fall, and the snow in the winter and early spring. I like seeing the sun hit the top of Mount Sunapee at dawn. I like seeing all the stars at night because there are no city lights to block them out. *reason*

Another reason I like living in the country is that I have the right atmosphere to do my writing, drawing, and painting. There are not many distractions, no noisy traffic, no crowds of people. My ideas have a nice place to grow just like the wildflowers that I see alongside the roads when I take an early morning walk. *reason*

In the winter, I like looking out and seeing the deer eating the leftover apples on the apple trees. And I have a whole flock of crows that live in the meadow all year. The way they walk and "talk" to each other keeps me smiling all day long.

342 A Published Model

I travel often and get to visit cities all over the world, but I'm always happy to get home to my house in the country. Nothing is nicer than to wake up early and have a cup of tea while looking out the window at the meadow. I watch my crows. I think about the day's work ahead. I am very happy.

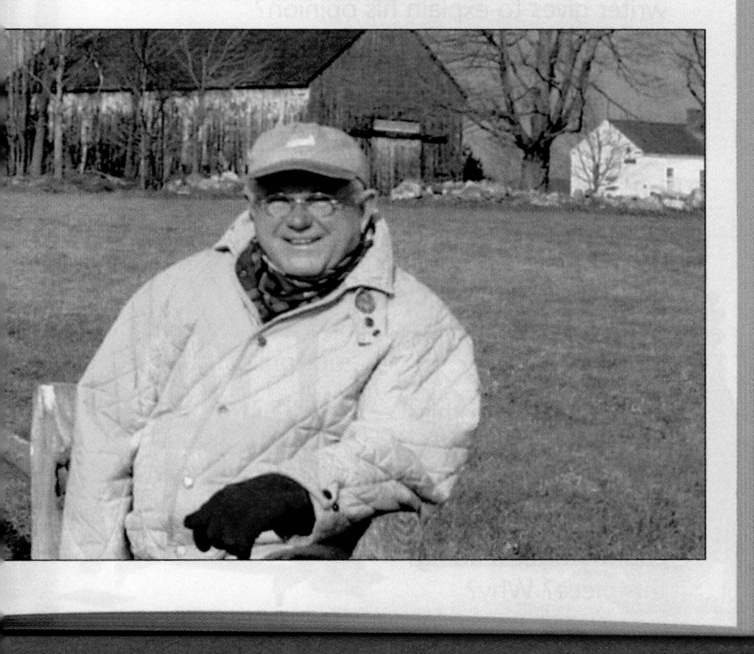

A Student Model: Working Draft

Lesson Objectives

Children will:
- read a working draft of a student-written opinion essay
- discuss the ways the model meets the criteria for a well-written opinion essay and ways that it could be improved

Focus on the Model

- Tell children that they will read a working draft of an opinion essay written by a real student, Phillip A. Jackson. Remind children that a working draft is a work in progress. This means that the writer writes his story without taking time for revisions, knowing that he will make revisions later.
- Have volunteers read the model aloud.

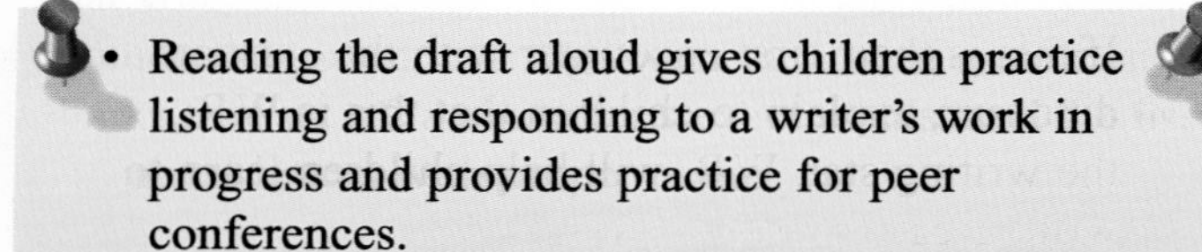

Alternatively students can listen to it read by a student (although not the student writer) on audiotape.

- Tell children to note which characteristics of a great opinion essay Phillip included. Explain that the speech balloons show W.R.'s thoughts about the opinion essay and that children will discuss his ideas after they read.

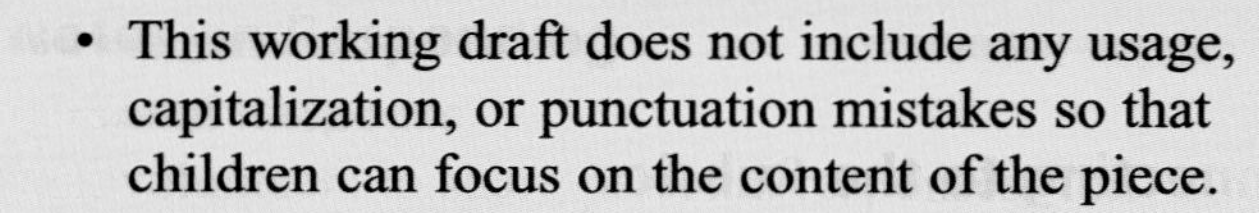

- Reading the draft aloud gives children practice listening and responding to a writer's work in progress and provides practice for peer conferences.
- This working draft does not include any usage, capitalization, or punctuation mistakes so that children can focus on the content of the piece.

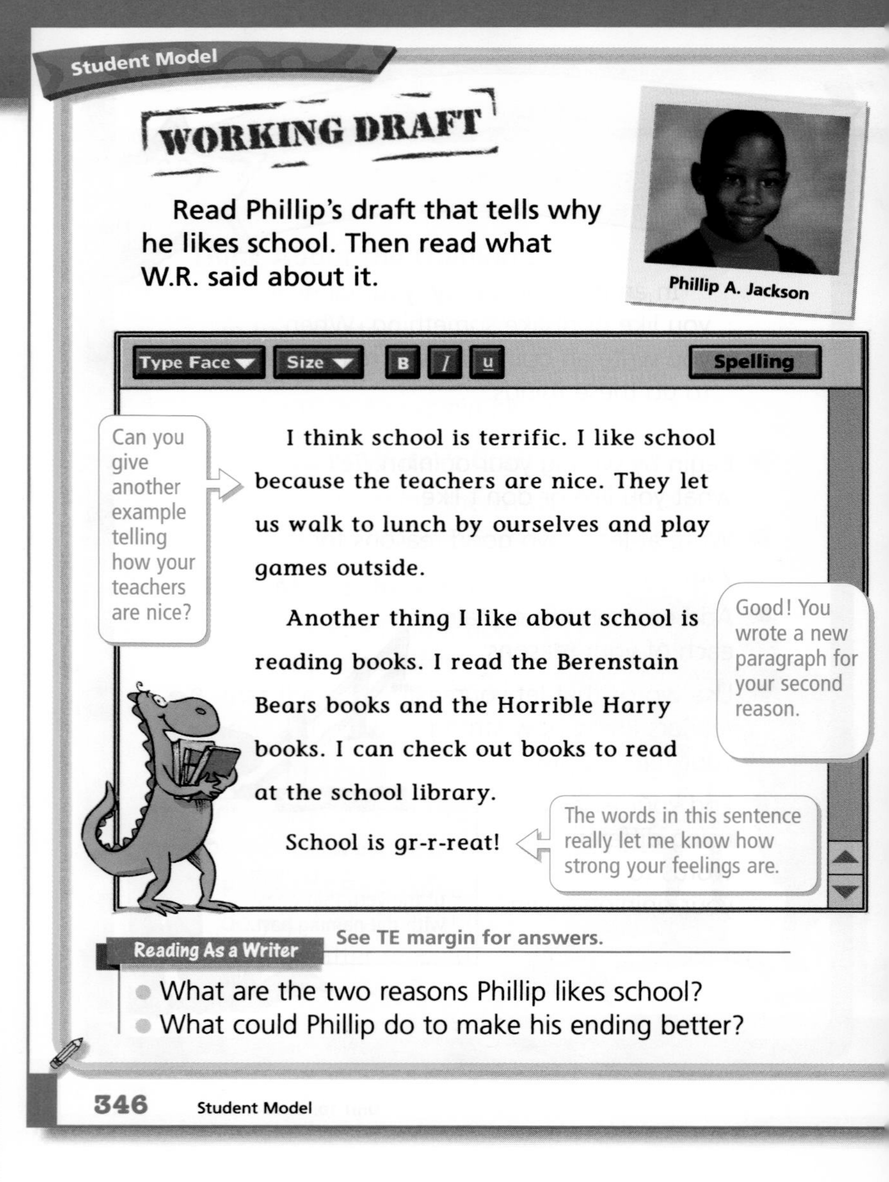

Answers to Reading As a Writer

- Phillip thinks the teachers are nice and he likes reading books.
- Phillip could tell his opinion again in a new way.

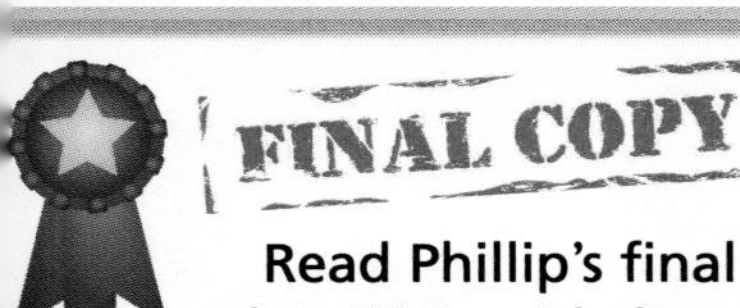

Read Phillip's final copy and what W.R. said about it.

Good! You began by writing your opinion clearly.

School Is Gr-r-reat!
by Phillip A. Jackson

I think school is terrific. First of all, I like school because the teachers are nice. They help us with our work. They also let us walk to lunch by ourselves and play games outside.

Beginning your sentence with these words helps me know that this is your first reason.

Another thing I like about school is reading books. I read books about the Berenstain Bears and Horrible Harry. I can check out books to read at the school library.

I really like school because of the nice teachers and the books I read. I think school is gr-r-reat!

Now your last paragraph really sums it all up!

Reading As a Writer See TE margin for answers.

- What example did Phillip add to help explain that the teachers are nice?
- What did Phillip add to make his last paragraph better?

See www.eduplace.com/kids/hme/ for more examples of student writing.

INTERNET CONNECTION Send your children to www.eduplace.com/kids/hme/ to see more models of student writing. You can also find and print these models at www.eduplace.com/rdg/hme/.

FOR STUDENTS ACQUIRING ENGLISH

Encourage children to list their opinions about school. Then have them compare these against Phillip's draft. Ask, "Are there places where your ideas fit in?" "Do they improve or clutter the draft?" "Is this a possible topic for you?"

A Student Model: Final Copy

Lesson Objectives

Children will:
- read a well-written final copy of a student's opinion essay
- note and compare the revisions that improved the first draft

Focus on the Model

SUMMARY OF REVISIONS In the final copy, Phillip added another example to support his first reason for liking school; he included an ending that retold his reasons in a different way. Blackline Master 10-1 provides a copy of the student's working draft, showing the revisions that were made.

Have volunteers read the model aloud. Alternatively, children can listen to it read by another student (although not the student writer) on audiotape.

Answers to Reading As a Writer
- They help us with our work.
- He retold what his opinion was and why.

Connecting to the Rubric

- Have children look again at the list of characteristics on page 345 and review with them how Phillip's final copy addressed each one.
- Point out that Phillip used the correct form of the verb that goes with the naming part.

More About Writer's Craft
- Discuss with children why Phillip wrote his essay in three paragraphs. (One paragraph tells why he thinks school is great, the next paragraph adds another reason why school is great, the last paragraph concludes the essay.)

Looking Ahead Tell children that they will next write their own opinion essays, using the writing process. As they go along, they will learn how to include good examples that support the reasons for their opinions.

Write an Opinion Essay

Lesson Objectives

Children will:
- list their ideas for audience, purpose, and publishing/sharing formats
- list ideas for an opinion essay
- choose an appropriate topic to write about

Start Thinking

Focus on Instruction

- Ask how an opinion essay written to your teacher might be different from one written to your best friend. (The teacher's might use more formal language.)
- Discuss how the purpose might affect the essay. (An essay written to persuade would include reasons and examples to persuade the audience.)
- Ask how including the essay on a poster might be different from writing it as a letter. (Posters would include visuals and be less personal.)

Choose a Topic

Focus on Instruction

Point out the Help Box to children for assistance in thinking of ideas. Draw children's attention to the Writing Prompts on page 360.

- Remind children to choose a topic that they feel strongly about.
- Review their final choices. If a topic seems too narrow, ask children to identify at least two reasons that back up their opinion.
- Students can write two points of view about their topics rather than just one if that matches the testing format in your state or district. The strategies for one point of view throughout the writing process can be applied to a second point of view as well.

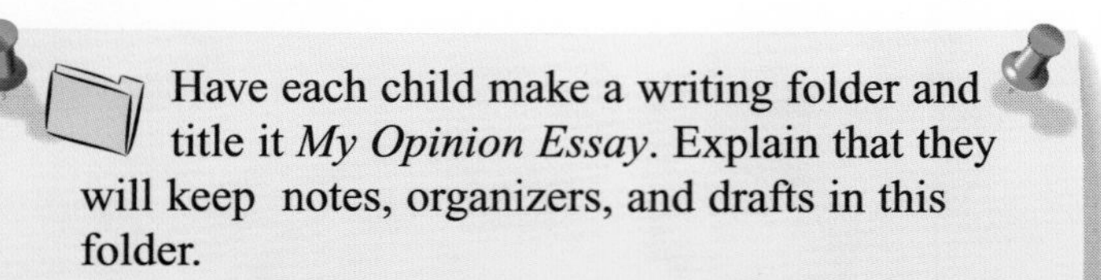

Have each child make a writing folder and title it *My Opinion Essay*. Explain that they will keep notes, organizers, and drafts in this folder.

- The topic discussion taps into children's oral language and helps them think about words and language to use when they write as well as elicit details.

SCHOOL-HOME CONNECTION Suggest that children discuss possible topics with family members.

Write an Opinion Essay

Choose Your Topic

1. **List** three things that you like a lot or that you don't like at all.

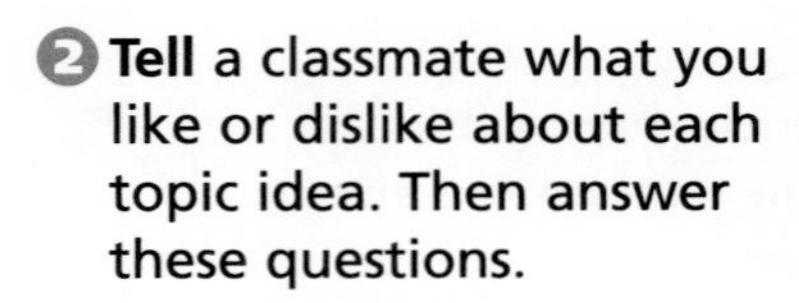

2. **Tell** a classmate what you like or dislike about each topic idea. Then answer these questions.
   - Which topic did you explain best?
   - Which topic do you have the strongest feelings about?
3. **Copy and complete** these sentences. Name your audience and topic.

   _____ will read or hear my opinion essay.

   I will write about _____.

Stuck for an Idea?

How about these?
- a subject in school
- foods
- sports or games
- holidays

See page 360 for more ideas.

Help with Choosing a Topic

MORE TOPIC IDEAS

Suggest that children:
- think of something they really like or dislike,
- look through magazines, newspapers, or websites on current events they find interesting, or
- jot down a few things they like best about: *school, neighborhood, family, friends.*

TECH TIP

Children can refer to Using the Computer on page H23.

PREWRITING DRAFTING REVISING PROOFREADING PUBLISHING

Explore Your Topic

1. **Think** about your topic. List reasons why you feel the way you do about your topic.
2. **Look** at the chart Phillip used to list the reasons he likes school.

Opinion Chart	
My opinion: I like school.	
Reason 1: nice teachers	Reason 2: reading books

3. **Make** a chart like the one Phillip made. Write your opinion and at least two reasons why you like or do not like your topic.
4. **Show** your chart to a classmate. Explain your reasons clearly. Do the reasons make sense to your classmate?
5. **Think** about what your classmate said. Make changes to your chart.

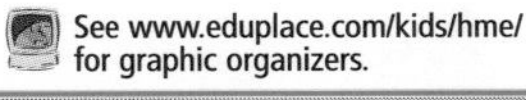
See www.eduplace.com/kids/hme/ for graphic organizers.

Help with Exploring the Topic

TECH TIP
To help children brainstorm reasons, have them type their opinion at the top of the page and then type as many reasons as they can think of beneath it. You may want to give children a time limit.

IDEAS FOR EXLORING
You can suggest these alternative ideas for exploring topics.
- Make a list instead of a chart.
- Work in small groups to think of reasons for each topic.

EXPLORING TWO POINTS OF VIEW
If you want children to express two viewpoints about their topics, suggest that they use a T-chart to help them list their reasons for each point of view.

WHY I LIKE CATS	WHY I DON'T LIKE CATS
• fun to play with	• jump on everything
• soft and cuddly	• wake me up a lot

Lesson Objectives

Children will:
- list reasons why they feel as they do about topic
- look at a modeled chart and create one
- share chart with partner and make revisions

Explore Your Topic

Focus on Instruction

- See Blackline Master 10-2 for a graphic organizer children can use to explore their topics. You can find other graphic organizers in the Tools and Tips section of the pupil book.
- Discuss with children the ideas in the Help Box on page 348. Tell them that ideas they feel strongly about work best. If they don't feel strongly about their topic, they may not come up with enough reasons to support it.
- Review each child's chart. Check that each reason is related to why they like or don't like their topic.

INTERNET CONNECTION Send your children to www.eduplace.com/kids/hme/ for graphic organizers. You can also find and print these organizers at www.eduplace.com/rdg/hme/.

FOR STUDENTS ACQUIRING ENGLISH
Without formulating or finalizing their topics yet, ask children to write freely for a few days about their topics. Challenge them to write lists, draw webs, and/or pictures, talk to friends and family, etc. Have them read poems, stories, or articles about their topic. Then they can begin to organize their material for writing.

Explaining with Examples

Lesson Objectives

Children will:
- identify modeled examples
- write examples to support reasons in their Opinion Chart

Focus on Instruction

- Ask children to tell titles of favorite books and movies. Write these on the board in two columns.
- Point to a title and ask volunteers why they liked the choice. Ask children to discuss a favorite part or character that tells more about their reason.
- Point out that the favorite books and movies are their *opinions*, the responses to why they liked them are their *reasons*, and their responses that tell more about a part or character are *examples*.

Try It Together

- Discuss the reasons children like recess.
- Have children elaborate by asking questions such as: What do you like to do at recess? Tell about a time when you did this. What can you do during recess that you can't do during class time? Tell about a time when you did this.

Plan Your Opinion Essay

- A copy of the organizer appears on Blackline Master 10-3. You can find other graphic organizers in the Tools and Tips section of the pupil book.
- Review children's completed charts to make sure there are examples for each reason and that everything relates to their opinion.

INTERNET CONNECTION Send your students to www.eduplace.com/kids/hme/ for graphic organizers. You can also find and print these organizers at www.eduplace.com/rdg/hme/.

FOR STUDENTS ACQUIRING ENGLISH

With all the information they have gathered and the thinking they have done, children should be able to select a number of examples to support their opinions. Suggest they look through all their information, circling or recopying each example they will use.

Focus Skill

Explaining with Examples

When you write an opinion, use good examples to explain each of your reasons.

Try It Together Answers will vary.

Why do you like recess? With your class, write some strong examples that explain each reason.

Plan Your Opinion Essay

1. **Look** at the examples Phillip added to his Opinion Chart to explain his reasons.

Opinion Chart	
My opinion: I like school.	
Reason 1: nice teachers	Reason 2: reading books
Example 1: They let us walk to lunch by ourselves.	Example 1: I read the Berenstain Bears and Horrible Harry books.
Example 2: They let us play games outside.	Example 2: I check books out at the library.

2. **Add** boxes to your Opinion Chart and write two examples to explain each reason.

See www.eduplace.com/kids/hme/ for graphic organizers.

Meeting Individual Needs

RETEACHING WORKBOOK, page 81

Explaining with Examples

Use examples to explain your opinions.
Opinion: I like ice hockey.
Reason: It's a fun and exciting game.
Example: My friends are on my team.
Example: We get to skate very fast.

Write the name of your favorite book. Tell one reason why you like it. Explain your reason with examples.

My Opinion: My favorite book is

Answers will vary.

Reason: I like it because

Example 1:

Example 2:

WORKBOOK PLUS, page 125

Explaining with Examples

My opinion: I think blue is the nicest color of all.
Reason: The color blue makes me feel relaxed.
Example 1: I am relaxed at the beach and blue makes me think of the ocean.
Example 2: I feel relaxed at my grandma's house because she has blue curtains.

Write an opinion about a food you do or do not like. Then write one reason why you feel the way you do. Write two examples that explain the reason. Answers will vary.

My Opinion:

Reason:

Example 1:

Example 2:

PREWRITING DRAFTING REVISING PROOFREADING PUBLISHING

Focus Skill

Openings and Closings

Your opinion essay needs a strong opening and closing. Your **opening** is how you start the essay. Your **closing** is how you end the essay.

Weak Opening	Strong Opening
I like Dallas.	Dallas is an exciting city.

Weak Closing	Strong Closing
So that's what I think about Dallas.	Dallas is a city with many interesting sights to see.

Try It Together Answers will vary.

With your class, choose a fun activity you have done together. Work together to write a strong opening and closing for an essay telling why you liked the activity.

Write Your Opening and Closing

1. **Write** a strong opening for your opinion essay.
2. **Write** a strong closing for your opinion essay. Tell your opinion again, using different words.

Openings and Closings

Lesson Objectives

Children will:

- write a strong opening for their opinion essay
- write a strong closing for their opinion essay

Focus on Instruction

- Ask children why it is important to write a strong beginning for their essay. (to grab reader's attention)
- Ask children why it is important to write a strong ending for their essay. (to remind the audience of the purpose)
- Ask if a writer were writing an opinion about why she loves basketball, should she begin with a sentence, such as I love basketball? (No, it's too weak.)
- Write the following sentence on the board: *Basketball is the best sport I know*. Then ask: Would the following sentence make a good closing for this opening? Why or why not? *Basketball is a good sport for exercise and excitement*. (Yes, it retells the main point in a different way.)

Try It Together

Have children work with partners to write a list of their partner's comments they think are useful. Remind them that they can use this list as a reference guide.

Write Your Opening and Closing

- Have children return to Phillip's final draft on page 347. Point out the short, exciting first sentence. Have children compare the new ending with the weak ending of the working draft.
- As children write their own openings and closings, have them ask what they could do to make them more interesting. Point out that there is more than one way to open or close a piece of writing. Children should choose the way that they feel would be most interesting for their audience.

FOR STUDENTS ACQUIRING ENGLISH

Before focussing on the openings and closings, help children number their facts in order by importance or by subject. Then show how these are written into paragraphs. The opening and closing are then finishing touches. Explain the phrase "jump right in" when discussing lively openings that absorb readers quickly.

Meeting Individual Needs

● RETEACHING WORKBOOK, page 82

Openings and Closings

A good opening starts the essay in an interesting way.
A good closing uses new words to retell the main point.

Weak Opening	Strong Opening
Swimming is nice.	Boy, do I like to swim!
Weak Closing	**Strong Closing**
That's why I like swimming.	Anyone can swim for fun and good exercise.

This paragraph has a weak opening and closing. Read the paragraph. Then write a strong opening and closing.

Littering is bad. Our school is a beautiful place. It looks messy when kids throw litter on the ground. When we throw our lunch wrappers in the trash, the playground and the halls look nice. We are proud of our school. That is why we should not litter.

Strong Opening

Sample opening: It makes me upset when kids litter at school.

Strong Closing

Sample closing: Everyone would be happier if we remembered not to litter.

▲■ WORKBOOK PLUS, page 126

Openings and Closings

Weak Opening	Strong Opening
I am writing about soccer.	I think soccer is a very cool sport.
Weak Closing	**Strong Closing**
I also like to play on a team.	Believe me, soccer is the greatest!

The opinion paragraph below needs an opening and a closing. Read the paragraph. Then write a strong opening and closing.

When you play basketball, no one stays still very long. Players have to dribble, pass, and run all the time. I also like basketball because I am good at it. I love the "swish" when I make a basket.

Strong Opening

Sample opening: What's so great about basketball? Listen carefully and you'll find out.

Strong Closing

Sample closing: Basketball really keeps you on your toes. That is what's so great about basketball.

Writing with Voice

Lesson Objective

Children will:
- write the body of their opinion essays

Focus on Instruction

Ask volunteers or the whole class to act out the sentences in the lesson. Have children discuss the feelings they expressed for each sentence. Write on the board the words that come up during the discussion.

Try It Together

- Write the following list of strong words on the board. Ask children to consider using them in the sentences:

excited	hurray	thrilled	special
terrific	fantastic	best	most

Write Your Opinion Essay

- Provide children with materials such as a thesaurus to help them choose strong words that add voice.
- Refer children to their Opinion Chart to help them keep track of their reasons and examples. Remind them that they should write two of each.

Drafting Reminders

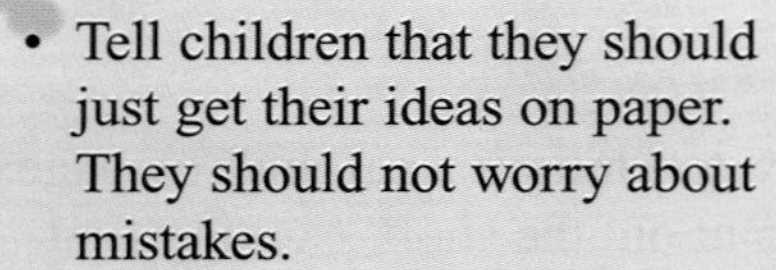

- Tell children that they should just get their ideas on paper. They should not worry about mistakes.
- Tell children if they don't know how to spell a word, they should spell it as best they can and go on. They can fix the spelling later.
- Tell children to skip every other line to leave room for changes.
- Remind children just to cross out words they don't like if they change their minds. They should not start over.

FOR STUDENTS ACQUIRING ENGLISH

Catchy openings and closings are a good place to show examples of voice. Challenge children to write in a completely different voice from the one that seems natural to them. If they are usually loud and funny, suggest they try writing quiet openings, and vice versa.

The Writing Process: PREWRITING | DRAFTING | REVISING | PROOFREADING | PUBLISHING

Focus Skill

Writing with Voice

In your opinion essay, use powerful words to show how strong your feelings are.

Weak Voice	Strong Voice
I like living in the country.	I live in the country, and I **love** it.
School is fun.	I think school is **terrific**.

Try It Together

Work with your class to rewrite the sentence below. Use words that will show your strong feelings.

I think spelling contests are fun.

Write Your Opinion Essay

1. **Begin** your opinion essay by copying your opening on another sheet of paper.
2. **Write** a paragraph to explain each reason in your Opinion Chart. Include examples to explain each reason.
3. **End** your essay by copying your closing.

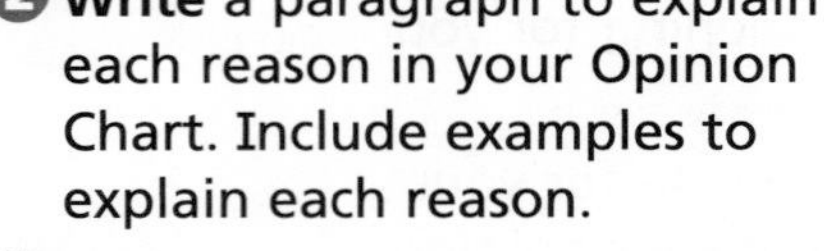

Meeting Individual Needs

● RETEACHING WORKBOOK, page 83

Writing with Voice

Use strong words to show your feelings.

Weak Voice	Strong Voice
The stories are good.	I think the Henry and Mudge stories are fantastic.

This paragraph about a funny book is dull and boring. Fix the underlined sentences by adding your own voice.

The book about puppies was a lot of fun to read. The smallest puppy was funny. He was a good friend. The mean puppy was not fun. Everyone should read this book.

Sample answers

The smallest puppy was very silly and made me smile.

The mean puppy made the other puppies and me very sad.

This is a great story with something for everyone to enjoy.

▲■ WORKBOOK PLUS, page 127

Writing with Voice

Weak Voice	Strong Voice
I go to Pinella Elementary. I like this school. The teachers are nice. My classmates are nice, too.	Pinella Elementary School is the best! The teachers help us with our work, and you can really tell they care.

The paragraph below is dull and boring. Rewrite it in your own voice. Use strong words that share an opinion.

People should treat animals kindly. Animals have feelings, too. People should take their dogs for a walk. People should brush their dogs and give them treats. Then the dogs will be happy. I feel strongly about this. Paragraphs will vary.

How Good Is Your Opinion Essay?

- **Read** your draft.
- **Copy** the sentences below that describe your essay.

Superstar

- My opening is interesting and tells my opinion clearly.
- I included at least two good reasons and some examples for my opinion.
- I used words that show my strong feelings.
- My closing retells my opinion.
- My writing has only a few mistakes.

Rising Star

- My opening could tell my opinion more clearly.
- I can add more reasons and examples for my opinion.
- I can use stronger words to show my feelings.
- My closing could retell my opinion better.
- My writing has many mistakes.

See www.eduplace.com/kids/hme/ to interact with this rubric.

How Good Is Your Opinion Essay?

Lesson Objective:

Children will:
- evaluate their opinion essays, using a rubric

Connecting to the Criteria

Have children reread the characteristics of an opinion essay listed on page 345. Then explain that the rubric shown on this page refers to those characteristics. Tell them that the rubric will help them decide which parts of their essays meet the standards of a great opinion essay and what parts they think still need more work.

Focus on Instruction

- Review the rubric with children. Have volunteers read aloud the pairs of related characteristics. Discuss the differences between the sentences in each pair.
- Blackline Master 10-4 provides a copy of the rubric as a checklist for children using the hardbound edition. Alternatively they can write the sentences that describe their essays.
- See the Teacher's Resource Book for scoring rubrics.

INTERNET CONNECTION Have children go to www.eduplace.com/kids/hme/ to use an interactive version of the rubric shown in the pupil book. Children will get feedback and support depending on how they mark the rubric items.

This page is also available as a poster.

Meeting Individual Needs

● RETEACHING WORKBOOK, page 84

Revising an Opinion Essay

Have I	yes
• stated my opinion clearly and in an interesting way?	☐
• written good reasons and examples?	☐
• used words that show my feelings?	☐
• told my opinion again at the end, using different words?	☐

Revise this paragraph to make it better. Check off each box to be sure. You can write your changes in the spaces above each line, on the sides, and below the paragraph.

I love big cities. ~~Big cities are fun.~~ There are so many different people. I heard people speaking Chinese and Greek. Each block has about ten restaurants, and each one serves a different kind of food. It's easy to get around in big cities. ~~I also like to ride buses.~~ Even if you don't drive, you can hop on a bus or train. I love big cities because there is so much happening. ~~Big cities are fun.~~

▲■ WORKBOOK PLUS, page 128

Revising an Opinion Essay

Have I	yes
• stated my opinion clearly and in an interesting way?	☐
• written good reasons and examples?	☐
• used words that show my feelings?	☐
• told my opinion again at the end, using different words?	☐

Revise this paragraph to make it better. Check off each box to be sure. You can write your changes in the spaces above each line, on the sides, and below the paragraph.

I think pizza is the perfect party food. ~~Pizza is party food because everyone likes it.~~ I don't know anyone who doesn't like pizza. You can add different things, like peppers or olives. Everyone can have what they like. Also, pizza doesn't cost a lot. One large pie feeds four people for only a few dollars each. Pizza has something for everyone. ~~That's why pizza is good.~~

FOR STUDENTS ACQUIRING ENGLISH

Before using the rubric in the pupil book, ask children to write a short sentence or two about how they think their opinion essay is going, what parts have been easy to write, what parts difficult, what parts need work and why, and what parts are great. Have a session in which each child shares his or her work at least once. Finally, ask students to consider whether their essay is moving toward being right for the audience and purpose they originally chose. Ask children, "If you were in the audience, what would you think of the essay?"

Lesson Objective

Children will:
- revise their working drafts, based on their evaluations

Revise Your Opinion Essay

Focus on Instruction

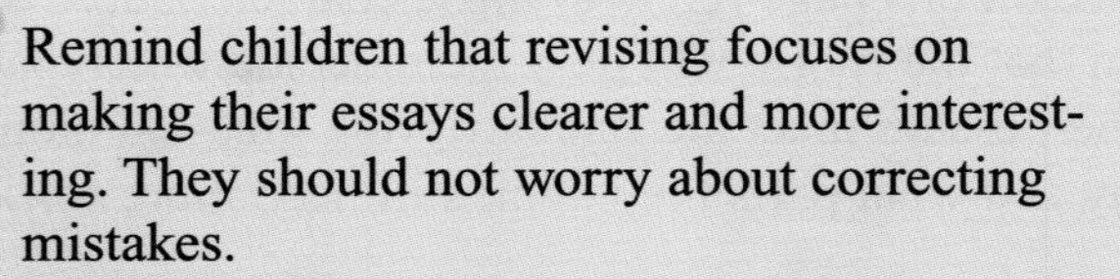

Revising Reminders

Remind children that revising focuses on making their essays clearer and more interesting. They should not worry about correcting mistakes.

- Review each child's evaluation of his or her opinion essay, and discuss what revisions the child could make to improve it. As they revise each part, have them check off the appropriate sentence from the rubric. When they are finished revising, ask them to read their essays again to be sure the papers are clear.

Revise Your Opinion Essay

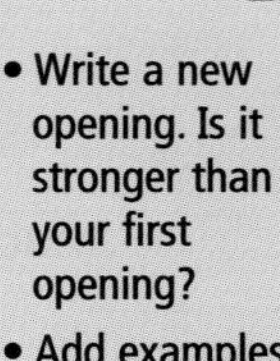

1. **Look** at the sentences from page 353 that you wrote about your opinion essay. What can you do to make your essay better?
2. **Have a writing conference.**

When You're the Writer
- Write one question that you have about your opinion essay.
- Share your essay with a classmate. Ask your question.

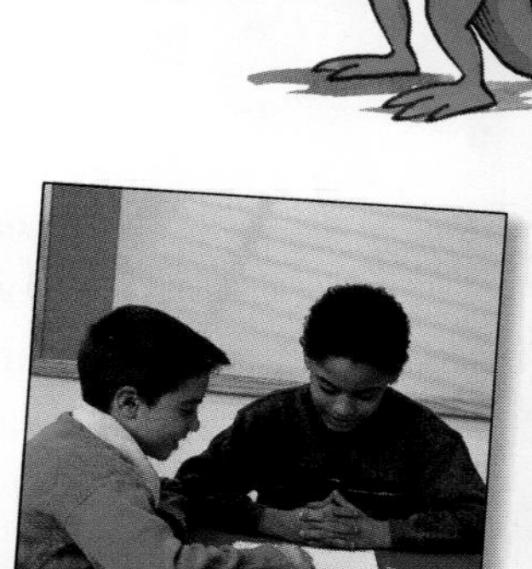

When You're the Listener
- Tell two things you like about the essay.
- Ask your classmate for more examples if you don't understand a reason.
- Look at the next page for more ideas.

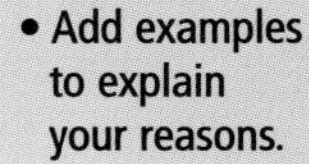

3. **Revise** your opinion essay. Think about what you and your classmate talked about. Make changes to your draft to make it better. The Revising Strategies on page 356 may help you.

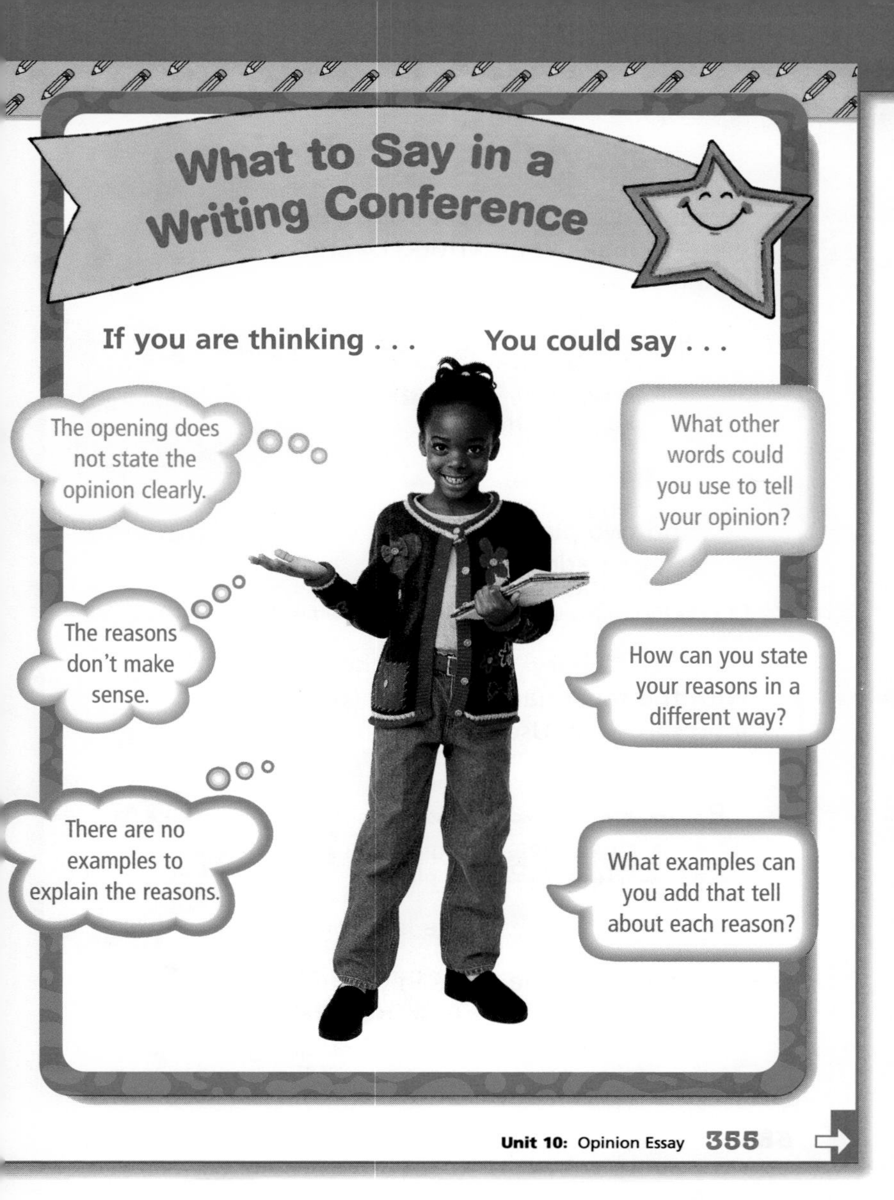

Help with Conferencing

ADDITIONAL CONFERENCING QUESTIONS

These questions may be useful during teacher-student conferences.

- Explain how you feel about your topic.
- Can you elaborate on your examples so your audiance can picture them clearly?
- How does this topic affect your life? Can you include those ideas in your ending?

EVALUATION TIP

Help refocus children who are having trouble by pairing them with those who are more comfortable with conferencing.

What to Say in a Writing Conference

Lesson Objectives

Children will:

- have a writing conference
- retell a spoken message by summarizing or clarifying

Read aloud and discuss with children the text in the thought and speech balloons. Explain that the thought balloons show what a listener might think while listening to an opinion essay. The speech balloons show what the listener could ask to help the writer know what parts might not be clear.

Writing Conference Reminders

- Tell children to read their papers aloud to their partners. Unclear handwriting and mistakes in spelling can interfere with the partner's ability to respond to the content of the paper.
- Tell children to do these things when they are the listeners:

  Always compliment the writer. Discuss possibilities, such as the reasons are strong or the examples are interesting.

  Retell what they have heard after listening to their partner's paper.
- Remind children to choose their words carefully. They don't want to make the writers feel bad.
- Direct children to speak softly if reading to a partner and louder if reading to a larger group.
- Tell children that they don't have to take all of their partner's suggestions.

 This page is also available as a poster.

- Children can use Blackline Master 10-5 during their writing conferences.

 **FOR STUDENTS ACQUIRING ENGLISH**

Conferencing is vital to help children become aware of the writing process. By simply reading aloud or seeing where someone loses interest, children can get a sense of where they need to correct grammatical errors or change content. Ask children to take notes as listeners and share them with you and their partners.

Revising Strategies

Lesson Objectives

Children will:
- use exact words to make their writing clearer
- combine short sentences to make one long sentence

Focus on Instruction

Word Choice
- Write the following sentence pairs on the board:

  I go to school early. I walk to school at 7:00 A.M.

  We play after school. My friends and I play basketball after school.
- Talk about the different images that come to mind in each sentence. Summarize with children that using exact words will help readers get a clearer picture.

Sentence Fluency
- Write the following sentences on the board:

  Running is easy to do.

  Running is good for you.

  Running is a lot of fun.
- Ask volunteers to suggest ways to make one long sentence from the three shorter ones. (Running is easy to do, good for you, and a lot of fun.)

Revising Strategies

Word Choice Write exact nouns, adjectives, and verbs to make your writing clearer.

I ~~like~~ love to ~~cook~~ bake with Grandma Ana.
We ~~make good things~~ bake tasty apple pies.

▶ Find two places in your essay to add exact words.

Use My First Thesaurus on page H45 to find exact words.

Sentence Fluency You can make short sentences with the same naming part into one long sentence. Use commas to do so.

Rex is the best dog! ~~Rex is cute.~~ Rex is cute, friendly, and playful.
~~Rex is friendly. Rex is playful.~~

▶ Try to find one place in your essay where you can join short sentences into one long one, using commas.

FOR STUDENTS ACQUIRING ENGLISH

Ask children to find and name weak words from their essays. List them on the board and have children work in small groups to find alternatives either from each other or by using the thesaurus. Some examples of weak words are *went*, *said*, *we*; strong replacements would be *hurried*, *shouted*, *the team*.

Meeting Individual Needs

● RETEACHING WORKBOOK, page 85

Revising Strategies: Word Choice

Use exact words to add clear details to sentences.

I ~~took~~ grabbed the ~~big~~ huge bike and ~~went~~ raced down the hill.

Read each sentence. Choose a more exact word to replace the underlined word. Write the new sentence.

asked	skipped	chicken	lovely

1. The girl went to town.
   The girl skipped to town.
2. He said, "Where are you going?
   He asked, "Where are you going?"
3. Bobby drew some good pictures.
   Bobby drew some lovely pictures.
4. I loved the food we ate for dinner.
   I loved the chicken we ate for dinner.

▲■ WORKBOOK PLUS, page 129

Revising Strategies: Word Choice

~~They went~~ Three boys rode to the ~~event~~ Harvest Fair.

Revise each sentence. Add exact nouns, adjectives, and verbs to make the sentences interesting. Sample answers

1. I think she works hard.
   I think my mom works really hard.
2. They went to a city.
   Dad and Grandpa traveled to Miami.
3. He liked the book.
   Marco enjoyed the funny book.
4. I liked the food we ate.
   I loved the delicious pasta we ate.

PREWRITING DRAFTING REVISING PROOFREADING PUBLISHING

Proofread Your Opinion Essay

1. **Proofread** your draft. Use the Proofreading Checklist and the Proofreading Marks.
2. **Use** a class dictionary to check spellings.

Proofreading Checklist

- Each sentence begins with a capital letter.
- Each sentence ends with the correct end mark.
- Each sentence has a naming part and an action part.
- Each word is spelled correctly.

Proofreading Marks

∧	Add	≡	Capital letter
⌐	Delete	/	Small letter
¶	Indent for new paragraph		

Using the Proofreading Marks

Soccer is great! it is so exciting when I scores a goal.

3. **Review** these rules before you proofread.

Grammar and Spelling Connections

Verbs and Naming Parts When you write a sentence, use the form of the verb that goes with the naming part.

Damon and Ed read books.

Chen reads the newspaper.

Final Consonant Sounds A final consonant sound may be spelled with two letters that are the same.

off fell class

See the Spelling Guide on page H40.

See www.eduplace.com/kids/hme/ for proofreading practice.

Help with Proofreading

MANAGEMENT TIPS

- Have each child keep a skill checklist of what he or she needs to proofread for.
- Keep a checklist of the revision directives on this page. Check to make sure that children have followed the suggestions by looking over their papers before they reprint a final neat copy.

TECH TIP

Children can change the color of those words that they are unsure of and then look them up in a dictionary.

Lesson Objective

Children will:
- proofread their opinion essay

Proofread Your Opinion Essay

Focus on Instruction

Proofreading Reminders

- Remind children that the proofreading stage is when they should correct capitalization, usage, punctuation, and spelling.
- Review with children how and when to use the proofreading marks.
- Have children use the Proofreading Checklist in the pupil book. Review and clarify each item in the checklist, using any related Grammar and Spelling Connections. If children need extra support, review the related grammar lessons with them.
- Provide dictionaries for children to check spellings. Tell them to circle any words they think are misspelled and check them in a dictionary after they have finished circling.
- For proofreading practice, see the usage and mechanics lessons in the Grammar units and the Mixed Review practice in each Grammar unit Checkup.

MEETING INDIVIDUAL NEEDS — FOR STUDENTS ACQUIRING ENGLISH

Remind children of their goals for this piece: "For whom are they writing?" "Why are they writing?" If a child cannot answer these questions, have the child read his or her piece aloud while other children help think of ways to make it more appropriate for the child's stated audience and purpose.

Opinion Essay

Lesson Objectives

Children will:

- make neat final copies of their opinion essays
- choose a way to publish or share their essays
- reflect on their writing experience
- evaluate the writing in comparison to others in their writing portfolio

Publish Your Opinion Essay

Focus on Instruction

- Have children decide how they will share their writing, as it may affect the form of their final copy.
- Instruct children to make neat corrections on their final copies, rather than recopy their papers again.
- Observe the way children hold their pencils and position their papers when they make their final copies. Check that they are gaining handwriting proficiency. Remind children to use word and letter spacing and margins to make their papers readable.
- For handwriting instruction and practice, see the Teacher's Resource Disk for printable blackline masters.

SCHOOL-HOME CONNECTION Suggest to children that they incorporate their essays into a family photo album.

Keeping a Writing Portfolio

A writing portfolio is where students can keep samples of their writing. Here are suggestions for creating and using writing portfolios.

- **Selection** A paper might be selected because it is
  - ✓ generally noteworthy
  - ✓ a good example of a particular criterion
  - ✓ an example of a certain kind of writing
  - ✓ from a certain time in the school year
  - ✓ a typical example of the student's work
- **Labeling:** For every paper, have students complete a cover sheet giving the title, date of completion, and reason for inclusion.
- **Review:** Have students remove papers that no longer reflect their best work or aren't needed as baselines.
- **Evaluation:** Review students' portfolios with them to discuss growth and areas that need improvement.

Publish Your Opinion Essay

1. **Make** a neat final copy of your opinion essay.
2. **Write** an interesting title.
3. **Look** at Ideas for Sharing on the next page.
4. **Publish** or share your essay in a way that works for your audience.

- Be sure you wrote all letters correctly and used good spacing. Check that you fixed every mistake.
- Begin the first, last, and each important word in your title with a capital letter.

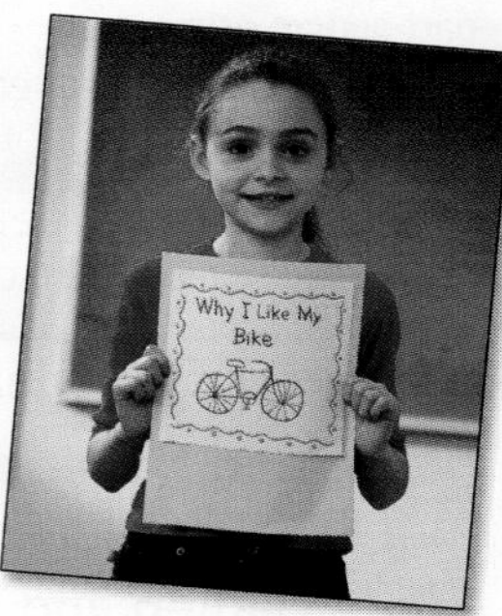

Reflect

Answer these questions about your opinion essay.

- What do you like most about your opinion essay? Why?
- What did you learn while writing your opinion essay?
- Do you like this paper better than other papers you have written? Why or why not?

Tech Tip
If you wrote your opinion essay on a computer, fix all mistakes. Then print out a final copy.

Ideas for Sharing

Write It

- Post your essay on your school's Internet site.
- Share your essay in a class newspaper or a school newsletter.

Say It

- Read your essay to members of your family. Discuss whether or not they agree.
- Send a recording of your essay to someone who might like to listen to it.

Show It

★ Display your essay on a poster. Add photos or drawings.

- Cut pictures from magazines. Make a collage to go with your essay.

Make sure you choose photos or drawings that really help to show your opinion.

Ideas for Sharing

- **School Internet Site** Suggest that children publish their essay on the school site and begin a student opinion page.

TECH TIP Have children choose several photos that they can scan to enhance the impact of their essays.

- **Class Newspaper** Children should set up their essays so that they are in the format of a newspaper article.

TECH TIP Help children format their essays into columns.

- **Read Aloud** Children can create a chart showing which family members agreed with their opinion and which did not.
- **Tape Record** Remind children to use appropriate volume and rate for the audience, purpose, and occasion.
- **Poster** Children can work in pairs to create their posters.
- **Collage** Children can make a collage of their own drawings instead of using pictures from magazines. Provide various art supplies for children to use.

This page is also available as a poster.

Writing Prompts

Objective

Children will:
- review prompts for choosing a topic or to practice for a writing test

Using the Prompts

You can use the prompts on this page in several ways.

- Ask children to review the prompts to help inspire them as they are choosing their topics for an opinion essay. Suggest that children use prompts that interest them which they can then use to brainstorm ideas for their topics.
- Choose a prompt to provide practice for a writing test. Use it with the Test Practice on the next page.
- Choose a prompt that fits with a related topic in another subject to write an opinion essay across the curriculum.

INTERNET CONNECTION Send your students to www.eduplace.com/kids/hme for more writing ideas. You can also find and print these prompts at www.eduplace.com/rdg/hme/.

FOR STUDENTS ACQUIRING ENGLISH

Some prompts that are especially useful with children learning English are: *What do you like best about the United States? What do you like best about your native country? What does the U.S. need to learn or know? What do you miss most about the country you came from? What do you miss the least?*

Assessment Link

Writing Prompts

Use these prompts for ideas or to practice for a test. Remember to include reasons and examples to explain your opinion.

1 What is your favorite animal? Write an opinion essay explaining why you like that animal.

2 Write an opinion essay about a chore you do not like to do.

Writing Across the Curriculum

3 **SOCIAL STUDIES**
Write an opinion essay about a place you visited. Tell what you liked and disliked about it.

4 **SCIENCE**
How do you feel about spiders? Write an opinion essay explaining how you feel about them.

5 **HEALTH**
What is your favorite dessert? Write an opinion essay explaining why you like it.

6 **LITERATURE**
Write an opinion essay about a character from a book. Tell what you like and dislike about the character.

See www.eduplace.com/kids/hme/ for more prompts.

Test Practice

In an opinion essay, you can write what you like about a topic.

Read this writing prompt.

> What is your favorite animal? Write an opinion essay explaining why you like that animal.

Follow these steps for writing to a prompt.

1. **Look** for clues that tell you what to write about. The words favorite animal, opinion essay, and like are clues.
2. **Look** for questions that you should answer. What question is in the prompt above?
3. **Plan** your writing. Use an Opinion Chart like the one on page 350.
4. **Look** at page 353. What makes a Superstar?
5. **Write** your opinion essay.

See www.eduplace.com/kids/hme/ for graphic organizers.

Test Practice

Objective

Children will:
- learn strategies for evaluating a writing prompt and writing an opinion essay for a test

Using the Test Practice

- Read through the page with children, discussing the strategies for evaluating and responding to a prompt to write an opinion essay.
- Before they write their practice test, review the rubric on page 353 with children.
- Have children write an opinion essay in response to the prompt on this page or to one of the prompts on the previous page. Impose time limitations or other qualifications specific to the testing requirements of your school.

FOR STUDENTS ACQUIRING ENGLISH

Make your expectations and grading standards very clear before children write. How will you determine a good essay? Invite children to help you brainstorm a simple rubric or grading system. Consider grading them individually, especially if there are children with varying levels of English proficiency.

Writing to Persuade

Lesson Objective

Children will:
- read a model of a persuasive essay and identify its parts

Focus on the Model

- Discuss with children the purpose of a persuasive essay. Explain that persuasive essays offer facts and examples to convince readers to think or act differently.
- Point out that a persuasive essay is writing that explains because it states an opinion and explains it.
- Tell the class that they will read a persuasive essay in which Maurice tries to convince his readers that everyone should help clean the local park.
- Point out the blue call outs. Explain that they highlight the different parts of a persuasive essay. Tell the class that they will learn about these parts as they read the essay.
- Ask volunteers to read the persuasive essay aloud. Each volunteer can read one paragraph.

Alternatively, children can listen to the model on audiotape.

Special Focus on Influencing

Writing to Persuade

When you write to persuade, you try to get your audience to do something. Read this **persuasive essay** that Maurice wrote and what W.R. said about it.

Why Everyone Should Help Clean Our Park

Everyone likes going to a park because it is so much fun there. Kids love to go to play, and grown-ups like to go for picnics and to be with family and friends. Nobody goes to our neighborhood park, though, because it is dirty. Everyone in our neighborhood should help clean up our park.

Your audience will know exactly what you want them to do. You stated your **goal** clearly.

A dirty park is not a beautiful place. Our park looks terrible because paper and litter are everywhere. People do not enjoy being there because it is such a mess.

A dirty park is unsafe. People don't want to go to a park where they have to worry about stepping on broken glass. Also, if we clean our park, parents will not have to worry about their children getting hurt.

These are strong **reasons** with good **facts** and **examples**.

The next time you visit our park, remember how important it is to make it clean. Do your part to help make our park a clean, beautiful, and safe place to be.

You **reminded** your audience of what they should do. You **summed up** your goal and your reasons.

Reading As a Writer See TE margin for answers.

- What is Maurice's **goal**?
- What two **reasons** does Maurice give to persuade people to clean up the park? What **facts** and **examples** does he write for each one?
- In which sentence does Maurice **remind** his **audience** of his goal?

Help with Writing a Persuasive Essay

MANAGEMENT TIP

If children are having difficulty understanding the concept of persuasion, have two volunteers role-play a persuasive discussion. As the volunteers make their arguments, point out the facts and examples they use to persuade others that their side deserves serious consideration.

Lesson Objective

Children will:

- read a model of a persuasive essay and identify its parts

How to Write to Persuade

Focus on Instruction

- Discuss with the class how the call outs help identify the important elements of a persuasive essay. Have volunteers answer the questions in the Reading As a Writer section.
- Explain that Maurice's opening is effective because he clearly states his main idea. This is his goal.
- Point out that each of the two body paragraphs begins with a topic sentence that states the main idea. Maurice also includes several sentences that explain and support the main ideas. He provides specific details and examples that help make his point.
- Discuss the elements in Maurice's closing sentence that make it a good conclusion.

Answers to Reading As a Writer

- Maurice wants everyone in the neighborhood to help clean up the park.
- Maurice's first reason is *It's not a beautiful place.* He backs this reason up with these facts: paper and litter; everyone does not enjoy being there. Maurice's second reason is *It's not safe.* He backs this reason up with these facts: stepping on broken glass; parents worrying about children getting hurt.
- Maurice sums up his goal in this sentence: "Do your part to help make our park a clean, beautiful, and safe place to be."

FOR STUDENTS ACQUIRING ENGLISH

Write *He persuaded me to go to the movies* on the board. Ask if anyone can explain what the verb *persuade* means. Look for synonyms such as *talk into*, *get someone to do something*, and *convince*. Ask children what they say to Mom and Dad, for example, when they want to persuade them. Then discuss a persuasive essay.

How to Write to Persuade *continued*

Lesson Objective

Children will:
- write a persuasive essay, focusing on choosing a goal

Focus on Instruction

- Discuss why people write persuasive pieces. Help children understand that it is a way for a writer to tell how he or she feels about something and to explain why others should feel the same way. Explain that writers use special words and phrases, such as *I feel* and *Don't you agree* to help meet the goal of the essay.
- Stress the importance of coming up with a goal that the writer finds interesting. Point out that this should be a goal that the reader will find important and interesting as well.
- Ask children to list goals that can be argued for and against and supported in various ways. One-sided issues should not be argued in a persuasive essay.
- Help children think about other viewpoints as they consider a goal they feel strongly about. Remind them that they can state that there is another point of view and then explain why they think their viewpoint is the better one.
- Have children discuss their goals with classmates. Tell them to discuss whether or not the goal is one-sided and if it will hold the interest of the reader.

How to Write to Persuade

1. **List** three goals that you feel strongly about.
2. **Talk** with a classmate. Answer these questions about each goal.
   - Do I feel strongly about this goal?
   - Who will read or hear my paper?
   - Can my audience really do what I want them to do?
   - Can I think of two strong reasons to help persuade my audience?
3. **Copy** and **complete** these sentences. Name your goal and your audience.

   I will write about _____.

   _____ will read or hear my essay.

Stuck for a Goal?

Here are some ideas to think about.
- My family should _____.
- The students in our school should _____.
- Our whole class should _____.

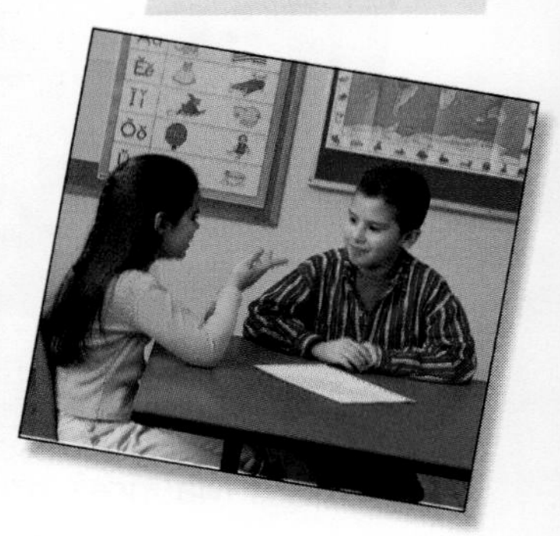

Help with Writing a Persuasive Essay

MORE TOPIC IDEAS

Suggest these ideas as possible goals for persuasive essays.
- Community: new stop signs; safer playground equipment, volunteer at animal shelter
- School: more/different after-school clubs; student art show; Field Day or other tournament

TECH TIP

If children are creating their persuasive essays on the computer, direct them to page H23 for information on using a computer for the writing process.

4 **Explore** your goal. Why do you think it is important? Why should your audience do what you suggest? Strong reasons will help you persuade your audience. Look at the web Maurice made to explore his goal.

Now make a web like the one Maurice did. Write your goal in the large circle. Think of two strong reasons for your goal. Write one reason in each of the smaller circles.

See www.eduplace.com/kids/hme/ for graphic organizers.

Lesson Objective

Children will:

- write a persuasive essay, focusing on reasons to support the goal

Focus on Instruction

- Point out that Maurice used a web to organize his reasons. Suggest that children list their reasons first and then choose their strongest reasons to put in their webs.
- Help children understand that strong reasons say more than "I just do/don't like it." Suggest that children test their reasons by restating them this way: *I feel this way because....*
- Have children share their reasons with classmates and discuss which reasons are stronger than others.

Help with Writing a Persuasive Essay

EVALUATION TIP

Review children's goal and reasons. Check to make sure the goals are suitable and children have cited strong reasons that adequately support their goals.

How to Write to Persuade *continued*

Lesson Objective

Children will:

- write a persuasive essay, focusing on supporting details

Focus on Instruction

- Discuss with children the difference between *facts* and *opinions*. Explain that facts can be checked to see if they are correct. *Opinions* cannot be correct or incorrect because they tell the writer's own feelings. Point out that opinions often use the phrases *I think* or *I believe* and words such as *good*, *best*, and *worst*.
- Tell children that if they use other sources such as articles and interviews to gather facts and examples to support their reasons, they should look out for opinion clue words. Stress that they should try to state only their own opinion, and use facts as support.
- Remind children to think about their audience as they explore facts, examples, and reasons. For example, how much do their readers know about the subject? Are they likely to agree or disagree with the goal?

Have each child make a folder for storing all notes, graphic organizers, and drafts for this assignment.

5 **Think** about your reasons. Facts or examples for each reason will make your goal even stronger. Look at the facts and examples Maurice added to his web.

Add to your web. Draw circles connected to each reason. Think of facts or examples for each one. Write one fact or example inside each circle.

Help with Writing a Persuasive Essay

TECH TIP

Children may use online sources to find facts and examples to support their goal. Guide children to find reliable, age-appropriate Web sites and show them how to download and print the information they find. Post a list of these sites as reference.

6 **Draft** your persuasive essay.

- Write a paragraph that states your goal in a clear and interesting way.
- Write one paragraph for each reason. Include your facts or examples.
- Write a paragraph that sums up your reasons. Remind your audience of what you want them to do.

7 **Look** at the checklist. What can you do to make your persuasive essay better?

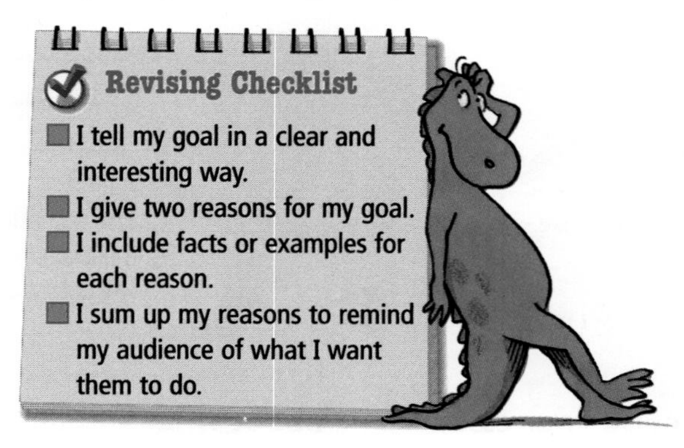

8 **Have** a writing conference. Take notes to remember your classmate's ideas.

Lesson Objectives

Children will:
- write the first draft of a persuasive essay
- revise a persuasive essay, using the Revising Checklist

Focus on Instruction

- Explain to children that they must state their goal somewhere in the first paragraph. This helps the reader know what kinds of information to look for.
- Emphasize the importance of using solid facts and examples to reinforce the writer's goal. Without this backup material, the essay will not meet its goal.
- As children revise their essays, remind them that the purpose of revising is to make their essay more persuasive and to make sure that their ideas are clear.
- Children should also make sure that every detail relates to the goal and there are sufficient details to persuade readers.
- Suggest that children underline each part of their paper that meets each item on the checklist. If they cannot locate the item, this is the time to add it.

Connecting to the Criteria

Have children review the characteristics of a good persuasive essay described in the Reading As a Writer section of this lesson. Explain that the Revising Checklist on this page will help them evaluate their persuasive essays in relation to those characteristics.

Help with Writing a Persuasive Essay

TECH TIP

Children may use bold type or a color to keep track of the items in their essays that meet the characteristics.

FOR STUDENTS ACQUIRING ENGLISH

First have the children work with partners or in small groups to write goals based on the models in the Help Box. Then talk about how to express a strong reason. Practice by presenting a goal children can relate to, such as *the class should take a field trip*, and having them present reasons orally. Help with language.

How to Write to Persuade *continued*

Lesson Objectives

Children will:
- discuss a persuasive essay in a writing conference
- proofread a persuasive essay

Revising Reminders

Remind children
- that they should speak clearly and slowly when they read their papers aloud to their writing conference partners;
- that any questions or comments from their writing partner are suggestions only. The writer should decide what changes to make.

Proofreading Reminders

- Review with children the Proofreading Checklist on page 367 and the use of proofreading marks.
- Tell children to circle any words they think are misspelled and check them in a dictionary.
- Remind children to refer to the Capitalization, Punctuation, and Usage Guide and to the Spelling Guidelines in the back of their books.
- Check children's proofread persuasive essays before they make their final copies.

FOR STUDENTS ACQUIRING ENGLISH

Make sure children understand that the first set of sentences shows what the listener might be thinking; the second set shows a more polite way to say these things. Have partners practice asking the polite questions. If needed, model appropriate intonation, volume, and body language, or have children role-play for the group

What to Say in a Writing Conference

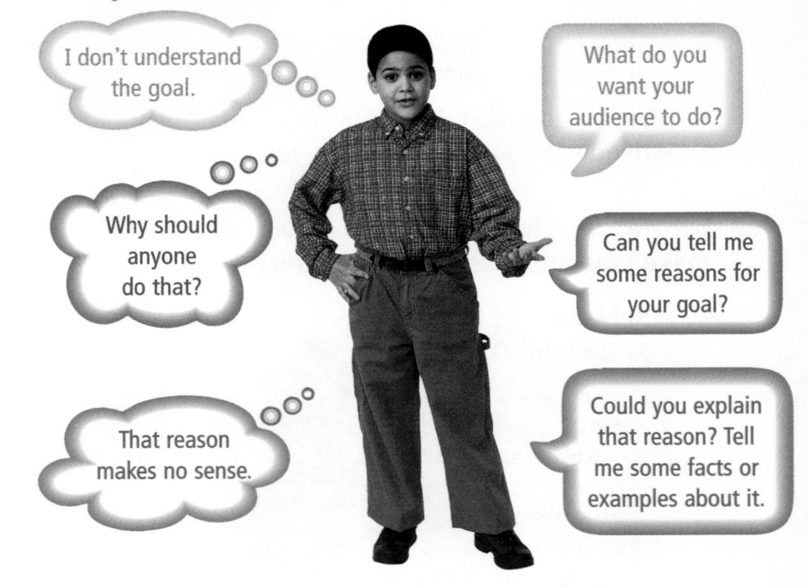

9. **Revise** your essay. Think about what you and your classmate talked about. Make changes to your essay.
10. **Proofread** your essay. Use the Proofreading Checklist on page 357. Use a class dictionary to check your spelling.

Help with Writing a Persuasive Essay

MORE CONFERENCING QUESTIONS

You may use these questions as you conference with children:
- Where do you state your goal?
- Who will be reading your persuasive essay? How do you think your reader will feel about your goal?
- Which details help support your goal in each paragraph? Which details don't?
- How does your closing sum up the goal and persuade your readers?

11 Publish or share your essay in a way that works for your goal and your audience. Make a neat final copy, using your best handwriting. Write an interesting title for your essay.

- ★ Present your essay to your audience as a speech. See Giving a Talk on pages 294–295 for tips.
- Publish your essay in a class newspaper or on your school's Web site.

Tech Tip
If you wrote your essay on a computer, fix every mistake. Then print out a final copy.

Help with Writing a Persuasive Essay

EVALUATION TIP
If possible, videotape children's presentations. Children can then view these later and use them for self-evaluation.

Lesson Objective

Children will:
- publish and share their final copies

Publishing Reminders

- Review with children their publishing plans to help them address any special requirements.
- Point out that if children find errors in their final copies, they can make neat corrections rather than rewrite the paper.
- Remind children to speak clearly when they present their persuasive essays to their audience. Point out that the volume and tone of their voices can help get their points across, and that their face and body movements are also important as their speak.

SCHOOL-HOME CONNECTION After children read their persuasive essays at home, have them discuss with family members which reasons they found most persuasive.

Discuss with each student whether this paper should go into the portfolio. Consider these possible reasons: (1) It is an especially good piece of writing; (2) it reflects a particular aspect of writing that the student did well; (3) it shows an aspect of writing that needs more work and could be used as a baseline for measuring growth.

Comparing Media

Lesson Objectives

Children will:
- think about different forms of media and how they provide information
- think about advertisements and how they use words, images, and music to persuade

Thinking About Media

Focus on Instruction

Before beginning this lesson, ask children what kinds of media they enjoy most and why. Brainstorm a list of the basic differences between printed media, the radio, and television. (Printed media has words and still pictures; radio has sound and spoken words only; television has moving pictures, sound, and both spoken and written words.)

Think and Discuss

- Point out the news stories in the text and ask volunteers which news report they prefer and why. Talk about facts and identify the facts in these news stories.
- Ask children to draw three new sketches with captions, showing how a magazine, radio program, and television program might report a new discovery in space. (Sample answer: The newspaper might run a long article with an interview with a scientist and one or two photographs; the radio might broadcast an interview with several scientists; the television might show photographs or computer images of the discovery and you might also see the astronauts or scientists at work.)

Comparing Media

Thinking About Media

Newspapers, radio, and television are all **media**. You can get news and information from different kinds of media. Each one gives news in a different way and can change how you feel and think about the news.

Think and Discuss

Look at the pictures above and think about the media. How are they the same? How are they different?

They all use words to report the news. Newspapers use pictures. Radio uses sound. Television uses both pictures and sound.

Thinking About Ads

Have you ever seen an ad for a toy and thought you just had to have it? Ads, or advertisements, are used to get people to buy or do something. You might see ads in magazines, on huge signs called billboards, or on television.

Ads use words and pictures that are attractive and eye-catching. Some ads also use sound. You might hear a tune you like that makes you remember the product in the ad.

Apply It

What do the magazine ad and billboard ad try to get people to do? Do you think the ads work? Why or why not?

visit Big Bend Park; Sample answer: Yes; they use words, pictures, color, kid's words

Thinking About Ads

Focus on Instruction

- Ask children to describe their favorite advertisements and tell why they like them. (Answers will vary.) Explain that artists and writers work hard to choose images, songs, and words that help people remember the ad and the product. Even if people don't buy the product, they may describe the ad to someone else and help advertise the product again.
- Explain that companies usually decide which media they will use by deciding how much they can spend. Television advertisements cost much more than magazine ads because they are harder to create. However, point out that commercials on television can also reach more people.
- Remind children that advertisements use persuasive writing and do not always tell the exact truth. An ad promising "the best time of your life," is exaggerating the fact that most people will have fun. Pictures can also stretch the truth. Food, toys, cars, and clothes might look better in an ad than in real life. Stress that children should be aware of specific clue words that help them recognize facts from nonfacts.

Apply It

- Focus children on the kinds of information conveyed by pictures, sounds, and images. Have volunteers tell why the speeding car might be more eye-catching than the still photograph.
- Ask children which advertisement they trust more and why. Which one might persuade them to do something?
- Extend the activity by asking small groups to sketch three designs for an advertisement. Have groups choose a toy, restaurant, or special place to advertise. Have each child sketch one design for a magazine ad, a radio spot, or a television ad. Ask groups to explain why they chose the words and images for each kind of media.

FOR STUDENTS ACQUIRING ENGLISH

Ask children to list the ways they or their parents get news. Then ask why they use this method. Ask them to list some positive and negative aspects of each news source. Then, if possible bring in age-appropriate TV and magazine ads for children to analyze.

About Tools and Tips

This part of the book includes valuable resources for instruction or reference.

Using Tools and Tips

You can use the resources in Tools and Tips at any time, either independently or in combination with lessons and features in the Grammar or Writing units. The Research and Study Strategies, Using Technology, Test-Taking Strategies, and Writer's Tools, sections provide instruction in these areas.

Draw children's attention to Guide to Capital Letters, Guide to Punctuation Marks, My First Thesaurus, the Spelling Guide, and the Grammar Glossary at the beginning of the year so that they can refer to them throughout the year as they work on their assignments.

Cross-references to lessons and sections in Tools and Tips are included in the body of the pupil book at particularly appropriate points of use.

Tools and Tips

ABC Order

The letters of the alphabet are in ABC order.

A B C D E F G H I J K L M

N O P Q R S T U V W X Y Z

Words can also be put in ABC order. Are these words in ABC order?

ant **b**ig **c**at

The words are in ABC order. Use the first letter of each word to put words in ABC order.

Try It Out

Speak Up Say these words in ABC order.

dog	**i**nk	**g**ame	**e**at

dog eat game ink

Write It 1–4. Now write the words in ABC order.

1. dog 2. eat 3. game 4. ink

Research and Study Strategies

ABC Order

Lesson Objective

Children will:
- alphabetize, using the first letter

Focus on Instruction

- Help children understand that ABC order is not just the entire alphabet. Say three letters in the middle of the alphabet, such as *g*, *h*, *i*, and ask volunteers to tell what the next letter would be.

Practice

- Encourage children to try to complete the activities without referring to the alphabet on the page.

ABC Order *continued*

On Your Own

1–8. Copy the alphabet. Write the missing letters.

A B C D E F G H I J K L M

N O P Q R S T U V W X Y Z

Write the words in each box in ABC order.

9. pet, open, nine — nine, open, pet

10. card, with, my, sky — card, my, sky, with

11. bear, map, hot — bear, hot, map

12. send, glass, hen, zoo — glass, hen, send, zoo

eel

octopus

shark

More Practice

A. Have children underline the word in each row that comes first in ABC order.

1. head feet arms
2. door key house
3. red brown green
4. cold hot warm
5. sky blue rain
6. color paint draw
7. hear talk smell
8. bear fox wolf

B. Have children write each group of three words in ABC order.

1. jay—tail—bird (bird—jay—tail)
2. wind—kite—fly (fly—kite—wind)
3. run—hop—walk (hop—run—walk)
4. pear—apple—banana (apple—banana—pear)
5. red—yellow—blue (blue—red—yellow)
6. car—bus—train (bus—car—train)

More ABC Order

You know that you look at the first letters of words to put them in ABC order.

Sometimes two words begin with the same letter. When this happens, look at the second letter in each word. Why does bat come before boy?

bat **bo**y **bu**g

Try It Out

Speak Up Say these words in ABC order.

sell	**sw**im	**sa**t	**sn**ow

sat sell snow swim

Write It 1–4. Now write the words in ABC order.

1. sat 2. sell 3. snow 4. swim

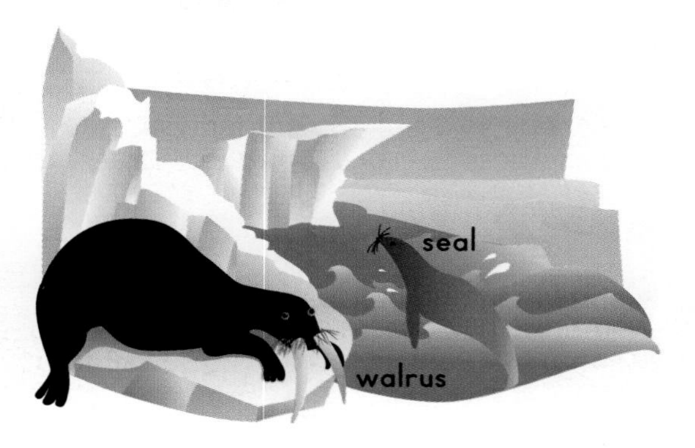

Research and Study Strategies

More ABC Order

Lesson Objective

Children will:

- alphabetize to the second letter

Focus on Instruction

- Have volunteers spell each of the example words (*bat*, *boy*, *bug*) and then tell which is the second letter. Write those three letters out of ABC order on the board and work together to alphabetize them.

Practice

- Suggest that children first write the words vertically on another piece of paper. This may help them see the letter order more easily.

More ABC Order *continued*

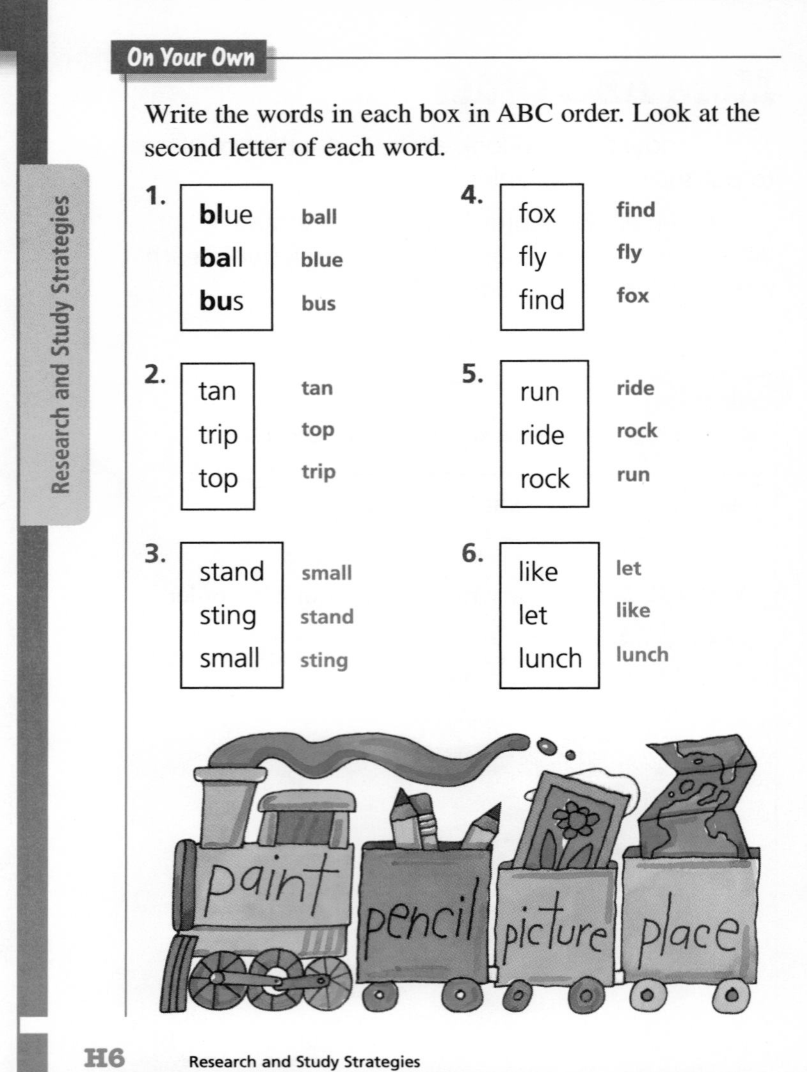

On Your Own

Write the words in each box in ABC order. Look at the second letter of each word.

1. **bl**ue, **ba**ll, **bu**s — ball, blue, bus
2. tan, trip, top — tan, top, trip
3. stand, sting, small — small, stand, sting
4. fox, fly, find — find, fly, fox
5. run, ride, rock — ride, rock, run
6. like, let, lunch — let, like, lunch

H6 Research and Study Strategies

More Practice

A. Have children write *yes* if the words are in ABC order. Have them write *no* if they are not.

1. deer, dog, duck (yes)
2. boat, blow, brave (no)
3. grow, glue, goat (no)
4. band, bell, block (yes)

B. Have children underline the word in each row that comes first in ABC order.

1. lamp, lunch, lock
2. star, sleep, sun
3. five, four, feet
4. paper, pen, print

C. Have children write each group of words in alphabetical order.

1. swim—sun—shine (shine—sun—swim)
2. his—head—hat (hat—head—his)
3. monkey—mice—mule (mice—monkey—mule)
4. elbow—ear—eye (ear—elbow—eye)
5. wind—water—weather (water—weather—wind)
6. pot—plant—pick (pick—plant—pot)

The Dictionary

A **dictionary** is a book about words. The words a dictionary tells about are in **dark print**. They are called **entry words**. Entry words are in ABC order.

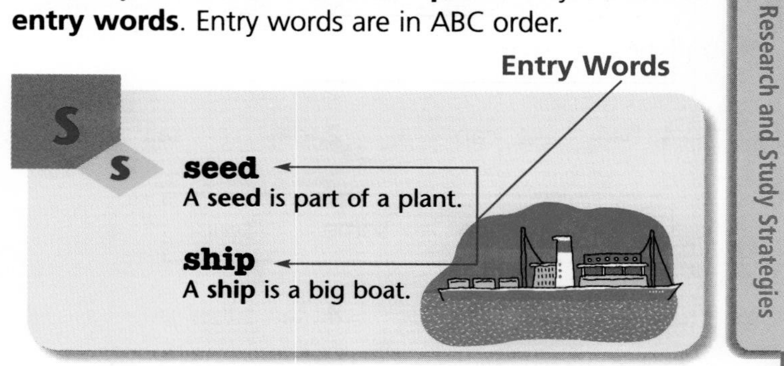

Try It Out

Speak Up Answer each question with a word from the Word Box.

and	dig
girl	now

1. Which word is between cap and fish? dig
2. Which word is between get and grew? girl
3. Which word is between mine and open? now
4. Which word is between air and boy? and

Write It 1–4. Now write the words.

1. dig 2. girl 3. now 4. and

The Dictionary

Lesson Objectives

Children will:
- identify entry words
- recognize that entry words in a dictionary are listed in alphabetical order

Focus on Instruction

- Before beginning the lesson, you may want to display a copy of a beginning dictionary. Ask volunteers to tell what they know about using a dictionary.
- Discuss when children might use a dictionary. Talk about times when they might have used a dictionary at home.

Practice

- Suggest that children say the letters of the alphabet that come between the first letters of the underlined words.

The Dictionary *continued*

Research and Study Strategies

On Your Own

Write the word from the Word Box that comes between each pair of entry words.

box	need	arm	eat

1. baby box cap **2.** day eat fall

school	sun	some	swim

3. see some stamp **4.** sad school seat

gym	give	grow	gave

5. get give glass **6.** good grow gull

money	noise	quack	rock

7. pear quack ride **8.** like money nice

crow	carry	clam	cent

9. chop clam corn **10.** copy crow cub

H8 Research and Study Strategies

More Practice

A. Have children tell whether they would look toward the front or toward the back of a dictionary in each of these situations:

1. You are looking for frost. You find lemon. (toward the front)
2. You are looking for palace. You find ladder. (toward the back)
3. You are looking for tractor. You find south. (toward the back)
4. You are looking for gallon. You find lion. (toward the front)

B. Have children look at each pair of entry words. Then have them underline the word in the row below that comes between those entry words.

1. box — dog
   child apple tail
2. rich — train
   prize sleep woods
3. ship — south
   saw swim slip
4. dear — drop
   dump door dark
5. pig — price
   plant put page

Finding Word Meanings

A dictionary tells the meanings of words. Look at the dictionary entry for mirror. What is the meaning of mirror?

Entry Word — Meaning

mirror

A **mirror** is piece of glass you can see yourself in.

a piece of glass you can see yourself in

Try It Out

Speak Up Tell the meaning of fog.

fog Fog is a cloud that is near the ground.

Fog is a cloud that is near the ground.

Write It Now write fog and its meaning. fog a cloud that is near the ground

Research and Study Strategies

Finding Word Meanings

Lesson Objective

Children will:

- use a dictionary to find the meaning of a word

Focus on Instruction

- Write a made-up word on the board and read it aloud. Help children read it aloud and then suggest meanings for the word.
- Choose one meaning and write it next to the new word. Help children understand that if this were a real word, the meaning would appear after it in a dictionary.

Finding Word Meanings *continued*

Research and Study Strategies

On Your Own

Write each word and its meaning. Use the dictionary meanings shown on this page.

1. storm **2.** stripe **3.** subway

storm

A **storm** is a strong wind with rain or snow.

a strong wind with rain or snow

stripe

A **stripe** is a wide line.

a wide line

subway

A **subway** is a train that travels underground through tunnels.

a train that travels underground through tunnels

More Practice

Have children use this sample dictionary page to answer the questions.

leaf
A **leaf** is a part of a plant.

lemon
A **lemon** is a kind of fruit.

line
A **line** is a long, thin mark.

long
Long is the opposite of short.

lunch
Lunch is a meal.

1. Which word means "a long, thin mark"? (*line*)
2. Which word means "a kind of fruit"? (*lemon*)
3. Which word means "a part of a plant"? (*leaf*)
4. Which word means "a meal"? (*lunch*)
5. Which word means the opposite of short? (*long*)

More Than One Meaning

One word can have more than one meaning. The dictionary explains each meaning. Each meaning is numbered.

How many dictionary meanings does the word wing have? two

wing

1. A **wing** is a part of a bird, a bat, and some insects.

2. A **wing** is a part of a plane. It sticks out like the wing of a bird.

Research and Study Strategies

Try It Out

Speak Up Tell which meaning of wing fits each sentence.

1. The bird hurt its wing. 1
2. I sat by a wing on the plane. 2
3. I can see the silver wings of the plane. 2
4. Bees have two pairs of wings. 1

Write It 1–4. Write each sentence. Then write **1** or **2** to show which meaning of wing fits the sentence.
See answers above.

More Than One Meaning

Lesson Objectives

Children will:

- recognize that more than one meaning may be given for an entry word
- choose the correct meaning for a word

Focus on Instruction

- Look again at the made-up word and definition you used for the previous lesson. Ask volunteers to make up two more definitions.
- Write these on the board and read all the definitions. Have other volunteers use the word in a sentence that tells each meaning. For example, if the made-up word is *pilko*, and one meaning is *a kind of sled*, a sentence might be *We used our new pilko to race down the snowy hill.*

Practice

- If children need extra support, you might read aloud the appropriate definitions before they begin each exercise.

More Than One Meaning *continued*

On Your Own

Write each sentence. Then write **1** or **2** to show which meaning of chest fits each sentence.

chest
1. The **chest** is a part of the body. It is below the shoulders and above the stomach.
2. A **chest** is a strong box.

1. Mother put the pictures in the chest. 2
2. Father is sunburned on his chest. 1
3. Ed has a pain in his chest. 1

Write each sentence. Then write **1** or **2** to show which meaning of spot fits each sentence.

spot
1. A **spot** is a small mark that is not the same color as the area around it.
2. A **spot** is a place.

4. Peter dropped the penny in this spot. 2
5. Lin got a black spot on her red dress. 1
6. The dog hid its bone in this spot. 2

More Practice

Have children study the dictionary meanings in the box. Then have them write *1* or *2* after each sentence below to show which meaning fits the sentence.

block
1. A **block** is part of a city street.
2. A **block** is a piece of wood.

horn
1. A **horn** is something you play to make music.
2. A **horn** is part of an animal's body.

orange
1. **Orange** is a color.
2. An **orange** is a kind of fruit.

1. All the houses on that block are white. (1)
2. The baby cried when I took away her block. (2)
3. The goat butted first with one horn and then with the other. (2)
4. Each child got a hat and a horn at the party. (1)
5. Jim picked an orange from the tree. (2)
6. To get orange, put some red paint into the yellow paint. (1)

Title Page and Table of Contents

The **title page** is the first important page in a book. It lists the book's title, author, and publisher.

The **table of contents** of a book shows the chapters, or parts, of the book. It shows the page where each chapter begins.

Research and Study Strategies

Try It Out

Speak Up Find the title page on the first page of this book. Say the title of this book. Houghton Mifflin English

Write It Look at the table of contents of the book below. It has three chapters. Write the answers to each question.

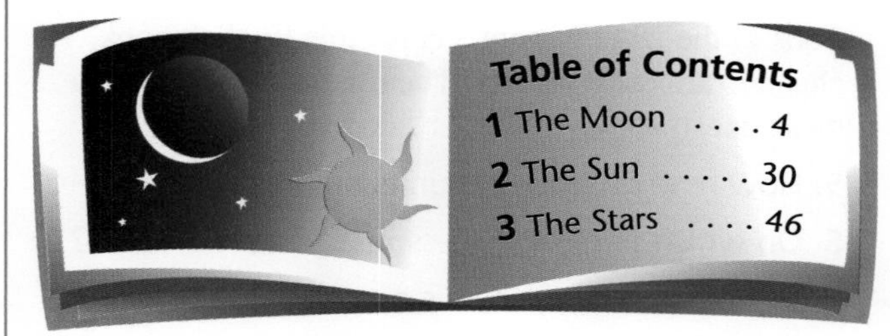

1. What is the title of Chapter 2? "The Sun"
2. On which page does Chapter 1 begin? 4
3. "The Stars" is the title of which chapter? 3

Title Page and Table of Contents

Lesson Objectives

Children will:

- use a title page to locate information
- use a table of contents to locate information in a book

Focus on Instruction

- Point out that the title is also on the cover of the book and often on the spine, or side, of the book.
- Help children understand that the *contents* is what something *contains*. Show an example such a box of crayons, and explain that the crayons are the *contents* of this box.

Practice

- Be sure children understand that one set of numbers is the chapter number and the other set tells the page number of the *first page* of the chapter.

Title Page and Table of Contents *continued*

On Your Own

Write the answers to the questions below. Use this table of contents.

Table of Contents

1. How many chapters are shown? 3
2. What is the title of Chapter 1? "Ants"
3. What is the title of Chapter 2? "Bees"
4. On which page does Chapter 3 begin? 28

Look at the table of contents for this English book. The chapters are called **units**. Then write the answers to these questions.

5. How many numbered units are in the book? 10
6. On which page does Lesson 1 of Unit 5 begin? 163
7. In Unit 9, what lesson is on page 301? Months

More Practice

Have children use this table of contents to answer the questions that follow.

Table of Contents

1. How many chapters does this book have? (three)
2. What is the title of Chapter 3? ("Your Teeth")
3. On which page does Chapter 1 begin? (page 5)
4. On which page does the chapter "Your Ears" begin? (page 11)
5. On which page does Chapter 3 begin? (page 17)

Using the Library

You can find books to read at your school or town library. A library is set up in a special way so that you can find the books you want quickly and easily.

Fiction One part of your library has fiction books. These are stories that are made up by an author. These books are put on the shelves in ABC order by the last names of the authors.

Nonfiction Another part of your library has nonfiction books. These books tell facts about real people, animals, places, and events. Nonfiction books are grouped by subjects such as science or history. They are given special numbers to help you find them.

Reference Reference books are found in one section. An atlas (a book of maps), a dictionary, and an encyclopedia are reference books. These may also be stored on CD-ROMs that can be used on a computer.

Using the Library

- This section explains the different types of materials in a library, including reference materials and how to locate them. Both electronic card catalogs and traditional card catalog are explained.
- To provide practice, select from the activities shown below on this and the following page. Write the activities on the chalkboard, on an overhead transparency, or make duplicate copies for distribution.
- Have children describe the layouts of local, school, or other libraries they have visited.

Practice

A. Have children write *fiction*, *nonfiction*, or *reference* to tell where in a library they would find each of the following books.

1. *Roberto Clemente*, by Jerry Bronfield, tells about the life of a famous baseball player. (nonfiction)
2. *Titch*, by Pat Hutchins, is a story about growing up. (fiction)
3. *Lucky Science*, by Royston M. and Jeanie Roberts, gives facts about scientific discoveries. (nonfiction)
4. *Information Please Kids' Almanac* contains facts about many subjects. (reference)
5. *Make Way for Ducklings*, by Robert McCloskey, is the story of a mother duck and her babies in the big city. (fiction)
6. *Kids On-Line* is a guide to Internet address for children. (reference)

B. Have children name the part of the library in which they would find these books.

1. *Goodnight Moon*, by Margaret Wise Brown, tells about a bunny and his bedtime. (fiction)
2. *The New Book of Knowledge* contains facts about many subjects. (reference)
3. *How a Book Is Made,* by Aliki, tells all the steps in publishing a book. (nonfiction)
4. *Swimmy,* by Leo Lionni tell the story of a little fish and his friends. (fiction)
5. *The Riddle Monster,* by Lisl Weil, is about a prince who meets a horrible monster. (fiction)

Using the Library *(continued)*

- Explain that fiction books will have letters representing the first letter of the author's last name. Nonfiction books will have numbers indicating the section in the nonfiction area of the library where the book can be located. Let children know that most libraries have the numbers of the sections posted at the end of each aisle.
- Point out that encyclopedia volumes are also arranged alphabetically.

Book-Finding Tools You can find books in the library by using a card catalog. A **card catalog** is a set of drawers with cards that list books in ABC order by the author's last name, the book title, or the subject.

Most libraries today have an **electronic catalog** stored on a computer. You can search for a book if you know either the book's title or author. You can also type in the name of the subject and find books about that subject.

Using an Encyclopedia

An encyclopedia is a set of books that gives information about many topics such as famous people, places, things, and events. The facts are found in pieces of writing called **articles**.

Encyclopedia articles are put in ABC order in books called **volumes**. Most volumes are labeled with one letter. Everything written about in that volume will begin with that letter. Some volumes may have more than one letter. There are also CD-ROM and online versions of encyclopedias.

Practice

Have children write each of the following titles with the author's name. Ask them to underline the title once. Then have them underline twice the word that helps them find the book in the library.

1. *Madeline*, by Ludwig Bemelmans (Madeline by Ludwig Bemelmans)
2. *Curious George*, by H.A. Rey (Curious George by H.A. Rey)
3. *Bedtime for Frances*, by Russell Hoban (Bedtime for Frances by Russell Hoban)
4. *Whose Mouse Are You*?, by Robert Kraus (Whose Mouse Are You? by Robert Kraus)

Using Visuals: Graphs

A **graph** is a drawing that shows information in picture form. It can help you understand and compare numbers of people or things.

A **bar graph** shows numbers, using colored boxes or bars. Look at this graph one class made showing their favorite fruits.

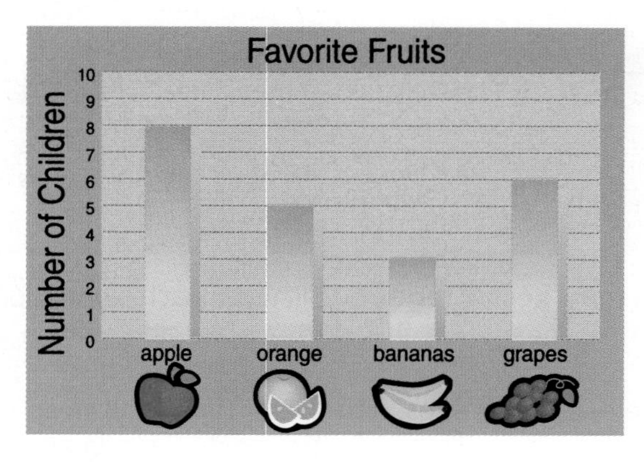

The **title** tells what the graph is about. The **labels** give more information. The label at the side shows the number of children. The labels under the bars or boxes show the different choices of favorite fruits.

To read this graph, look at the number beside the line that the top of each bar reaches.

Research and Study Strategies

Using Visuals: Graphs

Using This Section

This section explains how to use graphs.

To provide practice, have children complete the graph activity on this page. Write the information on the chalkboard, on an overhead transparency, or make duplicate copies for distribution.

Practice

Have children use the bar graph above to answer the following questions.

1. How many kinds of fruit are shown? (4)
2. What is this graph about? (Favorite Fruits)
3. Which fruit do the fewest children like? (bananas)
4. Which fruit is the favorite of six children? (grapes)
5. How many children like apples? (8)
6. What fruit would you add to the graph? (Answers will vary.)
7. How many of your classmates like this fruit? (Answers will vary.)
8. Is this more or less than the number for oranges? (Answers will vary.)

Using Visuals: Maps

Using This Section

This section explains how to use maps.

To provide practice, have children complete the map activities on this page. Write the information on the chalkboard, on an overhead transparency, or make duplicate copies for distribution.

Using Visuals: Maps

A **map** is a simple drawing showing all or part of a place. You may have seen a road map or world map with the outlines of countries. The map below shows most of North America.

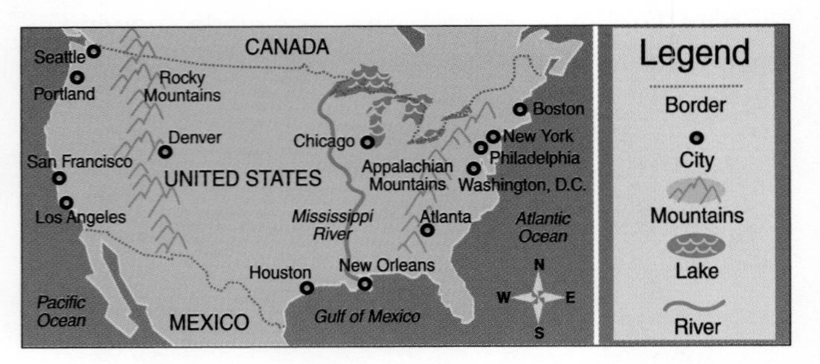

A **map key** or **legend** tells what each symbol on the map means. On this map, a black and orange dot stands for a city. The blue areas and lines show water—lakes, oceans, and rivers. The red dotted lines show where the United States meets Canada and Mexico. Small triangles show mountains.

The **compass rose** beside the legend shows directions on a map—north (**N**), south (**S**), east (**E**), and west (**W**).

Practice

Have children use the map above to answer the following questions.

1. Which country is north of the United States? (Canada)
2. Which city is south of Seattle? (Portland)
3. Name the two mountains on the map. (Appalachian Mountains, Rocky Mountains)
4. Which river is shown? (Mississippi)
5. Which is the closest city to the west of New Orleans? (Houston)
6. Is the Pacific Ocean to the east or west? (west)
7. Which city on the map is farthest north? (Seattle)
8. Which country is south of the United States? (Mexico)

Open-Response Questions

On some tests, you must read a paragraph or story and then write one or two complete sentences to answer a question about it. Remember these tips to help you write a good answer.

Tips for Answering an Open-Response Question

1. Read the question carefully. Try to use part of the question in your answer.
2. Think about what you read. What words, sentences, or ideas might answer the question?
3. Answer only the question that is asked.
4. Write your answer neatly in complete sentences.

Read the book summary below. Write sentences telling why the little house was unhappy.

A little house lived way out in the quiet country. It liked to watch the days and seasons come and go.

Then one day builders came. They built roads, houses, stores, and tall buildings. It became noisy and crowded all around the little house. The little house was now living in a city!

The city was too bright and noisy. Nobody noticed the little house anymore. It was squeezed between bigger buildings. The little house was unhappy.

Open-Response Questions

Lesson Objective:

Children will:

- analyze answers to a test prompt based on guidelines

Focus on Instruction

- Discuss the tips and the example question. Examine why each item in the Tips list is important.
- If children need extra support, read the passage aloud after they have had time to read it silently.

Open-Response Questions *continued*

Think and Discuss

Ask volunteers to read each of the test scorers' paragraphs aloud. Work together to identify the cited words and phrases in Answers 1 and 2.

Practice

The Personal Response questions at the end of each published model and the Critical Thinking questions afford additional opportunity for children to practice writing open-response answers. When used as practice, suggest that children review the Tips on page H19 before they begin their responses.

Think and Discuss Read these two answers to the question. Which one is a better answer? Why?

Answer 1

The little house liked living in the country. Then they built things all around the house I would like to live in the country.

Answer 2

The little house was unhappy because it wanted to live in the country and not in a crowded city. The little house was sad because nobody noticed it.

In the **first answer**, the writer does not tell why the little house was unhappy but instead tells what happens. The writer also gives information that the question does not ask for. The answer ends with a run-on sentence.

In the **second answer**, the writer uses words from the question. The writer uses information from the book summary to explain why the little house is unhappy. Only information that is asked for is given. The writer uses capital letters and end marks correctly to write two complete sentences.

Computer Talk and Technology Terms

CD-ROM a round disk on which numbers, words, and images can be stored and then read, heard, or viewed on a computer

cursor a marker on a computer screen, which may or may not flash, that shows where information can be entered

data the basic information that you get from a computer or that can be put into and understood by a computer

disk a magnetic object on which computer programs and data can be stored

document a piece of writing that you create on a computer

floppy disk a small plastic disk that is used to store computer data

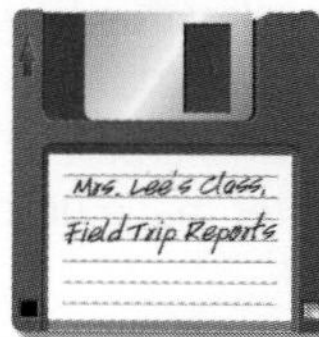

font any one of many styles of letters that a computer can make

Times
Courier
Helvetica

hard copy information from a computer that is printed on paper

hard drive a large disk inside the computer that holds more data and works faster than a floppy disk

hardware the parts of a computer including the keyboard, monitor, memory, and printer

Using Technology

Computer Talk and Technology Terms

Using This Page

This page and page H22 present common technology terms. If children are just learning about using computers, draw their attention to these pages as a helpful resource.

Computer Talk and Technology Terms
continued

Computer Talk and Technology Terms continued

Using Technology

Internet a large computer network that connects computers around the world

key any button on a keyboard with a letter, number, word, or symbol

keyboard the part of the computer made up of a set of keys

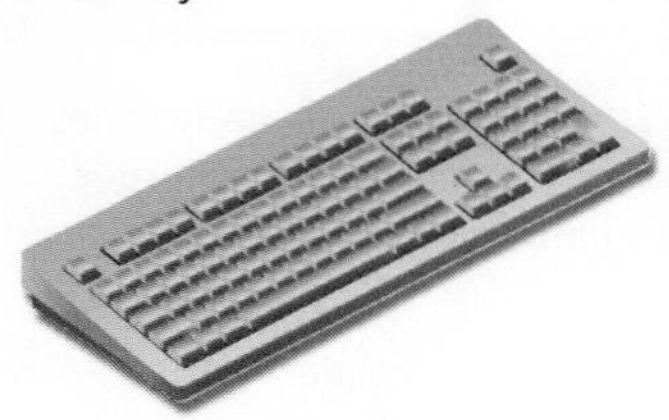

memory the part of the computer in which information is stored

menu a list of choices within a computer program that are usually shown on the screen

modem a machine that allows computers to communicate with other computers over telephone lines

monitor the part of the computer that shows the information on a screen

mouse the part of a computer that you move with your hand to move the cursor around the screen and make choices

printer the part of the computer that puts information on paper

software programs that let people do things such as type, play games, and draw pictures on computers

Using a Computer

A computer is an amazing tool! Read these pages to find out about some of the things you can do with it.

Games for Learning

Do you know that there are many games on CD-ROM and floppy disk that can help you learn? Some Web sites on the Internet also have games that you can open and play.

There are computer games that can help you become a better writer, review letters and sounds, practice math skills and problem solving, and learn about people and places.

Drawing and Writing

Have you ever written a story or a poem that you wanted to illustrate? You can use a computer to draw pictures and diagrams to go with your writing.

Some computer software gives you space to write and to draw a picture. Other programs let you insert a drawing, a diagram, or a chart anywhere within your writing. You can also choose a picture from a list to put into your document.

Using a Computer

Using This Page

This page presents an overview of some of the ways children can use a computer to enhance basic academic skills and to take advantage of the creative possibilities available through software and computer features.

If a computer is accessible, use this opportunity to demonstrate any available content-area games and creative software.

The Internet

Using This Page

This page provides an overview of ideas for using the Internet to learn information, to support school assignments, and to communicate with others. It also includes tips for using the Internet effectively. If children have access to the Internet in your class or school, discuss this page early in the school year. Another good time to review this page with children is while they are doing research for a research report.

INTERNET CONNECTION Send your children to www.eduplace.com/kids/hme/ for language arts activities and models. They will also find Internet links to sites with information about different topics to help with research reports.

Using a Computer continued

Using Technology

The Internet

The **Internet** is a network of computers from all over the world. It connects people, classrooms, companies, libraries, museums, and other interesting places. Here are some of the many things you can do on the Internet.

- Use a search tool to help you find Internet sites on topics that interest you. Type in a key word or phrase about your topic.
- Connect to the World Wide Web. You can find lots of information in places called Web sites. Each Web site has its own address.

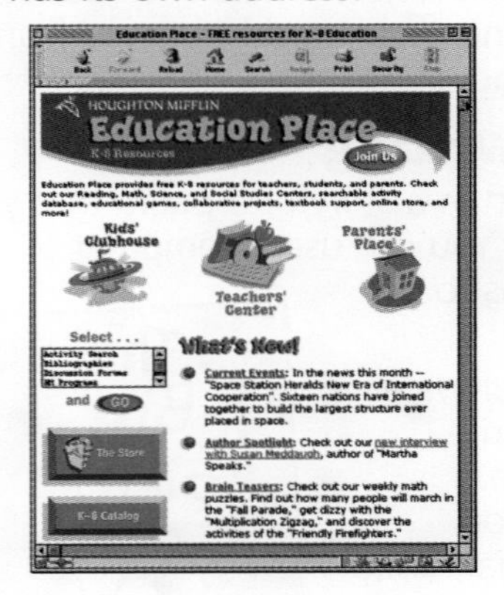

Tech Tip
Visit us on the Internet at www.eduplace.com.

- Send e-mail to your friends or family. See Using E-mail on the next page for more tips.
- Create your own Web page. Design the page, write the text, and choose links to other sites.

Using E-mail

E-mail is a great way to write and receive messages quickly from people all over the world. Read the message below.

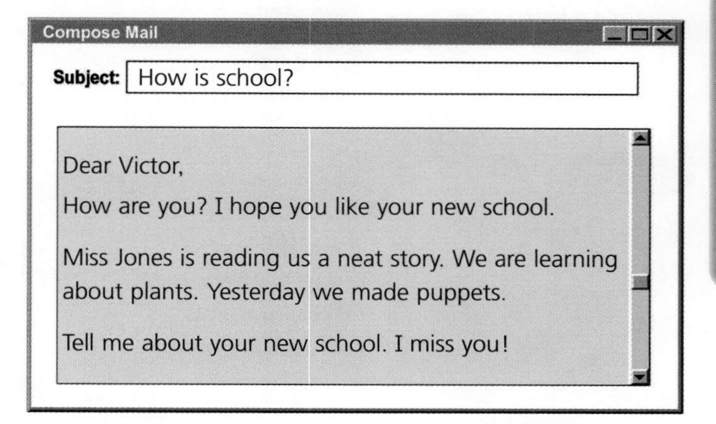

Compose Mail

Subject: How is school?

Dear Victor,

How are you? I hope you like your new school.

Miss Jones is reading us a neat story. We are learning about plants. Yesterday we made puppets.

Tell me about your new school. I miss you!

E-mail Tips

- Type a title in the subject line.
- Keep your paragraphs short.
- Skip a line instead of indenting when you begin a new paragraph. Your message will be easier to read.
- Do not use special type such as italics or underlining. It may not show up on the other person's screen.
- Follow the rules of good writing.
- Proofread your message. Check for missing capital letters and end marks. Fix all spelling mistakes.

Using E-mail

Using This Page

This page provides helpful information about constructing e-mail messages to promote easy readability and understanding of the content. It also addresses the differences between formal and informal e-mails and the issue of correctness. If children are using e-mail in the classroom, draw their attention to this page when you introduce the e-mail activities.

Another good time to discuss this page would be in combination with the Special Focus feature on writing friendly letters. When used in tandem with the friendly letter feature, be sure to point out the differences between the two types of letters.

Computers and the Writing Process

Using This Section

This section provides tips for taking advantage of the features of a computer and available software to help with the writing process stages of prewriting, drafting, revising, proofreading, and publishing. If children have access to a computer for writing, draw their attention to these pages at the beginning of the first writing assignment and remind children to try different ideas over the course of the year to find ones that are helpful to them.

Another way to use this section is to review the suggestions for each writing stage as children are about to work through that stage of the process. Encourage them to try one of the ideas and to discuss which suggestions they found most helpful.

Computers and the Writing Process

Try writing your next story, letter, report, or poem on a computer. Read these pages to learn how.

Choose New Folder from the menu of your writing software. Give your folder a name.

PREWRITING

List your topic or story ideas in a new document.

Word Processor- STORY IDEAS
File Edit View Insert Format Help
Story Ideas
a day at the beach
talking animals
kids finding gold
a class with no teacher

Discuss your ideas with a classmate. Add new ideas to your list. Then choose your topic.

Explore your topic. Add details you would like to include in your writing. Save your document in your folder.

Create a story map or other graphic organizer that you can use to help you plan your writing. See page H31 for help with using graphic organizers.

DRAFTING

Print out your prewriting documents. Use them as you write your working draft.

Open a new document and name it Working Draft.

Set your computer for double spacing. This will give you room between lines to write your changes after you print your document.

Type your thoughts as you think of them. Do not worry about completing your sentences or grouping ideas together. You can make changes later.

Using Technology

Tools and Tips H27

Computers and the Writing Process *continued*

Computers and the Writing Process continued

REVISING

Have a conference with a classmate. Print your working draft. Read your draft aloud and discuss any questions or problems. Take notes to remember your classmate's ideas.

Remember to save your working draft and place it in your folder.

Open your working draft and choose Save As from the menu. This makes a second copy of your document. Name this document Second Draft.

Make changes to your writing. Add, cut, or move words and sentences. Use commands from the menu or special keys on the keyboard to help you do this.

Copy	copies text you select
Cut	removes text you select
Delete key	removes text letter by letter
Paste	puts copied or cut text into a document
Return key	moves the cursor to the next line
Save	saves your changes
Shift key	lets you type a capital letter
Spelling	starts the spelling tool

Using Technology

H28 Using Technology

PROOFREADING

Proofread your sentences by turning them into a list.

- Place the cursor after each end mark and press Return.
- Fix sentences that are either too long or too short, do not begin with capital letters, or do not end correctly.
- After you proofread, just delete the extra returns.

A spelling tool can help you proofread your writing. However, it cannot find and fix some mistakes.

- It cannot tell the difference between words that sound the same but are spelled differently such as tale and tail.
- It cannot find a mistake that is the correct spelling of another word. For example, you type hid but want hide.
- It does not know if two words should be one word such as mail box.

Think of a spelling tool as a proofreading partner!

Choose Save As from the menu. Name this new document Final Copy.

Using Technology

Computers and the Writing Process *continued*

Computers and the Writing Process continued

PUBLISHING

Choose letter styles and type sizes that you like and that can be easily read.

Add artwork to your final copy. Use page breaks so that a small part or paragraph is on each page. Then use computer clip art or a drawing program. You can also print the pages and draw or paste pictures on them.

Print your final copy. Then place the document in your writing folder on the computer.

Graphic Organizers

You may have many ideas for a story or report. Which one will you write about? What will you write about your topic? How can you organize your ideas before you write? These graphic organizers can help!

Idea Wheel

Use an **idea wheel** to help you think of ideas to write about. In each section, write or draw ideas of people, animals, places, or things that you could write about.

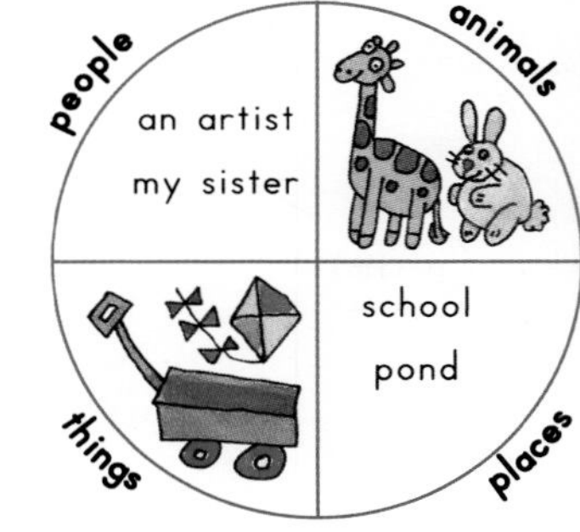

Describing Wheel

Use a **describing wheel** to write details about someone, something, or someplace. Write your topic in the middle of the wheel. List describing words that tell about your topic in the spaces between the spokes.

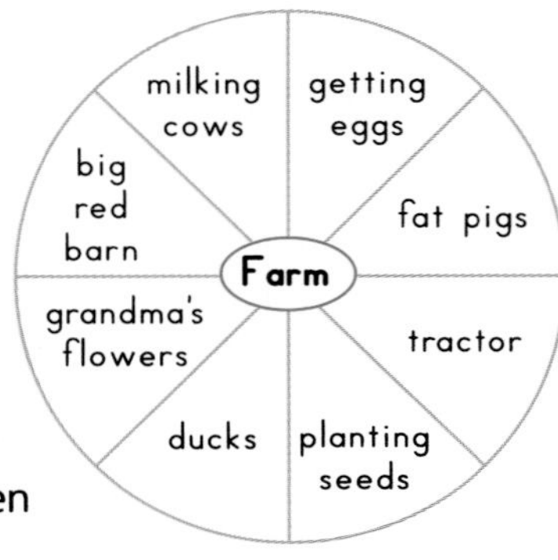

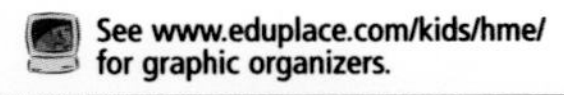
See www.eduplace.com/kids/hme/ for graphic organizers.

Writer's Tools

Graphic Organizers

Using the Graphic Organizers

This section presents a variety of graphic organizers that children can use to help them plan their writing. Some of these organizers are used in lessons within the book; others are additional options.

Each organizer is named, described, and modeled. The description suggests types of writing for which that organizer would be particularly useful.

Here are suggestions for using this section with children.

- Introduce and review the section with children so that they can use it independently when they need an organizer to help them with their writing.
- Periodically choose an organizer, and use it with children in a shared writing activity.
- Help children select organizers from this section to use in exploring or planning any writing activity in this book.

Graphic Organizers *continued*

Word Web

Use a **word web** to organize your details about a topic. Write your topic in a circle in the middle of the page. Then write details about your topic around it. Circle each detail. Draw a line from the circled detail to the topic in the middle.

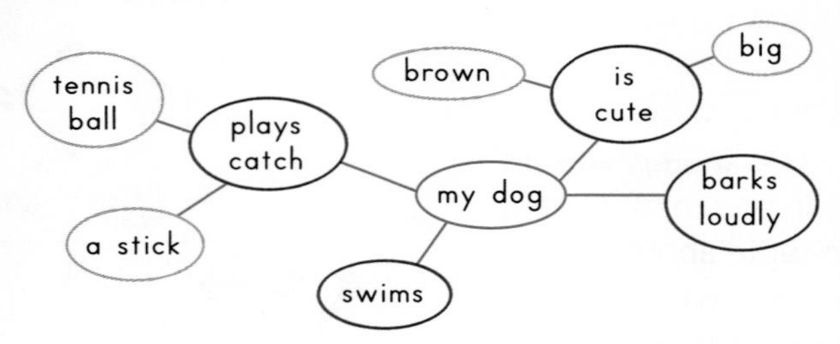

Tree Chart

Use a **tree chart** to show a topic and its details. Write the topic or main idea on the trunk. Write the details on the branches. Add as many branches as you need.

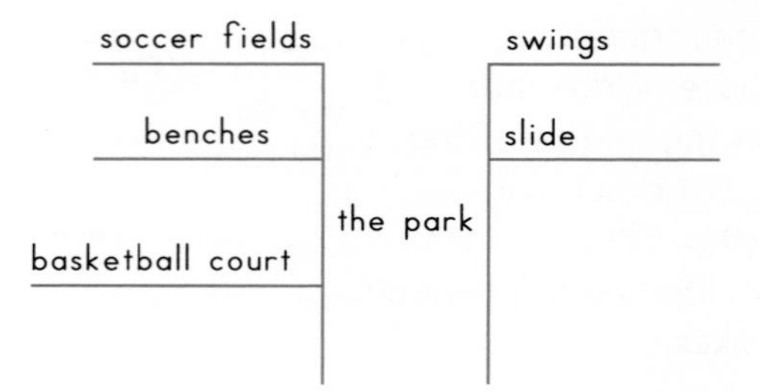

H32 Writer's Tools

Story Map

Use a **story map** to help you plan your story. In the Beginning box, name the main characters, write where and when your story will take place, and tell what the problem is. In the Middle box, write what will happen in your story and how the characters are working to solve the problem. In the End box, write how the problem is solved.

Beginning
cat, dog, animal friends
in the woods
summer
Cat falls into deep hole.

Middle
The dog asks friends how to get the cat out. They try to help.

End
They use a ladder to get the cat out of the hole. The friends have a party.

Writer's Tools

Five W's Chart

Use a **five W's chart** to list important details about an event. Your readers will want to know who, what, when, where, and why.

Five W's Chart	
What happened?	a puppet show
Who was there?	Ms. Rowe's class
Why did it happen?	to tell some fairy tales
When did it happen?	Tuesday at 10 o'clock
Where did it happen?	in room 8

Graphic Organizers *continued*

Spider Map

Use a spider map to list ideas and details about a topic. Write the topic in the center circle. Write main ideas on lines that go out from the center circle. Then write details that support each main idea.

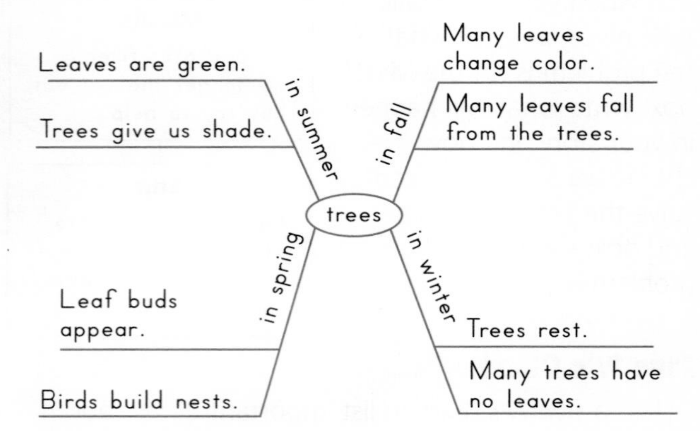

Sequence Chart

Use a **Sequence Chart** to help you put in order the steps for instructions or the events for a story.

Sequence Chart	
Topic	Planting Seeds
First	Dig holes in the dirt.
Next	Put the seeds in each hole.
Last	Cover the seeds with dirt and water them.

H34 Writer's Tools

Grammar, Usage, and Mechanics Terms

action part
the part of a sentence that tells what the naming part did or does

Andre **wrote a story**.
We **walk to school**.

adjective
a word that describes how someone or something looks, tastes, smells, sounds, or feels

The **tall** man walks **two** dogs in the **big** park.
The **red** roses smell **sweet** and feel **smooth**.

adverb
a word that describes a verb by telling how, when, or where

Ed ate **quickly**.
I rode my bike **today**.
My dog went **out**.

apostrophe
(') a mark added to nouns to show ownership
This mark is also used in place of missing letters in a contraction.

Lynn's cat purred softly.
The twins' room is messy.
The baby isn't asleep yet.

Grammar Glossary

Grammar, Usage, and Mechanics Terms

Using the Grammar Glossary

The Grammar Glossary provides an alphabetized list of grammar terms used in this book. Draw children's attention to this section, and tell them to refer to it if they forget the meaning of grammar terms that have been previously introduced and defined.

Grammar, Usage, and Mechanics Terms
continued

capital letter
an uppercase letter that is used to begin a sentence, a special noun, the first word in a quotation, and the first, last, and each important word in a book title

Most winters are warm in **F**lorida.
Scott asked, "**W**here does **A**nna live?"
Carmen read **T**he **B**ig **B**alloon **R**ace.

comma
(**,**) a mark used in dates, between a city or town and state, in quotations, and after words in a series

Zach was born on March 23**,** 1993.
He lives in Austin**,** Texas.
Inez asked**,** "Do you see a cat**,** a dog**,** and a bird?"

command
a sentence that tells someone to do something
It begins with a capital letter and ends with a period.

Clean your room.

complete sentence
a sentence that has a naming part and an action part

The children | swim in the pool.

contraction
a short way of writing two words
An apostrophe shows where letters were left out.

The word **doesn't** is the contraction for does not.

H36 Grammar Glossary

exclamation and exclamation point
a sentence that shows strong feeling; it begins with a capital letter and ends with an exclamation point (**!**).

I won! Please hurry!

helping verbs has and have
verbs that help other verbs show actions that happened in the past

Abby **has** given me a gift.
We **have** seen the beavers at Long Pond.

naming part
the part of a sentence that tells who or what did or does something

Dad fished in the stream. **The book** falls off the bed.

noun
a word that names a person, an animal, a place, or a thing

The **children** rode on the **bus**.
Four **frogs** jumped out of the **pond**.

period
(.) a mark used to end a telling sentence or a command

Dinosaurs are no longer living**.** Open the window**.**

pronoun
a word that takes the place of one or more nouns

Pedro and Callie play soccer. **They** are on the same team.
Kate studied stars. **She** learned about hot gases.

Grammar, Usage, and Mechanics Terms
continued

question and question mark
a sentence that asks something; it begins with a capital letter and ends with a question mark (**?**).

How old are you?

quotation marks
(**" "**) marks used to begin and end a person's exact words

Shawn said, **"**Let's play tag.**"**
Suki asked, **"**What is for lunch?**"**

run-on sentence
two sentences that have been incorrectly joined together as one sentence
It should be written as two shorter sentences, each with a naming part and an action part.

Ali lost her book a friend found it. (wrong)
Ali lost her book. A friend found it. (right)

sentence
a group of words that tells or asks what someone or something did or does
It begins with a capital letter and ends with a period, a question mark, or an exclamation point.

Nan read a book. Can you draw? I won a prize!

special adjectives a and an
They come before nouns that name one.

An insect walked on **a** leaf.

special noun
a noun that names a special person, animal, place, or thing
A special noun begins with a capital letter.

Corey e-mails his friend.
I patted my kitten, **Midnight**.
We went to the zoo in **San Diego**.
I saw the **Statue of Liberty**.

telling sentence
a sentence that tells something
It begins with a capital letter and ends with a period.

Mike likes to swim.
Jasmine learned to ski.

title
a word or abbreviation that can be used before a person's name
A title is also used to name a book.

Miss Ramon is sick today.
She wants to call **Dr.** Harding.
My favorite book is **James and the Giant Peach**.

verb
a word that shows action or being now or in the past

Pablo **hits** the baseball.
Ling **kicked** the soccer ball.
Tony **is** the winner of today's race.
Mandy **was** the winner last week.

Grammar Glossary

Words Often Misspelled

About the List

This list includes 60 words commonly misspelled by children in the primary grades. The words have been organized alphabetically for easy reference. Encourage children to refer to this list when proofreading their writing.

Words Often Misspelled

You use many of the words on this page in your writing. Check this list if you cannot think of the spelling for a word you need. The words are in ABC order.

A
again
always
am
and
are

B
because
before

C
cannot
coming
could

D
down

F
family
for
friend
from

G
getting
girl
goes
going

H
have
here
how

I
I'm
it
it's

K
knew
know

L
letter
little

N
name
new
now

O
on
other
our
outside

P
pretty

R
really
right

S
said
school
some
something
started

T
that's
their
there
through
time
tried

V
very

W
want
was
went
were
where
would
write

Y
you
your

Spelling Guidelines

1. A **short vowel** sound may be spelled **a**, **e**, **i**, **o**, or **u**.

   hat pet pin top fun bag ten mix fox mud

2. The long **a** sound may be spelled **ai**, **ay**, or **a**-consonant-**e**.

   mail train way play made ate

3. The long **e** sound may be spelled **e**, **ee**, or **ea**. At the end of a two-syllable word, it may be spelled **y**.

   be we keep green read clean many happy

4. The long **i** sound may be spelled **i**, **y**, **igh**, or **i**-consonant-**e**.

   find kind fly sky high light nine five

5. The long **o** sound may be spelled **o**, **oa**, **ow**, or **o**-consonant-**e**.

   go cold boat coat slow show those home

6. The long **u** sound may be spelled **u**-consonant-**e**.

   cute use mule huge

7. The vowel sounds in **moon** and **book** may be spelled **oo**.

   food room look good

8. The vowel sound in **town** and **out** may be spelled **ow** or **ou**.

   cow now brown mouse house found

Spelling Guide

Spelling Guidelines

Using the Guidelines

This section of the Spelling Guide includes spelling generalizations that are developmentally appropriate for children in the primary grades. Examples are included for each generalization that shows the most common spelling patterns for that generalization. Encourage children to refer to these guidelines and examples as they proofread.

If you find that a child is having trouble with a particular word or a certain spelling principle, find the appropriate spelling generalization and discuss it with the child. The child could then copy the generalization and the examples into a personal proofreading list or a writing notebook or staple it to his or her writing folder for easy reference when proofreading.

Spelling Guidelines *continued*

9. The vowel sound in **fog**, **paw**, and **call** may be spelled **o**, **aw**, or **a** before **ll**.

   d**o**g l**o**g s**aw** dr**aw** b**all** sm**all**

10. The vowel + **r** sounds may be spelled **ar**, **or**, or **ore**.

    arm c**ar** f**or** b**or**n m**ore** st**ore**

11. The sound at the end of **flower** is a vowel + **r** sound. This sound is spelled **er**.

    sist**er** aft**er** fath**er** ov**er** bett**er** wat**er**

12. Two consonant letters whose sounds are blended together are called a **consonant cluster**.
    A **consonant cluster** may be spelled **br**, **gl**, **st**, **tr**, **cl**, and **sw** at the beginning of words or **st** and **xt** at the end of words.

    brave **gl**ad **st**ep **tr**ip **cl**ub **sw**im ne**st** lo**st** ne**xt**

13. Some words end with consonant sounds spelled **nd**, **ng**, and **nk**. You hear the sounds of **n** and **d** in words that end with **nd**. You may not hear the **n** sound in words that end with **ng** or **nk**.

    e**nd** ha**nd** ki**ng** bri**ng** thi**nk** tha**nk**

14. The sound that begins **when** may be spelled **wh**.
    The sound that begins **then** and ends **teeth** may be spelled **th**.

    which **wh**eel **wh**at **wh**ile **th**an **th**em wi**th** bo**th**

15. The sound that begins **sheep** and ends **wish** may be spelled **sh**. The sound that begins **chase** and ends **much** may be spelled **ch**.

ship	wa**sh**	**ch**op	ea**ch**

16. The consonant sound at the end of **stick**, **speak** and **lake** may be spelled **ck** or **k**.

ki**ck**	ro**ck**	as**k**	for**k**	ba**k**e	hi**k**e

17. A final consonant sound may be spelled with the **same two letters**.

wi**ll**	o**ff**	a**dd**	e**gg**	dre**ss**

18. Some words have the vowel-consonant-**e** pattern. The **final e** in these words is **dropped** before **ed** or **ing** is added.

us**e**	hop**e**	rid**e**	lik**e**	nam**e**	clos**e**
using	hoping	riding	liked	named	closed

19. Some words end with a short vowel sound followed by one consonant. The **final consonant** in these words is usually **doubled** before **ed** or **ing** is added.

hu**g**	ge**t**	ru**n**	sto**p**	ba**t**	gra**b**
hu**gg**ing	ge**tt**ing	ru**nn**ing	sto**pp**ed	ba**tt**ed	gra**bb**ed

20. To name more than one, add **s** to most words. Add **es** to words that end with **s**, **x**, **sh**, or **ch**.

day**s**	thing**s**	dress**es**	box**es**	dish**es**	inch**es**

Spelling Guide

Spelling Guidelines *continued*

Spelling Guide

21. **Homophones** are words that **sound alike** but do not have the same spelling or meaning.

plain	road	tail	hole
plane	rode	tale	whole

22. A **compound word** is a word that is made up of two shorter words.

bedtime anyone maybe bathtub upon into

23. A **contraction** is a short way of writing two words. An apostrophe (') takes the place of the letter or letters that are left out.

I'll we've you're don't doesn't isn't can't

H44 Spelling Guide

How to Use This Thesaurus

A thesaurus can help you find just the right words to use when you write. Imagine you wrote this sentence.

My birthday gift came in a **big** box.

You decide that big doesn't tell how big the box really was. You need a more exact word. What can you do? You can look in this thesaurus to find other words for big.

1. First, find the word big. Remember that the entry words in a thesaurus are in ABC order. Since big begins with b, you would look in the section with B words.

B

big having great size

The elephant is so **big**!

huge

large

2. Next, read the meaning of the word big.
3. Then read the sample sentence. You can see that huge and large are words you could use in place of big.
4. Last, rewrite your sentence, using a more exact word.

Here is an example.

Your first sentence: My birthday gift came in a **big** box.

Your new sentence: My birthday gift came in a **huge** box.

My First Thesaurus

How to Use this Thesaurus

Lesson Objective

Children will:

- use a thesaurus to find synonyms or replacement words

Introducing My First Thesaurus

This introduction explains how to use the My First Thesaurus Index as well as show how the entries in the thesaurus are organized. Review this introduction with children prior to their using My First Thesaurus. Use the Practice exercises with children as guided practice prior to their using My First Thesaurus independently.

Focus on Instruction

- Point out that My First Thesaurus is like a dictionary in three ways: the entry words are alphabetized; each word is defined; each word is followed by synonyms.
- Call children's attention to the synonyms for *big*—huge, large—and help them understand that while main entry words are listed in alphabetical order, the synonyms are not listed alphabetically.

Practice

- Divide the class into two teams. Then write the words *wet*, *silly*, *pat*, and *now* on the chalkboard. Choose three children from each team. All six children will look up the first word. The first child will write the definition; the second will write the synonyms; the third will write a sentence using one of the synonyms. Repeat the process for the rest of the words.
- Have children rewrite the following sentences, changing the underlined word to a synonym they find in My First Thesaurus.

  That is a good picture.

  The brave child didn't cry when she bumped her head.

  Jack decided to run to my house.

My First Thesaurus

My First Thesaurus

My First Thesaurus

A

afraid filled with fear

The bird is **afraid** of the cat.

frightened
scared

argue to have a quarrel

They **argue** about the treat.

disagree
squabble

WORD BANK: Action Words		
Use strong action words like these when you write.		
climb	march	skip
crawl	ride	slide
dance	roll	walk

B

big having great size

That elephant is so **big!**

huge
large

brave facing danger or pain without fear

You are very **brave**, Mr. Bear.

bold
courageous
fearless

H46 My First Thesaurus

C

choose to pick out, after thinking about what is best

I will **choose** a dress to wear.

decide on
select

cold having no warmth

The wind is **cold** today.

chilly
freezing
frosty

cry to shed tears because of sadness or pain

Please don't **cry**, Little Bear.

sob
wail
weep

D

do to carry out an act

I will **do** my work now.

complete
finish

E

eat to take food into the body

They **eat** the corn.

consume
dine on
gobble up
munch

My First Thesaurus *continued*

F

WORD BANK: Words That Tell How Things Feel		
Use words like these to tell how things feel.		
cold	hard	soft
crumbly	rough	sticky
dry	smooth	warm

find to get something by looking for it

Will she **find** the kitten?

- discover
- locate
- spot

fun a good time

Playing soccer is **fun**!

- enjoyable
- entertaining

G

go to pass from one place to another

I will **go** as fast as I can.

- advance
- move on
- progress

good having fine qualities

That is a **good** sand castle!

- terrific
- wonderful

H

happy feeling pleasure

I was **happy** to see Uncle Ken.

delighted

glad

help to do what is needed or useful

I **help** Mrs. Wills.

aid

assist

lend a hand to

J

WORD BANK: Jobs		
Use words like these to tell about people's jobs.		
bus driver	doctor	police officer
carpenter	firefighter	teacher
chef	nurse	

jump to spring into the air

Teeny and Tiny like to **jump**!

hop

leap

K

keep to put something in a safe or handy place

I **keep** my bones here.

save

store

My First Thesaurus *continued*

My First Thesaurus

L

laugh to make sounds to show that something is funny
Bear's costume made her **laugh**.
chuckle
giggle
howl

little small in size or amount
Abby has a **little** house.
miniature
tiny
wee

look to see
We **look** at a big lion.
gaze
peek
stare

M

mad feeling and showing anger
Why does Hen seem so **mad**?
angry
bitter
cross

make to form, shape, or put together
Ben and Tim **make** a fort.
build
construct
create

H50 My First Thesaurus

N

near close to

Our house is **near** the beach.
by
next to

nice kind and thoughtful

Fran is a **nice** person.
gentle
good
sweet

now at the present time

You must get on the bus **now**.
at once
immediately
right away

P

pat to tap gently with an open hand

I love to **pat** the puppy.
pet
stroke

WORD BANK: People		
Use words like these to name people.		
aunt	child	mother
boy	father	sister
brother	girl	uncle

My First Thesaurus *continued*

WORD BANK: Places		
Use words like these to name places.		
city	mountain	school
country	ocean	store
house	park	zoo
lake		

pretty pleasing to the eye

These are such **pretty** flowers.

- beautiful
- lovely

put to move something to a certain spot

Put the dishes on the table.

- Lay
- Place
- Set

Q

quick very fast

Jill is **quick** at math.

- speedy
- swift

quiet with little or no noise

We were **quiet** in the library.

- hushed
- silent

R

rain to fall in drops of water from the clouds

It will **rain** soon.

- pour
- shower

ring a clear sound like that made by a bell

The loud **ring** woke up Yukio.

- clang
- gong
- jingle

run to move quickly on foot

They will **run** around the track.

- dash
- race
- sprint

S

sad with no happiness or joy

Penny Pig is **sad** about her hat.

- gloomy
- unhappy

WORD BANK: Smell

Use these words to tell how something smells.

clean	fresh	stinky
fishy	salty	sweet
flowery	smoky	

My First Thesaurus

My First Thesaurus *continued*

My First Thesaurus

said spoke aloud

Elli **said**, "I love my kitten."
- declared
- stated
- exclaimed

shine to give off light

The stars **shine** in the sky.
- glow
- sparkle
- twinkle

silly not serious

That is a very **silly** hat.
- amusing
- foolish
- funny

smart having a quick mind

Paula is **smart** in science.
- bright
- clever
- intelligent

WORD BANK: Sound

Use these words to tell how animals and things sound.

barking	noisy	soft
cackling	purring	squeaky
clanging	quacking	whistling
mooing		

H54 My First Thesaurus

stop to bring or come to a halt

When will the noise **stop**?

cease
end
finish

strange not usual

His coat is **strange**.

odd
unusual
weird

My First Thesaurus

T

WORD BANK: Taste		
Use these words to tell how something tastes.		
bitter	sweet	sour
spicy	salty	yummy
fruity	tart	

trip a passing from one place to another

They took a **trip** across the sea.

journey
voyage

try to make an effort to do something

Anna will **try** to win the race.

attempt
strive

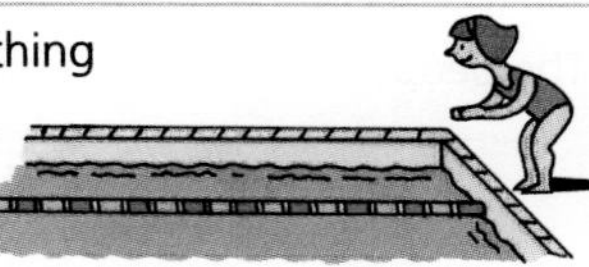

My First Thesaurus *continued*

U

under lower than

The mouse is **under** the lion's paw.

below
beneath

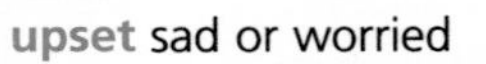

upset sad or worried

Dad was **upset** when we were late.

disturbed
nervous

W

wash to clean using water and soap

It's time to **wash** the dog.

bathe
scrub

wet being covered with a liquid

The **wet** bathing suits must hang to dry.

moist
soaked

Y

yell to call out in a loud voice

The people at the game **yell**.

scream
holler
shout

Guide to Capital Letters

When to Use a Capital Letter	
	To begin a sentence Today is my birthday. How old are you? Please cut the cake. It was a great party!
	With the name of a special person, animal, place, or thing Mary has a dog named Spike. She lives in Canton.
	With the pronoun I Janey and I played tag.
	With the names of the days of the week Monday Saturday
	With the names of holidays Flag Day Valentine's Day
	With the names of months January July
	With titles of people Mr. Adams Ms. Wong Mrs. Lee Dr. Sanchez Miss Jones
	The first word, last word, and each important word in a book title The Cat in the Hat Ira Sleeps Over
	To begin the greeting or closing in a letter Dear Grandma, Your friend,
	To begin the first word of a speaker's exact words Jenny said, "Sing a song with me."

Guide to Capital Letters

Guide to Capital Letters and Punctuation Marks

Using This Guide

The Guide to Capital Letters and the Guide to Punctuation Marks on pages H58–H59 provide easy references for children to check when to use capital letters and punctuation marks, based on the skills taught in the pupil book.

Draw children's attention to these two charts. Encourage children to refer to these pages when proofreading their compositions before making their final copies.

Guide to Capital Letters and Punctuation Marks *continued*

Guide to Punctuation Marks

Guide to Punctuation Marks

End marks	**Period** **After a telling sentence** Jimmy plays baseball.
	Question mark **After a question** Did he hit the ball today?
	Period **After a command** Keep your eye on the ball.
	Exclamation point **After an exclamation** He hit a home run!
Comma	**After the greeting in a letter** Dear Jody,
	After the closing in a letter Your pal,
	Between the day and year in a date May 15, 2004
	Between the names of a town and a state Buffalo, New York
Apostrophe	**To show who owns something** Mary's hat three girls' hats
	To take the place of letters in a contraction is not isn't cannot can't
Period	**After some titles of people** Mr. Kenney Mrs. Ramos Ms. Carter Dr. Johnson
Underline	**Under book titles** The Three Little Pigs
Quotation Marks	**Around a speaker's exact words** Bill said, "I saw a funny show."

Index

Index

Lesson Objective

Children will:

- use an index

Focus on Instruction

- Explain that an index helps a reader find information in a nonfiction book. Tell children that the index lists each topic in the book individually. It doesn't show the larger sections such as chapters or units. Ask children when they might want to use an index to find information. (when looking for facts about a particular topic)
- Point out that the main word in the topic of the entry is usually in dark type. Explain that some topics have more information about the copy listed below the entry. Point out that these elements are indented below the main entry word.
- Have children look at the first page of the index. Help them recognize that the entries are listed in ABC order. Tell children that the numbers following the key words or less important words and phrases are page numbers.
- Have children find the entry *Brainstorming*. Tell them that this entry has a cross reference —*See* Prewriting—which sends the reader to another entry that may have the information. Explain that if children look for a term in the index and they don't find it, they should try to think of a similar term and look there.
- Have children use the index to find the following information.

1. On what pages would you find information about a class story? (14-24)
2. What are the types of letters? (friendly, invitation, thank you)
3. On which page would children find information about fact and opinion? (230)
4. What are the subtopics for the main topic *Sequence*? (in instructions, in a story)
5. Where would you find information about indenting paragraphs? (24)
6. What word would you look under to find information about words such as *don't* and *isn't?* (contractions)

I-2 INDEX

Index

Index

Index

S

V

W

INDEX I-11

Acknowledgments *continued*

"Mushrooms Are Umbrellas" by Arnold Spilka. Copyright ©1994 by Arnold Spilka. Used by permission of Marian Reiner for the author.

"My Glider" from A PIZZA THE SIZE OF THE SUN by Jack Prelutsky. Text copyright ©1996 by Jack Prelutsky. Used by permission of HarperCollins Publishers.

"Wind Song" from I FEEL THE SAME WAY by Lilian Moore. Copyright ©1967, 1995 by Lilian Moore. Used by permission of Marian Reiner for the author.

Book Report

I'M TOO BIG (JE SUIS TROP GROS) by Lone Morton, pictures by Steve Weatherill. Published 1994 by arrangement with Barron's Educational Series, Inc., Hauppauge, NY.

Student Handbook

Definitions of "chest," "fog," "mirror," "seed," "ship," "spot," "storm," "stripe," "subway," and "wing" from the HOUGHTON MIFFLIN PRIMARY DICTIONARY. Copyright ©1989 by Houghton Mifflin Company. Reproduced by permission from the HOUGHTON MIFFLIN PRIMARY DICTIONARY.

One Minute Warm-up

2/1 BEDTIME FOR FRANCES by Russell Hoban, pictures by Garth Williams, published by HarperCollins Publishers, 1960. Used by permission.

2/1 CLAP YOUR HANDS by Lorinda Byran Cauley, published by PaperStar Books, 1992. Used by permission.

2/1 GOLDILOCKS AND THE THREE BEARS retold and illustrated by James Marshall, published by Dial Books for Young Readers, 1988. Used by permission.

2/1 MR. PUTTER AND TABBY FLY THE PLANE by Cynthia Rylant, illustrated by Arthur Howard, published by Harcourt Brace & Company, 1997. Used by permission.

2/1 MRS. BROWN WENT TO TOWN by Wong Herbert Yee, published by Houghton Mifflin Company, 1996. Used by permission.

2/3 A BIRTHDAY BASKET FOR TÍA by Pat Mora, illustrated by Cecily Lang. Text copyright ©1992 by Pat Mora. Illustrations copyright ©1992 by Cecily Lang. Reprinted with the permission of Simon & Schuster Books for Young Readers, an imprint of Simon & Schuster Children's Publishing Division.

2/3 ABUELA by Arthur Dorros, illustrated by Elisa Kleven, published by Dutton Children's Books, 1991. Used by permission.

2/3 AUNT FLOSSIE'S HATS (AND CRAB CAKES LATER) by Elizabeth Fitzgerald Howard, paintings by James Ransome, published by Clarion Books, 1991. Used by permission.

2/3 CHILDREN AROUND THE WORLD by Lynda Snowdon, published by Macmillan Children's Books, 1982. Used by permission.

2/3 JULIUS by Angela Johnson, pictures by Dav Pilkey, published by Orchard Books, 1993. Used by permission.

2/3 HAPPY BIRTHDAY, DANNY AND THE DINOSAUR! story and pictures by Syd Hoff, published by HarperCollins Publishers, 1995. Used by permission.

2/5 MAC & MARIE & THE TRAIN TOSS SURPRISE by Elizabeth Fitzgerald Howard, illustrated Gail Gordon Carter. Illustration copyright©1993 by Gail Gordon Carter. Used with permission of the Author and BookStop Literary Agency. All rights reserved.

Acknowledgments *continued*

2/5 OLLY'S POLLIWOGS by Anne & Harlow Rockwell. Copyright ©1970 by Anne and Harlow Rockwell. First published by Doubleday & Co. Reprinted by permission of Curtis Brown Ltd.

2/5 THE SEASHORE BOOK by Charlotte Zolotow, paintings by Wendell Minor, published by HarperCollins Publishers, 1992. Used by permission.

2/7 NOW WE CAN HAVE A WEDDING! by Judy Cox, illustrated by DyAnne DiSalvo-Ryan, published by Holiday House, 1998. Used by permission.

2/9 A YEAR FOR KIKO by Ferida Wolff, illustrated by Joung Un Kim, published by Houghton Mifflin Company, 1997. Used by permission.

2/9 BABY RATTLESNAKE as told by Te Ata, adapted by Lynn Moroney, illustrated by Mira Reisberg. Story copyright ©1989 by Lynn Moroney. Pictures ©1989 by Mira Reisberg. Reprinted with permission of the publisher, Children's Book Press, San Francisco, CA.

2/9 MISS NELSON IS MISSING! by Harry Allard, illustrated by James Marshall, published by Houghton Mifflin Company, 1977. Used by permission.

2/9 ONE GIANT LEAP: THE STORY OF NEIL ARMSTRONG by Don Brown, published by Houghton Mifflin Company, 1998. Used by permission.

Student Writing Model Contributors

Celsey Bédard, Maurice Bonar, Christine Guzman, Matthew Hodges, Phillip A. Jackson, Candice Lubin, Sarah Rose Manning, Kelly O'Masta, Adam Pynn.

Credits

Illustrations

Andrea Arroyo: 49, 192, 240 (t), 241, 247 (t), 256, 320 **Bernard Adnet:** 33, 173 (t), 307 (t) **Christiane Beauregard:** 257, 288, 289, H5, H13 **Elizabeth Brandt:** 300 (bkgrd.) **Dan Brawner:** 95, 96 **Lizi Boyd:** 46, 240 (b), 248 (b) **Liz Callen:** 10, 47 (m & b), 50, 57, 148, 172, 184 (b), 195, 201, 213, 215 (b), 237, 239 (t), 249 (t), 291, 293, 319 (m), 331, 338, H3, H4, H6, H31 **John Cymerman:** 53, 54 Linda Davick: 47 (t), 186 (t), 254 (t), 319 (t), H7, H9, H10 **Chris Demarest:** 29 (t), 38 (t), 39, 58, 160, 168, 263, 314, 326, 329, 332 **Dorothy Donohue:** 31 (t), 177, 182 (t) **Daniel Dumont:** 316 **Tuko Fujisaki:** 55, 187, 321 **Lee Glynn:** 86, 87, 176 (b), 246, 298, 306 (bkgrd.), 313 (t), H17, H18 **Kristen Goeters:** 64-65, 66 **Myron Grossman:** 41, 181, 183, 215 (t), 299 (b), 307 (b), H11, H12 **Tim Haggerty:** 179, 200, 203, 297, 299 (t), 308 (t) **Jennifer Beck Harris:** 27, 43, 82, 95, 156, 166, 167 (b), 170, 174, 176 (t), 180, 182 (b), 184 (t), 224, 247 (b), 249 (b), 286, 304, 315 (b), 318, 360, H23 **Eileen Hine:** H45–H56 **John Hovell:** 32 (bkgrd.), 36, 38 (b), 42, 46 (bkgrd.), 59, 94 (b), 172 (bkgrd.), 208, 242 (b), 244 (b), 250 (bkgrd.), 252 (bkgrd.), 310, H21, H22, H27 **Benrei Huang:** 44 (t), 330 **Anne Kennedy:** 6, 12, 13, 15, 16, 19, 21, 23, 25, 67–70, 75–78, 80, 81, 83–86, 89, 91, 139–144, 146–150, 152–155, 157–159, 209–211, 214, 216–220, 222, 223, 225–232, 234, 235, 237, 271–274, 276, 279–282, 284, 285, 287, 290, 292, 295, 345–349, 351–359, 361–364, 366, 367, H20, H25, H26, H27, H28, H29, H30

Credits *continued*

Illustrations *continued*

Jared Lee: 261 **Andy Levine:** 29 (b), 37, 45 **Cynthia Malaran:** 254 (b), 255, 319 (b) **Claude Martinot:** 30 (t), 32 **Ferris Nicolais:** 302, 306, 312, 318 **Tim Nihoff:** 28, 40, 165, 193, 305, 309 (t), 315 (t) **Diane Paterson:** 72, 88, 90, 161, 167 (t), 186 (m), 194, 202, 204, 205, 220, 225, 233, 235, 262, 265, 327, 335, H15, H16 **Chris Reed:** 31 (b), 152, 185, 188, 234, 236, 242 (t), 264, 313 (b), 370, 371, H47–H56 **Tim Robinson:** 244 (t), 248 (t), 302 (bkgrd.), 316 (bkgrd.) **Ellen Sasaki:** 173 (b), 239 (b) Michael Sloan: 243, 249 (m) **Jackie Snider:** 30 (b), 34, 94 (t), 96, 337 **George Ulrich:** 277, 311 **Ted Williams:** 40 (bkgrd.), 44 (b); bkgrd. for: 68, 69, 74, 78, 79, 84, 140–143, 152, 153, 158, 164, 168, 170, 174, 178, 184, 185, 210, 211, 221, 226, 227, 231, 253, 272, 273, 282, 283, 308 (b), 312, 356, 357, 362.

Photographs

Cover Photograph: Douglas E. Walker/Masterfile

Fine Art: 82 National Museum of American Art, Washington, D.C./Art Resource **156** Peter Ralston/Charles Scribner's Sons **286** National Gallery, London, UK/The Bridgeman Art Library.

Getting Started: 1 (tl) Kit Kittle/Corbis **1** (tm) Lawrence Migdale/Mira **1** (tr) Ron Watts/Corbis **1** (bl) Lawrence Migdale/Mira **1** (bm) Photodisc **1** (br) Mark Tomalty/Masterfile **2–5, 7, 8, 14, 18, 20, 22, 24** Joel Benjamin **9** (tl) Don Stevenson/Mira **9 (tr)** Erika Stone/Mira **9** (bl & br) Lawrence Migdale/Mira **11** all images Photodisc. **Unit 1: 26** Daniel J. Cox/Tony Stone Images **30** Photodisc **35 (tl)** Tim Davis/Tony Stone Images **35 (tr)** Kennan Ward/Corbis **35** (bl) Tim Davis/Tony Stone Images **35** (br) Renée Lynn/Tony Stone Images **36** Norman Myers/Bruce Coleman, Inc. **39** Stephen Krasemann/Tony Stone Images **42** Robert Carr/Bruce Coleman, Inc. **48** Jeff Greenberg/Rainbow/PNI **56** Jim Cummins/FPG **60** Martin Rogers/Prism/FPG **61** Stephen Frisch/Stock-Boston. **Unit 2: 62** Alan Hicks/Tony Stone Images **71, 74, 77, 80, 81** Ken Karp. **Unit 3:** 92 Ed Honowitz/Tony Stone Images **93** Harry DiOrio/The Image Works **99** Lawrence Migdale/Stock, Boston **100** Myrleen Ferguson/PhotoEdit **102** AJA Productions/Image Bank **103** (middle, l. to r.): Jose Carrillo/PhotoEdit, Arthur Tilley/FPG, Michael Newman/PhotoEdit, Bruce Byers/FPG, Barros & Barros/Image Bank, Stephen Simpson/FPG **103 (bottom, l. to r.):** Steve Skjold/PhotoEdit, Art Tilley/FPG, Lawrence Migdale/Stock Boston **105** Jeff Isaac Greenberg/Photo Researchers **106** Renée Lynn/Photo Researchers **111** Myrleen Ferguson/PhotoEdit **113** Myrleen Ferguson/PhotoEdit **114** (t) Hans Reinhard/Bruce Coleman, Inc. **114 (b)** Christine Steimer/OKAPIA/Photo Researchers, Inc. **115** Lawrence Migdale/Tony Stone Images **117 (l)** Alan & Sandy Carey/Photo Researchers, Inc. **117 (r) R.** Hutchings/PhotoEdit **118** Donna Day/Tony Stone Images **120** Michael Newman/PhotoEdit. **Unit 4: 134** Ron Chapple/FPG **145, 146, 147, 151, 155** Ken Karp. **Unit 5: 162** Chip Simons/FPG **163** Bill Bachman/Photo Researches, Inc. **164** William Whitehurst/The Stock Market **164 (tl & tr)** William Whitehurst/The Stock Market **164 (l)** Keith Gunnar/Bruce Coleman **164 (r)** Martin Rogers/Tony Stone Images **165** Bob Daemmrich/ The Image Works **169** Robin Smith/ **170** Chip Simons/FPG **171** Stephen Simpson/FPG **174** Lawrence Migdale/Photo Researchers, Inc. **175** Jeanne Drake/ Tony Stone Images **177** Tom Prettyman/ Photo Edit **178** Margaret Miller/Photo Researchers, Inc. **179** Michael Newman/Photo Edit **185** Hans Reinhard/Bruce Coleman, Inc. **186** Turner & Devries/Image Bank **189** Chuck Place/Stock Boston **196** Alan Hicks/Tony Stone Images **197** Gary A. Conner/PhotoEdit **198** Frank Fournier/The Stock Market

Credits ***continued***

Photographs ***continued***

199 Tom Stewart/The Stock Market. **Unit 6: 206** G. & V. Chapman/The Image Bank **212, 216, 219, 223, 228, 230, 233** Ken Karp **231** Buddy Mays/Corbis. **Unit 7: 238** Index Stock Imagery **241** Adamsmith Productions/Corbis **243** James L. Amos/Corbis **245 (l)** Tetsu Yamazaki/International Stock **245 (m)** Patrice Ceisel/Stock Boston **245 (r)** Sunstar/International Stock **250** C. Carton/Bruce Coleman, Inc. **251 (t)** E.R. Degginger/Photo Researchers **251 (r)** Nikolas Konstantinou/Tony Stone Images **251 (l)** Andrew Wood/Photo Researchers **252** M. Kahl/Photo Researchers **253 (l)** Robert Brenner/PhotoEdit **253 (r)** Robert Brenner/PhotoEdit **254** Tom Young/The Stock Market. **Unit 8: 266** Douglas E. Walker/Masterfile **275, 278, 281, 284, 285, 292, 294** Ken Karp. **Unit 9: 296** Ariel Skelley/The Stock Market **297** Jonathan Nourok/PhotoEdit **300** Tom Hussey/Image Bank **301** Myrleen Ferguson/PhotoEdit **302** Russell D. Curtis/Bruce Coleman, Inc. **303** Richard Price/FPG 304 Michael Heron/Stock Market **305** Merritt Vincent/PhotoEdit **317** Art Wolfe/Tony Stone Images **328** David Young-Wolff/PhotoEdit/PNI **333** Dan Tardif/The Stock Market **334** Ariel Skelley/The Stock Market **336** Ken Chernus/FPG **339** Douglas Faulkner/The Stock Market. **Unit 10: 340** Stuart Westmorland/Tony Stone Images **341, 342-343** Suki Coughlin **344** Mario D. Mercado **348, 350, 352, 354, 355, 356, 358, 359, 364, 368, 369** Ken Karp **363** Photodisc.